# The Character of Economic Thought, Economic Characters, and Economic Institutions

# The Character of Economic Thought, Economic Characters, and Economic Institutions

Selected Essays by Mark Perlman

*Ann Arbor*

THE UNIVERSITY OF MICHIGAN PRESS

1999   1998   1997   1996      4   3   2   1

*A CIP catalog record for this book is available from the British Library.*

Library of Congress Cataloging-in-Publication Data

Perlman, Mark.
    The character of economic thought, economic characters, and economic institutions / selected essays by Mark Perlman.
        p.   cm.
    Includes bibliographical references.
    ISBN 0-472-10711-9 (alk. paper)
    1. Economics.   2. Economics—History.   3. Economics—Philosophy.
4. Economists.   5. Labor movement—History.   6. United States—
Economic conditions.   I. Title.
HB34.P423   1996
330—dc20                                                      96-7707
                                                                 CIP

*Dedicated to my memories of my grandparents*
*Samuel and Dora Ticktin Shaber*
*Mordecai and Pauline Blankstein Perlman*
*and*
*to my hopes for my grandchildren*
*David, Justin, Daniel, and Alexandra Williams,*
*the children of Kenneth and Abigail Perlman Williams*

# Contents

CHAPTER 1

# Introduction: What Makes My Mind Tick

*Mark Perlman*

Doubtless there are many purposes for editing a collection of one's essays, particularly when the span of time of their preparation covers more than 40 years. In the end perhaps the most obvious purpose is to describe what one did with those decades and begin to explain why. I will come to the description a bit later, but here I will focus on why things were done the way they were. Many academics believe that their thoughts were responses to ideas and even to the influences of ideas as propounded by their teachers and other great persons. Yet, while I am more than willing to admit that my life has been shaped by others, including great teachers handling great ideas, in looking back, what has principally shaped my adult life was a series of institutional questions that I perceived, sometimes conventionally, but more than occasionally idiosyncratically.

I have always been as interested in *how to teach*—that is, in how to influence others—as I have been in *what to teach*. This trait I share with Adam Smith, who was more of a rhetorician than either an economist or a philosopher. To teach, one has to understand the constraints in the learner's mind. Many of these constraints are institutional, by which I mean (to paraphrase John R. Commons) collective thought shaping individual choices. This introductory chapter, accordingly, is my own analysis (buried in the narrative) of what has made my mind work.

## Physical Survival and Emotional Shaping

Surely the dominant institution that shaped my conscious thinking and my life was the fact of Hitler's Germany. Although I was born and largely raised a native of Wisconsin, I lived in Cardiff, Wales, in late 1938 and early 1939, and the Munich Agreement exacerbated the all-too-evident insecurities that a Jewish faculty-child living in a semihostile Madison, Wisconsin, had. Whatever, I recall the unanticipated feeling of profound relief when, shortly after one o'clock, I heard the special news bulletin on the radio of the attack on Pearl Harbor. Up to that moment I had lived with an immense fear that nothing could stop the Nazis. Of course, my analysis was, as we say these days, macro; from the micro standpoint I still felt doomed, since I assumed correctly that I would soon be in the army and assumed incorrectly that, what with my size and physical ineptitude, I would probably be killed. That I was not killed I ascribe to the bombing of Nagasaki: contrary to current revisionism, the reason that the Japanese surrendered was neither their economic exhaustion nor the bombing of Hiroshima. It was the second bomb that did it; contemporary and later apologists notwithstanding.

## My Family Background

I eschew most discussion of my childhood, which was then more than now clearly atypical. I was my parents' second child (both sons). My father, Selig Perlman, was a major figure on the world academic scene. My mother, Eva Shaber Perlman, died in her 36th year. She left a strong positive impression in both the Jewish and non-Jewish Madison community. My father then married my mother's younger sister, and there were two children (both girls) from that marriage. My older brother, later a research biochemist, was at ten better prepared to handle the death of our mother than I was at six. He appreciated and could articulate the dimensions of the loss; the event of her death took me before I could define where my own interests had to be protected, and I grew up in my father and aunt/stepmother's home feeling not only that I was unfortunately complicating their lives, but that I owed them something for taking care of me. My brother resisted feeling the same way—he believed that his rights were prior to my aunt/stepmother's, a view he did not hesitate to proffer. But for reasons that do my insight little credit, I never availed myself of his line, ". . . if Mother hadn't died, I could have had . . ." Instead, I tried to ingratiate myself with my father, for whom I became briefly something of an alter ego.

Thus, a second factor in my development was my mother's premature death and my attempts to become close to my father. He was a superb teacher, but also someone insulated with an observable layer of self-concern, albeit usually termed by him as *Weltschmerz*. But however he chose to define it, he still used this as a way to place his emotional needs up front, center stage. In my boyhood I must have spent a minimum of three hours each week in one-on-one sessions listening to him discuss the way as well as the substance of how he interpreted events. It was an overwhelming, if European-Jewish-style, intellectual relationship—a brilliant father and an admiring son; and neither ever forgot who was the father and who was the student. While he was quick to identify whatever originality I may have had, there was little equality in the debating. His way of teaching me was to ask me what I thought, listen to my reply without interruption, consider my answer, and then go on to show how that answer could either be reinforced or be negated. He exhibited an infinite patience in leading me through historical databases, analytical routines, and discussions of appropriate rhetoric. By the time I was his teaching assistant at the University of Wisconsin, we talked on professional matters well over two hours every day. He was a historian, not only of the labor movement (which was the basis of his fame), but also of philosophy, political science, and literature. A one-time medical student, he remained interested all of his life in the evolution of biological science, a discipline which stressed the process of mutation, not equilibration, as its principal analytical mode. He characterized this combination of interests in history and in mutation as an *institutional* or *organic* approach to thinking. His data bank seemed all but inexhaustible. For him, analysis or theory was not in and of itself something aesthetically elegant. Rather, it was merely a step to understanding pressures for change juxtaposed with pressures for continuity.

In his twenties, John Stuart Mill came to regard his father's domination of his mind with anger and repugnance. I was clearly far less prescient than the younger Mill, and all that I can truly say is that I was well into my late thirties before I even began to realize that, unlike his explanation of external events, my father's interpretation of personal events was not necessarily to be my own. Unlike John Stuart Mill, I was never strong enough in mind to be able to detach myself that completely from the impact of my father's influence. He died when I was 35.

Life in his household was intellectually exciting, but only if a child were prepared to listen and participate as an adult. Few of his many visitors (academic and occasionally political) were so awe-inspiring as to make me mute (not infrequently to my parents' articulated embarrassment); my siblings chose not only to be mute, but also generally absent. Given my interests, the nine years I spent in my father's home between my 12th and 24th year (I was in the army between 1943 and 1946) are a good part of my lifetime's intellectual treasure.

## My General Educational Preparation and the Irrational Rush to Complete It

The formal facts of my academic life included a preliminary education in the school systems of Madison, Wisconsin (with one intellectually splendid year at the Cardiff, Wales, High School for Boys), baccalaureate and master's degrees in 1947 from the University of Wisconsin, and a doctorate in 1950 from Columbia University. I enlisted in the United States Army in late 1942 and was called up early in 1943. I returned to civilian life in March 1946. During the 1947–48 academic year I taught full-time at Princeton University.[1]

---

1. I served as a preceptor for David A. MacCabe (Labor Economics), Ansley Coale (Probability Statistics), J. Douglas Brown (Social Security), and Paul Strayer (Introduction to Economics). I sat in on courses with Jacob Viner, who in his aggressive way was really very kind

Thus, if one considers the period between 1941, when I entered the University of Wisconsin as a freshman, and 1950, when I was awarded my doctorate—a span of nine and a half years, with three years spent in the army and one spent as a full-time teacher at Princeton—the three degrees were accomplished in five and one-half years, much too short a time to do properly what I set out to accomplish. But I was of the World War II academic cohort, and we hustled with time and took unnecessary and unwise intellectual chances.

I decided early on that I would become a professor and would try to succeed in my father's field. Even more, I became more imbued than I realized, until the end of my teaching career, with the importance of a high-pressure undergraduate education, one involving considerable contact with very capable thinkers. My father was unwilling to educate his children anywhere but at the University of Wisconsin (his university), and it was only after I took both a baccalaureate and a master's degree under his tutelage that he agreed the time had come for me to study elsewhere. But while I was at Wisconsin I had some magnificent personal (one-on-one) instruction: from Merle Curti (the social historian), from John Gaus (the political scientist), from Ed Witte (father of the American Social Security system), from Willard Hurst (the legal historian), from Ruth Wallerstein (the preeminent seventeenth-century English literature scholar), and from Roberto Lopez and Charles Edson (both first-rate historians with marvelous gifts for generalization).

My two Wisconsin degrees were awarded in 1947, and in the autumn of that year I went to Princeton, where I had taken a position as a full-time instructor, but where in fact I learned a fair amount from the lectures given by Jacob Viner,[2] somewhat less from Frank Dunstone Graham, and no small

---

to me, and Frank Dunstone Graham. My memories of Princeton vary: on the one hand, Paul Strayer (a wonderful man who died young) used as one textbook in an elementary course Hicks and Hart, *The Social Framework,* at a time when national accounting was still all but unknown to academic economists. On the other hand, I recall having a brief romance with a young lady at the Institute for Advanced Study and discovering its cafeteria. The romance quickly paled, but my love affair with that cafeteria (its menu and its prices) persisted. I found myself occasionally eating with a somewhat hard-to-understand scientist, whom others seemed to treat with self-imposed distance. I, however, found him delightful, and once began to argue with him about how few atom bombs it would take to destroy the American chemical industry, largely centered in northern New Jersey. After I had assured him that Ansley Coale, whose dissertational research on the subject contained such a calculation, was a very careful workman with wartime experience at the M.I.T. radiation labs, I decided to introduce myself and inquire his name. He was a mumbler, and I had to ask him to repeat it twice. When that proved inadequate I asked him to spell it. B-O-H-R—Niels Bohr, he said. I was so humiliated by my chutzpah that I did not return to that, my favorite cafeteria, until 1981 when I was a member of the Institute.

2. Jacob Viner made an indelible impression on all of his students. In a 1992 review of some of Viner's last essays, I wrote

Jacob Viner, long-time coprincipal economist (with Frank Knight) and contending

amount from conversations with two much younger men, Ansley Coale and Harvey Leibenstein.[3]

Princeton, with its emphasis on style and form, was clearly not to my academic taste. The Dean of the Faculty for whom I served as a preceptor, J. Douglas Brown, put the matter best when he said, "Perlman, you are not prepared to learn anything in the labor field besides what your father believes in. Get out of his field or go away." I transferred to Columbia in the autumn of 1948, where I taught half-time (one course each semester) and managed to zip

---

polymath (with almost everyone) at the University of Chicago (off and on from 1916 until 1946) and thereafter Princeton resident-guru to the scholarly learned in academia until his death in 1970, wrote well and much. Trained first at McGill and then at Harvard under Taussig, Viner was the teacher of economic price theory and international economics at Chicago, advisor to the Treasury, specifically, and to the federal government, generally, during the 1930s and 1940s, and scholar *par excellence* for all of his professional life. He was a man of indefatigable energy, unlimited curiosity, amazing self-confidence, and what seemed (at least to his students) witty and cruel bumptuosity.

Those of us who are lucky enough to remember Viner both as a teacher and as friend are wont to wonder how anyone who could be so devastating in the classroom could be so warm and charming in the salon. My judgment is that Viner, contrary to most current pedagogic practice, believed in the efficacy of adrenalin—his own and particularly his students'. Something of a truly compulsive talker, Viner believed in true competition for the leadership of every salon—and he was indefatigable in preparing for each opportunity and for exercising his considerable wit in capturing the podium, real or imagined. It has been said that he envied Lionel Robbins's abilities as an after-dinner speaker (just as Robbins is supposed to have envied the range of Viner's erudition), but if so, their envies were misplaced: on both scores Robbins was a "First," and so was Viner. . . .

Irwin's choice of Viner's 1950 Brown University Convocation address on scholarship and graduate education is, for my taste, quintessential Viner. It explains what we, who knew him also in the salon, saw in him: style, erudition, breadth of interest, wisdom, and even a great deal of tolerance for whimsy of mind and character. It is a charmingly worded essay on the differences between learning, knowledge, and scholarship. In this lecture he sought by example to show how important the manifestation of judgment and humor are essential to intercourse and really to the necessities of rhetoric, and how important rhetoric is in the scheme of things—particularly when it came to understanding individual greed and ego in the advancement of general social purpose. . . .

Viner, no doubt having practiced on a real matched fighter (Thorstein Veblen), liked to tease me (clearly not much of a match) about whether American Institutional Economics with its emphasis on time and place made any noticeable contributions to economics; if I had had the wit I would have asked him if he was really above contextual analysis, why did he spend so much time studying context. But, as it was, I could do no better than cite the old-fashioned welfare economics, which he told me was not much in the way of *economics,* as such (Review of *Essays on the Intellectual History of Economics,* by Jacob Viner, *Jour. Hist. Econ. Thought,* 14:116–18.)

---

3. Harvey Leibenstein was one of the few authentic near-geniuses of my cohort. He pursued important work in development economics, demographic economics, and micro-economic theory. His professional career was abruptly ended in an auto crash that effectively destroyed his mind, although the body lingered on for almost a decade.

through a year of studies in residence before I left to do my dissertation abroad. The details of that year in New York are unimportant except to report that I began the courtship of Naomi Waxman and that, as part of the post–World War II veterans' rush, I spent far too little time absorbing the intellectual atmosphere associated with graduate student fellowship.

There were many major events that dominated thinking in the late 1940s. Of course, the advent of the cold war explains why I, myself, wanted to get on with life; few of us ex-GIs had much confidence that peace would last, and unlike later generations who questioned their personal responsibility for making America militarily successful, my generation saw military service as not only patriotic, but something we somehow personally owed our chums who had been killed in World War II.

America was in a kind of turmoil associated with what in retrospect now seems hard to explain. The GI Bill had initially been viewed as a simple boondoggle (like the much maligned "Hoover" Veterans' Bonus), but by 1948 it was evident that postwar America, fueled in part by legislation, was "flying." We believed that the growth in economic output, no doubt associated with a disciplined skilled labor force and the availability of considerable capital, would run around 4 to 6 percent per year, in real terms, and that of that amount no less than 2 to 4 percentage points could be associated with a partly inexplicable "residual productivity growth." So magnificent a phenomenon led most working people to expect regular and marvelous annual wage-rate increases. Given everything, their expectations were almost regularly realized, but not without a stately minuet of strikes in the basic industries, the convening of "fact-finding panels," and the finding of such facts as would justify wage-rate increases.

### My Dissertational Project: Applying a Theory of Judicial Notice

Doubtless influenced by my training in labor economics and one aspect of law (the judicial interpretation of the legislative process) at Wisconsin (Selig Perlman, Edwin E. Witte, and Willard Hurst) and by Carter Goodrich and Paul Brissenden at Columbia, I chose to do my dissertation on an Australian labor relations topic. My motive was shaped by my desire to work with Goodrich (who had done a major seminal article on Australia some 20 years earlier) and with Brissenden (who was something of a saintly figure). I applied for and was given a research training grant by Paul Webbink at the Social Science Research Council; my sponsors were Goodrich, Brissenden, Arthur Frank Burns, and John Maurice Clark, as well as Edwin Witte and Merle Curti from Wisconsin. I mention Webbink because he has been far too easily forgotten; he was the person who was Simon Kuznets's impresario in the development of the American social accounting system, as well as the administrative figure behind Kuznets's later work on economic growth. When I was interviewed by Webbink, I had no idea of his own historical significance; but I remember telling others how impressed I was with his capacity to listen, to absorb what I was trying to say, and then to help me clarify and assign priority to my thoughts. I told him that I wanted to compare the Australian labor relations system (depending upon compulsory arbitration) with the American free-wheeling system, which eschewed judicial interposition.

As I knew almost nothing about Australia when I got there in early November 1949, I gave myself an intensive but extremely brief reading course on Australian history and then turned to looking at the way that the Arbitration Court operated. Subtlety was never my long suit, and I found myself asking the Court's judges what I now realize were such grossly impertinent questions as what personal reservations caused each to disagree with his brethren-on-the-bench, and what each thought kept the others from seeing the appropriate point. I usually had prepared myself well regarding the facts of the cases, and to my continuing amazement I found the judges ready, even eager, to talk. In particular I knew the facts of the cases in the pastoral (wool-raising and shearing) industry, the metal trade (metal working) industry, and the stevedoring industry. What I learned from the judges was that each of these industries was significantly different. In the first (the pastoral), the employers were in bitter competition, and the union was greatly divided between the interests of the elite shearers and the unskilled sheep station workers. In the second (metal working), each side of the industry was tightly organized—the monolithic Amalgamated Engineering Union faced the tightly organized Metal Trades Employers' Association. And, in the last (the stevedoring), the union was tightly controlled by its leadership (politically Communist, but insofar as the court was concerned that was pretty much of an irrelevance), while the employers were divided between coastal shippers (who faced competition from the railroads and truckers and for whom Australian stevedoring charges could determine firms' survival or bankruptcy) and overseas shippers (who faced no competition from Australian railroads and truckers, and for whom Australian stevedoring charges were trivial compared to their need to get their ships in and out of Australian ports quickly). The overseas shippers were thus willing to give the union pretty much anything if time in Australian ports could be minimized.

In studying legislatures and courts, perceptive students become aware that no one ever really asks where legislatures come by their ideas, but courts are supposed to derive their information from five sources: (1) the examination and cross-examination of witnesses; (2) constitutional authorizations pertaining to judicial powers; (3) positive legislation that meets judicial standards for clarity and constitutionality; (4) legal precedent as defined in the common law and through *stare decisis* as seen in each court's own jurisdiction; and (5) a nebulous thing that the judges, themselves, define as "common knowledge." This last is called *judicial notice,* and Willard Hurst has suggested in several of his lectures that it is a Pandora's box that clever judges use to twist a clear "the-law-is-an-ass" situation into something truly appropriate.

I appropriated his point to explain when and how the arbitration court was successful.[4] When the parties were both disunited the judges actually seemed to use a vastly expanded judicial notice to establish the facts—in other words, a judge would replace testimony and cross-examination with the product of his own reading and thinking (a kind of procedure that Louis Brandeis advocated). A judge's sanction was that if he were challenged he would expose the contestants to questions showing their own organizational frailty.

By contrast, when each of the parties did have its act together, the judge minimized the insinuation of his own views and gave opinions based on the other four sources. His sanction was to threaten the parties with the usual legal obstacle course—"take what comes from your testimony and accept it, or go ahead and appeal and see what all of the litigation will give you." (In one wonderful case, Mr. Justice O'Mara, usually a clever practitioner of this ploy, tried to get judicially over-tough and in the end had to admit from his bench that it was apparent that the arbitration system needed the Amalgamated Engineering Union more than the union seemed to need the court.)

In the instance where each of the litigants preferred different approaches (the ship owners wanted the judge to find the facts for himself because they could not agree on what they really wanted and the stevedores wanted conventional testimony and cross-examination), the court repeatedly foundered.

In the course of my extended talks with the arbitration court judges, one, Mr. Justice Alfred William Foster, invited to our lunch his close friend and mentor, Mr. Justice John Vincent Barry (later Sir John Barry) of the Supreme Court of Victoria. Barry and I left Foster after eating sandwiches in his chambers and spent the rest of the day talking. I recall arguing with him that private monopolies were more responsive to corrective criticism than public monopolies were (*Quis custodiet ipsos custodes*). That he was impressed (and, incidentally, had never heard of my father) I doubtless found flattering. Anyway, from that chance luncheon there developed the great intellectual friendship of my life. Barry, then a widower with two adolescent children, was an indefatigable letter writer. He matched me letter for letter. He had a historical sense that equaled anything I had ever seen: his awareness and feeling for nuances in words reflected his Irish cultural heritage, and his ideas on

---

4. The gist of these distinctions is explained, with the actual case material, in my *Judges in Industry: A Study of Labour Arbitration in Australia.* Melbourne: Melbourne University Press, 1954.

penology were not merely intellectual fantasies coming from his voracious reading, but many of them had actually been experimentally tried from his bench. His views on the relationships between biological advances and equity law were eventually both taken to the High Court and appealed to the Law Lords in the London Privy Council (he was initially overruled, but by now his views are canon). A marvelously organized and brilliant man, Barry was a wonderful challenger of most of my conservative views. In the early 1950s he was an advocate of abortion-on-demand; I thought that it was too profound a cultural question to admit of easy dispensation. He was an early advocate of environmentalism; I thought it a trendy enthusiasm. He was the preeminent civil libertarian in Australia; I had and still have reservations about the dangers of expression of hateful comments (the English legal maxim, "the greater the truth the greater the libel" always made sense to me, and I share the British view that the test for libel is the intent to harm, not the falsity of the statement). Barry sharpened my thoughts more than he dominated them, however. In truth it was a wonderful relationship because, while I was always ready to give him an opportunity to lay out systematically his thoughts (as I should have been), he took my objections seriously, and in virtually every one of our contacts I came away consciously wiser than I had been.

He remarried in 1951 (we had met in 1950) and I tended to regard myself (no doubt presumptuously) as what the Jews call *Ben Bayit,* "son of the household." Never lacking much in the way of brashness when it came to doing something I thought socially useful, upon my return from Australia in April 1950 I visited the Carnegie Corporation and proposed that it finance a trip to America for him. It did, he came, and his Australian reputation stretched to his becoming world-famous as a criminologist. From 1950 until his death in 1969 I participated in a weekly debate with the best-read man, quite probably the man with the most catholic knowledge, and one of the most generous souls I have ever met.

Barry sponsored the publication of my dissertation. He proposed as readers Richard Eggleston KC (longtime university chancellor and later Mr. Justice Sir Richard Eggleston) and Professor Zelman Cowan (later Sir Zelman Cowan, Governor General of Australia, provost of Oriol College, Oxford, and president of the British Press Council). These two brilliant men, both lawyers, were unbelievably generous: Eggleston offered to write an introduction for the book, and Cowan did for a complete stranger what I still cannot comprehend—he edited the manuscript to get rid of its legal errors, its ambiguities, and many of its stylistic *gaucheries.*

Later (in 1954) Eggleston was instrumental in having the 1904 act creating the arbitration system declared *ultra vires* (unconstitutional). In the 1954 *Boilermakers' Union* case the Australian High Court overwhelmingly (seven to one) bought Eggleston's point; he handled the brief of the president of the Boilermakers' Union, who had been jailed by Justice Foster for well-documented contempt-of-court offenses. Eggleston argued that the Arbitration Court, since its inception in 1904, had unconstitutionally mixed the legislative and the judicial roles, a view that clearly paralleled what I had originally noted in my dissertation. I was later told secondhand (that is, by someone who had been present) that the former Chief Justice, Sir William Latham, when questioned about my work—the product of a hardly mature economist— reacted so violently to this parallelism that it seemed apparent to all at that dinner save him that I had "discovered" the law even before the Court had. The Menzies government took the case on appeal to the Privy Council (that avenue then existed). (Eggleston passed through the United States on his way back to Australia to see me after arguing before their Lordships.) The Privy Council accepted his view, and I was briefly infamous in Australia. But I am getting away from my story.

In due course (December 1950) I defended my dissertation. My examin- ing committee included Carter Goodrich (my nomimal supervisor), David Truman (the political scientist), Leo Wolman, Arthur R. Burns, some histo- rian whose name I have mercifully forgotten, and George J. Stigler.[5] The defense went swimmingly, although the historian said all too pompously, "Perlman, you write in the tradition of Adam Smith, but not as well." Before I could think of what to reply, Professor Truman, who had previously assessed the dissertation in superlatives, remarked dryly, "Yes, he also writes in the language of Shakespeare, but not nearly so well." A few days later I deposited the manuscript in the Columbia University Library and even asked (person- ally, it turned out) General Eisenhower, then about to leave Columbia Univer- sity to set up NATO, to sign my diploma. He did.

### Getting along on the Job

Upon receiving my doctorate I taught for twelve months (starting in January 1951) at the University of Hawaii,[6] and then went to a temporary position at Cor-

---

5. Stigler had earlier (October 1949) given me a very rough time in my economic theory field examinations; the examiner was to have been John Maurice Clark, but the new chairman, James Waterhouse Angell (who had replaced Goodrich), decided to experiment, and I was the first and only victim. After that first bitter examination (Stigler had voted against my being passed) I recall actually saying to Stigler, "What do I have to do to get past you, memorize your god- damned text?" Stigler replied imperturbably, "That should do for starters, but you will probably have to do even more." Yet, during my defense (December 1950) Stigler and I developed a mutual regard for one another. Many years later, when writing a memorial about Stigler for the *Economic Journal,* I observed that he suffered fools more gladly than those he did not consider fools, but rather ill-prepared. People like me got "the treatment," but I was surely the better for it, and my appreciation of his focus on catallactics was greatly sharpened.

6. During my year in Hawaii I wrote several essays. I was able to use papers from my

nell. That initial one-semester appointment was extended, over no small amount of opposition from within the faculty (the issue was a desire to have an avowed socialist on the faculty), to a three-year assistant professorship. I have always taken lecturing very seriously, in that I believe that one lectures not only to convey data and constructs, but also to show why and where one applies both. A lecture should reflect the organic nature of the lecturer's thinking process.

At Cornell I taught a couple of courses, one of which was on the literature describing labor unionism. What evolved was my second book, *Theories of Labor Unionism,* which was neither the panegyric to nor the bitter dismissal of my father's *A Theory of the Labor Movement,* which I suppose that my sponsor and my critics really wanted. For the most part the book was well-reviewed, although I did note two lines of criticism that I had not really anticipated. One line was that the literature I reviewed was, itself, not "close to the level of historical fact," a view that my father had known from the beginning would be his reservation. The other, coming from an economic historian with a personal history of conversions from one truth (Marxism) to another (neoclassical economics), offered the judgment that I really did not know what a theory was. Of course, he was right; no one knows what a theory is, if knowing what a theory is gives you a key to truth such that you can unlock everyone's mind. When I read his review I wondered just how my colleague Fritz Machlup (to be mentioned in the following) would respond. Machlup's reaction was reassuring: "The man's a fool; indeed, the very worst kind, a wise fool," he said. "There are numerous irrelevant interpretations of what a theory ought to be; the real issue is what a theory is *supposed* to do. Moreover, your book provides a taxonomy, and that is where most thinking and then theorizing has to start." But that was several years after I had left Cornell.

My Cornell experience involved me in a problem which, drawing upon von Gierke's idea called *Genossenschaft*[7] (fellowship or brotherhood), came

---

students in a class in labor history to ferret out the references. What impressed me most was how much more concerned the workers were with *Genossenschaft,* membership-grouping, in this instance ethnic, than in a real economic class struggle. I do not recall ever being able to use undergraduates for such purposes after that. I discovered in 1951 what is now generally known: the children of immigrants from the Orient (then as now) combine occasional brilliance with almost invariable careful, hard work.

7. Otto von Gierke, a historian of the German government, explores this as an evolutionary idea. His research, based on medieval and later data, saw informal groups, which started as voluntary associations, eventually developing internal rules and in time becoming the effective political government. These internal rules often specified who was eligible for membership. The medieval guilds were one example of this kind of organization. They had complex rules for admission to membership. On one of my travels I was told, for example, that the reason that Jews in Amsterdam went into diamond cutting and book printing was simply because these technologies came after the period of guild hegemony, and Jews were accordingly not subject to the usual guild exclusionary rules.

to fascinate me. What constitutes and who determines a group's boundaries? Being both overconfident in my views of things and insensitive to what I was doing to the interests of others, I learned about *Genossenschaft* the hard way. It was clear that among the assistant professors I was probably the most respected teacher, and I certainly published more than the others put together, but it also became apparent even to me (and that unwillingly) that at Cornell I "just did not fit in." That was reason enough for leaving. "Fitting-in," or becoming a member of the *Genossenschaft,* is very much the "name" of any social struggle, and although one who "holds property" may buck the system for a time, "fitting-in," whether it is a religious, political, or even a cultural test, has long been the active bugaboo of social success. It is *the* general academic problem, with the actual terms of membership in the *Genossenschaft* varying—one may be inadmissible because of the wrong race, the wrong sex, the wrong politics, the wrong age, the wrong jargon, the wrong value system, or even the wrong level of mediocrity.[8] At Cornell I failed the "level of mediocrity" test.

Harvard's John Dunlop (later an unusually conscientious secretary of labor who resigned when President Ford found it politically expedient to annul a moral commitment made to him) came to my rescue and arranged for a comfortable stipend for me to write a history of the International Association of Machinists. George Heberton Evans, Jr. later hired me as assistant professor of political economy at Hopkins.

About Dunlop I will say that he had all of the qualities of Ed Witte—he was indefatigable as a teacher and as a public servant, he was thoroughly well-informed, and he was totally committed to his work and to the institutions that supported him. In addition, he was thoroughly trained as an economic theorist, with inter alia "credentials" coming from the great Maynard Keynes. I always found him straightforward, well informed, and kindly. My personal acquaintanceship with my father's teacher, John R. Commons, was slight, but John Dunlop seems to me to have been cut from the same cloth. True, he may lack some of Commons's complex spark of originality and genius, but neither is he burdened with Commons's neuroticism nor with his inability to turn brilliant generalizations into forceful abstractions. Commons's forte was a knowledge of history; Dunlop's is of sociology. Commons read German fluently; from my standpoint, it is unfortunate that Dunlop does not read Italian, because were he able to, like John Hicks, he could have chosen Pareto as an intellectual mentor and ridden that line of genius to even greater fame as an economic theorist. As it is, he knows Pareto's translated works well, and is one of the few American economic theorists to have begun

8. When I once remarked to my father that David Hume claimed that the basic sense was the sense of smell, he replied that while that may have been true of eighteenth-century Edinburgh (about that, he said that he knew not), in twentieth-century Madison, he had found it to be the sense of envy—one failed entry into the *Genossenschaft* if one were too able.

to mine the treasures in *Trattato de Sociologia Generale* (translated as *Mind and Society*). Dunlop's interest in economics focused on what gave labor institutions their stability and what worked to destroy them. Whenever I have talked to him, I have marveled at the degree to which he and my father set up their analysis in the same way.[9] Both saw labor movements as conservative (when the workers had anything real to lose). Both were true pragmatists; among the various tests to be applied before judgments were made was the test of workability. Both embraced nominalism (going from the specific to generalizations) rather than the method of medieval realism (applying abstractions to concrete situations). Both were students of the uses of language to highlight or to shade meanings.

It was my experience at Hopkins, however, that reshaped my thinking more. After my move to Baltimore in 1955, I became devoted to two quite different men, both historical luminaries: Fritz Machlup and Simon Kuznets. Each was conscious of the sensitivities of the other, and each used me to "test" the other's reaction to proposals before they were publicly stated. As I wrote several essays (two reproduced here) concerning the work of these great and dear friends, I shall not give attention to their magnificent perceptions of economics in this chapter. Suffice it to say that the happiest academic years of my life were the few when they were together at Hopkins, and that their intellectual guidance and subsequent personal-professional friendship I greatly treasure. My appointment to Hopkins had been made in Machlup's absence from Baltimore, and I suspect that much of his warmth for me was his discovery that I had great eagerness to learn about the Austrian economic tradition; he had supposed that I was "anti-theory," only to learn that I was all for the subject, providing it was not advanced as a religion. Machlup was a Hayekian, and like Hayek he had his own reservations about economic theory as "scientism." While Fritz lacked Lionel Robbins's patrician lordliness, the two men were much alike—they were aesthetes, compulsively hardworking, and above all else curiously tolerant and generous.

Kuznets was only in some senses their type. Also an aesthete with regard to art and music, Simon had fantastic breadth of historical and literary knowledge, a grasp of the principles underlying statistical technique, and a general economic imaginativeness. Like my father, he had had a czarist *gymnasium* education, had turned as a high school student to *Bundist*[10] socialism as a

---

9. Of course their ways of looking at the American labor movement were somewhat different. My father's fascination was with the craft unions; Dunlop, coming to maturity in a later period, studied both craft and successful industrial unions.

10. The *Bund*, the translation of its full title being "The General Jewish Workers' Union in Lithuania, Poland and Russia," at the time these men were youths was a political movement in czarist Russia. It was part of the group making up the *Menshevik* (that is, the anti-Bolshevik) wing of the Marxian spectrum. The *Bundists* were secularists (anti-Jewish religious orthodoxy) seeking political recognition of Jews as full citizens (albeit with recognition of their Jewish

definition of problems, and had emigrated to America, where, fortuitously, he had been chosen by a great empiricist (Wesley Clair Mitchell) as his special student. I saw a fair amount of Kuznets even after he went to Harvard. Listening to Simon was a joy. Moreover, he and I often differed in interpretations. I recall once when he was arguing that the modern world was the result of technological changes in the cotton weaving and iron industries, I argued that it was more likely the extension of the market (a point I discovered much later that Viner had made in his Earlham lectures). He and I were each holding tight when he asked me why I was so adamant. Embarrassed, I answered that he argued just about on a par with my father, but that he didn't put me down as my father did; and I still entertained a hope that I could persuade him.

It is in the chapter on his work on national economic accounts where the magnificence of his genius comes across. In my judgment, he and his student, Robert Nathan, did measurably more to shape the world's destiny before and during World War II than any other economist in history has ever done. Men like Smith, Malthus, and Keynes did much to shape ideas; but Kuznets truly caused epochal history.[11] I have met a great many wonderful and a great many truly brilliant men, but, in terms of makers of history, none was like Simon Kuznets.

## My Interest in Public Health and Economic Growth

Some time late in the winter of 1959–60 Hopkins was asked to staff a team investigating the record of a wartime U.S.-Brazilian agency, the *Servicio Especial della Saudia Publica,* which had sought to foster improved public health (largely preventive medical) services. The team's leader was Abel Wolman, a legendary individual who had done most of the work in establish-

---

national status) and were passively, and more often actively, anti-Zionist; they wanted democratic reforms to replace the official autocracy of the czarist system. What is more important than the details of their projected reforms was their outlook. They believed that capitalism set worker against worker; that great inequalities of wealth and income set class against class; and that the czarist government's official anti-Semitism exacerbated anti-Jewish feelings, themselves largely caused by the Orthodox and Roman Catholic churches and particularly by the vicissitudes of the business cycle. After World War I the *Bund* became a major Jewish political party, particularly active in combatting the official anti-Semitism of the Polish government during the 1930s. The party was disbanded by the Communists after World War II.

11. From 1933 to 1935 Nathan, under Kuznets's general direction, designed the basic national income accounts of the United States. Then Kuznets turned to studying gross capital formation in the United States, particularly in manufacturing industry. After Pearl Harbor, Nathan, by then director of planning for the War Production Board, brought Kuznets to Washington. Their collaboration resulted in a completely new concept of ordering war materiel—in about four years military output went from a mere 4 percent to a gigantic 48 percent of the nation's gross national product. Their wartime collaboration was initially resisted by the army general staff, and they resigned in disgust. But Ferdinand Eberstadt, an investment banker, managed to persuade Henry Stimson, the secretary of war, of the correctness of their system. It was adopted.

ing a sanitary engineering academic profession in the world. Kuznets had initially been asked to join the team, but he had little or no interest in the travel, indeed in the questions, involved. These questions were whether expenditure on public health investment programs could be justified on economic grounds. Absent Kuznets, then me. And that is how I came to consider the bases for investment in public health. I spent about a month traveling with Wolman, from whom I learned a great deal about the actual methods of epidemiology, about the facts of disease transmission, and about the problems of intercultural communication. After that I traveled in Brazil for about another month alone, but with a vast sum of money put aside for my education. I recall chartering small airplanes to fly me about the Amazon Valley and to one or more points in the state of Minas Gerias.

Ours was an energetic and friendly team: besides Wolman the other members were Timothy D. Baker, M.D., and Margaret Bright, a sociologist. I drafted much of the report; in it I presented my own "theory" of economic development, with the health of entrepreneurs being in some senses the most fragile variable. Later, Baker and I did a book on the supply and demand for health services in Taiwan in which we actually collected a stratified random sample of household consumption data, which we then used as the principal economic independent variable. After I left Hopkins and went to the University of Pittsburgh, Baker and I tried to collaborate on a further study of the relationship between health and economic development, but I had lost my faith in our earlier results and had begun to argue that health was a final, not an intermediate, product—or to put the matter in its worst light, investment in health programs really could not be justified in terms of speeding economic growth.

This eventual conclusion likely soured my colleagues, who preferred to think that virtue and success should be constant companions. Nonetheless, early on (as those things go) I was writing in the Health Economics field; indeed, I wrote numerous articles and edited three books on the topic. For the most part, my interest was not in the popular question of how to improve health care delivery, but in broader economic questions like when and how to invest in public health, particularly in disease prevention facilities. Nevertheless, it was my experience in Brazil that was key, and it led me to wonder about the mechanism of economic growth. I fancied that economists handled the mechanism too abstractly; from a macro standpoint almost anything could be considered *abstractly* as either a simple fixed or variable factor. My view was that studying the economic process required a set of foci on several *concrete* factor markets: (1) *land and other natural resources,* (2) the availability of *water and power,* (3) the cost of *transportation,* (4) the availability and spectrum of *labor skills,* (5) the sum of *capital*—that is, control of scale and production time, including technology, (6) *managerial talent,* and (7) access to effective *markets.*

In recent years my reading has led me to wonder about the meaning of economic growth. I now conclude that it is a murky concept quite capable of four different definitions, involving rising per capita consumption, rising national gross domestic product, falling levels of unemployment, and higher levels of national domestic investment. But in 1960 I was quite fired up with what the team had been doing, and was pleased, nay overjoyed, when Ernest Stebbins, dean of the faculty of the School of Hygiene, offered me a supplementary appointment (with summer pay) on his faculty. He told me that when queried about my credentials he explained to the school's advisory board that I was the most "Compleat Hypochondriack" that he had ever known—not only did I know the symptoms of diseases that he had never heard of, but I had personally experienced them!

I returned from Brazil to Hopkins in September 1960 just delighted with life. I became interested in urban economic problems, just then emerging as an important focal point. Harvey Perloff of Resources for the Future and its Committee on Urban Economics asked me if I would do an essay on defining urban problems. I presumed what he had in mind was doing for that emerging discipline what economists had done for the study of labor institutions—something that was academically known as "labor problems." I prepared such an essay, and it was used to stimulate a group to undertake separate essays. In retrospect, I think that Perloff erred: while he may have wanted a study of urban problems, what the profession wanted was econometric studies that offered positive and mensurable criteria for policy choices. My tie with Resources for the Future was of limited duration, but I enjoyed the association. Perloff's eventual choice was to sponsor econometric studies, something more numerical and seemingly scientific. Yet, for all of their appearance of numerical accuracy, we still have not really defined the sources of, much less the cures for, urban malaise, of which blight is only the most obvious frustration.

During the ensuing 1960–61 academic year, the Hopkins Department of Political Economy quickly disintegrated. Evsey Domar had already left, and Richard Musgrave had replaced him. Simon Kuznets, who had turned down a Harvard offer in 1959–60, accepted it when it was renewed. And Richard Musgrave, believing that Fritz Machlup's brand of economic theory, focused as it was on separate theories (each with its own methodology) of relative prices, incomes, and employment, was conceptually out of date, counseled George Heberton Evans (by this time dean of the faculty as well as departmental chairman) to encourage Machlup to leave.

When Machlup was suddenly offered the successorship to Jacob Viner at Princeton (Ragner Nurske had already accepted the post, but died suddenly before he could take it up), Evans did as Musgrave counseled. By going to the provost saying that Evans's decision was flawed, I then probably fouled my own nest. [12] Anyway, the events played out. Kuznets went to Harvard, Machlup to Princeton, and then, after a bit, Musgrave also went to Princeton. Evans brought in a new team, with Carl Christ as impresario. The criterion for membership in the new *Genossenschaft* was econometric analysis and presentation—again quite possibly the wrong level of mediocrity or the wrong religion (numeracy can be a religion).

## The Pittsburgh Years

I looked around for alternative offers, and the one that I took was a professorship at Pittsburgh, where I have remained until now. I had asked for and been granted an appointment specifying that I could teach economic history as well as labor economics. I should mention here that upon my arrival in Pittsburgh there was a sudden need to staff an advanced course in the history of economic thought. As it was easier to replace me temporarily in the labor field, I concentrated on the other two. But I was unwilling to leave the labor field, and I had what I thought was an inspiration. I had agreed to work with Edgar M. Hoover on a research project involving the relationship between fertility control programs and economic development, and I proposed to Hoover that if he would teach a lecture course on demographic economics (which I could take more or less as a student), I would prepare myself to take it over in a year or two. Thus, in the autumn of 1964 I began an intensive reading course in demographic economics, and by the autumn of 1965 I was teaching American economic history, demographic economics (with Hoover), and the history of economic thought. I will say more later about my own academic work during the 30 years I was at Pittsburgh, but here I turn to two major responsibilities I undertook in the 1960s.

By 1965 the University of Pittsburgh's administration was in deep financial trouble, and Benjamin Chinitz, the departmental chairman who had hired me and a long-time collaborator of Hoover's, despaired of his program surviving. He resigned suddenly to take a political position in the Johnson administration. In the absence of anyone presumed to be a fitter candidate, I became chairman, a position I retained for about five years, also resigning suddenly

---

12. Machlup was long unaware of my presumptuous intervention. Several years later (the last time we talked—he and his wife, Mitzi, stayed with me in Vienna in 1982) I mentioned it to him. He said nothing in immediate response, but the next day he mentioned to me en passant that he felt that he owed me no thanks—I did what I did not for him, but because I had moral principles. One respects (and does not thank) those whose principles motivate their actions, he commented. I felt his compliment could not have been improved upon. (Again, for readers interested in Machlup's career and life, see chap. 18 herein.) During that visit he insisted upon telling me and a visitor he had never previously met the "these days not so unusual" story of his birth and upbringing, saying that the editors of the *New Encyclopedia of the Social Sciences* had foolishly bowdlerized John Chipman's article about him.

when the newly appointed dean of the Faculty of Arts and Sciences found my hard-line administrative posture (it was the era of anti-Vietnam radicalism) unacceptable. However, in 1969 I was appointed University Professor of Economics, a title which was supposed to indicate breadth of interest spanning two or more disciplines—in my case economics, history, and public health.

## What Should an Economics Department Be?

As a departmental chairman, I thought that my principal duty was to build a teaching department, one that taught undergraduates how to think and express themselves in serious economic terms and graduates how to do responsible, competent research and express it in terms, if possible, simultaneously understandable by both college graduates and holders of doctorates in economics. I favored each faculty member handling each term three moderately sized classes (with quiz sections to supervise writing and testing), and I used the argument that as a department we were generating sufficient "shadow-revenue" for all of us to have what was then an uncommon amount of money for faculty research assistance as well as seminar speakers. Thus, I sought generous administrative support for my colleagues' professional development, and I wanted the senior administrators to know and to appreciate just what each person was doing. One such effort involved my drafting a congratulatory letter, summarizing the principal findings, which was then sent by the vice chancellor every time a significant article or book was published. I recall that my most perceptive colleague accused me of some minor duplicity in these efforts, saying, "Mark, do you think me so naive as not to realize that the letter from the vice chancellor was really written by you?" My reply was that as the vice chancellor was a contracting officer, he had the habit of reading very carefully only what he signed; accordingly, the one best way to get him to grasp just what was going on in the department was to give him something to sign.

When I became chairman I put in place my version of a system based on tenure and as much merit and mature judgment as was civilized and possible. I started by trying to get those already on the scene to focus attention on the departmental and personal aspects of their own performance. As I have noted, I assumed, really without thinking much about it, that professors should teach a lot. Their "bread and butter" came from teaching undergraduates; they had a duty to teach research methods and to supervise the research efforts of advanced students. Whatever creative research they wanted to undertake should generally be done only after their teaching responsibilities had been met. When it came to new hires (and in those days chairmen and deans usually made most of the decisions), my plan had an equal opportunity aspect, and since there was still institutional prejudice against blacks and women (which I clearly eschewed) we managed to hire *and promote* some exceptional people.

Yet, among those I hired were several whose perception of what economics was about, as well as their priorities with regard to academic responsibility, differed markedly from mine. I will come to the differences in their ideas about economics later, but here I focus on our differences regarding academic responsibility. I eventually (less quickly than should have been the case) came to realize that many of my colleagues believed in the "marketing of their own careers," and sought to pursue policies intended to maximize their alternative offers. They pointed out that research, as seen in the output of articles, *and surely not undergraduate teaching* was what "paid off." Insofar as teaching was concerned, most were prepared—if required to teach at all— to teach only graduate courses employing the going "professionalese" (shades of Molière's *Les Précieuses Ridicules*) and were more concerned with what was abstractly stylish than with studying directly how men went about earning their livings. For many of them (to quote Viner), "Economics is what economists do," which, in practice, meant that whatever they chose to do was accordingly economics.

In the 1960s, production functions enjoyed *le succès fou*. Later it was the Quantity Theory of Money, followed after a few years by Rational Expectations. More recently, Game Theory (in its third or fourth incarnation, including Experimental Economics), has become all the rage. I do not wish to suggest that my perception of economic theory involved no more than organizing the presentation of a mixture of Marshall-Joan Robinson-Chamberlin and Keynes and Musgrave-Ackley macroeconomics plus Hicks-Samuelson general equilibrium into quasi-integrated set of ideas, which could then be rather loosely jammed into what Clapham originally termed a "box of tools." This box contained intellectual implements to be applied selectively to policy problems and historical materials, sometimes referred to applied subfields. Indeed, shortly after I became chairman I invited G. L. S. Shackle, whose interpretation of Keynesianism was non-Hicksian, to spend a semester with us "to teach us (the faculty) about uncertainty," then emerging as a fashionable focal point. He came and gave two superb sets of lectures—one achieved fame as *The Years of High Theory*.

Thus began my relationship with Shackle, which flowered over the remaining years of his long life. I count him as one of my most insightful mentors, and I have selected in this collection a single, but to me very meaningful, piece referring to his work and to him. It is my review of his *Imagination and the Nature of Choice,* a book that he undertook, as he notes in the introduction, at my suggestion. I also thought that the links between economics and such disciplines as epidemiology, operations research, philosophy, political science, and sociology ought to be explored. In retrospect, I did not see the fascination of linkages between economics and very advanced mathematics (like chaos theory), which was particularly blind of me since I had had some awareness of the work done in mathematical statistics, but it surely did not register as it should have. In a tribute to Shackle I confessed that what I knew of uncertainty I had originally gotten from reading Knight; I was far less aware of Maynard Keynes's work on subjective probability (to say nothing of Savage's major contributions) than I should have been.

## How to Create a Journal

When I first arrived at Hopkins I discovered that the department, which was with but a single exception composed of mutually admiring colleagues, lunched together almost daily, but on Wednesdays we spent part of the time discussing annotations of books prepared by Edith Penrose, a Machlup *protégé* as well as something of a literary stylist. Machlup had managed to find funding to publish the *Economics Library Selection Lists,* which originally paid for and evaluated the books that the editor (then Dr. Penrose) selected. In time the funds grew thinner, and the books were donated by publishers seeking listings. After Dr. Penrose left Hopkins to take a readership at the University of London School of Oriental Studies, the publication had several fine editors, including Eileen Springer. About the time I left Hopkins, interest in it ceased, and the new chairman offered the publication to me as part of my "dowry" in my new "marriage."

During the period when I was departmental chairman, I had some discussions with Milton Friedman, then president of the American Economic Association, about the founding of a new type of academic economics journal, the *Journal of Economic Literature.* Insofar as I am aware, my name had been brought to Friedman's attention by both Fritz Machlup and George Stigler.

Friedman asked me what I thought should be included, and my plan involved commissioned survey articles on the broad developments in sub-fields, commissioned essays reflecting personal thoughts about the development of the academic economics profession and its literature, book reviews of about 200 to 225 books, and annotations of about 1,200 to 1,400 new books each year (the last being an expansion of the ideas explicit in the *Economics Selection Lists*). Friedman wanted the new journal also to offer reference to the contents of around 200 academic economics journals in a four-tiered classificatory matrix, as well as author-presented brief (100-word) abstracts of about one-quarter of the journals. The two ideas were merged, and my wife, Naomi, and I undertook the task jointly. Of course, we had the help of a small staff (including specifically a copy editor, as well as help from two of my then junior colleagues who supervised graduate students handling the classification of journal articles).

I had my own views about journal editing and remained managing editor for something just over 49 issues; these opinions were summarized in my valedictory issue and are presented in this volume. But it is pertinent to add to what I mentioned there. First of all, it was a splendid opportunity to get good scholars to undertake the kind of *refereed* expository studies that I relished.[13] It was a way to learn the high points about areas which I had no time to study. Many ideas about topics were my own, some came from the eventual authors, and I was ever alert to suggestions, particularly from professional colleagues like Machlup, Wilfred Prest, James Tobin, and William Fellner. One of my first ideas when I took up the editorship was to approach Anne Krueger about an article describing the going issues on balance-of-payment theory. When I told Wilfred Prest about Anne's willingness, he suggested that I seek out Geoffrey Harcourt in Adelaide to explain the lines of argument in the re-switching controversy between Cambridge-on-the-Cam and Cambridge-on-the-Charles. Others whom I contacted were: Jacob Mincer, to explain what he saw as the potential of the human capital approach to studying the operation of labor markets; Bruce Johnston on structural transformation of agriculture in developing countries; Eirik Furubotn and Svetovar Pejovich on recent adaptations of the theory of property rights; Raymond Mikesell and James E. Zinser on the savings function in developing countries; Gerald Goldstein and Leon Moses on urban economics as a field; Robert Ferber on consumer economics as a field; Robert Stern on international trade policy as it was actually developing; Edwin Burmeister on the neo-Austrian theories of capital; Ray Marshall on the economics of racial discrimination; Morton Kamien and Nancy Schwartz on innovation and market structure; Michael J. Greenwood on the literature on migration; E. Roy Weintraub on the tie between micro- and macroeconomics as seen in the literature; George M. von Furstenberg and Burton Malkiel on government and capital formation; Helmut Frisch on inflation theory; Ewald Nowatny on inflation and taxation; Gian Singh Sahota on theories of personal income distribution; Anthony M. Santomero and John J. Seater on the inflation-unemployment trade-off in the literature; Robert Clark, Juanita Kreps, and Joseph Spengler on the economics of an aging population; Robert Ferber and Werner Z. Hirsch on systematic social experimentation with economic policy; Amartya Sen on the literature about the welfare basis

---

13. Sir Zelman Cowan (mentioned earlier), when governor-general of Australia, was asked to give a tremendous number of speeches. Like mine, his interests are catholic, and I well recall his telling me how pleased he was to be able to use the talent of the Commonwealth Scientific Industrial Research Organization as his tutors. I was pleased to tell him that I had had a similar set of experiences, albeit not as preparation for my own speaking engagements.

of real income distribution; William S. Comanor and Thomas A. Wilson on advertising and competition; Jack Hirshleifer and John G. Riley on uncertainty and information; Ryuzo Sato and Rama Ramachandran on the impact of technical progress; Todd Sandler and John T. Tschirhart on the economic theory of clubs; and Bela Gold on size, scale, and returns. This list is not complete, but it does offer a good look at the kind of things that intrigued me.

I also commissioned a large number of personal reaction articles. Among these I remember with particular vividness two articles by Allan Meltzer (one on intermediation and the other on Keynes); two by Harvey Leibenstein; three by Paul Samuelson; one by Abram Bergson; one on Japanese Marxism by Thomas T. Sekine; one on disequilibrium and coping with uncertainty by Theodore W. Schultz, several on Keynes by Abba Lerner, G. L. S. Shackle, Alan Coddington, Walter S. Salant, and Richard Kahn; two by William Fellner on macroeconomic policy; one on rational expectations by Robert E. Lucas, Jr. and another by Brian Kantor; one by Joan Robinson giving her second thoughts on a personal research agenda; one by Gary Becker on altruism; one by Richard Stone commenting on Dennison's accounting for the growth slowup; and above all else two by Oskar Morgenstern: one on his complaints about modern economic theory and the other about his collaboration with John von Neumann. Perhaps the one I best remember for the tone it set was "A Curmudgeon's Guide to Microeconomics" by Martin Shubik.

Of course I enjoyed reading the annotations of virtually every economics book printed in English, as well as the reviews of about 15 percent of them, which I commissioned. Choosing which books to review (as well as the reviewers) bothered me a great deal. I told Friedman from the start that one advantage of the annotation process was that books that were not reviewed at length would still be described.

When we started the journal, the American Economic Association's secretary-treasurer was Harold F. Williamson of Northwestern University. He had "inherited" the job from George Washington Bell, who as treasurer had invested the association's funds most wisely. Williamson was a Harvard Ph.D., an economic historian of note (also the author of a popular text on American economic history), and he ran the American Economic Association's office with diplomatic skill. The association has a fascinating history. Founded in 1885, in its first incarnation its self-defined task was to stress the disadvantages of laissez-faire and the advantages of the responsible state. The early founders were strongly influenced by the Bismarckian Hohenzollern German experience. For their troubles, they were shunned by several of the leading American theorists. However, peace was made in the 1890s, and it was agreed that the association might discuss, *but would never endorse,* any legislative course of action. During the Vietnam War years the progressive wing repeatedly sought to get association endorsement for its anti–U.S. government position, but because of that phrase in the charter no vote could ever be taken—not that there was any reluctance on the part of the "peaceniks" to spend hours in useless debate at the annual meetings.

Over the years the association experimented with publications, and starting in 1910 it brought out the *American Economic Review;* in 1969 it brought out the much larger and more expensive-to-produce *Journal of Economic Literature;* and more recently it has produced a third journal, the *Journal of Economic Perspectives.* After World War II the association expanded considerably. By the early 1960s it was operating with a large surplus. The old political division could still be seen, and there was a tendency to alternate as president someone of a conservative and someone of a progressive persuasion. By and large, the crucible of conservativism was the University of Chicago and the crucibles of progressivism were Harvard and Columbia Universities. (I use the term *crucible* to indicate where the people tended to be trained—not necessarily where they taught. Tobin, one of the major progressives, taught at Yale, albeit he was Harvard-trained.) Michigan, Wisconsin, and Berkeley tended to be "progressive."

Of the various presidents of the association with whom I dealt as the journal's managing editor, there were a couple who, although distinguished scholars in one way or another, were simply difficult persons; many who were interesting and often quite helpful (Friedman, Wassily Leontief, John Kenneth Galbraith, Arthur Lewis, and Gardner Ackley—to name several who come easily to mind); quite a few who seemed to me to be intuitively brilliant (Kenneth Arrow, Friedman, Lawrence Klein, and James Tobin—to mention but four); and one who simply "wowed" me. That was William Fellner, a man with whom whenever I spent an hour I came away with an insight that I believed I would never have otherwise acquired. It was a quality I found in my father, in John Vincent Barry, in Richard Eggleston and Zelman Cowan, in Fritz Machlup and Simon Kuznets. Others who have had it, and whom I have not yet mentioned, were G. L. S. Shackle, Arthur Frank Burns, Shigeto Tsuru, Joan Robinson, Herbert Giersch, Harvey Leibenstein, and Alan Coddington.

Being a journal editor, particularly of a journal with a circulation well in excess of 23,000 copies, gave me a kind of entrée which was like a dream. My correspondence with different authors and reviewers was only a part of it;[14] the discussions about content and style often spilled over into all sorts of fields and interests. I enjoyed the job thoroughly, but I was always worried

---

14. My professional correspondence, of extreme bulk (my diligent secretaries found the filing system so useful that they were loathe to throw any letter out if they thought that at some time it could be retrieved [that took two minutes] and referred to), is in the special collections unit at the Duke University Library; it is divided between letters as the *Journal of Economic Literature* editor and all other professional letters.

that I was having too much fun, and that my liking for the personal contacts was numbing my editorial sensitivities. I decided that ten or eleven years was the maximum tenure that a founding editor should have (presumably non-founding editors should have shorter tenures). George Borts, managing editor of the *American Economic Review,* and I had both been appointed at the same time by Milton Friedman, and the other, more progressive, wing of the association may have wanted its turn. In any event, we both resigned (I stayed on until Moses Abramovitz, my own chosen successor as managing editor, had completed his term as president of the association).

There were several personal spin-offs from my editorship of the *Journal of Economic Literature.* During the early 1970s I organized (with the help of a Pitt colleague, Dr. Arnold Kroner), a "prestige giveaway" publication for the United States Information Agency, the *Portfolio on International Economic Perspectives,* which contained reprints of articles from a myriad of American magazines and journals, as well as selected reprinted book reviews. In the late 1970s Dr. Colin Day, then of the Cambridge University Press, asked me to edit (I suggested Professor Phyllis Deane as coeditor) the Cambridge Surveys of Economic Literature, which drew on many of the authors who had written survey articles for the *Journal of Economic Literature,* as well as others. The list of that series' books comes to over 20. I particularly recall talking with Mark Blaug about a book on methodology in economics, which I correctly predicted would be a best-seller. In recent years the Cambridge University Press has launched a second, companion, series, the Cambridge University Surveys of Economic and Political Institutions, with the first three books being a splendid review of the postwar German economy, *The Fading Miracle: Four Decades of Market Economy in Germany* by Herbert Giersch and two young associates (Karl-Heinz Pacqué and Holger Schmieding); a brilliant interpretation of the postwar Japanese experience, *Japan's Capitalism: Creative Defeat and Beyond,* by Shigeto Tsuru; and a speculative view of the U.S. economy as it enters the twenty-first century by Nicholas Spulber. I also took up editing for the International Joseph A. Schumpeter Society and the *Journal of Evolutionary Economics,* as well as the Great Economists of the Twentieth Century series for Edward Elgar, Publishers.

## My Research Interests in Recent Years

### Demographic Economics

I have already mentioned my work for Harvey Perloff of the Resources for the Future. He had asked me to write an essay on my perception of urban economic labor problems. From this there stemmed a conference at which a number of papers were presented. My essay was included as an appendix in that volume. Perloff then asked that I write a second essay outlining a policy prescription. Insofar as I can infer, that essay was a bust. Presented in the autumn of 1962, it had several themes, which were seen more as wrong than as premature. For one thing, I thought that structural unemployment was becoming a major concern, and that the federal government was going to be forced into becoming "the employer of last resort." For another thing, I was critical of the way jobs were classified, arguing that pigeonholing by the kinds of skills involved overlooked a much more basic problem facing the unemployed: what to do in order to maintain not skill classification, but wage-group classification. While there were other points relating to the relationship between economic and sociological categories, what I most remember was the misery I felt in November 1962 when Neil Chamberlain in kindly but firm terms dismissed my effort as a set of pipe dreams. Perloff did not publish that essay. Of course, by November 1963 Lyndon Johnson had become president, and he labored to create governmentally Wallas's Great Society, something that envisioned the government as the employer of last resort. But from the experience I concluded that trying to do work in urban labor problems, particularly by relying upon my knowledge of market institutions, was not going to be easy.

Much worried about the future of my research interests, I consulted Simon Kuznets, by that time already at Harvard. Simon's advice was somewhat delphic, but I decided that he thought that my having a better knowledge of demographic analysis would stand me in good stead were I to want to do work in public health or in urban economic analysis. Fortunately, as I have noted, I found at Pitt a congenial colleague, Edgar M. Hoover, who offered to tutor me (in the guise of our jointly taught course) in demographic economics. As a consequence my interest in labor moved from industrial relations to the institutional determinants of labor supply and the demand for aggregate product. He and I collaborated on several projects (which by the terms of intellectual trade made me the great recipient). Initially we were supported by a grant from the Planned Parenthood Federation, and although we were assured of complete intellectual freedom relating to our results, the federation leaders were clearly disappointed when our final report suggested that a diminution in the number of births would not be without serious economic consequences. After that, he and I undertook a study for the Agency for International Development concerning some hypotheticals as applied to Pakistan, where we purported to find that a reduction in the number of births could make Pakistan able to generate enough capital to meet its own developmental needs. Insofar as I recall, the Pakistanis were thrilled with our results; not because they had any intention of relying on their own capital for economic development (meaning increased per capita consumption), but rather because they saw a hope that they could spend more on their military.

Hoover and I differed slightly on one important assumption. He believed that fertility control programs would work in all sectors of the population. I thought that such programs, if officially favored, might well work best in just that portion of the population from which future entrepreneurs would come. My concerns about inadequate natality among the educated and social leadership probably were self-generated. The Holocaust gave me profound emotional fears that certain cultures, not committed to large families, would easily disappear, and that to the disadvantage of civilization as I knew it. This was also the view of Simon Kuznets, Harvey Leibenstein, and Julius Simon. In recent years, when the burden of an aging population seems to be upon us, there is more tolerance for the position we took than before. But our fears for refugees and our concern for having enough skilled workers has made all of us enthusiastic about easy immigration policies.

My work in demographic economics tended to focus more on the facts of increasing life expectancy than on the problems of reducing natality. I wrote several papers reflecting this concern. One point that stands out is that intellectuals have always seemed to have a predilection for encouraging the "unwashed" to limit their procreative propensities, a point I made in several different contexts.

### What about Macroeconomic Problems?

During the mid-1970s one of my colleagues at Pitt, Marina von Neumann Whitman, had seen considerable government service, and eventually became a member of the Council of Economic Advisers. When it came time for her to return to academia, I (probably along with many others) urged the appointment of William Fellner as her successor. I recall telling her sometime around 1972 that I had the impression that the Nixon administration was going to need someone with the reputation for probity, and that that was Fellner's long suit. (Fellner had known Marina from her infancy, and when the time came that I had to decide whether or not to print Oskar Morgenstern's essay on his own role in the creation of game theory, Fellner was the critical referee—particularly after he told me that he and John von Neumann had been engineering students together in Zurich, had disliked the lectures, and had between themselves decided to attend the economics courses. He offered the view that he, more than anyone else, knew von Neumann's span of interest in matters economic, and that "Johnnie would have granted every point *and more* that Oskar had claimed".) Whatever else, Fellner radiated personal integrity, broad scholarship, imagination, and careful generosity. When he went to the American Enterprise Institute (after his White House service), he offered me a regular spot as a contributor to his annual book of essays on macroeconomics.

In all, I wrote five essays for him before he died. The first was a survey of the debate about productivity measurement and change in which I sought to integrate my understanding of what productivity change involved on the microlevel with demographic changes. The second described the principal demographic changes that had been occurring since 1957 or so and that were all but unrecognized as late as 1980. The third dealt with popular expectations about the delivery of medical care, productivity gains in that sector, and why costs could not really be contained. The fourth dealt with expectations, tax policy, and regional (state) economic growth. The last dealt with what had been happening in the area of labor relations.

One theme that can be found in these essays is my view that the federal government usually achieved its policy objectives but generally was blind to the problems its success engendered. Shades of Willard Hurst's lectures: "what was the problem, what was the solution, and what problems did the solution engender?" Another theme is that certain forces, usually tied to personal expectations, could not really be thwarted for very long. One was the immigration of the ambitious poor from areas of stagnation to areas of opportunity; another was the desire for good quality, inexpensive goods and services.

Coming from the progressive state of Wisconsin I had been taught since childhood that central governments could and should exercise protective responsibility for those unable to handle the uncontrollable economic vicissitudes of their lives. To effect this purpose, governments had to have control over their tax base. For that reason, as a student I had great doubts about the long-run implications of free-trade policies. But during the 1980s it began to seem to me that the taste for good quality, inexpensive goods and services had become so general and so strong that trade restrictions were no longer politically feasible. My consequent worries about what to do about the tax base clearly emerged. The first instance was in a paper, deemed "politically incorrect" at the time, on what Giersch and others had been advocating, and the other was a series of books that bear my name as coeditor, but which really bear the organizational genius of Claude Barfield and Christopher DeMuth of the American Enterprise Institute. I should add that when in 1988 the University of Pittsburgh sought to celebrate its 200th anniversary, I asked Arthur Frank Burns, Lewis Branscomb (then the chief scientist of the IBM Corporation), Yotaro Kobayashi (president of Fuji-Xerox), and Jagdish Bhagwati (Columbia University) to prepare formal papers on the world integration of factor markets, and I was not only pleased with the result (also published by the American Enterprise Institute), but came to the conclusion that for political, but not necessarily for macroeconomic, reasons, the urge for free trade of both factors and products was proving to be irresistible. I still do not begin to fathom how national states can finance their social welfare programs if they have no control over the location of industry within *and particularly without* their borders. But true to the principles laid out for me by Shackle, the real measure of the greatness of man is his inventiveness, and I do not completely despair.

## The History of Economic Thought

On the first day of classes at Pitt in 1963, Asher Isaacs (whom I had never met) died suddenly in his office; I agreed immediately to pick up his required course in the history of economic thought in addition to my course on American economic history and my course in labor economics. Over the years I gave this two-semester course many times, not only because it seemed desirable to have the material taught to Ph.D. candidates, but also because I thought that all undergraduate students seeking economics honors degrees ought to know something about the crucibles of their cultural legacy.

In 1977 I began to be active in the History of Economics Society (I had been a founding member, but had taken no role). I helped Helmut Frisch organize an international meeting in Vienna honoring Joseph A. Schumpeter, and we agreed that I would present a paper on the evolution of Schumpeter's thinking about economic analysis. When I became president of the society, I used the opportunity to suggest that the study of what underlay the evolution of various types of economic thinking was a companion topic to the study of economic methodology. Several of my essays in this area are included in this volume. In general, my views have been that one can compare various approaches to the study of economic thought. Among these are approaches that build on differences in the Aristotelian-Aquinas legacy and the Talmudic-Aristotelian-Maimonides legacy, the former seeing scarcity of goods and services as the unique assumption of economic analysis, the latter seeing scarcity of goods, services, *and information* as the assumption at the core of the topic. I am also interested in three modern approaches to the topic, using the methods of Karl Pribram, Wesley Clair Mitchell, and Joseph Schumpeter as exemplars.

There is a story that Clare Boothe Luce, a convert to Catholicism, while serving as American Ambassador to Rome once lectured Pope Pius XII on the evils of communism; it is said that he replied with patience, "Madam Ambassador, I have always been a Catholic." The relevance of this anecdote is that I have always been a student of the history, including the evolution, of ideas, of cultures, and of institutions. I recall being asked whether I was a Schumpeterian or an institutionalist, and while I aver in an essay not included in this volume that the differences between the economic sociology of Schumpeter and of the Commons institutionalists are more talked about than real, I recall Richard Arena (of Nice) saying, "But you are a historian of thought. You are not allied with any school." As I was pondering, I realized that he was correct. I was raised in an environment that was both interested in and skeptical of the assertions made by any prophet preaching salvation-by-school; at times, however, I have inevitably envied "born-again economists." Like George Schultz, I have always wanted (but failed) to be as sure of anything as some economists are. I recall telling some academic colleagues that as I am a rather conventional Conservative Jew (a middle path between the Orthodox, who seek to preserve the customs of the Middle Ages, and the Reform Jews, who find most of the tribal identification rituals arcane and too quaint to be observed), I find my identification in my religious and national identifications, and I don't look for my significance in either my politics or even my professional alliances. I repeat: I recognize that, in truth, I accept myself as a historian of economic thought and institutions and I eschew generalizing and then defending ideologically what I find in my studies.

Perhaps it follows that my inability to identify my professional economic alliances is accompanied by a skepticism about just how truth is (or should be) identified. Even before Donald McCloskey summarized his position stressing that economics was not scientific truth so much as it was rhetoric, that is, the art of persuading, I had written in a review (actually cited by McCloskey) that economists were advocates, not true scientists or (I might add in retrospect) real evangelists. As advocates we tailor our arguments to the minds of our clients—for some empirical observation works best; for others it is the test of immanent criticism. For me the test which carries the most weight is some kind of congruity with my patristic (cultural) legacy, a legacy combining a traditional Jewish view that man should be compared to animals,[15] not to God; that the historical accounting unit is even more the family than it is the individual; that the greatness of America has been not so much its material wealth as the openness of its social structure; and that personal indifference is the greatest of human failings.

## Summing Up: The Importance of Teaching

My upbringing was in an academic household—one which stressed that the teacher has not taught until the student has learned. Early on the problems of

---

15. To have one's behavior compared to an animal's is among the least flattering things that can be done within the Jewish context. This point is particularly subtly made in Genesis 22:5, where a line is drawn between the moral levels of different kinds of men:

> [Abraham] said to his [two accompanying servants], "Stay here with the Ass while I and the boy go [to the top of Mount Moriah where the drama of the sacrifice of Isaac was to take place]."

The principal Jewish perception of sin is that the target appropriate for humans has been missed, rather than some venal or mortal offense has been posted to the individual's "divine credit balance."

teaching became involved in the framework of most of my value systems, systems which depended upon the concentration of the mind.[16] With this background I have had a profound respect for the places of memorized databases in one's mind. Indeed, much of the problem of early education is how to use the memorizing ability efficiently. One must memorize language, dates, philosophical concepts, theological truths, and even most emotional references. I was similarly impressed with the need to learn how to analyze. This was done by imitation: one memorized theorems and then tried them out on corollaries. One memorized others' efforts at generalizing and then experimented both on generalizing and on abstraction on one's own. In the end, one seeks to emulate neither Bacon's ant nor his spider, but Bacon's bee, "which selects its nectar carefully and processes it into sweet honey."

Another factor in my analytical process was a basic belief that one could not anticipate the uses to which one's teaching and writings would or could be put. Someone once wrote that a rational author would gladly trade 1,000 readers at the year of publication for 100 readers 10 years later, and a mere 10 readers 100 years later. Thus when my dissertation produced an idea that ended up in a major Australian High Court case, then appealed to the Law Lords of the Queen's Privy Council, I was flattered but I hardly believed that my having a star, much less a rising star, was certain. It is perhaps for this reason that much of my teaching and written work strived to be no more than "my level best" (to use the phrase of my Cardiff headmaster; getting "your level best" out promptly took priority over endless revision with a hope for the achievement of perfection).

It is within this context that I have become agitated about what we are teaching our best students. This is the concern expressed in the opening chapter of this collection, drawing upon the topic (and criticizing the conclusions) of Charles Snow's Reid Lecture on "The Two Cultures." Where Snow thought that science was the key to the future and that study of the past was a

---

16. I am wont to tell my students who doubt that nothing can be better for children than gentleness about my strongest memory of my mother (who died five months after the incident involved in this story). I recall coming home from first grade on a Tuesday in October 1929 and her asking me how well the reading was coming. I replied that I found it too hard—the other children could read the word on the card that Miss Scarseth (the teacher) held up, but I couldn't. She then said, "There are those who read with their eyes and those who read with their ears; you read with your ears and by Friday you will be able to read." I remember that Tuesday to Friday as a period of real horror. I was scolded; I was shaken; I was spanked; I was sent to my bedroom; but by Friday I could tell Miss Scarseth, when she asked me why I could read "phone" while no one else in the class could, "Because *ph, gh,* and *f* all make the same *f-sound.*" Mother, an experienced first-grade teacher, had no doubts about the need to make students governable before you could make them take pride in achievement. The conclusion is that with adrenalin one learns—with enough adrenalin one may well learn what had been impossible on Tuesday could become routine by Friday.

sort of dilettantism, I believe that one studies science to learn about things, but one must study the humanities to learn how men think and derive their conclusions from both the cultural legacies and their scientific and nonscientific observations. Of course, underlying my view is the conviction that economic principles are not in the Lavoisier/Priestly tradition of paradigmatic foundations. About virtually all economic propositions reasonable men can differ, largely because those propositions rest on empirical rather than purely logical foundations. These days, physicists are not as sure about their "laws" as they once were,[17] and I have always thought that economists were advocates, not "true scientists," whose work would always stand the test of truth. Some of my writings anticipated the direction, but not the integrated evidence and analytical beauty of Donald McCloskey's views about rhetoric.

I have been a university teacher for almost 50 years, and in that time universities have seemingly shed their commitment to explaining value systems in terms of civilizations. Such moves have seemed to me to be a pedagogical disaster. I have never believed that a student had to *accept* a system, but he surely had to *grasp* it. When I was younger, English departments were the guardians of culture. I always felt that the English culture was quite warped in several critical areas—indeed, pedagogy in the French Lycées and the German *Gymnasia* was better. But the English experience was the foundation of much American law; Protestantism and the Old Testament were the foundations of much American political theory; and Shakespeare was the architect of much of our language. In any case, these were the things that should be stressed in an undergraduate liberal education, and any education was incomplete if the student was inarticulate in both writing and speech.

During my three decades at Pitt I supervised well more than three dozen dissertational students. After a bit, I developed a system. Generally, each student took about six months to discover his/her topic, and thereafter he/she was to present about ten pages every fortnight for group criticism. The critics were required to say something, and it became apparent that blood drawn by any of them would be reciprocated when they had their turns to present something. Consequently, there was much behind-the-scenes mutual preparation, and the critics usually explained why they thought the author was on to something good. And, since the author had already incorporated many of their better points, he/she usually was. The system worked, and I not only enjoyed

---

17. During my time at Princeton University I had a brief interchange at a party with John von Neumann. He remarked that we had met once before, and in the course of our pleasantries he asked me what my "field" was. When I replied, "Economics," his reaction was to comment that it really was quite an advanced subject, ". . . more so, than physics, [perhaps]." I responded that his assessment ran contrary to common thought. And, as I recall, his final point, before turning to some other guest, was that economists realized how little they really knew about the foundations of their theories—not so the physicists, who thought little about such things.

those seminars immensely, but the speed with which dissertations were completed was unusual. As I recall, only one student never finished his dissertation. My view was that a dissertation was to be a professionally competent research job. If it managed to offer something truly original and correct it was to be published; otherwise not.

I was also stimulated by my undergraduate honors students. Undergraduates, particularly senior year honors students, put up with relatively little cant and even less useless repetition; boredom was shown by absence from class.[18] As time went on, however, I came to feel that my students were coming to class less and less well prepared. Eventually, I took to giving them my typed-up lectures just before the previous lecture so that they would be ready for discussion. In the discussions I tried to point out how my "potatoes" were cooked, and even if they were small they were still fresh (my father's phrase).

For over 45 years I was ready to join battle and argue that while there was likely some excellent reason to see just what was involved in "how people went about their daily lives making their living" by examining the problem from a wide variety of perspectives, the professional eye should never wander far from that "ball." When I no longer felt the fight either winnable or worth the candle, I realized that my retirement time had come. I retired at 70 with no significant regrets.

All of which brings me back to my opening thoughts. Why should one want to bring together a collection selected from over 40 years of writing? Let me eschew the obvious and shallow reasons. As I have noted, we study the past in order to study the evolution of the mind of man. And if it is true, as Protagoras wrote, that man is the measure of all things, and it is one's own mind that does the initial measuring, then how better to see the spark of one's own thought within the context of one's own patristic legacy than by tracing for oneself what one has believed—insights and blunders together.

---

18. My father used to say that bravery was so rare among his colleagues that its exhibition was always perceived as historic; students, however, spoke out. Toward the end of my years at Pitt, I became convinced that real bravery among my colleagues was still very rare, but that students no longer spoke out. I tried to encourage the latter to pursue the advocacy of their interests, but to no avail. It was not so with me; I recall in my senior year at high school my math teacher told me that I was the most arrogant student she had ever had, and she had been teaching nigh onto 30 years. My reply, as I have been recently reminded by a classmate who was there, was, "Mrs. Cowles: For a guy who's chosen last for every sports team and who hears those who have to carry him on their team groan, I tell you that my problem isn't arrogance; that just is not the word you're groping for." Perhaps my generation was not easy to handle, but we were diligent and articulate. (Indeed, I do not recall that my answer was treated as chutzpa so much as it was taken as an acceptable, sharp retort to an out-of-line aside. As I recall, Mrs. Cowles, aunt of my closest friend, had no trouble giving me the only B+'s I got in senior high school; her nephew was grateful for the C she gave him.)

# Part 1
# On Economic Literature
# and Literary Economics

CHAPTER 2

## Snow's *Two Cultures* Reconsidered:
## Why Study the Past?

*A liberal education is not an intermediate, but an end, product. The difficulty is that it has to compete with other end products like examinations to enter professional and graduate schools, to say nothing of trade professions like accounting. However, in this essay, written when I was close to retirement and organized as a criticism of Charles (Lord) Snow's famous Rede Lecture, I seek to persuade young economists to study the humanities and social sciences.*

*After identifying Snow's argument and Leavis's criticisms of it, I turn to the American university tradition (different from Oxbridge's) generally, and to education in economics, specifically. What follows is the story of the impact of the study of the economics of time-and-place context, largely forged in the decades between the two world wars, on the outcome of war materiel supply during the period 1942–45. My conclusion is that the quest for positivism and an attendant neglect of the study of the record of how decisions are made make for intellectual sterility.*

*This is an effort to generalize on what I now think is the task and purpose of a good education. It can be contrasted with Chapter 25, written in 1952–53, which, as I will note, I trot out as a quasi-conscious effort to show what my legacy had done for me when I was finishing my formal education.*

**The Problem of the Two Cultures: Scientific Economics
and/or Economic History**

The Two Cultures

It has been almost a commonplace that Sir Charles Snow delivered the BBC-commissioned Rede Lecture at Cambridge in 1959 (see Snow 1964). Entitled "The Two Cultures," it was a review of his life's experience, an experience which had offered him, a writer of conventional novels and essays, what he termed "a ringside view of one of the most wonderful creative periods of all physics" (1959, p. 1).

---

This chapter has not been previously published. The essay was offered as a lecture to the Pittsburgh chapter of the National Association of Scholars.

Obviously, what Snow was trying to accomplish was not only to urge greater communication between those who call themselves scientists and those who call themselves intellectuals, but to tilt the discussion towards the philosophers-intellectuals taking greater notice of scientific achievement. The repetition of such a word as 'intellectual' was, itself, considered churlish by some—early on he quotes G. H. Hardy, the mathematician, "Have you noticed how the word 'intellectual' is used nowadays? There seems to be a new definition which certainly doesn't include Rutherford or Eddington or Dirac or Adrian or me. It does seem rather odd, don't y' know" (Snow 1964, p. 4).

Just how churlish Snow's views were became part of modern British cultural history. In his effort to explain why scientists look at the world different from the way that the (literary) intellectuals do, Snow managed even to offend both. Snow (a sometime Fellow of Christ's College) was in due course vehemently (perhaps viciously) attacked by one of Britain's leading literary critics, Dr. F. P. Leavis, at the time the Cambridge University Reader in English and a Fellow of Downing College. He was also criticized by scientists such as Michael Yudkin, a Cambridge biochemist. Leavis gave the 1962 Richmond Lecture, an "in college," privately endowed essay; entitled "Two Cultures? The Significance of C. P. Snow," it contained an acerbic attack on Snow, opening with the sentences:

> If confidence in oneself as a master-mind, qualified by capacity, insight and knowledge to pronounce authoritatively on the frightening problems of our civilisation is genius, then there can be no doubt about Sir Charles Snow's. He has no hesitations.

The plane of Leavis's criticism continued downward. In the end, there was a court suit with F. P. Leavis involving defamation of character. Debates about what is smart, who is right, and does the phrase, "we die alone," mean anything apparently lead to charges of the use of semantic vitriol, with the barristers and the judges ultimately getting involved to their combined profit and embarrassment.

And it was not the humanists, alone, who attacked him. As I have noted, Dr. Michael Yudkin inveighed against him, as well. His essay, "Sir Charles Snow's Rede Lecture," was published with Leavis's aforementioned Richmond Lecture and a special Prefatory Note in 1962 in England and in America in 1963.

The whole conflict was analyzed by Professor Lionel Trilling, whose respect for Leavis was great (Trilling 1962). Yet Snow, albeit his case was poorly and probably erroneously put, was in some popular sense vindicated. Everyone agrees that there ought to be more communication between scientists and philosophers, but the burden for improvement is said to rest on the philosophers.

Possibly I should therefore know better than to consider combat, even mock-combat, on that same field of battle. Caution is hardly one of my stronger virtues; so I must hope that I can count on the reader's tolerance. Here, I want to apply what I thought Snow undertook to identify as the tension between the "forward looking scientists" (his phrase, meaning physicists and chemists) and the backward looking literary intellectuals (including historians of the modern era).

## Application of the Problem

It is frequently observed by young people that although potential employers advise them to get a "solid liberal education," when it comes to being hired, those who have detailed credentials in accounting and/or engineering not only get the jobs but also get well paid, to boot. Perhaps this observation should be amended so that if one has a "solid liberal education" *as well as* either detailed credentials in accounting and/or engineering one is likely to be preferred to one who lacks the "solid liberal education" background. Similarly, I find that my colleagues and I, when it comes to hiring or promoting, give only lip service to the virtues of cultural understanding, and particularly to the principle that we ought to be willing and able to teach cultural understanding. Like Hamlet and Snow, they think that the real things in this world do not "pertain to your philosophy."

What I propose to talk about this evening is the evolution of economics as a discipline, as a profession, and as a body of information, particularly as it has shed its earlier moral philosophy and its subsequent "solid liberal education" background and has substituted for the cultural fellowship they once offered a tight marriage to the "queen of the sciences." My thinking operates within the environment of the contemporary American university, and it focusses on the complementarities, supplementarities, and contradictions within the current, bitter, even devastating conflict between Charles Snow's "two cultures," found in modern economics. In the case at hand, it is the inherent conflict between scientific methods, stressing analysis at a point in time or space, and the less "rigorous" (meaning specific and formal) historical methods, stressing the general roles of evolutionary adaptation.

### The American University as the Context

The American *collegiate* tradition should be understood for all of the complicated things it is. Many writers, even to this day, claim to see its origin in Oxbridge, but they should know better. Our historically most elite universities have always had something of a Puritan, rather than a Cavalier, flavor to their purpose. Charles Webster has chronicled in his *The Great Instauration* the rise and fall of the Puritan experience at Oxbridge (Webster 1976 as well as my review: Perlman 1976); what he does not stress (but I have) is that Harvard and Yale (to say nothing of William and Mary, Columbia, and Princeton) were designed to train "problem solvers" as well as to keep "the brightest and/or best placed young men" on this side of the Atlantic. Occasionally, parents of the young men (as well as the American professors) developed "delusions of respectability," and urged that these colleges train their young to be gentlemen, but, almost invariably, there was on the immediate scene a flow of real Oxonians and Cantabrigians, each of whom was likely willing, able, and eager to remind those with these pretensions of the cultural (to say nothing of the social) verities.

True, Harvard and the others may have thought that they stressed "basic education," but the truth is that their young men were being prepared to become clergymen-social workers, lawyers, doctors, and the like; few of them expected to be gentlemen, or as we economists like to put it (in oxymoron fashion), "pure rentiers."

By the time we come to the epoch of the great "state-related" universities, such as North Carolina, Pennsylvania, Virginia, Michigan, and Wisconsin, emphasis on professional and professional-type training was clearly dominant (see Barber, William J. 1988 as well as my review: Perlman 1990). It was dominant (in my judgement, at least) for exactly the reason mentioned at the opening of this talk—occupational preparation and/or training paid off; those who had it rose to positions of responsibility and those who lacked it often suffered accordingly.

It is almost a commonplace that the prototype modern American university follows not the Cardinal John Henry Newman University College, but the Johns Hopkins University model, with the latter's emphasis on student brilliance, professorial specialization, and graduate training, particularly for scientific research. If its founding president was a generalist its second president was a chemist—incidentally, one of the discoverers of saccharine. One does not have to try hard to find literature explaining that the model for the Hopkins approach was the University of Berlin (of the 1840s, the 1880s, and beyond) and not either Oxbridge nor any of the other Berlin Continental universities during that same period. Harvard (under Charles Eliot), Columbia (under Nicholas Murray Butler), and Princeton (under Thomas Woodrow Wilson) all sought to give dual focus to the training their schools gave to young men. One side of their effort was the traditional medieval Continental tradition, as adapted by the Oxbridge; they insisted on a traditional variety of breadth (including a modernized version of the *trivium* (grammar, rhetoric and logic) and the *quadrivium* (arithmetic, geometry, astronomy and music)). The other was to touch on social problem-solving (as seen in the Puritan heritage) and contemporary science (including empirical observation). Whatever else, the fact is that by the 1950s, only at most four generations after the Hopkins mold had become something of a standard, post-graduate education became the touchstone for intellectual achievement; the collegiate baccalaureate degree was necessary but clearly no longer sufficient. What was needed more and more was graduate scientific education, a mode that increasingly focussed on abstraction. It was, to use Snow's phrase, "forward- rather than backward-looking." Until the late 1950s Hopkins still required evidence of cultural breadth among its PhDs; thereafter, specialization was enough.

*The Two Cultures in Economics*
Among the first professional lecturers in economics were Thomas Robert Malthus (who taught at an "academy" organized by the British East India Company) and Nassau Senior (who was the first Drummond Professor of Political Economy at Oxford; he was reelected to the then five-year chair about two decades later). One can mention others, but in the early years of the academic discipline of economics, the emphasis was on the Malthusian split between (1) models (of which the first edition of his *Essay on Population* is a splendid early example) and (2) recognition of empirical observation (of which the later evolution of his population work and his *Principles of Economics* are also fine examples). Senior, an unusually well-read man, in his early lectures to the Oxford undergraduates talked in terms of abstract principles (akin to models), but in his professional life he was regularly a member of Royal Commissions and his empiric knowledge of the details of English cotton-spinners' lives is ample evidence that in adult practice, "principles were not enough."

As I do not wish to devote time at this point of this evening's talk to a discussion of the polarization of economics between those who were in the tradition of Cartesian (usually mathematical) models/graph displays and those in the tradition of Francis Bacon's scientific empiricism, let me pause only to mention that it was the redoubtable Alfred Marshall whose appointment to the University of Cambridge signalled the full "coming of age" to the economics discipline. It took him more than a decade to achieve his goal, the tripos in economics. The time as well as the politicking required is not part of my story. What is, however, was his fight to keep economic history in the tripos. William Cunningham, a King's College (London) professor who established economic history as a separate academic discipline, did battle with Marshall, who, at least in his arguments, argued persuasively that without the economic history component, the economics tripos would likely become arid, even sterile (Groenewegen 1988).

It is commonly said (and believed by many, including myself) that the

Oxbridge undergraduate economics training remains superior to virtually all American undergraduate economics training. This situation doubtless exists for many reasons, including factors like the quality of the students involved as well as a commitment to undergraduate tutoring and the like; but what I am really saying is that those who hold this view just happen to like the desired product. An Oxbridge undergraduate economics training involves some of the things which Snow thought were impediments to the solution to his question about the two cultures. The Oxbridge types are supposed to know humanities as well as science.

In America, our undergraduate economics training goal has increasingly become a "head-start" program for post-graduate studies, the market smiling most favorably on those that are scientific. That is so because there is a virtually universal admission that an undergraduate degree is precious little vocational preparation. It may be one of the better ways to spend one's time until admission to a graduate economics department, or more likely a law school, is available (Barber 1988; Perlman 1990).

But, if a need for post-graduate education became the rule, just what that post-graduate education was to be become, by the 1880s, the operative question. At Hopkins in the 1880s the fight was between the careers of its brilliant professor of astronomy, Simon Newcomb, and its entrepreneurial associate professor of economics, Richard T. Ely. Newcomb saw economics developing as a set of formal (meaning logical, and therefore, mathematical) constructs which could be used to understand processes; the concepts of stock and flow, often attributed to Yale's Irving Fisher, came to Fisher (as he dutifully recounted) from Newcomb. Ely, by way of contrast, wanted students to master the empirical, including the cultural-moral (for this read 'ethico-sociological') context surrounding the explicit economic question. It was, as I mention to tie my points together, an anticipation of the conflict between Snow's two cultures; and the academy came to belong to Newcomb and those who shared his views. Why?

Newcomb and Fisher were possibly abler men; it is also true that what they set out to do was less complicated, and perhaps for that reason, too, they were more successful. In any event, Ely left Hopkins and went to Wisconsin, where in time he attracted two of his Hopkins students, John R. Commons and Edward Alsworth Ross, who in time devised what they called "an institutional" approach to the study of economics. That institutional approach is one in which historical facts are assembled (as in the original Baconian tradition), then sorted (the catchy Wisconsin phrase was "fearlessly winnowed and sifted"), and from them generalizations are derived. With these generalizations it was possible to devise political, legal, and even more basic juridical constructs capable of resolving social tensions and, in time, creating new facts, facts more to the economists' preference.

Wisconsin institutionalism depended upon "episodic empiricism"; that is, their data were court cases involving analysis of the evidence submitted and the evolution of the judgments that followed. Whatever else, their findings seemed fuzzy, and if they produced legislation, it was not hard to argue that legislation was not scientific and was something which should be left to lesser minds. Theirs was not the only institutional approach; there were others, some good and some truly bad. I think one of the better ones was the "quantitative empiricism" developed by Wesley Clair Mitchell. His data were originally the changing prices of gold (in dollars) over decades of time, but he stretched his analysis to develop a most elaborate set of definitions and constructs describing the nature and, eventually after a great deal of careful pondering, the spectrum of likely causes of business cycles. Mitchell dealt in numbers, although those who know how he arrived at them will be the first to insist that he did not see anything precise about them.

Mitchell believed that scientific economic theory, as it had developed, was, at best, a set of idiosyncratic personal explanations for various institutional (that is, contextual) changes. He was indefatigable in his research efforts and, in his striving, for quantitative relevance and accuracy. His analytical tools were seemingly unsophisticated—as though he was ready to socialize with the "Queen of the Sciences," but neither to live with her nor surely to marry her. Mitchell, every bit as cultured a man as has been seen in the economics profession, was not enamored of scientific abstraction; yet, insofar as economics deals with quantifiable concepts, he is more responsible for their precise development than any one else.

By way of contrast to the Wisconsin economic history tradition, there was the Irving Fisher tradition; it focussed much less on the context of historical events and more on the romance with that "Queen." In the period of my own career the progeny of that romance, particularly those who begat Paul Samuelson and those whom he begat, swelled their numbers. Samuelson, himself, as a begat and as a begetter, stressed the tradition of the romance (to use his phrase, Mathematics is not [as Josiah Willard Gibbs, Fisher's teacher, had said] "a language;" rather, mathematics is [to use Samuelson's own phrase] "language, [itself]." Samuelson, the text book writer, however, continued to offer both cultures.

In any event, during the period when I was educated as a professional economist, there was internecine war between the "scientific theorists" and the historico-sociological contextual "institutionalists." The battle went nominally, but not easily, to the swift; giving an indication of the way the Snow-Leavis battle was to settle, Cartesian scientific economics has emerged as the victor over historico-empiricism.

Yet, all of this is surely not to admit that the war really was lost. The "institutionalists" created modern national income analysis, a basically contextual device, which became the basis for the rapid and thorough conversion of the American economy to war-time material manufacture during the years 1942 through 1945.

What happened there is worth a summary. Simon Kuznets, one of Mitchell's students and collaborators, sketched out in the early 1930s the principles of modern national income accounting in a commissioned article for the Seligman *Encyclopaedia of the Social Sciences*. Through fortuitous circumstances, his approach was grasped by Paul Webbink, administrative assistant to Senator Robert M. LaFollette, Jr. Webbink persuaded the Senator, the Senator the Congress, to direct the new (post-1933) Secretary of Commerce to implement the sketch. The Secretary repaired to Mitchell for advice, and Professor Kuznets, working part-time (one day a week) with two erstwhile students, Robert Nathan and Milton Gilbert, published in 1935 the accounts for 1932, 1933, and 1934.

Kuznets went on to other things, including the picking up of an uncompleted study of capital formation in the United States.

In 1942, Robert Nathan, who headed the planning committee of the War Production Board, asked Kuznets to join him in Washington. Together they mapped out a strategy for converting the American economy to a war-machine; the story of that effort is remarkable because they won the strategic war although in the process they were personally repudiated on the tactical level. The delicious details of that experience I have recounted elsewhere; it is not relevant to our story, this evening (Perlman 1987).

By 1946 the "institutional"-approach was firmly established in the Department of Commerce, albeit not to Kuznets' personal satisfaction. Kuznets thought that the Department's analysts had carelessly reformulated his system to accommodate the contemporary Keynesian model, and in the process had frozen it. He attacked their work in 1948 and was never reconciled to what Gilbert and others had done.

Thus, the Mitchellian quantitative empiricism got whatever cachet the historical method achieved within economics. The episodic empiricism approach was dwarfed by the other's achievements. And that was perhaps a pity, since quantitative empiricism could (and tended to) attract what Francis Bacon called "empirical ants who collect and collect and collect." Mitchell and Kuznets, to mention but the two whom I have already identified, were, themselves, not only historically and comparatively multi-cultured, but they decried excessive attention to sheer number-crunching at the expense of future blue-print drawing.

Let us return, for a moment, to the other camp, the "scientific theorists." They pursued their goals, and by the late 1930s were developing new forms of math which seemed applicable to economic problems. Ordinal ranking analysis was complemented by cardinal ranking analysis. Traditional linear algebra incorporated more and more matrix algebra; and linear programming, itself a major breakthrough, was succeeded by dynamic non-linear programming. Von Neumann's adaptation of the theory of binary numbers to the principle of the magnetic core led to the high speed computer which could (and did) process not only vast amounts of quantitative data, but which could (and did) solve lengthy purely mathematical problems.

In any event, by the early 1960s, the "scientific theorists" had developed a magnificent set of analytical tools, the complexity and subtlety of which even dwarfed what Samuelson's generation had known. This dwarfing was at once both a scientific achievement and an economic problem. It was a scientific achievement because it permitted a wide-scale graduate-student level analytical sophistication far beyond what all but the most prescient scholars in the 1940s had dreamed feasible for themselves, alone.

But, it has become (in my view) an economic problem because its very sophistication requires the allocation of so much time that the graduate students, seeking to complete their professional training before they are out of their late twenties, have had to eschew first a bit, and then almost all, training in the contextual historic-social institutionalism. Snow's dilemma is upon us.

## The Two-Cultures Problem in Our Universities, Generally, and in Economics, Specifically

I have thus suggested how and why economics has tended to become "scientific," rather than jointly "scientific" and "historico-institutional-cultural." I have indicated that whatever else, the principal cause was the economic problem of too many things (varieties of knowledge) for too few resources (time). One could learn formalism, even if with difficulty, over a few years' time. To develop an adequate historical base took much longer; it also took a great many different skills.

We come now to the operative question; is it possible to set up a curriculum which is "balanced" between analytical rigor and historical knowledge?

From an analytical standpoint, there are exogenous considerations. First, the schooling process can be reconsidered so that the length of training time (that is, really, the number of hours) can be expanded. Precollege students in most industrialized countries do not work the 40-hour, 5-day week. In France they work closer to the 45-hour, 5½ day week. They do not have as much vacation time, and what they do have is spread out somewhat more evenly. So one solution is to require more time.

Another is to accept the principle that educational tracking is, if not socially desirable, functionally necessary. There is, it seems to me, little problem about what each track requires, and relatively little problem about how candidates for each track can be initially (and, if necessary, remedially) identified. What is the big problem is the general or popular will to do so. But, what is not done generally or popularly can still be done, as, indeed, it is. In an open society like ours, there are always new groups who are seeking excellence and achievement by pursuing through long hours and "survival of the most adaptive" individual success. Once, as one of my friends at Princeton told me, the brightest boys were "young Jews;" now, she tells me, they are "Oriental girls."

What we do not ourselves train for completely can still be ours. The inflow of ambitious, very hard-working immigrants (students and others) may serve to mitigate the general results of over-specialized training.

But, at best, these are not the preferred solutions to the problem. Rather, it would be more desirable to reassert the necessity for those whose training specializes in either the "scientific culture" or the "historico-institutional culture," to have training in the other, as well.

What that actually means for economists is that mathematics is really what Gibbs called it, "a language." But it should be necessary for economists to know other languages, as well, and I do not mean only English. Knowledge of language is not simply knowledge of semantics (although that capacity should never be down-played); it should be knowledge of differing cultures. Not all cultures are equally useful for our purposes; whatever may be the great attraction of Asian cultures, knowledge of them is not a substitute for knowledge of European cultures. A complement, surely; but not a substitute. Knowledge of philosophy is not a substitute for knowledge of religion;[1] again, a complement, surely; but not a substitute. A capacity for individual imaginative experimentation must be shaped; so, too, must a capacity for individual imaginative reflection. In practice what I mean is that the design of experiments under supervision should be accompanied by tutoring on what one has found and to where it leads.

Snow's point was that the great challenge of our time is the integrating of the two cultures on terms putting the burden on the historians. I think that his point is generally regarded as true (as well as specifically true for economists), but that that will have little effective meaning until it is done in each of the disciplines, generally, and among economists, explicitly. What Snow saw as the general scholarly problem, one affecting the sciences and the humanities, I suggest is perhaps the major specific problem for economics. But, he puts the burden on the wrong side.

---

1. For those who worry about such things, I am not a natural-born decrier of John Henry Newman's views on the university as being a center for all knowledge. Indeed, if I wanted to be a purist (a luxury not many of us can afford), I would argue that drawing a line between religion and the state can in the last analysis only be the creation of a mirage. As I am not a purist, I aver that one pretends to draw such a line, because "without it" tests on our tolerance have proven over time to be too great to be borne. Nonetheless, I am always shocked to hear philosophers (who ought to know better) decry any knowledge of theology.

All of the foregoing, aside from the facts (something others call trivia), is so well-known that it has become a commonplace. But as such it gets only lip-service. My colleagues in economics, like the potential employers mentioned at the beginning of this talk, call for academics with perspective, breadth, and a cultural orientation. But, when it comes to hiring and promoting, what counts is whether the candidate is on the way to becoming a recognized scientific specialist—whether his/her name and articles are in the leading "esoteric" journals. In other words, in spite of our cry that we admire all scholarship, the only kind that we hire is specialized—indeed, the more, the better. When we promote, we count not so much teaching as writing, and not writing, as such, but writing in the "leading ten journals." As the Founding Managing Editor of one of those journals, I know the others well. Mine has been the eclectic journal; the others have become increasingly specialized and formal.

I suggest that the mission of this organization is to take up the Snow-Leavis battle, or at least the battle that each thought he was fighting. What we need to consider less are our ideological differences about what we think; what we need to consider more are why and particularly how we think what we do. I believe that one can abstract from ideology only about as much as one can abstract from life; but I also hold that it is possible for me to be interested in others' ideology even without accepting or rejecting it. More basic than ideology may be methods of thinking, since what one believes may well be the result of how one defines problems, selects proofs, and the like. Thus, to put my whole talk in a nutshell, one should not try to smooth over the differences between scientific economic analysis and the historico-institutional-cultural method of economic history; one should accept the differences for what they are and work both sides of the economics "avenue of thought." The crisis we face is not so much a battle of ideology as a battle of inter-cultural communication. And the battleground is not simply a matter of separating truth from fallacy, but the more difficult one of identifying the foundations of wisdom and appointing people who are wise.

It seems like such an obvious point that I apologize again for raising it. On the other hand, however obvious that point is, it is arcane if we perceive academic excellence in terms of cultural specialization and infinite subdivision.

REFERENCES

Barber, William J. [ed.] (1988). *Breaking the Academic Mould: Economists and American Higher Learning in the Nineteenth Century.* Middletown, CT: Wesleyan University Press.
Leavis, F. R. [1962] (1963). *Two Cultures? The Significance of C. P. Snow:* With an Essay on Sir Charles Snow's Rede Lecture. New York: Random House.

Groenewegen, Peter D. (1988). "Alfred Marshall and the establishment of the Cambridge Economics Tripos," *History of Political Economy*. 20 (Winter), pp. 627–67.

Perlman, Mark (1976). Review of Webster, Charles. *The Great Instauration*: Science, Medicine, and Reform, in *Journal of Economic Literature* 14 (1976), 1289–91.

——— (1987). "Political Purpose and the National Accounts." In Alonso, William A. and Starr, Paul. *The Politics of Numbers*. New York City: Russell Sage for the National Committee for Research on the 1980 Census.

——— (1990). Review of Barber, William J. [ed.] (1988). *Breaking the Academic Mould*: Economists and American Higher Learning in the Nineteenth Century, in *History of Political Economy* (Spring).

Snow, C. P. (1976). *The Two Cultures; And A Second Look*. An Expanded Version of the [1959] 'Two Cultures and the Scientific Revolution'. Cambridge: Cambridge University Press.

Trilling, Lionel (1962). "Science, Literature, and Culture," *Commentary*, vol. 33, pp. 461–77.

Webster, Charles (1976). *The Great Instauration: Science, Medicine, and Reform*. New York: Holmes & Meier.

CHAPTER 3

# On the Editing of American Economic Journals: Some Comments on the Earlier Journals and the Lessons Suggested

*The four parts of this essay deal, respectively, with (a) a synoptic history of the early economics journals in the English-speaking world, stressing why and how they came into being first in America and then in Britain; (b) some generalizations about the supply and demand characteristics for professional journals; (c) an essay on varieties of the editor's role; and (d) my views of the "have been" and "could be" roles of such journals. I was gratified afterward to see that John Hey, editor of the prestigious* Economic Journal, *changed his journal in the direction I had had in mind.*

In many ways the end of the American Civil War and the following decade of Reconstruction date the emergence of that new intellectual-social order which most of the world now recognizes as American. While one should resist the temptation of facile "painting with a broom," I would argue that the same national forces which produced modern economic data collection and analysis as worked out initially by the Census and the Treasury and eventually by the federal (Department of Labor's) Bureau of Labor Statistics and even the (Department of Commerce's) Bureau of Economic Analysis also worked to create the other, more academic, side of professional economics. Whatever else these forces were, they included the identification of a set of social phenomena which economists defined as the heart of their professional concern, a knowledge of a "package" of constructs and data sets which they asserted that journeyman status in the profession required, and a set of quasi-formal tests which aspiring applicants for professional status had to "pass."

The teaching degree was enhanced, and, following the German model, became synonymous with what had been the research degree (PhD). This new "license" required the writing (and occasionally) the publication of a scholarly tome (a book, if you will). But, as time was to show, the publication of books (if not ever abandoned) was too cumbersome and time-consuming to permit

---

*Economic Notes* 20 (1991): 159–72.

the adept statement of a view and even demonstrate one's intellectual adeptness. The profession did the obvious thing, it looked for, discovered, and appropriated a supplementary medium, professional economic journals. There had been in the seventeenth century English tradition weekly and monthly journals of opinion of which the 1712–14 (intermittently) *Spectator* [papers] are a good example. In time, some of these journals of opinion refocussed, but quite possibly because of the idiosyncratic experiences of some of the leading figures on the American scene. It has been canon to suggest that the 1880s was a decade when the academic American economics profession seemingly looked to Imperial Germany for intellectual leadership. It found not only established research degrees in the profession; it also found the PhD's most obvious by-product, the professional journal. Schmoller's *Jahrbucher* served as the chronicler of the German economists' thinking; it was, in and of itself, of professional interest, but unlike such earlier belles-lettres-publications-with-a-policy-twist like the British liberal *Edinburgh Review* or the British *Tory Fortnightly Review,* or even eclectic, if idiosyncratic, quarterlies like the *North American Review,* the *Jahrbucher* aspired to be scientific even as much as it aspired to be wise.

All of this canon has been laid out by a brace of such eminent economists and historians ranging from Joseph Dorfman (1949) to William Barber and Associates (1988). They note that the professional study of economics in academia became institutionalized by name in the United States during the 1880s and 1890s, when there emerged a body of ideas, sets of data, and methods of analysis which became a common requirement for those who described themselves as economists. That is not to say that there was necessarily much agreement with regard to the priorities or even the rightness or wrongness of these three elements, but the important thing is that economics came to differentiate itself from moral philosophy (its historic source) and from anthropology, history, political science, social psychology, and sociology (its epistemological siblings). Instead if anything, the discipline was intent upon discovering how its unique, if prosaic, personality could be put to recognizable public and certainly private use. Economics had not yet become visibly involved with its present romances with matrix algebra, set theory, and today's leading charmer, symbolic logic. Indeed, in the 1880s and 1890s, its affinity for the calculus was kept largely hidden, and was an indulgence which was permitted only to cranks of one sort or another. Problems of a differentiated rhetoric were generally in the future; what was in the then present were the age-old concerns about what was going on, why, what could be done about it, and how. What should also be realized is that the speed of this professionalization of economics was remarkable not only from the standpoint of changes in university curricula, but even more by the rapid proliferation of professional economics journals, perhaps established in the mold of Schmoller's *Jahrbucher.* These journals gave more than mere place-focus to the new subject. In their selection of authors and much later their specialized rhetoric, their editors shaped the thinking of academic economists.

## A. A Synoptic History of Some of the Earlier Economics Journals

The first of these new journals was the *Quarterly Journal of Economics,* which appeared in 1886 at Harvard. The *Political Science Quarterly* appeared the following year in 1887 at Columbia University. *The British academics were to emulate them;* Marshall and Edgeworth established the *Economic Journal* in 1891.

1892 was the bumper year for the appearance of economics journals in America with the establishment of *The Annals of the American Academy of Political and Social Science* at the University of Pennsylvania, the *Yale Review* (old series) in New Haven, and the *Journal of Political Economy* at the University of Chicago.

This sudden increase of space available to academic economists resulted, in my judgement at least, in amazingly few dull or bad articles. Part of the explanation is that what was new was mostly the *venue;* what had already been established was the form, with the old venue being publications like the *North American Review.*

Although James Laurence Laughlin, a junior faculty member at the time, was apparently the one who organized the resources which produced the *Quarterly Journal of Economics* at Harvard, it was Charles F. Dunbar who became the pace-setting editor from 1886–1896.[1] At Columbia the responsibility for its new journal, the *Political Science Quarterly,* was spread among several men; and the new journal, then as even now, reflected the diversity of their disciplines as well as the spectrum of underlying policy opinions.

The other pace-setting journal was also founded by Laughlin, who had left Harvard shortly after his founding of the *Quarterly Journal of Economics* to go into the insurance business, from whence he soon departed to occupy the chairmanship at Cornell. From there he soon moved to the chairmanship at the new department at the University of Chicago, where he immediately founded the *Journal of Political Economy,* of which he remained its editor until 1916! As for some of the other new journals, one can report that most responsible for Pennsylvania's *Annals* . . . were Edmund Janes James and Simon Patten, and the two who most strongly shaped the *Yale Review* were Arthur

---

1. Dunbar was succeeded by Frank W. Taussig, who remained editor until 1937.

Twining Hadley and Henry Farnham (although Irving Fisher did serve later on the editorial board). These new academic editors were men of imagination, and relying on several already seasoned authors they commissioned and/or accepted articles offering much information, a variety of analytical methods, and, in many instances, significant felicity of style.

The new academic professional organization, the American Economic Association, published regularly, but its prototype was the very long essay or, the dissertational short book. It was not until 1910 that the Association created its own quarterly journal. Yale took the occasion to transform the *Yale Review* from its focus on economic topics to something more along the lines of belles lettres.

If one peruses the early issues of each of these journals, it is clear that discussions of policy issues predominated, with each journal titled to the mix favored by the editor. Dunbar was a moderate, as between laisser-faire and governmental regulation of the economy. Laughlin was not a moderate on that score; moreover he was vitally committed to a "sound money" (anti-inflationary) preference. Yet, what may have given them their initial distinctive influence (which came quickly) was the professional quality of certain of the substantive published debates, on monetary, tax, or trade policies.

Yet, before I proceed I should stress that the point that I make must be put into carefully-stated perspective. Noting how the tilt began towards abstraction and "scientific economics," it is true that the great mass of articles until well after World War II were largely descriptively devoted to problems of public policy. The *Quarterly Journal of Economics* and the *Journal of Political Economy,* if admittedly the pace setters for American professional economics, traditionally devoted most of their space to what we would now call normative discussions about questions of policy.

No small part of the reasons for the mix may well have been the personal interests of their creative editors, the now all-too easily forgotten Charles Dunbar, long-time architect of economics at Harvard, and Laughlin who has been described by Professor Dorfman as the voice of conservative reaction, but who was nonetheless the protector of Thorstein Veblen at Chicago. There may have been other factors as well—Harvard has had a Puritan tradition of discussing publicly organized social solutions for social problems. Indeed, that consideration has not only long given a peculiar cachet to Harvard's charisma, but it serves to contrast Laughlin's and Chicago's long-established emphasis on private (i.e. market) solutions to social problems (which was originally seen as in some way tied up with the business practices of Chicago's great benefactor) with the established harvardian "on-the-one-hand, and then on-the-other-hand approach" of reasonableness as superior to pure ratiocinative logic.

Fairly early on, however, Dunbar came to discover an editor's dream author, John Bates Clark, an academic who had taught at Carleton College (Minnesota), Smith and Amherst Colleges (Massachusetts) and who much later taught at Columbia University. Bates Clark wrote regularly (better than one major article per year). Each was long, original, and usually provocative; moreover his articles were eminently readable, and he did not hesitate to engage in gentlemanly (but firm) dueling. His foil turned out initially to be an Austrian provincial professor, Eugen von Boehm-Bawerk (Innsbruck), at a time previous to the beginning of his great academic cum public servant career in Vienna. The contest dealt with matters of economic *theory* (not *policy*). It was their varying views on the true nature of *capital,* something which both Clark and Boehm-Bawerk believed had been ill-handled by the classical school.

After a bit, Francis Ysidro Edgeworth, the editor of the new *Economic Journal* discovered and nurtured another editor's dream author, Irving Fisher the Yale *Wunderkind* (who was the protege of the great American mathematical physicist, Josiah Willard Gibbs), to join the battle of which Dunbar had been the initial impresario. Fisher not only wrote regularly and delivered on time but as a rhetorician he seemed unusually able to convert the battle to a contest on the field of his preferred choice. While Fisher initially attacked Bates Clark, he managed somehow to redefine the issue from Clark's ambiguous, if rich foundation to some crystal-clear points for which he established priority in the discipline. Discussion of statics and dynamics was subordinated to discussion of stocks and flows. Methods of defining and then measuring physical capital and human capital came to replace Bates Clark's interest in expanding Locke's labor theory of value to explain (and probably justify) the legitimacy of the capitalist's role in and share of the economic process.

About a decade later the battle, again involving Clark, Boehm-Bawerk and Fisher, was resumed. However, two new would-be champions emerged: Charles Tuttle (Wabash University) and Frank Fetter (Stanford, Cornell, and later Princeton). Afterwards, the battle lapsed for almost a quarter of a century, but emerged again in the 1930s when Kenneth Boulding, Frank Knight, Friedrich Hayek, Fritz Machlup and Nicholas Kaldor exchanged thrusts. In the 1950s the battle was taken up once more—this time principally between the intrepid, impatient Joan Robinson (University of Cambridge) and the good-humored, if less than fully patient, Robert M. Solow (Massachusetts Institute of Technology).

Elsewhere in this issue I have provided a lengthy summary of the way that Dunbar and later Taussig used the debate on the nature of capital to turn the academic spotlight on their *Quarterly Journal of Economics,* and how Edgeworth successfully sought to join the battle, using Fisher (Perlman 1991). That I discuss this lengthy episode reflects my judgement that it made their journals the pacesetters in the period of their editorships. I could, without difficulty, show how then as well as in the 1930s the editor of the *Journal of Political Economy* managed to do much the same with the series of articles by Kenneth Boulding, Frank Knight, and, Friedrich Hayek disputing capital theory, and how the editor of the *Economica* and other journals sought to get into the act much as Edgeworth had tried to use Fisher's comments at the end of the last century.

As this article is not on the evolution of capital theory, I will say little about the substance of that attraction-getting debate; yet, it is relevant to comment on the principles involved, and how they shifted the discourse to what is currently the "preferred tenor" of journal articles—that between generalization and abstraction, the tilt is increasingly towards the latter. The wide-ranging debate on the nature of capital theory, carried on in an informed analytical way, used in a barbed way the language of the leading literary/public policy journals, for example Boehm-Bawerk first seeming to bow low in respect to Clark's style, but then to comment *hardly sotto voce* that scientific arguments cannot be won by the clever use of metaphor. That play remains to this day a sign of disengagement (cf. the controversy over the Donald McCloskey–raised "storm" about rhetoric!).

Competition between these journals led to their refocussing. Two in particular, refused to focus predominantly on economic analytics. As I have already suggested, Columbia's *Political Science Quarterly* always took an eclectic view of what its focus ought to be, and moved quickly to the practice of political economy as seen through the science of politics, and Pennsylvania's *Annals* moved to special issues focussed on a very large spectrum of topics, each topic being handled by different writers commissioned to give their explicit views.

The *Yale Review* suffered somewhat from a peculiar form of editorial schizophrenia. Fisher, the sharpest analyst at Yale, seemed to reserve his choice pieces for the British *Economic Journal,* with Henry Farnham and Arthur Twining Hadley pursuing their interest focussing on the traditional teaching views of economists and policy choices. The American Economic Association, having tried for over two decades to develop a research outlet which would involve the bulk of the membership, decided, that the commissioning of selected studies was not the appropriate avenue, and, to establish a new journal, the *American Economic Review* reflecting differences of economic opinion. Farnham and Hadley abandoned the claims of the *Yale Review* to economists' job-territory. While their decision probably made sense, a quick perusal comparing the contents of the *Yale Review* (old series) and the new *American Economic Review* will show that the quality of the articles did not improve, although the drainage basin from which the new American Economic Association's review drew its pieces was far larger.

I turn now to the objective factors which underpin the editor's problem as a merchandiser.

## B. Factors Shaping the Demand and Supply
## Characteristics of Economics Journals

It takes no great wit to realize that an editor has to be concerned with the demand for and the supply of his product. If the demand stems from a sub-disciplinary or an "interest-oriented" group (as in sound money, pro-labor union, anti-monopoly), any editor is likely to play to themes interesting that group. Playing to themes is, as Professor Slichter of Harvard used to say about public speeches, "give them something they expect, but also something they did not expect; and give them something that they will like, but also give them something which will anger them." Too much of what is expected and liked will lead to boredom; too much of what is unexpected and infuriating will lead to loss of reader interest. The question then turns to how to approach one's readers.

In this area there is the question of language. Language as Hobbes noted long ago is the means people have for relating to each other. What they relate is mutual experience mutually communicated. Simple intellectual curiosity has to be relied upon to get Parties A, B, and C to relate to their own activities, the experiences of Parties D, E, and F. A common language is the necessary denominator. But, which language is the most common language is what the editor has to discover. In a culture where there is a common literary experience, certain poetic and prose classics (the Bible, Dante, Shakespeare, Molière, Tolstoy, and Dickens) offer the preferred language. In a culture where these classics are no longer accepted as such, there emerged the need for a new rhetorical common denominator. Schumpeter suggested two; one was a common ideology (however specified); the other was a formalized medium—mathematics being the one which Descartes had thought the lowest effective common denominator.

*Ideology and Professional Economics.* Thus it is that these two media have come to be significant claimants. The *Journal of Political Economy,* for example, has pioneered the use of the ideology of the self-regulating market as the key to the minds of many of its readers, just as other journals have used the ideology of the philosophy of science to be the key opening the minds of their potential readers. But, ideology is also a matter of metaphor and experience; so descriptive material laid out with a broader or a more precise brush can do wonders in attracting attention, particularly when what is being described can be related to some politico-ideological issue. Among economists who have done this spectacularly as books are Mandeville (*The Grumbling Hive*), Defoe (*Robinson Crusoe*), Swift (*A Modest Proposal*), Veblen (*The Theory of the Business Enterprise*), Friedman and Stigler (*Roofs vs. Ceilings*), and Galbraith (*The Industrial State*). Many articles on the comparative virtues (often confusing a dynamic with a static assumption) of the advantages of free trade attract and hold journal readers.

Scientific methods, as such, are fair media, serving as a sweetened fly-paper which catch minds-on-the-wing. Discussions of appropriate methodology (the science of selecting preferred criteria relating to persuasion), if not handled at too abstract a level, often seem to reinforce persuasion.

"*Success is in the Rhetoric.*" This leads to the second medium, the use of deductive proof. As Descartes noted, mathematics is believed to be the linguistic linkage between the "sciences." For a long while, limitations associated with the lack of advance of the frontier of mathematics led to frustration, even denial, that Descartes was correct. How to handle probability distributions and their impact on empirical work emerged rather markedly after World War I, and the era of the virtually exclusive dominance of the calculus seems to have ended in the mid-1950s, with dynamic linear programming and advanced matrix algebra being illustrations of these fast-breaking innovations.

The editor's problems in this approach involved working within the limitations of the two new ideological *succès foux,* free trade with open markets, and the socially responsible society; as well as the improving mathematical competence of the academic Toms, Dicks, and Harrys.

In the United States there have been several marked ideological changes since World War II. Okun's 1975 lectures on Equity and Growth are not only evidence of this kind of change, but subsequent fascination with his lectures intensifies the continuing interest.

Thus I suggest that the supply and demand of articles in journals reflect current ideological trends and the form of the rhetoric reflects the now universal requirement that graduate economists have certain types of mathematical language skills. The readers reflect this change, and those who would publish and thereby show nominal leadership must take these things into account.

But, there is more to the change. Since World War II quantitative data series and econometric testing have become the basis of observation and the preferred method of proof. That the data series are often inadequately examined, and the results using econometric testing have not been preferable to the results using older statistical methods is probably true; yet the audience neither thinks so or even demands discussion of them.

In sum, one cannot really escape the easy conclusion that the older Austrians were right; the market is dominated by the subjective expectations of the consumer. But, as I have suggested, the supplier can shape the consumer's preference schedule by means of advertising and other forms of "education."

In some of the *Newsletters,* circulated with the recent issues of the *Economic Journal,* there has been a continuing discussion of who should be the intended audience for the Royal Economic Society's journal. This discussion started with Sir Austin Robinson's criticism (1990) of a Policy Forum paper by Ruth Towse and Mark Blaug (Towse and Blaug 1990) in which Robinson interpreted the Towse-Blaug admittedly qualified definition of professional economists (those with the equivalent of a PhD in the subject) as too academically specialized. As I read both the original paper and Robinson's comment on it, I see less disagreement than a mutually shared quandary since both parties (Towse-Blaug and Robinson) were clear that the spectrum of those calling themselves economics-trained and/or economics-professionals are the likely target for the *Economic Journal*. But, Robinson's comment is that the *Journal* ought to have considerable general material for those whose interests are not totally riveted to specialized "doctoral-dissertation-type" topics, however à la mode they may be.

One answer, or at least a statement formulated as an answer, is given by J. Richard Aronson, a professor at Lehigh University (Pennsylvania, USA). Although he appears to be "carrying water on both shoulders," he specifically recommends that:

> the world's most prestigious journals (the *American Economic Review*, the *Economic Journal*, and the *Journal of Finance*) are the appropriate outlets for our most sophisticated research and by definition, this work is complicated and not easily understood by the general practitioner . . .
> . . . In the US the *Journal of Economic Literature* and *Journal of Economic Perspectives* provide important information in language a generalist can understand . . .
> . . . (Aronson 1990, p. 16).

I note that Aronson carried water on both shoulders because while, he seemingly argues that prestigious journals ought to be at the intellectual frontier (presumably catering to the needs of the pioneers amongst us), he also thinks that the *Economic Journal* ought to be both prestigious *and readable*. Aronson goes on to note that the editor of the *Economic Journal* is now in the business of commissioning survey articles which expand the proportion of his journal's space which the general practitioner can handle.

As this topic of editing a high-circulation professional association journal is one to which I had earlier contributed considerable time and thought, I repeat my 1980 assessment of my experience:

> There is no doubt in my mind that if Molière were alive today and were aware of what is going on in economics that he would observe that the language of abstraction is the passion of the trained economist. The question, of course, is not really whether abstraction is desirable or undesirable. The question is not really about the existence of abstraction but about the level of it. Insofar as we train our young people in mathematical expression, there is a propensity to have a high level of abstrac-

tion. That is what mathematics is supposed to do; that is what it does (Perlman 1981, p. 2).

For those who edit journals, abstraction serves an additional purpose. It tends to make the expression of thoughts terse. If a picture is supposed to replace a thousand words it is quite likely that five good difference equations could replace a thousand pictures.

Consequently we have created a passion for *curricula vitae* with bibliographies of large numbers of short (mathematized) items. Formal statements seem to replace the need for detailed descriptions. What we have ended up with is a profession that specializes in journal articles rather than books, a generation that wields neat sets of brackets rather than one that turns a clever phrase. True, such a development reduces printing costs; it is likely, however, that it does not increase readership . . .

. . . I think that the survey articles (a form I promoted from the very first) seem to have caught on. Some, perhaps, tended to be overly technical; others, perhaps, too prosaic. Judging from the readership surveys that have been commissioned and from the demand for the expansion of the survey articles into books published by commercial or semi-commercial firms . . . , I think that the idea of the survey has been fully justified (pp. 2–3).

But, it was my final points which remain most relevant now: . . . the American Economic Association is a unit made up of a variety of subfield specialists, different generations with different kinds of training, persons of greatly varying ideological preferences, individuals with markedly different methodological choices, and a lot of Indians and a lot of would-be chiefs. When Professor Samuelson concluded his American Economic Association Presidential Address, he observed that what we economists work for is the applause of our fellows. But I rather fancy that what interests one segment of the profession bores another. Fortunately, the membership of the American Economic Association by and large is not intolerant and they suffer their periods of boredom patiently (p. 4).

May I sum up my thought: The points are: (1) that journal editors must offer their potential buyers (or society members) something to preserve hope that the journal will prove interesting enough to read; (2) that while Professor Aronson has a point that publication in the most prestigious journals should exist as a way to indicate professional sophistication, he should also realize that for the most part the most sophisticated scholars will already have read and commented on those articles during the long period of idea gestation and journal composition and printing; and (3) that the measure of journal editorship success can best be seen *ex post,* not by following a simple *ex ante* formula.

A popular novelist/essayist once remarked that any rational author should be willing to trade 1,000 readers at the time of publication for 100 readers ten years later or 10 readers 100 years later. While the numbers of entries in the citation index, particularly a year or two after an article comes out, could be a measure of its long haul value to the profession, it may be really more a measure of fashion than value. The true measure of value can only be retrospective—and, even then, with a threshold of about 10 years. Such judgements are the special province of the historians of ideas.

## C. Varieties of Editoring

At the end of my period of *Journal of Economic Literature* editorial steward-ship I reported that I thought that there were two styles of editing:

> . . . One puts a nominal emphasis on the process of editorial choice as a [competitive rationing] process; the editor receives the manuscripts (or . . . commissions them), chooses appropriate referees, sends the manu-scripts to the referees, and lets the referees make such suggestions as they think appropriate and carry the burden of the final selection process.
>
> The other . . . is for the editor to judge the manuscripts. In this in-stance he uses referees to expose to critical review those manuscripts that the editor thinks interesting. The referee's opinions should be transmitted to the author but with the view that the referee was not always chosen for his impartial qualities. 'You might as well know what your worst critic will say when the manuscript comes to the light of day.' Then this editor works with the author to tighten up loose points, to illuminate or elimi-nate irrelevancies; but in the end to let the author's neck stick out. In the first instance the editor tries to be *hors de combat;* in the second he assumes that the readers want interesting material, even if a scrap is involved. In the former case, the process of refereeing should be opti-mally double blind; . . . In the latter . . . [i]t is important for the referee to know who the author is, since part of the mission is to present a provocative paper. Identification of the author often helps the referee realize just why the paper is supposed to be provocative . . . [When the author knows] who his referees were . . . [he often reasons thus]: "If Professor R—, an avowed admirer, thinks that this essay is not vintage me, perhaps I don't want to print it. Such has been the reaction of any number of [would be] authors (Perlman, 1981, p. 2).

But I would go on to say that what has to be added to my earlier remarks are statements pertaining to choices about editorial creativity. We tend easily to remember editors who failed to appreciate *and give recognition* to brilliance (cf. McCulloch's treatment of Malthus, Edgeworth's towards Barone, May-

nard Keynes's delay in printing Kalecki, etc. etc.) and to attribute to them
decisions based on jealousy, politics or hurt feelings. The other side of this
coin is the reluctance of an editor to encourage discussion lest it be considered
too wild. I recall one of Seymour Harris's colleagues, when denigrating
Harris's lack of originality, adding that Harris did not have any capacity
whatsoever for bringing out a *boring* issue of the *Review of Economics and
Statistics*. In many instances what Harris did was to urge effectively provocative statements; it kept the readers reactive as respondents and as subscribers,
all the while.

Let me extend this point. Provocativeness takes several forms. Clearly
selection of author and subject matter is one. Style and form (as any student of
Swift, Defoe, or even Stephen Leacock of McGill clearly appreciates) are
obviously a second. But, efficiency as seen in time of publication turnaround
is yet another; the fact that Milton Gilbert had previously been editor of the
*Survey of Current Business* and that he retained the managerial clout to get
immediate turnaround time explains why that otherwise prosaically heavy
government publication became, during World War II, the provocative vehicle
showing anew each month additional recent evidence of the transformation of
a peacetime to a wartime economy in the magic mirror of macroeconomic
studies.

### D. The "Have Been" and "Could Be" Role of Economics Journals

In sum, economics journals have been sometimes more or sometimes less
successful vehicles for bending the economics profession's general and specific activities relating to disciplinary content and style. Some have served to
identify "distinction" or sophistication. Others have served as necessary vehicles or means for the promotion of persons or ideas. Each and all of these
things they can continue to be.

Among the responsibilities which economics journals have not undertaken, however, are the semantic duties of the French Academy, the principal
function of which is to police language usage. Few journals pay more than lip-
service in attributing much value to bibliographic and statistical checking.
Even fewer attribute much value to expository balance and style, be it prose or
mathematical.

Nor is any economics journal any longer undertaking obituary biographies so that not only the profession's candidates for "the pantheon of heroes"
are no longer celebrated, but also that the essential qualities of heroism are
infrequently identified. Laziness and/or fear of the "cult of the individual" has
led a discipline which has always been concerned about incentive processes to
forget that obituaries serve specific creative-incentive functions.

Finally, technological change may be close to the point of destroying the journal system as we have known it. If printing costs continue to soar and xerography and satellite transmission costs continue to shrink, where will there be effective demand to permit the publications of journals to continue?

REFERENCES

J. R. Aronson (1990), "The Royal Economic Society Information Service," *Newsletter*, 71 (September), pp. 15–16.
W. Barber ed. (1988), *Breaking the Academic Mould: Economists and American Higher Learning in the Nineteenth Century*, Middletown, CT: Wesleyan University Press.
J. Dorfman (1949), *The Economic Mind in American Civilization, Volume III: 1865–1918*, New York: The Viking Press.
A. M. Okun (1975), *Equality and Efficiency: The Big Tradeoff*, Washington, DC: Brookings Institution.
M. Perlman (1981), "Editor's Note," *Journal of Economic Literature* 19, pp. 1–4.
M. Perlman (1991). "Early Capital Theory in the Economics Journals: A Study of Imputed Induced Demand." *This journal.*
A. [Sir] Robinson [E. A. G.]. " The Royal Economic Society Information Service", *Newsletter*, 69 (Mar), pp. 16–19.
R. Towse - M. Blaug (1990). "The Current State of the British Economics Profession." *Economic Journal* 100, pp. 227–36.

ABSTRACT

Examining particularly the contents and policies of Harvard's pioneering *Quarterly Journal of Economics* and five other early journals, this article explores the success of these professional journals. The answer lies in the provision of a few provocative articles and ensuing discussions. What made articles provocative? Brilliant, sustained originality, phrased in an appropriate rhetoric. What is appropriate rhetoric? Mostly a controversial (but partly acceptable) ideology (e.g. limited state intervention vs. the free market; sound money vs. inflationary redistribution) and a comprehensible linguistic vehicle (e.g. relevant and illuminating analogies vs. formalized, specified statements). Quick turn-around time and overwhelming relevance, too (as in the case of the *Survey of Current Business* during and after World War II), has been another factor.

**Part 2
History of
Economic Thought**

**A. General Essays**

CHAPTER 4

# Perceptions of Our Discipline: Three
# Magisterial Treatments of the Evolution
# of Economic Thought

*How three scholars interpret the history of a modern discipline became the
introductory subject of my 1985 Presidential Address to the History of Economics Society. The three were Wesley Clair Mitchell, Joseph A. Schumpeter,
and Karl Pribram. I then sought to discuss why such a comparative approach,
rather than using a survey derived from Popperian methodology, made sense
to me. Of the three, I had met only Schumpeter, who, at the time of our
meeting, did not overwhelm me. Later, when Helmut Frisch asked me to write
a paper on Schumpeter's approach to the History of Thought (Perlman,
1982c), I became intrigued with the assumptions to be gleaned from his
unfinished chef d'oeuvre,* The History of Economic Analysis. *That paper led
me to reorganize my graduate course on the subject, and the outcome will
appear as a two-volume study. This essay was not the first wherein I suggested
that Popperian methodology was not the only way to adjudge economic ideas
(see "Reflections on Methodology, Persuasion, and Machlup" 1978d).* [1]

I have taken as the subject of this presidential address a consideration of the
dynamics (that is, what shapes the future direction) of the *professional* discipline of economics. From a conceptual standpoint, I feel most comfortable
with our dating the latter part of the nineteenth century, surely during the
1870s, as the time when what had been a general, and perhaps even gentlemanly, subject became a professional discipline.

For purposes of our discussion I shall use an abridged definition of
"professional discipline," namely, "a shared perception of a body of knowledge, including sets of questions, data and analytical methods, common to
those who are identified as and/or identify themselves as members of that
profession." Thus, what we are basically considering at this time is how that
body of knowledge identified as economics was and continues to be reshaped.

*Bulletin of the History of Economics Society* (Winter 1986): 9–28.

Analyzing that reshaping process is, according to my view, what the sub-discipline of the history of economics is all about.

Our point of departure is to examine *ad seriatim* three quite different treatments of the history of economic thought in order to suggest alternative perceptions of the causes for change in the delimitors of our professional knowledge. We then turn to assessing the three treatments. The paper concludes by suggesting an alternative to methodology [cf. Perlman, 1978] or to "rhetoric" [cf. McCloskey, 1983] as the basis for the functional delimitors of the agreed-upon body of our professional knowledge.

It is said of Franz Liszt and Arthur Rubenstein, both concert pianists of the greatest distinction, that "they often missed some of the notes." Thus, one can be authoritative without always being accurate. And so it is with the three treatments which I identify as magisterial; the posthumous books on the history of economic thought by Schumpeter [1954], Mitchell [1967 and 1969], and Pribram [1983]. To be magisterial is to be authoritative, and each achieves magisterial status because of the distinctive and comprehensive originality of each author's perception of intellectual evolution, rather than because of chronological scope, accuracy, even polish. In short, I view each of these studies as simultaneously grand (in the most approbative sense), yet flawed. Each is like an Old Testament hero, touched by something miraculous, yet, nonetheless, mortal and "morally" imperfect. The purpose of this paper is not to focus on their flaws but to contrast the ways in which each has achieved *chef-d'oeuvre* standing. And, from those comparisons, I think that we can say some things worthwhile (and perhaps even new) about the ways we do and ought to view our subject.

Let us then turn initially to considering the three works.

### Wesley Clair Mitchell

Insofar as most of us recall Wesley Clair Mitchell, most of us perceive him as having been above all an unusually careful collector of business cycle data.[2] Yet, few generalizations could be so devoid of insight, to say nothing of accuracy. He defined the business cycle itself, devised and tested the concept measurements; and created the bases for the present body of empirical data. His approach became the matrix for everyone else's work in business cycles. He offered a methodological view which was seminal to modern economic empiricism. Yet, prior to these efforts at business cycle definition and measurement was his unusual work as a monetary economist [Mitchell, 1896, 1903, 1904, and 1908], where after he demonstrated the intellectual inadequacy of Irving Fisher's perception of the quantity theory of money, he went on to develop his own theories of role of the monetary instrument in macroeconomic activity and of cost-price transmission of the business cycle [Mitchell, 1913]. Few economists have so completely changed and expanded their areas of expertise; indeed, only Milton Friedman, one of the last to join the Mitchell group, comes to mind as comparable to Mitchell, and Friedman went from statistics to an interest in monetarism while Mitchell had gone in just the opposite direction.[3]

Even a brief perusal of Mitchell's bibliography [Mitchell, 1952, pp. 343–66] reveals how vital was his interest in the evolution of economic theory. His volume of collected essays, *The Backward Art of Spending Money* [Mitchell, 1934] reprints only a portion of these essays, but even there the power as well as the catholicity of his interest in economic theory is manifest, as indeed is the skillfulness of his analytical assessments. In particular, I direct attention to his 1917 essay on "Wieser's Theory of Social Economics" [Mitchell, 1917], which combines a thorough and sympathetic review of the book with some penetrating and sharp criticisms of the Austrian school's insistence upon self-limitations, namely a refusal to examine the operating principles of the individual's subjective process.[4]

For a variety of reasons it makes for efficiency and good sense to turn to the published version of Professor Joseph Dorfman's edition of the John Meyer and others' sets of lecture notes, which were drawn from several different years of Mitchell's Columbia University course, "Types of Economic Theory" [Mitchell, 1967 and 1969].

*A Reader's Guide to Mitchell's "Types of Economic Theory."* The two volumes are not divided into "parts" or "sections," only 22 chapters, each focused on one or more topics. In the Dorfman version, however, 34 pages are devoted to a general orientation to the subject.

Mitchell's opening discussion is of "Adam Smith and how political economy came to be systematized in England," and covers about 136 pages. It leans very heavily on Smith's own writing and very little on Smith's natural law and physiocratic precursors. It is very "United Kingdom-oriented," and although it does mention Smith's earlier book, the *Theory of Moral Sentiments* (1759), it does not do so in great detail. Early on, Mitchell says:

> Economists like to speak of economics as a science, and of Adam Smith as the father of political economy. In their more careful moments, they have perhaps some reservations about both remarks. They know that Adam Smith was preceded by Quesnay; that Quesnay was preceded by Cantillon; that Cantillon was preceded by a whole group of at least half-enlightened mercantilist writers upon public policy. Yet when all these deductions are made, it remains a fact that the *Wealth of Nations* was in a genuine sense the start, the foundation of modern economics (1967, p. 145).

Such was the enunciated position in Mitchell's approach; such clearly could not have been the view of the others, Schumpeter and Pribram, who identified the beginning of economics with Plato and Aristotle and had a very different view of Smith.

The next section (4.4 percent of the whole) of Mitchell's treatment focuses on Bentham and utilitarianism. There then follows a very short, only 26 pages, discussion of "Malthus and the empirical trend." While much of this discussion is on Population Malthus, Mitchell, himself, seemed more impressed by Malthus's theory of "general overproduction" or underconsumption, found in the 1820 *Principles of Political Economy*.

Not surprisingly, there follows a lengthy (120 page) chapter on "David Ricardo and the making of classical political economy," containing not only an explanation of what Ricardo thought, including some of the changes in his thinking, but also a good deal of economic history. It also contains several rather interesting assessments of Ricardo by others, *e.g.* Walter Bagehot. Most of all, it tries to put Ricardo's own views, particularly with regard to his intellectual relationship with Malthus, into a context easily grasped by American students with some knowledge of Regency Britain. It is quite clear that Mitchell was neither an avid admirer of Ricardo nor of classical economics. Skeptical as he was about finding essential truths or universal insights in the classical tradition, Mitchell, the historian, was certainly ready to give the Ricardian group "high marks" for reflecting as well as shaping events. The three chapters following the one on Ricardo run to a lengthy 223 pages and are entitled, "The new social sciences at work: The philosophical radicals," "Political economy in the days of its triumph," and "John Stuart Mill and the humanization of classical economics."

My reading of the last, the chapter on Mill, yields a judgment that Mitchell assessed Mill's conversion from Benthamite utilitarianism to ethical socialism to be an important development in the history of economic thought. It was not merely one man's "born again" revelation; it revealed an insider's assessment of the heartlessness of the historical consequences of the social policies derived from classical economics. While the quintessential personalness of this change is something I fancy many modern scholars might find cloying or sentimental, rather than monumental, Mitchell judged Mill to be a humanitarian of epic proportion even if he were less than an original scholar. I read many current writers' (as well as Schumpeter's and Pribram's) verdict as something more favorable, namely, that Mill had originality as well as that rare kind of grasp (unknown to most Englishmen), and, the breadth of philosophical (as distinct from historical) vision reserved to those on anyone's international list of all-time wise men (what Schumpeter called "consultant administrators"). My conclusion, put bluntly, is that what Mitchell most admired in J. S. Mill leaves many relatively cold; and what enthuses them,

Mitchell did not value highly. Strange that the admiration expresses itself in such extreme differences.

Mitchell then turned to the great reformers of method: Jevons, Menger, and Walras. To them he devoted only 110 pages, with the largest share going to Jevons. (Schumpeter put Jevons as the least of the three.)

After that comes a chapter on Alfred Marshall, again another 110 pages. My reading of Mitchell's view is that Mitchell believed that Marshall, not J. S. Mill, was the wisest of the English contributors: Marshall's definition of economics suggested a realistic science (although all of his analyses rest on some simplifying assumptions), while Mill preferred his political economy to be highly abstract. Marshall, contrastingly, asserted that he was talking about real men, while Mill explicitly used an artificial definition of man—a being animated solely by desire for wealth, aversion to labor, and a preference for present rather than future enjoyment. Marshall agreed with Schmoller that the economist must use both deduction and induction, while Mill advised that political economy must rely mainly upon the deductive method, although conclusions should be verified by "specific experience." Marshall held that money is the center around which economic science clusters, while Mill holds that "money is a thing of indifference," exercising no influence upon human behavior except when "it gets out of order" (Mitchell, 1969, p. 217). As I will indicate later, Schumpeter had rather mixed judgements about Marshall; my inference is that Mitchell did not. Again, a major distinguishing difference.

At this point in the text, Mitchell turned to a discussion of American economists with a 30 page chapter on "The development of American economics and the role of J. B. Clark." Then follows a larger (50 page) chapter on "Frank A. Fetter and the American psychological school." Fetter was influenced by J. B. Clark, by Simon Patten (University of Pennsylvania) and, of course, by the Austrians, particularly von Boehm-Bawerk. Then follows a reasonably long chapter on Herbert J. Davenport, whose abstract, price-oriented economics was the subject of a fair amount of evaluational disparagement:

> In other words, [Davenport] supposes prices to exist for other articles in indefinite number in the very process of explaining the price at which any given article will be supplied. To repeat what I said at the beginning, the theorist finds his price analysis is itself circuitous—he explains prices by prices. The price of one thing is in very large measure explained by the prices of other things. If his pecuniary analysis is both superficial and circuitous, where does he stand? (Mitchell, 1969, p. 341).

And, Mitchell's answer tended to be human desires, productive capacity, and instrumental equipment (technology).

After that comes a brief chapter on von Wieser and a slightly longer chapter (41 pages) on "The pure economics of Joseph Alois Schumpeter and Vilfredo Pareto." His work on Schumpeter does not mention Schumpeter's interest in the history of economic thought; rather it focuses on Schumpeter's *The Nature and Main Content of Theoretical Economics* (1908) and Schumpeter's *Theory of Economic Development* (1912). Pareto is treated somewhat more briefly than Schumpeter, but not necessarily any more gently. In many senses Mitchell apparently believes that Schumpeter's theoretical ideal was better handled by Pareto than by Schumpeter (Mitchell, 1969, p. 412).

The next chapter, "The mathematical approach of Gustav Cassel" is very short, only 31 pages. There is then a chapter on the American monetary economist, Benjamin McAlester Anderson, Jr. After that, a short chapter on John A. Hobson and the rise of British welfare economics.

Mitchell was, himself, an American institutionalist. Part of the origins of American institutionalism are to be found in the German historical school, and the nineteenth chapter is on von Schmoller. It is principally in this context that Mitchell reveals his judgements of Marx. He compares Schmoller as an economic historian adversely to Marx. Following, there is a very long chapter on Mitchell's own teacher, Thorstein Veblen. To Mitchell, Veblen was the basic American institutionalist, and although Mitchell was appropriately respectful towards Veblen and certainly intrigued by the originality of Veblen's interpretations, I do not think that Mitchell felt himself in any sense constrained by Veblen's conclusions. Indeed, Mitchell immediately turned with almost unrestrained enthusiasm to the work of Professor John R. Commons, another kind of American institutionalist.[5] The volume then ends with almost 60 pages of retrospective and then prospective conclusions.

*Summary of Mitchell's Approach.* Mitchell, for his own personal reasons, sought to use the history of the discipline to show that the binding elements in both the discipline and in economic history, itself, were "exogenous" historical continuities, by far the great majority of which were clearly associated with the evolution of industrial society. As such, then, upon empirical examination theoretical truths tend to be all too ephemeral in terms of time and place. Economics, as he came to perceive the discipline, was not a history of the refinement of any abstractions, but the record of almost idiosyncratic interpretations by key individuals of exogenous events according to a combination of their own priorities and the technical language which they had inherited (but which they did not always use consistently).

Accordingly, Mitchell saw no purpose in dividing the history of economic thought into basic chronological periods; rather, he favored a division into "formative types," each being something of a personal rationalized response to a set of historical events. He put his emphasis on individuals as the architects of each of these types. Economic truths, as he saw them, thus, seem to have been highly relative and were (as well as are) in good measure based on the subjective values of the analysts. Episodes revealing the priority system of the key individual had their essential place. Although it is stylish these days to decry the role of anecdote and casual observation in serious discussion, this position is not truly consistent with Mitchell's approach, even though he seems to have been quite a reserved, non-gossipy type. Facile abstractions and their careless use were Mitchell's bugaboos. The danger to economics lay not so much in boring specificity as in carelessly specified models, which could all too easily turn something useful into a very dangerous tool; abstraction, at its worst, could be crude "excogitation," which permitted, even encouraged, analysts to try to plant their feet "firmly in mid-air," the least useful of all possible stances.

## Karl Pribram

We come now to the most recently published of the three magisterial treatments, the one by Karl Pribram [1983].

Pribram was only secondarily an academic, although the positions he held in no sense should suggest any lack of major academic recognition. A student of von Wieser in Prague (where Pribram was born), his education there and his outlook as an economist were clearly Austrian, as his relatively brief experience as a student at the University of Berlin clearly showed.[6] In any event, he then went to Vienna where he polished his views and was for a time (1917, when von Wieser was in the cabinet), the latter's academic deputy.

In the post-World War I period he participated in the drawing up of the Austrian social security system, an experience which led to his becoming Chief of the International Labor Organization's Department of Research and Statistics. Throughout his life he was a prolific writer on many topics, including the importance of eliminating trade barriers and the need for governmentally designed actuarially-sound social security systems. In 1928 he became professor at Frankfurt and entered vigorously into worldwide academic activities. He was a major participant at the famous University of Chicago June 1931 seminar with Maynard Keynes and E. J. Phelan (then Secretary General of the ILO).

Fearful of his future in Germany, he left the University of Frankfurt at the end of 1933 to accept a temporary position at the Brookings Institution. Two years later he joined the staff of the American Social Security Board, where he remained until 1942. Thereafter, he worked for the United States Tariff Commission until his retirement in 1952. During the 1940s he remained prolific as an author, particularly on topics dealing with social security, international trade policy, and as time passed with methodological questions, including several works on statistics and econometrics. The present book is mostly a product of his retirement. He did not finish the manuscript completely, but it was in a more polished form at the time of his death (at ninety-five in 1973) than seems to have been the case with the other two works we are considering.

*A Reader's Guide to Pribram.* Pribram's approach is more firmly fixed in the Carl Mengerian subjectivist tradition than I would have thought possible. It is entirely a study of ideas, not people nor the impact of any exogenous historical events. The period Pribram treats is from Aquinas until the post World War II scene, which he trisects with the divisions taking place at the time of the emergence of English classical economics (about 1800) and after World War I (1918). The pre-classical period (Book One) takes up about 23 percent of the study, the period between 1800 and 1918 (Book Two) about 40 percent, and the remainder (Book Three) about 37 percent.

In organizing his interpretation, Pribram devoted the first two of 11 parts (as distinct from the "books," referred to immediately above) to the active Thomistic tradition and then to its breakdown, taking some effort to discuss the impact of Spanish theology on the latter. The second part, "The Development of [Roger] Baconian and Cartesian Economics," introduces what he considered to be the principal tension in the development of the discipline; it covers the periods associated with mercantilism and cameralism, physiocracy and Adam Smith. He emphasized the distinction between the Descartian[7] model-building and the alternative of organizing empirical or cognitive data into a meaningful system. The former stresses the uses of syllogisms and mathematics; the latter some form of direct observation and the [Francis] Baconian scientific method. This is the particularly seminal section of his interpretation; it is the largest in his study and takes up about 20 percent of the whole.

Pribram's second "book," "Conflicting Economic Doctrines, 1800–1918," is divided into four more parts. The first (Part III) focuses on the utilitarian tradition, building on Bentham and Ricardo but also including the extension of the Smithian tradition to the European Continent and to America. The second deals with the growth of nineteenth century romantic organic nationalism, in some measure identified in Pribram's mind with Kantian and "NeoKantian" philosophy, and afterwards with such German writers as Sombart and Weber. The third considers Marxian dialecticism. The fourth (Part VI) takes up three schools of marginalism (Jevonian or utilitarian, Walrasian or mathematical, and Mengerian or psychological) as well as some *sequelae* like the American pro-marginalist and anti-marginalist or institutionalist writers.

"Book Three" is divided into five sections, carrying some of the earlier discussion into the post-1918 world. Section VII (the first of these five) deals with the decline of romantic "organicism" and its transformation into national totalitarianisms. Section VIII covers the degeneration of the dialectic into "Bolshevist Economics." Section IX, the third largest section of the book (14 percent) takes up "hypothetical economics,"[8] or what is the current American "mainline" activity, albeit that its eventual popularity may not have been obvious during the period when Pribram was doing most of his research and writing. Section X is on the Keynesian general disequilibrium approach, the topic which seemed to have emerged as dominant during Pribram's actual career. The final section (Part XI) deals with international relations; as such it offers an important, even if not the dominant, insight into Pribram's priorities. Pribram's work was done prior to, during, and immediately after the Second World War; consequently, he stressed the division between romantic nationalism and Marxism. This is a second and clearly lesser division in his analytical schema.

I have described Pribram (actually von Wieser's student) as more Mengerian than I thought it possible for anyone to be; yet, he possessed a subjectivism that he adapted intellectually to the political events of the inter-War and immediate post-World War II period. That he concluded his work with a discussion of Keynesian autarkic models and with the emerging studies of international relations, identifies the dominant ideas of the end of his career period, just as his clear preference for Descartian model-building reflects the earlier Austrian economics training he had received. His focus on the power of romantic organicism (Fascism and Nazism) and on dialecticism (Bolshevism) also reflects the 1930s, World War II, and the Cold War.[9]

Generally, as I have noted, Pribram's principal theme was that there has been throughout the development of the discipline of the history of economic thinking a tension between theorizing and observation. Theorizing involves reliance upon intellectual constructs, early examples of which include Platonic perceptions and Aristotelian deductions. Contrastingly, observation involves horrendous problems of interpersonal comparisons relating to cognition.

After Aquinas's efforts at fusing the two approaches, his effort was seen to have failed with the Dominicans preferring the method of Platonic "essentialism" (Pribram's phrase), and the Franciscans preferring reliance upon cognitive description. By the Renaissance the tension was described differently, although it had not, in fact, changed. Rene Descartes and his school developed a systematic way of creating models which served to identify intellectual "realities" and which had certain logical (mathematical) properties permitting deduction and transformation. By then Roger Bacon (Pribram's hero/anti-hero) had also introduced an alternative method of "observation-hypothetical statement-more observation . . . tentative conclusion."

According to Pribram, Isaac Newton's efforts at trying to fuse the latter two, although initially accepted, were soon ignored on the Continent, where the emphasis on historicism and that kind of qualitative assessment of events achieved a foothold in German universities. Pribram saw the development of British classical economics as principally an offshoot of Benthamite utilitarianism (an intellectualized idea-set if ever there was one), not as an effort to achieve certain specific socio-legislative reforms—Terence Hutchison's judgements to the contrary notwithstanding [Hutchison, 1978, p. 45].

The Continental thinkers worked in the more rarefied and, consequently, more nearly perfect Descartian tradition—witness the emergence, flowering, and eventual persuasive dominance of the Austrian contribution.

Time does not permit a thorough exposition of the Pribram judgements, but on the whole his scheme fits the medieval and post-medieval periods best; it also explains the Austrian tradition, but in effect, it eschews all efforts to understand either institutionalism as a systematic method of perceiving the evolution of the economics discipline or the shift of emphasis from model-building as an explanatory end-in-itself to policy prescription as the professional economists' essential objective. Those who have reviewed his book seem to me to be obviously uncomfortable with his approach, but this lack of acceptance says more about the reviewers and their training than it does about Pribram's contribution. It is almost impossible for those who are trained to think in terms of policy formation to use rarefied criteria like those involved in handling Platonic essentials for making assessments; how does one for example, really dismiss the usual charge of triviality made about Aquinas's own dissertation involving the corporal nature of ideas [and angels]—"How many angels can sit on the head of a pin?"

## Joseph Alois Schumpeter

The initial quintessential element of Schumpeter's interpretation of the history of economic analysis, possibly attributable to Luigi Cossa [Cossa, 1893],[10] starts with a division of the emergence of our discipline into four parts. The first dealt with moral philosophy and stretched from Hellenistic Athens through 18th century Edinburgh, from Plato to Smith or as he phrased it (in part) from the concept of golden men to "Scottish wooded philosophers." The second dealt with the classical school, running from approximately 1790 (Bentham/?) until 1870. The third was the emergence of "a spectrum of [specialized] schools," including the German Historical, the marginal utility and marginal product, the Marxian, the American historical, the Marshallian neoclassical, and that of the Lausanne general static equilibrium tradition. The fourth was to be in the future, the appearance of a dynamic general equilibrium fusion, something only partly described, including a formal (mathematical) approach, capable of integrating some sociological and historical trends into the analytical process. What one can see here is a reluctant embrace of the view that economics was much less a science than he had supposed when he wrote his original treatise on substance and method [Schumpeter, 1912]. His phrase, "the Filiation of Scientific Ideas—the process by which men's efforts to understand economic phenomena produce, improve, and pull down analytic structures in an unending sequence" [Schumpeter, 1954, p. 6], identifies his initial goal, but as he wrote he discovered that it worked less well in economics than "it has in almost all [other fields]." He put the matter more strongly a few pages later on when he noted that economics was not that kind of science (defined as "tooled knowledge") like acoustics, rather, like medicine it is ill-defined [1954, pp. 9–10]. Nonetheless, even if the product is not truly scientific *"either by subject or method,"* the mind-set of the economist is scientific, and that is what counts [1954, p. 10; italics in the original]. What then follows is that economics, as such, has critically important historical, statistical, theoretical [sic], sociological, and political dimensions. The Filiation of Scientific Ideas, his original lodestar, apparently had to be abandoned, and the goal of "The Development of Economics as a Science" (the starting point in his 1912 work), is replaced by a chronicle of the history of economists' thinking. Earlier, I put it that the younger Schumpeter promised his readers a *wertfrei* and *zeitfrei* goal, a goal which the older man realized he, himself, could not reach [Perlman, 1981, p. 145].

And what about the history of economists' thinking—the one thing which Schumpeter eventually believed he could produce? Schumpeter asserted that writers in the field tended to be judged as partisan pamphleteers, representing special economic interests, or consultant administrators (his version, perhaps, of Plato's golden men). The former suggested a disorderly and inefficient set of sellers in the marketplace of ideas; the latter was a set of balanced and immutable purveyors of truth. Thus, the era of moral philosophy ends up with a clattering confusion of self-interested assertions or a dilution of the great Hellenic conceptions to the point of Scottish "woodenness."

His discussion of the second period is seemingly more precise insofar as he identifies the classical school with 12 separate attributes. That precision of approach gets lost when he comes to his third period. This period deals with a variety of schools. Each school looks at different as well as the same explicit and methodologically implicit phenomena and derives its own definition of economics. The final period, the dynamic theory of general equilibrium, is presented as a Holy Grail, not as an achieved level, although perhaps he might have seen his erstwhile student, Samuelson, as the likely *cicerone,* rather than Keynes, whose pretensions to the role he had examined, and not surprisingly, had dismissed.

*Schumpeter's Definition of the Topic.* Let me start by admitting that I am unable to present a clear delimitation or definition of Schumpeter's perception of the history of economic thinking. As noted in his 1912 essay Schumpeter had described the topic as "The development of economics as a science" and had suggested that it had two halves. One was purely philosophical learning for its own sake and, as such, was intellectually integrated and coherent; the other centered on the "scribblings," to paraphrase Gibbon's potential patron, of the intellectual servants or hirelings of special economic interest groups. Yet, once having identified these two approaches or sets of products, Schumpeter, I believe, backed away from the implications of the distinction. But he did not abandon this early division, perhaps because of the pedagogical neatness of what he was proposing; and even if in practice this division does not work out perfectly, its pedagogical utility remains.

In Chapter 1 of his posthumous *History of Economic Analysis* HEA [Schumpeter, 1954],[11] there is a rather brilliant if unsuccessful, effort at reconfirming his 1912 approach to the development of economics as a science:

> By History of Economic Analysis I mean the history of the intellectual efforts that men have made in order to *understand* economic phenomena or, which comes to the same thing, the history of the analytic or scientific aspects of economic thought (1954, p. 3).

However, the older Schumpeter then explains why he pursued the study of the "history of economics" (sic); and in so styling the topic, he has already moved from discussing the history of a science to the more pedestrian history of a discipline. How does he justify this sleight of hand? He suggests that virtually all modern work combines some current institutional overtones which must be compared to earlier manifestations of the same idea in order to be purged of their time-limited characteristics. What he seems to have wanted most was to treat his topic as an exercise in epistemics, that is an exercise in the theory of theories, using economic thought as exemplar material, while admitting that in its details it differs from the "purer" sciences.

There is a contradiction between the simplicity of outline that Schumpeter originally suggested in 1912 as his topic (the discovery of straightforward, universal, scientific economic principles), and what he then went on ultimately to present in 1954, namely, a more conventional circuitry, full of the interactions of men, ideas, and events. Thus, I conclude that the differences between Schumpeter's approach to the topic of the history of our discipline and the approach of many others are not as startling as he wanted them to be. But, if I mark him down on the score of originality, I mark him up on the score of qualitative execution. What he did was not so different from others' efforts, it was just better.

From the panoramic standpoint, Schumpeter relied only in the first approximation on a chronological presentation of ideas and writings. In practice he tended to depart from the strictly chronological in order to pursue the evolution of an idea. Moreover, Schumpeter seemed not only unable to resist the temptation, but also to be actually eager, to include discursions into other disciplines. Most of these discursions were in the disciplines of moral, ethical, and historical philosophy; they did not consciously focus on the relationship between historical events and ideas (as Wesley Clair Mitchell preferred to do) or on the pleasurable, if not actually Elysian, fields of aesthetics.

Schumpeter was a great name-, title-, and adjective-dropper. The vastness of his bibliographic recall all but boggles the mind. Quick metaphor and the studied simile brighten up the page; on many occasions they were also used to blacken the character. Whatever the relation of the intent to the result, they seem to give his writing a highly personal flavor.

*A Reader's Guide to Schumpeter's Thinking on the History of Economics.* Schumpeter's two books, the 1912 *Epochen* (EDM) and his 1954 posthumous *History of Economic Analysis* (HEA), did three things. They tried to show how the history of economists' serious thinking should lead to a dynamic general equilibrium system, that is, to a general system which if it does not have a precise teleological goal, does have an identifiable dialectical pattern. Secondly, they show that the rhythm of philosophical thought served to shape a more stable understanding of the future than did the compilation of a record of partisans' rationalizations. The goal of the "consultant administrator" (as noted earlier, his version of Plato's Golden Man) is in several senses superior to particularistic "pamphleteers"—clearly an anti-Mandeville kind of view towards the conflict or the competition among ideas. And finally, the books suggest that economics as a discipline is a subset of epistemology, not a simple one-discipline social studies exercise.

The most important thing to grasp in Schumpeter's work is the change in his thinking. In EDM he starts by contrasting the "consultant administrator" with the "pamphleteer." Or to concretize, he contrasted thinkers of the calibre of Aristotle and von Pufendorf and Turgot against mere "pamphleteers" like Barbon, North, and Misselden. Even more strongly stated is the comparison of that "compiler," Adam Smith, with the creative Physiocrats (whose virtue was their perception of economics as a circular system that is, as a self-contained or balanced aquarium). Smith's *Wealth of Nations* (1776), he suggests, contained no new perceptions; worse yet, it was a politician's cookbook, no less and no more. It was not inspired. Nor was he taken with the aesthetics or style of Smith's writing.

From there, Schumpeter goes on to discuss the classical system which he believed was at its creative peak for "ten to fifteen years" after the 1817 appearance of Ricardo's *Principles* and which ended with a final burst of splendor with the similar work by John Stuart Mill in 1848. As noted above, he lays out his thinking in 12 numbered points. The first deals with the identification of the period. The second suggests that doctrines, not persons, are the "heroes." The third observes that the initial success of the classicists with regard to policies led them to fractionate, and in so doing they tended to lose sight of the "grand scheme" and to become somewhat less impressive, to become "pamphleteers." This transformation from philosophers to pamphleteers (many writings taking the form of textbooks and catechisms) led to a further narrowing of vision and, in sum, to a loss of any tie to an epistemological grand scheme. The fifth point discusses who dominated the profession in various countries—in Germany it was the professors, in France the merchants, in the United Kingdom the Benthamite utilitarians. He was particularly fascinated with these Benthamite utilitarians because while they were very versatile they relied principally on a provincial knowledge of British history. I infer that he was disturbed that they were not particularly well versed in moral philosophy.

The sixth point stresses that the classicists preferred an *a priori* method; however, they really were ignorant of its limitations. The seventh point tried to come to grips with cultural economic sociology, which had, over time, diluted much of the initial scientific thrust of the classical tradition. The eighth point relates to the peculiar sociological schema of the classical economists, who viewed nations as hierarchically organized, with three classes (the landowners, the workers, and the capitalists). This attitude was presented as an immutable and inevitable social structure with each of these classes basing its actions on a rather narrowly defined self-interest. The implication is that the particularistic pamphleteer mentality replaced the wiser general philosophical one. The ninth point was that the classicists' perceptions of what economic theory was supposed to be about were largely circumscribed by the first and second books of the *Wealth of Nations*. The tenth point was that price determination was at the center of their thinking. The eleventh point was that their best work was on the theory of distribution, where they did a good but not complete job. And the twelfth point was that as a group they tended to eschew discussion of the theory of money, although John Stuart Mill, himself, did have a quantity theory of money. This treatment of the classical economists amounts to approximately three-eighths of the early book (EDM).

Schumpeter then went on to the era of schools and of the subdisciplines, where his concern centered on the dangers of slogans, easy formulas, and on an excessive fascination with "policy implications."[12] His treatment of the early German historical school was comprehensive, although he believed that a historical element must be balanced by a theoretical element. But if he was no "Austrian" in terms of the lineup associated with the famous *Methodenstreit,* his identification of the British disciples of the German historical school (namely, Cliffe Leslie, J. K. Ingram, and Sir William Ashley) as "irrational," says something very important.[13] He condemned the roles they played in limiting epistemological growth. He also discusses the intellectual conflict the French economists had with the French sociological tradition. He then turned to the *Methodenstreit,* itself, and noted that the issue was not really abstraction versus empirical fact, but was a conflict about the role of free trade and tariffs. In other words, it related not to a higher-order, nominally epistemological issue, but to a lower-order pamphleteering kind of thing. There follows a discussion of the mathematical method, an epistemologically high-order topic, for which he had an obvious respect. He listed among the principal contributions those of Whewell, Cournot, Jevons, Marshall, Edgeworth, Fisher, Auspitz, and Lieben.

Not content to leave the historical school with a listing of names and intellectual ties, he returned to assess it. He believed that it gave economics a perception of reality, that it stressed the unity of social activities, and that it identified the place that anti-rationalism[14] had in the development of social organization. At its best, it stressed evolution, while the more traditional classical economists focused on statics. He was particularly careful to point out the historical school's interest in correlations (suggesting relationships without identifiable cause-effect sequences). And finally influenced as he now was by Marxism, he stresses the organic point of view which the historical school also emphasized.

From there he turned to the burst of theorizing after 1870. He mentioned the earlier precursors of this group (in his later work [HEA] he was to call them "men who wrote beyond their time"), and he identified specifically the contributions of Menger, Jevons, Walras, von Boehm-Bawerk, and von Wieser. He noted how freely and widely the marginal method was employed, and he particularly noted the development of a new theory of price.

Many years later when writing the *History of Economic Analysis,* he followed the pattern generally suggested in *Economic Doctrine and Method.* The HEA is organized in five parts. Part 1 (3.7 percent of the book) is the imperfect delineation of what Schumpeter thought he was doing. It reflected the conflict between "science and ideology," where he tried to establish a distinction but did not succeed. In the four chapters of this part there are 22 sections. Each section is a related but not smoothly flowing set of observations. My own judgement is that his approach reflected a desire to implant a sense of cause and effect as seen by the physicists of his time, but that he realized that perceptions are grasped by ideologically conditioned minds. In other words, little in economics starts really *tabula rasa,* and the best that one can do is to examine continuously one's conclusions and to see whether one has unconscious or unarticulated premises that shape them. But in dealing with unarticulated or emotional premises (which certainly one may be easily able to discern in others), the problems remain. Can one "correct" in oneself the effects of these premises? If so, how? He does not tell us.

Part 2 of the *History of Economic Analysis* is slightly more than a quarter of the book. It is the summary of the struggle between the "consultant administrators" (those aspiring to a broad-gauge view) and the particularistic advocates, still rather sneeringly referred to as "pamphleteers." Truth, or better yet, scientific truth stretches to the horizons in all directions—the historical, the spectrum of disciplines, and in all political and ideological directions (up, down, right, left, the progressive as well as the traditional spheres of culture). "Pamphleteers," by way of contrast, want only to fight tactical and not strategic battles.

As before, Schumpeter's approach seemingly employed chronological sequence, but only as a first approximation. The sequence is Aristotle, the Church Fathers, natural law and those who apply it to problems of production, distribution, and exchange (the last being the economists). In Schumpeter's view the great philosophical breakthrough for economists remained the physiocrats' perception of circularity. The key names were: Boisguillebert, Cantillon, Quesnay, and Turgot. Smith's name then tagged along!

Money and value were studied and were well understood, even by modern standards. Smith lost this thread when he came to weaving the *Wealth of Nations,* and the classical rug merchants thought it might be done without. Schumpeter, of course, dissented.

Part 2 concludes with a grudging review of the truths employed and presumably in some senses discovered by the "pamphleteers." In this sense, Schumpeter differs very markedly from Jacob Viner and Lionel Robbins, who saw in the "pamphleteer's" activities the basis of a truly competitive market of ideas.

Part 3 covers the classical period but also identifies those who transcended it. It is almost a third of the book and provides a very concise statement of an important era. It ties classical economics to other partial intellectual systems prevalent at the time. While it does so in something of a chronological sequence, the stress is on breadth rather than on the historical order; he mentioned the romantic movement, developments in sociology, an enthusiasm for evolutionism, concern with human psychology, development of logic and epistemology, and a new "theology" (pre-Marxian socialism). He balanced the darker Ricardian beginnings of the classical era with a rather admiring view of John Stuart Mill's culminatory contribution. Given Schumpeter's assessment that the classicists were only talented specialists, I find his a balanced evaluation. The treatment focused mostly on England and its English intellectual experiences, but it does include other topics; there is a particularly fine discussion of the Marxian system, even though Marx, himself, is relegated to something less than the heroic role.

The fourth part of the book (eight chapters and an appendix on "The theory of utility") is on the era of schools. It is again about a third of the book. I think it is the best of the various parts. It starts with long sections (about 18 percent of the whole) on what was going on in other areas—social policy formation, other disciplines (history, sociology, psychology), and how these activities affected mainstream economics. Schumpeter then went on to his three "greats"—Jevons, Menger, and Walras. His lesser greats, including the Marshallians (certain key inventors and their discoveries) and men such as Pareto, certain Americans, and some Marxians, each of whom is mentioned rather superficially.

The "consultant administrators" of this era are generally of a historically lesser calibre. Of them, Marshall, is the best but with a personal perception of dynamics as being no more than a commitment to progress. Marshall's vision was essentially inherited from John Stuart Mill. Schumpeter's appreciation of Mill, who by historical standards was one of Britain's broader-gauge states-men-philosophers (hence a "consultant administrator"), revealed a great deal about Schumpeter and his value scheme. Mill was hardly an innovator of analytical technique, although there was a streak of originality in some of his expository material (e.g. the stationary state). But he was a philosopher with breadth, and that is what counted most. Schumpeter saw the period as full of progress, but most of the progress was in the perfection of technique and in the specialization in subfields.

The important part of this section is Chapter 7 and its appendix on equilibrium analysis. Although only one-eighth of the book, Chapter 7 con-tains Schumpeter's assessment of the accomplishments of this critical turning point. His judgements are placed in the perspective of the problems of the era and the practical type of work carried out in attempts to solve them—work on credit and business cycles. This chapter and its appendix summarize the great advances—advances in concepts and application. But eschewed completely are the contributions of Wesley Clair Mitchell and Frank Knight, however. I find these omissions intellectually inexplicable.

The book concludes with a fifth part, which traces the breakdown of the Marshallian tradition. It identifies also the unfulfilled quest for a dynamic theory of general equilibrium. It does mention, but only briefly, research on statistical material with some attention being paid to business cycles. There is a full-scale and rather ill-focused attack on Keynes's *General Theory*.

At best, the book ends in speculation. Yet, it must be remembered that Schumpeter was writing prior to the era of much modern mathematics and the capacity to process data with the high-speed computer. This portion of the book (being the last) may have been given less attention because it was so difficult; moreover, one should not forget that the book, itself, was unfinished before he died.

In an earlier essay I compared Schumpeter to Mitchell along four lines:

1. Schumpeter fancied economics as a subset of epistemology. Mitchell saw economics as part of the historical conflict between different economic and intellectual factions.
2. Modern economics in Schumpeter's view drew on the western culture's essential antecedents, which suggested that one ought to start, at least, with the Hellenistic philosophers. Mitchell, more "modern history minded" saw the quintessential watershed as the industrial revolution; one could really neglect the expressers of most ideas prior to Smith since what was so omitted would surface in the post-Smith writers.
3. Schumpeter was more confident (1912) than he later became (1954) that there were truly scientific immutable principles in the economics discipline, but he never completely lost faith even if he could not discover the full set, others would. Mitchell's survey of economics had as one of its principal findings that all economic ideas related to economic institutions and that the latter were quite likely universally evolutionary. Hence, it followed that one freed oneself from the tyranny of any theory by observing its origins, its halcyon period, and its seemingly inevitable decay.
4. Schumpeter's erudition embraced not only English but also a good many elements of [European] Continental thinking. Mitchell's erudition was much more specific to the United States's culture and its British antecedents.

To these I can add:

5. Pribram's Mengerian (Austrian) subjectivism and unconscious association with the problems of the post-World War II situation offers us an effort to see economics as essentially dependent only upon the evolution of the conflict between ideas. The important "tension-sets" are medieval nominalism and medieval realism, seventeenth century Descartian theorizing against Francis Bacon's quasi-empiric scientific method, nineteenth century romantic organicism and dialectical materialism, and twentieth century autarkic economic planning and international economic interdependency. Sources of these "tension-sets" are essentially philosophic, or if one pursues the topic, epistemological; they are not historical in the political or socio-economic sense, nor are they perceived as personally idiosyncratic in the individualistic sense.

## Conclusions

### History of Economic Thought and Methodology

Our own discipline, the history of economic thought, is frequently asserted to be one part of an intellectual duet; the "twin" or "soul-mate" is said to be the study of economic methodology. Much of the recent and innovative work in the history of economic thought has been an effort to try to categorize the contributions of various writers along the lines of the method preferred by each. In some senses, the *exemplar* of this approach is the Pribram treatment.

Methodology, as a subject, is the study of the criteria one employs to prove the validity of a scientific proposition. Indeed, many try to broaden the concept of methodology to prove the validity (*i.e.* confirm the truth) of all propositions. Recently Donald McCloskey has chosen to attack contemporary economists' statements, including mainline economics by asserting that as a subject it is not sufficiently scientific to stand the various tests of rigorous methodology. His reasoned argument ultimately comes to the point of asserting that our contemporary profession really enjoys not a sense of common test, but a sense of common expression, "rhetoric." In part, his argument rests upon the view that each period (possibly even less than a generation) has its own preferred language as well as methods for demonstrating what it has to say.

By way of contrast, although I agree with McCloskey that a particular period may have its favorite or dominant style, I have maintained for some time that individual preferences for different intellectual approaches persist throughout time [Perlman, 1978]. Some have preferred to use logic, and the test of their thinking tends to follow the procedures of immanent criticism. Are the premises consistent, does the major proposition cover the case of the minor proposition, and is the conclusion specified as to its being necessary and/or sufficient?

Others distrust use of the syllogism because they are unsure of their capacity to offer complete statements. (My students are aware of the "Bentham" ploy, wherein one asserts that Proposition X "can only be challenged on seven grounds," that because examination of the seven grounds does not mar the proposition, the proposition must, therefore, be true. One trouble often is that Bentham or, more likely, Bentham's audience was unaware that there were more than the seven challenges, with the result that they, and only possibly he, were gulled. This experience need not occur very often before the "student" comes to distrust his own use and/or acceptance of the deductive method.) In that event, the "student" may turn to the cognitive senses as a surer method for identifying truthful statements. Empiricism has its attractive side; obviously it has similar difficulties, particularly among those whose capacity to observe (including inference of what goes on beneath that which is immediately visible) is limited.

Others prefer something besides deduction or induction; occasionally it is reliance upon a dialecticism, consistent with an underlying sense that things constantly change, according to some overall rule. If this dialecticism appeals to some, a romanticism appeals to others. And in many cases what some really seem to want is a *mélange* of one or more of the foregoing, a *mélange* which is consistent with the general cultural priorities.

My point was that within any given society and/or at any given time individuals' preferences regarding methods and tests vary. Accordingly, what may be persuasive to one, might well not be persuasive to another. And while one can insist pedogogically that there is a single "right" criterion, and that part of the training of students is to educate them to the importance of acceptance of that criterion, the result may well be far more "intellectual" than it is truly effective. Styles (in terms of particular eras or times) in our profession vary not only because of the coming and going of charismatic leaders (*e.g.* Ricardo, Marshall, Friedman, and John Muth), but also because of compositional quantitative changes among the followers.

### Perceptions of the Dynamics of the Discipline

We come now to the point of this whole exercise. What these three magisterial treatments offer us are two things. One is three quite different ways of perceiving how the body of our discipline has developed. And in discussing them in some detail, I have tried to show how each can be seen and ultimately analyzed on its own terms. Implicit is my view, that each is capable of restatement within its own confines, such that the restatement takes into account new material. For example, our current understanding of the technology, the infra-structure, and the various kinds of redistributive effects of the industrialization process is much more detailed than anything which Mitchell had available to himself. Thus, even for those working within the principally historic framework one can now do better than Mitchell could.

Similarly, the rigor of the immanent criticism of each of the six post-medieval traditions which Pribram ultimately identified (Descartian *a priorism,* Baconian empiricism, Romantic nationalism, dialectical materialism, Keynesian planning, and economic interdependency) has in some senses matured since the time of his analysis. Even the first two, which he handled with most care, are far richer in analytical content than he understood. Studies of each figure he analyzed have been and probably can be more thoroughly

developed than he found them to be. His analyses of the other four were
limited by the contemporaneous state of the relevant idea sets.

If the impact of exogenous disciplines on economics is great, as Schumpeter came to believe, then the developments in each during the almost half
century since he worked suggests directions for future efforts. One has only to
look at developments in mathematics during and since the Second World War
to perceive great changes—and think, then, what those changes have meant
for economics.

Accordingly, one of our tasks as historians of economic thought seems to
me to be clearly something deeper than either the reciting of narrative *Geschichte* (which is *not* to say that "getting the story correct is unimportant") or
the application of any single methodological criterion.

But, there is, I think, a second, perhaps even more important message
which I seek to give. What I think even more important than showing how
each set of interpretations depends upon its own kind of organic thinking, is
the point that this kind of an approach is an alternative to "grading" early
writers on their *methodology*.

We start by recognizing that the topic of economics is not only seen but
necessarily must be analyzed by different sets of eyes and brains, and each
surveys the material, including the many facets, making up its growth by
pulling it together with different epistemological priorities. The task of the
historian of economic thought, then, is to record for the larger discipline (*i.e.*
economics) what shapes that development. In so doing, we offer those working in the larger discipline some sense of perspective, namely protection from
the silliness of believing that any particular idea currently enjoying *un succès
fou* need be truly revelational. In practice we can even show today's "experts"
that "rational expectations," as a "divine" gift has its antecedents in other
disciplines, and even in the economics discipline itself. Indeed, the kind of
narrowing of the surveying of the field (which it represents) is an old procedure, well-known of old to the weavers of the fabric of general historical
events.

What does all of this mean? Obviously, the purposes of this address have
been to argue that if methodological debate has its limited useful purposes,
our role as historians of economic thought goes well beyond our classifying
individuals and groups of individuals according to some methodological matrix. And in the effort to offer something more, let us not try to tax our
imaginations unduly. It is enough to recognize what is magisterial and to
realize that a comparison of authorities offers us much of what we need. In
brief, our principal tasks include using our own "masters" to offer various
matrices, and then employing those matrices in teaching our colleagues where
their ideas come from, where attacks on their ideas are likely to originate, and

most of all *why* the quest for interpretations is so complicated, and, in the end, so critically important.


NOTES


1. This paper has been drawn from several sources including an essay I prepared for a 1980 Vienna conference [Perlman, 1982], a forthcoming book review in the *Eastern Economic Journal,* and an essay presented at the 1985 Pittsburgh Eastern Economic Association meetings. Numerous people have commented on these several papers; among them I would express particular thanks for help given by Professors Nicholas Balabkins, William Fellner, Helmut Frisch, Fritz Machlup, Warren Samuels, and Wolfgang Stolper. My wife, Naomi Perlman, also helped in the preparation of these papers; her aid is, as ever, gratefully acknowledged.

2. Professor Koopmans' attack on Mitchell's work is, it seems to me, clearly responsible for most people's total misunderstanding of Mitchell's vast contributions [Koopmans, 1946]. Koopmans must have known virtually nothing of Mitchell's multitudinous writings and chose to use Mitchell (and Arthur F. Burns) as strawmen targets for emotional reasons. The kindest interpretation that I can offer is that Koopmans, asked to review a book he, himself, found boring, decided that he needed to "anthropromorphize" a target. It is all too evident that he knew not a whit about Wesley Clair Mitchell's profound interest in *a priori* theorizing, including such things as a sponsorship of the translation of the von Wieser *Social Economics* [see Mitchell, 1925]. This was no case of "Homer nodding;" Homer was having a nightmare.

3. For some inexplicable reason there is no intellectual biography of Friedman easily available. Considering his monumental contributions to statistical methods, to several aspects of contemporary theories of relative prices and incomes, to methodology, to economic history, to monetary economics (and that is to say nothing of his serving as a living and moving target for legions of bitter critics), one would think that there ought to be a ready market for such an effort.

4. Mitchell was well-read in the German and Austrian literature, coming out in much of his time. His interest in Austrian economics was great. He had respect for their work on the role of subjectivism, but he criticized their unwillingness to study how the subjective process actually worked [*cf.* Perlman, 1986].

5. There are several strands to American institutionalism. Veblen's drew heavily on clinical and "instinctive" psychology. Mitchell's stressed several methods then and later associated with statistical inference. Commons's approach involved a keen interest in the social theories of such nineteenth century writers, Germans like Otto von Gierke and English writers like Frederic Maitland. Several other institutionalists like John Maurice Clark and John Kenneth Galbraith focussed on social aspects of the market process. What differentiated Mitchell from several (but not all) of the others was his mastery of "orthodox" theory, prior to his attacking it.

6. There is in the 1983 volume a biographical essay about Pribram presumably

written in large part by his widow, Edith Kornai Pribram [Pribram, 1983, pp. xix–xlvii].

7. The usual adjective is "cartesian," but I find that its use leads students to expect graphic coordinates. What *I* want to stress is the use of internally consistent models, and for that reason I have employed a neologism/?, "descartian."

8. "Hypothetical economics" seems to involve phrasing questions in the form of a statement and subjecting the statement to the test of immanent criticism or some test of statistical inference.

9. Professor Lawrence Moss, who played a significant role in preparing the volume for publication, wrote an unpublished essay as a projected introduction to the book. One point he stressed was the impact of actual political events on Pribram's own perception of the discipline. Pribram's commitment to historical theorizing notwithstanding, Pribram saw the conflict between romantic nationalism (*i.e.* Fascism and Nazism) and dialectical materialism (*e.g.* Bolshevism) as long-run phenomena. Homer must have nodded.

10. Luigi Cossa is yet another scholar whose work is too little appreciated. His impact on our sub-discipline (history of economic thought) was tremendous. Jevons, himself, translated and had published the second edition of Cossa's *Introduction to the Study of Political Economy.* Cossa's personal library is now at the University of Bergamo.

11. The point is that the manuscript was far from finished when Schumpeter died. What was eventually published represents the efforts of a great many individuals trying to give the book coherence.

12. *Cf.* Hutchison, 1977.

13. *Cf.* Elster, 1979.

14. Irrational and anti-rational are not quite the same thing. The former suggests an approach which is devoid of cause-effect and/or logical sequence. Most aesthetic values seem to me to be irrational, although not the worse for what they lack. On the other hand, that which is anti-rational is meant to reject reason, not to "rise above it."

REFERENCES

Cossa, Luigi (1893). *An Introduction to the Study of Political Economy.* (Revised from his original [1876] and revised versions of *Guido allo studio dell' economia politica* by the author and translated from the Italian by Louis Dyer.) London and New York, Macmillan, 1893.

Elster, Jon (1979). *Ulysses and the Sirens: Studies in Rationality and Irrationality.* Cambridge: Cambridge University Press, 1979.

Hutchison, Terence W. (1977). *Knowledge and Ignorance in Economics.* Chicago: University of Chicago Press, 1977.

———. (1978). *On Revolutions and Progress in Economic Knowledge.* Cambridge: Cambridge University Press, 1978.

Koopmans, Tjalling Charles (1947). "Measurement without Theory," *Rev. Econ. Stat.,* 29 (1947), 161–72.

Machlup, Fritz (1982). *Knowledge: Its Creation, Distribution, and Economic Signifi-cance*, Volume II, "The Branches of Learning." Princeton: Princeton University Press, 1982.

McCloskey, Donald N. (1983). "The Rhetoric of Economics," *Jour. Econ. Lit.*, 21 (1983), 481–517.

Mitchell, Wesley Clair (1896). "The Quantity Theory of the Value of Money," *Jour. Pol. Econ.*, vol. 4, 139–65.

———. (1903). *A History of the Greenbacks, with Special Reference to the Economic Consequences of Their Issue: 1862–65.* (The Decennial Publications of the University of Chicago, 2d. Series, vol. 9) University of Chicago Press, 1903.

———. (1904). "The Real Issues in the Quantity Theory of Money Controversy," *Jour. Pol. Econ.* vol. 5 (1904), 403–8.

———. (1908). *Gold, Prices, and Wages under the Greenback Standard.* (University of California Publications in Economics, vol. 1). Berkeley: University of California Press, 1908.

———. (1913). *Business Cycle.* (Memoirs of the University of California, vol. 3). Berkeley: University of California Press, 1913. [New edition of Part III published with title *Business Cycles and Their Causes.* Berkeley: University of California Press, 1941].

———. (1917). "Wieser's Theory of Social Economics," *Pol. Sci. Quart.*, vol. 32, pp. 95–118. [Reprinted in *The Backward Art of Spending Money,* 1937, pp. 225–57].

———. (1927). Foreword to Friedrich von Wieser's *Social Economics* (translated by A. Ford Hinrichs). New York: Adelphi, 1927.

———. (1937). *The Backward Art of Spending Money and Other Essays.* New York: McGraw-Hill, 1937.

[Mitchell, Wesley Clair] (1952). *Wesley Clair Mitchell: 'The Economic Scientist'.* Edited by Arthur F. Burns. New York: National Bureau of Economic Research, 1952.

———. (1967 and 1969). *Types of Economic Theory: From Mercantilism to Institu-tionalism.* Edited with an Introduction by Joseph Dorfman. New York: Kelley, vol. 1, 1967; vol. 2, 1969.

Perlman, Mark (1978). "Reflections on Methodology and Persuasion," in [Machlup, Fritz]. *Breadth and Depth in Economics.* Edited by Jacob S. Dreyer. Lexington, Mass. and Toronto: Health-Lexington, 1978, pp. 37–45.

———. (1986). "Subjectivism and American Institutionalism," in a forthcoming but as yet unannounced *Festschrift* edited by Israel Kirzner.

Pribram, Karl (1983). *A History of Economic Reasoning.* Baltimore: Johns Hopkins University Press, 1983.

Schumpeter, Joseph A. (1912). *Epochen der Dogmen- und der Methodengeschichte.* J. C. B. Mohr, (Paul Siebeck) verlag, 1912 (English edition entitled *Economic Doctrine and Method: An Historical Sketch.* Translated by R. Aris. London: Allen & Unwin, 1954).

———. (1954). *History of Economic Analysis.* New York: Oxford University Press, 1954.

# CHAPTER 5

## *The Fable of the Bees,* Considered Anew

*When in 1987 Horst-Klaus Recktenwald asked if I would like to participate in his facsimile editions of the economics classics, he suggested that I might like to undertake an essay on Mandeville's classic (1714) edition. I undertook to discuss in turn: (1) Viner's and Hayek's contrary views about the book and what we knew about Mandeville, the man; (2) a summary of the 1705 original poem's principal argument, the history of its publication and its eventual expansion into a two-volume effort, and a detailed discussion of the various things Mandeville appended to the 1705 poem, ranging from essays on charity schools and the desirability of such things as brothels to the litigation involved in the 1714 edition; (3) five quite different interpretations, drawn from the secondary literature and my own analysis, of what Mandeville may have been up to; and (4) a summary of Mandeville's "anachronistic" economic insights. This chapter, previously available only in German (as translated and slightly shortened by Professor Recktenwald), was great fun to research and to write. My only difficulty was that ultimately I really could not decide which of the five interpretations I, myself, found most convincing. To my amazement, Recktenwald then remarked that that was a typical Perlman outcome.*

> O Lord, I will dispute with thee, for thou are just;
>   yes, I will plead my case before thee.
> Why do the wicked prosper
>   and traitors live at ease?
> Thou has planted them their roots strike deep,
>   they grow up and bear fruit.
> Thou art ever on their lips,
>   yet far from their hearts.
> But thou knowest me, O Lord, thou seest me;
>   thou dost test my devotion to thyself.
> Drag them away like sheep to the shambles;
>   set them apart for the day of slaughter
>                               Jeremiah 12:1–3

---

An English version of this chapter has not been previously published, although a German version appeared in Friedrich von Hayek, Mark Perlman, and Frederick B. Kaye, *Bernard de Mandevilles Leben und Werk* (Düsseldorf/-Darmstadt [FRG] Verlag Wirtschaft und Finanzen GMBH [Ein Unternehman der Verlagsgruppe Handelsblatt] 1990), 65–107.

**Introduction**

The Book's Unique Place

Few books have been so stigmatized, not only initially but also over the succeeding 250 years, as Bernard de Mandeville's *Fable of the Bees*. Is there any other book which another major author—much less so Jovian a figure as Adam Smith—denounced as "wholly pernicious," a phrase intended as an ultimate in terms of scorn in order to distance his own all-too-similar views (Smith 1759)? Yet, *The Fable of the Bees* has had its significance justified and then rejustified by generations of critical acclaim, and this series editor's decision to include it among the economics classics asserts anew the tremendous hold it has had on creative thinking in economics, as well as in other disciplines. Likely there is no other such "ancient" work in the economics discipline in which contemporary writers are still discovering critical insights on the nature of individualism (Hayek 1948). Professor Hayek's major lecture two decades ago before the British Academy is substantial further proof of just this point (Hayek 1967).[1]

In this lecture I try to identify Mandeville's nominal argument and the numerous interpretative problems associated with the content and style of his message, and to suggest reasons for the timelessness of the book's appeal (cf. Sprague 1967).

We know relatively little about Mandeville's personality. Focus must be on the book, not on Bernard de Mandeville, the author. His style probably combines some sarcasm and irony, satire and cynicism, understatement and overstatement, paradox and dual truths. It has always been more or less hard to identify which of these he was employing—wouldn't it have been simpler if punctuation marks were available to identify each? Consequently, inference about his motives is not persuasive, and there has been much confusion about what he may have meant to convey. On this point Hayek parted company with Professor Jacob Viner, whom he explicitly had previously regarded as the expert on canon (cf. Viner [1953] 1958; Rosenberg 1963; Hayek 1967). Yet only part of the difference between the two men seems to have been the product of inference; more of the problem seems to be purely philosophical— that is, whether or not those who address questions in the secular mode are *prima facie* antireligious (Viner 1978, 121). The real point is that an absence of unity about Mandeville's true meaning has given rise to contradictory seminal interpretations.

---

1. Hayek credits others for predating his views. In particular, he lauds Albert Schatz's book on the origins of individualism (Schatz 1907).

## Mandeville, the Man

We know that Mandeville was born in Rotterdam in 1670, was educated both as a philosopher and as a physician at Leyden, and, following in his father's path, took up practice as a physician specializing in nervous and stomach disorder (then termed "hypo-chondriak and hysterick passions"). Hayek likens his practice to modern psychiatry. After some travel in Europe, he emigrated to London and married a Miss Ruth Elizabeth Laurence in 1698–99.

Mostly, he seems to have practiced medicine and written several social tracts as well as scientific papers. Along the way he seems to have developed politically influential friendships (including a significant one with a Lord Chancellor, the Earl of Macclesfield). We have it on Benjamin Franklin's word[2] that he was a good talker and companion (Franklin [1791–93] 1964, 97).

Early on, even at the age of 15 (in 1685), Mandeville had become something of a writer, eventually both on medical and philosophical topics. F. W. Kaye, surely one of the most comprehensive students of Mandeville,[3] lists a minimum of 17 books known to have been written by him, as well as at least 5 more possibly having him as the author (Kaye 1924, vol. 1, xxx–xxxii).

While little has been reported directly about his intellectual interests,[4] two facets seem to be relevant. The first of these is that he had a dominant commitment to observation, that is, to the empirical method. Combined with his interest in the practice of a branch of medicine greatly committed to observing the psychological causes of physical distress,[5] this preference for describing things as they are, rather than as others think they ought to be, made him a critic of chains of transcendental (Platonic) thought (Rousseau 1975). The second facet is that Mandeville was more impressed with man's

---

2. At the time that he met Mandeville, Franklin was very young (probably 19), but he was mature. In 1725 he had written and published a pamphlet (later disavowed), *A Dissertation on Liberty and Necessity*. That pamphlet came to the attention of William Lyons, a surgeon and author of a book, *The Infallibility of Human Judgment,* who took the young Franklin to the Horn Pale-Ale House, where he met Mandeville and enjoyed his entertaining company. He was much, although not totally, influenced by Mandeville's Hobbesian materialism, by his literary style, and by his attitudes toward the lazy poor (Aldridge 1965, 63,199).

3. The prototype treatment of any economist or writer on economic subjects must be the Kaye edition of *The Fable of the Bees*. Virtually all writers on Mandeville, fortunately sooner rather than later, pay almost unlimited tribute to Kaye's scholarship. That this two-volume study has been out of print for decades is a great pity.

4. Kaye has assembled a great many inferences about Mandeville's interests, personality, and friendships (Kaye, vol. 1, xvii–xxxii).

5. Hayek refers to his practice as psychiatry (Hayek, 1967, 140).

propensity for rationalizing than with his propensity for reasoning. The philosophical bases for this latter quality as they affected his work were derived
from Hobbes and Erasmus, but it is possibly his knowledge of, and preference
for, the works of that presciently modern and tolerant thinker, Pierre Bayle,
which explains this facet best.[6] Mandeville died at Hackney, near London, on
21 January 1733.

The book at hand, *The Fable of the Bees,* his most controversial work,
took more than 25 years to develop into its ultimate form.

## The Content of the Book and the History of
## Its Publication

### The Poem's Argument and the Paradox

In its earliest and simplest form, the book is built around a short poem, of
doubtful literary quality,[7] first published anonymously in 1705. Entitled in
that initial form, *The Grumbling Hive: or, Knaves Turn'd Honest,* it describes
allegorically the history of a beehive. In actuality, the poem lays out judgmen-
tally the moral outrage of Mandeville's England (a view of the English culture
as seen from his London).

Mandeville starts his poem's argument by identifying the beehive with a
human nation. In his description he enumerates a comprehensive list of thoroughly corrupted professions or callings, each of which, nonetheless, actively
claims full commitment to religious piety. Mandeville's initial shocker is his
argument that, in spite of this widespread corruption and hypocrisy, the beehive's economy prospers—indeed, prospers at a level well beyond any previously known.

Mandeville then chooses to show what happens when hypocrisy is erased
and religious piety takes the upper hand. The hypocrites' prayers for morality
have been answered by Jove, who, choosing to mix things up properly, grants

---

6. Cf. particularly Kaye 1924, vol. 1, xxxviii–cxiii; M. R. Jack 1975, E. D. James 1975;
Philip Pinkus 1975; and Hector Monro 1975, particularly 249–67.

7. The quality of the poem (the later prose is clearly better) is a matter of taste. Albert
Schatz, whose admiration for Mandeville's work was truly tremendous, in describing the poem
wrote, "Il y raconte, *en assez mauvais vers,* l'histoire d'une ruche d'abeilles . . ." (Schatz 1907,
61, emphasis added). Or consider Eli Heckscher's assessment, "The poetry is incredibly bad from
the literary point of view, but the author's mental dexterity—though more particularly his more
comprehensive observations in prose—has made the work exceptionally illuminating"
(Heckscher 1934, vol. 2, 119). There is the contrary assessment by F. B. Kaye, "[one] is most
struck at first by the freshness of his style. . . . [A] style in which the most idiomatic and homely
vigour is combined with sophisticated control of rhythm and tone . . . retaining all the easy flow
of familiar speech and yet with a constant oratorical note. No style of the age has retained more of
the breath of life. It is more forceful and vivid than Addison's" (Kaye 1924, vol. 1, xxxviii). It is
possible that Kaye has the prose in the later essays, but not the poetry, in mind.

them their avowed wish. Moral virtue immediately and universally replaces the previous outrage. Corruption and hypocrisy disappear. However, as this new era of private virtue is established, Mandeville introduces his second shocker. As a consequence of the new morality, national economic depression completely replaces the previous national prosperity.

Mandeville's conclusion, one he makes explicit in the poem's closing *Moral,* is that while private immorality is consistent with public economic prosperity, private virtue is not. Quite the contrary, there is a functional contradiction between Christian morality and economic success. But just what this conclusion implies is somewhat unclear.[8] First, he could have meant that, given a morally virtuous community, economic success was then impossible; thus it was preferable to abandon economic success as a goal. Second, he could have meant that economic prosperity was so important an end that it was wise to abandon the search for community virtue. Or, third, he could have simply stated his proposition as a paradox. It is hard to argue that he favored the first, and although some, like Professor Viner, have often suggested that it may have been no more than the third, I think it probable that Mandeville meant the second.[9] But this implies a sharp distinction between private and social virtue.

In its original 1705 anonymous six-penny quarto of 26 pages, the poem stood by itself.[10] It was printed for Sam Ballard and sold by A. Baldwin. Kaye reports that "The piece took, for a pirated edition was soon printed, and 'cry'd about the Streets in a Half-Penny Sheet'" (Kaye 1924, vol. 1, xxxiii).

## The History of the Book

The book, *The Fable of the Bees,* however, goes considerably beyond the poem. Its initial appearance as a one-volume book (here contrasted with the appearance of just the poem) was in 1714.[11] *It is this first edition that is*

---

8. I am indebted to Professor Rescher for suggesting the phrasing of the different interpretations in this fashion.

9. This point was developed in extensio by a Spanish writer, Fernandez Florez, in a 1926 allegorical novel, *Las siete columnas* (Florez 1926). The argument, as summarized by Pozo and Samuels (no date), is that Satan, for personal egotistical reasons, is led to abjure the seven deadly sins. What results is not bliss but "poverty, economic depression and squalor" (pp. 11ff.). Whether Florez had read anything by or actually knew of Mandeville is unknown; according to Pozo and Samuels, the excellent translation by Mitchell (1934) does reflect the translator's knowledge of Mandeville.

10. There was no identification on the title page of the author; indeed, that lack of specific attribution continued through all of the editions in Mandeville's own lifetime. However, such lack of author identification may have been custom and/or modesty.

11. The University of London Goldsmiths' Library has two 1714 "editions"; presumably both are "first." They are listed in the Goldsmiths' Library catalog as numbers 5094 and 5095 (Goldsmiths' Library 1970).

*published here in facsimile.* Besides reprinting the original poem, this 1714
edition offered 20 general commentaries ("Remarks") on specific lines
and/or couplets from the poem, as well as an essay, "An Enquiry into the
Origin of Moral Virtue." This last addressed the problem of the govern-
ability of men.

The second edition came out in 1723 and contained all parts of the 1714
edition, with some changes in the original wording of the poem, some extensive revisions to the aforementioned 20 *Remarks*, 2 new *Remarks*, two additional essays—"An Essay on Charity and Charity Schools" and "A Search
into the Nature of Society"—plus the *Index*.[12] I find this index (as well as
those found in later editions also of Part 2) of particular interest, because each
puts the various points that Mandeville made into his own categorical pigeonholes.

As Mandeville himself wrote, it was the 1723 second edition that precip-
itated the beginning of the widespread public denunciation (Kaye 1924, vol.
1, 409). A grand jury of Middlesex moved a presentment calling it "a public
nuisance." The charges were five: (1) the book denied the Trinity and introduced the Arian heresy; (2) the book denied Providence and affirmed "an
absolute Fate"; (3) the book reviled the clergy and "by the Libertinism of [its]
Opinions [it] may encourage and draw others into . . . Immoralities of . . .
Practice"; (4) "That a General Libertinism may the more effectually be established, the *Universities* are decried, and all *Instructions of Youth* in the Principles of the Christian Religion are exploded with the greatest Malice and
Falsity;" and (5) In order to achieve these vile ends "studied Artifices and
invented Colours have been made use of to run down Religion and Virtue as
*prejudicial* to Society, and detrimental to the State; and to recommend Luxury,
Avarice, Price, and all kind of Vices, as being necessary to *Publick Welfare*"
(Kaye 1924, vol. 1, 383–86, italics in the original).[13] Mandeville thought the
instigator to be a Baron Carteret, who then wrote a note further denouncing
the book; that note appeared in *The London Journal* on 27 July 1723. Mandeville replied to this latter attack with his, "An Abusive Letter to Lord C." His
reply (where he seems to have at last identified himself in print as the author),
was published in *The London Journal* of 10 August 1723. In it Mandeville
asserted that the book was "designed for the Entertainment of People of
Knowledge and Education. . . . It is a Book of severe and exalted Morality
. . ." (Kaye 1924, vol. 1, 404–5). In subsequent editions, that is, printings
starting with the "third" edition of 1724, Mandeville included the grand jury
presentment, a copy of the abusive letter to Lord C., and his reply all under
the title, "A Vindication of the Book" (see Kaye 1924, vol. 1, 15, 383–412).

---

12. Cf. Goldsmiths' Library catalog no. 6178 (Goldsmiths' Library 1970).
13. Particularly offensive to the grand jury seems to have been Mandeville's tolerant, even
benign, treatment of whoring and whores (Cook 1975).

In 1728 a "fifth" edition appeared;[14] like some (but not all) of the immediately prior versions, J. Tonson was the London publisher. In 1732 J. Tonson sold a "sixth" edition, still containing, more or less, the contents of the 1724 edition, the one augmented with the grand jury indictment and its *sequelae*. Prepared by the author before his death (21 January 1732), it is the one on which most subsequent critical analysis has been focused. This sixth edition, consisting of much more than the 1705 original verse, contained:

1. A 1724 revision of a 1723 preface
2. The original poem, with some small but not insignificant changes in the wording
3. "An Enquiry into the Origin of Moral Virtue" (an essay apparently written during or before 1724)
4. Twenty-four *Remarks*. Most of these *Remarks* had been published with the 1714 revision of the poem
5. An essay, "An Essay on Charity and Charity-Schools"
6. An essay, "A Search into the Nature of Society"
7. An essay, "A Vindication of the Book, from the Aspersions contain'd in a Presentment of the Grand Jury of *Middlesex* and An Abusive Letter to Lord C."

During all or part of the period after 1723, Mandeville was working on a second volume entitled *Fable of the Bees, Part II*. Published separately in 1729,[15] it had its own preface and contained six dialogues, as well as Mandeville's own index for it. It, too, went through revisions in 1730 and 1733. Its contents are a refutation of the criticisms of the *Fable* generally, and of the author specifically. The dialogue form was again a manifestation of Mandeville's literary virtuosity.

In 1732 Mandeville again attacked his critics, in this instance George Bishop Berkeley, with his final effort, *A Letter to Dion, Occasion'd by his Book call'd Alciphron or The Minute Philosopher*. This essay has not been published as part of the *Fable* editions. Nonetheless, it was used by Professor Viner ([1953] 1958) to substantiate his interpretation of Mandeville's true meaning (the one challenged by Hayek); this is discussed below.

In 1733 (after Mandeville's death), the two volumes were merged, and the set of two volumes, more or less the way we know it now, was published.

---

14. There are problems distinguishing the appropriate identification number for each edition. Kaye offers a comprehensive listing of each edition, but it still has gaps. One trouble was that in the eighteenth century small print runs, widespread book pirating, and authors' desire for anonymity make accuracy of numbering editions difficult (see Kaye 1924, vol. 1, xxxiii–xxxvii and vol. 2, 386–400).

15. Listed as № 6642 in the London Goldsmiths' Catalog (Goldsmiths' Library 1970).

## The Contents of the First Edition within the Context of the Later Editions

As noted already, the first edition of the book contained the poem (described above), an essay on the nature of moral virtue, and twenty commentaries or "Remarks." What follows here, however, are brief summaries of the original contents plus the additions in volume one as they were included in the final two-volume work.

*An Enquiry into the Origin of Moral Virtue.* The immediate need of the leadership of any society is to keep its members governable. As these members are self-willed and full of selfish passions, all sorts of artifices tend to be employed by those leaders to counter the natural centrifugal forces, as unleashed by the members' imperfect natures. Mandeville easily sees that the act of governing, itself, encourages, indeed requires, the construction of a comprehensive pseudomorality, offering the governed social structure and personal purpose.[16]

Just how much Mandeville had in mind in the way of a comprehensive discussion of morality is far from clear. Professor Hirschman (1977, 17–19) has pointed out that all of his examples, the foci of his interest, really pertain to only one human passion, the desire for material goods.[17] And thus, one can easily conclude that he was interested in economic success first, and in morality second. In this sense, his was a more specialized form of iconoclasm than were the widely focused iconoclasms of Voltaire, Paine, and LaMettrie; rather, his iconoclasm was the obverse of Rousseau's, who felt that giving economic success priority was wrong because such success was always built on a foundation of evil.[18] Another difficulty in interpreting Mandeville is determining whether he was advocating strong governmental controls of economic life, as both Professors Heckscher and Viner believe, or whether he

---

16. Anyone looking for a precursor to Marx's historical materialism, the theory that each era creates a social value system to make its governing duties easier, has no difficulty in recognizing Mandeville's assertion of the same thought (cf. Dumont 1977). Of course, Mandeville's social structure is *not* based on control of the means of production, as Marx's was; but Mandeville's perception of the uses of pseudovalue systems in the relationship between the governing group and the governed is clear.

17. Hirschman's treatment of Mandeville and Smith is exemplary; as I understand his view, what he points out is that although Smith explicitly attacked Mandeville in the last edition of the *Theory of Moral Sentiments,* what Smith had done in the *Wealth of Nations* was simply to use the same *simplice* perception of man's nature (*homo economicus*) as Mandeville had. More to the point, those who hold that the *Theory of Moral Sentiments* is the broader-based of Smith's two major books can see that Smith emulated the Mandeville rhetorical framework while later going on to lambast that kind of error. For drawing this point to the surface of my memory, I must thank Professor Sonya Gold.

18. Again, for this point I express thanks to Professor Rescher.

was advocating only the government's setting of the "rules of the game," as Hayek, Chalk, and Rosenberg seem to think. This will be discussed in the following.

*The Remarks.* These, which give meaning to the poem, are critical because they were Mandeville's often inflammatory commentaries or expansions of the meaning of various selected lines of the poem. Mandeville, choosing to explain the conflict between what he saw and what others (and possibly he, as well) thought moral, seemingly left little to inference—although, as we shall see, good, even great, scholars seem to have their difficulties in understanding his purported meaning. In exquisite prose and explicit detail, but also with general accuracy, Mandeville relies on his acumen as a physician with trained powers of direct and indirect observation,[19] as well as on his apparent understanding of Christian morality, particularly as perceived by early eighteenth-century British divines, to paint his paradoxes.

While it would be useful to summarize each, I shall confine my comments to those *Remarks* involving economics. In the last part of this, my introduction, I shall try to summarize "Mandeville's economics."

> *Remark A:*[20] Whilst others follow'd Mysteries,
>   To which few Folks bind 'Prentices;

Here he develops his theory of choice of occupation and job selection, choices where interested individuals (as well as a wise parent) detachedly take into account the child's abilities and interests as well as the position's status, its pecuniary utilities and disutilities, and its income potential.[21]

> *Remark B:* These were called Knaves; but, bar the Name
>   The grave Industrious were the Same.

Mandeville observes that in trade, buyers and sellers have differences in their subjective utility functions and the amount of information available to each, with the result that their trading positions are affected, and the buyers often claim that the seller has employed deception.

---

19. See footnote 51, for some discussion of empiricism.

20. Wherever possible all of the quotations of lines come from the 1714 first edition. This is the accompanying essay to the edition printed in facsimile. Where material was added in later editions I have used quotations from Kaye 1924, vol. 1.

21. Clearly central to Mandeville's concern is the role of expectations. Fulfilled expectations were the goal; shortfall was the cause of personal frustration and eventual social disharmony.

*Remark C:* The Soldiers, that were forc'd to fight,
If they surviv'd, got Honour by't.

This is a discourse on honor and shame, neither of which is, as commonly believed, ordained by God. Honor is mostly the good opinion of others, as shame also mostly reflects others' opinions. Neither is purely subjective; they each reflect communications between people rather than purely personal (in one person's mind) assessments. This remark was lengthened in the 1723 edition. The addition inter alia describes in clinical detail what we would now call the physiological symptoms of a neurotic response.

Of particular importance to the Mandeville *Weltanschauung,* this remark stresses that what are commonly called virtues or moral faults can have three sources: what is ordained in heaven, levels of conduct that society forces on the individual, and the individual's own conscience.

*Remark D:* For there was not a Bee but would
Get more, I won't say, than he should;
But than, &c.

Self-esteem, seen as an innate desire to self-aggrandize one's gains, is often offset immediately (and it would seem briefly) by sellers when they realize how resentful the buyers are upon perceiving that the sellers have made gains. This meanness of the buyers' spirits has a souring effect on any honesty in interpersonal transactions, and may in the long run be matched by the sellers' enthusiasm for telling the world how he gulled the buyer. Whether and how this boastful aspect is covered up is simply a matter of idiosyncratic style.

*Remark E:* ——As your Gamesters do,
Who, tho' at fair Play, ne'er will own
Before the Losers what they've won.

Winners initially deny their gains and losers initially exaggerate their losses; later the winners move to exaggerating their gains and the losers laugh and make little of their losses.[22]

*Remark F:* And Virtue, who from Politicks
Had learn'd a Thousand cunning Tricks,
Was, by their happy Influence
Made Friends with Vice.—

---

22. Something akin to this distinction was presented only a few years later (1738) as Daniel Bernouilli's "St. Petersburg paradox"; more recently Twersky and Kahneman have identified this point as the "framing problem" (1974).

Any distinction between virtue and vice pales before the "fact" that virtue is often the product of vice. Industrious good people often earn their livelihoods from activities supported by others' vices, or by expenditures based solely on pride and luxury.

*Remark G:* The worst of all the Multitude
　　　　　　Did something for the Common Good.

The explicit paradox is that vice (seen in "Thieves and House-breakers") creates work opportunity for virtuous workers such as ironsmiths. Originally no more than a paragraph long, this Remark was expanded greatly, and in its longer form it emphasized the virtuous and beneficent social effects of the "employment multiplier." The highwayman (a villain) gives money to a harlot (also a villain), but from that point on when she gives that money to a mercer, to a shoemaker, to a draper, and so on, and each of them gives it to other virtuous workmen, it can then be seen that the original vice is now fueling virtue. Mandeville repeats the point when applying it to the drinking of gin; a loathsome habit, it nonetheless gives employment to many.

*Remark H:* Parties directly opposite,
　　　　　　Assist each other, as 'twere for spight.

This remark observes that the presence of wickedness can bring forth its own reform, that is, "Nothing was more instrumental in forwarding the Reformation, than the Sloth and stupidity of the *Roman* Clergy; yet the same Reformation has rous'd 'em from the Laziness and Ignorance then labour'd under" (p. 63). Upon closer investigation, however, that inherent wickedness-reform relationship is seen to be a necessary part of public policy formulation.

*Remark I:* The Root of Evil, Avarice,
　　　　　　That damn'd ill-natur'd baneful Vice,
　　　　　　Was Slave to Prodigality.

This Remark and the next are interdependent. Here Mandeville discusses avarice, hoarding, and dissipation of funds. Without avarice, there could be no funds to dissipate; yet, without dissipation, avarice would freeze economic activity. Hoarding by some makes money scarce for the rest. Prodigality (purposive expenditure), not dissipation, is advanced as the essential correction to avarice.

*Remark K:*[23] That noble Sin——

---

23. There was no J in the numbering system.

Mandeville argues that prodigality is what "makes the Chimney smoke, and all the Tradesmen smile" (p. 74). Frugality, on the other hand, is a "mean starving Virtue" (p. 76), suitable only for small societies of good peaceful men, content to be poor. In a large growing nation, frugality falls far short of the socially more advantageous of the two vices (avarice and prodigality) working together in combination. From the Keynesian standpoint, what Mandeville argues is the relatedness between saving (the results of avarice) and profitable investment (usually the by-product of a prodigality leading men to consume more than the bare minimum). "I look upon Avarice and Prodigality in the Society as I do upon two contrary Poysons in Physick. . . . They may assist each other, and often make a good Medicine between them" (p. 79).

*Remark L:* ———While Luxury
Employ'd a Million of the Poor, &c.

A lengthy remark in which Mandeville first dismisses the idea of luxury as a pejorative, noting both the point that employment benefits from the production of luxuries and the point that what are luxuries to some are necessities to others. Second, Mandeville is clearly embracing a view that is heretical to eighteenth-century mercantilism. As against the classical mercantilist bullion view, he stresses that for countries not possessing or owning gold and silver mines, expansion of international trade over time is most desirable, but can be possible only if the import-export accounts are balanced. With "a wise Administration all People may swim in as much foreign luxury as their [export] Product can purchase, without being improverish'd by it" (p. 97). He adds that the use of luxuries will not interfere with the ability of the military forces. True luxury, he concludes, promotes not debility but splendor, and splendor is a state not to be deprecated.

*Remark M:* And odious Pride a Million more.

Here we find a lengthy commentary stressing that it is pride, not humility, that serves as the key and necessary social incentive. Like prodigality, individuals' pride, morally base as it may be, is what produces socioeconomic success. Economies lacking the presence of individual pride invariably stagnate; those present individual pride, flourish.

*Remark N:*[24] Envy itself, and Vanity,
Were Ministers of Industry.

---

24. This Remark was added in the 1723 edition. This and later additions, of course, changed the numbering scheme for the following Remarks.

Here Mandeville discusses envy, an emotion that all men possess, but that due to hypocrisy they hide, even from themselves. As we all wish the best for ourselves, we grieve when someone else possesses anything we would like to have but lack. We also feel anger toward the owners. Envy often leads to emulation of the successful ones and thus to hard work to achieve the same rewards.

*Remark N [Later O]:*[25] Real Pleasures, Comforts, Ease.

Here the argument becomes an exhaustive attack on the clergy (including the religious orders) who make a shibboleth of extolling the point that self-denial is the crucible for all virtue. Mandeville maintains that the real pleasures of mankind are based on worldly and sensual cognition, not on transcendental meditation. His judgment is tied to an empirical, not to an abstract-theoretical, method, although he uses not only his own observations but his knowledge of historical and philosophical treatments of topics as well. Examples of the latter are variously his contrasting of the Epicureans with the romantic Stoics and the "literary" incident between the cynic, Diogenes, and Alexander the Great (pp. 126–27). Yet, toward the end of this lengthy attack he does "admit" to at least one presumed observed exception to his rule: "Thus I have prov'd, that the real Pleasures of all Men in Nature are worldly and sensual, if we judge them from their Practice; I say all Men *in Nature,* because Devout Christians who alone are to be excepted here, being regenerated, and preternaturally assisted by the Divine Grace, cannot be said to be in Nature" (p. 138). It may simply be irony.

*Remark O [later P]:* ——The very Poor
Liv'd better than the Rich before.

This comment comprises a discourse on how much economic progress has benefited the poor and also discusses how much this same progress has impaired individuals' capacities for empathy.[26] Higher living standards lead not only to non–pain-causing use of animals (shorn wool) or vegetable-grown clothing; they also lead to the consumption of animal meat, the slaughtering of which causes death and, Mandeville thought, much pain. It is the egoism of man which argues that everything has its purpose, of which the consumption of the flesh of animals, fish, and crustaceans is an example. The comment

---

25. This appears as Remark N in the 1714 facsimile edition.

26. This is seemingly a reference to the analysis of rising standards of living. Mandeville noted that historically what earlier had been luxuries often became necessities for later generations.

closes with an explicit attack on Descartes, who reasoned irresponsibly (rather than carefully observed) that animals did not feel pain.[27]

> *Remark P [later Q]:* ————For frugally
> They now liv'd on their Salary.

This is a lengthy discussion of the role of frugality in national economic development. It draws considerably on Mandeville's interpretive histories of contemporary Netherlands (including both Belgium and Holland) and Spain. The Dutch became frugal when they were oppressed by Spanish rule and burdened by very heavy taxes on food and other necessities. Dutch wealth, however, stemmed not from their frugality but from their trade. Spain, on the other hand, had been a rich country, but the influx of precious metals from the New World led people to cease to work productively—"[T]heir Industry forsook them. The Farmer left his Plough, the Mechanick his Tools, the Merchant his Compting-house, and everybody scorning to work, took Pleasure and turn'd Gentleman. . . . [The Spanish] from a rich, acute, diligent, and laborious, bec[a]me a slow, idle, proud and beggarly People; so much for *Spain*" (pp. 176–78). Possession of great bullion reserves is not, Mandeville avers, a blessing; it can be a disaster: "[T]he Enjoyment of all Societies will ever depend upon the Fruits of the Earth, and the Labour of the People; both which joined togethr are a more certain, a more inexhaustible, and a more real Treasure, than the Gold *Brazil,* or the Silver of *Potosi*" (Mandeville 1714, 178–79).

Thus, frugality, in and of itself, Mandeville asserts, leads nowhere; but frugality, as a means to satisfying such base passions as covetousness and envy, selfishness and military aggressiveness, is a necessary although not a sufficient condition for economic prosperity.

There are two other points. The first deals with stimulating workers' energies: lacking pride or avarice, workers have "nothing to stir them up to be serviceable but their Wants. . . . The only thing then that can render the labouring Man industrious, is a moderate quantity of Money; for as too little will, according as his Temper is, either dispirit or make him Desperate, so too much will him Insolent and Lazy" (Mandeville 1714, 175).

The other point can be found in the original version (Mandeville 1714, 174–75), but was supplemented in the 1723 edition (Kaye 1924, vol. 1, 193). Mandeville notes strongly that the amount of coin needed in a country is a

---

27. Mandeville had written in 1689 (at age 19) a college thesis, *Disputa Philosophica de Bruntorum Operationibus,* and in 1691 a tract, *Disputatio Medica de Chylosi Vitiata,* based on Descartes' view (F. B. Kaye, 1924, vol. 1, 181n.1). This repudiation seems to me to be more than a coincidence. Mandeville came to appreciate that because he had to believe what he, himself, had witnessed and not what others had asserted, he was in the experiential and/or empirical tradition of Bacon and Hobbes, not in the rational Cartesian tradition.

function of the number to be employed and their wages. This is an early perception of the need for liquidity as a determinant of the necessary quantity of money, a point sometimes called the "real balance" or the "Pigou effect."[28]

*Remark R [later S]:*  No Limner for his Art is fam'd,
                        Stone-cutters, Carvers are not nam'd.

As Mandeville saw his world, it was the demand for buildings and housing that most stimulated the domestic side of prosperity. Frugality in this sector presaged unemployment.

*Added Remark T:* ———To live great,
                    Had made her Husband rob the State.

The strength of wives' demands for luxury and variety results in a demand for additional production. Mandeville observes that "a considerable Portion of what the Prosperity of *London* and Trade in general . . . and all the worldly Interest of the Nation consist in, depends entirely on the Deceit and vile Stratagems of Women . . ." (Kaye 1924, vol 1., 228). Thus, once again it is not frugality and similar virtues which fuel the system. This Remark did not appear in the 1714 edition.

*Remark S [later V]:*[29] Content, the Bane of Industry.

Mandeville defends his designation of contentment, rather than laziness, as "the Bane of Industry." He defines a lazy person as one who, having no other employment, refuses to do any business or service "which he ought to do for himself or others" (p. 215). A man who refuses to perform a service for a payment which he regards as too little is not lazy. Contentment is a situation where men are satisfied with the station that they are in, and Mandeville concludes that laziness and contentment are either very close, or if not, contentment is more contrary to industriousness than laziness.

*Remark T [later X]:* To make a great an Honest Hive.

Mandeville repeats that what people desire is the satisfaction of their pleasures. Discussing Sparta he wrote, "there never was a Nation whose Greatness was more empty than theirs" (p. 225), and he emphasized that

---

28. The real balance effect was part of the Pigovian "oral tradition," although Dennis Robertson attributed it to Maynard Keynes (Robertson 1926, 50n).

29. There never was a Remark U.

although Sparta had been a mighty power, the harshness of life would thoroughly repel Englishmen.

*Remark V [later Y]:*[30] T' enjoy the World's Conveniencies.

While a lesser part of this Remark appeared in the 1714 edition, it was greatly expanded to provide a defense against the critics of that edition; the following comments come from the last edition. The critics had held that the excessive luxury he advocated would lead to national ruin. Mandeville pointed out that he had shown the limits that effectively constrained luxury. This he did by maintaining that he had set out, even in that first edition, five absolute maxims: (1) The poor must be made to work: it is prudent to relieve their poverty, but folly to cure it (cf. Mandeville 1714, 175–76 and Furniss [1920] 1965); (2) Agriculture and fishing should be promoted to make food, and thereby the cost of labor, cheap (cf. Mandeville 1714, 178); (3) "Ignorance . . . [is] a necessary Ingredient in the Mixture of Society: from all of which it is manifest . . . that Luxury was [not] to be made general through every part of a Kingdom" (cf. Mandeville 1714, 77 and Kaye 1924, vol. 1, 249); (4) "Property should be well-secured, justice impartially administred, and in every thing the Interest of the Nation taken care of" (Kaye 1924, vol. 1, 249, but cf. Mandeville 1714, 87); and (5) the legislature must see that yearly imports never exceed exports (cf. Mandeville 1714, 86–87). He concludes with the point that avarice and prodigality, working in tandem, are necessary to any successful society: "National Frugality there never was nor never will be without a National Necessity" (Kaye 1924, vol. 1, 251). "Sumptuary Laws,"[31] he added, "may be of use to an indigent Country, after great Calamities of War, Pestilence, or Famine, when Work has stood still, and the Labour of the Poor been interrupted; but to introduce them into an opulent Kingdom is the wrong way . . ." (Kaye 1924, vol. 1, 251).

*An Essay on Charity and Charity Schools.* In this essay Mandeville moved from the more-or-less general to the more-or-less specific.

Just as in our own times enthusiasm for supervised early education of the children of the poor has been seen as the way to cut the cycle of poverty, so in the early eighteenth century there was a similar enthusiasm for church-run charity schools. Such schools were supposed to be benevolent and purely altruistic answers to the vices found among the children of the working poor.

---

30. Virtually all of this Remark was added in the 1723 edition.

31. These were laws that limited consumption of goods to parties of higher social order. Economists, often thinking *post hoc ergo propter hoc,* tend to view this kind of legislation as having the purpose of reducing domestic consumption. Historians also appreciate that much of the motivation for these laws was to conserve the relative social status of the political and economic aristocracy.

Mandeville attacked the establishment of these schools on two scores. First, he argued that they were hardly examples of pure altruism because those who founded them did so not to solve social problems so much as to aggrandize their own moral reputations. Second, he held that the education given the young "scholars" served to increase their expectations beyond what the market had to offer them. Thus, it frustrated them and likely ruined them as workers.

In his presentation Mandeville took the opportunity to deride the altruistic pretensions of those who supported the schools. Charity, he held, is the altruistic things we do for those who are not friends or persons related to or dependent upon us. Charity is not engendered by empathy, compassion, or pity, each of which is something quite different, due to motivations and consequences. As for motivations, his point is that when one gives to a beggar or charity for a similar immediate purpose, one is moved to assuage one's conscience. As such, then, the gift is not disinterested; one is mostly removing an internal pain. And, as for consequences, it is consequences for the donor, not the recipient, that seem to matter.

One's empathy, he noted, is generally inverse to the distance from the observed.[32] In his discussion of pity he points out that pity is responsible for "more Mischief in the World than what is excited by the Tenderness of Parents . . ." (Kaye 1924, vol. 1, 260). The conclusion related to this point is that "Pride and Vanity have built more Hospitals than all the Virtues together" (Kaye 1924, vol. 1, 261).

The focus then shifts to the second argument. It is that schooling for its own sake engenders habits contrary to workmanship and individual responsibility. Schools exist not for any supposed social benefits associated with workers becoming educated above their station and expectations; instead, they exist to appease the considerable vanity and self-love of the schools' founders and other benefactors.

As I read the essay what comes through, besides an undiluted, almost sophomoric, cynicism is a total unawareness of the social benefits of a literate labor force. Mandeville's conclusion here is not only shocking, but it seems to me it could be incredibly wrong. Perhaps some of the sting of this criticism can and should be dismissed, however, when one hears repeatedly even now that in some contemporary developing countries (e.g., India, Bangladesh, and Pakistan) too many students take or are given higher education[33] and are thus exposed to expectations which can never be realized.

---

32. Cf. Adam Smith's theme in *The Theory of Moral Sentiments* (1759, Part I, Section 1, chap. 1).

33. One of my students from the People's Republic of China, Mr. Dingbo Xu, has corrected my perception by noting that it is not higher education itself, but the wrong kind of higher education, which creates the problem.

*A Search into the Nature of Society.*[34] This is a lengthy attack on the system of sentimental morality offered by Anthony Ashley Cooper, later the third Earl of Shaftesbury. Cooper, whose work was an answer to Hobbes, asserted that every normal man had a moral sense. Mandeville's reply attacked Shaftesbury's Platonic position, which proposed a single answer to all moral questions. Mandeville started with a thorough review of the empirical evidence and rejected the simplicity of the Shaftesbury position. Mandeville then went on to his own belief that it is the presence and necessity of dealing with evil, not good, that binds society together and derivatively produces what desirable consequences there are.

Mandeville's preference for the empirical method, of course, puts his argument on a different plane from that which Cooper, a Platonist, proposed. As such, the differences in their methods made their positions irreconcilable.

What Mandeville concluded, which was consistent with his general theme, could not be anything but abrasive. In asserting that good does not produce good but rather that evil produces good, Mandeville seemed to be going beyond the recitation of a paradox. He was saying that the Great Satan, not God, the epitome of good, was the font of *social* (perhaps as distinct from personal or private) virtue;[35] it was classical Manichaeism.

*A Vindication of the Book, from the Aspersions Contain'd in a Presentment of the Grand Jury of Middlesex and An Abusive Letter to Lord C.* Explicitly stating that it was necessary to identify them to those who had not had the opportunity to read the Fable, this started with a George Bernard Shaw-like recitation of all of the alleged evils in the work, reproducing verbatim the Middlesex Grand Jury's indictment as well as several screeds, printed in the *Evening-Post*. The essence of his argument is then reproduced:

> I flatter my self to have demonstrated, that neither the Friendly Qualities and kind Affections that are natural to Man, nor the real Virtues he is capable of acquiring by Reason and Self-denial, are the Foundations of Society; but that what we call Evil in this World, Moral as well as Natural, is the grand Principle that makes sociable Creatures; the solid Basis the Life and Support of all Trades and Employments without Exception; That there we must look for the true Origin of all Arts and Sciences; and that the Moment Evil ceases, the Society must be spoiled, if not totally dissolved (Kaye 1924, vol. 1, 402).

---

34. This was added in the 1723 (second) edition.

35. One wonders whether John Milton, in his obvious but denied admiration of the Prince of Darkness, could have been guilty of the same charge. Professor Tobias tells me that this idea has usually been credited to William Blake, who wrote well after Mandeville.

However, despite all he has written, Mandeville adds a clarifying quali-fication, which should have done much to stem the flow of criticism. Evil, he adds at length, is imperfection—not only moral imperfection but imperfection of inadequacy: "*Evil* . . . I would have taught them . . . [is] every Defect, every Want . . . [and] that on the Multiplicity of those Wants depended all those mutual Services which the individual Members of Society pay to one another; and that consequently, the greater the Variety there was of Wants, the larger Number of Individuals might find their private Interest in labouring for the good of others" (Kaye 1924, vol. 1, 402–3).

The book, he averred, was meant to entertain "People of Knowledge and Education." It is, he wrote,

> a Book of severe and exalted Morality, that contains a strict Test of Virtue, an infallible Touchstone to distinguish the real from the counter-feited, and shews many Actions to be faulty that are palmed upon the World for good ones: It describes the Nature and Symptoms of human Passions, detects their Force, and Disguises; and traces Selflove in its darkest Recesses. (Kaye 1924, vol. 1, 404–5)

So much for his explicit evaluation of the book. How did others assess it?

## Five Principal Interpretative Assessments of the Book's Message Based on the Criticism of It in Its Final Form

The first edition received neither reviews nor any mentions. However, as noted above, of even more interest to us than the specific harsh criticisms, which were elicited by the later editions, is the wide spectrum of and ulti-mately favorable commentary that the final two-volume work eventually prompted.

What now follows is an effort to arrange these comments, pro and con, into the smallest number of categories. Invariably the act of pigeonholing is one of personal taste.

### Lines of Critical Assessment

These five categories identify the books as

1. An application and an extension of Hobbes's conclusions and method.
2. An irresponsible, anti-Christian intellectual satirical romp.
3. An exercise in seventeenth-century mercantilism and secularism.

4. A truly modern-type Christian tract, discoursing on the mystery of how "God works His wond'rous ways."
5. The cornerstone of the British Utilitarian tradition.

## The Fable of Bees as a Hobbesian Exercise

This is ethically the most neutral of the assessments. It is the view that Mandeville's efforts can best be grasped as his attempt to offer an extension of the principal political theory argument found in Hobbes's *Leviathan.* Although Hobbes had offered a plethora of ideas, two seem relevant here. Hobbes had argued that the methodology of discovery was empirical observation, as refined first in the brain and then further constrained by the rules of interpersonal communication, principally language. With this concept Mandeville had no trouble; he grasped the empirical method with both hands.

Hobbes's second relevant point was that the social and governmental process represented man's capacity to reason applied to brute force. The Hobbesian social contract was necessary lest men out of sheer fear kill one another off. The Hobbesian government contract gave the monopoly of force to the sovereign, who had to deliver law and order or suffer dethronement as a consequence.

Mandeville, it was argued, went beyond Hobbes and suggested that morality (as practiced, rather than as preached) and the network of social or institutional arrangements pertaining to production, consumption, and exchange simply served to establish the government contract. Thus, the book represents a generalized reply to the attacks on the Hobbesian formulation by such Christians as Joseph Bishop Butler and Anthony Ashley Cooper, Lord Shaftesbury.

Recall what Hobbes had offered. It was, first, an empirical rather than a Platonic method. And, second, it presented an argument that the organization, in fact, of society was based on pragmatic (even opportunistic) ethics rather than on Christian religious revelation.

It was Hobbes's attack on the religious dogma (the sources of ethical order) which shocked the clerics. Some responded with new religious answers. Joseph Bishop Butler promised to give a Christian answer to the method and the conclusions offered by Hobbes, albeit softened but not reversed by Locke. Butler's answer involved an appeal to the use of reason (not as rigorous as Descartes', but of that genre). This perception of reason asserted that one could accept Christianity without having to swallow superrational assumptions, including explicitly revelation. Whether Bishop Butler was successful may be another matter and does not concern us directly here, but the indirect effect of his work was to differentiate reason from faith.

Another clerical answer was offered by Anthony Ashley Cooper, something of a golden boy—one born into truly the leading intellectual and politically powerful English family. Cooper had actually been tutored by John Locke and supervised at Cambridge by John Austin. He was persuaded neither that man was basically a brute, nor that life was really "brutish, knavish, and short." Like the prophet Elijah, he believed that in every normal man's heart, irrespective of personal experience and including cultural conditioning, there was "a still, small voice," counseling morality.[36] Like the five senses, morality came as "standard equipment." Hence, this still, small voice was morality based on a cognitive sense or, if you please, it was "sentimental morality."

Was Mandeville's the Hobbesian riposte to the Anglican swipe?[37] What he offered was an extension and (in that sense) a defense of Hobbes's argument and his method. The attack on Shaftesbury focuses on Shaftesbury's preference for Platonic thinking, rather than empirical observation. The attack on Shaftesbury, nonetheless, was more apparent than it was real (cf. Primer 1975b). Mandeville was, when all is said and done, not prepared to argue that man was completely immoral and that there could be no inner voice of moral restraint. All he argued was that such an inner voice was hardly "standard equipment." It certainly could not be counted upon as an observable fact. Moreover, when it does surface, its existence hardly solves all social problems (as Shaftesbury and Butler seemingly thought it would).

## The *Fable of the Bees* as an Anti-Christian Satire

*The Book as a Satire.* In very recent times there has been an effort to explain the book as an exercise in satire, although admittedly a less skillful satire than Jonathan Swift's (Adolph 1975; Pinkus 1975; Monro 1975). This argument is predicated on the twin assumptions that Mandeville had a coherent unambiguous message attacking the very conceptualization of the Christian virtues,

---

36. Cf. Smith's dispassionate observer (Smith, 1759, Part I, Section I, chap. 4), which is not exactly the same thing because Cooper's morality was not that cerebral. But, then again, Smith's preference for dispassionate evaluations may have been a product of his own self-delusion. Hume thought so.

37. Professor Rescher probably disagrees with my interpretation, but our differences go to Hobbes, not to Mandeville. Rescher holds that Hobbes argued that if God had not invented morality, man would have had to—so important is it to the processes of social control. Mandeville does not dispute that God invented morality, he just claims that morality has nothing to do with community prosperity. Rescher's view is that Hobbes's concern was not with the impact of morality on economic life (indeed, there is no suggestion that Hobbes saw any conflict between community morality and community prosperity), but with the origins of morality. Of his point, I am clearly unsure; however, from the standpoints of preferring observation rather than pure reason (what I call a preference for empiricism), Hobbes and Mandeville are alike. And they shared the honors of being the "bad boys" of their time.

and rhetorically, the way he chose to proceed was to use rigorous language, although tongue-in-cheek. With regard to the former, Mandeville repeatedly asserted that he believed that the Christian virtues were individually desirable, even if their implementation was other than genuinely motivated.

The usual satirical rhetoric differed from his because satire generally employs hyperbole, irony, and/or sarcasm and rarely explicitly condemns. Consider the case of Swift (Pinkus 1975). While Swift's lines of condemnation involved both indirection and subtlety, his use of the *Yahoos* as a critical device was possible because of the misuse of reason, and he presented a subtle paradox in a satirical fashion.

What was lacking in Mandeville's rhetorical style, however, was any dimension of sarcasm or irony (Adolph 1975). His paradox does not lend itself to irony. The ironist means the opposite of what he says; irony is usually indirect (Adolph 1975). Mandeville, by way of contrast, was very direct and meant exactly what he wrote. If what Mandeville intended was satire, it seemingly lacked the usual, perhaps the necessary, irony.

Instead, what seems to have surfaced was a kind of crude cynicism. Monro, in keeping with the later 1953 Viner assessment (discussed below) holds that Mandeville was "at best an easy-going man of the world, at worst a profligate, a cynic, a [born] scoffer at all virtue and religion" (Monro 1975, 1). And that he may well have been. Cynicism is heady stuff, and possibly in his effort to be a satirist Mandeville rushed or fell into an unsophisticated cynicism. On the whole, I conclude that the verdict for the case that the *Fable of the Bees* was satire is, at best, nonpersuasive. At worst, it is anachronistic and/or disingenuous.

*The Anti-Christian Aspect.* What makes an idea un-Christian or anti-Christian depends in no small degree on the context of the times. Recall that the poem was attacked during a period when not only was Western Christian orthodoxy (the Roman Catholic and the Church of England clergies) reeling from almost continual attacks on the role their hierarchies played, and when Unitarianism and Deism, to say nothing of rationalism and "secularism," were increasingly fashionable among the reading public. What stands out in the attacks on the poem for its anti-Christian message generally was the point that it was not the paradox (the conflict between personal righteousness and social welfare), but its underlying theme (there is no positive effective social significance to personal piety), which was meant to and truly did offend. What offended the orthodox the most was not Mandeville's asserted view that man was not perfectible (which would clearly have been bad enough), but his view that the perfectability of man was not only *not* essential to the improvement of society, but that such a change (the Christian ideal) was, from the standpoint of public policy, actually contraindicated. That it was the clergy and its allies which went on the attack makes sense when we recall that the hope for the

Christian moral perfection of man was, then as now, the raison d'être for the church and its clergy.

The earliest and most popular lines of Christian orthodox attack on the *Fable . . .* in the early years centered on two points. No one in this group seems to have imagined, much less suggested, that Mandeville's posture was tongue-in-cheek when he wrote about the goodness of the Christian virtues. Rather, they accepted Mandeville as a *rigorist* (one who accepts the conventional perceptions of virtue as divinely revealed). This is the position basic to F. W. Kaye's interpretation of Mandeville. Viner ([1953] 1958) came to dispute it, as did Rashid (1985).

The two points the seventeenth-century critics usually dealt with were something other. The one used by William Law, in his criticisms, was that Mandeville seemingly rejected the *binding* truth that God's *twin* gifts to man were (1) Christian revelation relating to the definition of virtue, and (2) ratiocinative reason. Law, also a rigorist, was unlike Mandeville in that he believed that, if man was currently imperfect, in the end he would be perfected. Law saw Mandeville as arguing the view that it was not possible for virtue to exist on this earth, and therefore "everything was an emptiness." Such skepticism might be tolerated in the reading of most of Ecclesiastes, but when all was said and done, Law's quandary was, "Of what purpose was Christ's crucifixion if man, himself, consciously and determinedly opposed his own salvation?"

The other line of orthodox argument was offered by George, Bishop Berkeley. It focused on Mandeville's perception of the uses of reason. Mandeville had asserted, it was noted, that reason had really nothing to do with Christian revelation and godly purpose; rather, according to Mandeville, reason, as he saw it being used, was principally an instrument for justifying man's (largely anti-Christian) passions. Mandeville's position seemingly denied the relevance of Augustinian determinism, which from the standpoint of the time was the "principal game in town." Bishop Berkeley, in his effort to show that the use of reason reinforced rather than diminished the role of revelation, assumed that only with the harmony of true reason and revelation could Christian virtue, the divine gift, be achieved. Scoffers like Mandeville, when they held that reason reinforced not revelation but man's passions (among which there were many that no one could consider to be virtuous), tarnished the nature and eventually the product of reason.[38]

Another line of Christian attack was one used by other Christian rationalists. They sought to blunt Mandeville's impact by showing simple errors in his logic. One such example was Francis Hutcheson, Smith's teacher and mentor. Hutcheson stressed that Mandeville (as well as a good many "Scotch [sic]

---

38. Mandeville's later (1732) *Letter to Dion* was his answer to Berkeley.

Presbyterians") erred when he asserted that the essence of Christian virtues was self-denial, and consequently virtuous acts could not yield sensuous satisfactions. It was not true, as Mandeville believed, that maximization of self-regard underlay all individual consciously good actions. Putting the matter in another way, the error was in the belief that anything enjoyable must, therefore, be sinful, and when Mandeville wrote that because all pleasures were not virtues, then all virtues had to be unpleasant. Mandeville's was a logical error—if all A's are not B's, it does not follow that all B's are not A's (Hutcheson 1750, 9, 81). Highlight this premise, the argument went, and the real thrust of Mandeville's case disappeared. Mandeville's adherents claim that Mandeville never made the assertion that all virtues were uncomfortable.

But was the work anti-Christian? In a world involved in the problems of the Thirty Years' War, one which was still unwilling to admit, much less accept, religious pluralism—even within sects of the same purported specific faith, any writing romping through the paradox between private vices and public benefits was, if full of no more than minor error, ipso facto anti-Christian in effect, even if not in intent.

In all, I am uncomfortable with any assessment of Mandeville's anti-Christian beliefs as simply or even principally a product of Epicurean and/or hedonic libertinism (Rashid 1985). I believe that insofar as Mandeville was anti-Christian, his attitude reflected a set of morality poses which were intended mostly for rhetorical purposes. If underneath he was ridiculing the Christian virtues—and suggesting nothing in their place—he was doing so with the mindset of an erstwhile medical student. Medical students are perceived as overly insensitive because they have seen too much human suffering and they handle it with a kind of grisly, epicurean humor. For me, the best direct explanation, from the religious standpoint, of Mandeville's handling of the paradox is to recall the historic tension between the clergy and the medical profession.

### The Fable of the Bees as a Seventeenth-Century Mercantilist and Secularist Tract

Because Mandeville wrote at a time when many were arguing the virtues of economic policies designed to magnify the powers of the nation-state, it has been canon to assert that he was a mercantilist writer. Admittedly, there can be no doubt that he was fascinated by *National Ökonomie,* both as a concept and as a set of policy problems. Having contempt for the intelligence and the stoical discipline of the working classes, he counseled low real wages for workers in order to drive them to be more productive. He also argued that countries without ownership of gold and silver mines ought to be worried about their trade balances. He was a bourgeois and not much of a respecter of the principle of noble privilege. These were the things which characterized most of the mercantilist writers of the seventeenth and eighteenth centuries and it is these things which have led Eli Heckscher and Jacob Viner, two of the greatest interpreters of mercantilist doctrine, to identify him quintessentially as a proponent of mercantilism (Heckscher 1934; Viner [1953] 1958, 1978). In his 1937 magnum opus, Viner had identified Mandeville as a forerunner of "individualism and laissez-faire" (99). This view Viner clearly abandoned in his essay on *A Letter to Dion*, where he explicitly labels Mandeville as "a convinced adherent of the prevailing mercantilism of his time" ([1953] 1958, 341).

But there is another side to the story. Mandeville was generally a foe of sumptuary legislation.[39] And he did appreciate that the *Lumpenproletariat* could and should aspire to more than bare survival; indeed, he made quite a point of what the self-pride of Dutch workmen did for their own productiveness and the prosperity of their nation. Thus, he saw the importance of growing income among workers and its impact on the growth of trade. He certainly advocated the lifting of trade restrictions within national boundaries. His was a reasonably sophisticated perception of the importance of positive trade balances (also true of many acknowledgedly mercantilist writers). His attitudes toward the "higher classes," if not more respectful on grounds of their moral qualities, did reflect a respect for their social power. And these were not the views of the typical mercantilist.

There has been a massive amount of literature during the past half century stressing that Mandeville is really the one who introduced the notion of individualism into the literature (but cf. Viner [1953] 1958, 340). Although this point is discussed in the following, it is pertinent here to stress that several writers, indeed more and more in recent decades, have argued that Mandeville's perception of the role of the state *put into the context of the thought of his time* essentially denied the basic "political state-building" premise of mercantilism. This point was developed and expanded into a major interpretation by Professor Albert Schatz (Schatz 1907), but his book was in French and seems to have commanded little or no attention in the English- and German-reading community.

It was F. W. Kaye whose brilliant edition of the *Fable* created the current century's enthusiasm for Mandeville. Nathan Rosenberg (1963), in a much-quoted article, explicitly attacked Professor Viner's assessment of Mandeville as a prototype mercantilist writer. Rosenberg's position had been anticipated in 1951 and was further developed by Alfred E. Chalk in 1966; indeed, it is not hard to make the case that Kaye in 1924 had seen the point, as well. However, instead of Schatz's interpretation (to which Hayek paid the greatest of personal tributes), it was Professor Hayek's 1966 eulogistic treatment of

---

39. Professor Viner's view was that many mercantilists opposed sumptuary legislation ([1953] 1958, 341).

Mandeville before the British Academy which stands as the principal modern Soviet-style rehabilitation of the nonmercantilist character of one long-deceased (Hayek 1967).

Yet, even more recently, Professor Rashid has written a meticulous summary of the whole debate. His conclusion is that Mandeville's economics were "just thrown in to defend his libertinism." (Rashid 1985, 327). Mandeville, Rashid concludes, was principally a defender of Epicurean libertinism.

If one wants to pin labels, Mandeville was far more a hard-grained secularist than a garden-variety mercantilist. And while most mercantilists were also somewhat secular, I conclude that Mandeville was principally a secularist and only somewhat a mercantilist, and a very limited mercantilist at that. This is clearly not the view of Eli Heckscher or of Jacob Viner. But, with all respect sincerely due to two scholars of the front rank, I think that within the context of his time the principal mercantilist writers would have assessed him to be more of an intellectual stranger than one of their band.

### The *Fable of the Bees* as a Premature Nineteenth-Century Christian Tract

The argument here is that the book was really the work of an unrecognized genius. What Mandeville wanted to show was that good came out of evil, a variant form of an eighteenth-century existentialism. It was a modern "God-works-in-His-mysterious-ways" kind of Christianity. Another, more basic way to see this approach is to argue that the relationship between evil and good is God's major mystery (cf. Monro 1975, 3, 249–67; Hutcheson 1750; Browning 1887;[40] and Selby-Bigge [1897] 1964).

What would favor this position is accepting the premise selected by Kaye and others that there was a genuine and clear Christian rigorism underneath all of Mandeville's strictures, and that, contrary to the Rashid and somewhat-qualified Viner views, Mandeville was not writing as a libertine.

My judgment, accepting some but not all of Monro's (1975) reasoning, is more to the eclectic. As already noted, even more than a purported or possible Christian rigorist, Mandeville was primarily a physician, a specialist in hypochondria and hysteria who accepted without illusions, albeit unwillingly, the world he found (cf. Mandeville 1730). That world preached a childlike faith in the example of self-denial.

Mandeville saw that private vices led to public welfare and private virtues led to economic stagnation. His problem was to square these results with

---

40. I find DeVane's point that Browning did not understand Mandeville nonpersuasive; I think that neither Mandeville nor Browning used DeVane's kind of rational framework in their thinking on the subject.

the teaching of private virtue. His answer seems to have been that God managed to achieved public welfare by bringing virtue out of evil. Mandeville's religious heterodoxy was, in his view, that the common or orthodox approach distorts true Christianity. Probably the essence of his religious truth was that the greatness of God is that He brings goodness out of evil— something that man, lacking that kind of Grace, cannot comprehend.[41] This approach, if Mandeville had it "prematurely," has appeal to those who see little good in organized religion, but who are also believers in a God who loves man; actually it surfaces in many places, of which Isaiah 42–50 is a fair example and Jeremiah 12:1 is an even better example.[42]

Monro (1975) does not accept this assessment, noting that the historical facts do not support it (it is ingenuous). He thinks that Mandeville wrote out of anger and true disillusionment. Not in full agreement with Monro, I see this not as Mandeville's moral confusion or religious heterodoxy, but rather as his having the typical physician's patience with man's foibles and as saying that sin does not bring down an end to the world—a "modernist" Christian "existentialism." This makes him a seer, the type of figure whom Schumpeter described as "writing before their time,"—that is, one who discovers truths that others do not grasp for centuries.

### The Fable of the Bees as a Premature Exercise in the Philosophy of Individualism

Within the past century the book has come to be considered in its own right a cornerstone of the Utilitarian cum nineteenth-century English "liberal" tradition. Albert Schatz, an economist particularly interested in the history of economic thought, traces the origins of British utilitarian individualism to Mandeville's *Fable of the Bees* (Schatz 1907). Professor Hayek, explicitly crediting Albert Schatz with this insight, argues that, while much of the current significance of the book remains ideological, the real (if uncredited) impact is mostly a matter of method. Mandeville, according to Hayek, is one of the founders of the English utilitarian tradition, a tradition that embraces experience first and reason only afterward.[43] This method is opposed to

---

41. St. Paul's position, as I understand it, was that evil men could prosper in this imperfect world, but that "after Judgment" they would suffer punishment and not be worthy to enter Paradise.

42. Of course, there is the old problem posed in the Book of Job. Professor Rescher put it to me wonderfully: Job's view is that personal virtue (true religiosity) yields no assurance of worldly success for individuals. God does not provide his faithful with earthly rewards. Mandeville's position is that the personal virtue (copy-book morality) of individuals is actually *inconsistent* with the worldly success of the group.

43. Both Schatz and Hayek give earlier credit to Hobbes, but each stresses that it was

methods that build initially on reason or that build first on revelation and then on reason.

Experience is perceived as being basically an individual's cognition. Thus the concept of individualism stems from personal empirical experience. What the *Fable of the Bees* offered was a view of the relationship between individuals and social progress. J. A. Maxwell (1951), in fleshing out this point, regards Mandeville's contribution as clearer in his later writings, particularly the second volume of the *Fable* and his *Letter to Dion*. Mandeville, he argues, is halfway between Hobbes and Rousseau. Hobbes's man is psychologically unchanged when he moves from the state of nature to society. Rousseau's man in society is different and on a higher plane than he is as a single individual. Mandeville's man seems to accept the Hobbes position from the standpoint of his theology, but in practice he seems to have moved toward Rousseau. The key, as I see Maxwell's suggestion, is to perceive that Mandeville had his own brand of utilitarianism, combining two subforms. There was the utilitarianism of the individual from the standpoint of his own moral world. There was also the utilitarianism of the privately moral statesman who, having to face the general populace's appetite for wickedness, had also to realize that passage of legislation could not eradicate wickedness, but it could minimize some deleterious effects.

What is more important than the reporting of paradoxes between the coexistence of personal morality and social progress, a point little considered, is that Mandeville's use of his own personal observation underlies both. In this present century, about 200 years after Mandeville wrote, there is a peculiar strength to this new interpretation. It reveals that not only do Mandeville's efforts at reconciling what others thought opposite continue; it suggests that the Mandeville "mother lode" is still being mined. Not bad for the "Hobbesian bad boy," whom Adam Smith called "pernicious!"

### A Summary of Mandeville's Economic Views

A final, but still important, query is whether Mandeville had only a series of insights or intuitions, an integrated set of testable economic views, or even a comprehensive gestalt from which a full economic theoretical system can be identified.

Of the wide range of his insights or intuitions there can be no doubt. These are listed in the following. That they went well beyond what we would today call economics is also clear. After all, what hits the eye first and foremost are his interests in ethics (morality) as well as his obvious fascina-

---

Mandeville, not Hobbes, who explicitly considered personal empiricism to be the way to study moral performance.

tion with the relationship between ethics-in-practice and eighteenth-century personal and social morality (cf. Harth 1970, 23ff.). Hayek, in spite of his great admiration for Mandeville's originality, thought his economic views rather thin, a judgment which Rashid's 1985 article summarizes.

I do not really concur: admittedly one cannot easily distill from his work, its substance, and its rhetoric an articulated set of testable economic ideas or, more rare, an identifiably personal and novel approach to the consideration of economic phenomena. Yet, can intuitive insights add up to analytical building blocks?[44]

Our query is whether Mandeville had an economic gestalt. At least ten sets of Mandeville's insights can be identified:

1. Much of Mandeville's interest was in the nature and consequences of *buyer and seller subjectivity* (cf. Remarks B and E). The role of bargaining, clearly central to his perception of the way the market (for him the economic) process operated, required considerable suppression of any public expression of personal (subjective) preferences. This lack of interpersonal openness was one aspect of individual hypocrisy; as such, that critical vice turned out to be a sociopolitical necessity, particularly in late Stuart and early Georgian England.[45]

---

44. By way of comparison, Smith knit together theories of comparative national wealth, of specialization of production, and of relative prices along with a value-loaded perception of the relative efficiency of market-driven rather than state-driven allocations. Hume worked out theoretically the basis for exchange rate fluctuations. And Ricardo worked out abstract principles explaining the power of the landholding class and the advantages of international specialization of production. Each of these was self-conscious regarding his economics and analytical system. Even Schumpeter's views on the causes of business cycles, the role of the entrepreneur in history, the effect of creative destruction, and the dynamic nature of the economics science add up to a gestalt, if not to an integrated theory. Not so Mandeville.

45. One of the noteworthy aspects of literary development between early Stuart and Georgian England was the "muddling up" of rhetoric. Francis Bacon's language still stands for me as a model of clarity, with intentional ambiguity existing only because of the complexity of the ideas. His literary secretary, at one time, was Thomas Hobbes. Bacon's lasting influence on Hobbes (apparent in any number of other ways) did not include rhetorical clarity as one of the major intended (wherever possible) virtues. And by the time that William Petty was writing, he thought it the better part of wisdom to eschew any publication (if it could be avoided). I attribute the principal reason for this "perceived decline" in rhetorical clarity to be the corrosive influence of decades of civil strife, war, and criminal prosecution. Toward the end of the seventeenth century many wise men measured their printed words carefully; indeed, if they were wise enough they avoided clarity by cumbersome syntax, by sarcasm, and by resort to fable or metaphor. By Mandeville's time such caution was less exercised; if one chose to write anonymously it was not out of personal fear (see fn. 10). As for the decline in the quality of British prose after Shakespeare's and Bacon's time, my colleague, Professor Tobias, suggests that my reaction is not

2. Mandeville, for all of his discursiveness about prodigality and dissipation, did see the complexities of the connection between the decision to save and the decision to invest (cf. Remarks I, K, P/Q, and −/T).

3. Mandeville, even at the risk of alienating all of his sophisticated if cynical audience (who usually were oriented to mercantilism), was presciently (pre-Sismondi and pre-Malthus) so *demand-management* oriented that it led him not only to "tolerate," but even to stress the consumption of sumptuaries.[46]

4. In practice his policies called for the *expansion of employment opportunities for low-level skill workers.*

5. Consistent with his commitment to employment opportunity, he favored the *production of labor-intensive products.* These he believed to be mostly luxury goods—hence his further defense of sumptuaries.[47]

6. In his discussion of the justification for producing luxury goods, he seems to have grasped *the fundamentals of the multiplier as it could be applied to trade, to income, and most of all to employment.*[48]

7. Almost as important as was his commitment to expansion of employment opportunity was his qualified commitment to understanding *the role of worker incentives;* thus, there was a supply-side to his economics, too (Remark P/Q).

---

shared by most literary experts. They identify Sir William Temple as the inventor of modern English prose, and he wrote before Mandeville; incidentally, Jonathan Swift was his secretary during various segments of the 1690s, when Temple's papers were being put together.

46. Although Maynard Keynes identified Bartholemy de Laffemas, Wilhelm von Schröder (he spelled it Schrötter), John Cary, and Nicholas Barbon as being the earliest to understand the ideas behind underconsumptionism, Keynes's enthusiasm for Mandeville's broader set of insights led him to quote the 1704 poem in extenso (Keynes [1936] 1973, 359–62). Part of Keynes's quotation in his 1936 *General Theory* is quoted in extenso as part of the front matter preceding this essay.

I have written elsewhere that I thought that Malthus's concern with agricultural employment opportunity, which underlay his interest in demand side-driven economies, was derived from a conviction that driving workers off the land would lead to social unrest (Perlman 1984). Mandeville's view did not pertain to agricultural labor alone; rather, it pertained to the social necessity of encouraging all families to support themselves by continuous labor market participation and, if possible, of achieving widespread household saving.

47. Smith and later Ricardo advocated policies which clearly took note of the burgeoning industrial revolution, a set of institutional changes which, for the most part, occurred after Mandeville's death.

48. I think that Sir James Steuart could be said to have intuitively grasped this same analytical point (1767, Bk I, chap. 6).

8. Like Dudley North, he favored *the freeing of trade,*[49] believing that it generally, even if indirectly, stimulated domestic prosperity and thus employment opportunity.

9. He seems to have grasped *the role of expectations in economic performance from the standpoints of both income and risk taking.*

10. He grasped some of the ideas inherent in the concept of *liquidity preference* (cf. Remark P/Q).

Professor Laurence Moss has argued that the Mandeville writings can be tied together. His rubrics are:

1. explanations of market behavior in terms of subjectivist categories of analysis,

2. the role markets play in reconciling subjective differences,

3. the interrelatedness among economic phenomena, and

4. [a coherent] economic policy (Moss 1986)

I think that one should go beyond Moss and recognize that Mandeville anticipated a wider variety of insights. From the first he seems to me to have had a many-faceted economic gestalt embracing individualism, utilitarianism, empiricism,[50] and a plethora of insights pertaining to behavioral psychology.

---

49. As I see the situation even today, there is a major difference between advocating the freeing of trade (when trade is far from free) and seriously advocating within the context of a nation-state world fully free trade. One is the becoming (which although philosophically quite complex has often been thought through); the other is the being (which is a world as yet unknown to us). This difference has not been recognized by most who write of the virtues of freeing trade as distinct from a world without economic borders. Both Dudley North and Mandeville wrote, admittedly not without qualifying contradictions, of the advantages of freeing trade (improving the openness of product markets). Yet anyone like Mandeville who is conscious of more than the single goal of product cheapness of price (goals like employment opportunity, changes in economic competitiveness, economic growth, etc.) must grasp the point that achieved total free trade *within the context of laissez-faire-laissez-passer* yields only cheapness of product price. This may be enough for some.

50. Just what empiricism embraces is far from obvious. Current usage among economists is to identify all who use cognitive data series (measured in number or in rank orders) as empiricists. These I call *quantitative empiricists,* and they are the primary type of economic empiricists today. For those who build their analyses on cognitive observation of differences in qualities or on historical events, I tend to use the label *episodic empiricists.* I believe that this second category is far from universally accepted, and I interpret Professor Recktenwald's comment to me that Mandeville was not a empiricist to mean that he, Recktenwald, does not accept the supplementary definition. Bacon, who got into the empiricism-defining act early on, likened the "empiric" philosophers to ants, which collected and collected; the comparative type were the "dogmatics," likened to spiders. The optimal philosophers, according to Bacon, those combining the empirical laboriousness of the ever-working ants and the beautiful cobwebs spun out of

But even if he could not or did not choose to put these ideas into a peculiarly economic framework, it can be done.

Mandeville did not perceive of his writings as economics or of himself as an economist. Like Molière's M. Jourdain, he may have been unaware that he was talking economics. But unlike M. Jourdain, he probably would have derived no pride in being told he was an economist, as such. Thus, his lack of a feel for either binding his views into an explicit comprehensive economics *Gestalt* or for a set of abstract analytical rules[51] suggests no more than he would have settled, at least, for being an amusing observer or, at most, for having made some contributions to moral philosophy.[52] No matter how he is interpreted, Mandeville was first and foremost a physician who was committed to the method of cognitive observation and to the process of trying to find regularities. What he added to economics was an effort to find reason in the social system. That effort was not successful, and it clearly irritated a great many of his contemporaries, although not all of his later readers.

REFERENCES

Adolph, Robert. 1975. "What pierces or strikes": Prose style in *The Fable of The Bees*. In Primer 1975a, 157–68.
Aldridge, Alfred Owen. 1965. *Benjamin Franklin: Philosopher and Man*. Philadelphia and New York: Lippincott.
Bacon, Francis. [1620] 1855. *Novum Organon*. Edited with English Notes and Appendices by Rev. G. W. Kitchin, M.A. Oxford.
Browning, Robert. 1887. *Parleying with Certain People of Importance in Their Day to Wit Bernard de Mandeville, Daniel Bartoli, Christopher Smar, Gearuge Bub Dodington, Franaacis Furini, Gerard de Lairesse, and Charles Avison: Introduced by a Dialogue between Apollo and the Fates; Concluded by Another between John Fust and His Friend*. Boston: Houghton, Mifflin and Company.
Chalk, Alfred E. 1966. Mandeville's *Fable of the bees: A reappraisal*. *Southern Economic Journal* 33:1–16.
Cook, Richard I. 1975. "The Great Leviathan of Lechery": Mandeville's *Modest defence of public stews* (1724). In Primer 1975a, 22–33.
DeVane, William Clyde. 1964. *Browning's Parleyings: The Autobiography of a Mind*. New York: Russell & Russell.

---

"nothing," were like bees, who chose their pollen carefully and processes it into sweetest nectar (Bacon [1620] 1855, 78). I am inclined to see the ratio of bees to the other two as very small, and in the economics profession, past and present, the ratio of spiders to ants as too large.

51. His aversion to quick and dirty abstractions was already noted.

52. Sir William Petty, who by any standard was a professional economist, was not so labeled. Adam Smith, writing almost two generations after Mandeville's time, wrote as a moral philosopher because he held that chair at the University of Glasgow. If the *Wealth of Nations* is regarded as professional economics the physiocrats should probably be credited with the identification of the profession, as such.

Dickinson, H. T. 1975. The Politics of Bernard Mandeville. In Primer 1975a, 80–97.

Dumont, Louis. 1977. *From Mandeville to Marx: The Genesis and Triumph of Economic Ideology.* Chicago: University of Chicago Press.

Franklin, Benjamin. [1791–93] 1964. *The Autobiography of Benjamin Franklin.* Edited by Leonard W. Labaree, et al. New Haven, Conn.: Yale University Press.

Furniss, Edgar. [1920] 1965. *The Position of the Labor in a System of Nationalism.* New York: Augustus Kelley.

Goldsmiths' Library. 1970. *Catalogue of the Goldsmiths' Library of Economic Literature.* Compiled by Margaret Canney and David Knott with an Introduction by J. H. P. Pafford. Vol. 1, printed books to 1800. Cambridge: Cambridge University Press.

Good, Stephen H. 1976. Introduction to *A Treatise of the Hypochondriack and Hysterick Disease*, by Bernard de Mandeville. New York: Scholars' Facsimiles & Reports.

Harth, Phillip. 1970. *The Fable of the Bees.* Edited with an Introduction by Philip Harth. Harmondsworth, Middlesex, England: Penguin.

Hayek, Friedrich. 1948. *Individualism and Economic Order.* Chicago: University of Chicago Press.

———. 1967. Dr. Bernard Mandeville. *Proceedings of the British Academy,* 125–41.

Heckscher, Eli. 1934. *Mercantilism.* Translated by Mendel Shapiro. London: George Allen & Unwin.

Hirschman, Albert O. 1977. *The Passions and the Interests: Political Arguments for Capitalism before its Triumph.* Princeton: Princeton University Press.

Hutcheson, Francis. 1750. *Reflections upon Laughter and Remarks upon the Fables of the Bees.* Glasgow: Printed by R. Uriel for Daniel Banter, Bookseller. (Garland Publishing, New York City, published a facsimile edition in 1971.)

Jack, M. R. 1975. In Primer 1975a, 34–42.

James, E. D. 1975. Faith, Sincerity, and Morality: Mandeville and Bayle. In Primer 1975a, 43–65.

Kaye, F. B., ed. 1924. *The Fable of the Bees: Or, Private Vices, Publick Benefits.* With a Commentary—Critical, Historical, and Explanatory by F. B. Kaye. Oxford: Clarendon Press.

Keynes, John Maynard. [1936] 1973. *The General Theory of Employment, Interest and Money.* London: Macmillan.

[Mandeville, Bernard de]. 1714. *The Fable of the Bees: Or Private Vices, Publick Benefits.* London: J. Roberts.

———. 1730. *A Treatise of the Hypochondriack and Hysterick Diseases.* (Scholars' Facsimiles & Reports, New York City, published a facsimile edition in 1976; it contains an introduction by Stephen H. Good.)

———. 1732. *A Letter to Dion.* (The Augustan Reprint Society published a facsimile edition in 1953; it contained an introduction by Jacob Viner.)

Maxwell, J. A. 1951. Ethics and politics in Mandeville. *Journal of the Royal Institute of Philosophy* 25:242–52.

Moss, Laurence S. 1987. The subjectivist mercantilism of Bernard Mandeville. *International Journal of Social Economics* 14:167–84. (One of two issues edited by J. C. O'Brien as a *Festschrift in honor of Anghel N. Rugina.*)

Monro, Hector. 1975. *The Ambivalence of Bernard Mandeville.* Oxford: Clarendon.

Perlman, Mark. 1984. L'audience de Malthus aux Etats-Unis comme économiste.

*Malthus hier et aujourd'hui.* Congres de demographie historique. Paris: Editions du CNRS.

Pinkus, Philip 1975. Mandeville's Paradox. In Primer 1975a, 193–212.

Pozo, Susan, and Warren J. Samuels. N.d. "Fernandez Florez's *Las siete columnas*: Mandeville Rehearsed." East Lansing: Michigan State University Department of Economics. Typescript.

Primer, Irwin, ed. 1962. *The Fable of the Bees or Private Vices, Publick Benefits.* Contains an introduction by Irwin Primer (pp. 1–17). New York: Capricorn.

———. 1975a. *Mandeville Studies: New Explorations in the Art and Thought of Dr. Bernard Mandeville (1670–1733).* The Hague: Martinus Nijhoff.

———. 1975b. "Mandeville and Shaftesbury: Some Facts and Problems." In Primer 1975a, 126–41.

Rashid, Selim. 1985. "Mandeville's *Fable*: Laissez-faire or libertinism?" *Eighteenth-Century Studies* 18 (Spring): 322.

Robertson, Dennis H. 1926. *Banking Policy and the Price Level.* London: P. S. King & Son.

Rosenberg, Nathan. 1963. "Mandeville and Laissez-faire. *Journal of the History of Ideas* 24:183–96.

Rousseau, G. S. 1975. "Mandeville and Europe: Medicine and philosophy." In Primer 1975a, 11–21.

Schatz, Albert. 1907. *L'individualisme économique et social: Ses origines, son evolution, ses formes contemporaines.*

Selby-Bigge, L. A., ed. [1897] 1964. *British Moralists, Being Selections from Writers Principally of the Eighteenth Century.* Indianapolis, New York: Bobbs-Merrill.

Smith, Adam. 1759. *The Theory of Moral Sentiments.* A photo-offset edition, based on the Henry G. Bohn London edition, was published in 1966 by Augustus M. Kelley, New York.

Sprague, Elmer. 1967. "Mandeville, Bernard." In *The Encyclopedia of Philosophy,* vols. 5 & 6, 147–49. New York: Collier Macmillan.

Steuart, Sir James. 1767. *An Inquiry into the Principles of Political Economy.* A truncated edition was published for the Scottish Economic Society in 1966 by Oliver & Boyd, Edinburgh and London. It was edited by Andrew S. Skinner, who also provided an introduction.

Twersky, A., and D. Kahneman. 1974. "Judgement under uncertainty: Heuristics and biases." *Science* 185:1124–31.

Viner, Jacob. 1937. *Studies in the Theory of International Trade.* New York: Harper & Bros.

———. [1953] 1958. "Introduction to Bernard Mandeville *Letter to Dion.*" Reprinted in *The Long View and the Short: Studies in Economic Theory and Policy.* Glencoe, Ill.: Free Press. [Also see Mandeville 1732.]

———. 1978. *Religious Thought and Economic Society: Four Chapters of an Unfinished Work by Jacob Viner.* Edited by Jacques Melitz and Donald Winch. Durham, N.C.: Duke University Press.

CHAPTER 6

# Rhetoric and Normativism: An Idiosyncratic Appraisal from the Standpoint of the History of Economic Thought, a Review Essay of Albert O. Hirschman's *The Rhetoric of Reaction* and Donald N. McCloskey's *If You're So Smart: The Narrative of Economic Expertise*

*Asked to review lesser books by two of the most literate economists currently writing, I used the opportunity to comment on the uses of economics as rhetoric. Much earlier I had written in another review that "economists are not experts, they are basically persuaders' advocates" (1978f, 585). The five parts of this Chapter take up, in turn: the authors; the place of each of the books in the author's bibliography; a discussion of the economists' hopes of or pretensions to being scientific; a summary of the three magisterial treatments described in Chapter 4; and some observations on the dependency of the addressor's rhetoric on the addressee's cultural framework; Finally, I discuss the reasons why we study the history of economic thinking, showing the multiple purposes (contradictions?) we harbor in our thinking. One such contradiction that I discuss briefly involves two seminal interpretations of the nature of God's punishment for Original Sin. The commonly perceived punishment was work and scarcity; the less common, but no less significant, was Shackelian uncertainty. Aristotelian rhetoric can be more than direct persuasion; it can be the tool linking the imagination to many levels of analysis.*

I think that there are two kinds of economics. One of them aims at precision, rigorousness, tidiness and the formulation of principles which will be permanently valid: an economic science. The other is, if you like, rhetorical. This word is often used disparagingly, but that is a modern unscholarly abuse. The rhetorician employs reason and appeals to logic, but he is a user of language at its full compass, where words are fingers touching the keyboard of a hearer's mind. I do not believe that human affairs can be

---

*Methodus* 5 (June 1993): 129–39.

exhibited as the infallible and invariable working of a closed and permanent system.
—G. L. Shackle (1983) p. 116

Eventually the purpose of this review article is to discuss just how scientific those in the profession should consider modern economics to be. The agreement between the authors of these two books that economics, whatever others pretend, is not a scientific, but a cultural or humanistic discipline, has long been my own position: "Economists' self-perception is as 'an expert'. But economists are not experts; they are basically persuaders."

## 1. About the Authors

Each is a prominent academic scholar, whose purpose in these books is to explain how economists actually ply their craft, not only when facing other economists, but also when dealing with would-be customers for economic ideas leading to policy.

Albert Hirschman's task in his *The Rhetoric of Reaction* is the more specific in that he describes how "the other side" has subverted "the story." A notable scholar of some considerable political experience, he was a pre-Nazi era German Social Democratic student, later served as professor at both Columbia and Harvard, and is currently Professor-Emeritus at the Institute of Advanced Study. His has been a life full of considerable personal risk (self-exiled early on from Weimar Germany and a War-time Resistance hero in France); he is a man whose personal norms have been tested by experience and emerged only after long and careful reflection. Moreover, Hirschman has made not one, but several, truly seminal contributions to contemporary economic theory—contributions which are conceptually broad and the significance of which has been accepted by virtually all positivist economists, certainly many of whom do not share his socio-political value commitments.

Donald McCloskey, a Harvard-trained economist-historian, yet one well-scarred by debating encounters while teaching at the University of Chicago, is a somewhat younger (but hardly young) scholar. He made his initial scholarly mark as an economic historian, and in the past decade he has created a niche as the leading commentator on the techniques and foibles of his fellow economists. His method is to analyze from the standpoint of rhetoric the literary gymnastics of the most usual forms of economic argumentation, and among his comparative advantages is a massive breadth of literary knowledge. (To my mind Hirschman may be one of the few remaining scholars whose reading can "trump" McCloskey's—Hirschman's literacy in German, French, Spanish, and English is of a quality matched insofar as I am aware by no one else currently in the profession). As one might expect, a large part of McCloskey's reading has been directed at formal questions of rhetorical efficiency (namely what are the standard lines of thinking used to persuade) rather than to the substance of the argumentation, itself.

## 2. About the Books

McCloskey's book begins by focusing on the consumption side of the rhetorical problem—what lines of argument seem best to influence the customer, or what are the techniques useful in persuading consumers to do what you want them to do (like eating carrots). Hirschman's, on the other hand, starts on the production side—what caveats must competent Social Democratic reformers offer in the way of negative "bites" (commercials) to offset the anticipated evil effects of the conservatives' or reactionaries' counter-offensives?

Hirschman's *The Rhetoric of Reaction* is a commentary on one side of the usual public social policy debate. Mostly analytical, the book presents *ad seriatim,* and in beautiful prose, three of the usual conservative rhetorical fearful postures, which the anti-democratic (read anti-socially liberal and responsible) economico-politicians have, alas, used all-too successfully during the past two centuries to thwart desirable reforms. These postures are: the masks of *perversity,* of *futility,* and of *jeopardy.*

*Perversity,* of course, suggests that attempts, particularly the ones motivated by benevolence, at bettering a situation will inevitably not only fail to better the situation, but instead, will only make it worse. Using several splendid examples drawn from social history (and Hirschman has a wonderfully easy familiarity with eighteenth and nineteenth century Continental [particularly French and German] writers), Hirschman emphasizes not only how failure is, thus, made to seem inevitable, but particularly how emotionally-engendered rightful efforts are seen to come to naught.

By way of contrast, *futility* does not depend upon a warm or forceful intention. Rather, it suggests the conclusion that reform efforts, however well conceived and effectively executed, will invariably fail, perhaps because of the perversity of the agents. Again, Hirschman draws on examples, but this time they derive from the analytical literature written by disillusioned anti-democratic geniuses like Gaetano Mosca and Vilfredo Pareto.

The *jeopardy* ploy is usually more complicated than the previous two. Here the posture is that not only will all efforts at reform fail and actually make things worse, but that they may so affect the original problem that total disaster, itself, becomes a high probability outcome (e.g. a Constitutional convention called to make only a limited number of amendments may lead to a disastrous reconsideration of the whole document, particularly the Bill of Rights). It is a sort of a "just-because-I-am-for-you-and-worry-about-you, I-fear-that-you-will-irretrievably-harm-yourself" kind of thing.

McCloskey's *If You're So Smart* is no composition of "danger signs" marking the course of professional discourse, so much as it is an effort to persuade his readers that even the most "scientific" of economists is really no more than skillful rhetorician, extracting his intellectual "rents" by posturing as a scientist (the most unchallengeable form of expert). He offers advice on how to tell stories like an economist (that is, how to posture)—how plots should be constructed, how to choose one's genre, and so forth. The book builds on his earlier, more self-consciously analytical 1983 article and 1985 book (both bearing the same title, *The Rhetoric of Economics*), wherein he classified, *inter alia,* the various argument techniques maintained as "scientific proofs" by several prominent current academics, including Gary Becker (1984) (the intermingling of two sets of metaphorical connotations as in "human capital"), Robert Fogel (a bagful of conventional rhetorical tricks), Milton Friedman (1953) (positivism as the very soul of economic truth), such Keynesians (as distinct from Maynard Keynes), as Irving Kravis and Robert Lipsey (1982) ("one statistical level of significance is good enough for us, you may prefer another"), John Muth (1961) (more or less, "one can use the law of large numbers to get reliable estimates of the future"), Paul Samuelson (1947) (an appeal to a variety of earlier authorities, not necessarily each of them being without blemish), and Robert Solow (1968) (an arsenal of irony, metaphor, metonymy and synecdoche).

### Assessment: The Books Viewed as Part of Each Author's Contribution

As noted, each man is a distinguished writer and scholar. Each book is eminently persuasive and, as such, truly valuable. Each book has a creative charm. Yet, neither book is truly the author's prime "vintage." Hirschman's earlier books on economic development are renowned for their analytical content; his somewhat later books commenting on the philosophic side of social development are even more so for the richness of their literary form (including virtually magnificent selections of quotations from eighteenth and nineteenth century French, German, and sometimes Spanish writers). *The Rhetoric of Reaction,* if viewed by itself, is exceedingly good, but Hirschman's standard is so high that it certainly does not match, much less tower above, his other works. Yet, if one reads this book, one would be led to read his others.

McCloskey's writings in economic history have been particularly rich. His decision to side-track that interest in favor of addressing the *Gesellschaft* on "how they do what they do, even were it done only semi-consciously," has given the profession pause as well as real benefit. But his major points were made earlier in the 1983 article, the 1984 book, and in a wonderfully clever

1985 exchange with Martin Hollis's, "The Emperor's Newest Clothes" as against "Sartorial Epistemology in Tatters: A Reply to Martin Hollis," in *Economics and Philosophy* (1985, pp. 128–37). This contribution does not seem as creative and therefore not as important as they were—or, from my standpoint, as rich as the work he has done (and I trust will do in the future) in economic history.

Yet, in this world where the shelf life of books in book stores is so short, one would be wise to secure these two—if for no other reason than the difficulty of getting earlier books by Hirschman and McCloskey. But, if one is prepared to rely upon libraries, some of each man's other contributions are richer. Richer? Well, as wines are often rated, (7 [tops] to 0 [no good]), I would say that for "human vineyards" that have harvested creative 6's and even perhaps a rare 7, this crop seems to me closer to a 4 or perhaps, generously put, a 5. I might add that there is nothing "wrong" with a "4 or perhaps a 5;" much of what I regularly chose to consume on a daily basis is a marginal 4 or even an inexpensive 3. But their 6's and their possible 7's had what were then novel bouquets. These books lack mostly that novel feature.

### 3. How Scientific Is Economics?

Having thus summarized the themes of both books, let me turn to the more basic topic, the one indicated in the opening paragraph. I begin with a brief, if obvious, analysis. There are, it seems to me, three main possibilities.

   a. Economics is a normatively-neutral science;
   b. Economics is really no more than a host of social priorities with some abstractly put "rules of thumb," which tend to be space- and/or time-constrained; or
   c. Economics is a combination of normatively neutral scientific principles (called "the Science of Economics") as applied to a particular cultural or institutional setting (called "Political Economy").

*"Normatively-Neutral"*

For some economists it has long been an assumption or even a dream that economics, as a discipline, fitted the *first* category. Did not Herschel and others use observed facts and pure reasoning (1) to explain why Jupiter wobbled, and (2) to pinpoint the position of Uranus? Is that not the way of science? Why should economics be different from physics? Given enough of the appropriate observed facts and adequate theoretical constructs, economics will eventually emulate physics and chemistry and (like Beethoven) achieve success, or, at least, its desired objective. This was the avowed goal of the

Cowles Commission, a creative group which pioneered in theoretical econometrics, when it existed originally in Boulder, later in Chicago, and for even much of its life in New Haven. There are many credos associated with members of this group, but Tjalling Koopmans's 1947 vehement attack on Wesley Clair Mitchell and Arthur F. Burns' "Measurement without Theory," is an exemplar of this view.

One of the leading economic methodologists, Sir Karl Popper (1962), even developed at the London School of Economics certain "rules" for identifying "scientific economic statements." First, in order to eschew tautologies, each statement or precept had to be in its original form "falsifiable," that is, subject to being proved wrong. Also, each should be phrased in the boldest or "wildest" form imaginable, subject to a high degree of falsifiability, as to be tentatively correct so long as not proved wrong; they are subsequently only corroborated, not confirmed. Third, while the statements should conform to observable reality, observation was admittedly full of statistical error; therefore, the test of immanent criticism was easier and more conclusive than the test of empirical checking. This emphasis on proof (be it logical or empirical) is important; science, unlike the humanities, must be open to full *objective, yet analytical,* examination. And because such is so, it seems to be in some important sense "hard and therefore superior" to humanistic or other cultural statements, which by comparison are "mushy and therefore inferior."

Yet, if economics were truly of the first category, i.e. were it a scientific discipline, economists should no more disagree on matters of common observation than do physicists or chemists. And since economists are virtually always found in such continual conflict on ordinary things, does that not suggest, even denote, that economics is not that much of a science? There is a commonly-voiced view that because economists are so frequently in conflict, which "certainly" would not be the case if they were true scientists, then one can only conclude that at a fundamental level economics is not that much of a science.

Answering this line of thought leads one to ask, "Under what conditions can scientists *legitimately* disagree?" Do the conflicts stem from poorer or better "facts" or from questions of poorer or better reasoning (poorer or better models)? If these are the causes of disagreement, then more carefully mined facts and better honed theories will eventually bring economics as a science "up to snuff." This view suggests that "it is all a matter of time; eventually the refined truth will emerge."

Yet, even here, some economic scientists have an interesting twist. Milton Friedman long ago offered a justification for his professional brethren in the form of the alternative line of reasoning of instrumentalism. "If my model (i.e. economic reasoning) leads me to predict successfully what will happen, what matters it operationally if my facts are or are not correct and clear and my analytical thinking neither direct nor true?" Accordingly, for many, influenced as they are by the doughty Friedman, scientific economics is defined simply by an instrumental test.

Of course, this first approach with its desire to make economics a science reflects an underlying attitude, probably but not necessarily contemptuous, towards disciplines which are less than scientific or even non-scientific. Long ago, Friedrich Hayek (1964) pilloried this theological "scientism," and I can recall hearing Ronald Coase relating the story of how he reminded (perhaps only once, but one hopes more frequently) Milton Friedman that his preference for positive (read "scientific") economics was, itself, no more than a normative statement.

## The Importance of Contextual Influence

Many economists and many who read economic literature harbor the *second* view; they not only doubt that economics can ever truly be a *real* science, if by a real science one means a discipline engendering time-less and space-unbound theories, but they think that such things are in and of themselves irrelevant. Economic thinking, say they, is invariably contextual, and much depends upon the way that questions are framed, the varying significance of the question as seen by all who discuss it, and most of all by the psychological "tricks" used in the discussion. Many of this ilk, authors like Hirschman and McCloskey, have abandoned the pretensions that economics is scientific, and are devoting themselves instead to the proposition that the test for persuasion is not "scientific hardness," but some form of interpersonal psychology. In hardly more than a word—they eschew abstraction, the necessary language of scientists.

What is at issue is the question of how necessary is abstract statement to scientific discussion? One of the more interesting histories of economic thought argues that it was Locke's ability to frame his economic propositions in the abstract, thus permitting their logic to be analyzed, which characterizes the birth of modern economics.

Yet, so long as the various forms of human psychology or even cellular biology have claims to "scientific status," the tightness of that analytical test seems to me to be excessive. Economics, as well as psychology and biology, has had difficulty with full description in the abstract. In sum, I do not buy the proposition that abstraction and science need to share a common territory or even a common border.

Nonetheless, I hasten to add that the majority of those currently serving as or being trained as professional economists, Hirschman and McCloskey notwithstanding, accept as an article of faith that to be scientific, economics must be expressible in abstract, value-free form. Further, if the applications of the abstraction lead to intellectual fracas, then the fracas may be otherwise, but the abstract statements, themselves, are what is scientific.

One way of approaching the position that economics is contextual is to note the use of *ad hominem* arguments as do Hirschman and McCloskey. The legend is that Daniel Webster, a Dartmouth alumnus, won the famous Dartmouth College Case by an argument clearly addressed to the prejudices and tastes of Chief Justice Marshall. As with Webster and many other Constitutional lawyers, many economists would admit that in the end it was the choice in framing the argument, rather than the argument itself, which matters. That was my position when I wrote in 1978 the sentence quoted in the first paragraph of this paper. What it involves is emphasis on the resonances that an argument can induce, seen in the delightful quotation of that master economist-rhetorician, G. L. S. Shackle. Economics, then, is mostly a matter of contextual analogy.

Granted this point, are there not "economic truths," valid irrespective of time and place, which must be seen in the light (or bearing the fruit) associated with a time and place? Of course, there are experiential "rules of thumb," which because they are familiar are accepted and always used, e.g. Gresham's Law that "bad money doth drive out good." The question is whether such rules of thumb are invariably true. While they may be generally true, there is always the problem of "believing in the emperor's clothes,"—that is, the problem of a "rule attaining truth through rote repetition." The truth may be hidden by custom, but it is truly and objectively always there: Winston Churchill's truth, he said, was so precious that it had always to be surrounded by handmaidens of falsehood.

### Measurement, Social Priorities, and Contextual Influences

In the next section I will turn to Wesley Clair Mitchell. Here let me note only that Mitchell argued two points: First, that insofar as science has to have abstract, universally-true theoretical constructs, economics would never qualify as a conventional science. As with Lord Kelvin, if science consists *mostly* of measurement of some form of cognitive phenomena, then as economic facts can be measured, economics should be called scientific. Where Mitchell came out was (1) that abstraction was not essential to a discipline being scientific—a position with which not very many economists currently seem to agree, but one which should still be considered; and (2) that economics was essentially a systematic effort to understand the socio-economic process as it developed in a particular society, in his example during the period of modern industrialization and conurbation development. In brief, a systematic approach was more basic to scientific inquiry than an abstract approach. Mitchell's economics systematically sought regularities. And, in the end, he seems to have become convinced that systematic investigation was invariably founded on the investigator's social and personal motives, definitions, measuring techniques, and in these senses upon the time and place of the investigator.

Mitchell even came to a conclusion that economic theory as we teach it (a mass of abstract principles) was mostly the abstract idiosyncratic statements made by the Fathers of the Profession. Admittedly I do some damage to Mitchell when I assert that he thought that the major scientific element in economics was in the training process of economists (teaching them to conceptualize and to verify through quantitative or episodic measurement), and that the subject itself was full of constantly shifting social values and moral priorities. That he called his regular lectures at Columbia University, "Formative Types of Economic Thinking," was intentional and descriptively correct of what he had in mind.

## Economics as an Amalgam of Principles Applied and Modified by Contextual Considerations

It should come as no surprise that the profession has been and is bifurcated between those who emphasize the "scientific" aspect—be it a matter of abstraction (e.g. model-building) or systematic observation and measuring—and those who assert that what is important is individual or social "problem-solving." Academic economists are usually of the former camp; business- and public affairs economists of the latter. The most that can be said, it seems to me, is that there are those who view the subject in one way, and those who view it the other. But, I think that we can do more than merely note the existence of this division. Let us look at the history of the discipline and see how it developed. It is to this last task that we turn, not because there is anything really conclusive in the discipline's history, but because the history (or rather, a comparison of certain interpretations of it) reveals the connection (*filiation* was the term used by Schumpeter) between stages of its intellectual development. While I am not ready to assert that the history of a science can be a conclusive way to study that science, I do believe that the history may reveal things, which when interpreted, offer important explanations.

## 4. Three Principal Interpretations of the Dynamics of the Economic Discipline

We come now to a discussion of what I make of the ways that economics as a discipline actually has developed. In a 1985 paper, I argued that how one put the whole business of economics together related not only to personal value priorities (to which I will turn next), but also to how serious scholars, who knew a great deal about the various writers, tried to understand the dynamics of the history of the discipline itself.

There I identified three magisterial treatments of the history of economic thought. I called them magisterial because they created frameworks which linked together interpretations over time and across other boundaries.

One approach I associated with Karl Pribram (1983), a von-Wieser trained man who became for the most part a civil servant in his later life. His history of thought stressed the continual tension between emphasis on Platonic realities and the Aristotelian effort to introduce observation to flesh out the Platonic transcendental realities. That tension surfaces again in the time of Bacon[1] and Descartes,[2] when the egg-chicken argument of which came first, the model or the confirming evidence, divided philosophers. Pribram argued that the conflict between Hegel and Kant was a successor to this original division; that Communism and Fascism were also juxtaposed in the same way; and that Keynesian macroeconomics (with its emphasis on "short-term" site and time problem solving) and American free-tradism (intellectually conceived and applied willy-nilly) are later manifestations of the old division. In a nutshell, this approach to the study of economics stresses the continuity of the tension between Platonic model building and the Aristotelian method of modifying models to approximate cognition. This approach asserts that the development of the economics discipline, through its many manifestations and incarnations, is essentially tied to an ages-old Greek philosophical preoccupation; one sees the intellectual future as an adaptation of the historical intellectual past.

A second approach I associated with Wesley Clair Mitchell (1967, 1969), whose fame has already been noted. Mitchell came to believe that modern economics was essentially a set of ideas reflecting certain conflicts engendered by the industrialization of western society and the kind of urbanization that went along with it. Mitchell certainly did not argue that economics came into being only after the Industrial Revolution; rather, he argued that what was relevant to modern society tended to remain on the surface, and that the relevance of what had disappeared tended to clutter unnecessarily library shelves and men's minds. Economics, to Mitchell, was clearly site- and time-bound; he was an institutionalist. Mitchell, as I have noted, stressed the primacy of observation, and when and if one chose to explain and link observations by means of a theoretical construct, that construct was likely idiosyncratic in nature—particularly with regard to time and place. Mitchell had great but not unlimited faith in numerical quantification; one of his major critics, the econometrician Tjalling Koopmans, claimed that Mitchell merely collected data but could not arrange it in meaningful, interpretive ways (Koopmans 1947). And while I think that Mitchell's skills and his perceptions were clearly time- and site-bound, today he would merely observe that what Koopmans said of his work should have been adjudged on terms of what was new and true; those parts of Koopmans' criticisms which were true were not new, and vice versa.

So much of my own treatment of the topic is tied to an institutionalism that I am hard put to adjudge just how I feel about the underlying validity of Mitchell's approach. It requires continuous updating—in some senses Pareto's observation about knowledge is fully consistent with the point I am making. Whatever else, this approach argues that a knowledge of economics starts with an appreciation of the cobweb of existing governing institutions which give rise to and are the result of technological and political changes.

A third approach to the history of economic thought I identified with Joseph A. Schumpeter (1954), whose work spanned a very long period. As a young man he drew heavily (and unacknowledgedly) on the work of an Italian scholar, Luigi Cossa; while engaged in that early work, Schumpeter was fascinated with the distinction between what he phrased as scientific economics and political economy (or sociological economics or even ideological economics). There is much to be said for Schumpeter's contributions, but the point I want to make here is that during the last decade or so of his life, he added an additional focus to his analysis of what economics was all about and how it developed.

In his unfinished *History of Economic Analysis,* he not only examined what the changes were, but questioned from where they came. In answering the latter question, he suggested that in part they were the result of a new data base (the kind of thing his rival, Mitchell, would have said was basic). In part, however, they came from other intellectual traditions—Newton's calculus placed emphasis on physical equilibrium; new philosophical schools (logical positivism) offered new kinds of economic thinking; different schools of historical interpretation offered not only new data bases but new analytical frameworks; and certainly the discovery of new statistical methods have played a strange role in interpreting what uncertainty is and how it may be handled.

Perhaps more to the point, Schumpeter counseled economists to study law, sociology, history, and even literature. The sources of understanding the changes in economic analysis, he clearly believed, came from the wealth of methods which these other disciplines offered, and also from the usually overlooked assumptions which tied other disciplines' methods to their techniques and findings.

Years ago Professor Einstein commented to a small group of us that "a great mathematician is someone who observes some ideas or phenomena he wants to explain, and then creates a math to explain it." Newton was a great mathematician, I aver, because he was trying to explain physics; von Neumann was a great mathematician because he was trying to explain how his father, an investment banker, combined concerns about maximization of profits with concerns about the minimization of risk. Economists closed-eye emulation of Newton (and his successors) has led them to look everywhere for equilibrium (Newton's perception of the basic problem of physics). Economists' closed-eye emulation of von Neumann (and his successors) has led them to conclude that the basic economic question is how to handle risk-management.

My summary here is that if we want to understand our discipline, in its own terms, we can profit from the magisterial interpretations of all three figures—and perhaps of others' whose work I have not discussed.

## 5. Getting Back to the Question of Rhetoric

Still, there is another avenue to travel. Let us admit that there may be validity in the realization that our own idiosyncratic cultural choices also shape our discipline. The study of these cultural choices is far from mechanical. To illustrate what I think is involved let me now turn to one additional point, a view fleshed out by Pareto.

### Our Patristic Traditions and What Their Study Teaches Us

What I turn to now is the influence of patristic thinking—that is, thinking along some paradigmatic lines determined by the cultural crucible in which the stuff of our minds is initially mixed.

The obvious question is what is meant by a Patristic approach? "Patristic" refers to "father," and like it or not "father" is generally interpreted as an authority figure. Theologians have observed that "mother" is a generosity figure. "Mother Earth" gives us the good things of life; the "Sky Father," to quote from one usual self-assertion, is ". . . a Man of War," or "I am a jealous God." Patristic approaches are basically the approaches of authority; "by what reason do you hold or believe or act or claim?" is the usual reference to the patristic approach.

The next obvious question is why do we bother with patristic approaches? Many modern types claim that they do not so bother; but irrespective of that claim, I think that we do have patristic elements almost irremediably built into our minds (our culture, for example), and that they not only set the stage for our civilization (which is not only the dominant one in the world and our own European patristic tradition, but is also the appropriate one for us to study in light of the need to grasp what a civilization is), but they make it all but impossible for us to escape what we are. One's patristic approach may do much to define the path to our rhetoric. As I see it, civilizations have at their heart sets of categorical imperatives (authorities or law codes, if you please); certainly interpretations of these codes evolve and how they evolve goes to the heart of the process of social dynamics. Here are two examples:

   a. The evolution inherent in the traditional basic Jewish question of "by what authority?" or, can matters involving ethics and ritual be redetermined, and
   b. The parameters and implications of the Augustinian Christian question of "how can God simultaneously condemn man for his sins when an omnipotent and an omniscient God controls man?"

Our own European patristic approaches were principally ethical, involving the rights and obligations between individuals and households. There were, however, theological imperatives (cf. the Hebraic emphasis on the Sabbath ("the earth belongs to God, but the Sabbath belongs to man"), the sabbatical year, the jubilee year, the residual property rights of the slave, and the Biblical (but not Greek) injunction of the necessary ennobling role of work.

### The Classical Greek Patristic Legacy

Generally this has been considered the role of key philosophers and philosophical schools, such as the cynics, the stoics, the epicureans, the pythagoreans, etc.

But, self-conscious economics began with Plato's *Republic,* as subsequently refined (if not watered down by an older, wiser man) in *The Laws* and later by Aristotle. Of Plato's contributions, none is more important than his avowed emphasis on the process of pure reasoning. Of course, he sipped from the institutional bottle (whenever he addressed particular problems or selected his examples, he was forced from pure abstractions to something more cognitively observable), but his reputation was built on his preference for abstraction—that is, for what today we would call modelling.[3]

Aristotle's approach, emphasizing the relationship between the economic running of households with political (community) necessities, was based as much or more on the observation of human habits and needs as it was on abstract reasoning. His advocacy of the efficiency-necessity of private property was based on observation. His rhetoric (stressing the role of and means for persuasion) makes him quite attractive, even now. Persuasion, of course, suggests personal growth, and he knew it—thus his system was not purely static.

Yet, for all of his observations based on cognition, Aristotle did have his "givens," among which was the truth that "money creates nothing; it merely reflects power relationships." Money, he argued, is simply an artifice and can be thoroughly manipulated by law.

While there were other Greek explicit contributors to what we have latched onto as part of the Patristic tradition, the need for brevity forces me to end that discussion at this point. But, to go on is not to abandon our interest in what the classical Greeks gave us. Among other things they stressed that the basic economic question related to the allocation of scarce resources. What they failed to give us, in some instances we got from other legacies—the Judeo-Christian, to mention but the strongest. Here, having mentioned that strange term, Judeo-Christian legacy, we must pause and ask just how the two are related. In part the relationship is chronological, the latter is said to have grown (in whole or in part) out of the former (like the English and the Americans, they are both united and divided by a common language). In part, the relationship focuses on monotheism and a single cosmic plan.

But, while they share a common history, their interpretations of that history differ. The names associated with the interpretations seem to me to be less important than the subtlety of differences, themselves; but for the Judeo tradition I suggest following the reasoning of Moses Maimonides (1135–1204), a practicing physician as well as a Jewish Aristotelian, and for the Christian the reasoning of Thomas Aquinas (1225–1274), a professor at the University of Paris and later acknowledged as a principal (Roman Catholic) Church Father and also an Aristotelian. Fortunately for us, one of the issues they handled was the principal nature and its origin of the essential *economic* problem. Let me start our consideration of this difficult question, "What is economics all about?" by asking what is the point of the shared Book of Genesis concerning the inadequacy of Man.[4] Apparently whatever were His expectations, God became disappointed with Man. Mankind (and particularly Woman, perhaps since men wrote up the history) did not live up to His expectations (what that says about omniscience and/or omnipotence may be other matters). In any case, humankind were informed that they had "fallen" from Grace, and they have been made to suffer ever since.

### Two Differing Interpretations of Patristic Priorities

From our analytical standpoint we now come to the two crucial questions:

a. What was the sin; and,
b. What was the punishment?

The sin seems to have been something combining (1) inability to leave good-enough alone, (2) greed involving things (something forbidden) and time (instant gratification), (3) excessive curiosity, (4) inability to follow precise directions, and (5) a willingness to be tempted, particularly when one could assert that 'one was only doing what everyone else (sic) was doing.'[5]

What interests us next is "What was the punishment?" Although purportedly a distinction was made between what happened to Man and Woman (differing sexual roles with Woman, the home-body, and Man the outside worker), the one clear answer, particularly as seen by Aquinas and by most economists ever since, was that man/woman were made to live in a world of scarcity—it would only be by the "sweat of the brow" and the labor of the back that life could be maintained, and even then it was of limited duration. Hence, it can be maintained that the economic problem, the absence of a plethora of goods and services, was/is God's curse on man. Man, by labor and by ingenuity, must strive to try (inevitably unsuccessfully) to overcome scarcity. The study of the economics of the production of goods and services, it follows, is the result of the original sin. Since Eve was the proximate cause of the Fall, and Eve represents sexual attraction or desire, some (particularly St. Paul, whose opinion of womankind is problematic) have considered that sexual attraction was in some way even more responsible for the Fall than anything else. Put crudely, even if economics is not a sexy subject, its origins were sexual.

It is the other analysis which may be novel, and I put it to you here. Scarcity may not have been the greatest punishment, because man could use his reason to allocate priorities and thereby overcome the greater disasters of scarcity. Scarcity simply means that one has to allocate between one's preferences. What was the greater, indeed the greatest punishment, was one even more basic to life. In Maimonides' view, God's real punishment was to push man beyond the limits of his reason. This point leads to the view that until the Fall, man *knew;* after the Fall he only had *opinions.*[6] Requisite to omnipotence is omniscience, and what man/woman lost was such limited claim to both which they might have had. In other words, what truly underlies the misery of scarcity is neither hunger nor thirst, but the lack of knowledge of what one's preference schedule will do to one's happiness. For if one had complete knowledge (including foreknowledge) one could compensate accordingly.

If one pursues Maimonides' line of inquiry, it seems that uncertainty (which is based on not only ignorance of what can be known, but also on the unknowable) is the real punishment of man/woman. Here it serves my purpose to point out that the concept of uncertainty can be seen, under most circumstances, to be not only an essential part of our patristic thinking, but also to be at the heart of hearts of the economics discipline.

## 6. Conclusion

So here we have it; we study the history of the discipline of economic science simply to see what, if anything (or things), served to unify, and in that sense partially clarify, the subject. From understanding our western cultural patristic heritage, we can immediately see that much of the division among economists relates to differences within the cultural heritage—are we concerned with rational rationing or are we concerned with superrational unknowledge, to use another of Shackle's phrases? No wonder economics is schizophrenic and the fraternity is rent with schisms—analyses started off from the first by going in quite opposite directions. Add to that the points made by Pribram, Mitchell, and Schumpeter about what shapes the discussion. Pribram looks back to the ancient conflict in thinking between Plato and his purported student, Aristotle. Mitchell looks back to the revolutions begun in the XVIII century when modern industrial specialization and urbanization came to dominate life and then thought. And Schumpeter, seeing his own answers, looks to epistemological developments, related but hardly confined to the ideas suggested by Pribram and Mitchell.

I believe that most of us have disordered minds, or minds sufficiently disordered that we have learned by experience not be averse to leaving a lot of strings loose. We study, and we ponder, and to some extent we can grasp others' ideas and proposals, and to quite a different (and usually lesser) extent we can disentangle explanations for our own preferences.

### What Do We Make of It All?

This lengthy paper started with the question of what economics was all about—was it really only cultural rhetoric or was it something different, a true science? One of my colleagues, a most distinguished game theorist, has often, when given the opportunity, pointed out to me that no real physicist really worries about the history of physics. History is a luxury reserved for those who want to study as unfocused a thing as the history and philosophy of science; it suffices for real physicists to know what is state-of-the-science truth now.

My answer, admittedly not persuasive to him (but it is to me) is that physics is about things; economics is about people. Things generally are stable; people virtually never are. One has to study the history of a discipline involving humans because the data are sufficiently unstable that their cause and effect relationships cannot really be defined. And because of that subjective element, economics is a different kind of science.

As my colleague is a game theorist, I go further and say that game theory has its own genesis, and for all of its supposed scientific nature and success, chess masters are still beating the computers. Even more powerful is the point that although we know far more than von Neumann believed anyone would have to know about the weather, we still cannot predict the weather well.

It is not for nothing that rhetoric was originally part of the *trivium;* rhetoric was the key which unlocked men's minds to reason. Thus, I argue that it is essential to study the history of the rhetoric of economics to understand what persuades more and what persuades less. Early on, one should get beyond the level of immanent criticism, a level which is very persuasive only to those whose intellectual operation is well within the bounds of the reason necessary to accept the argument. Language, as Hobbes pointed out "in the beginning of modern times" is the means of transmitting ideas, and ideas, themselves, are the product not only of cognition but also of intellectual compression within the brain.

How does one study the rhetoric of economics? Admittedly, one can learn some things from the likes of the two books by Hirschman and McCloskey. Yet, I aver that economists have also to understand that what persuades one may not persuade another; what it took to convince Aquinas may still convince any number of like-minded types, but whatever that was, it did not persuade Hobbes or Mandeville or Smith. And what persuaded Smith surely did not persuade Cournot or Jevons; and what persuaded Pareto does not seemingly persuade Arrow. What sets each group apart has not been anything so simple as the *method* of their thinking; rather it is the set of criteria to which their thinking gives priority.

Methodology, we tire of repeating to those who will never learn, is not the study of method, but the study of reasons for selecting the criteria which a particular method is supposed to satisfy. To identify the parameters of an appropriate method is no more than to talk to those already converted. How little credit we do to our powers of persuasion if we can do no more than repeat the argument which captured us. Our difficult task is to grasp the foundations of the thought process—and I suggest that our patrician legacies serve as fine, if often confused, examples of that.

In the end, it comes down to this. We study the history of economic thought to grasp the rhetoric of economics, that is, what lines of reasoning (thought identification) have been used to make woven intellectual tapestries have meaning to different viewers. Knowing a variety of types of formative thought (Mitchell's term for the study of the history of economic thought) is the way to learn how others have calculated and will likely calculate in the future. Then we should phrase what we want to demonstrate according to criteria meaningful to them.

One data bank on that information is the history of economic thought, and although the path is a long and discursive one, there is no short royal turnpike to the answer.

Catallactics (the study of prices and quantities) and, more basically and therefore far harder, the study of what forms *value* is the heart and the goal of one tradition. The Common Law was said to reveal the life history of the English people; accordingly, the history of our discipline is more likely to reveal the many things for which we have been looking—quite aside from the rigor of any of the answers we think we have discovered. Or, to put the matter in a nutshell, seeking the appropriate question is more important than developing answers.

But, in seeking the basic economic question, I suggest we find a very interesting conflict between the patristic legacy which sees economics as the study of the rationing of scarce means, given fully understood and defined ends, and the patristic legacy which says that economics is merely a systematic effort at trying to cope with what cannot really be known. That is, with what Shackle and others call unknowledge—in a world where choices have to be made.

Let me now flesh-out my own judgement. Insofar as I am aware there are, *inter alia,* two principal paradigms in economics. Each stems from our "Western" patristic tradition. One lays the foundations for a belief that economics deals with the allocation of scarce resources; the other for the belief that economics has to handle the unknowable as well as the knowable. When one studies the history of the discipline—the search for understanding—one quickly discovers that these paradigms, seemingly unrelated, draw their answers from the same stock of inputs. It behooves us, consequently, to study this data bank.

NOTES

I note the pleasure I have received from Dr. Charles McCann in a series of discussions about rhetoric and hermeneutics. He and Mr. Morgan Marietta also reviewed the manuscript, for which I thank them.

1. Pribram thought that the Franciscan scholar-monk Roger Bacon was the best example of the Aristotelian approach; I would have thought, particularly in terms of the Anglo-American tradition, that a better case could be made for Francis Bacon.

2. While Descartes is my preferred choice others think that a better case could be made for Leibnitz or Kant.

3. Plato's system was based on a division of activity (the usual point is to call it division of labor, but since the best of all activities was not work [something distasteful] but things valued in the doing as well as in the consequence, the verbal emphasis is worth noting).

His preferred system, the one run by philosophers, who were more committed to social efficiency than to personal probity, had only community property for themselves. For lesser types, the need for appealing their smaller minds might make personal property rights the appropriate kind of incentive or opiate, however ownership was not a right, simply a means necessary until men were properly educated.

Plato's approach was not developmental; it was static. It stressed the coordination and planning of the use of resources.

4. An even earlier major point is that everything is said to have had a prior cause, with the Prime Cause being God.

5. Cf. Genesis, 3; 9–12, 16, 17. "[9] But the Lord God called to the man and said

to him, "Where are you?" [10] He replied, "I heard the sound as you were walking the garden, and I was afraid because I was naked, and I hid myself." [11] God answered, "Who told you that you were naked? Have you eaten from the tree which I forbade you?" [12] The man said, "The woman you gave me for a companion, she gave me fruit from the tree and I ate." [*Note: the story as recalled suggests that Adam was dependent upon Eve (for what?), and the price of that dependency was to be agreeable to Eve ("it was really all her fault—I only did what You [God] had laid out for me").*] [16] To the woman he said: I will increase your labour and your groaning, and in labour you shall bear children. You shall feel an urge for your husband, and he shall be your master. [17] And to the man he said: Because you have listened to your wife and have eaten from the tree which I forbade you, accursed shall be the ground on your account. With labour you shall win your food from it all the days of your life. It will grow thorns and thistles for you, none but wild plants for you to eat. You shall gain your bread by the sweat of your brow until you return to the ground; for from it you were taken. Dust you are, to dust you shall return." [*Again, for those civil libertarians amongst us, kindly note that God forced Adam to testify against himself? Who says that the Bill of Rights is an inherent aspect of divine justice? Far from it, in the Last Judgement, pleading the Fifth won't do at all.*]

6. This point is to be found through an expansion of the thinking of Maimonides (*Guide of the Perplexed*, see Chapter 2); his question is what was the state of man's knowledge before and after the Fall. The line of his argument is that man did not have any worries before the Fall, because everything was taken care of. The Fall, coming about only because God had told man to avoid just one thing which man then did not avoid, led to man no longer being taken care of, and man, having become mortal, having to spend his days worrying about the unknown. Where once man could count on a certain future, now man had to worry about the unknown, about which he could only have limited expectations. Maimonides (1135–1204), a native of Cordoba (Spain), spent the greatest part of his career in Cairo, where he was the Court physician. Maimonides is one of the great Aristotelians, and although much of his theology was considered questionable by Thomas of Aquinas, Aquinas had little trouble with Maimonides' Aristotelianism.

REFERENCES

Becker, Gary (1964). *Human Capital*. New York: Columbia University Press.

Burns, Arthur F. and Mitchell, Wesley Clair (1946). *Measuring Business Cycles*. New York: National Bureau of Economic Research.

Fogel, Robert William (1964). *Railroads and American Economic Growth*. Baltimore: Johns Hopkins University Press.

Friedman, Milton (1953). *Essay in Positive Economics*. Chicago: University of Chicago Press.

Hayek, Friedrich (1967). *Studies in Philosophy, Politics, and Economics*. London: Routledge & Kegan Paul.

Koopmans, Tjalling (1947). *Review of Economic Statistics* xxix, 161–72.

Kravis, Irving R. and Lipsey, Richard C. (1982). "The Location of Overseas Production and Production for Export by U.S. Multinational Firms," *Journal of International Economics,* 21.

McCloskey, Donald N. (1983). "The Rhetoric of Economics," *Journal of Economic Literature,* vol. xxi, 481–517.

———. (1985). *The Rhetoric of Economics.* Madison: University of Wisconsin Press.

Mitchell, Wesley Clair (1967, 1969). *Types of Economic Theory: From Mercantilism to Institutionalism.* Two vols. Edited with an Introduction by Joseph Dorfman. New York: Augustus M. Kelley.

Muth, John F. (1961). "Rational Expectations and the Theory of Price Movements," *Econometrica* 29, 315–35.

Pareto, Vilfredo (1935). *The Mind and Society,* being a translation of *Trattato de Sociologia Generale.* New York: Harcourt, Brace and Company.

———. *Manual of Economics* (1977), being a translation of *Manuale d'economia politica.* New York: Augustus Kelley.

Popper, Karl (1962). *Conjectures and Refutations: The Growth of Scientific Knowledge.* New York: Basic Books.

Pribram, Karl (1983). *A History of Economic Reasoning.* Baltimore: Johns Hopkins University Press.

Samuelson, Paul Anthony (1947). *Foundations of Economic Analysis.* Cambridge, MA: Harvard University Press.

Schumpeter, Joseph Alois (1954). *History of Economic Analysis.* New York: Oxford.

Shackle, George L. S. (1983). "A Student's Pilgrimage," *Banco Nazionale di Lavoro,* 107–16.

Solow, Robert (1968). See Zellner, Arnold [ed.]. *Readings in Statistics and Econometrics.* Boston: Little, Brown, pp. 349f.

## CHAPTER 7

# Early Capital Theory in the Economics Journals: A Study of Imputed Induced Demand

*John Maurice Clark, the son of John Bates Clark, was my teacher at Columbia. His views of the evolution of economic thought surely must have shaped mine. And his assessment of the evolution of his father's thinking was revelational to me. Here was a son, clearly devoted to his father's work and memory, who thought his earlier work was better (in the sense of being truly original) than that done later (even though the latter had been, in some major sense, influenced by the son). Clark's collection of early essays, the 1886* Philosophy of Wealth, *and his subsequent writings for the American Economic Association and the* Quarterly Journal of Economics *were chosen as foil by Eugen von Boehm-Bawerk. The sophisticated Austrian, however, failed to dent Clark's calm, perhaps even his consciousness. These exchanges and the next stage of the debate involving Irving Fisher, Frank Fetter, and others, are the subject of this chapter.*

*This essay was a by-product of Chapter 3 of this volume. Here I seek to explain: (1) The background of John Bates Clark's theory of capital, including his orientation to Lockean thinking; (2) his conflicts with Eugen von Boehm-Bawerk on both capital and interest; (3) his shift in 1899 to statics in the* Distribution of Wealth; *(4) a detailed summary of the entry of Irving Fisher and Frank A. Fetter into the debate; (5) a partial effort to rehabilitate the original Clarkian position by Charles A. Tuttle with a heavy-gun rejoinder by Fisher; and (6) a swinging free-for-all between Clark and Boehm-Bawerk. Here I recount early battles in a long war. After this "smoke" cleared there were renewed engagements involving Kenneth Boulding, Nicholas Kaldor, Frank Knight, and Friedrich Hayek in the 1930s and Joan Robinson, Paul A. Samuelson, and Robert M. Solow in the 1950s. I see the war as a staged play, with each set of battles being an act. Here I present only Acts 1 and 2.*

Elsewhere I have noted that one of the instruments of success for journal editors is to find stimulating controversies which attract contributors, sub-

---

*Economic Notes by Monte dei Paschi di Siena* 20, no. 1 (1991): 58–88.

scribers and other readers (Perlman 1991). What follows here is a survey of one of the controversies which Charles Dunbar and others unearthed in the early years of the American *Quarterly Journal of Economics* and the *Journal of Political Economy,* and the British *Economic Journal.* In that same article I mentioned that in the 1880s professional economics journals came to share the venue with books.

One way to look at the history I am about to relate is to imagine that what we have is simply a group of competitive playwrites at work: I recount the story accordingly.

**Prologue**

To introduce the story adequately, one must first know a few things about the author John Bates Clark, who may or may not have posed the original problem, but who certainly proposed an answer which stimulated the controversy. A dominant problem in Clark's professorial career involved rationales for the social rights of various economic classes. What he took as his initial theme was the basis for a reasonable and logical formulation of the right to a place at the social bargaining table of the owners of capital. Briefly put, he asked: "Why are not only laborers and entrepreneurs but those whom Marx snarled were 'capitalists' essential to all economic processes?" And, "Is there anything special about capitalists which gave them their uniqueness aside from their holding, according to the institutions of the time, scarce resources?"

Clark's initial posture was as a moral philosopher, and he saw his principal role as the employer of persuasive morality in the discussion. Having been educated in Germany and having taken a leading role in the formation of the more-or-less anti-pure-laissez-faire American Economic Association, he had long entertained a fascination about capitalists, particularly why they as well as landlords and workers were entitled to any part of the social product. Furthermore, he lived at a time when an aggressive new economic class, the parvenu capitalist, was emerging: seemingly it had cynically rejected any obligation to exercise traditional *noblesse oblige,* and its open avowal of economic power and slavish emulation of the worst of eighteenth century English and French aristocratic consumptionism was aesthetically and socially as well as morally distasteful to a kindly man of simple tastes and personal self-discipline.

Clark understood well the role of property rights in America, and the claim of landed property owners he grasped fully—if for no other reason than he had first hand experience with farming and with small-scale, property-owning farmers. He also had no trouble understanding the importance of labor; to which was added a conviction that workers were not doomed by some Iron Law of Wages to no more than subsistence. In this sense his

Christian Socialism, something which his son John Maurice Clark thought stayed with him in some form all of his life, suggested that inter-group understanding and cooperation could smooth the essential inequities of social bargaining power. His question was why should those who merely advance capital be entitled to a share—and, as events were progressing, an unseemly large share—of the social product.

To understand Clark one has to grasp the essentials of the British and particularly the American political experience (for a contrary view see Homan, 1928, Chapter 1). It goes back to Thomas Hobbes's seminal 1651 book, *The Leviathan,* which (1) introduced empiricism as *the* method of discovering the sources of truth and (2) the ideas that without a social contract every man feared every other man, and (3) without an effective (meaning functioning) government contract the social contract would not be enforced. Hobbes, who had been tutor to Charles II, was not a believer in the Divine Right of Kings theory because his empirical method (observation) had led him to judge that the largest portion of right was clearly might.

Much of the next 150 years was spent in answering Hobbes's assertion that force was at the heart of any system of government, and that government alone (the monopoly of force) is what saves men from the rapacious greed and brutality of other men. For our purposes John Locke's answer is the most trenchant. The Lockean argument involved many things, of which I mention principally two; the unalienable right to property, and the property right being based on previous labor-input. No supporter of the ecclesiastical hierarchy, Locke thought that the individual dealt directly with his God and that God had given every man three intertwined undeniable rights—life, liberty, and property. Life is so basic, that no threat is worth voluntarily yielding one's life. Liberty, he defined as the right to move "horizontally" from an unpleasant society or situation to one of one's preference; only slaves lack this right, and Locke was not, in principle at least, sympathetic to slavery. But it is understanding the unalienable right to hold property, essentially the transmutation of one's personality through labor into things, which gives the individual a property claim to the things.

Locke held that the property right was coequal to the other two since without property no man could effectively—to say nothing of financially— enjoy the other two. Moreover, in suggesting that the original source of the property right was associated with the intermingling of one's labor with things, he made work (so repugnant to Plato) the cornerstone of man's achievement. Labor-input was the source of the property right.[1] As one can

---

1. The Roman (or earlier dominant) view was that the property right was accorded to the discoverer or the first one who claimed the right; later it was amended to incorporate the notion that rights, as such, derived from society, and if the courts held that yours was the prior claim,

quickly see, the Lockean perception of the relationship between labor and property was immediately applicable in the case of British colonists taking unimproved land in the New World.[2]

Locke is the grandfather of not only the formal structure of the American political system, but in a metaphorical sense he is also the grandmother—since the finer things of our culture (always identified when possible with Grandma), namely the nobility of work, the rights of labor, and the importance of enjoying the fruits of one's labor (particularly those sold for money or traded for other property) remains even now the name of the principal game in the land.

We now can return fully to John Bates Clark. In his early essays, written earlier for the *New Englander*,[3] which were combined in his 1885 book, *The Philosophy of Wealth,* Clark wrestled with the question of whether the return to capital, particularly as held by non-workers, had a rationale as simple as the return to labor.

In time, Clark was to decide and to preach that the holding of wealth as capital (meaning something other than realty) was as justified in terms of original rights to say nothing of being socially necessary, as holding realty, and that the historic rational justification for paying a return to landholders (rents) should be used exactly to explain the paying of a return (profits) to other forms of property including capital-holders. But, the simplicity of that argument came about a decade later, and it came by way of a long series of journal articles.

What Clark had to deal with first was the actual nature of wealth. In Clark's lexicon "wealth" was essentially individual and tied up with ownership; yet, he suggested externalities—that the well-being which wealth created often spread to others in the community (e.g. a beautiful home gave satisfaction not only to the owner but also to his neighbors). Wealth was well-being, but well-being obtained externally (from outside) to the recipient.

---

yours was the right. By contrast, there is a certain biblical logic to the Lockean view: In the beginning—so to paraphrase another basic document—there was the land (meaning resources) and there was man. "By the sweat of his brow" man fashioned the resources and thus they became his. In the course of time these improved or fashioned resources were bought and sold, but insofar as anyone improved resources not thereafter considered part his, that person had to be compensated for that labor (as a quitclaim)—otherwise the product was partly owned by anyone who had added to the fashioning of it.

2. Locke's argument fitted in beautifully with his position that since the indigenous Americans (the red Indians) had not invested any personal labor in the land, that land was without any owner. Locke, as the friend and employee of Lord Shaftesbury, wrote the Constitution of the Colony of South Carolina, a colonial settlement largely undertaken by the Cooper (the Lords Shaftesbury) family.

3. One of the serious magazines which characterized the intellectual frontier of clear-thinking intellectual discussion before, during, and after the American Civil War.

Wealth could possess a flow of pleasures associated with things material, objective, useful, and appropriable. *Human knowledge, however, does not really come under this definition of wealth, because knowledge is part of man, himself, not something which can be totally separated from him, when that knowledge is appropriated.*[4]

> All forms of labor create wealth; yet for every product nature furnishes the substance and man only the modes. One class of laborers create . . . the attribute of appropriability; the other general class create the attribute of utility (1885, p. 15).

Such a concept as "non-productive labor" was, the masters to the contrary notwithstanding, an error—a non-starter. Not all wealth creates labor, but only labor, as such, can create wealth.

Clark paired his views on wealth with another defined concept, the "philosophy of value", which was simply "a measure of utility". Utility, however, as he phrased it was a social rather than an individual valuation—utility was worth what it brought on the market.[5] *Yet, underlying all of these points was his moral commitment to social responsibility,* a point which went beyond Locke's system of individual rights and was the basis for Clark's Christian morality: What is ordinarily termed a good bargain for the individual is, morally, a bad bargain. Yet, Clark did not condemn out of hand something like speculation; for that worked to the social advantage of progress—the speculative merchant was being rewarded for his time and place preference. When it came to the market, Clark wrote of "effective utility" or "social effective utility"—precisely what Jevons (whose work, if he had read, he had not read all that well) meant by "final degree of utility" and as "marginal utility", the phrase now used.

While Clark stressed the virtues of open competition, not all competition met the test of openness. As for social justice and markets, Clark observed that labor by and large faces unequal terms in dealing with employers. It is best that laborers combine in their bargaining, but preferably they should combine not along trades of skill lines, but as workers dealing with a mutual employer. He endorsed the all-embracing Knights of Labor rather than the particularistic trade unions.

---

4. Accordingly human capital (meaning saliable knowledge and/or skills resident in the individual's mind) was an oxymoron—if it was human (resident in the body), it could not be capital.

5. This view that values to have any practical meaning must be essentially social rather than subjectively personal is where the study of institutions, economic or otherwise, must start. Cf. T. H. Green's 1880 views as seen in his *Lectures on the Principle of Political Obligation* is a timely example of Clark's kind of thinking.

The book was generally well-received, and it came out with some revisions and a new introduction in a second edition in 1886. Yet, there were influential dissidents. For example, Arthur T. Hadley, then professor at Yale (later he was its president), while admitting that Clark was himself a "sound" thinker, attacked the pernicious socialism, albeit Christian socialism, inherent in Clark's formulation. Hadley felt that Clark should have *and had not* explicitly disavowed the interpretation of the Lockean view that (1) labor is the source of all wealth or (2) trade involved one party invariably exploiting the other (Dorfman, 1949, 194–6).

**Act 1: Scene 1**

In 1888 Clark, taking some note of his critics, moved to refocus his analysis; in this instance he shed from his writings (but not really from his beliefs) an explicit commitment to social reform. It was a lengthy essay published by the American Economic Association in its Official Publications.[6] Shorn of his Christian socialist leanings, this article stands out as a scientific defense of the need for capitalists as economic functionaries. Clark's case is made on the necessity for private property in land; he considers private property in chattels as no different.

This essay is important because Clark introduces capital as a split concept. The way he prefers to split it is to claim that there is an abstract fund of control over resources. It possesses and perhaps embodies, to use his phrase, 'effective social utility' and ". . . The destiny of [this capital fund] is to migrate through an endless series of outward forms". It was a right which took alternately forms of fixed things and liquidity.

Against this were concrete *but limited in their life* examples of this fund. These were the "fixed things", the capital goods which we all easily identify. As the capital good is used, it transmits part of its material quality into the products so manufactured, but the right of the owner remained.

To understand Clark, one has always to recall that while he was all but innocent of any training in mathematics and he fancied himself a keen observer of the world about him, he nonetheless preferred the *a priori* method because it gave him firm answers. He was hardly an autodidact (he had studied in America, Germany, and Switzerland), yet his was a very original

---

6. When it came to publications the American Economic Association has tried several different modes. In its earliest years it published some essays (really dissertations) reflecting Richard Ely's enthusiasms. Later it published book-length articles, of which Clark's is a prime example. Eventually in 1910, it undertook the publication of the *American Economic Review* and from 1969 and 1987 other journals like the *Journal of Economic Literature* and the *Journal of Economic Perspectives,* respectively.

mind. Many of his creative distinctions (e.g. statics vs. dynamics, capital vs. capital goods, absolute utility vs. effective utility) were, he realized, purely definitional. But in actual rhetorical use, these terms were chosen to clarify and integrate (processes he favored), yet, beneath everything there was a profound conviction that the meaning of and institutions controlling life could not be fully simplified. His distinction between the abstract capital fund and concrete capital goods seems to me to come from a general perception that a labor input and the eventual property right were in some underlying sense parallel to the right of property and the right for a property income. His actual example was the comparison of cultures which can endure even though individuals within a culture invariably die. The importance is not the use of the culture analogy, but the point that a given thing may have disparate sides. Thus, Clark wrestled with the question of whether the return to capital, particularly as held by non-workers, had a rationale as simple as the return to labor.

Our scene closes with the point being urged that the study of economic capital was not only a study of what capital does (namely serve as a concrete input into the productive process), but a study of what capital is (an organic force with an independent life, although perhaps no soul, of its own).

## Act 1: Scene 2

The other giant to be considered imminently will be seen to be Eugen von Boehm-Bawerk, at the time a professor at Innsbruck (in the Tyrol), but even then on his way to Vienna where he had two simultaneous and unusually distinguished careers as professor of economics and Finance Minister of the Austrian-Hungarian dual monarchy. But, his importance for us is best grasped when it is realized that he was seen as the champion of a new way of looking at economics, a way different in form and in principle from the British tradition of Ricardo as interpreted by John Stuart Mill.

In October 1888 Charles Dunbar printed as the lead article in the third volume of the *Quarterly Journal of Economics* a lengthy survey essay, "The Austrian Economists and Their View of Value" by James Bonar (1888a), one of that select few (British) civil servants who has left a major mark on academic scholarship in economics.[7] Our interest in Bonar centers here only

---

7. Bonar (1852–1941), worked both in Britain and in Ottawa (where he was Deputy Master of the Royal Mint). He is renowned for his scholarly contributions to the study of Smith and Malthus, which earned him most of the credits rewarded by honorary degrees from Glasgow and Cambridge. Like Smith he took his first degree from Glasgow and was a Snell Exhibitioner at Oxford.

on his acknowledged role as the introducer into English literature of the significance of the Austrian school of economics.[8]

Starting with a full description of the anti-utilitarian nature of the Mengerian approach to economics, Bonar ascribes to the Austrians a willingness to come to grips with measuring value in use, rather than simply value in exchange. He finds that Boehm-Bawerk's work clears up errors in Menger, particularly with Menger's apparent belief that the value of anything was determined by the price of the last item bought. The market reflects degrees of value attributed by the last buyer and last seller: each is willing *in his own mind* to exchange money and the good for possession of that n-th item.

Values of inferior goods are determined by the imputed prices of superior goods. Capital, thus, becomes associated with what its products will bring first within the minds of the buyers and sellers and then with the iteration as seen in the n-th transaction. But, the role of alternatives is also important. To Bonar price is clearly not value; value can exist without price:

> The service . . . that Jevons and the Austrians have rendered . . . seems to be . . . not the . . . introduction of "subjective value" . . ., but the clearer definition of it. . . . [T]he notion of "final utility" throws light rather on the nature than on the causes of value (p. 26).

Three months later (by then 1889) Dunbar published in the *Quarterly Journal of Economics* Bonar's enthusiastic descriptive review of the 1888 or 1889[9] German edition of Eugen von Boehm-Bawerk's *The Positive Theory of Capital,* which was itself the second part of a project (Bonar, 1888b).[10] Interest is not a reward for time, alone. It could be a reward for abstinence, but probably is not. What interest involves is a recognition of risk and uncertainty (although these terms were not applied to Clark's point until a couple of generations later when Frank H. Knight used them.)

In 1891 Macmillan eventually (not that much time had passed) published William Smart's English translation of the 1888 *Eugen von Boehm-Bawerk's The Positive Theory of Capital.* This is the edition which when it came on the

---

8. I acknowledge that William Smart, the first holder of the Adam Smith Chair in Economics at Glasgow, also has a strong claim to being the British St. Paul of this missionary effort. But, Smart's initial efforts (and in the long run even more significant than Higgs's) relate to his translations of the Austrian economists. The success of movements apparently need translators like St. Jerome (*Eusebius Hieronymus*) and John Wycliffe, too. In Edgeworth's review (see fn. 4, above), Edgeworth praises Smart's earlier translation of Boehm Bawerk's *Capital and Interest* and urges him to translate *The Positive Theory of Capital.* Smart did so.

9. The printing which Bonar reviewed apparently came out in 1889. However, Smart, who translated it, based his translation on a printing which came out in 1888.

10. The first part was the 1884 *Kapital und Kapitalzins. Erste Abteilung: Geschichte und Kritik der Kapitalzins-Theorien.*

English-speaking scene became the solid link in the development of capital theory. Smart's Translator's Preface contains a useful comparison of four existing *and erroneous* interpretations of interest as well as Boehm-Bawerk's correct version. One, the *Productivity interpretation:*

> attribute[s] the existence of interest to the productive power of capital . . . [and it confuses] quantity of product with value of product, either in the way of tacitly assuming the identity of the two, or of failing to show any necessary connection between them. . . . Capital is productive, but interest is not its product (p. v).

The second is the *Use* interpretation:

> "Interest is the price paid for the use of capital", . . . [and this interpretation is] shown to base interest, which is notoriously an income obtained from all kinds of capital, on an analogy drawn from one special kind of capital, viz., durable goods. The idea that the *use* of capital is something distinct from the *using-up* of capital, and interest something different from the price of the principal, becomes untenable when the true economic nature of the 'good' is understood as the sum of its material uses or services (p.v.; italics in the original).

The third is the *Abstinence* theory which confuses

> the origin and accumulation of capital with the source and cause of interest. Abstinence will account for the owner having a sum to lend, but it will not account for that sum growing 3% [sic] larger in a year's time (p. vi).

The fourth was the *Socialist or Exploitation* interpretation.

Boehm-Bawerk's fifth was a *Conquest of Time* interpretation; it involved a complex point that man worked for consumption and saving purposes. That which was put aside for saving was essentially intended to increase (not merely to maintain the present level for the future) future levels of consumption. Technological improvement (lower unit-output cost) could be purchased at the expense of lengthening the time of the production process. Capital when increased produces with other given inputs disproportionately more. Interest allows the entrepreneur to get capital for a longer period of process-time and to employ a superior technology (again, unit out-put cost is lowered); interest is the price of time.

In 1891, Clark, writing in the *Quarterly Journal of Economics,* condensed and extended his argument about capital. In a way, it is the clearest statement of his original basic position, which he was later to modify and refine. Values, Clark held, were essentially social and organic in nature. And while values took specific forms, they also possessed a certain élan vital (what Henri Bergson held to be the creative element in all organisms and thus responsible for evolution):

> Capital may be studied from two points of view. . . . In formal definitions a concrete view has been taken, and capital has been treated as a mass of instruments for aiding labor. . . . In the actual treatment of the subject capital has been regarded in a way that is more in harmony with practical thought. It has been considered abstractly, as a fund or quantity of wealth devoted to productive uses . . .
>
> Both views are essential in economic analysis: the common and practical though abstract view is the more serviceable in the solution of problems of distribution. Capital, itself, is in reality one and the same thing in whichever way it is treated (p. 300) . . .
>
> As the capital that figures in our present problem is the pure social fund of productive wealth, so the labor in our problem is a corresponding fund of human energy. . . . Workers are distinct from work. For the purpose of a study of distribution they are related to it as capitalists are related to capital (p. 302) . . .
>
> Abstractly regarded, labor is this fund of pure energy itself, as changeful in its forms as is pure capital.
>
> As a fund, it is kept intact by the young generation of workers, who come upon the scene and take the places of the older ones who depart. Laborers are perishable, but social labor is continuous . . . The parallelism between capital pure and concrete, on the one hand, and labor pure and concrete, on the other is fact of primary importance (p. 303).

Clark's theme was augmented slightly in an article he published later in 1893 in the *Yale Review*:

> A perfectly reasonable being would make no difference between a present good and a future one merely because of the intervening time. Uncertainties count . . .
>
> With men whose altruism is imperfect, the fact that the benefits resulting from saving accrue mainly to other tells against this process. With men whose reason is imperfect, the mere lapse of time is a consideration . . .
>
> It is wrong to say that at the point of cessation, the personal cost of creating capital equals the personal gains accruing to the owner in consequence of it. Two opposing motives for action are at the point in equilib-

rium. One is the definite personal sacrifice involved in abstinence. The other is an endless series of gains incapable of exact measurement and extending through unknown generations. Not simple is the action of time in the calculations of the capitalist. *That on which the effect of time is observable is not so much gains as motives* (pp. 314–15, emphasis added).

Boehm-Bawerk chose to do battle with all of his critics, self-described or fancied (and we have mentioned only Clark); it became not only a lengthy three-part series of articles published in Dunbar's *Quarterly Journal of Economics* in 1895 and 1896 (Boehm-Bawerk, 1895a, 1895b, and 1896), but he actually slipped in a separate article on some more of his ideas during that time (Boehm-Bawerk, 1895c). Even though that lengthy Boehm-Bawerk three-part manuscript replied to several critics (Walker, 1892; White, 1892; Bilgram, 1891; Hawley, 1892), several but not all of whose articles had been written in the *Quarterly Journal of Economics*, the principal focus of his attack was Clark's assessment.[11] Boehm-Bawerk opened by mentioning his satisfaction that so many Americans have received favorably his views (1895a). He then matches, and perhaps, exceeds Clark's efforts at left-handed compliments. Clark's criticisms should be turned on his own work, for Boehm-Bawerk's argument really applies well to the illustration which Clark had used to fault the argument. Clark had suggested that present goods could not really be compared to future goods, because present and future did not permit comparisons (much in the sense that a later Supreme Court held that equal but separate education was an oxymoron). Boehm-Bawerk said that he never had claimed that the two were equal except in the subjective thinking of the decision-maker.

Having warmed himself up with his defense, Boehm-Bawerk then goes on the attack. To use the figure of speech, popularized much later, Boehm-Bawerk argues that capital is either a concept or a form—if it is a concept it is malleable like *putty,* if it is a form it is fixed as in *clay.* It must be one or the other. And Clark is trying to claim that it can be both. "A theory," he writes, "not borne out by the facts cannot be saved by a metaphor, not even by a metaphor so ingenious and alluring as Professor Clark's . . ." (p. 128).

---

11. The later articles in this series, although related, are not trenchant to our story. The second essay, appearing in April 1895, attacks General Walker's 1892 (two issue-long criticism of this approach). And the third, in the January 1896 issue, attacks Horace White, Hugo Bilgram, and MacVane (Harvard) at considerable length and Frederick Hawley with a short but more blistering dismissal. Their criticisms which had appeared earlier and his replies are of antiquarian interest, but I skip them here in order to shorten an already too-long treatment (Boehm Bawerk, 1895b, 1896).

**Act 1: Scene 3**

However, Clark quickly returned to Boehm-Bawerk in the April 1895 issue in a respectful but clearly general two-pronged attack, "The Origin of Interest" (Clark, 1895a). Boehm-Bawerk, he believes, wants to study not capital, but capital goods. And, the lengthening of the production process may be a sufficient but it certainly is not a necessary aspect of reducing costs.

Given the opportunity Boehm-Bawerk came back immediately (the next issue [July]) with a stringent statement touching on these points and suggesting that Professor Clark has not read the book with sufficient attention to detail (1895c).

Clark took up his pen again (1895b, but also see 1895a). His article, "Real Issues Concerning Interest", opens with:

> Professor v. Boehm-Bawerk is entitled to the last word in the pending discussion. I will neither repeat my former argument nor extend it, but will gladly accept the verdict to which readers may be led by a study of the discussion already published. It is desirable, however, that unnecessary misunderstanding should be removed (Clark, 1895b, p. 98).

Warming to the opportunity "not to have the last word", he goes on with a patient and somewhat less than blistering appraisal of Boehm-Bawerk's *The Positive Theory of Capital*. His complaint was that Boehm-Bawerk wanted to talk about specifics (capital goods) rather than the general concept ("[capital] in its entirety") (Clark, 1895a). He numbers four points: Boehm-Bawerk misquotes him; Clark holds to an abstinence theory of the origin of capital (Boehm-Bawerk has no such theory rather the origin of capital is the unspent unnecessary property of capital holders); Clark thinks that the capitalist must in some sense abstain from spending (Boehm-Bawerk seems to think otherwise); and, Clark is not persuaded that roundaboutness is a necessary condition for decreasing unit costs (Clark 1895b).

Clark then went on to other business, publishing it in the *Quarterly Journal of Economics*.[12]

---

12. In the next few months (April) Clark digressed and published in the *Quarterly Journal of Economics* one of his most original papers (1894), "A Universal Law of Economic Variations". It anticipates (1) more modern work on the point that goods are bought for the consumption services they are believed to render (bundles of services, as it were), (2) there is a difference in impact between changes in prices and changes in incomes, marginal analysis deals with discontinuous as well as continuous functions, (3) and marginal product does not directly set wage rates because it concentrates on logical ordering not on historical ordering. Finally, for one not schooled in the intricacies of finer maths and geometries, he nonetheless introduces a 3-dimensional graph.

**Act 1: Scene 4**

In 1899 Clark published his second book, *The Distribution of Wealth*. It dealt only with economic statics, but he promised in the Preface "a later volume on the dynamics of distribution" (Clark 1899, p. ix). He refers generally to contributions made by Marshall, Francis A. Walker, Hadley, Taussig, Smart, Hobson, MacFarlane, Stuart Wood, and Herbert M. Thompson. He thanks Franklin H. Giddings (cf. 1888) and Simon Patten (cf. 1888) specifically. Reference to Boehm-Bawerk is simply as an antagonist, and clearly not as the only one. Henry George was every bit as great an antagonist, since George thought that value was ultimately set *only* by the costs of marginal, or no-rent, land. And Clark's hero, sung here for the first time, is Johann von Thuenen.[13]

This is the volume in which Clark lays out clearly his perception of marginal productivity being the ultimate determiner of returns to each of the factors of production—labor and capital (including land). "It is the productivity of labor . . . that sets the *ultimate* standard of wages" (cf. Clark 1899, p. xvii, emphasis added).

He is concerned with "Catallactics, the term once suggested as a title for the whole of scientific economic science, . . . treat[ing] of phenomena that are attributable to exchange only (Clark 1899, p. 52). If societies are, as he believes and asserts, essentially dynamic, "The imaginary static world, reveals certain forces of real life acting alone".

Chapters IX through XIII start by reviewing his dual perception of capital as a permanent "fund" and capital as specifics—in the form of capital goods. Then he turns to fixed and circulating capital, which pertain to the former—fixed capital is active, circulating capital is passive. Just as capital has a permanent fund aspect, so does the labor force (his term is "social labor"). Wages are worked out in a static analysis by adding increments of labor to a fixed amount of capital.

Space here precludes a detailed examination of his argument, but it is pertinent to note that he ends by saying that while applications of static analysis are theoretically interesting, the real (observable) world depends upon dynamic analysis. He virtually treats this not at all. Edgeworth gave the

---

A second and third article, appearing in October 1898 (Clark, 1898) and January 1899 (Clark, 1899a) in the *Quarterly Journal of Economics* under the titles, "The Future of Economic Theory" and "Natural Divisions in Economic Theory," are unsung institutional economics classics. Clark copes with varieties of theoretical expectations and criteria—from the standpoints of both economic statics and economic dynamics.

13. Von Thuenen, who is the originator of a modern theory of uncertainty (one could cite Cantillon, as well, however) becomes Frank H. Knight's Lochinvar in a later battle on capital theory in the 1930s.

book a respectful but far from critical evaluation in the *Economic Journal* (Edgeworth, 1900).

The point of the foregoing is not simply that Clark attacked, using such rhetorical devices as the "back-handed compliment" and insisting that Boehm-Bawerk should not be allowed to define the field, but that Boehm-Bawerk replied with vigor. Clark felt that Boehm-Bawerk had over-simplified the topic, made it mechanical rather than organic, and *had succeeded* in deflecting economics from what Clark thought a truer course.[14] From the standpoint of an insightful observer of this play, the first act ends with Clark's rhetoric quite strong, Clark's institutionalism seeming more than a bit misty, because it really depends upon economic dynamics (which he does no more than identify), and Boehm-Bawerk's ratiocinative discussion, with no distinction between statics and dynamics, seeming much clearer. That observer however could likely have wondered whether (1) Clark had asked a good question but found the answering of it succinctly too difficult for the moment, and (2) whether Boehm-Bawerk, whose argument seemed much clearer, had set up and knocked over quite deftly what is a large but, nonetheless still, a straw man.

### Act 2: Scene 1

As one might expect the battle was joined by younger expositors. Two are particularly worth noting. The first is the disciplined, imaginative, and indomitable Irving Fisher;[15] the second is Frank A. Fetter, whose interests in the

---

14. In 1892 Clark sent, according to Professor Dorfman (see Dorfman 1949, Appendix No. 3, p.v.), an amusing postcard to William A. Folwell (of the University of Minnesota):

Nov. 12, 1892

How is this"
*Individual* subjective value = condition of competition; Competition = mechanism of adjustment of ratios of exchange ("objective value")
Ratios of exchange express *social* subjective value
Gulf between subjective and objective values not bridged by Austrians, except by B. Bawerk, and by him thus:

15. Again, we have no time to treat Fisher's education involving virtual tutorship by Yale's great Willard Gibbs. Suffice it to note that Fisher's first book was reviewed by Clark at the invitation of Francis Ysidro Edgeworth, the editor of the British *Economic Journal* (Clark, 1896). Fisher, himself, had traveled in England and Europe and apparently had made a lasting reputation as being brilliant. Fisher was heralded by Edgeworth in reviewing his second book as the greatest

basics of psychology were coupled with his commitments to catallactics, logic, and synthesis. The others may seem now to have been less noteworthy, but as we are comparing them to giants we ought not to dismiss Charles Tuttle and Herbert Davenport as trivial, which they were clearly anything but.

About this time around 1895–96 Fisher wrote for Edgeworth's *Economic Journal*[16] three truly brilliant articles on capital; they were far more than summaries of the Clark-Boehm-Bawerk debate.[17] Indeed, what he did was to lay out quite a new approach of his own. Yet, he built his contribution by relying on the history of economic thought. By going back in the history of economics writings (and he was meticulous in crediting as many of his fore-runners as he could) he lists in the first article, published in 1896 as "What Is Capital?", the views of a group of authorities: Turgot, Smith, Ricardo, Senior, J. S. Mill, Klein-Waechter, Boehm-Bawerk, Marx, McCulloch, Knies, Hermann, Walras, Jevons, MacLeod, and Bates Clark (Fisher 1896).

He then traced the use and misuse of the concept of capital from the time of Turgot ("accumulated values") through Bates Clark ("effective social utility"). He finds most of these not only incomplete but often wrong. Wealth and capital are not synonymous. Wealth is a stock; interest and/or income is a rate of flow. The concepts of stocks and flows he credits to Simon Newcomb. Capital is a stock, but not all wealth relates to that stock. He uses the analogy of a lake and a river (Physics gets into his game!). He senses that Turgot, who saw all set-aside wealth as the origins of capital, had the best view. Smith was off-track when he lumped anything involved in a flow, like bringing a revenue into being, tied up with one's capital stock. Much of consumption is tied into uses of capital and revenue, as well—one can pay one's current expenses out of revenue or out of stock. In the end Smith "defines capital as that portion of stock not devoted to immediate consumption" (p. 521).

Fisher credited Boehm-Bawerk with shifting the tide of capital from interest to production. His view is that interest in the end must ultimately be paid out of profits, not out of capital accumulation. He argues that Smith held that productive wages were paid out of a capital fund and that unproductive wages out of a revenue, and that for Smith any increase in capital expanded

---

of his generation in mathematical economics (Edgeworth, 1898). Perhaps it is for those reasons that Fisher wrote (and Edgeworth highlighted) his great treatment of capital theory for Edgeworth's journal.

16. Edgeworth had been quite taken with Fisher, and had reviewed Fisher's first publication, an edition of Cournot (Edgeworth, 1898).

17. Edgeworth, himself, had reviewed Boehm-Bawerk's *Positive Theory* (1894a). It seems to me to have been quite a respectful review, even if Edgeworth's endorsement was somewhat less than total. Boehm-Bawerk thought otherwise, and replied at some length to Edgeworth (Boehm-Bawerk, 1894), and Edgeworth retorted (1894b). Edgeworth also personally reviewed Clark's *Distribution of Wealth . . .* (Edgeworth, 1900).

employment and wages. Ricardo and James Mill/McCulloch picked up and expanded this confusion.

He suggested that it was Charles Morrison, who started the salvage of the Wages Fund confusion by introducing the rate of turnover. And he credited Simon Newcomb as being the real burier of that wrong-headed doctrine. Newcomb had held that any fund had to be replenished or otherwise it would be dissipated.[18] Consequently, the wages fund had to be constantly replenished. Why Marshall neglected to pursue the clarity of this distinction Fisher does not know. Perhaps it was because Marshall "conceives of income as a flow of pleasure rather than of goods" (p. 527). Taussig picked up from Marshall. It is with the two Walrases that the point is finally clarified (p. 528). But, Leon Walras stripped capital of its attribute of productivity, and replaced it with mere fecundity. Walras also preferred "land, man, and capital". Even Pareto is confused when he argues that capital, even when used, can be replaced—but why not then food as capital?

In this article Fisher particularly focussed on John Bates Clark's approach, which Fisher argued agglomerates too much under capital and in the process loses operational significance. In the end it was Edwin Cannan who comes out as Fisher's Lochinvar. The difference between capital and income is one of time-relation. Income relates to a period of time; capital to a point in time. "[i]ncome is a flow of *pleasure;* capital is a stock of *things* (p. 534). But Cannan foundered on the problem of adding income (the double counting problem). Fisher concludes that locating the path of the movement of goods in the production process is "the work done by money" (p. 534).

In Fisher's second article, printed in the same journal in June 1897 as "Senses of 'Capital'" (Fisher, 1897a), Clark's name, although mentioned is not prominently displayed, yet, it was basically an attack on Clark's work. Clark sees capital as a kind of power source, where Fisher, building mostly on the stock-flow concept, thinks it the agglomerate of things and services.

Clark's is not the only kind of confusion. Fisher finds four "sorts of stock:" "wealth-capital, wealth-capital-value, property-capital and property-capital value" (p. 201). The first is what most economists mean; the second is what Bates Clark means, the third is what Henry Dunning MacLeod says (1891), and the fourth is what the business man has in mind.

Fisher then seeks to disentangle wealth from property, and quantities from values. "Taken literally, the formula for wealth includes man himself" (p. 201). It is here where he seems to move towards Petty's concept of human capital, although that exposition actually is not worked out in this article.

---

18. Fisher's obituary of Simon Newcomb is an example of judicious total praise (Fisher 1909b).

Property is really not a thing, but a right. "Goodwill" is essentially a series of promises to perform.

If quantities are the primary magnitudes, they derive much of their significance when a price vector is attached.

> The aggregate of wealth is therefore not a sum but an *inventory*. . . .
> A "sum of wealth" is meaningless (p. 204). The most natural classifica-
> tion of capital in its first sense is into "human capital", land capital, and
> . . . products. This is the classification of Walras. . . . Another impor-
> tant classification is into business capital and private or personal capital.
> Such and other distinction of classification . . . are of undoubted
> importance in descriptive economics. It seems certain . . . that the *con-
> ception* of capital useful in economic analysis is not to be sought in that
> direction (p. 212–13).

Fisher's third article (1897b), "The Role of Capital in Economic Theory", both summarizes and goes on.

> [c]apital is . . . a stock of wealth of any kind existing at an *instant of
> time*. Its peculiarity lies in its relation to time, not in any characteristics
> of the goods composing it. It is correlative to income, or more precisely,
> to economic "flows" through a *period* of time. Since the time-distinction
> between "stock" and "flow" applies to the value of wealth, as well as to
> wealth itself, and also to property and its value, the term capital is
> conveniently extended so as to cover four separate but cognate senses,
> viz: (1) a stock of wealth, such as the number of pounds of meat in a
> storehouse; (2) a stock of property, such as the number of railway shares
> owned by a particular individual at a particular time; (3) the value of
> stocks of wealth, as the value of a factory plant; (4) the value of stocks of
> property, as the value of a bank's assets. The "capitalization" or "capital
> stock" of a business concern comes under the fourth head (p. 511).
> . . . If wealth denotes "useful appropriated material object" and prop-
> erty "rights in wealth", or more explicit "rights to the *services* (or uses)
> of wealth", then wealth and property are correlative terms, the total of
> capital-wealth and capital-property are co-extensive, and the totals of
> capital-wealth-value and capital-property-value are equal (p. 511–12).
> The theory of capital, however, has to do not so much with the rela-
> tions between the four senses of capital, as with the relations between
> "capital and income: between economic stocks and flows. These rela-
> tions, involving as they do the study of the time element in economic
> science, opens up a vast field only parts of which have been explored.

The study seems naturally to group itself about three heads: (1) The relations between capital and the outflow which exhausts it and the inflow which replenishes it; (2) the relations between capital and income exchanged against each other; and (3) the relations between capital and the flow of services which it renders. The first sort of relation is exemplified in the connections between a stove-dealer's stock and the annual number of stoves which enter and leave his warehouse; the second is seen in the exchange of a consignment of stoves for a periodical payment of money; and the third, in the connection between the stock which the deal carries and the profits which he wins thereby. Among the important economic problems under these three heads may be especially mentioned, under (1) the problem of "saving", under (2) the theory of interest, and under (3) the problem of "income" and its distribution (p. 512).

There then follows something of a discussion about movement. Movement can be changes in physical form, changes in ownership, and as between locations (sites).

Saving does not increase capital—saving may lead to investment which is a net inflow of capital. But this shift must be seen against time. The calculus lends itself beautifully to this transformation.

$$C' = C + A - S$$

or

$$C' - C = A - S$$

and,

$$(C' - C)/t = A/t - S/t$$

which then becomes $dC/dt = dA/dt - dS/dt$, or

$$c = a - s$$

He then puts this in as percentage rates:

$$(C' - C)/Ct = A/Ct - S/Ct$$

and

$$c/C = a/C - S/C \text{ or } \gamma = \alpha - \sigma$$

Time becomes the reciprocal of a the percentage rate A/Ct. The reciprocal of the *time of turnover* is the *rate of turnover*. From this he goes into examples showing how money is the mirror of three basic classes of transactions: money, bank deposits, and "goods". As each can be traded against each, there are, therefore, six kinds of transactions.

Here he derives his quantity theory, laid out as

$$MV + DU = PT \text{ with } (D = \text{Deposits, and}$$

$$U = \text{Velocity of Deposits})$$

This led into a discussion of aggregation and deriving means. The next part (Part II) goes into an endorsement of Boehm-Bawerk's view that interest is the price of time, not simply the price of money.

Boehm-Bawerk reached a correct theory of interest only by abandoning his elaborately prepared definition of capital. Every careful reader of the *Positive Theory* must have remarked that "an exchange of present against future goods" is not restricted to any particular sort of goods. . . . In respect Rae, the chief anticipator of Boehm-Bawerk, was more consistent. Though he uses the word stock instead of capital, he expressly applied the theory to all stock (p. 523).

Fisher stresses that transactions go two ways, and that some transactions have two parts (what is paid during the period and what is paid at the end of the period); much of the criticism of Boehm-Bawerk he thinks ties to an erroneous insistence that what exchanges at the end is different in quality from what went on earlier (time preference and the superiority of present goods); but in both instances money is money (everything gets converted into it).

The third part (Part III of the third article) gets onto services. Fisher's first point is that goods really are intermediate to services, since in the end it is the service, not the material good, which is what the customer seeks from any good. Services by their nature must be flows. Whether any particular service is for consumption, for investment, or for both, has been, he reflects, a source of a great deal of confusion. One then goes on to figuring the value of the service during the useful life of a thing. The time path will, of course, depend upon the thing (fruit trees have a different service pattern than let us say a man's suit). Also, if one has to replenish the thing, the service it performs has to be balanced by the disservice (the wearing out and replenishing) involved. He extends this idea to the disservice of having to keep a cash reserve (a liquidity, if you will).

A confusion results when one puts the value of things which are instantly and totally consumed at their price. The more general and preferable rule is to see that their consumption, too, has a time path, but perceived as only an instantaneous one. Their value then is their cost less their disservice cost over an interval approaching 0. The problem of double counting has to be ever kept in mind. A grove of trees costing 1,000 and yielding an annual income varying from −20 to +63 should have its costs and income capitalized.

Fisher points out that a twist occurs when one considers as capital things, which necessarily have both an initial cost and an income stream. Yet, if one considers human services as an income stream, one should have no trouble measuring the value of a purported initial cost even if there was no property ownership involved. The proper way of measuring the value of all capital is to capitalize the income stream. Thus, it is proper to capitalize human incomes to ascertain the value of that human capital.

This first scene of the second act has the most electricity; Fisher emerges as the new voice and, quite possibly as Joseph A. Schumpeter suggested and James Tobin believes, the real Lochinvar (Tobin, 1985). His argument had substance; more than that (which the others had as well) it had a form and built-in-self-delineator. He asked only good questions, but he limited himself to those good questions which he could clearly answer. From the standpoint of a journeyman, this was a masterpiece. But it was Fisher's capacity to limit himself to what he could do very well, that is also particularly to be noted. But, there were then (and are still) questioners.

### Act 2: Scene 2

As we have already heard, there were others who joined the battle. In some instances they were admirers of Clark and sought to break spears on his behalf. Others may have been drawn to the philosophical framework which Clark embraced and sought to keep the discipline from breaking away from its moral philosophy roots. In any event, let us turn first to another name which had then more or less just come on the scene. It was Frank A. Fetter (then at Stanford, later at Cornell, and 'finally' at Princeton). In a *Quarterly Journal of Economics* article in November 1900 Fetter was intrigued with Boehm-Bawerk's approach, and, in particular, with the brilliancy of Boehm-Bawerk's insights about capital and the 'errors' in his insights about interest. Boehm-Bawerk had attacked the idea of each factor getting rewarded by the market value of its marginal product; Boehm-Bawerk's pejorative phrase was 'the marginal product theory of interest'.

Yet, before he could attack Boehm-Bawerk (whose work he seemed to assert started the whole debate, a view with which I disagree) Fetter took pains to praise and then condemn Clark—praised him for his fresh originality, condemned him for wooly-headed thinking.

While he considered Fisher to be the third of these 'greats', what emerges most clearly was that he hardly saw Fisher as having advanced thinking very much; Fisher's contribution had, to use Francis Bacon's metaphor, merely "cast light" rather than having truly "borne fruit".

## Act 2: Scene 3

The second party in this renewed dialogue was Charles A. Tuttle (Wabash College, Indiana), whose three articles in the *Quarterly Journal of Economics* appeared in 1901, 1903, and 1904. Starting with the first in the February 1901 issue, Tuttle who was trying to pursue (rehabilitate/?) the lines of argument and/or thinking which Clark had initially presented when his *Philosophy of Wealth* was clearly at the forefront of his thinking (Tuttle, 1901). Tuttle's major effort it must be seen, was not to break spears on Clark's behalf— indeed, much of the article is critical of Clark's expository choices. Rather, Tuttle's mission was to go back to what he thought Clark had originally tried (should have tried again/?) to argue; that started from a concern with the definition and nature of economic *value*. Tuttle was prominent among those who claim that prices can explain only prices—two prices are neither cause and effect nor any general tie to value. Value is, to use his phrase, a "[general] relation between commodities and man" (Tuttle, 1901, p. 236). As one might consequently expect, Tuttle's approach is to argue that economics is a subject which must deal with the complexities of human values, man going about earning a living; it does not admit of a 'royal road':

> . . . It has been our aim to make clear by the light of the fundamental and universal economic principle, that value is not, in any scientific sense of the term, a "ratio of exchange", that it is not "power-in-exchange", or "purchasing power", or "the quantity of some other thing or of things in general". One cannot get a conception of value, from either the individual or the social point of view, by an objective comparison of specific economic goods,—for example, a pair of shoes and a barrel of flour. To determine the social value of a given pair of shoes, a measurement of its social "effective utility" becomes necessary. . . . The social value of an article, then, in a given market, expresses quantitatively the weal-relation of society to that article, under actual circumstances. . . . (Tuttle, 1901 p. 231).

## Act 2: Scene 4

In Fetter's next article, appearing in the *Quarterly Journal of Economics* in May 1901, "The Passing of the Old Rent Concept", he appeared to pull himself away from Clark in the direction of Boehm-Bawerk. Clark, as you will recall, thought that the distinction between land and capital was more apparent than real; Fetter thought that capital had a time-dimension which land did not. Rents, as such, Fetter sees, are a general phenomenon ("general surplus" was his phrase) and not limited to land. But at the end Fetter credits Clark, not Boehm-Bawerk, with the critical change:

> The use of the term, "rent" for any surplus above "real" cost is out of harmony with the conception of rent as a regularly occuring income, and with the practical needs of a money economy in which the concept must be employed.
>
> The doctrine of quasi-rents, involving the idea that no income, or share, enters into market prices in short periods, cannot stand. On the other hand, the recognition that there is no difference in short periods between land and other wealth in relation to market values is a great advance.
>
> The relation which rare and not easily producible appliances have to market price over long periods of time is of just the opposite character from that asserted. The less capable of increase particular appliances are, the greater income they yield, the more therefore it "enters into price" as the demand for their products increases.
>
> The need for a new concept of rent which will evade the difficulties of the old is evident.* [Here he credits John Bates Clark's "notable essay"]. The way is prepared for it by the break-down of the old and the patent difficulties of the substitutes that have been presented. (Fetter, 1901, p. 455).

The following year Fetter's article, "The 'Roundabout Process' in the Interest Theory", was published in the *Quarterly Journal of Economics*. His verdict is that Boehm-Bawerk, Fetter concludes, has never rejected Clark's productivity theory of interest; rather, his 'roundabout theory of interest' is merely a special case (Fetter, 1902).

### Act 2: Scene 5

We now return to Tuttle whose focus is on wealth and capital, to him hardly synonymous. In the second of his articles, this one published in 1903, Tuttle argues that wealth is broad and contains much that is not capital; capital, on the other hand, is "surplus wealth as a possession" (Tuttle 1903, p. 58), and is traceable to Turgot, although it was erroneously side-tracked by Smith, but not by Say (ibid., p. 67–68).

> . . . Capital, according to our conception, is not land, buildings, machines, materials or workshops. The distinction between a thing and

its value must be kept always in mind. Capital is not a concrete material article. Specific economic goods—a McCormick reaper and binder, for example—cannot be expressed in dollars and cents. Economic goods may serve as an investment for capital, but they are not capital. By way of illustration, take a given horse; its value is five hundred dollars, its weight two thousand pounds, its height seventeen hands. Who would say that the horse and its weight or its height or its value were one and the same thing. As the weight of a horse is the measure of one physical property, and the height of another, so the value is the measure of the economic quality of effective utility. Capital then, is a fund of value,— *surplus wealth as a possession,*—and not a material products or an aggregate of such products (ibid., p. 61–62).

Clark's usage of words in his *Distribution of Wealth* remained

"careless . . . [and] lacks the definiteness that a scientific treatise should have. Janus-like, he seems to be looking at the same time back to the concrete capital concept of Adam Smith . . . and forward in the direction of the common, practical conception of business life" (ibid., p. 88).

This article concludes with an attack on Fetter's 1901 article, where Fetter criticizes Clark on the one hand for over-abstraction and Boehm-Bawerk, on the other, for having two capital concepts.

At this point Fisher reentered the fray. He is clearly responding to Tuttle's second (1903) article, and while he comments briefly that he finds some merit in it, he turns quickly to his task of explaining his position, either once again or, *as is more probable,* as modified. Fisher relies on the stock-flow distinction, which he notes that neither Fetter nor Marshall (who had written in the *Economic Journal* in 1898) had accepted as vital. But, it is vital, as everyone from Turgot's time on should have realized.

It ought now to be clear what the course of history has been. Business and popular usage has preserved a very consistent tradition from 1678[19]— when capital meant, among other things, "all goods which are possessed"— to 1883[20], when it still meant "the net worth of a party" (Fisher 1904, 400–401).

Yet, Fisher notes that Fetter has used his (Fisher's preferred) definition. It

---

19. Fisher has found several very early definitions. This one, which he treats as authoritative, is from Dufresne du Cange, Glossarium—and Fisher writes in a footnote it was quoted by Umfenbach in his *Das Kapital in seinere Kulturbedeutung* (Wuerzburg, 1879, p. 32).

20. Here Fisher refers in the text to P. L. Simmonds (Fisher, 1904, p. 395).

was in a paper given to the American Economic Association in December 1903.[21]

As for Tuttle, his definition of wealth as surplus is both too broad and too limited (Fisher, 1904, p. 403–4). Moreover, Fisher holds that the noun, surplus, already has too many connotations.

In November 1904, again in the *Quarterly Journal of Economics,* Tuttle returned to do battle. It is principally an answer to Fisher's May of-the-same-year article, mentioned immediately above, and serves as both a specific and a general attack.

Tuttle's specific line of attack is that Fisher employs the standpoint of a mathematician when treating what is essentially a problem in moral philosophy. Specifically, after quoting William James, he says,

> . . . The economic present is a period rather than a point of time. The economic present is a species of what the psychologist calls the "specious present". The economic present is not a period, but it is period of sufficient definiteness in each man's consciousness to serve as the basis for the organization and administration of his individual household. It is not an absolute period, and, accordingly, its duration cannot be given as so many hours, or days, or weeks, or months. . . . Its duration depends largely on the individual's economic condition,—his mode of economic activity and the length of the production period, the conditions under which the work is done and the terms of payment, the scope of his mental grasp and the character of the individual system to which he belongs (Tuttle, 1904 p. 86).

Then taking Fisher up on Fisher's preferred grounds, the history of the usage by such eminent economists as Turgot and Smith, he asserts that Fisher, in the general needs to specify terms according to his mathematical bent, interprets both Turgot and Smith wrongly. This article becomes an unusual example of economists pitting lexicographers against each other, derivations of definitions against other derivations, and so forth.

### Act 2: Scene 6

Fisher's reply, published in the next issue (February 1905) was to decry Tuttle's willingness to accept vagueness in definitions. For reasons obvious to any mathematically-minded type, Fisher prefers an imposed semantic discipline.

---

21. The proceedings of the American Economic Association annual meetings were not systematically published at the time.

## Act 2: Scene 7

In 1906 Fisher published his *The Nature of Capital and Interest,* a book of over 400 pages. Frank A. Fetter was the reviewer for the *Journal of Political Economy* (Fetter 1907). It is lengthy (30 pages) and both respectful but not ground-yielding. Fetter employs the Tuttle approach—words as they have been historically used in the literature cannot be made specific simply to accommodate the mathematical mind. Fetter refers not so much to ambiguity or sloppiness as to the point that some concepts apparently defy the kind of specification which he understands mathematics requires. The review ends by a ringing endorsement of the originality of John Bates Clark and Simon Patten whose "sounder and tested fruits . . . [have been] so thoroughly . . . [adapted as] a part of our thought, that they now seem simple truths" (Fetter 1907, p. 146).

   Naturally Fisher responded to this review. It was published in the *Journal of Political Economy* as a mere Note, but is no less than 14 printed pages. Fisher's point is that Fetter approached his book with his mind made up on the question of semantic discipline, and that if one wants to know what Fisher thinks one should look at Fisher's book, not the misinterpretation represented as Fisher's book by Fetter (Fisher, 1907).

## Act 2: Scene 8

While all of the debate with Fisher was going on, Boehm-Bawerk's admirers were not idle. In the May 1902 issue of the *Quarterly Journal of Economics,* Herbert Davenport published an article on semantic discipline and its application to the terminology of the Austrian school (Davenport, 1902). What stands out is that in his view the Austrian marginal analysis has swept the American academy, but the common usage of the term, *marginal analysis,* is confusing. Davenport sets out to distinguish (1) *utility,* (2) *marginal utility,* and (3) *marginal relative utility.* Only the last refers to a theory of general value. Davenport's contribution is the idea of tying the derived phrase, *marginal relative utility,* to his new term, *marginal sacrifice.* In this way he thinks that he has offered a tie between the Clarkian concept of an organic capital fund and the concrete capital goods which the Austrians focussed upon (Davenport, 1902).[22]

---

22. Davenport pursued this line of attack in the *Journal of Political Economy,* two years later. Taking up the term, *capital,* as used primarily in the English literature (e.g. Nassau Senior), he considers how the concept of capital as a competitive element emerges in the economics literature. In this discussion he attempts insofar as he can to merge his views with Fetter and Fisher but avers that as between them, he sides with Fisher more than Fetter (Davenport, 1904).

There had been a slight delay while Boehm-Bawerk gathered his forces; no doubt part of the reason is that Boehm-Bawerk was serving as the Minister of Finance for Austria-Hungary as well as trying to keep his hand in at the University of Vienna. In time, however he struck out in the *Quarterly Journal of Economics* (in November 1906 and February 1907) taking in his sweep the works of Clark, Carver, Cassel, Seager, Fetter, and Seligman. We confine our examination to what he has to say about Clark, specifically, except to note that he approved of Fetter more than the others.

The point of departure is Clark's "new" book, *The Distribution of Wealth.* His respect for Clark as a rhetorician is more than apparent, but he and Clark must live in disagreement. Part of what separates them is that Clark seems more impressed with trying to divine an unmanageable truth than he is in finding something serviceable but limited. Clark's insistence upon dividing the concept of capital between a fund and capital goods is essentially not serviceable, whatever other virtues it may seem to have. Clark seems to agree and not to agree that capital cannot be "in a disembodied state". And when Clark tries to define a functional middle ground between his permanent fund and concrete capital goods, his effort "is simply an error". Clark's assertion that capital can be putty is wrong: "Clark's perfect and absolute mobility is, to put it plainly, perfectly and absolutely false".

In the February 1907 article, Boehm-Bawerk expands his criticisms of perceiving interest as the productivity return for capital. From the pedagogic, the logic, and the practical senses, the return to capital must be a cost, rather than a rent. And this truth exists not only for static, but also for dynamic analysis. In the end Clark has made capital as mystical a source of value as Marx made labor.

Clark's reply to these two articles is in the May 1907 issue of the *Quarterly Journal of Economics.* There are no backhanded compliments; Clark like Boehm-Bawerk appears to realize that neither can persuade the other, and that neither is persuasive to everyone.

> . . . As a general criticism Minister von Boehm-Bawerk accuses me as liming to "sow with capital goods and reap with capital". Construed as I should construe them, these words afford a good description of what practical men are doing and of what a theorist has to study and describe. The men make instruments and set them working, which is sowing with capital goods. They keep the stock of instruments intact, and thus enable

---

Davenport's book, *Value and Distribution: A Critical and Constructive Study,* was published in 1908. Fisher reviewed it for the *Journal of Political Economy,* giving it very high marks. Fisher's principal caveat was that Davenport's treatment of the theory of interest was inconsistent with his (Fisher's) and accordingly misguided (Fisher, 1908).

the products of all industry of to-day to emerge to-day in useful forms; and thus they reap with capital (Clark, 1907, pp. 368–9).

Clark concludes that their differences relate to varying levels of abstraction in their respective arguments.

Boehm-Bawerk did, indeed, seek to have that last word. In the November 1907 issue of the *Quarterly Journal of Economics* he turns to listing the changes in Clark's position from the time that their differences first became apparent. Clark now admits, he says, that capital must be the summation of goods—not the mystical fund, or to use the phrase Clark employed, "embodied value, as a permanent value in a shifting corporeal embodiment". Boehm-Bawerk finds himself particularly vexed by the success of Clark's rhetorical use of metaphor—surely a suggestion of Boehm-Bawerk's own frustration with his own choices of metaphor. Further, Boehm-Bawerk gropes for something missing in the Clarkian explanation of the decision process—how do people know when there is so much for the present that is unknowable? The concept for which he gropes is, of course, expectations (the ex ante version of being clever), but the word does not come to his mind. Worst of all, Clark describes rather than explains—that is the charge that the theorist invariably makes of those whom he holds to be non-theorists. What seems so maddening to Boehm-Bawerk is Clark's apparent (to him) insistence that all decisions are made for the moment at hand; what went on earlier in the production process is a given unexaminable prologue and as it cannot be changed we move from what we have, from where we are. Where Boehm-Bawerk sees the past as a series of imputations, Clark does not seem to take the past into active account.

. . . Nearly all theories of distribution, and more particularly, the theory of my distinguished opponent, rest the claims of the several producers on some sort of relation to the product whose existence is due to them. The fundamental ground of justification is not that the immediate present decides as to the distribution of those things which at this same present are available. This perhaps would be the method of distribution of a band of robbers, who proceed at once to the division of the booty between them. Distribution, in its economic sense, takes place among those who have taken part in the creation of the product and in such quotas as correspond to their contribution. No one has stated this principle more distinctly than Professor Clark himself. The gist of his whole theory of distribution is that each factor of production reaps that which is due to its contribution to the joint product.

I ask, is it in any way possible to deny or disprove that the coat ready to-day has been created partly by the farmer who bred the sheep, the spinner, the weaver, and so on? This is surely so, notwithstanding certain peculiar views of Professor Clark's, . . . Is it not always the fruit of a process of production which runs through time and in which the cooperating factors succeed each other? And, this being the case, must not the operation gone through for the completion of a consumable commodity be necessarily of the "past" kind,—in the case of the coat, everything except the very last stitch of the tailor? . . . And is not, then, a theory which bases distribution on the contributions of the factors of production necessarily deprived of its foundation if the contributions of the past are disregarded merely because they are past?

Professor Clark speaks of a mixture of periods. Now what is the period to be whose limits we are to regard with such scrupulous respect? Literally one day, that "today" of which Professor Clark so often speaks? Or, perhaps a longer period? A week? A month? A year? Is there any essential difference between the nature of the contributions from the labor of yesterday and that of last week or of last year? Does not each of these labors contribute to the joint product, and must not each one of them, in precisely the same day, be incorporated in an "existing capital good?" (Boehm-Bawerk, 1907b, pp. 40–42).

### Epilogue

Here the curtain falls on the second act. There is a long time-interlude between this point and the third act which involved Gifford, Boulding, Knight, von Hayek, Machlup, and Kaldor in the 1930s. The latest (and surely not the last act) is post-World War II and the principal playwriters were Joan Robinson, Robert Solow, and Paul Samuelson.

One important point growing out of these two acts is, as I have indicated, substantive; it shows how great and almost-great minds managed to forge an idea. It also shows the importance of how an idea is framed, since, as I clearly believe, it was Fisher who emerged as the clearest of the playwrites. Fisher's virtue was not that he promised the most (I think that Clark did), but that both delivered more than anyone else, and Fisher delivered closer to his promise more than anyone else.

While I could point to other things in the early years of journals which explain their gradual rise to dominance as the medium of idea-expression, I think that Fisher is our prototype. He wrote concisely, even beautifully. His prose examples were the best, and his introduction of math (in that sense an index of the rigor of his argument) was a quantum jump from what the others offered.

As one can see when the debate reemerged in the 1930s and the 1950s, some of the lines of battle were by then traditional (permissible levels of abstraction); but, others, particularly Knight, managed to go beyond Fisher in the framing act—Knight introduced the role of expectations, a contribution that prompted a wholly new set of thoughts.

ABSTRACT

Tracing the topic in early English-language journals, the article illustrates how John Bates Clark's and Eugen von Böhm Bawerk's early efforts sparked a professional journal intellectual conflagration in the 1880s, and throughout the 1890s, and how first Irving Fisher (starting in the 1890s) and then Frank A. Fetter, Charles Tuttle, and Herbert Davenport (in the next decade) further engaged in battle. Clark's were deep, perhaps scientifically unanswerable, structural—and morality questions; Böhm Bawerk offered an original, if partly flawed, system; Fisher offered limited, but analytically brilliant, constructs; but, as each was addressing slightly different points, agreement was never achieved. Outside of this article's ambit were the debate continuations in the 1930s (Knight, Hayek, etc.) and in the 1950s (the two Cambridges controversy).

REFERENCES

E. von Boehm-Bawerk ([1888] 1891), *The Positive Theory of Capital*, Translated with a Preface and Analysis by William Smart, London and New York, Macmillan.

E. von Boehm-Bawerk (1894), *"One Word More on the Ultimate Standard of Value"*. *Economic Journal* 4, (Dec), pp. 719–24.

E. von Boehm-Bawerk (1895a), "The Positive Theory of Capital and Its Critics: I. Professor Clark's View on the Genesis of Capital", *Quarterly Journal of Economics* 9, (January), pp. 113–31.

E. von Boehm-Bawerk (1895b), "The Positive Theory of Capital and Its Critics: II. General Walker Against Capital and Interest", *Quarterly Journal of Economics* 9, (April), pp. 235–56.

E. von Boehm-Bawerk (1895c), "The Origin of Interest", *Quarterly Journal of Economics* 9, (Jul), pp. 380–87.

E. von Boehm-Bawerk (1896), "The Positive Theory of Capital and Its Critics: III. The View of Mr. White, Mr. Bilgram, Professor MacVane, and Mr. Hawley", *Quarterly Journal of Economics* 10, (January), pp. 121–55.

E. von Boehm-Bawerk (1906), "Capital and Interest Once More: I. Capital vs. Capital Goods", *Quarterly Journal of Economics* 21, (Nov), pp. 1–21.

E. von Boehm-Bawerk (1907a), "Capital and Interest Once More: II A Relapse to the Productivity Theory", *Quarterly Journal of Economics* 21, pp. 247–370.

E. von Boehm-Bawerk (1907b), "The Nature of Capital: A Rejoinder", *Quarterly Journal of Economics* 22, (Nov), pp. 28–47.

H. Bilgram (1891), "The Interest Controversy", *Quarterly Journal of Economics* 5, pp. 375–77.

J. Bonar (1888a), "The Austrian Economists and Their View of Value", *Quarterly Journal of Economics* 33, pp. 1–31.

J. Bonar (1888b), "The Positive Theory of Capital", a review article, *Quarterly Journal of Economics* 3, pp. 336–51.

J. B. Clark (1885), *The Philosophy of Wealth: Economic Principles Newly Formulated*, Boston: Ginn & Company.

J. B. Clark (1888), "Capital and Its Earnings", *American Economic Association* 2, pp. 88–149.

J. B. Clark (1891a), "Distribution as Determined by A Law of Rent", *Quarterly Journal of Economics* 5, pp. 289–318.

J. B. Clark (1891b), "The Statics and the Dynamics of Distribution", *Quarterly Journal of Economics* 6, pp. 111–119.

J. B. Clark (1893), "The Genesis of Capital", *Yale Rev.* 2, pp. 302–15.

J. B. Clark (1895a), "The Origin of Interest" *Quarterly Journal of Economics* 9, (April), pp. 257–78.

J. B. Clark (1895b), "Real Issue Concerning Interest", *Quarterly Journal Economics* 10, (Oct), pp. 98–102.

J. B. Clark (1896), Review of Irving Fisher, "Appreciation and Interest: A Study of the Influence of Monetary Appreciation and Depreciation on the Rate of Interest, with Applications to the Bimetallic Controversy and the Theory of Interest", *Economic Journal* 6, pp. 569–70.

J. B. Clark (1899), *The Distribution of Wealth: A Theory of Wages, Interest, and Profits*, Macmillan, New York.

J. B. Clark (1898), "The Future of Economic Theory", *Quarterly Journal of Economics* 13, (Oct), pp. 1–14.

J. B. Clark (1899a), "Natural Divisions in Economic Theory", *Quarterly Journal of Economics* 13, (Jan), pp. 187–203.

J. B. Clark (1899b), *The Distribution of Wealth*, Macmillan, New York.

J. B. Clark (1901), "Wages and Interest as Determined by Marginal productivity", *Journal of Political Economy* 10, (Dec), pp. 105–09.

J. B. Clark (1907), "Concerning the Nature of Capital: A Reply", *Quarterly Journal of Economics* 21, (May), pp. 351–70.

H. J. Davenport (1894), "The Formula of Sacrifice", *Journal of Political Economy* 2, (Sep), pp. 561–73.

H. J. Davenport (1902), "Proposed Modifications in Austrian Theory and Terminology", *Quarterly Journal of Economic* 16, (May), pp. 355–84.

H. J. Davenport (1904), "Capital as a Competitive Concept", *Journal of Political Economy* 13, (Dec), pp. 31–47.

J. Dorfman (1949), *The Economic Mind in American Civilization: Volume Three, 1865–1918*, The Viking Press, New York.

F. Y. Edgeworth (1892), Review of Eugen von Boehm-Bawerk, *The Positive Theory of Capital* in the *Economic Journal* 2, pp. 328–337.

F. Y. Edgeworth (1894a), "Professor Boehm-Bawerk on the Ultimate Standard of Value", *Economic Journal* 4, pp. 518–21.

F. Y. Edgeworth (1894b), "One Word More on the Ultimate Standard of Value: Reply", *Economic Journal* 4, pp. 724–25.

F. Y. Edgeworth (1898), Review of Augustin Cournot's *Researches into the Mathe-*

*matical Principle of the Theory of Wealth* (1838), translated by Nathaniel T. Bacon; with a Bibliography of Mathematical Economics by Irving Fisher, and Irving Fisher's, *A Brief Introduction to the Infinitesimal Calculus, designed to aid in reading Mathematical Economics and Statistics* (n.d.[sic]), *Economic Journal* 8.

F. Y. Edgeworth (1900), Review of John Bates Clark's *The Distribution of Wealth, Economic Journal* 10, pp. 534–38.

F. A. Fetter (1900), "Recent Discussion of the Old Rent Concept", *Quarterly Journal of Economics* 15, (Nov), pp. 1–45.

F. A. Fetter (1901), "The Passing of the Old Rent Concept", *Quarterly Journal of Economics* 15, (May), pp. 416–55.

F. A. Fetter (1902), "The 'Roundabout Process' in the Interest Theory", *Quarterly Journal of Economics* 17, (Nov), pp. 163–80.

F. A. Fetter (1907), "The Nature of Capital and Income", *Journal of Political Economy* 15, (Mar), pp. 129–48.

I. Fisher (1896), "What is Capital?" *Economic Journal* 6, pp. 509–34.

I. Fisher (1897a), "Senses of Capital", *Economic Journal* 7, pp. 199–213.

I. Fisher (1897b), "The Role of Capital in Economic Theory", *Economic Journal* 7, pp. 511–37.

I. Fisher (1904), "Precedents for Defining Capital", *Quarterly Journal of Economics* 18, (May), pp. 386–408.

I. Fisher (1905), "Professor Tuttle's Capital Concept", *Quarterly Journal of Economics* 19, (Feb), pp. 309–12.

I. Fisher (1907), "Professor Fetter on Capital and Income", *Journal of Political Economy* 15, pp. 421–34.

I. Fisher (1908), "Davenport's Value and Distribution", *Journal of Political Economy* 16, (Dec), pp. 661–679.

I. Fisher (1909), "A Reply to Critics", *Quarterly Journal of Economics* 23, (May), pp. 536–41.

I. Fisher (1913), "The Impatience Theory of Interest", *American Economic Review* 3, (Sep), pp. 610–18.

F. B. Hawley (1892), "The Fundamental Error of *Kapital und Kapitalzins*", *Quarterly Journal of Economics* 6, pp. 280–307.

P. T. Homan (1928), *Contemporary Economic Thought*, Harper & Bros., New York.

H. D. McLeod (1963). *A Dictionary of Political Economy.*

S. M. MacVane (1890), "Boehm-Bawerk on Value and Wages", *Quarterly Journal of Economics* 5, pp. 24–43.

S. M. MacVane (1892), "Capital and Interest", *6, Quarterly Journal of Economics,* pp. 129–50.

S. M. MacVane (1893), "Marginal Utility and Value", *Quarterly Journal of Economics* 7, pp. 255–85.

M. Perlman (1991), "On the Editing of American Economics Journals: Some Comments on the Earliest Journals and the Lessons Suggested", This journal.

J. Tobin (1985), "Neoclassical Theory in American: J. B. Clark and Fisher" *American Economic Review Dir.* 75. (Dec), pp. 28–38.

C. A. Tuttle (1901), "The Fundamental Economic Principle", *Quarterly Journal of Economics* 15, (Feb), pp. 218–53.

C. A. Tuttle (1903), "The Real Capital Concept", *Quarterly Journal of Economics* 18, (Nov), pp. 54–96.

C. A. Tuttle (1904), "The Fundamental Notion of Capital, Once More", *Quarterly Journal of Economics* 19, (Nov), pp. 81–110.

F. A. Walker (1892), "Dr. Boehm-Bawerk's Theory of Interest", *Quarterly Journal of Economics* 6, pp. 399–416.

H. White (1892), "Boehm-Bawerk on Capital", *Political Science Quarterly* 7, pp. 133–48.

CHAPTER 8

# The Historical Bias Implicit in Shackelian Uncertainty: A Review of *Imagination and the Nature of Choice,* by G. L. S. Shackle

*Because I had always thought Kenneth Boulding to be an economist with an unusual taste for literary style and a feeling for imaginative thinking, I chose him to review Shackle's* Epistemics and Economics *for the* Journal of Economic Literature. *Boulding agreed, but after paying tribute to the artistry of Shackle's language, he went on to say that he would be terribly uncomfortable living in a world of Shackelian uncertainty. Shackle, deeply disappointed with Boulding's review, turned to me and asked what I thought he could do to explain, once again, that his system was hardly bleak. I proposed that George write what turned out to be* Imagination and the Nature of Choice, *saying that I, myself would review it and try my hand at persuading those sharing Boulding's fear. In this review I quote at length a personal letter to me, giving George's description of what he thought his basic contribution to be, and go on to assert that the unknowable in terms of time has a historically friendly bias, called "technological innovation."*

Many economists not only think, but actually assert *as an axiom,* that ours is a *policy science;* perhaps we economists are, as Professor Thomas Mayer once remarked, like engineers, who purportedly feel humiliated when they have to acknowledge a lack of competence to answer a straightforward question. Physicists by contrast, Mayer asserts, are not so policy oriented and can admit to being ignorant about most things, and even when they do assert competence, they are ever aware of the time and space limitations constraints. A decade of embarrassment about our use of the term "fine tuning," however, may have done much to remind us what the Greeks meant by *hubris.* In that case, the discipline may now be more ready than previously to consider Shackle's comprehensive message, a message that never attempts to get to the policy level.

*Journal of Economic Literature* 18 (March 1980): 115–18.

That message, as worked out in several books, is a basically different perception of what economists should *ultimately* offer as their contribution to wisdom. *Ultimately* because Shackle, unlike most "heterodox" types, does not denounce economic theory as useless within the context of analysis of the past, or even as a means for understanding the logic of contemporary relationships. The distinction between the conventional "scientific view" of the economist's world and Shackle's "view" is that the former stresses that we as a profession are seeking to reveal the laws according to which the system normally works (or tends to work), subject to mischievous shocks, serving to spice things up a bit. The system, so the conventional view has it, has a built-in tendency to stability (except for those mischievous shocks); indeed, there may be more than one stable equilibrium and the economist, if skilled, is able to maneuver society into an optimum equilibrium. Shackle's "view," by way of contrast, is that there is no long-term tendency to stability and that we as a profession should not count upon discovering laws that govern the future. Instead we should study the details of the "game" so that we can respond to omnipresent shocks (not mischievous but an inherent element in the system) and, insofar as man and God build the world together, we can "dish out a few, too."[1] Shackle's latest book is about the nature of free choice, true uncertainty, the limited uses of probability, and of the saving factor, human imagination. This book, I believe, caps the evolution of his philosophical speculation, first set in motion when the author, at the time a mature graduate student at the London School of Economics, sought to integrate the subjective economics of the Austrian School, the *ex ante/ex post* analytical time constructs then being introduced by Gunnar Myrdal, and the ambiguities about decision-making simultaneously presented in chapters 1 and 6 of Keynes's *Treatise on Probability* (1921).

Before going on, let me add that Shackle is one of the few real literary stylists now writing in economics. The care with which he chooses exactly the appropriate word, his capacity to construct beautifully balanced sentences, his patience with the pedagogic problems of communication are all so well developed that no one who has read any reasonable segment of his writings ever emerges without comments akin to awe. His *Years of High Theory* (1967), I think, is a leading candidate for the "best written" economics text of the

---

1. This bit of "irreverance" is Perlman, not Shackle. *Aficionados* of Talmudic lore will recognize the resemblance to the case of Rabbi Eliezer ben Hyrcanus (*Baba Mezia* 59 B). Non-*aficionados* can get the gist of the point in the observation that Elijah (the intermediary between God and man), so the report goes, revealed that God wept with gratitude when He realized that the majority in the rabbinical academy were *not* swayed by Heaven-inspired miracles, since it (the majority) was quoting His law (Book of Deuteronomy 30:12) in their ploy against Him.

decade of the 1960's. Yet, even with his clarity of exposition, with all his mastery of the tools (including the mathematical) of our "trade," Shackle's is not a classroom, much less a household, name. Why? The answer to my mind is simply because he, in spite of all his adeptness, wrestles with championship problems and plays in a game that he is never likely to finish. His question is so "hard" that many do not wait for the answer because they instinctively conclude there is none.

As I have noted, this book is the capstone of a lengthy inquiry, an inquiry that began with his dissertation, *Expectations, Investment, and Income* (1938). There he decided that uncertainty was for most economists an unsolved (or as he once put it in a letter to me [11 June 1975], "a missolved") problem. Logically, it comes to, "How can uncertainty be turned into certainty, how can un-knowledge be turned into knowledge?" The answer, to anticipate the bottom line, is "the creative imagination."

His second book, *Expectations in Economics,* published in 1949, lays out the essential Shackle. I once asked him to summarize his scheme; his answer is, I think, definitive:

> [The 1949 book] contains my suggestion of a measure of the standing (seriousness, claim to epistemic[2] respectability) of hypotheses, able to be assigned to the members of a list of hypotheses (suggested answers to some question) recognized to be uncompletable and potentially indefinitely extensible. That is to say, I wished to escape from the logic that compels probabilities assigned to the members of a complete list of rival answers to some one question to add up to unity. The escape consists in saying that, in the most general context, the list of suggested answers cannot be deemed completable. Thus we need a measure of standing that need not, must not and cannot have its degrees; respectively assigned to different answers, added together. The next step is to flesh-out these bones with some psychic content. My suggestion was potential surprise. It will be *zero* for answers (hypotheses) assigned the highest standing and an arbitrary absolute maximum for lowest standing (entire rejection). Standing is thus represented inversely by a formal measure which increases in the opposite sense to those measures of it which represent degrees of positive confidence in the hypotheses. (What sense does it make to have positive confidence in rival, mutually exclusive hypotheses?) Standing is represented by degrees of *dis*belief. The problem is thus solved by inverting it, a respectable ploy for problem-solving as Jacobi (I think) declared. It remains to seek some formally respectable or

---

2. Epistemic, a term used by some psychologists, is "the theory of thoughts."

dissectible basis for potential surprise itself. Potential surprise will only be zero if the assessor knows of no principle or circumstance which is incompatible or incongruous with the truth of the hypothesis. It will attain its utmost degree if there is present to the assessor's thought some fatal obstacle to the truth of the hypothesis. Thus potential surprise offers an (inverse) expression of *possibility*. We may consider that "perfectly possible" and "perfectly impossible" are the only levels which have meaning. To me it seems permissible to define intermediate levels, "imperfect possibility."

This scheme of ideas is what I would put in place of all meanings of "probability," including Keynes's "degree of rational belief." Keynes himself refers in the *General Theory* (page 148) to his *Treatise on Probability*, but in the end, especially in the QJE, he rejected probability as irrelevant, without however, suggesting anything in place of it. My endeavor to fill the vacuum is *not* another attempt to show that irremediable lack of knowledge (of time-to-come) can be remedied by some gimmick. It can, I think, be *exploited* (in the interest of a good state of mind) but not in any way which would satisfy men's notion of being masters of their fate.

Thus did Shackle (as distinct from Frank Knight) initially move to suggest how one comes to cope with uncertainty, insofar as one can cope. Like Knight, Shackle's system "tilts" not towards equilibrium (*cf.* Marshall) but towards disequilibrium.

Because Shackle writes principally for economists, he has allocated considerable effort for devising a history of ideas framework broad enough to include the kind of open-ended speculation that he feels is the best that mortals can attain. Shackle's erstwhile mentor, Professor Hayek, was of the Austrian tradition, and Shackle has always had a keen interest in the role of time. But to Shackle, time is many things—not only a dimension for "roundaboutness" to work itself through; it is also (and more importantly) a dimension over which mortals have no firm grasp. Time and reason, he notes, are polar extremes—reason is based on the knowable; time (seen in his way) can and usually does hold surprises. These unpredictable surprises are the uncertainty that is the setting of his contribution.[3]

As Shackle's ideas have ultimately coalesced, they cluster around the nature of choice. Having concluded that speculation but real choice (which for

---

3. Most of those who currently incorporate "uncertainty" into economics treat it as risk and assign a probability to the unknown. Characteristically, they assume that one can estimate *ex ante* all of the possible states of the world and their likelihoods.

purposes of the discussion involves the unknowable future) is the most that man can expect, Shackle has tried to focus on the means for selection of choice, which in his system comes to a reliance upon the imagination. "Imagination, the source and business of original thought," he writes, "is the indispensable resource of non-determinism. . . . If men are essentially free, they are essentially creative in a fundamental sense. That sense confronts thought with a *ne plus ultra*" (p. 7). Of course, choice is *not* restricted to a menu of specified outcomes; nor is it clear that anything selected from that menu will necessarily arrive as perceived or as ordered. Here the rational expectations group and Shackle take alternative forks in the road.

What Professor Shackle has done in this latest volume is to present 24 short related essays on the roles that probability, knowledge and ignorance, time, and imagination play in the human choice process. One reason for reading this book is that Shackle has laid out in 24 *pensées* how a creative imagination sorts out its choices and the coherence of the way it works. As I see it, Shackle's free choice is similar to St. Augustine's free will, which in Shackle's view contains cultural and experiential elements. At its core the essential freedom of that choice is the teaser that God gives to man, individually.

Professor Theodore Schultz, in what I thought was a most perceptive essay in this *Journal* (1975), really offers the explicit point subsumed in the Shackle argument. Schultz noted that what economic education was all about was the ability to recognize disequilibrium when it occurs and to imagine appropriate new tactics and/or strategies. In Shackle's scheme the facts of the disequilibrium are a "kaleidoscopic field of events," perceived as the *News;* the appropriate reaction Shackle would call the "Imagined deemed Possible."

This book offers Shackle's integrated theme—with consciousness extended beyond the certain mind and the imagination used to reduce the emotions of uncertainty in dealing with the future. The task involves the description and explanation of the field and the incorporation of the *News* into the prior scheme. This revised or new scheme is then applied in imagining the courses and consequences of action, the assignment of epistemic priorities to sequels, the choice among the bundles of sequels (each belonging to some symbolically identified course of action). The whole is offered as a unity, a tying together of ideas.

When, in 1973, Professor Boulding reviewed *Epistemics and Economics* in this *Journal,* he concluded that, "Shackle's view leads only to total despair; to me he seems right only when he asserts that about some (and fortunately a limited number of) things, there is true uncertainty" (1973, pp. 1373–74). I would guess that what separates the Shackle and Boulding perceptions is a curious inversion of "Jacob's capacity to wrestle with the Angel." Shackle is profoundly aware of man's ability to handle uncertainty and is consciously less afraid of Destiny's possible cruel grip on man. Shackle suggests, as I read him, that man's capacity to sort out and absorb feedback is God's saving gift.

This book is the latest effort to flesh-out the Shackle system; it is not one with which to start one's study of Shackle. Nor can this review serve as more than a taste of the real thing. But the book does buttress the scheme of the argument for those who have grasped it in the earlier expositions (*cf.* 1972). If its appearance (as well as this reviewer's obvious enthusiasm) brings a few more to this aspect of our scholarly tradition, the cause of wisdom may well have been served. It is not necessary to attempt answers *only* to those questions where answers are known to exist. The dialogue between man and God (fate, if you prefer) may well be just that; perhaps man's imagination serves as a stimulus as well as a response.

If Shackle seems to be outside of the usual English Classical/Neoclassical/Keynesian—General Equilibrium—Macroeconomics sequence, it is only because we will it to be so. Because some or all of those in this rich tradition appeared to focus on tendencies towards equilibrium, we have willed equilibrium to be at the center of the natural order of things. The probable truth is that they didn't; the certain historical fact is that it isn't.

REFERENCES

Boulding, Kenneth. "Book Review of *Epistemics & Economics*, by G. L. S. Shackle," *J. Econ. Lit.*, Dec. 1973, 11(4), pp. 1373–74.
Keynes, John Maynard. *A treatise on probability.* London: Macmillan, 1921.
Shackle, G. L. S. *Expectations, investment, and income.* Oxford: Oxford University Press, 1938; reprinted Oxford: Clarendon Press, 1968.
———. *Expectations in economics.* Cambridge: Cambridge University Press, [1949] 1952.
———. *The years of high theory: Invention and tradition in economic thought, 1926–1939.* Cambridge: Cambridge University Press, 1967.
———. *Epistemics & economics: A critique of economic doctrine.* New York and London: Cambridge University Press, 1972.
Schultz, Theodore W. "The Value of the Ability to Deal with Disequilibria," *J. Econ. Lit.*, Sept. 1975, 13(3), pp. 827–46.

CHAPTER 9

# On Schumpeter's *History of Economic Analysis,* 40 Years After

*Alan Jarvis of Routledge, London, deciding to undertake a reprinting of Schumpeter's magisterial* History of Economic Analysis, *offered me the delightful opportunity to write an interpretive essay as the reprint's introduction. This chapter covers not only the history of Schumpeter's treatment of ideas, the unfinished nature of this presentation, and the largely favorable reviews it received upon publication, but also my effort to reflect what the meanings of those reviews were, and how I would assess the book's thrust some 40 years after it was first published. Oxford University Press reprinted the book in 1995 for the American market, incorporating this Introduction. My own thoughts are that the book is clearly magisterial, but that Schumpeter strangely not only omitted all discussion of those doing economic sociology (an approach that he advocated strongly in the early chapters), but also clearly skirted any treatment of the nature of true value theory. "Without a vision, the people are lost," was surely a sentiment he espoused, but when it comes down to it, he really didn't offer his readers much, if any. I arranged this introduction in five parts: (1) Schumpeter's place in the histories of economic thought picture; (2) the place of this book in his life; (3) the book's organization; (4) reviewers' views of the book; and (5) my own assessment as different from those mentioned in the previous part.*

*There is, as we shall see, much in this book which is redundant, irrelevant, cryptic, strongly biased, paradoxical, or otherwise unhelpful or even harmful to understanding. When all this is set aside, there still remains enough to constitute, by a wide margin, the most constructive, the most original, the most learned, and the most brilliant contribution to the history of the analytical phases of our discipline which has ever been made. (Viner 1954, pp. 894–5).*

---

First appeared as "Introduction," in *History of Economic Analysis* by Joseph A. Schumpeter, (London: Routledge, [1954] 1994, xvii–xxxix; New York: Oxford University Press [1954] 1995, xvii–xxxix).

Thanks are owed to several friends who have read and corrected the manuscript: Professors A. W. Coats, Warren Samuels, Yuichi Shionoya, Richard Swedberg and Shigeto Tsuro, and Dr. Charles McCann.

179

## I. Putting Schumpeter and Histories of Economic Thought in Perspective

1.1 Schumpeter was a man of many interests as well as talents. Beyond that he had, certainly as a young man, monumental ambitions. It is not appropriate in this essay to devote much space to the journey of his life; fortunately there are now available not only the 1950 insightful memorials by his colleagues, particularly the one by Gottfried Haberler,[1] a massive as well as a magnificent piece of bibliographical scholarship on what he wrote, who wrote about him, and with whom was he most frequently compared by Massimo M. Augello (1990),[2] but also three recent (1991) and assuredly major biographies of the man. *Schumpeter, A Biography* by Richard Swedberg contains a particularly carefully balanced, scholarly assessment of Schumpeter's four or five major efforts as well as an intriguing general account of the times and environments in which he lived. Swedberg discusses *ad seriatim* the various decades of Schumpeter's life and work, and if he attempts to explain the man, he does so only by inference.

The second biography is different. *Opening Doors: The Life and Work of Joseph Schumpeter* by Robert Loring Allen has more of the characteristics of James Boswell's *The Life of Samuel Johnson, LL.D*, or Samuel Pepys' *Diary* (1815). Benefitting greatly from the massive, scholarly, even daunting[3] task of deciphering Schumpeter's personal diaries undertaken by Mrs. Erica Mattschnigg Gershenkron,[4] Allen interpreted the often elliptical, if not actually obscure, materials. Unlike Swedberg (a sociologist), Allen (an economist) was a much-impressed, even overwhelmed, Schumpeter student. Allen documents much of what Swedberg could do no more than infer.

The third biography, *Joseph Schumpeter: Scholar, Teacher, and Politician* by Edward März, a Viennese Marxian historian, eschews not only discussion of Schumpeter, the idiosyncratic individual, but virtually all mention of Schumpeter's historico-cultural-epistemological interests. März's effort is to fit Schumpeter into the ranks of latter-day Marxians, an interesting effort but one hardly germane to what we are interested in. For that reason,

---

1. This essay appeared originally in the *Quarterly Journal of Economics*. It was reprinted in Seymour Harris's edited volume, *Schumpeter, Social Scientists* (Harris, 1951) and again in Haberler (1993). The 1951 volume also contained essays by 16 leading economists, including *inter alia* Ragnar Frisch, Arthur Smithies, Paul A. Samuelson, Jan Tinbergen, and Fritz Machlup.

2. Augello cites 260 works (including articles and books translated into languages other than the original) by Schumpeter and 1916 works on Schumpeter. Augello's own generalizations or findings are in a comprehensive 93-page essay, replete with valuational (that is, Augello's straightforward evaluations) notes. I am not aware of a comparable task done recently by any economist on an economist.

3. The task was daunting because much was written, even scribbled, in an archaic German shorthand.

4. I am indebted to Professor Yuichi Shionoya for this information and other points, too.

what follows is based in large measure on the memorials and the other two studies.

1.2 I believe that Schumpeter's intellectual efforts centered on five (possibly four and a half) major projects. I would classify the first burst of effort (including three books) as at least two major projects, one involving the nature of economic theory and economic science and the other concentrating on the nature and sources of economic development. The first surfaced in the 1908 *Das Wesen und der Hauptinhalt der theoretischen Nationalökonomie (The Nature and Essence of Theoretical Economics)* and to a lesser degree in the 1914 *Der Dogmen- und Methodengeschichte (Economic Method and Doctrine: An Historical Sketch)*[5]; the second in the 1911 *Theorie der wirtschaftlichen Entwicklung (The Theory of Economic Development)*.

His next (I would term it the third) major effort involved a book on money (partly written but never published by him although it did appear in 1970 as *Das Wesen des Geldes*[6]) and his 1939 two-volume *Business Cycles*. This generally unsuccessful effort paralleled Maynard Keynes's 1930 abortive *Treatise on Money* and his thoroughly successful 1936 *General Theory of Employment, Interest, and Money*.

Schumpeter did not think that his *Capitalism, Socialism, and Democracy* was a major effort; indeed he 'often called it a "pot-boiler"' (Allen, 1992, II, p. 133). Others have not shared that assessment, and it may well be termed Effort 'Three and a Half' or even Four.

His fifth effort involved his interpretation of the filiation of ideas in the development of economic theory. This effort surfaced initially with his 1914 *Epochen der Dogmen- und Methodengeschichte* (translated later as *Economic Doctrine and Method: An Historical Sketch*) and was unfinished when he died, but the outline of the corpus appeared as *History of Economic Analysis* (1954). I would also include in this fifth effort another posthumous collection, *Ten Great Economists* (1954), which contains polished essays.

1.3 The unfinished *History of Economic Analysis (HEA)* is the most significant part of the fifth and last of Schumpeter's great projects. To some, its development represents the somber reflections of an older scholar, one embittered by personal, career, and character tragedies. To others, it is the quintessential, if uncompleted, final great professional *tour d'horizon* of the leading practiced academic professional economics visionary of the twentieth century. And for still others it is the wisest compendium of names and titles ever

---

5. This book was essentially the basis for the last effort. However, as Schumpeter thought all study of economic theory involves knowledge of its origins, at the time (pre-World War I) he linked the two.

6. Edited and introduced by F. K. Mann. Göttingen: Vandenhöck & Ruprecht, 1970, pp. xxvii, 341.

published in English (and possibly in all other languages) in the long history of the discipline.

1.4 In the past there have been many treatments of the history of the discipline employed as explanations of the development of economic theory. Indeed, one way to explain the emergence of the Smithian and Ricardian virtual hegemony was simply to recount how Smith had fused earlier writings, rejected some, and made others canon. Ricardo, referring to Smith's 1776 economics masterpiece,[7] offered a tighter type of reasoning, and thus it seemed classical economics was assembled, if not actually born.[8] The official 'registry of birth,' as seen by the British, was undoubtedly John Ramsay McCulloch's *The Literature of Political Economy* (1840), just as Jérôme-Adolphe Blanqui's *Histoire de l'économie politique en Europe*[9] (1838) could be said to have been an even earlier French claim—of course making McCulloch's either a collateral, if lesser, relative or simply a Pretender.

There is a German lineage, as well. Wilhelm Georg Friedrich Roscher first brought out his *Geschichte der Englischen Volkswirtschaftslehre* (1851) and then later in 1874 his *Geschichte der Nationalökonomie in Deutschland,* and his student, Gyula Kautz, published in 1860 *Die Geschichtliche Entwicklung der Nationalökonomie und Ihrer Literatur.* One could go on, but it suffices to indicate that not only Marx treated the history of economics in *Das Kapital* (particularly in Volume One, 1867) but that object of Marxian scorn, Eugen Karl Dühring, published a positivist *Kritische Geschichte der Nationalökonomie und der Sozialismus* in 1871.

From a more 'modern' standpoint, I am tempted first to point to William Stanley Jevons' decision to commission a translation of Luigi Cossa's *Guido allo Studio dell'Economia Politica* (1875) as our 'cornerstone.' Cossa was so pleased with Jevons' request that he expanded and partially rewrote his first edition for that translation. So it was that the 1876 second edition with a Preface by Jevons (and not published in Italian until the next year, 1877!) became the template for many of the analytical history of economics texts which followed.[10]

Until Schumpeter's 1954 *History of Economic Analysis* appeared, American (and presumably British) economics graduate students generally referred

---

7. The earlier (1759), masterpiece was the more carefully written, *The Theory of Moral Sentiments*.

8. A more properly systematic approach is to refer to that collector's 'gem of a servant,' *The History of Economic Thought and Analysis* (1973) by Emma Fundaburk, to consider the wealth of efforts at synthesizing the various approaches.

9. This book went through several successive editions. The fifth French edition is dated 1882, and there was a translation into English of the fourth French edition (1880).

10. The well-known text by Charles Gide and Charles Rist, *A History of Economic Doctrines,* was not published until 1915.

to several 'old standbys:' Eric Roll's strange mixture of pro- and then a-Marxian (to coin a neologism) *A History of Economic Thought* (particularly the post-World War II 2nd [1946] and 3rd [1954] editions) and Charles Gide and Charles Rist *A History of Economic Doctrines from the Time of the Physiocrats until the Present Day* (translated into English in 1948 from the several [2nd, 6th, and 7th] French editions). More recently, that is, within the last 20 years, Mark Blaug's *Economic Theory in Retrospect* and *The New Palgrave* have been the principal authorities for graduate students. For economics undergraduate students there was Alexander Gray's excellently composed *The Development of Economic Doctrine: An Introductory Survey* (1931) and Henry W. Spiegel's *The Growth of Economic Thought* (1971). More advanced scholars relied on monographs on writers, schools, periods, and sub-sets of the topic (e.g., monetary theory, etc.). None of the foregoing, however, is, in my view, magisterial—none attempts to synthesize a vision.

Since the appearance of the *History of Economic Analysis* two other particularly authoritative works have appeared: Wesley Clair Mitchell's *Types of Economic Theory: From Mercantilism to Institutionalism* as edited by Joseph Dorfman (1967, 1969)[11] and Karl Pribram's *A History of Economic Reasoning* (1983). Neither attempted to synthesize a vision, although each sought to present an organizing theme, itself a 'Whiggish' interpretation (I would not consider such interpretations really to be visions). I shall compare their major approaches below.

The most important thing about Schumpeter's *History of Economic Analysis* is its impact on the profession. Unfinished and published with obvious and identified lacunae, it can not serve as a good reference guide. Yet, reference is regularly made to it. Why? Although I will expand on this point later, let me say here only that it offers a complex but not-quite-idiosyncratic vision of economics.

Schumpeter knew Continental sources, with which most British- and American-trained economists may have had some familiarity, but certainly had not studied in any rigorous way. Schumpeter had had an excellent *Gymnasium* education, giving him a familiarity with Greek and Latin philosophical schools, and a working knowledge of German, French, Italian, English, and some ability to read other European languages. Schumpeter's coming of age in the overcharged last decade of the declining Hapsburg Monarchy, and his knowing personally the leading economists in his own country and in Germany, France, Britain and America, plus his ambitious, possibly arrogant, showmanship, gave him both a sophistication and a range of personal contacts

---

11. The basic manuscript was the result of a student's shorthand notes; in that form it was sold in 1949 by Augustus Kelley, Bookseller (New York) with Mrs. Mitchell's permission (extended to a very limited number of sets) as *Lecture Notes on Types of Economic Theory: From Mercantilism to Institutionalism.* Dorfman corrected and greatly expanded the material.

that no other major historian of the whole discipline has had. Moreover, he generalized easily and often imaginatively. Most of all, he escaped the usual constraints of having been educated within the bounds of British Utilitarianism, and even though for much of his life he apparently had a weakness for the effortless superiority of the English gentleman-scholar, he was in the important sense an intellectually superbly equipped outsider.

1.5 In sum, then, the importance of the book is that it gives a vision of the development of the economics discipline, a vision created by an unusually well-read 'outsider' (from the standpoint of most British and American-trained professional economists) at a time when he shunned most professional company and was driven by a personal ambition work ethic to complete a monumental effort explaining the relationship between what he called the economic science and not only other sciences but also other social studies and philosophical disciplines. Flawed by its incompleteness (due to the author's sudden death), there is, nonetheless, nothing else like it in the English language; and even when one turns to other cultures, nothing has appeared which has its appeal, if not its scope. Most of all, it is the product of an imaginative mind embittered by a World War in which his adopted country, perhaps misled by an ubiquitous Anglo-Saxon cultural penumbra (which he came to despise), was seemingly fighting the wrong enemy. The book stands as a challenge (perhaps if it had been finished it would have been as a rejection) to the way Anglo-American economists were accustomed to looking at themselves and their craft.

## II. The Book's Part in Schumpeter's Life

2.1 Just why Schumpeter undertook to write the 1914 *Der Dogmen- und Methodengeschichte* seems to me to be less of a mystery than is the slant of its contents. He was at the time a young man, perceived both by the world and by himself as a *Wunderkind*. It was part of his judgement as well, perhaps, of his conceit, that he wanted to lay out a schema for the understanding of the development of the economics discipline, both as a science and as practiced as an art. Assertive in tone, it reflects an intellectual confidence that was as yet essentially untouched by any serious career failures. But, if Schumpeter was unscarred, he certainly was aware that others had been. Of them, according to Swedberg (1991, pp. 91–3), he was greatly concerned about the opinions of Max Weber, whose efforts to combine an overly abstract theoretical science of economics with a comparably over-detailed history of events and policies had resulted in a new 'discipline,'—*Sozialökonomie*.

Opportunity came to please him in the form of a request from Weber, himself, to prepare a history of the subject of economic theory. Weber was undertaking the organization and publication of a deliberately important collective handbook, *Grundriss der Sozialökonomie*. The other selected authors were two eminent older scholars, Karl Bücher and Friedrich von Wieser. Their presence, plus his own desire to ingratiate himself with Weber[12], doubtless affected the rhetoric in the book. And while it retains a nominal tolerance for a kind of historical approach, it seems to me to be clear that this was a concession to Weber's feelings and was more of a courtesy than a fully sincere opinion. At that time, Schumpeter was generally putting his chips on abstract theory.

This earlier book went untranslated into English until after Schumpeter's death, but for most of the history of economics *aficionados* of the inter-Wars period, its existence and (for those who could read German, its contents) assured Schumpeter of an extra degree of professional standing. Yet, Schumpeter himself seems to have regarded it as evidence of an unfinished product. Space limitations do not permit much dwelling on its contents (cf. Perlman, 1982), but at the time he wrote it he was intent upon (1) drawing a distinction between scientific economics and political economy; (2) showing how British classical economics was giving way to 'schools of economic thought;' (3) indicating that the future of economic analysis lay in the tradition of Walrasian general equilibrium analysis, albeit in a 'dynamic rather than a static form;' and (4) insisting that the filiation of ideas as well as economic policy rested best in the minds and hands of a disinterested cultural elite.

2.2 By the 1940s Schumpeter was estranged from many of his Harvard colleagues. It is popularly believed that this breach came about because of World War II and the alliance between the Western democracies and Stalin's Soviet Union. More than fifty years after the event, it is hard to reconstruct the many feelings influencing the situation. Loring Allen suggests that the alienation may have had an earlier source in Schumpeter's ambivalence regarding anti-Semitism and the Nazis; but many of Allen's judgements seem to me to be facile and too easily based on hearsay as well as *post hoc, ergo propter hoc* assessments. But, whatever the cause, Schumpeter withdrew from Cambridge and concentrated on reformulating his ideas about the historical development of the discipline. When the war ended, Schumpeter reemerged from his cocoon, but he was never the caterpillar, much less the butterfly, he had been as a young man. He wrote brilliant essays on Irving Fisher and Maynard Keynes; both of them were published posthumously in *Ten Great Economists*

---

12. It succeeded: Weber became a strong admirer and a supporter when it came to Schumpeter's applying for chairs. Swedberg reports, however, that the two once avoided coming to blows only by Weber's stomping out of a coffee house. What caused such violence? Schumpeter was fascinated by what was going on in the Soviet Union, and seemingly endorsed Leninism, as practiced. Weber, incensed by Schumpeter's indifference to human cruelty, could not restrain himself (Swedberg, 1991, pp. 92–3).

(*TGE*), surpassing his analysis in the *HEA*. He served as President of the American Economic Association in 1948 and in that capacity delivered an address on 'Science and Ideology'. More to our point, he was asked to deliver, *inter alia,* a eulogy of Wesley Clair Mitchell just after the latter's death (in 1950). It was a strange, idiosyncratic performance, but, for the record, the written essay, finished just before Schumpeter's own death, if effusive is also wise. The *History of Economic Analysis* seems to have been largely the product of the bitter years leading to and during the War. Swedberg relates how Schumpeter proposed the volume to the Oxford University Press, and from the first it was conceived as a vision, a massive treatment of the emergence of the scientific discipline. But, like many last great works of artists and other writers, it seems to have been cursed by an evil star. What was written was done so by a depressed author. It was unfinished when he died, and his devoted student and third wife, Elizabeth Boody Schumpeter, who had brought out of chaos what order there had been during the years from around 1938 onwards, sought to polish the manuscript as best she could and to integrate as much as possible.

The task was extremely difficult. Schumpeter's writing method was disordered. Major bits and large pieces were to be found in three different studies, and it was not always clear which had been written first and which later. Much was written in an archaic German shorthand. However, she persevered.

But the evil star's curse on the project followed her as well. She suffered a malignancy during the months when she could work on the book, and she died well before it came out. Several Harvard colleagues did what they could to complete her task, but committees rarely can do as well as a single individual and, as I have indicated, Elizabeth Schumpeter's own knowledge of the vision, surely greater than anyone else's, was far greater than theirs.

Elizabeth Schumpeter also proposed the printing of a collection of his essentially obituary essays on key economists, essays running from 1914 until no less than a fortnight before his death. Her selection (*TGE*) combines a judgement regarding market taste (which may explain the lengthy essay on Marx coming first) and one reflecting Schumpeter's regard for the eminence of the ten 'greats' (Marx, Walras, Carl Menger, Marshall, Pareto, von Böhm Bawerk, Taussig, Fisher, Mitchell, and Keynes) plus three appended short pieces on Knapp, von Wieser, and von Bortkiewicz.

*Ten Great Economists* I find is worth noting particularly because of its lengthy analysis of Pareto's work. It is canon that Schumpeter thought Walras the greatest economist in the history of the profession. I suggest that a less conventional view is also worth considering. In the end he admired Pareto as much or more. At the very 'least,' Pareto was the worldly St. Paul to Walras's spiritual Jesus.

## III. How the Book Is Organized

3.1 In the *HEA* Schumpeter sets out to explain how the discipline should be perceived. Part I (3.7 percent of the pages) as it appears seems to me to be the most important. In his 1914 study, *Der Dogmen- und Methodengeschichte,* which was long on self-conscious organization,[13] Schumpeter's themes involve a distinction between 'science' (e.g., scientific economics) and econopolitical programs (political economy), and contrast the roles played by disinterested 'consultant administrators' as distinct from venal pamphleteers (cf. Perlman, 1983). The older Schumpeter set out in the *HEA* to do something far more sophisticated. He sought to explain economics in terms of the dynamics of the sociology of knowledge rather than under the more usual rubric, classical epistemology. I feel that his exposition would possibly have been pedagogically easier had he chosen to tie his thoughts to Pareto's *Trattato di Sociologia Generale,* with its distinction between rational and nonrational systems. But their goals involving theory as a means to understanding human meanings were similar and Schumpeter, in explaining ultimately what shaped economics (and by economics he clearly meant economic theorizing), stated quite flatly that first one had to know economic history[14] and statistical display and analysis.[15] Given that background, one was then ready to study theory. Schumpeter took pains to explain that much writing passing for theory was irrelevant and even jejune; theorists poisoned their own well by making foolish condemnations of empirical details and extravagant claims relating to their own progress and prowess. Many theorists were intentionally ignorant of the fact that the best theorists (like Newton) were skeptical (with reason) of being classified by theorists as theorists.

Nonetheless, Schumpeter's rule of thumb was that abstract rules were to be derived from and then tested against observed data. Although he refers to Marshall as a leader in the practice of 'scientific economics' (1954, p. 21), it is also even more true that Schumpeter abhorred the tendency of Marshall and the Marshallians to bend their analysis in the name of ideologies such as free trade, utilitarianism, and so forth.

In a significant sense, Part I of the *History of Economic Analysis* seems to have been laid out as a major contribution. However, as it was unfinished, it

---

13. Jacob Viner observed that this book was along the lines of the Cossa study (1954, p. 898).

14. Swedberg notes the influence of Max Weber (Swedberg 1991, p. 184).

15. Schumpeter's view was similar to Lord Kelvin's; science involved measurement, even if it was not measurement, itself. Schumpeter, alert to Hayek's disparagement of *scientism,* was amenable to every discipline developing its own ordering of *knowledge* (not *learning*), and specifically physics (Schumpeter 1954, pp. 16–18).

suffers seriously from omissions. What Schumpeter had to say about his bugaboo—ideology—and his Golden Fleece—a scientific economics—can be inferred from the written version of his 1948 Presidential Address. But what he had meant to say about his coming to grips with the meaning of Weber's *Sozialökonomie* is not adequately specified, and in his conscious eschewing of Pareto's sociological system (as we will note below, his long essay on Pareto was written during the last months of his life) his views are left for me, at least—up in the air.

3.2 Part II reflects Schumpeter's greatest relative strengths. It involves about a quarter of the book's pages, and it takes up *ad seriatim* first the contrasting seminal contributions of Plato and Aristotle and the amazing lack of analytical material associated with Republican and Imperial Rome before turning to a splendid survey of the Christian and Natural Law writers. The third chapter of this part is a reprise of his 1914 theme of the consultant administrators and the pamphleteers—the former groped for a vision, the latter for reward. His treatment of Smith is insightful but, nonetheless, harsh. Praise, such as he gave it in this chapter to the English, was reserved for Josiah Child.

The fourth chapter is more generous in tone; in it Schumpeter's identification of the qualities of the hero becomes apparent. What impressed him most was the hero's ability to build an original system rather than merely to introduce a mechanism of thought. Taking up William Petty and his associates, Boisguillebert, Cantillon, Quesnay and his associates, and Turgot, Schumpeter, the first President of the Econometric[16] Society, eventually added (in pencil) Turgot's name to one chapter's original title, *The Econometricians*.

There follow three chapters focussed on specific topics and subtopics; suffice it here to list only the topics: (5) Population, Returns, Wages, and Employment; (6) Value and Money, and (7) The 'Mercantilist' Literature. They contain much informative information—names, titles, dates, and, most of all, the tracing of the filiation of ideas, but they are mostly descriptive. Schumpeter, quite naturally, 'graded' the names—among those getting 'firsts' or 'very high seconds' were Botero, Serra and Misselden, Steuart, and perhaps Hume. For many, the most useful thing about this part is the integration of Continental names (with what is for many readers limited to English) the British names.

3.3 Part III covers economics between 1790 and 1870. The initial three chapters cover the plan of the analysis, a bird's-eye view of the economic history of the period, and a marvelous survey of the dominant idea-sets of that

---

16. Schumpeter thought the word, *Econometrics*, philologically ignorant, '. . . it ought to be either Ecometrics or Economometrics' (Schumpeter 1954, p. 209).

era. Again, Schumpeter 'reviews the troops' (his phrase), and identifies his heroes, including Longfield and von Thünen, Cournot, J. S. Mill, Say, and Sismondi. Schumpeter then devotes most of a chapter (5) to J. S. Mill. In chapter 6 Schumpeter synthesizes British Classical Economics, using Senior's four postulates (rational maximization, the Malthusian Law, diminishing returns in agriculture, and increasing returns in industry) as a convenient reference point or point of intellectual departure. From there he continues in the integration of Ricardian and Marxian thinking, Say's Law of Markets, and the concern with production and distribution. Both chapter 6 and its sequel (7), 'Money, Credit, and Cycles' are English-experience oriented.

Schumpeter's treatment of British Utilitarianism is worth specific mention. He accepts its centrality in the development of the British classical system, but he does not accept its validity. Accordingly, it should come as no surprise that neither Mandeville[17] nor Bentham has a tablet, much less a memorial, in his Pantheon.

3.4 Whereas it took three chapters of about 84 pages in Part III to introduce the intellectual background (the sociology of ideas) for the period 1790 to 1870, it took four chapters but fewer pages (about 74) to introduce the intellectual background for the period 'From 1870 to 1914 and later' in Part IV. Even so, this Part is the one giving full geographical sweep. Taking up developments in theory in Britain (he concentrates far more on Marshall than on Jevons or Edgeworth), France, Germany and Austria, Italy, the Netherlands and Scandinavia, the United States, and finally in 'Marxism' (if not a land, certainly a 'cloud' of its own), he sets the stage for what he really wants to discuss. Chapter 6 is on the Marshallian system; chapter 7 is on the evolution of equilibrium analysis (partial equilibrium being seen as the product of Cournot and Marshall; general equilibrium, albeit static, as principally the product of Walras). Chapter 8 takes up applications as seen in the treatment of Money, Credit, and Cycles.

Schumpeter mentions with enthusiasm his colleague Haberler, and with less enthusiasm his contemporary, Maynard Keynes.[18] Bates Clark and Wesley Clair Mitchell[19] get short shrift.[20] Irving Fisher (on balance) is treated

---

17. Hardly mentioned (two slim references). Hayek, by way of contrast, makes Mandeville's role seminal in the development of individualism, utilitarianism, and even in the self-regulating market. (See Hayek, 1967, Perlman, 1990, and 5.6 below.)

18. Schumpeter's treatment of Keynes, always something of a touchy subject, is most conscientiously handled in a critical but yet balanced manner in *Ten Great Economists* (Schumpeter, 1951, pp. 260–91).

19. See 2.2, above for reference to a much more thorough assessment of Mitchell.

20. Mitchell paired Schumpeter and Pareto in his lectures. Even so, the topic was not one of Mitchell's 'favorites' (Mitchell, 1969, chapter 15).

with qualified enthusiasm and at some, if limited, length.[21] Instead, he sets out to glorify Walras, and as I have mentioned earlier and will mention again below, he eschewed most but not all lengthy discussion of Pareto. As Schumpeter was a man hardly consumed with modesty, false or otherwise, it is puzzling why he did not mention any of his own contributions; perhaps that was to be left to the last.

In my judgement, Part 4—because it was to lay the foundations for an understanding of the meaning of dynamic general equilibrium analysis—needed much more work. My guess is that, given the time, Schumpeter could have greatly expanded and improved its exposition. But, I also believe that given the state of mathematics during the period before 1960 and his own reluctance to get involved in further studies in mathematics, this section was bound to have been limited.

3.5 Part V was to be 'A Sketch of Modern Developments.' As the manuscript was left, it had a truncated statement of his plan, a comparison of the Marshallian-Wicksellian (an essentially partial equilibrium analysis) approach, a discussion of 'totalitarian economics' (Germany, Italy, and Russia), some thoughts about dynamics and business-cycle research, and a slightly polished assessment of Keynes's impact on the profession.[22] This Part, clearly intended to be ultimately no more than a 'sketch', is too unfinished to be of concern to anyone but those interested only in very preliminary drawings.

## IV. The Reactions to the Theses in the Book

4.0 The appearance of the book about four years after Schumpeter's death may have affected its reception, but we know for a fact that it produced a number of unusually long book review essays. Virtually everyone thought it monumental—in its purpose, if not in its delivery. Most, but not all,[23] of the leading journals reviewed it, usually choosing a well established scholar[24] to assess Schumpeter's vision of what a massive assessment of the development of economics should be. Most reviewers did not hesitate to assess it relatively passionately—the reviews appeared for the most part long after Schumpeter's death and the book was considered so important that no attention was paid to the *nil nisi bonum* rule.

Briefly put, all the reviewers were in some senses impressed, even awed,

---

21. Again, duty overcame the sequence of writing discipline. In *Ten Great Economists* there is a generous memorial essay on Mitchell, written just before Schumpeter's own death.

22. See 3.4 for reference to a longer, and presumably written later, essay on Keynes.

23. The *Economic Journal*, for instance, promised to review it, but I cannot find the review in the journal, Loring Allen's reference to the contrary notwithstanding (1991, pp. 215, 218).

24. *Economica*, by way of contrast, turned to the then very young A. W. Coats to write a review. He did a discerning job.

by the vision and the massive detail (however imperfect it was left). But many of the reviewers were put off by Schumpeter's evident anti-British (usually meaning anti-Utilitarianism) judgements. Most reviewers swallowed hard his lauding of his Continental heroes, but most of them, lacking his first-hand familiarity with the texts, were in no strong position really to complain. One reviewer, Ronald Meek (1957), took him to task for oversimplifying, indeed bending, the Marxian concept of the institutional nature of social value (social *mores*) creation.

4.1 George Stigler's review in the *Journal of Political Economy* was unusual in that he was led to question from the first why anyone should want to 'write on such a scale' (p. 344). While Stigler expressed his amazement at Schumpeter's obvious erudition, he also thought that many of Schumpeter's derived generalizations (e.g. economists are slow to embrace new ideas) were clearly wrong (ibid.). He found the exposition so truncated that he often could not really understand just what Schumpeter had in mind.[25] His criticisms were even more directed to the vision than they were to the execution.

But, Stigler also had rare praise for Schumpeter:

> There is splendor in Schumpeter's contempt for those who explain and appraise theories by the venal motives that their authors conceivably nurtured. There is intellectual chivalry in his attempts to divorce the quality of the analyses from the policies to which they were married. There is magnanimity and generosity in the treatment of almost every minor economist, and of course these are the ones who need such treatment. And there is wit . . . (p. 345)

4.2 Another Chicago economist, Frank Knight (himself no mean historian of economic thought) had what seem to me to be among the most trenchant criticisms of the book. Although he ended his lengthy essay with a sort of 'if-cats-can-look-at-kings' apology, his review, appearing in the *Southern Economic Journal*, was clearly admonitory on several grounds. He took care to notice that if Schumpeter was willing to start with the Babylonians, albeit with only a brief reference, he surely should have been able to make some, even if limited, references to Indian (and presumably other Asian) sources as well. Knight's point was that Schumpeter's book was limited to Western economic thinking, but that even there, Schumpeter failed a real test.

Like several others, Knight noted the anti-British feeling in Schumpeter's mind-set. Unlike all the others, however, he noted strongly Schumpeter's

---

25. 'When Mill's fundamental propositions on capital or Böhm-Bawerk's three grounds for the emergence of interest are disposed of in a page or two, not even the expert can claim a full understanding of Schumpeter's position' (p. 344).

clear neglect of the Protestant (and explicitly the Old Testament) impact on economic thinking. He explicitly distrusted Schumpeter's sense of hero-worship—Schumpeter scored individuals on scales of originality and personal endowment—of course, absent personal moral qualities. Knight chose to soften that criticism by adding the paradox that if he had to trust anyone's judgements, Schumpeter's would have been among the more reliable.

Most interesting to me, however, was Knight's observation relating to Schumpeter's limited appreciation of the fact that different societies had different 'utility functions' (to employ an accepted neologism). Individualism emerges late in the historical game. And:

> Primitive ideas were, necessarily, oriented to *order*, not to Freedom and Progress. But under primitive conditions the activities of the money-lender (even the merchant) can be profoundly disturbing, disastrous. And medieval society had powerful additional 'reasons' in a theory of society centered on 'salvation,' to be achieved through an orthodox creed and ritual in the custody of a divinely commissioned absolute authority. (p. 267, emphasis in the original)

4.3 Three English writers sought to target his anti-British judgements and their implications. I turn first to I. M. D. Little, then to Lionel Robbins, and finally to Mark Blaug, whose assessment of the book is probably the most carefully reasoned.

While Little's principal interest seems to lie in criticizing Schumpeter's discomfort with welfare economics, I thought his strongest criticism was reserved for Schumpeter's virtually total neglect of the influence of Thomas Hobbes on whatever came afterwards. Hobbes, Little believes (and I share this view), offered economists along with others the paradigmatical problem; the efforts of most English theorists sought either to deny or to resolve that problem. From Hobbes comes the streams of thought emerging as individualism, empiricism, and eventually utilitarianism. But, as Schumpeter's interpretation does not stress the Hobbes connection, Schumpeter would have little or no reason to employ Hobbes as the hinge between the medieval traditions and what I tend to call the modern.

Lionel Robbins first took pains to indicate how beautifully prepared Schumpeter had been by his connections and training in Vienna (then bathed in intellectual sunshine) to undertake the task of writing a massive (too massive, in Robbins' opinion (Robbins, 1955, p. 4)) treatise on the whole subject of economics. After the usual bows in the direction of some personal *nil nisi bonum* rule, Robbins got down to his task.

Robbins, like Schumpeter, was a man of great culture, wide reading, and many friendships. Unlike Schumpeter, Robbins harbored virtually no religious sympathies. Instead, he was a Common Sense Englishman with faith in the perfectibility of man through study and the uses of reason; in short, he embraced British Utilitarianism, something which Schumpeter did not accept either as a workable philosophy or, even less, as a substitute for religious convictions. Thus, much of Schumpeter's erudition, based as it was on a sophisticated Continental Catholicism, not only left Robbins cold, but clearly he paid no attention to it.

In general, Robbins thought that Schumpeter's bias against classical economics reflected the feelings of someone outside the 'true' Utilitarian tradition. Robbins wrote that Schumpeter's perception of the influence of Bentham's and James Mills' Utilitarianism was distorted; most English writers were more balanced in their assumptions of the meaning and consequence of that doctrine.

However, it is when Robbins sets out to demolish Schumpeter's scaler system of hero ratings that he scores his truest hits. Robbins's approach is to attack *first* the textual validity of Schumpeter's assertions (1) of Smith's place in the scheme of things, (2) of Ricardo's influence, (3) of Cournot's analytical skills, and (4) of Marshall's writings and influence, and *second* to demonstrate that Schumpeter's treatment of Walras was biased in the other direction. Schumpeter, according to Robbins, clearly did not apply the same rigor in assessing Walras as he did elsewhere (Robbins 1955, pp. 4–5).

Clearly what Robbins dismissed was the basic Schumpeterian schema, which separated what went earlier from the economics of the British classical school—giving to the former the split between real philosopher/theologians and mere pamphleteers. The main casualty was Adam Smith's reputation: put against such philosopher/theologians as Plato, Aristotle, and Aquinas, Smith becomes a small potato. Schumpeter's implication (never really stated) that Ricardo had a good bit of the pamphleteer in his writings, tended further to denigrate his opinion of the majesty of the British contribution. But it would be an error to conclude that the thoughtful Robbins was unimpressed with what Schumpeter had to say in 400 pages about the classical British tradition.

Robbins lauded Schumpeter's treatment of economics since 1870, but noted rather trenchantly that in contrast to Schumpeter's rule, individual writers, not the schools of thought, are what is to be judged. It is in this sense that Robbins thought that Schumpeter clearly underrated Marshall and treated a supposed neglect by Marshall of Jevons, of von Thünen, and of Cournot and Dupuit with scorn. He thought that Schumpeter's treatment of Walras was designed so as to protect both himself and Walras from criticisms that Edgeworth and Marshall were Walras's betters both with regard to vision and to technical detail.[26]

---

26. Later, when Lionel Robbins (1955) was to suggest that he disputed Schumpeter's ranking Walras ahead of Ricardo, I think that Lord Robbins missed the underlying point. Ricardo's substance was based squarely on a Benthamite pedestal displaying at best only one

While Robbins chose to end his essay with a pastoral reminiscence of his last meeting with Schumpeter, the important thing is the thrust of an Englishman against someone who may have been an Anglophile in his youth (prior to World War I), but who was very different in his maturity and old age.[27]

Somewhat later on, Mark Blaug was to put this line of criticism in a different way, but with much more precision and clearly more bite. In his authoritative statement-cum-textbook (1963, etc.), Blaug takes most of Schumpeter's assertions about what he set out to do and then measures them against what he actually did. Of course, it was the same with Schumpeter as with many others: the reach was greater than the grasp. Most importantly, Blaug struck at Schumpeter's belief that ideology could be separated from science. But Blaug's blow, unlike Ronald Meek's (to which we will come shortly), was not aimed with the view that one's directions are shaped by one's environment; rather, where Schumpeter asserted that in the making of theory, particularly when it dealt with statistical factual observation, one could strip from the science one's ideological commitments, Blaug asserts that the stripping occurs when one sees the results of the true scientific applications only after testing the constructs under differing conditions. Blaug, something of a Popperian, is also something of a logician; and between the two, Blaug fashions his measuring rod. Blaug, like Schumpeter, does not suffer from observable doubt; nonetheless, in my judgement, he offers, scattered throughout his book, the most penetrating, detailed analyses of Schumpeter's treatise.

4.4 Another critical attack came, as one might expect, from the Marxian corner, in the person of Ronald Meek. Published in the *Scottish Journal of Political Economy* in 1957, Meek's essay, 'Is Economics Biased? A Heretical View of a Leading Thesis in Schumpeter's *History*,' attacks frontally Schumpeter's problem of separating science and ideology, and in so doing turns to the thorny issue of whether the filiation of ideas invariably leads to progress. Meek understands Schumpeter's fascination with Marxism, but insists that it was so endowed with a visceral distaste for Marx that Schumpeter was rendered unreliable in making his judgements. Marx had argued that economics was making scientific progress until the 1830s and then went off on a bourgeois kick.

---

limited aspect of human *frailty-cum-choice,* while Walras's substance was based on the greater foundation of mathematical logic and the Cartesian perception of cosmic system.

27. The pastoral reference is to the last time when Schumpeter and Robbins met; it was 'a lovely day in June [in the middle 1930s] . . . and, as we glided down the Thames between Twickenham and Datchet, I can still see him, cheerfully ensconced in the prow of our ship, surrounded by the eager spirits of the day, Nicky Kaldor, Abba Lerner, Victor Edelberg, Ursala Hicks-Webb, as she then was, the master-organizer of the party—the four fingers and the thumb of each hand pressed against those of the other, discoursing with urbanity and wit on theorems and personalities' (p. 22).

Marxians argue, writes Meek, that during the Patristic-Scholastic phase the writings tended to identify what prices ought to be; during the Neo-Scholastic-Mercantilist phase the writings tended to explain why things sold at the prices they did, and in the classical stage the writings tended to identify the competitive equilibrium and the amount of labor power consumed in the manufacture of goods. Schumpeter, by contrast, thought that the Patristic-Scholastic writers had developed a theory of utility and scarcity. What emerged afterwards contained much side-tracking as well as clear error.

Meek's argument is most clearly appreciated when it comes to consideration of marginal analysis, something which Schumpeter thought was real science and ideologically neutral. Meek thinks that marginal analysis reflects the nexus between men (the producers) and goods, whereas the earlier classical analysis reflected the nexus between men (the workers) and the owners. Consequently, there was no great advance with the advent of marginal analysis; if anything, it led to the examination of things other than what was important—namely social relationships and the production process.

4.5 Having thus laid out several lines of criticism of Schumpeter's book, let me turn to one of the more masterful reviews, that of Jacob Viner which stresses the virtues of the work:

> It is when Schumpeter is dealing with authors whose analytical quality he rates highly and whose economic analysis constituted a complex and coordinated system that he rises to his highest level in his book. His reports of these systems are magnificent feats of summarization. In outlining the analytical framework of these systems, moreover, he brings clearly into the light the fullness of their achievement and enables us to read these authors henceforth with deeper understanding and appreciation. It is the substantial portions of the book which he devotes to exposition, appraisal, and praise of the economic analysis of Cantillon, Quesnay, Marx, Jevons, Menger and Böhm-Bawerk, Cournot, and Walras—and less enthusiastically, Adam Smith, Marshall, and Fisher—which constitute its most valuable contribution. *Nowhere else, I think, in the literature of our discipline, can one find, within comparable limitations of space, as brilliant, and as self-effacing, exposition by one economist, himself a master, of the analytical achievements of other economists.* (p. 899, emphasis added).

The foregoing is not presented as though Viner did not have major disagreements, which are presented logically and comprehensively. I still find Viner's case against Schumpeter's treatment of Ricardo the best yet.

4.6 Limitations of space preclude any more than the merest reference to O. H. Taylor's (Schumpeter's colleague who regularly had taught the History of Economic Thought at Harvard) generally laudatory review in the *Review of Economics and Statistics,* or G. B. Richardson's critical and laudatory essay in the *Oxford Economic Papers,* or of a 1956 general review essay (containing other books as well) by V. W. Bladen in the *Canadian Journal of Economics and Political Science.*

I am left, however, to report just one additional criticism, to be found in Arnold Heertje's biography of Schumpeter in *The New Palgrave.*

> Reading Schumpeter, one realizes that his lasting significance stems from historical description and non-mathematical theoretical analysis. His inability to put his ideas about the development of economic life into a mathematical form may eventually change our assessment of him. But whatever the final evaluation of Schumpeter may be, it cannot be denied that he gave new direction to the development of economic science by posing some entirely new questions. Schumpeter's preoccupation with the dynamics of economic life broke the spell of the static approach to economic problems.
>
> Throughout his life Schumpeter was an *enfant terrible,* who was always ready to take extreme positions for the sake of argument, and often seized the chance to irritate people. But he was also a giant on whose shoulders many later scholars contributing to economic science stood. As an economist he is no longer in the shadow of Keynes, but in the centre of the economic scene, both in the theoretical and empirical sense. (Heertje, 1987, at p. 266).

## V. My Assessment of the Book

5.1 What is outstanding in this work in my estimation is first the scope of Schumpeter's vision and secondly the evidence of breadth of execution. I believe that since its publication, two, perhaps three, other books offering a vision of comparable (but not necessarily of equal) scope have appeared. They are works by Ben B. Seligman (1962), Wesley Clair Mitchell (1967, 1969), and Karl Pribram (1983). The latter two were also published posthumously, but the material they were based upon was more complete than was the case here.

5.2 The Seligman book studies the history of economics from the standpoint of an increasing emphasis on analytical (meaning generally geometric and algebraic) technique. As a study, I think it reflects a dismay (perhaps even a disillusionment) about the directions that economics has taken, particularly since the dominant influence of Paul A. Samuelson's 1947 *The Foundations of Economic Analysis*. It is a readable book, but its vision is narrowly reactive, and I think that the mere mention of it suffices for our purposes.

**5.3** The Mitchell study, *Types of Economic Theory: From Mercantilism to Institutionalism,* on the other hand, is magisterial. In its form it is a well-revised transcript of a student's shorthand transcription of several sets of Mitchell's lecture notes by Joseph Dorfman, the noted historian of American economics.[28] Mitchell's approach, reduced here almost to the point of triviality, is an interpretation of how economic thinking mirrored society's adaptation principally to the phenomena of modern (post-Industrial Revolution) industrialization and modern industrialized urban life.[29] Economic theory, in Mitchell's mature and considered judgement, was essentially a set of somewhat idiosyncratic explanations by a group of bright economists seeking to explain in terms familiar to themselves empirical phenomena associated with the aforementioned social processes. In common with Schumpeter, Mitchell thought theory was about meanings, usually of observable phenomena.

**5.4** I believe that Pribram's book, *A History of Economic Reasoning,* is another example of a magisterial interpretation. Pribram's approach, also reduced to something approaching triviality, is that from the time of Plato until the present, economics, as a type of thinking, has sought to harmonize two quite opposing methods, *a priorism* and empiricism. Such was the problem faced by Aristotle in contemplating Plato's *essences;* such was the problem faced by the Franciscan, Roger Bacon,[30] in facing the Dominicans and what later became the Cartesian influence; such was the division between the 19th-century Kantians and the Hegelians, the division between the Communists and the Fascists during the 1930s, and such has been the division between the internationalists (the American post-World War II Free Traders) and the 'autarkic nationalists' (meaning the Keynesian-influenced British).

**5.5** What Schumpeter offered in the *History of Economic Analysis,* again reduced to something almost approaching triviality, is the view that under-

---

28. I have not included any discussion of Dorfman's five-volume encyclopedic masterpiece, *The Economic Mind in American Civilization,* principally because it deals only with the evolution of thought within a geographically determined framework. Nonetheless, it serves as the prototypical factual summary of the evolution of the discipline.

29. Mitchell, himself, did not focus consciously on the process of modern urbanization, but I believe that a sophisticated reading of what he covered also included that phenomenon, even if not consciously articulated.

30. Perhaps because I am better versed in English secular literature than I am in Latin theological literature, I prefer as the prototype not Roger Bacon (1214–94) but Francis Bacon (1561–1626).

standing economic phenomena, after abstracting what one understood from ideological preferences, depends in large part on the epistemological methods one employs, but that each of these methods has its own historico-sociological experience. He came, particularly in his later years, to the view that one has to appreciate the way that what one borrows affects whatever one has. As I interpret this point my example is that in employing the calculus, economists borrowed a method originally designed for physical mechanics, and that the physics discipline's fascination with explaining the equilibrium of forces was translated in economics into a fascination with a static equilibrium, not at all suited for a process which was essentially biological, organic, and ever-mutating.[31] When Schumpeter wrote of dynamic general equilibrium he had in mind something quite different from a 'Newtonian'-Golden Fleece. Pribram, also educated at the University of Vienna (he was von Wieser's principal assistant), like Schumpeter expressed the view that British and American economics was seriously constrained by the influence of Benthamite utilitarianism.

5.6 I come now to my own principal criticism of what Schumpeter offered us, namely his vision. Blaug's careful reading of what Schumpeter promised and what he delivered shows that they were not the same. Query, if one is the more important than the other, is the delivery *necessarily* the basis for the ultimate assessment? If so, then one does not understand the unique place of visions. But, will any dream do? Not likely! What sets Schumpeter's dream above the others' is the multiplicity and complexities of its parts.

But, assuming that Schumpeter sought to offer a vision, how can his vision be judged? Hayek, in some senses a product of the same Viennese *Gymnasium*-mold which produced Schumpeter, offers the beginnings of an interesting comparison and ultimate criticism. Hayek came to embrace the complex paradigm of individualism-utilitarianism. Accordingly, had he written of Schumpeter's vision, he probably would have said (no doubt politely) that Schumpeter had it wrong.

But Hayek's enthusiasm for the individualism-utilitarianism paradigm, emphasizing in his economics the centrality of Mandeville (Hayek, 1967a), Smith, J. S. Mill and personal liberty, brings to my mind the question of

---

31. There are several ways of viewing the process of looking for equilibrium. One, the Newtonian, is *determinate*: if Jupiter wobbles, one can ultimately not only figure out why, but should be able to confirm the source through cognition (albeit with a better telescope). The second one, which can be termed *agricultural*, postulates that by controlling the inputs, the output can be determined within limits (e.g. change the temperature, and the tomatoes will come to market sooner or later). The third approach, the *Shackelian*, suggests that there is no way to determine equilibrium; in the struggle between well-matched adversaries there is no way to predict whether there will be an outcome, much less what it involves.

various possible alternative paradigms. I mention but three: the centrality of scarcity, the centrality of uncertainty, and the centrality of essential (i.e. stable) moral imperatives (i.e. values).

As we have seen, Schumpeter rejected the paradigm of individualism-utilitarianism (and personal liberty). He did not seriously consider the paradigm of uncertainty. But, in the absence of any other specification, it seems to me he was groping for some paradigm of fundamental social morality. He was easily side-tracked, and spent too much effort decrying ideology (although he never decried theology).

Ronald Meek noted in his Marxian interpretation that prior to the classical tradition, economics dealt with social (by which I suspect he might have meant stable imperatives) issues[32] like the relationship between workers and their lords. He went on to say that during the classical period that paradigmatic interest shifted away from a historically appropriate discussion about classes, people and social organization to an historically inappropriate nexus between producers and goods. My suggestion is that the vision that Schumpeter really sought was one involving something akin to a theological paradigm—integrating fundamental, non-changing, ethical and social values and the dynamic workings of an evolutionary economy.

By fundamental human and social values, I mean an absolute, true system which was exogenous to time and place. It was for this reason that so much of Schumpeter's interest focussed on medieval writers and Natural Law, but his own remarriage after his divorce alienated him from the religion of his ancestors. Loring Allen asserts that while Schumpeter seemed to believe that *conventional* religious beliefs were for mortals lesser than he, he became increasingly mystical as he grew older—to the point of writing to and talking with his dead mother and his dead second wife (Allen, 1991, I, pp. 223–7; II 58–9). My own assessment differs from Allen's, who like many modern scientists offer their discussions and judgements of concepts of religion and religiosity on narrow, somewhat formalistic and institutionalized planes. Schumpeter, in my view, had a strong religious nature, albeit one not categorized among the 'going-organized' religions. His second marriage after a divorce may have put him outside of the Roman Catholic flock, but his devotion to the souls of his dead mother and second wife are considerable evidence that something of his earlier religious conditioning remained.

When he was a younger man he had thought of science as furnishing answers covering all topics. By the time he had gotten to this work, he had less faith in science (note his bow to Hayek's crusade against Scientism: Schumpeter 1954, p. 17), replacing it with an interest in historical sociology. My point is simply that his sense of vision, great by comparative standards,

---

32. Within a dialectical stream, of course.

was nonetheless admittedly incomplete. On the one hand there was from his religiosity a sense of timeless all-encompassing truth which included but transcended science, for science was the name given to marvelous sets of analytical tools, when perfected perhaps also timeless in nature, but certainly never as grand as the basic vision itself. On the other, there was historical sociology, which gave a system to the bodies of material, including methods of exposition, relating to ever-changing societies.

I think there was genius in Schumpeter's linkage of science and greater truth, but he knew of a flaw as well. He was aware that scientific advance in one area not only could be translated to work in other areas, but that in the process more was transferred than merely the scientific method. The original area had its own *Gestalt,* and the transference often brought along pieces of that original *Gestalt,* which could be essentially alien to the new area. Newton, one of the inventors of the calculus, was a physicist interested in mechanics and therefore concerned with equilibrium. Economists, appreciating the potential of the calculus, often were unaware that they were applying a physics-derived technique to a socio-biological type discipline, where the one important truth was not equilibrium but constant mutation.[33]

Thus, I conclude that Schumpeter wanted a vision which embraced and bound together the permanent and exogenous with the sociological-transitory and indigenous, and he failed to find it. Had he chosen to build on the American Institutionalist writers like Commons and Mitchell as exemplars of the sociological-transitory with their inability to find the timeless truth, he could have shown the dilemma from the non-'theoretical' side.[34] Unlike many of the theorists of his time, Schumpeter expressed some, if limited, respect for what they were trying to do; but, he did not go on to say what should have been said: (*a*) that they did not see beyond the Hobbes-Locke individualist-utilitarian paradigm, and (*b*) that their ignorance of Pareto's work on non-rational systems made their work far more barren theoretically than it should have been.

---

33. This is Perlman's example, not Schumpeter's. But, I have found it pedagogically useful when explaining how Schumpeter's broader vision as put forth in Part I of the *HEA* went beyond the earlier lesser vision found in *EDM*.

34. Schumpeter's neglect of the American Institutionalists may have had any number of causes: (1) His department at Harvard was divided between the 'mid-westerners' and the 'Europeans.' He was a principal among the latter, and his Harvard 'mid-western' colleagues were, by and large, Institutionalists. (2) Part of the 'in-snobbery' or 'intellectually-correct' professional posturing of that and many other periods was to deprecate sociology and historico-political analysis. (3) He might have gotten around to this material had he lived longer. (4) Not having read the material in detail or having had the time to integrate it (the Institutional writers were poor at integration), Schumpeter concluded (I would say erroneously) that the American Institutional analysis was likely provincial or perhaps, if one wanted to be generous, pretty much limited to societies embracing the Utilitarian paradigm.

Perhaps had Schumpeter lived longer, he might have tidied up his presentation. But, as it was published, it is that incompleteness of his vision, rather than Blaug's 'inadequate-delivery' criticisms, which is the critical one. Like many Old Testament figures, Schumpeter was magnificent, but flawed; like them, he had a great vision, but only of less than perfect proportions. As with Einstein, Schumpeter failed to find his unified theory, but like Einstein he believed that there must be one somewhere.

I once described the Schumpeter, Mitchell and Pribram treatments thus:

> It is said of Franz Liszt and Arthur Rubenstein, both concert pianists of the greatest distinction, that 'they often missed some of the notes.' Thus, one can be authoritative without always being accurate. . . . To be magisterial is to be authoritative, and each [of the three authors, Schumpeter, Mitchell, and Pribram] achieves magisterial status because of the distinctive and comprehensive originality of . . . perception of intellectual evolution, rather than of chronological scope, accuracy, even polish. (Perlman, 1986, p. 9)

Schumpeter's was the bravest of those visions; the most comprehensive of those dreams.

Why? Because, as Robbins and virtually everyone else wrote, Schumpeter had read more, more widely, and more imaginatively than had any of the others. In the words of Viner:

> This is a book written in the polymath manner by perhaps the last of the great polymaths. . . . Schumpeter did possess learning and skills manifestly exceeding in range those displayed by any other economist of his or our time, and that in this book he applied these endowments to the enlightenment of his readers with a brilliance and a virtuosity which excite and dazzle even when they fail wholly to persuade. (1954, p. 894)

REFERENCES

Augello, Massimo M. (1990). *Joseph Alois Schumpeter: A Reference Guide*. Berlin: Springer-Verlag.
Allen, Robert Loring (1991). *Opening Doors: The Life and Work of Joseph Schumpeter*. New Brunswick, NJ: Transaction Publishers.
Bladen, V. W. (1956). 'Schumpeter's *History of Economic Analysis* and some Related Books.' *Canadian Journal of Economics and Political Science*, 22, 103–15.
Blanqui, Jérôme-Adolphe (1838). *Histoire de l'Économie Politique en Europe*.
Blaug, Mark (1985). *Economic Theory in Retrospect*, fourth edition. New York and

202 Economic Thought, Characters, and Institutions

Cambridge: Cambridge University Press. The earlier editions were published by Irwin in 1962 and 1968, and by Cambridge University Press in 1978.

Cossa, Luigi (1875). *Guido allo Studio dell'Economia Politica* A second edition, first published in English as *An Introduction to the Study of Political Economy* with a Preface by William Stanley Jevons in 1876.

Dorfman, Joseph (1946–49). *The Economic Mind in American Civilization.* In five volumes. New York: Viking.

Dühring, Eugen Karl (1871). *Kritische Geschichte der Nationalökonomie und der Sozialismus.*

Gide, Charles and Charles Rist (1948). *A History of Economic Doctrines from the Time of the Physiocrats until the Present Day.*

Gray, Alexander (1931). *The Development of Economic Doctrine: An Introductory Survey.* London: Longmans, Green.

Haberler, Gottfried (1951). 'Joseph Alois Schumpeter, 1883–1950,' *Quarterly Journal of Economics,* 64, 333–72.

——. (1993). *The Liberal Economic Order.* Edited by Anthony Y. C. Koo. Aldershot, Hants, United Kingdom: Edward Elgar.

Harris, Seymour Edwin, (ed.) (1951). *Schumpeter, Social Scientist.* Cambridge, MA: Harvard University.

Hayek, Friedrich (1967a). 'Dr Bernard Mandeville,' *Proceedings of the British Academy,* pp. 125–41.

——. (1976b). Review of Joseph A. Schumpeter's *History of Economic Analysis,* in *Studies in Philosophy, Politics, and Economics,* Chicago: University of Chicago Press. This is an abridged version of what had appeared in the *Freeman* in 1954.

Heertje, Arnold (1987). *The New Palgrave,* vol. 4, pp. 263–6.

Kautz, Gyula (1860). *Die Geschichtliche Entwicklung der Nationalökonomie und Ihrer Literatur.*

Knight, Frank H. (1954). 'Schumpeter's History of Economics.' *Southern Journal of Economics,* 21, 261–72.

Little, I. M. D. (1955). 'Essays in Bibliography and Criticism XXXI. History of Economic Analysis.' *Economic History Review: Series 2,* 10, 91–8.

Marx, Karl (1867). *Das Kapital.*

März, Edward (1991). *Schumpeter: Scholar, Teacher, and Politician.* New Haven, CT: Yale University Press.

McCulloch, John Ramsay (1845). *The Literature of Political Economy: A Classified Catalogue: Select publication in the different departments of that science with historical, critical, and bibliographical notes.* London: Longman, Brown, Green, and Longmans.

Meek, Ronald (1957). 'Is Economics Biased? A Heretical View of a Leading Thesis in Schumpeter's *History.' Scottish Journal of Political Economy,* 1–17.

Mitchell, Wesley Clair (1949). 'Lecture Notes on Types of Economic Theory: From Mercantilism to Institutionalism.' Sold by Augustus Kelley, Bookseller, New York.

——. (1967 and 1969). *Types of Economic Theory: From Mercantilism to Institutionalism.* Edited with an Introduction by Joseph Dorfman. New York: Kelley.

Perlman, Mark (1982). 'Schumpeter as a Historian of Economic Thought,' in Helmut Frisch (ed.), *Schumpeterian Economics*, Eastbourne, East Sussex, England: Praeger, 1981, pp. 143–61.

———. (1986). 'Perceptions of Our Discipline: Three Magisterial Interpretations of the History of Economic Thought.' *History of Economics Society Bulletin*, Winter Issue, pp. 9–28.

———. (1990). 'Die Bienen-Fabel: Eine moderne Würdigung,' in von Hayek, Friedrich A., Perlman, Mark, and Kaye, Frederick B. *Bernard de Mandevilles Leben und Werk*. Düsseldorf: Verlagsgruppe Handelsblatt.

Pribram, Karl (1993). *A History of Economic Reasoning*. Baltimore: Johns Hopkins University Press.

Richardson, G. B. (1955). 'Schumpeter's *History of Economic Analysis*.' *Oxford Economic Papers* 7, 136–50.

Robbins, Lionel (1955). 'Schumpeter's *History of Economic Analysis*.' *Quarterly Journal of Economics*, 44, 1–22.

Roll, Eric (Lord Roll of Ipsden) (1938). *A History of Economic Thought*. London: Faber and Faber.

Roscher, Wilhelm Georg Friedrich (1851). *Geschichte der Englishen Volkswirtschafts-lehre*.

———. (1874). *Geschichte der Nationalökonomie in Deutschland*.

Samuelson, Paul A. (1947). *Foundations of Economic Analysis*. Cambridge: Harvard University Press.

Schumpeter, Joseph A. (1908). *Das Wesen und der Hauptinhalt der theoretischen Nationalökonomie (The Nature and Essence of Theoretical Economics)*. Munich and Leipzig (Duncker & Humblot).

———. (1912[35]). *Theorie der wirtschaftlichen Entwicklung (The Theory of Economic Development)*. Leipzig: Duncker & Humblot. There is an English translation by Redvers Opie of the second (1926) revised edition: *The Theory of Economic Development: An Inquiry into Profits, Capital, Credit, Interest, and the Business Cycle*. Cambridge: Harvard University Press, 1934.

———. (1914). *Epochen der Dogmen- und Methodengeschichte*. Tübingen: J. C. B. Mohr. There is an English translation by R. Aris: *Economic Doctrine and Method: An Historical Sketch*. New York: Oxford University Press, 1954.

———. (1939). *Business Cycles: A Theoretical and Statistical Analysis of the Capitalist Process*, in two volumes. New York: McGraw-Hill.

———. (1942). *Capitalism, Socialism, and Democracy*. New York: Harper.

———. (1949). 'Science and Ideology,' *American Economic Review*, 39, 345–59.

———. (1951). *Ten Great Economists from Marx to Keynes*. New York: Oxford University Press.

———. (1954). *History of Economic Analysis*. New York: Oxford University Press.

Spiegel, Henry (1971). *The Growth of Economic Thought*. Durham, NC: Duke University Press.

Swedberg, Richard (1991). *Schumpeter: A Biography*. Princeton: Princeton University Press.

---

35. Swedberg (1991, p. 240) reports that the book actually appeared in 1911.

Stark, W. (1959). 'The "Classical Situation" in Political Economy.' *Kyklos,* 12, 57–65.

Stigler, George J. (1954). 'Schumpeter's *History of Economic Analysis.' Journal of Political Economy,* 82, 344–5.

Taylor, O. H. (1955). 'Schumpeter's *History of Economic Analysis.' Review of Economics and Statistics,* 37, 12–21.

Viner, Jacob (1954). 'Schumpeter's *History of Economic Analysis:* A Review Article.' *American Economic Review* 44, 894–910.

# B. Essays on American Institutionalism

CHAPTER 10

# Political Purpose and the National Accounts

*In chapter 1, textual footnote 11 I have already indicated much of the histori-*
*cal gist of this chapter. After Kuznets went to Harvard in 1961, I visited him*
*quite regularly; the visits became somewhat more frequent during the period*
*of his retirement. As I had with my father, I repeatedly asked him about his*
*life's experiences and the lessons he drew from them.*

*When he was at Hopkins he and his wife, Edith, were splendid hosts, and*
*Naomi and I met many of their visitors, including Paul Webbink and Selma*
*and Raymond Goldsmith. Once I asked him about the basis of his relationship*
*with Webbink, and that led to talk about his establishment of the American*
*system of national income accounting and his tie with Robert R. Nathan.*
*Nathan having been brought into the picture, there was over the years a long*
*discussion of their World War II experience with the War Production Board.*
*After the 1980 Decennial Census, the Russell Sage Foundation commissioned*
*several interpretive studies, and William A. Alonso and Paul Starr, the editors*
*of one of them, asked me to suggest a topic. This chapter was the result. Built*
*around Kuznets's story of his development of an idea in an article on National*
*Income, written for the 1933* Encyclopaedia of the Social Sciences, *and going*
*back to predecessor efforts to measure the distribution of income, the essay*
*traces Kuznets's career during the 1930s and early 1940s, culminating with*
*his disavowal of what the Department of Commerce had done with that idea.*

Economic data are constantly used in the interpretation of economic events
and the formulation of economic policies by both government and the private
sector. But which data are collected and how they are manipulated and analyzed depend on the underlying objectives of a statistical system. If and
when the purposes of a system are redefined, new objectives may require
different choices in data collection and analysis.

First appeared in *The Politics of Numbers*, William Alonso and Paul Starr, eds. (New York:
Russell Sage, 1987) 133–51.

This chapter is part of a larger project on the American contribution to modern empirical
economics. That project has been supported by grants given by The Institute for Advanced Study,
where I was a Member during the 1981–82 academic year, and by the Rockefeller Foundation's
research program at the Villa Serbelloni (Bellagio, Lake Como, Italy), where I was a Resident
Scholar during April–May 1983. It is a pleasant duty to acknowledge their interest and help.

This chapter takes as a case study the growth of national income accounting in the United States from 1933 to the present, focusing on its intellectual origins and changes in objectives during the formative period 1933 to 1948. It is not presented as a comprehensive history of the construction of the national accounts since several excellent histories are already available.[1] I stress as my theme the several shifts in the main uses for which our accounting system has been designed. My interest is to identify changes in the socioeconomic philosophical choices underlying the measurement of national income.

My point of departure is the recognition that those who participated in designing the national accounts, beginning in 1933, have had, at different times, distinct and partially conflicting objectives. Economists have wanted variously to use the national accounts to measure or identify: (1) the distribution of income and of the costs of government; (2) the extent of unused capacity in various sectors of the economy; (3) the sources of economic growth; (4) pecuniary well-being; and (5) the fluctuations of the business cycle so as to design economic stabilization policies.

---

1. In 1980 the U.S. Department of Commerce published *Reflections of America: Commemorating the Statistical Abstract Centennial*. Within it there are several short chapters dealing with various aspects of economic materials as they emerged in the Statistical Abstracts; in particular, see John Kenneth Galbraith, "The National Accounts: Arrival and Impact," pp. 75–80.

There are several excellent histories of the development of the American government's interest in statistical material. Among the best is the one by Joseph W. Duncan and William C. Shelton, *Revolution in United States Government Statistics, 1926–1976* (Washington, D.C.: U.S. Department of Commerce, Office of Federal Statistical Policy and Standards, 1978), which covers in detail and with apparent accuracy much of the material I summarize here. What it does not do, and what I shall undertake, is to discuss the foregone choices made by the designers of our national account system. But it goes far beyond my efforts in describing the variety of social, including economic, statistics that the federal government has undertaken. It was followed by a second volume, intended to peer into the future, Duncan and Shelton, *A Framework for Planning U.S. Federal Statistics for the 1980's Government Statistics, 1926–1976* (Washington, D.C.: U.S. Department of Commerce, Office of Federal Statistical Policy and Standards, 1978).

There are also two indispensable summary histories of the American experience in the development of its present national accounting institutions. The first is by Carol S. Carson, "The History of the United States National and Product Accounts: The Development of an Analytical Tool," *Review of Income and Wealth* 21 (June 1975):153–81. A second is by John W. Kendrick, "The Historical Development of National Income Accounts," *History of Political Economy* 2 (Fall 1970):284–315, which goes back to before the period covered by Carson. But I have found no historic treatment, particularly with the fascinating early English experiments, that begins to touch the quality of "The Use of National Income Statistics in English Economic Thought in the Seventeenth and Eighteenth Centuries," chap. 2 of George Jaszi, "The Concept of National Income and National Product with Special Reference to Government Transactions" (Ph.D. diss., Harvard University, 1946). Another useful account is by Richard Ruggles, "The United States National Income Accounts, 1947–1977: Their Conceptual Basis and Evolution," in Murray F. Foss, ed., *The U.S. National Income and Product Accounts: Selected Topics* (Chicago: University of Chicago Press, 1983).

This discussion of the changes in the principal purposes of national accounting aims to bring out the choices that were faced, the alternatives accepted and rejected, and what the cost of the decisions may have been.

## Origins of National Income Measurement in the United States

Although a few studies of national income and wealth appeared in the midnineteenth century, the first modern study was published in 1896 by Charles B. Spahr, a writer on economic topics. Socialism and the distribution of income and taxation were timely topics, and Spahr's approach carries the appropriate hallmarks. In estimating the distribution of American income and wealth during the 1880s and 1890s, he wanted to determine whether the working classes bore the heaviest burden in financing government. On the basis of his findings he argues that because of regressive taxation, a large and growing share of the cost of the federal government was borne by the laboring class.[2]

Spahr's pro-working class, if not actually socialist, conclusions helped to stimulate a lengthy 1915 study for the period 1850–1910 by Willford Isbell King at the University of Wisconsin. Although King was primarily interested in measuring changes in the distribution of income and wealth, his work reflected the prewar concern that the shift in origins of immigrants to the United States meant the defeat of the Jeffersonian ideal of economic equality. King's conclusions, as I read them, were simultaneously antimonopolist and Malthusian. First, he noted the tremendous growth of manufacturing and other economic output. Second, he concluded that concentration of income was even greater than when Spahr had written, but that much of the change had come at the expense not of the poor but of the middle classes. However, the propensity of the poor (and I interpret this to mean particularly the immigrant poor) to have excessively large families was likely to keep them impoverished, even as average incomes rose.

King's interest in economic class structure continued after he moved to New York University, and when the National Bureau of Economic Research (NBER) was established in 1920, he became one of its earliest professional associates. He undertook to measure national income and its distribution, using estimates from the sources of production. Oswald W. Knauth, another of the early NBER associates, undertook similar measurements, using distributed and undistributed incomes. As the results from the two methods for the period 1909–19 appeared to be the same (within about 7 percent), King and

---

2. This is discussed rather fully in Paul Studenski, *The Income of Nations*, vol. 1 (New York: New York University Press, 1961), pp. 132–34.

Knauth were satisfied that their findings were correct. Published in 1921–22, these findings stressed that concentration of wealth had diminished during the wartime period. King found that the top 5 percent of the population were receiving less of the total national dividend than at the time of his 1915 study. The middle classes seemed to be moving toward greater equality of income.

In an effort to extend his conclusions, King decided to include estimates of unrealized capital gains as an element of income. This decision led to a conflict with several other economists working on the measurement of national income; among these was Sir Josiah Stamp, an English economist. In the exchanges between them, King lost the capital gains battle and apparently much of his professional standing in the subfield of national accounts. In any event, the NBER decided to reform its approach to national income accounting. At this point Simon Kuznets entered the scene. Lest we lose sight too soon of King and his interest, it is worth stressing that his approach to national accounts, unlike Spahr's, focused on the size distribution of income (even more than wealth). What reduced King's influence were his limitations as a statistician, specifically, his reliance upon too-fragile data and his apparent inability to conceptualize alternative approaches to his problem.[3] By 1931, when Kuznets took over the national income work of the NBER, he was already a recognized and, for his age, seasoned scholar. Like Spahr, he had a strong interest in the economics of social class relations.[4] He had by this time written several major works. In the most important, *Seasonal Variations in Industry and Trade* (1933), Kuznets thoroughly analyzed the reliability of available data as well as the problem of choosing the optimal techniques of statistical manipulation. The study provides an imaginative discussion of the underlying political question about which social classes bore the costs and gained the benefits of seasonality in manufacturing.

In his work on national accounts, Kuznets was initially concerned with the same questions that had interested both Spahr and King: (1) whether the poor and the wage workers were bearing a disproportionate (and possibly growing) share of the costs of an industrial society; and (2) whether workers' incomes were rising in relative or in absolute terms. But Kuznets's interests went beyond theirs to the causes of economic growth. Briefly put, as much as he was interested in the old socialist questions about the burdens of the working class, Kuznets was equally and even more interested in the Schumpeterian problem of the triggers of economic growth.

3. King continued his work in the area, even under NBER sponsorship. See Willford Isbell King, *The National Income and Its Purchasing Power* (New York: National Bureau of Economic Research, 1930).

4. See Mark Perlman, "Jews and Contributions to Economics: A Bicentennial Review," *Judaism* 25 (Summer 1976):301–311.

Kuznets's initial explicit work in national accounts is to be found in his article, "National Income." His opening statement is worth quoting because it illustrates the breadth of his ultimate objective:

National Income may be defined *provisionally* as the net total of commodities and services (economic goods) produced by the people comprising a nation; as the total of such goods received by the nation's individual members in return for their assistance in producing commodities and services; as the total of goods consumed by these individuals out of the receipts thus earned; or, finally as the net total of desirable events enjoyed by the same individuals in their double capacity as producers and consumers. Defined in any one of these fashions national income is the end product of a country's economic activity, reflecting the combined play of economic forces and serving to appraise the prevailing economic organization in terms of its returns.[5]

Kuznets then turns his attention to the uses of such information. These include measuring: (1) the comparative productivity of nations; (2) per capita welfare; (3) the constancy of income flow (another per capita welfare consideration); (4) the rate of growth of the nation's economy, if the analysis were maintained over sufficient time; (5) the distribution of income among social classes; and (6) the division of income between consumption and other uses.

Pointing out some difficulties in using available figures, Kuznets accepted as a necessary compromise the idea that national income accounting nets to cruder approximations of income received or consumed. He then asks where the summary of "the combined play of economic forces" might best be seen. Is it at the levels of production, distribution, or consumption? This became his principal operative question. True, each level allows for measurement, but what best measures our objective? Is it mostly an effort merely to summarize the production process, or to appraise its organization, possibly for reasons of augmenting output? Kuznets apparently concluded that income received by individuals "after it leaves the productive units proper and before it has been diverted into the various channels of consumption" provides the best and most versatile measure for the analysis of both welfare and growth.

Among the measurement problems Kuznets faced, none was more difficult than measuring the value of the multifarious activities of government. The economy can be perceived as an interplay of production and consumption forces. On the consumption side are things directly consumed (final product), indirectly consumed (intermediate product), and deferred for later consump-

---

5. Simon Kuznets, "National Income," *Encyclopedia of the Social Sciences*, vol. 11, pp. 205–224 (New York: Macmillan, 1933), p. 205.

tion (inventories, consumer durables, or consumption hoards). On the production side, the evaluation is more or less straightforward in the private sector; the price paid by the buyer is the value of the product or the service. But the question becomes thornier when dealing with such complex institutional realities as the government and the banking system. How does one price those services of the government for which no payment seems to be made? The technique has been to argue that they are worth what is paid for them; but what is paid for them is not for the output but for the input. As the economic role of government expands, the assumption that the value of the output is defined by the cost of the input affects an increasingly important part of our totals.

Ultimately, Kuznets gets to the accounting problem in differentiating between physical and human capital (of course, the latter term was then not in current use). The value of the output of the former is affected by depreciation (even by obsolescence), but it is not easy to find a comparable method for evaluating the changes in the "remaining productive value" of the individual. One can see the value of one's physical capital being diminished as it is being transferred to output. Can one say the same for labor? To Kuznets, as I read his 1933 work, the answer is clearly *no*. But Kuznets's answer, as I understand it, does not satisfy him.

Two additional points should be stressed: Kuznets was critically concerned about the role of economic organization and the societal importance of the distribution of family income. He wanted most to stress his interests in income distribution, economic growth, and the roles played by banking and particularly government institutions in stimulating economic growth. Kuznets did not focus on economic stabilization as an area of comparable importance.

### National Accounting Becomes a Government Function

In June 1932 the U.S. Senate passed a resolution requesting the secretary of commerce "to report . . . estimates of the total national income of the United States for each of the calendar years of 1929, 1930, and 1931." The resolution specified that the work was to be done by the Bureau of Foreign and Domestic Commerce (BFDC). It soon became clear that the bureau's personnel was inadequate to the task. The secretary turned for help to Wesley Clair Mitchell, head of the NBER, who asked Kuznets, now professor of statistics at the University of Pennsylvania, to oversee the establishment of a cadre to organize the new statistical system. Thus, for about two years after January 1933 he was in weekly contact with the department's statistical data-processing unit. In January 1934 Kuznets submitted a 261-page report, which included material for the unasked-for year 1932 as well.

Thus, the first set of governmental accounts came out. Kuznets, however, left the BFDC, returning to the National Bureau where he maintained his interest in national accounts. After an internal struggle, the BFDC did get the national accounting program operationally established.[6] It was Robert F. Martin who stressed that regular and prompt publication of these accounts permitted their use for multiple purposes. He argued that the administration needed accurate and adequately classified national income data in order to design appropriate welfare and economic recovery programs; that the Internal Revenue Service needed such data for making projections, based on a variety of changes in the tax laws; that these data were invaluable to business for market analysis and to scholars for research; and that only the federal government had the resources essential to the checking (thereby insuring the reliability) of the vast amount of data involved. Thus developed an identifiable new objective for national income accounting, namely, an equitable, efficient, reliable, and speedy numbers supply, essential to the experimental functions associated with economic reform through legislative action.

Martin left the BFDC shortly after the report came out and was replaced by one of Kuznets's University of Pennsylvania graduate students, Robert R. Nathan.[7] Nathan's staff, again very small, produced two bulletins: *National Income in the United States 1929–35* (1936), and *National Income in the United States 1929–1936* (1937). The previous format and emphases remained, the only major innovation being revision of some of the earlier estimates. One of the major problems of any government statistical agency is the necessity of getting its data out quickly; speed and accuracy are basically trade-offs, and the obvious solution is not to hold up publication but to publish later revised figures when the corrections become available. By 1937, national income figures began to be published in preliminary *monthly* form. The monthly data were regarded as essential for estimating current and near-future purchasing power and for inferring near-future levels of business output, including the demand for employment.

---

6. Duncan and Shelton, *Revolution,* quote Carol S. Carson, "The History of the United States Income and Products Accounts," as the basis for a lengthy account of bureaucratic infighting about the regularization of the national accounts research work in the Department of Commerce. The problems were apparently legion: (1) Congress had not appropriated funds, (2) Kuznets and those whom he had brought into the effort did not remain with the Commerce Department's Bureau of Foreign and Domestic Commerce (BFDC); (3) the secretary had little sympathy for the effort and refused to allocate funds for printing an updated version (including data for 1933). These 1933 data did appear in the department's *Survey of Current Business,* in the January, August, and November 1935 issues and in the July 1936 issue. The BFDC, largely under the leadership of Willard Thorp and Robert F. Martin, and aided by Winfield Riefler, chairman of the Central Statistical Board, did get the program institutionalized and congressionally funded.

7. Martin went to the National Industrial Conference Board ". . . where he was a frequent critic of the Department of Commerce figures." Duncan and Shelton, *Revolution,* p. 80.

In retrospect, we see that three somewhat unrelated developments occurred during this period. Together they shifted the national accounts system significantly from the broad outlines of Kuznets's 1933 blueprint and from the contextual composition of the 1934 publication. The first was the passage in 1935 of the Social Security Act, which called for massive employee and employer contributions to retirement funds. Combined with welfare (relief) payments and the one-time payment of World War I bonuses to veterans, these transfers put a strain on the simplicity of Kuznets's 1933 definition of payments to business firms and individuals for goods and services provided. The Kuznets definition was accordingly modified, this being the first of several major movements away from his 1933 architectural blueprint.

The second was the publication in 1936 of Maynard Keynes's *The General Theory of Employment, Interest, and Money,* which triggered a major professional effort at redesigning macroeconomic (a word then all but unknown) policies for full-employment stabilization. Looking back, we see clearly that the Keynesian formulation offered a theoretical system, and thereafter many, indeed most, of those who worked on the national accounts wanted their work to reflect and to be integratable with what the Keynesian analysis offered. Kuznets's blueprint did not begin to offer a well-knit theoretical system; indeed, anyone familiar with Kuznets's work recognized his preference for empirical rather than *a priori* research.[8] Thus, with the appearance of a *theory,* certainly something easier to grasp than an endless literature of historical generalizations, the Kuznets-NBER influence among the national-income specialists first acquired a rival in Keynes and later lost considerable ground.

The third major factor entering the stage in this period was the obvious failure of the 1936 business revival, signaled by the business recession of 1937–38, an event that seemed to confirm the fear that the country faced a period of indefinite economic stagnation and large-scale unemployment. This fear so dominated the thinking of the period that the principal focus of the whole accounting system fastened on measuring consumer purchasing power as the means to economic recovery.

Federal peacetime deficit financing, though known to and employed by President Herbert Hoover, had also been well advertised as the principal hallmark of the New Deal recovery program, even before Keynes's book appeared. In Washington, "pump-priming" had become by 1937 a regular if not exactly a successful policy. This perception, later synthesized by Abba Lerner and others as a program of "functional finance," was at the time being

---

8. There was an exchange of correspondence (April through August 1936) between Kuznets and Keynes after the publication of Keynes's *The General Theory of Employment, Interest and Money.* The letters dealt with Keynes's mishandling of data on capital formation. (*The Collected Writings of John Maynard Keynes,* XXIX pp. 188–206).

touted in Washington by Professor Alvin Hansen of Harvard and Lauchlin Currie, assistant director of research and statistics at the Federal Reserve Board. In any case, the kind of economy for which Kuznets's 1933 blueprint had been drawn was less and less the actual case. By the mid- and late 1930s, the federal government's role in the economy had expanded, and whether the Kuznets 1933 perception could have been implemented is now a moot question. In practice, the government's various roles in the economy were held to be *sui generis,* and all its economic activities were segregated for accounting purposes.

As already mentioned, by 1937 monthly national income estimates were being made and published. Another change occurring during this same period was the disaggregation of national accounts by state. Duncan and Shelton report that this series attracted immediate and vast business interest, and by October 1938 the estimates included: (1) the addition of direct relief payments and the veterans' bonus; (2) the deduction of the workers' contribution to the Social Security funds; and (3) the addition of payments from these same funds.[9] What was now being emphasized was the frequent measurement of short-period changes of potential purchasing power by local area.

Emphasis on measuring purchasing power, the principal Keynesian key to unlocking the door to economic recovery, took other forms as well. After several somewhat unsuccessful efforts, the Commerce Department in 1941 began to publish reports on retail sales, manufacturers' inventories, orders, and shipments. The department also took into account Kuznets's own post-1934 work on commodity flows and capital formation. The goal here was further to improve the quality of the consumer expenditure data.

At this point two shifts could clearly be seen. The first was the rapid emergence of a wholly new set of economic problems. The characteristic Depression crisis of overproduction was replaced rapidly by the 1938–40 rearmament crisis of underproduction; chronic unemployment was giving way to the specter of price inflation. The other shift was more personal. Kuznets's one-time student, Milton Gilbert, took over the leadership of the whole national economic account effort.

For expository purposes I discuss the Gilbertian influence first. Gilbert, unlike his immediate predecessors, not only felt thoroughly qualified to take charge of the national accounts program; he also decided to change the focus of its presentation to make it readily adaptable to the incoming Keynesian macroeconomic mode. In brief, the new format was a standardized report meant to mirror at short intervals (not impeded by delayed preparation) the economy as it was actually operating, from the standpoint of both its immediate past and the quickly developing inflationary pressures. With the *tour*

---

9. Duncan and Shelton, *Revolution.*

*d'horizon* offered by the mirror, policies could be quickly modified as their shortcomings became evident.

It is important to stress that at about this time the British, under the leadership of James Meade and Richard Stone, were compiling for Churchill's war cabinet an accounts system that would reveal any possible slack areas that could be filled with orders for war material. In his biography of Maynard Keynes, Roy Harrod describes the origins of this wartime attempt to assess the economic capabilities of the British economy.[10] These origins, in Harrod's view, lay with E. A. G. Robinson's efforts to implement Keynes's *How to Pay for the War*. Robinson brought together Meade and Lionel Robbins, the former something of a Keynesian (although in truth many of the so-called Keynesian principles Meade had anticipated before 1936). Meade was then paired with Stone, and in the winter of 1940–41 the two rushed through an analysis of income and expenditure, published at the time of the 1941 budget.[11] The English developments influenced American events, but what was happening on the American side proceeded almost completely independently.

The American events of the period 1940–42 are remarkable for many reasons. Talent was quickly identified and employed; new concepts were quickly developed and discussed; and the national accounts system as we know it seemed to emerge almost overnight. True, in a general academic way, the British in some sense were leading the way; the publication in 1940 of John R. Hicks's "The Valuation of the Social Income" opened the eyes of the profession to the wholly new set of wartime "overconsumption" problems. Hicks's terminology was not completely new, although his use of the term *gross national product* (initially used in a slightly different sense by Clark Warburton in 1934) gave a completely different slant to the national income analysis routine. GNP was defined as national income plus business taxes plus depreciation and other capital charges. It included not only civilian economic activity but also government expenditures, which in wartime were particularly important. Hicks's paper introduced the basic equation:

$$GNP = C + I + G$$

where $C$ stands for consumption, $I$ for investment, and $G$ for government expenditure.

---

10. Roy Forbes Harrod, *The Life of John Maynard Keynes* (New York: Kelley, 1969).

11. Stone (now Sir Richard) and Meade have individually recounted to me the skimpiness of the resources allocated to them by the Treasury in the first stages of their efforts. Initially denied even a calculator, they were able to proceed only because Stone, very much the junior of the two, owned a hand-operated model. Their stories of Meade's looking up the numbers and Stone's pushing the buttons and turning the crank, only to discover empirically that comparative advantage lay in the reversal of the assignments, emphasizes more than anything else the magnificence of their achievement.

While the British were making these innovations, developments in the United States led to the formation of the now-familiar national accounts system. Robert R. Nathan and Simon Kuznets, at that time both employed at the War Production Board, were responsible for estimating how quickly and to what levels the economy would be able to switch to war production.[12] The accomplishments of the Kuznets-Nathan group during the less than two years between 1941 and 1943 are awe-inspiring. The board had informed the White House that the maximum output goals for 1942 would amount to about 40,000 tanks and about 50,000 airplanes. The day after receiving these estimates, President Roosevelt informed the Congress that his goal was 60,000 planes for 1942 and no less than 125,000 for 1943. He "upped" the tank promise for 1942 from 40,000 to 45,000 and for 1943 he "promised" 75,000. And he revised the output of merchant shipping, which the board had thought would amount to 7 million tons in 1942, to 8 million tons for that year and an all but unbelievable 20 million tons in 1943. Such promises gave rise to two related problems: Were the plans *feasible,* and what would be their *inflationary* impact?

The effort by Nathan and Kuznets to work out the principles of American military procurement planning was to become one of the great technical triumphs in the history of the economics discipline. The Nathan-Kuznets group estimated how and where the American economy could summon the resources to meet the new targets. In effect, it was telling the armed forces

---

12. On January 16, 1942, the president created the War Production Board, with Donald M. Nelson as its chairman. Nelson set up several staff (advisory) bodies that reported directly to him and whose duties were to advise him with regard to the actual orders his office was issuing concerning production allocation priorities. One of these advisory committees was the Office of Progress Reports, headed by Stacy May. Another, set up in February 1942, was the Planning Committee, its chairman was Robert Nathan. In May 1942 Nathan asked Kuznets to join him. Kuznets had previously been working with the statistical group, an association he managed to continue. Somewhat earlier (before the Japanese attack on Pearl Harbor), the administration had felt the pressure, largely focused by a French refugee, Jean Monnet (who was an official on the joint Anglo-French purchasing commission), to formulate an overall production program designed to achieve military victory in Europe. By the end of September 1941, even before the United States was formally at war, the administration established a $150 billion Victory Program, which was targeted for achievement of its goal and invasion of the European continent by mid-1943. The Victory Program gave rise to the feasibility and the inflationary gap questions. The events of Pearl Harbor, of course, changed the previous plans. The goals were revised upward, thus exacerbating the twin problems of feasibility and inflation. In due course, Kuznets prepared and Nathan sent several memoranda to Nelson regarding the achievable limits. These memoranda were subjected to what eventually was harsh criticism. The history of the bureaucratic skirmishing is well detailed in John E. Brigante, "The Feasibility Dispute: Determination of War Production Objectives for 1942 and 1943" (Washington, D.C.: Committee on Public Administration Cases, 1950). In the end, there were several historically important results; the critical one was that the Kuznets-Nathan approach was accepted by the military not only for the prosecution of World War II but also for its future military planning.

that military procurement was a "science." To ask for too little was to prolong the conflict; to ask for too much was to inflate costs without producing significantly more. To look to the wrong sectors was to hamper technological innovation; to look to the right sectors was to minimize the pecuniary and nonpecuniary costs of the war. Anyone who thinks that the armed forces, particularly the army, were willing students has only to look at the narrative of John Brigante. But anyone who concludes that the lesson cannot be successfully taught has only to look at the record. The War Production Board, over violent opposition and at the cost of the physical and emotional exhaustion of Nathan and Kuznets, managed to show how the goals could be achieved. This they did by relying on the national accounts system, as then produced by the Commerce Department, and on the accounts for capital formation that Kuznets had developed. What they helped to accomplish for 1942 was the expansion of national output by $17 billion through (1) more intensive use of the existing plant (for example, lengthening the work week by eliminating overtime pay for anything less than forty-five hours per week); (2) the transfer to war-related purposes of $7 billion worth of resources normally devoted to civilian capital formation (for example, residential or commercial construction); (3) depleting accumulated inventories (mostly consumer goods) in the amount of $4.5 billion; (4) reducing consumer demand by $7 billion by increasing taxation (not a signal success) and by consumer goods rationing; and (5) a variety of other, somewhat smaller, shifts designed to release resources.

As mentioned, Gilbert had taken charge of the national income accounts program in 1941. His acknowledgment of Kuznets's ideas, added to his grasp of what Meade and Stone were doing in Britain, led to the development of a new blueprint. His plan reflected not only the omnipresent specter of American defense preparations but also the Keynesian macroeconomic theoretical system, with its emphasis on postwar full-employment, compensatory government investment if necessary, and a federal program of income redistribution. In 1942 Gilbert published two critically important expository articles, using the national income/gross national product approach to explain both the wartime production allocation problem and the likely impact of the proposed solutions. His "War Expenditure and National Production" is an educational *tour de force,* including a projection of gross national product to fiscal 1943 in 1941 prices. In December 1941, he had laid out much of this analysis in a paper read before the American Statistical Association. Both works drew heavily on "The Construction of Tables of National Income, Expenditure, Savings, and Investment," published by Meade and Stone in 1941. Gilbert made two major contributions to the program. First, he was integrating actual recent numerical estimates with a Keynesian theoretical analysis to answer such timely questions as (1) how the peacetime economy could be converted to war purposes with the least inflationary impact; and (2) how the essential needs of the civilian economy could be successfully protected from wartime demands. Second, he was using the *Survey of Current Business,* with its fast printing turnaround time, to explain immediately the economics of the current war-production effort. [13]

National income accounting during these wartime years had as its avowed purpose the reallocation of productive resources and encouragement of certain areas of economic growth needed to win the war. But scarcely concealed by this purpose was Gilbert's continuing pedagogical effort to provide a set of national accounts mirroring the economy to show what government policy was doing and what, perhaps, it could do. War exigencies led the national accounts far from the types of objectives that either Spahr or King had had in mind.

One point should be added, indeed, stressed. The Commerce Department officials were greatly influenced by the English macroeconomic theory formulated largely by Keynes and the social accounting system worked out first by Meade and Stone and then largely refined by Stone. Hicks's *The Social Framework,* first published in 1942, helped to popularize national accounting. In 1945 the publication of an American edition under the adapted title, *The Social Framework of the American Economy,* capped the transformation of the discipline, which had so recently depended on Marshall's *Principles of Economics* plus the modifications regarding deviations from competition introduced by Edward Chamberlin and Joan Robinson.

The postwar growth of the American economy reinforced the economics profession's great confidence in the scientific basis of its discipline. That confidence reflected a well-grounded satisfaction that the newly developed expertise displayed by economists, achieved at forced draft, could make it not only possible but also almost easy to avert the economic disaster of the 1930s. The war experience had shown that economists like Gilbert and his associates, to say nothing of the more senior architects like Kuznets and Nathan, apparently could bring order out of chaos and organize quickly the material require-

---

13. In all, the *Survey of Current Business* published the new research results including articles on changes in consumer income and expenditure (Bangs, 1942); on the gross flow of finished commodities and new construction (Shaw, 1942); on surveying the gross national product, 1929–41 (Gilbert and Bangs, 1942); on quarterly estimates of construction (Klein, 1942); on corporate profits and national income by quarters, 1938–42 (Smith and Merwin, 1942); on the distributive costs of consumption commodities (Fowler and Shaw, 1942); on the distribution of income payments by state, 1929–41 (Creamer and Merwin, 1942); on reviewing the national income and the war effort for the first half of 1942 (Gilbert and Bangs, 1942b); on estimating national business inventories, 1928–41 (Hance, 1942); on consumer expenditures for selected groups of services, 1929–41 (Denison, 1942); on monthly dividend payments, 1941–42 (Smith, 1942); and a general recapitulation of the 1942 national income and national product (Gilbert and Jaszi, 1943).

ments for victory. If the war gave the medical profession antibiotics, it gave economists new tools and techniques and comparable optimism about what their future role would be. Immediately at the war's end, the American group on national income accounting turned to preparing an integrated set of accounts. It appeared in a supplement to the July 1947 *Survey of Current Business* under the title, "National Income and Product Statistics of the United States, 1929–46." Its publication seemed like the keystone to the economists' arch—theory and observation now fit neatly together.

The 1947 publication drew heavily on Richard Stone's systematizing of social accounts. Using the form of traditional double-entry bookkeeping, it introduced several elements that were not strictly a debit-asset comparison. The supplement was a lengthy document with forty-two annual tables (covering more or less completely the data for the years 1929–46), five quarterly tables for 1939–46, and a monthly table for 1929–46. An industry breakdown included twenty tables in manufacturing and an additional thirty-seven in other areas. Care was taken to explain thoroughly the sources of the data. In addition, the data were presented so that for the first time it was possible "to compare corporate profits with wages, salaries and supplements paid by corporations." The whole was displayed in six basic tables, called (in the tradition of double-entry bookkeeping) "T-accounts": National Income and Product Account; Consolidated Business Income and Product Account; Consolidated Government Receipts and Expenditures Account; Rest of the World Account; Personal Income and Expenditure Account; and Gross Saving and Investment Account.

The 1947 study was widely hailed and extensively reviewed. But it met with serious criticism from the original architect, Kuznets. In a lengthy critique published in 1948, Kuznets repeated his position that any "view of national income as a *net* product total . . . can be defined only in relation to *some end-goal of economic activity.*" But the Commerce Department did not clearly define the end-goal.

Kuznets's approach is characteristically historical. From the time of Quesnay the conventional approach had been to perceive a country's economy as an aggregation of component sectors connected by continuous flow relationships. Kuznets writes:

> One may therefore ask, what is the specific advantage of the approach via a system of economic or social accounts? How does it help a student who is already aware of the desirability of presenting not merely single national totals but of articulating them by significant components at different stages of economic circulation? Does a system of accounts help the student deal with the vexing problems of scope, netness, and con-

sistency of valuation that must be resolved when national income is defined as a measure of an economy's *net product?*[14]

Having thus put the question, Kuznets finds that a simple answer, given what the group has done, is improbable. The difficulty is the ambiguity of their use of the term "account." On some occasions they have used it in the conventional, narrow sense of debits contrasted with assets; on other occasions, they have used it to "connect" two separate estimates of some entity like gross national product. In the end he concludes:

> There is little in the technique of the system of accounts in and of itself to help us determine the proper scope of national income and the observable flows that represent net yields and those which, from the standpoint of the national economy, represent costs; . . . and the significant sectors to be distinguished at any level of economic circulation. Indeed, examination of the report fails to convey the impression that the setting up of the accounts assisted in any way in solving these problems of definition and distribution. On the contrary, the impression is that these problems were solved without benefit of the system of accounts, and that the system of accounts was constructed to fit the solutions. Consequently, the statement in the report that "the accounts . . . show . . . how the whole is derived as the sum of the parts" . . . cannot be intended to imply that the cast of the accounts determined in any way either the parts or the whole.[15]

Kuznets is clearly not overwhelmed by the technique of setting up T-accounts. They are at best a neutral means to illustrate what one wants to show:

> Providing one exercises full freedom in deciding what is a transactor group, what is a transaction, and what the economic meaning of a transaction is from the viewpoint of the economy at large, a set of accounts is like a blank notebook: One can write in it anything one wishes. And this is in fact what the report does: It recognizes families living in their own houses as transactor groups, although it excludes illegal firms which are more obviously a group of transactors; it classifies retention of product by farmers as a transaction, but does not classify tax collection by government as a transaction representing charges for services rendered. One

---

14. Kuznets, *Income*, pp. 151–152.
15. Kuznets, *Income*, p. 153.

may agree with these decisions or not; there is no sign that the system of accounts affected them in any way.[16]

I read the Kuznets review principally as the assessment by an economic institutionalist about the Procrustean effect that economic theory seems always to have had. And it is precisely this point that must not be buried as the data collection and data presentation processes proceed.

My conclusion would be different were the system of accounts to stand not for merely another way of casting statistical tables, but for something more substantial—the corpus of accounts as they are *in fact* formulated and used by business enterprises and other economic institutions. If one were willing to accept the judgments of the various economic units as to what they think their net income or product is, as expressed in their accounts, one could resolve many conceptual and classification problems. *But obviously no such acceptance is feasible when the definition and distribution of national income is governed by some theoretical concept of the operation of the economy.*[17]

Withal, however, Kuznets has to admit that the national income experts cannot in fact accept the businessmen's estimates; they have, instead, to try to fashion more stable measures than the latter would give them. What seems to bother him is that what these experts have fashioned relied too heavily on the Keynesian *a priorism,* and too little on their own independent work. This is a matter of judgment. Kuznets's unchanging essential definition remains:

The final goal of economic activity is provision of goods to consumers, that final products are those turned out during the year to flow either to consumers or to capital stock (for the ultimate benefit of future consumers), and that everything else, by the nature of the case, is intermediate product whose inclusion in the output total would constitute duplication.[18]

But Kuznets makes his complaint most strongly about the way that Gilbert et al. have handled the governmental account, something so complicated that it should not be swept under a single rubric (or carpet). He argues that inclusion of government goods "that are to be consumed either by business enterprises or by society at large for shoring up its own organizational

16. Kuznets, *Income,* p. 153.
17. Kuznets, *Income,* p. 153. Emphasis added.
18. Kuznets, *Income,* p. 156.

structure . . . involves duplication. . . . The total we are seeking is that of *product,* of the end-result of activity—not of the volume of *activity* itself."[19]

Kuznets's review then treats in detail the handling of product totals and the national income total. He stresses the changes that this report introduces from his earlier 1934 Commerce Department work. He notes his differences from the English group's work and also takes care to identify how much of the deviation of the 1947 practice was introduced to handle the special case of a war economy. Both of the factors had, he allows, their one-time reasons. His point is, however, that those reasons impede rather than contribute to the understanding of the growth and operation of the economy under more normal conditions. In the end, Kuznets's position is that many of the changes are matters of arbitrary judgment, and what has been lost is the connective link with the history of the efforts to measure the dynamic qualities of national economic growth; who bears the burdens and why; and the many efforts made in the 1920s at the NBER to determine whether different approaches would lead to substantially different answers. In his assessment, the new system veiled the real pecuniary transactions in the economy. The institutionalization of the accounting system was purchased at the expense of considering the ever-changing philosophical underpinnings that constituted the essential purpose for the exercise.

Thereafter, Kuznets turns to discussing the impact of the group's revisions from the figures he had earlier derived in order "to show the changes in the magnitudes of major components of the national totals both on the income flow and the final product approaches" and to make some comments about the margins of error associated with the new figures.

And what was their reply? Gilbert and his associates open by agreeing with Kuznets that no system of accounts will in itself answer all of the questions that rightly should be asked. But they go on immediately to assert that what they have produced is superior to anything previous (including specifically Kuznets's own 1941 *National Income and Its Composition*). They justify their work on pragmatic grounds, which they appear to believe is a criterion that Kuznets would accept. There are five reasons for what they have done: (1) their system reveals clearly the structure of the economy; (2) it forces consistency and thus aids in the handling of socioeconomic policy problems; (3) it parallels pedagogical material currently in use; (4) its framework is sufficiently flexible to permit further improvements; (5) it provides material in such a way that most conclusions can be achieved by alternative routes, thus making checking possible.

From the standpoint of our original question, the Commerce group's objectives seem far more short-run and ahistorical than the kinds of things that

---

19. Kuznets, *Income,* p. 156–157.

had earlier attracted Spahr, King, and Kuznets. Specifically, Gilbert and his colleagues, as Gilbert wrote in 1945, were "not trying to measure welfare but the value of production from a business point of view." And while there have been many changes in the national accounting system since 1948, the changes have occurred within the framework of the 1940s.

Kuznets's criticism reflected an articulated doubt about the implicitly Procrustean nature of the Keynesian theoretical system. Most economists, trained along Keynesian lines, would not have shared Kuznets's reservations, at least not until the early 1970s, when the era of fine-tuning was over along with the general belief that the Keynesian system contained the solution to all important macroeconomic problems.

But it is not the loss of supreme confidence in the perfection of macro-economic theory, as worked out since the 1936 Keynes formulation, that explains the shifts in the national accounts since 1947. In the ensuing years, the accounts underwent refinements as well as extensions into new areas, or, more precisely put, began to include the careful measurement of additional national economic phenomena, such as income distribution by size of share and changes in labor and total factor productivity.

While several committees from time to time have advised the national income unit on how and why it ought to change its procedures, the unit has largely pursued its 1948 pattern. From the standpoint of the set of questions put at the beginning of this chapter, the point is clear. We have institutionalized and expanded a national accounting system to offer us answers to many of the various questions that prompted work in national income measurement. We have surely improved the coverage of data as well as their quality, but whether the project can ever be properly finished remains a moot point. Kuznets's original view, that the end-goals essentially determined the statistical means, remains viable. Surely the failure in recent years of our capacities to measure the benefits of pollution control, affirmative action, and better occupational safety standards, to say nothing of controlling the costs of entitlement programs, suggests that we know a good deal less than we thought. The loss of confidence in macroeconomic forecasting, even in the relevance of macroeconomic descriptions, is evidence of this judgment. On the other hand, there are those like Richard and Nancy Ruggles who are confident that a unique social accounting system will produce answers to all of the questions:

> It is now generally recognized that national accounts have three major functions: They serve as the coordinating and integrating framework for all economic statistics; they give timely and reliable key indicators on the performance of the economy; and they illuminate the relationships among the sectors of the economy that are fundamental to an understand-

ing of its functioning. During the past two decades, both the availability of data for national accounting systems and the uses of these systems have grown. . . . At the same time, the increasing complexity of economic and social problems has led to more sophisticated types of analysis. . . . The emphasis of policy and analytic interest has changed for an exclusive focus on aggregate output to questions of distribution, and to social, as well as purely economic concerns. This changing emphasis has significantly broadened the range of data for which national accounts can serve as a framework, while the rapidly increasing and complexity of the data have intensified the need for a broader framework.[20]

In sum, if there is a lesson to the history of the national accounts, it is that much is to be gained by looking not only at the finished product but also at the original architectural plans. The building process, by its very nature, modifies the original vision. Whether these modifications, created by choice or by the exigencies of the moment, should remain as dominant decisions may be the real question. If so, it can be answered only by the appearance of a new master architect, conscious and capable of perceiving and designing new answers not only to the old questions but also to those that are emerging.

---

20. Richard Ruggles and Nancy D. Ruggles, "Integrated Economic Accounts for the United States, 1947–80," *Survey of Current Business* (May 1982), vol. 62.

CHAPTER 11

# Understanding the "Old"
# American Institutionalism

*This chapter, originally presented as a paper to the Charles Gide Society's 1992 meeting in Marseilles, offers my explanation of what Bates Clark and three others (Veblen, Mitchell, and Commons) were trying to do in their efforts to establish what Commons was later to call institutionalism. The paradigms about which economic orthodoxy had been built involved Locke's political and economic answers to Hobbes, namely limited government; the inalienable individual rights of life, liberty, and estate (sometimes referred to as property); and the source of ownership through the act of physical production (i.e., labor). I believe that these four Americans sought to supplement the Lockean outlook by offering companion paradigms. One such paradigm was the unavoidable role of capital; another was a derivative of Shaftesbury's Moral Sense, in this instance having to do with the nature of individual motivation; and a third focused on Genossenschaft, suggesting that the right of entry into the bargaining process of the market, itself, involved paradigmatic interpretations. Combinations of these sets of ideas became the principal heterodoxy in American academic economics during the inter–World War years.*

The "older" American Institutional Economics is often perceived and described (cf. Samuels, [1987c]), particularly by those who neither know or want to know much about it, as monolithically mostly anti-abstract theory, but such is a silly judgement, and has too often been made by people who ought to know better. For the more serious, it is traditional to identify three kinds of "old school" American institutionalism: Veblenian, Mitchellian, and Commonsonian. Each of these is related, but it is an error to lump them. My main intent here is to show from what each was generated and how their impacts were primarily directed at diverse groups within and without academia.

   The principal underlying premise for all of them was that the study of economic relationships was of a "long run" nature, and each was contextually, that is time and space, bound. All three writers were American midwestern-

*Revue d'Economie Politique* 102 (1992):281–95.

ers, and each was clearly a product of the economic civilization which had emerged in the decades after the American Civil War during a time when the priority of an economic need for union over a political tradition of voluntary state federalism was accepted as obvious.

By present standards each was nationalistically optimistic; for them America was a bold experiment in the absorption of European immigrants, acculturation to what they perceived as an English Common Law (preferably Whig) heritage, and a land of close to infinite moral improvement. Their basic political culture they saw as an outgrowth of English political experience during the seventeenth century.

### John Bates Clark, the "Abraham" of American Economics

The dominant imaginative figure in their economics education was John Bates Clark,[1] preeminent as an American economic philosopher and Theorist. Bates Clark was a man of two sides; the student of the nature of capital, and the student of Catallactics. Clark was actually the dominant pedagogue in Thorstein Veblen's own schooling, and as Mitchell was one of Veblen's students and friends, the filiation of the Clarkian sets of ideas can be reasonably suggested. I recently discussed Clark's impact on Commons' thinking and I refer you to that article to explain the details of that connection (Perlman [1991a]).

Clark's work in the 1880s and 1890s, during the most intellectually formative years of the three, involved rationales for the rights of various social classes at the social bargaining table (where distribution takes place). Briefly put, he asked: "Why were not only laborers and entrepreneurs but those whom Marx snarled were 'capitalists' essential to all economic processes?" Or, "Was there anything special about capitalists which gave them their uniqueness aside from their holding, according to the institutions of the time, scarce resources?"

Clark, by nature a moral philosopher, saw his principal role as the employer of persuasive morality in the discussion of certain economic rights. Educated in Bismarckian Germany, with all of its paternalistic plans for social welfare, and a founder in 1885 of the anti-pure-laissez-faire American Economic Association, he seems to have been fascinated with capitalists, a distasteful aggressive parvenu class, which had seemingly cynically rejected any obligation to exercise any traditional *noblesse oblige,* and, instead, openly avowed exercising its economic power with and its slavish emulation of the

---

1. For a life of John Bates Clark, see Dewey (1987).

worst of eighteenth century English and French aristocratic consumptionism. They were both aesthetically and morally distasteful to a kindly man of simple tastes and personal self-discipline. Why, he seemed to ask, were they as well as landlords and workers entitled to any part of the social product? His question was why should those who merely advance capital be entitled to a share (progressively large) of the social product.

Clark understood well the historic importance of the role of property rights in America. He had no trouble understanding the importance of labor; to which was added a conviction that workers were not doomed by some Iron Law of Wages to no more than subsistence. And he grasped fully the claim of landed property owners. His innate Christian Socialism suggested to him that intergroup understanding and cooperation could smooth the essential inequities of social bargaining power.

To understand Clark, one has to grasp the essentials of the British and particularly the American political experience (for a contrary view see Homan [1928], Chapter 1). It goes back to Thomas Hobbes' seminal book, *The Leviathan*, which introduced (1) empiricism as *the* method of discovering the sources of truth, (2) the idea that without a social contract every man feared every other man, and (3) the premise that without an effective (meaning functioning) government contract the social contract would not be enforced. Hobbes, who had been tutor to Charles II, was not a believer in the Divine Right of Kings theory because his empirical method (observation) had led him to judge that the largest portion of right was clearly might.

Much of the next 150 years was spent in answering Hobbes's assertion that force was the heart of any system of government, and that government alone (the monopoly of force) is what saves men from the rapacious greed and brutality of other men. For our purposes John Locke's answer is the most trenchant. While the Lockean argument involved many things, of which I mention principally two; (*a*) the unalienable right to property (estate) and, (*b*) the property right being based on previous individual labor-input. No supporter of the ecclesiastical hierarchy, Locke thought that the individual dealt directly with his God, and that God had given every man three intertwined undeniable rights—life, liberty, and property. Life is so basic, that no threat is worth voluntarily yielding one's life. Liberty, he defined as the right to move "horizontally" from an unpleasant society or situation to one of one's preference; only slaves lack this right, and Locke was not sympathetic to slavery.

Locke held that the property right was coequal to the other two since without property no one man could effectively enjoy the other two. Moreover, in suggesting that the original source of the property right was associated with the intermingling of one's labor with things, he made work (so repugnant to Plato) the cornerstone of man's achievement. Labor-input was the source of the property right.[2] As one can quickly see, the Lockean perception of the relationship between labor and property was immediately applicable in the case of British colonists taking unimproved land in the New World.[3]

Locke is not only the grandfather of the formal structure of the American political system, but in a metaphorical sense he is also the grandmother of (some of the finer things of our culture) the nobility of work, the rights of labor, and the importance of enjoying the fruits of one's labor. Even now the Lockean system remains the name of the principal game in the land.

### Thorstein Veblen's Interpretation and Legacy[4]

By way of contrast, Veblen thought that the emphasis should be on an essentially instrumentalist right to create goods and services. He approved of and stressed the 'engineers', not the 'merchants' mentality; the paramountcy of making things, not the making of money. The Lockean tradition, as he perceived the pecuniary society, may have served as an earlier American *Zeitgeist,* but he wanted this engineering creativity to serve as the present and future *Zeitgeist.* To that end his system tried to explain the psychology of the individual and the behavioral relationship between groups making up society. One cannot do brief justice to the subtlety of Veblen's reasoning, but in general he thought the ordinary man was endowed with four instincts: The acquisitive (self-centered); the parental (the non-self-centered and generous); workmanship (the one denoting pride in creation and competency); and, idle curiosity (the one tying imagination to workmanship). Left to his own devices the typical man, "personally ploughing his Candidian field", set out to improve his lot, particularly aggrandize his acreage. If for institutional reasons he was not able to advertise his success by greater investment in acreage, he was wont to advertise by more noticeable consumption.

The simple elements of this schema plus the imaginative use of pseudo-

---

2. The Roman (or earlier dominant) view was that the property right was accorded to the discoverer or the first one who claimed the right; later it was amended to incorporate the notion that rights derived from society, if the courts held that yours was the prior claim, were your right. There is a certain biblical logic to the Lockean view: In the beginning there was the land (meaning resources) and there was man. "By the sweat of his brow" man fashioned the resources and thus they became his. In the course of time these improved or fashioned resources were bought and sold, but insofar as anyone improved resources not thereafter considered part his, that person had to be compensated by for that labor (as a quitclaim)—otherwise the product was partly owned by anyone who had added to the fashioning of it.

3. Locke's argument fitted in beautifully with his position that since the Native Americans had not invested any personal labor in the land, that land was without any owner. Locke, as the friend and employee of Lord Shaftesbury, wrote the Constitution of the Colony of South Carolina, a colonial settlement largely undertaken by the Cooper (the Lords Shaftesbury) family.

4. For a description of Veblen's life and ideas, see Dorfman (1934) and Sowell (1987).

"scientific" rhetoric caught the eye of many, in and out of academia, who were puzzled and disgusted with the excesses which they associated with a pecuniary free enterprise system and, in practice, to comparative excesses in consumption. This social irresponsibility inspired many to form a Veblen cult.

But there was more to that intellectual reaction than merely a cult. Veblen, himself, had initiated and eventually published a comparative study of industrial control decision-making and industrial control in Imperial (Hohenzollern) Germany and the United States (Veblen [1915]). Of the many disciples of the Veblenian tradition, probably none surpassed Adolph Berle, a lawyer and Gardner Means, an economist, who collaborated on the "jewel of the Veblenian crown", *The Modern Industrial Corporation and Private Property*. Published in 1932, and going beyond the basic Veblen schema, it asserted that no longer were the corporate property owners those who ran things and benefitted from their property rights; rather, it was the managerial class, who using "Other Peoples Money" (the title of one of Louis Brandeis's books attacking monopoly power), paid themselves so well that they enjoyed virtually unlimited luxuries of economic goods and social power. Berle was to play an important role in the Roosevelt Administrations of the 1930s, as well as the Temporary National Economic Commission of 1938–1940, devoted to illuminating the degree of interactive corporative leadership, and proved to be one logical outcome of the 1932 book.

Arthur Robert Burns's scholarly 1936 *The Decline of Competition,* and Walton Hamilton and Associates 1938 *Price and Price Policies,* are other critical linkages in the Veblenian tradition, albeit developing analytical frameworks (and even some conclusions) which are not truly envisaged in Veblen's original works. Much of the work going into and the theoretical results coming out of the 1938 Temporary National Economic Commission, was Veblenian. In the 1940s the leading Veblenian was Clarence Ayers,[5] professor of economics at Texas, Austin. There are many today still writing in the tradition; surely John Kenneth Galbraith is a, if not the, paramount example.

One element of Veblen's original approach was his interest in behavioral psychology. The writers whose works I have just cited did not build on that block. Now, a new set of writers, probably not conscious of their legacy from Veblen (and through him to Smith of the Theory of Moral Sentiments and Mandeville and Locke and Hobbes), are creating a new literature, Experimental Economics, which is an effort to approach production and distribution and even the handling of uncertainty from the standpoint of cognitive psychology. In time, they, too will suggest some form of lineal descent from Veblen.

---

5. For a biography of Clarence Ayers, see Samuels (1987a).

### Wesley Clair Mitchell and the School of Modern American Macroeconomic Analysis

Wesley Clair Mitchell[6] enrolled in the first class at the modern American University of Chicago and was its first PhD in economics. There, he studied with Veblen, but his mentor was James Laurence Laughlin,[7] the Department's founder and chairman. Laughlin, preeminently interested in sound money, wanted Mitchell, also working in monetary economics, to assess the validity of Irving Fisher's statement of the quantity theory of money (MV = PT). Using empirical data, Mitchell concluded the 1879 legalization of American Civil War Greenbacks as authorized in 1873, had no perceptible effect on the American price level; ergo Fisher erred, a conclusion satisfactory to Laughlin. More impressive, however, was that Mitchell was not satisfied and went on to explore what did cause price fluctuations. From his detailed analysis of variations in the output, employment levels (hours worked), and prices of specific industries, he constructed statistical charts showing variations. These variations, termed by him "specific cycles", when agglomerated (and this was an artistic study even more than it was one of scientific mechanics) and adjusted for longer than seven year movements (called trends), were termed the business cycle. The business cycle could be dated in terms of peaks, troughs, and points of inflection, and measured in terms of duration. They could also be measured in terms of amplitude (differences between adjoining peaks and troughs) and, the relationship in terms of leads, lags, and amplitudes between specific cycles and the business cycle could be studied to determine regularities.

Mitchell's post-doctoral research dealt with these changes and his findings were published in 1913; the analytical section of that book, Part III, has been republished numerous times under the title, *Business Cycles*. He went on to publish considerably more; two of his best known treatises were the 1927 *Business Cycles: The Problem and Its Setting,* and (with Arthur F. Burns) *Measuring Business Cycles.* But, Mitchell was interested in generalizing upon his professional perception. Profoundly devoted to empiricism, he worried about the relationship between cognition and cogitation. At Columbia University he gave a lengthy course on "Formative Types of Economic Thought," in which he reviewed his extensive knowledge of post-Industrial Revolution economic writings, both empirical and theoretical, and tried to bring some

---

6. By far the best biography of him is the one written in 1953 by his wife, Lucy Sprague Mitchell (a preeminent educator in her own right), *Two Lives: The Story of Wesley Clair Mitchell and Myself.* A knowledge of its contents offers some unusual material, since Mitchell at a critical point in his long and difficult courtship of Miss Sprague wrote several detailed letters highly analytical of what interested him in economics and why.

7. For a life of Laughlin, see Friedman (1987).

personal order out of what he assessed to be professional chaos. These lectures were recorded, and after he died one of his colleagues, Joseph Dorfman (the principal biographer of Veblen) edited them; they remain available in two volumes (Mitchell [1967, 1969]).

In 1920 Mitchell founded the National Bureau of Economic Research, where his impact, seen among those whom he trained and with whom he collaborated, reads inter alia like a list of the American Empiric Economic Academic Greats: Simon Kuznets, Arthur Frank Burns, Milton Friedman, George Stigler, Raymond Saulnier, Moses Abramovitz, Geoffrey Moore, and Solomon Fabricant.

Kuznets,[8] in particular, went on to create a system of national income accounts which serves as the heart of the American system of national accounting (Kuznets [1933a] and Perlman [1987]). Subsequently, Kuznets's 1937 and 1938 studies of American gross capital formation served as the basis for much of the pioneering work he did in converting the American peacetime economy manufacturing to wartime material production (see Perlman [1987] and Brigante [1950]).

Mitchell's studies on the self-generative qualities of specific industry cycles as well as on many areas of measurement including not only those mentioned above, but questions of appropriate index number construction, and definitions of price changes, gave him a much undeserved reputation for dogged fact-gathering, yet, nothing could be further from the truth. It is in his 1937 collection, *The Backward Art of Spending Money,* and in his 1967 and 1969 *Types of Economic Thinking* that one best comes to grips with his perception of what institutional economics principally was.

For Mitchell institutional economics was the study of historical context as the basis for and background of the interpretation of economic (production and distribution) phenomena. The study of historical context involved measurement of relevant variables or their proxies. Measurement while quantitative, was never mechanical; the investigator always had to seek the significance, which Mitchell thought was a cultural phenomenon. To Mitchell most economic theories were simply a set of idiosyncratic explanations of economic events. As they were idiosyncratic they reflected essentially personally-imagined constructs, the relevance of which would ebb and flow even as they were made quantitatively more reliable.

In my mind, Mitchell's preferred successor, Arthur Frank Burns, is likely a more accurate reflection of Mitchell's institutionalism than was Kuznets. Burns's meticulousness regarding data collection and interpretation, his preference for careful and generally small generalizations, and his emphasis on personal intellectual caution at the expense of imaginative creative-

---

8. For a brief biography, see Easterlin (1987).

ness typify Mitchell's own perception of the principal nature of institutionalism. Yet, my perception of Mitchell's essential institutionalism includes Kuznets' contributions. Mitchell and certainly Burns were sophisticated in terms of American and possibly Anglo-American culture; Kuznets' Jewish and Tsarist-Russian cultural roots were on a much broader scale. Accordingly, the comparative yet creative work on national income popularized by Henry Rosovsky and Phyllis Deane, the empiric yet hypothesis-fiddling work done by Richard E. Easterlin, and the kinds of things which Oded Stark and Julian Simon have been doing in demographic economics are well within the Mitchellian strand of institutional economics.

## John Rogers Commons: Institutionalism Based on the Process of Social Bargaining

John Rogers Commons's was a career failure until his appointment, at the age of 42, at Wisconsin in 1904.[9] Early on, he had been fascinated with questions of socio-economic conflict, and in one of my studies of him I list his intellectual development as having gone through four phases: (1) Christian Socialist, (2) quasi-Marxian socialist, (3) Maitland-like legal history, and (4) a self-conscious effort at formulating his own economic institutionalism. Here, our concern is with the last two.

After repeated academic dismissals, Commons, who had studied with the German-educated Christian Socialist Richard T. Ely at Hopkins, was brought by Ely to Wisconsin to administer a Bureau of Industrial Economics, funds for which had been procured for Ely by John Bates Clark. Out of this grew two massive documentary studies. The first, the 10-volume *Documentary History of American Industrial Society,* published in 1910–1911, was an edited collection of records, many of which were legal, describing social conflicts. Commons wrote several truly seminal essays introducing the various sections of this critical contribution. These essays are efforts at understanding the origins, character, and flaws in social interaction on the American economic scene. Rejecting intellectuals' idealism in favor of the grassroots level of "practical" (meaning personally and yet generous) idealism and noting that American workers were made beholden to the industrial system (not necessarily by the fact of capitalists' ownership of the means of production) by the depersonalized nature of external competition (both in the labor factor market and in the product markets), he worked out his own intellectual answer as to why the economy operates, and to some limited extent what palliatives could be introduced to counter the excessive burdens the system put on labor.

---

9. For a discussion of Commons's career and some of his ideas, see Perlman (1958) and Samuels (1958b).

Commons was at Wisconsin during the heyday of the La Follette political reform movement. With the legendary Charles McCarthy,[10] Commons went on to design legislative reforms which both thought would not only palliate the evils of industrial accidents and cyclical unemployment, but which would meet the until-then irrepressible constitutional provisions precluding state interference into the right of individual free contract. The critical initial mechanism was the design and then operation of the Wisconsin Industrial Commission, a government body with mandated advisory groups coming from the leadership of capital and the leadership of labor. Their plan worked, and after some waffling the courts upheld the formula.

While many believe that Commons, because of his being aided by money in part raised by Bates Clark and having directed the writing of the history of organized American labor (Commons and Associates [1918]), was essentially a social reformer, I hold that this was not Commons' personal perception of himself. He was persuaded that his mission was to show how through episodic empiricism (that is, the study of the resolution of specific conflict situations) the American economic system really worked. For a man who had great success in designing governmental programs, he had relatively little faith in any magic associated with some intellectual (and surely legal) assertion of governmental power, unless it were backed by sheer force, and that he believed would prove only to be temporary (cf. Commons [1919–1921]). Rather, he thought that the leadership of capital and the leadership of labor would develop a capacity to govern industry wisely and each specific leadership would be able to educate and control the excesses of its own clientele. He favored "voluntaristic industrial government," not "government in industry," and he sought to lay out both the patterns which had emerged in his America and how he had discerned what those patterns were. The first, "industrial government," depended upon some *elan vital,* which the accountants and he came to call "goodwill." Goodwill was a possible institutional product of a long series of group interactions. Drawing on Maine and Maitland, he saw not contract (which cannot be effectively enforced in the face of social hatred) but growing specified agreement replacing traditional status. Collective bargaining was a process; and if "labor contracts" were the name of the result of each stage, the term "contract" was used in a special sense. Implicit contract is the phrase now more popularly adopted. Much of the work of Ronald Coase and Oliver Williamson is a reconstruction and extension of what Commons described as his results. However, Commons was interested as much in empiric method as he was in the social engineering results associated with his name. His best writing illustrating his method was in the latter chapters of his 1924 *Legal Foundations of Capitalism.* He wrote two books on his method, *Institu-*

---

10. For a biography of Charles McCarthy, see Fitzpatrick (1944).

*tional Economics* in 1934, and *The Economics of Collective Action* (in my view better entitled, "Investigational Economics") published posthumously in 1950. Both are self-conscious efforts to return the study of economics to an interest in the communications devices which parties, active in factor- and product-markets, construct and modify in their attempts to signal desires for change.

### Criticisms of American Institutionalism

We have neither the space nor any need to survey all of the criticisms, a good many of which were focussed on what was perceived as the "institutional-ists'" scornful assessment of mainstream economic theoretical analysis. Suffice it to say that what has now turned up as Cartesian theory was seen by all three as intellectual games, perhaps worthy of firstrate minds, but certainly of little interest to them.

Rather, they focussed on using some form of empiricism to establish their concepts. Excogitation (what Francis Bacon once termed the "spider spinning glorious webs out of its own mind") was to be avoided; accordingly, they eschewed abstractions.

The major criticism of Veblen was that he was destructive. He was not interested in catallactics; he was scornful of trying to make economics into a bench science; and he, personally a loner holding preference for argumentation and differentiation, passed a long career flouting social and professional norms. His rebelliousness was attractive to some; to most it was sophomoric.

The major criticism of Mitchell was that he was like Bacon's ant, only interested in accumulating mountains of data and trying to package them. Tjalling Koopmans, in a famous 1946 review article, lambasted Mitchell for eschewing scientific (abstract) analysis. Just as cats can look at kings, I will assert that Koopmans erred; I ascribe the target and the tone of his essay as principally an effort to dethrone statistical indexing and to enthrone in its place econometric modelling.

Mitchell admitted his respect for abstractions; he just was not convinced that any of the economic abstract theory that was being distributed as universal wisdom justified its claim. While any perusal of his personal record will reveal how ambitious he could be, that same perusal will also reveal how intellectually careful and modest he was.

The major criticism of Commons was that his investigational system eschewed catallactics, commonly perceived as a study of exchange from the standpoint of prices.

The three were lumped together because they were seen as self-conscious attacks on Marshallian neo-classical economics. Elsewhere I have argued that lumping was an error, since only Veblen's work fell into that category (Perlman [1977]). If there are two sides of economics, the "inside" and the "outside," I judge that their being lumped together was mostly a matter of their being on the "outside."

But, their individual sources were different. Veblen wrote in the tradition of the late seventeenth and early eighteenth century moral philosophers. He should be compared positively to Mandeville and negatively to Lord Shaftesbury or the earlier *Theory of Moral Sentiments* Smith. Veblen sought to show the contradictions seen in his contemporary social intercourse and the judgements about it. At this, Mandeville was his better, and I think that H. L. Mencken his inferior.

Mitchell's sources dealt with the great advances in statistical methodology of the turn of the 20th century. Less imbued with anger at the going American social system than Veblen and suffering no personal discriminatory experiences which could have caused that bitterness, Mitchell was trying to call shots as he saw them, particularly as he understood the contemporary development of statistical inference and method. Mitchell was so skeptical of the universalities of economic theory, that he doubtless thought Koopmans' attack naive. When and if econometric modelling came up with results which were head-and-shoulders better than sheer indexing and simple probability inference, I think that he would have been ready to accept it, albeit with a persistent but not aggressive skepticism.

I believe that the obvious initial source of Commons's institutionalism was the same vein as Bates Clark's *Philosophy of Wealth,* but Commons went well beyond Clark because Commons replaced Clark's Christian Socialist morality with a rhetorically tedious but nonetheless brilliant episodic empiricism. Commons's later sources were an autodidactic legal training, one based on examination of historical prose (cf. Commons [1924]). One of the classics in his world was Oliver Wendell Holmes Jr., *The Common Law.* Had he read and incorporated parts of Pareto's *Tratto di Sociologia Generale* (translated as *The Mind in Society*), his institutionalism would have become an orthodoxy in sociology, where perhaps it more rightly belongs.

## The Results

Veblen's impact was to formulate a line of social criticism directed at the pomposity of the economics profession and particularly its self-defined "scientific" advocacy of Catallactics. Catallactics is not only a study of the pecuniary economic system, but it is a study which sometimes assumes and almost invariably concludes that the free market allocation solves the least bad of all problems. As we are once again living in an era which asserts that free markets are the least bad approach, we are once again likely to have an epidemic of individuals writing in the Veblenian tradition which accepts the fact of a pecuniary as well as a real economy, but which stresses that the pecuniary economy is essentially non-productive. This issue of productive vs. non-productive goods and services is one which Catallactics, by its very nature (which instrumentally defines value as price), denies. Bates Clark always argued that prices explain prices; prices do not explain value. As long as Bates Clark's view survives, whether it prevails or not, there is thus one good reason for the Veblenian line to flourish.

But there is more to the Veblenian tradition than elements of social criticism. It is a tradition with its own rhetoric and taste for that rhetoric. The rhetoric is in line with the words of the Book of Ecclesiastes, which, as all of us professors know, is the one which young intellectuals first come to love. Don McCloskey is only among the most recent to stress the overwhelming role of rhetoric; I would argue that the power of rhetoric is what interested Adam Smith most, and it was the pithiness of his social criticism, found in those excellently phrased first chapters of the *Wealth of Nations,* which made it the inspiring tract that it became. So, too, with Veblen.

It is hard to overestimate Mitchell's impact. He gave material form to the soul of macroeconomic analysis. Ideas cast no shadows; numbers, when tied to ideas, do. Mitchell, like Jacob, begot numerous intellectual sons: Arthur Burns and business cycle measurement, Solomon Fabricant and productivity analysis; Milton Friedman and Anna Schwartz and a form of monetary analysis, and so forth. Principal amongst those whom Mitchell begot was Simon Kuznets, whose fecundity is legendary. Also there was Robert Nathan and Milton Gilbert and modern national income analysis, Robert Nathan and modern wartime reallocation analysis, Richard Easterlin and Oded Stark and modern demographic empirical analysis, Jacob Schmookler and modern numerical analysis of the patents, numerous students and a variety of measures of income distribution by size, and even more students, including the brilliant if independent-minded Walt Rostow and the J-shaped economic growth curve. By now Mitchell's own begats are mostly history and the begetting has become so frequent and has passed through so many generations that his seed is becoming as numerous as the sands on the beach.

Commons's fecundity took a different form. His work on the *Weltanschauung* of organized labor was extended principally by Selig Perlman 1928 (Perlman and Taft [1935]); of recent years it has resurfaced as the largely Marxian reaction to the Perlman-Commons tradition and has come under fire by "grandchildren", who want to know what their socialist parents so disliked about their bourgeois grandparents. That the Selig Perlman *A Theory of the Labor Movement* remained in print for over half a century is one thing; that it has recently been the focal point of a featured discussion of labor history in the *American Historical Review,* is quite another. In that sense this aspect of Commons's institutionalism still lives and to some limited degree thrives.

Commons's work on industrial accident insurance led in the 1930s to the Paul Rauschenbush Wisconsin system of experience-rated unemployment insurance. Within a quinquennium the Wisconsin system had gone national under the American Social Security System (engineered and administered by such Commons begats as Edwin Witte, Arthur Altmeyer, and Wilbur Cohen). It also took form in Commons's designing of systems of public utility discriminatory rate regulation (extended through Martin Glaeser, who in turn begot a series of regulators), and his work on the monitoring of governmental expenditure (he had established in Milwaukee the prototype of what has now become the federal Office of the Budget).

Currently the most noticeable of the Commons's offspring is the work being done on economic contracting. While it is true that Ronald Coase's work on public goods can be said to have precedents in the work of Commons, closer to the original Commons set of ideas is the work of Oliver Williamson on implied and explicit contracts.

Commons's efforts at establishing a methodological school of institutional economics at the University of Wisconsin thrived for the better part of half a century; in the latter part of that period it was located in the Department of Agricultural Economics, not in the Department of Economics. The kinds of things done by Douglass North and by Rudolph Richter and Erik Furubotn, often designated as neo-Institutionalism, assume that Commons was more anti-Catallactics than in point of fact he was; he was not anti-, rather he was uninterested.

BIBLIOGRAPHY

Berle A. A. and Gardner M. [1932], *The Modern Corporation and Private Property*, New York, Macmillan.
Brigante John E. [1950], The Feasibility Dispute: Determination of War Production Objectives for 1942 and 1943, Washington Committee on Public Administration Cases.
Burns A. R. [1936], *The Decline of Competition*, New York, McGraw-Hill.
Commons J.-R. [1979], *Industrial Goodwill*, New York, McGraw-Hill.
Commons J.-R. [1921], *Industrial Government*, New York, Macmillan.
Commons J.-R. [1924], *The Legal Foundations of Capitalism*, New York, Macmillan.
Commons J.-R. [1934], *Institutional Economics*, New York, Macmillan.
Commons J.-R. [1950], *The Economics of Collective Action*, New York, Macmillan.
Commons John R. and Associates [1919], *History of Labour in the United States*, 2 vol., New York, Macmillan.
Dorfman J. [1934], *Thorstein Veblen and His America*, New York, Viking.
Fitzpatrick Ed. [1944], *McCarthy of Wisconsin*, New York, Columbia University Press.

Friedman Milton, Laurence J. [1987], *The New Palgrave: A Dictionary of Economics*, vol. 3, p. 139–140.

Hamilton Walton and Associates [1938], *Price and Price Policies*.

Homan P. T. [1928], *Contemporary Economic Thought*, New York, Harper & Bros.

Kuznets Simon S. [1933a], National Income, *Encyclopedia of the Social Sciences*, vol. 11, p. 205–224, New York, Macmillan.

Kuznets Simon S. [1934], *National Income, 1929–1932, Senate Document no. 174, 73rd Congress, 2nd Session, Washington, G.P.O.*

Kuznets Simon S. [1937], *National Income and Capital Formation, 1919–1935*, New York, National Bureau of Economic Research.

Kuznets Simon S. [1938], *Commodity Flow and Capital Formation*, New York, National Bureau of Economic Research.

Koopmans T. [1947], Measurement without Theory, *Rev. Econ. Stat.* 29, 161–172.

Mitchell L. S. [1953], *Two Lives: The Story of Wesley Clair Mitchell and Myself*, New York, Simon & Schuster.

Mitchell Wesley Clair [1912], *Business Cycles and their Causes*, Berkeley, University of California Press. Part III, alone, was republished several times under this title (University of California Press [1941]).

Mitchell Wesley Clair [1927], *Business Cycles: The Problem and Its Setting*, New York, National Bureau of Economic Research.

Mitchell Wesley Clair and Burns, Frank A. [1946], *Measuring Business Cycles*, New York, National Bureau of Economic Research.

Mitchell Wesley Clair [1967, 1969], *Types of Economic Theory: From Mercantilism to Institutionalism*, 2 vol., Edited with an Introduction by Joseph Dorfman, New York, Augustus M. Kelley.

Perlman M. [1976], Jews and Contributions to Economics: A Bicentennial Review, *Judaism*, 25, 301–311.

Perlman M. [1977]. Orthodoxy and Heterodoxy in Economics: A Retrospective View of Experiences in Britain and the U.S.A., *Zeit. fuer Nationaloekonomie*, 37, 151–164.

Perlman M. [1991a], 'Early' Capital Theory in the Economics Journals: A Study of Imputed Induced Demand, *Note Economiche*, vol. 20, p. 58–88.

Perlman S. [1928], *A Theory of the Labor Movement*, New York, Macmillan.

Perlman S. and Philip T. [1935], *History of Labor in the United States, 1896–1932*, vol. 4, New York, Macmillan.

Samuels Warren J. [1987a], Ayers, Clarence Edwin, *The New Palgrave: A Dictionary of Economics*, vol. 1, p. 165.

Samuels Warren J. [1987b], Commons John R. *The New Palgrave: A Dictionary of Economics*, vol. 1, p. 506.

Samuels Warren J. [1987c], "Institutional Economic," *The New Palgrave: A Dictionary of Economics*, vol. 2, p. 864–866.

Sowell T. and Veblen Thorstein [1987], *The New Palgrave: A Dictionary of Economics*, vol. 7, p. 799–800.

Veblen Thorstein [1923], *Imperial Germany and the Industrial Revolution*.

CHAPTER 12

# Orthodoxy and Heterodoxy in Economics: A Retrospective View of Experiences in Britain and the USA

*This chapter, written while I spent a Fellowship semester at the University of Cambridge, reflects my growing perception of just what Marshall's impact had been when he set up the Economics Tripos. Both Marshall and such American institutionalists as Veblen, Mitchell, and Commons were reacting to the orthodoxy of John Stuart Mill. They clearly trusted their senses of empirical observations (leading to generalizations) much more than they did their capacity for linking syllogisms (leading to abstractions). The later, post-Marshallian/Pigovian Cantabrigian tradition shifted to ratiocinative modeling. In America, the impact of National Bureau number collecting worked to destroy the hegemony of ratiocinative model building. Written as the Invited Lecture at the 1977 Riverside, California, meeting of the History of Economics Society, its brevity is ascribable to the conditions of its presentation.*

## 1. Introduction

One main thrust of this essay's argument is that the three great figures of American Institutionalism, Thorstein Veblen, Wesley Clair Mitchell and John Rogers Commons, should most properly be seen as a reaction to the economic orthodoxy prevailing in their relative youth. As such, they should most appropriately be compared to Alfred Marshall, whose own work was also, as I see it, a reaction to that same orthodoxy. Veblen, Mitchell and Commons did not undertake to provide a comprehensive treatment of the discipline of economics; instead their work, individually, focused on several aspects of the orthodox tradition but lacked the sweep of Marshall's now somewhat ignored (if not actually discredited) *Principles of Economics*. I shall somewhat later in this paper explain why I think that, aside from his own inherent abilities, Marshall's handling of the orthodox tradition took a different form from those of the three aforementioned American Institutionalists.

The orthodoxy these Institutionalists opposed included a dislike for the simplicity of John Stuart Mill's ethical hedonism or, as he called it, his

*Zeitschrift für Nationalökonomie* 37 (1977):151–64.

"utilitarianism". Mill had, it is clear, departed considerably from his early Benthamite perceptions of utilitarianism, but even in spite of the modifications which Mill had made to the original Benthamite doctrine, the criticism was that Mill had not gone far enough. The American Institutionalists also felt negatively and strongly about Mill's reliance upon deduction, yet anyone who supposes that Mill did not use induction as well is innocent of the subject. Rather, as in the case of white corpuscles and red corpuscles, the problem was that there was too little induction compared to the frequency and rigor of deduction. So, much of the criticism of orthodoxy was directed at the basic premise of classical Benthamite economics (utilitarianism) as modified by John Stuart Mill, and at the deductive method, which Mill preferred to use. The American Institutionalists, however, went beyond these criticisms and, quite erroneously, I think, attacked all formalism, which I think they associated with rigor and therethrough with mathematics. Jevons attacked Mill's subject matter and method, but Jevons's attack by way of contrast did embrace mathematical formalism—while the three Americans apparently eschewed the calculus. In all, for reasons that I will try to explain later, the American Institutionalists quite clearly did not feel sympathetic to the Jevons approach. I do not think they were as hostile to the Marshall approach as later generations thought they were. Of that I will say more later.

There was a strong American orthodoxy, which still embraced the classical tradition of Mill, both with regard to his perception of utilitarianism as the basic rationale of economics and with regard to his mix of deduction and induction. That hard core American respectability included Simon Newcomb of Johns Hopkins, Arthur Hadley of Yale, J. Lawrence Laughlin of Chicago, and some earlier figures like William Sumner of Yale. The three American Institutionalists clearly attacked this group. There is a popular view that their attack was phrased in terms of criticism of the free market. I think this criticism is malfocused; an earlier generation of American heterodox economists (Richard T. Ely, Henry Carter Adams, Edwin R. A. Seligman and even John Bates Clark) had attacked excessive reliance upon this free market when they founded the American Economic Association. However, the most that can be said about the impact on Institutionalism of this earlier generation of American greats was that they were the teachers of the three principal Institutionalists. Their students, the three American Institutionalists, did not seem to me to focus on *laissez-faire* as the principal evil of orthodoxy. The evil of orthodoxy as seen by the three was Mill's utilitarianism, Mill's preference for deduction over induction, and what they thought was an emerging excessive mathematical formalism. They did have some feeling, these three, that there was something compellingly unique and free about American economics. They had not escaped completely Walt Whitman's and others' faith that America offered a special kind of freedom to the mind as well as to the body. In this sense, I think the three suffered from an excessive provincialism. They also probably shared a "reverse commitment" to Hohenzollern German social reform. Both Veblen and Commons had worked for the United States Industrial Commission, and both were keenly conscious of the possibilities of political leadership in economic development.[1] None of the three had been educated at the more "pro-English" of the American universities. Only Mitchell (who had studied with Veblen at Chicago) had had easy sailing in his collegiate and university careers. Thus only he was conditioned to have an easy sympathy with the American academic system as it then existed.

I mention this point because I think each of them thought of London and conventional economics as more or less synonymous. I find little evidence that any of them was aware of what was happening in Cambridge (where great things were happening), and I do find considerable evidence that Veblen and Commons both had a predisposition to be sympathetic to what was happening at the University of Berlin and to the kinds of social reform that the various Hohenzollern governments were discussing and in large measure implementing.

## 2. Generalizing about American Institutionalists

Differences within the group were very great. What most united the three was a sense of being on the outside. To discuss the internal differences I find it useful to think of economics as a discipline having three aspects (a sense of question, a body of data and a concern with analytical technique); each of these three leading men (Veblen, Mitchell and Commons) handled each of these aspects in his way.

How did each handle the question of *laissez-faire?* Only Veblen clearly attacked the Mandeville *Fable of the Bees* prototype. Mitchell was for the most part a political conservative, and although at one point he may have been relatively critical of excessive reliance upon the market system (particularly during the Great Depression), he was in no sense part of the conventional antimarket crusade. Commons, quite interestingly, believed in monopolistic competition; indeed, the willingness of some to lump Commons with Brandeis as sharing a mutual distrust of big business is something for which I find virtually no evidence.

How did each perceive the question of the psychology of decisionmaking? According to my reading, Veblen really belonged to the level of the literature of the Sentimental Moralists. Although he decried the antiquarian

---

1. There is, to my knowledge, no real history of this amazing intellectual effort. I did, however, describe briefly its genesis, the contents of its voluminous output, and its lack of apparent results in my Labor Union Theories in America: Background and Development, Westport 1976 (second edition), pp. 264–79.

nature of eighteenth century values (and I might add that his criticism of this period was by assertion rather than by any effective proof), it is apparent that he was not particularly aware of developments within the field of *Gestalt* psychology, to say nothing of the later developments that led to Watsonian behaviorism. Indeed, it is rather remarkable how little Veblen seemed to know about the contemporary developments in psychology, which had occurred and were occurring in Baltimore and Harvard under Peirce and William James. Commons was interested in the evolution of group values; indeed, he defined institutionalism as "collective choice in control of individual choice". But, Commons was not *au courant* with developments in social psychology. If anything, he seems to have been relatively skeptical about the discipline of psychology offering very much to economics. His strong personal friendship with Frank Fetter suggests that he was not alien to the idea of fusing economics and psychology, but he certainly did not stress it.[2] Wesley Clair Mitchell clearly recognized the importance of psychology in the decision-making process, but I think that his delightful essay, "Backward Art of Spending Money", in spite of its wonderful title, raises only very interesting and critical questions. Unfortunately, the title suggests only a value judgement and the essay is not strong on answers.

Thus, on the whole the three did not share strong enthusiasm for attacking *laissez-faire,* nor did they approach the question of the psychology of decision-making as a group or even frontally. So much, then, for unanimity of approach regarding the sense of question.

What about data? Veblen is really not very hortatory on the topic, although his Industrial Commission work apparently gave him a feel for "the facts". He was an arranger of factual evidence much in the sense that a barrister organizes evidence in the preparation of a persuasive argument. The barrister's technique stresses the marshalling of facts, not so much for purposes of revealing the complex truth as for the purpose of suggesting an inexorable and unavoidable conclusion. I would think (as I shall mention immediately after this point) that Veblen was far more interested in persuasion than he was in stressing the importance of facts in whatever form they appear. Mitchell, by way of contrast, saw data as quantitative measurement revealing a unified complex truth. In a great sense Mitchell's approach is part of the American traditional culture, where display of information was regarded as sufficient to answer all queries. The American national census is probably the earliest of record. These censuses achieved levels of great importance in the nineteenth century. The DeBow census of 1830 is an excellent piece of work.

---

2. Cf. M. Perlman, ibid., pp. 187–88 and also M. Perlman: Some Reflections on Theorizing about Industrial Relations, in N. Morris and M. Perlman (eds.): Law and Crime: Essays in Honor of Sir John Barry, New York, London and Paris 1972, pp. 181–209.

Moreover, Carroll Davidson Wright developed a data-providing institution (the Bureau of Labor Statistics) which went far beyond the decennial censuses in presenting factual information. Mitchell, as I note, stressed the importance of systematic regular data. He liked quantification in the same sense that a great many natural scientists say they like quantification—"science is measurement", and his perception of himself was as a scientist.

Commons to a large extent shared Mitchell's views; it is a matter of record that Commons constructed the first American wholesale price index. But Commons went on to use qualitative or episodic data (court records, etc.) as well as quantitative data. Commons' reliance upon court records was not drawn from the American tradition; I think it quite clear that he got his ideas regarding this matter from the work of Frederic Maitland, Downing Professor of Law at Cambridge University.

One thing they had in common: all three American Institutionalists seemed to eschew substituting numerical examples for actual data, probably because they thought it introduced an artificial abstractionism, which they distrusted. In so doing I think they were clearly turning their back on the kind of argumentation that Ricardo and Böhm-Bawerk favored. Perhaps Ricardo favored this kind of argumentation because harder data were not available. Their distrust of artificial abstractionism extended, I believe and as I mentioned previously, to Jevons' use of the calculus.

What about techniques? I think it important to recognize that Veblen used ironical juxtaposition as a way for making his points. He was quite good at it. Good as he was, I do not think he was as good as Jonathan Swift, who also used the same technique. It is true that Swift's ironical juxtapositions usually dealt with theological perceptions of morality, whereas Veblen's often focussed on the cumbersome language of contemporary biology and theology. But as a technique it was effective then, and it is effective now. Veblen has remained a popular writer, and his intellectual descendant, John Kenneth Galbraith, is probably now the most widely read American economist.

Mitchell used tabular display, but his quantitative tabular display relied almost entirely on very simple statistical measures of central tendency, scatter, time leads and lags, and correlation. His distrust of economic theory was legendary. And in time it led to Tjalling Koopmans' famous 1947 attack, entitled "Measurement Without Theory".[3] This is not to suggest that between 1912 and 1947 the Mitchell group relied on simple statistical measurement and on tabular display. Quite the contrary. Witness the plethora of theoretical concepts, not based purely on statistical measurement, developed by John

---

3. T. Koopmans: Measurement Without Theory, Review of Economics and Statistics *XXIX* (1947), pp. 161–72 and his reply to R. Vining: Methodological Issues in Quantitative Economics, Review of Economics and Statistics *XXXI* (1949), pp. 77–86 entitled: A Reply, *ibid.*, pp. 86–91 and then Vining's A Rejoinder, *ibid.*, pp. 91–94.

Maurice Clark, Simon Kuznets, Arthur F. Burns, Moses Abramovitz and Solomon Fabricant—to mention but a few. However, the great leap forward with regard to the processing of data did not come in Mitchell's time. I suspect that it was not simply the impact of European econometricians (in contrast with nativist American statisticians) which accounts for the many changes that have occurred in the last 30 years. It was also the great expansion of government data collecting, particularly with the use of scientifically designed samples, and above all the availability of high speed computer processing time, which accounts for the rise of modern American econometrics. Putting the matter bluntly, the European discipline of econometrics using the solid foundations of an American penchant for systematic data collection made use of the high speed computer (largely developed by a European in America) to present the world with the contemporary American form of economic analysis, the data-tested theory as yet unfalsified. Had the leadership of the National Bureau of Economics in 1947 seen what was occurring, they would have recognized Koopmans' assault as the Battle of Hastings; the subsequent appointment more than two decades later of John Meyer as its President was the consequent coronation.

Commons used the method of the historical analog, which I mentioned that I believe he got from Maitland. Where did Maitland get it? There are some who believe that Maitland was reacting largely to the historical work of Sir Henry Maine. Others, probably more perceptive, accept Maitland's assertion that he got his ideas from Paul (later Sir Paul) Vinogradof, a Russian legal historian who ultimately became Regius Professor of Law at Oxford.

As I review what has been written, I am impressed with the diffusion of generalization that can be made about the American Institutionalists. They were all reacting to orthodoxy, but the object of their attack was not *laissez-faire* capitalism. If anything, orthodoxy was utilitarianism and an excessive dependence upon the method of deduction. But in their attacks on utilitarianism and the method of deduction they varied. Their ignoring of developments in the field of psychology also largely unites them; it also serves as a basis of criticism of their work. There is one other point about them, which is often overlooked. They had mutual experiences. Both Veblen and Commons had studied at Hopkins (one having left because he failed), and both came to regard their teacher at Johns Hopkins, Richard T. Ely, as less than profound. Veblen taught Mitchell at Chicago. Mitchell and Commons apparently had great respect for each other. Commons actually was one of the directors of Mitchell's National Bureau of Economic Research, and Mitchell made gallant efforts to explain Commons to the profession in his reviews of Commons' seminal books[4] as well as a rather interesting and inspiring effort to explain

---

4. Cf. his review: Commons on the Legal Foundations of Capitalism, American Economic Review *XIV* (1924), pp. 253 ff.

Commons to his students (as revealed in Mitchell's lecture notes on the formative types of economic thought).[5] If these three got along reasonably well, it is not clear that their successors did. But there were conflicts in each of the three camps, too. The strong generalization that emerges is that the American Institutionalists were more united in what they were against than in what they were for in the sense that we can see what they disliked. Further, none made much of an attempt to organize a comprehensive formulation of what he advocated. Veblen specialized in "creative destruction". Commons was more interested in improving society by means of educated legislative reform than he was in developing a coherent discipline of economics. If anything, his aspirations for creating a coherent discipline relate to combining what was known about the theory of public administration with what was known about the theory of the evolution of legal instruments within the context of what was economically feasible. As for Mitchell, I think he was probably the most successful of the three, but only in the sense that his creation, the National Bureau of Economic Research, became a viable continuing institution. Yet, in the process it shifted from his perception of statistical analysis and was, as I have mentioned, taken over by the econometricians who, fortified by better data than Mitchell was ever able to get and a vastly improved technology, produced what the world today knows as American orthodox economics.

## 3. Parallel Developments in the English Cambridge

English economics was dominated by developments in London during the last 70 to 90 years of the nineteenth century, but the reaction to the orthodox economics took place, however, not so much in London but in Cambridge. There had been instruction in economics on the university level at Cambridge University as early as 1816 when George Pryne undertook to lecture (without pecuniary remuneration). He became the first Professor of Political Economy in 1828. Notwithstanding Pryne, the old classical tradition at Cambridge was at its peak during the tenure of Henry Fawcett, appointed Professor in 1863. Fawcett is a particularly worthy individual because he had overcome a great handicap, blindness. Wounded by his father in 1858 in a hunting accident, Fawcett drove himself through sheer will-power to a life of full activity. He wrote several books, stood for Parliament many times, was actually elected to Parliament (where he served as Minister). Personalities aside, the key generalization is that both Pryne and Fawcett were rather conventional, traditional classical economists. Fawcett was a friend and admirer of John Stuart Mill, and as Mill wavered in his own devotion to Benthamite utilitarianism, so did

---

5. W. C. Mitchell: Types of Economic Theory: From Mercantilism to Institutionalism, edited by J. Dorfman, New York 1967–69. See vol. 2, pp. 701–36.

Fawcett. Fawcett's opposition to religious test acts at Cambridge parallels Mill's own views on the subject.

There was a great deal going on at Cambridge aside from Fawcett's economics, which had implications for the future development of economics there. The traditional *triposes* (curricula) had been in classics or in mathematics. However, a new generation of scholars had discovered empirical techniques in biology, chemistry and physics. Their enthusiasm for their findings led them not only to challenge the hold that theology and mathematics had on the structure of the curriculum, but also to have considerable doubts regarding the whole social climate that awarded these conventions their preeminence. Everywhere there was dissatisfaction with the curriculum. The immensely unpleasant and no less gifted Master of Trinity, William Whewell, sought reform in order to stave off (as it turned out unsuccessfully) a Royal Commission. He enlisted the Prince Consort as his ally. Thus, voices for curricular reform were heard first from the "right" (meaning such as Whewell) and then from the "left" (meaning the new generation of natural scientists). A group of young Fellows (Dons) not only churned up this wave but also "rode it to success". Sheldon Rothblatt has written one of several rather interesting analyses of the changes that occurred.[6] The key figures, none an economist but who were crucial to the development of the discipline of economics at Cambridge, include Henry Sidgwick (Professor of Moral Philosophy and one of the critically significant influences in developing the "new" Cambridge University), F. D. Maurice (an apparently universally beloved Low Churchman whose personality did much to hold the group together—incidentally, he was the great grandfather of Professor Joan Robinson) and the aforementioned Frederic Maitland. It was a strained group because each wrestled lengthily with his own conscience.

Rothblatt recalls how Sidgwick opposed Whewell's criticisms of Mill's utilitarianism until he realized that what he disliked was not the product of Whewell's mind but Whewell's personality. Whewell, a man who had done important works on winds and tides, had written an insightful book, *The History of the Inductive Sciences*. The book was tolerantly, even admiringly, reviewed by Mill, but the import of the book was clearly anti-utilitarianism. Indeed, Whewell offered a different measure of value as well as a mechanism for implementing this measure. The mechanism was intuition; intuitionism stressed some cultural control over the individual in lieu of the total control of the felicific calculus.

As time developed, Sidgwick opposed the views of Henry Fawcett. When the time came for Fawcett's replacement, Sidgwick and John Neville

6. S. Rothblatt: The Revolution of the Dons: Cambridge and Society in Victorian England. London 1968.

Keynes (the father of John Maynard Keynes) played critical roles in the selection of Alfred Marshall, a St. Johns (Cambridge) graduate and, at the time, Principal of the University of Bristol. Marshall's mission was to make Cambridge economics "modern"; he was to create a *tripos* in economics, and that curriculum was to depend less upon deduction and more upon induction; it was to require study of actual market and socio-political behavior. But it was also to be more quantitatively systematic in its observations than "the less science-inspired Philosophy-Politics-Economics program at Oxford, set up considerably later by Roy Harrod and others."

John Whitaker has recently published a splendid essay introducing the early works of Marshall.[7] To my mind, Marshall undertook a task identical with that of the American Institutionalists. His position and previous equipment, however, were much different. He was Professor of Political Economy in *the* great scientific university, then at the beginning of its modern preeminence. At Cambridge he was allied with potentially powerful and intellectually most creative scholars. Not least among them was Frederic Maitland, who had originally been a student of Sidgwick and who had been brought back to Cambridge (from London where he was a barrister) to develop the discipline of legal history. Maitland used as his source material English county and other land documents, as well as what judicial records he could find to construct new theories of socioeconomic development. Also, as a result of Sidgwick's persuasion, Maitland undertook a translation and thorough examination of Otto von Gierke's work on the structure of the Middle Ages. What Maitland found was that economic institutions created material records, which could be combed to understand the evolutionary nature of the social control process. Maitland's work in the Seldon Society is what is best known to most current scholars. However, his influence on Commons (in particular) just cannot be overstressed. Maitland offered a basis for understanding the way economies grew. Commons read Maitland; Marshall worked alongside of him.

Recently a paper, "The English Historical School of Economics and the Emergence of Economic History in England", was written by Gerard N. Koot. Koot argues convincingly that Marshall opposed the development of an independent discipline of economic history,[8] because its proponent, Cunningham, who had been defeated by Marshall in the competition for the chair in political economy, would have thus left economics to become too formal (perhaps sterile) a subject or discipline. It was the bitterness of the conflict between these men and its reverberations with regard to the work of Sir

---

7. See A. Marshall: Early Economic Writings of Alfred Marshall, 1867–1890. Edited and with an Introduction by J. K. Whitaker. Two volumes, London 1975.

8. Paper given at the History of Economics Society meetings, Riverside, California, March 1977. The author is at Southern Massachusetts State University.

William Ashley and the Socialist economic historians at the London School of Economics that had tended to hide the tremendous commitment Marshall, himself, had to historical techniques. One has only to glance briefly at his great work *Industry and Trade* to perceive how thoroughly dependent Marshall was on historical materials.

The important point, however, is not that Marshall relied upon historical material but that Marshall relied very heavily on empiricism. And while it is true that Marshall has a brilliant Mathematical Appendix, anticipating most of his later critics, to his *Principles of Economics,* the key appendix was the one on methodology where induction is stressed.

Marshall elected to retire prematurely. Professor Ronald Coase has recently published a history of Marshall's intervention in the selection of Arthur C. Pigou over Foxwell as his successor.[9] Professor Sir Austin Robinson has told me that he thinks that Coase misunderstands the reasons for the intervention. Marshall believed that Foxwell lacked both the intellectual power and the necessary personality to guide the development of the economics *tripos* within the Cambridge scientific scene. Marshall believed that the *tripos* needed the leadership of an individual who would be neither the tool of those adhering to economic classicism nor of those who would be urging some aspect of the anti-theoretical German historical school.

It is an unfortunate part of our current tradition that Marshall represents the "dead hand of the past"; such was the assertion of Keynes. It seems to me there is plenty of evidence to the contrary. Marshall, himself, publicly urged Keynes to make the Marshall *Principles of Economics* outdated. Moreover, Marshall's characterization as a "neoclassicist" has come to mean many things to many people. Neoclassicism today apparently refers to the kind of economics taught by Samuelson and his associates in Cambridge, U.S.A. Lost in all the current controversy is the underlying point; Marshall was selected as a worthy adversary of the Mill's classical economics.

How does Marshall compare with the three American Institutionalists? He was much more of a synthesizer than any of them was. I do not think that his understanding of psychology was any more profound than any of theirs, but he cursed the lacunae less. He was capable of more formalism than any of them was—after all, he was well trained in math, particularly the calculus. But he did not choose to pursue his mathematical formulations, and I think there is considerable evidence that he would have viewed with some reservations his discipline moving in the direction of Samuelson's *Foundations.* . . .

Like Mitchell and Commons, Marshall had great entrepreneurial talents, but they went into the establishment of a curriculum rather than to the found-

---

9. R. Coase: The Appointment of Pigou as Marshall's Successor, Journal of Law and Economics *XV* (1972), pp. 473–485.

ing of an institution devoted to the collection of economic data (that was in the tradition of the German institutes) or like Commons into the development of broad socio-economic legislative changes.

## 4. Some Conclusions

At the outset I mentioned that one main thrust of this paper was to show that the great American heterodox economists—Veblen, Mitchell and Commons, were reacting to the elements of Millsian orthodoxy which also prompted a group at Cambridge University to select Alfred Marshall to found the new *tripos* in economics. Marshall's achievement was, I believe, academically more comprehensive than the combined efforts of the American three.

If so, why?

First, because Marshall worked in an intellectually more stimulating atmosphere—an atmosphere stressing intuition and empiricism, analysis and synthesis as found in a variety of scientific disciplines.

Second, because Marshall did not eschew completely the formalism that all four initially thought too strong. Indeed, it turns out that Marshall's analytical errors pertaining to the prose discussion of increasing returns to scale (and ultimately pointed out by a later Cantabrigian, Piero Sraffa),[10] were "covered" in his formal Mathematical Appendix. I suspect that the American three lacked the expertise to handle formalism, which explains why they did not undertake the kind of thing, which perhaps "saved" Marshall.

Third, because within the group of Marshall's immediate and later second generation groups of successors there were those like Pigou and Keynes, Robertson and E. A. G. Robinson, Stone and Meade, who sought to keep the delicate balance between the two types of empiricism and formal analysis.

In time, however, formalism seems to have all but swamped the Cambridge scene, which suggests one of the reasons for the fractionation of the current faculty in Cambridge.

In America, however, the Institutionalist revolt produced quite another tradition, not always as academic (in the sense of the academy), but no less pervasive and certainly no less persuasive. Commons' efforts were memorialized by the enactment of a massive legislation program, including public utility pricing patterns, social security laws (workmen's accident compensation, superannuation and unemployment insurance, and labor relations codes) and public budgeting institutions. All these, however, lacked a formal or theoretical side.

---

10. P. Sraffa: The Laws of Returns Under Competitive Conditions, Economic Journal *XXXVI* (1926), pp. 535–550.

On the historical side, however, the Commons tradition produced several generations of social historians, including Selig Perlman, Philip Taft, Walter Galenson and my own works. Most but not all of these, however, moved from using legal materials—possibly because other documentation was either more easily at hand or was believed to be of a superior relevance. Yet even here there was a studied eschewal of formal analysis—it is amusing to note that the initial clarion call for cliometrics seemingly suggested Selig Perlman's work on the nature of unionism as an alternative point of departure to the Ulrich Phillips' thesis pertaining to slavery and the (American) Civil War. To the extent that the cliometricians did not provide formalism however, the Commons' historical tradition still lacks it.

Mitchell's National Bureau, on the other hand, did clearly acquire the mathematical, particularly the theoretical aspect. Introduced, in some instances over Mitchell's own resistance (cf. Milton Friedman's doctoral work in the 1930's on the consumption function, which faced, so I am told, formidable opposition within the Bureau's own group), but later through the powerful intervention of the Ford Foundation hierarchy in the appointment of an econometrician as the Bureau's President, theoretical formalism of the Bureau's mode became the synthesis and, as such, the new American orthodoxy.

Only Veblen's plea for more psychology in economics has gone largely unheeded. Recently Professor Herbert Simon seems to me to have confirmed this point just as A. W. Coats established it a generation ago.[11]

Let me terminate this paper with the following additional thoughts.

a. The American Institutionalists and the English Marshall fought excessive deduction (which meant excessive formalism); from the standpoint of what they had in mind, Marshall's Methodological Appendix makes their point best.
b. Their heterodoxy swamped the old orthodoxy and certainly in the case of Mitchell's direct National Bureau heirs, the old heterodoxy seems to have all but become the new orthodoxy.
c. Neither the American three nor the Marshallian tradition at Cambridge has offered anything comparable to the unifying psychological principle of Utilitarianism, which all were intent on replacing. Indeed, the modern theory of demand is essentially *a priori*, which is just their originating point of criticism. *Plus ça change, plus c'est presque la même chose.*

---

11. H. A. Simon: From Substantive to Procedural Rationality, in S. J. Latsis (ed.): Method and Appraisal in Economics, Cambridge 1976, pp. 129–148 and A. W. Coats: Economics and Psychology: The Death and Resurrection of a Research Programme, ibid., pp. 43–64.

# CHAPTER 13

# Hayek, Purposes of the Economic Market, and Institutionalist Traditions

*Like many of my generation, I read both William Beveridge's* Full Employment in a Free Society *and Hayek's* The Road to Serfdom *while in military service during World War II. My reaction was typical: Hayek was a reactionary—his ideas were simply the rationale of the Vested Interests. However, the year I spent as my father's graduate assistant led me to become skeptical about the prospects for economic and political growth and social stability in a centrally planned, full-employment economy.*

*By the time I came to know Fritz Machlup at Hopkins, I was well on the way first to considering and then to admiring the institutionalist artistry in Hayek's post–World War II writings. Machlup's reputation prior to 1962 as being simply a theorist of the ardent Austrian variety belied his commitment to social justice. Through him and through Herbert Giersch, I began to appreciate Hayek as both exemplar modern Utilitarian-individualist and a philosopher having both the wit and the imagination to integrate into economic orthodoxy the Commons' organic substance, "Industrial Goodwill."*

*The centrality of market transactions is a major theme in economic literature. Too much attention has been paid to the catallactics side; too little to the conventions according to which a market operates. In this chapter I consider the variety of purposes for which markets are established, and Hayek's shift in emphasis from seeing the market as a vehicle for free souls to express their longings and deal their assets to seeing the market as a process that shapes the expression of willingness to buy and to sell. Hayek then moved to quench the fires devoted to excessive focus on equilibration as the key market process. Ultimately, he came to stress the market's primary role as being the exchange of information. After this discussion, I then move to several writers I consider institutionalist in their treatment (A. C. Pigou*

From Stephen Frowen (ed.), *Hayek, The Economist and Social Philosopher: A Critical Retrospect* (London: Macmillan, forthcoming).

I acknowledge the great assistance given me by Dr. Charles Robert McCann, whose views on this topic were somewhat different from my own, but we have compromised—perhaps at a point closer to his position than I realize (or as he says, "would like").

*[malgré lui], J. M. Clark, Ronald Coase, and John R. Commons. Their resulting insights were similar; what differed were their philosophical foundations—Hayek's was Kantian; the others' were Hegelian.*

*This chapter was significantly shaped by my collaboration with one of my best Ph.D. students, Dr. Charles R. McCann, who is something of a Libertarian. As a student I was always skeptical of what my most admired professors told me, but I still listened to them; now that I am an emeritus, I am skeptical of what my prize students tell me, but I still listen to them.*

## The Problem and Line of Thought

While we are celebrating the anniversary of the death of Friedrich Hayek, one of the unique aspects of his life is that his active career covered more than 60 years. Such a lengthy period of intellectual output is virtually unique; some, for example, Isaac Newton, approached the same time span of achievement, but Newton, unlike Hayek, outlived his creativity, as well as the beneficent effects of his influence.

There has long been a purported conflict between economic theorists, particularly of the line from which Hayek stemmed, and the "empirically oriented socioeconomic" Institutionalists of which Wesley Clair Mitchell, John R. Commons, and John Maurice Clark were exemplars.[1] Schumpeter noted some of the flaws in such a division (Schumpeter 1954, 431n, 507, 819–20, 823n, 875, but see particularly 954), and I wrote more directly to just this point (Perlman 1986, 268–80). One intention of this chapter is to consider the nature of the tie between Hayekian theorizing and American institutionalism, as well as the factors that separate the two approaches to economic analysis. The tie is there, expressions of intellectual animosity to the contrary notwithstanding.

But if there be such a tie, why then the animosity? The second intention of this chapter is to illustrate how the two "groups" (Hayek being perceived as the "theorist") came to miss the parallelism of their interests and conclusions, and to misunderstand the fact that each one's destination was the same.

---

1. As used, the term *economic theorist* relates to a general preference for dealing more or less logically with abstractions. Use of the term *empiricist* is somewhat harder to define. Surely those who measure observable quantities are empiricists. Yet I also believe that those who compare historical episodes (episodic empiricists) should be so characterized. The line between these two categories is fuzzier than most individuals who ally themselves with one approach or the other realize. While there are some really deduced economic principles, most were observed cognitively at one time or another. And even the most convinced empiricist, when it comes to setting up categories, does employ logic in defining their boundaries.

## The Economic Market and Its Purpose

In *The New Palgrave,* there are almost 25 double-columned pages devoted to the topic of the market. These articles approach the subject from the standpoints of (1) market failure, (2) marketing boards, (3) market period, (4) marketplaces, (5) market price, (6) market share, (7) market socialism, (8) market structure, (9) market structure and innovation, and (10) market value and market price. One could readily comment, as the author of the topic of marketplaces, Polly Hill, indeed does, that

> economists have displayed little interest in market places, as distinct from market principles, having condescendingly passed the subject to economic historians . . . ; their disdain has now become absolute in the sense that their exceedingly numerous publications on "marketing" never include the "place" in their indexes. This is odd since market places, especially those handling livestock or wholesaling meat . . . are far from being defunct institutions in Europe. . . . (Hill 1987, 332)

The market is seen as so basic an element in economics that it is its structural principles, rather than its significance, which have become the Golden Fleece for economic theorists. As Hill quite rightly notes, the institutional details of specific markets contain much that is revealing. In this essay, an exercise in speculation, the focus is not on the details, but rather on the question of the purpose of the market.

To inquire as to the purpose of the market may seem to some to be an exercise in futility; after all, has not the topic been exhausted? We know that markets are places where one exchanges goods or services for other goods or services, goods or services for money, or goods or services for credit. Yet the point is that there is still much to be gained by studying the purpose of the market. Economists sell themselves short intellectually, and underestimate their analytical abilities, if all they see in an economic market is a venue for exchange. The market serves a variety of other, typically neglected, functions, not all economic, but rather a great deal being moral, social, and political. Likewise, the study of markets cannot be confined to the purely pragmatic, but must encompass the theoretical, moral, empirical, and sociological.

Examples of market types are the following:

1. Obviously the most blatant test of a market is whether transactions take place. Transactions, in their purest form, are sealed bids made by prospective buyers and submitted to prospective sellers. This is the

process of *tâtonnement*, meaning literally to "grope one's way," a process which some economists possessed of tunnel vision believe is subjectively nonexperiential. This "groping", they believe, is achievable without cost or risk, that is, the transactions take place in a sterile environment wherein the participants are completely devoid of the fear of failure. The actor is completely skilled in the maneuvers, despite the blindness brought about by the sealed bids, he never loses patience, and always arrives at the place he so chooses.

2. A second form of market type is one often associated with *le sentier*. This type differs from *tâtonnement* in that the "groping" is associated more closely with the actual situation, whereby the actors are fraught with fear and are not absolved from considering the costs of their actions. The actor may quite often fall down, struggle and tire, lose patience, and be compelled to accept a settlement (read "price") that is less than optimal. The actor may be a seller or a buyer; if both seller and buyer are engaged in the market under the conditions of *le sentier*, the seemingly perfect efficiency of *tâtonnement* disappears, replaced by bluffs and other elements of strategic posturing.

3. Participation in the market, most obvious under conditions of perfect competition, leads suppliers (sellers) to consider the arrangement of their input costs according to the principle of least-cost combinations. Böhm-Bawerk's period of production, Marshall's short and long runs, recent work on the varieties of portfolio composition, and the familiar switching-reswitching controversy are all subsumed under this rubric. The modal blind man looking at an elephant "sees" this market as a model of allocative efficiency, and as a guarantor of price efficiency. Depending upon when and where we as economists were trained, this *Gestalt* was offered us under the label of Böhm-Bawerk, Marshall, Friedrich Lutz, Modigliani and Merton Miller, Tobin, Harry Markowitz, William F. Sharpe, and so on.

4. Conversely, participation in the market can be interpreted as the result of educating or advertising.[2] The intention of entering the market is gauged and judged. Education or advertising results in standardization of product, which itself usually results in the long run in scale economies and lowest prices, purchased at the cost of customizing preferences. In any event, the market perceived in this way amounts to what Alfred Marshall called the "secular shift." Great economic "revolutions" such as those brought about by the shift to steam, the shift to electricity, the shift to electronics, and the shift to computers and computerized information depended for their success on education,

---

2. I educate, he advertises; I lead, he bullies; I propose, he seduces.

seductive advertising, or a bit of both. This aspect of the market may be, to quote Winston Churchill, "its finest hour."

5. George Shackle once remarked that exchange did not require the presence of at least two parties; all that was required was one. To Shackle, exchange was choice, and everyone is engaged in the making of choices virtually every waking hour of the day. Thus the Shackelian market decision could take place subjectively within the recesses of the individual mind. However, these could be seen only when the individual actually acted, and so revealed through his choice the market decision.

As we shall shortly note, the writings of Hayek offer an interpretation much akin to that of Shackle, his student. But Hayek went even further, as he saw the market not as a place where goods and services were traded (objectively or subjectively), but as a venue for the exchange of information.

## Hayek and the Purpose of the Market

Hayek's writings on the market, its structure, meaning, and purpose, show not so much an evolution of thought, as his position early on was sufficiently developed intellectually, as they do a refinement and change in emphasis. We will examine this refinement of Hayek's thesis through a look at four of his numerous articles on the subject, written from 1933 to 1946. They will be presented in the order of their appearance.

Hayek's 1933 "The Trend of Economic Thinking" marked one of his earliest discussions of the concept of the competitive market and the functions it serves. In this discussion, generally overlooked as a progenitor of Hayekian ideas in the area, Hayek presented, along with a cogent refutation of socialism and centralized planning, an argument for the economic viability of institutions, the manner of their generation, and the important role they serve in the market.

Attempts by economists to understand in an empirical sense the subject matter of their discipline have all, according to Hayek, led to the realization that rational planning is not the agency responsible for the allocation of resources or the coordination of plans among the individual actors in the economy. The vehicle responsible for this coordination is one which is, for the most part, a mystery in its origination, and most certainly not the result of deliberate design. What empirical economic analyses of the competitive market structure proved was the contrary proposition, namely,

that changes implied, and made necessary, by changes in our wishes, or in the available means, were brought about without anybody realising their necessity. In short, it showed that an immensely complicated mechanism existed, worked and solved problems, frequently by means which proved to be the only possible means by which the result could be accomplished, but which could not possibly be the result of deliberate regulation because nobody understood them. Even now, when we begin to understand their working, we discover again and again that necessary functions are discharged by spontaneous institutions. If we tried to run the system by deliberate regulation, we should have to invent such institutions, and yet at first we did not even understand them when we saw them. (Hayek 1933, 129–30)

The failure of the perfect competition models is that they postulate the market instead of accepting its spontaneous development.

That institutions, of which the market is undoubtedly the single most important, develop spontaneously is not an idea with which most neoclassical and even Marxian economists are comfortable. That these institutions are not the product of human design and invention is disturbing; even more so is the realization that these institutions develop and flourish absent our knowledge of their genesis. Hayek attributed this deficiency on the part of economists to their inability to define adequately and label this attribute of the market. All we know for certain about these institutions is "that they perform a necessary *function*." (ibid., 130)

One of the errors economists make, notes Hayek, is in assuming that only rational intention and design can create a functioning, purposeful system. They refuse to accept that order can be produced from chaos without the guidance of a rational, omnipotent, calculating hand. This "anthropomorphic" attitude pervades the discipline; it is so entrenched that it taints the way in which economists view the market process, and by extension, the policy prescriptions they advance based upon this view.

This is probably the *last* remnant of that primitive attitude which made us invest with a human mind everything that moved and changed in a way adapted to perpetuate itself or its kind. . . . [W]e still refuse to recognise that the spontaneous interplay of the actions of individuals may produce something which is not the deliberate object of their actions but an organism in which every part performs a necessary function for the continuance of the whole, without any human mind having devised it. (ibid., 130)

Once economists accept that the intervention of a calculating planner is not a prerequisite for the establishment of a coordination system, and that institutions are the result not of conscious creation but of uncoordinated individual human activity (i.e., the result of "blind chance"), only then can they accept that economics has something to offer.[3]

Thus Hayek was led to his principal charge against economic planning. The sine qua non of the planner is to allocate so as to achieve a more efficient result than could be provided by the haphazard process of the competitive market. However, to do so requires that the planner be placed in the ironic situation of having to *emulate* the functioning of the market, for in no case will the planner be able to better the efficiencies thus obtained: "the wisest thing he [the planner] could do would be to bring about, by delicate regulation, what is accomplished spontaneously by competition." (ibid., 132)

Having thus demonstrated that the competitive solution is efficient, and that the institutions generated by the unplanned, chaotic, and in general incomprehensible interactions of individuals in the marketplace were necessary, Hayek next turned his attention to a different but related question, this concerning the role of knowledge in the market. It was with the publication of his 1937 *Economica* article, "Economics and Knowledge," that the foundations of the Hayekian theory of the market and the central role in this theory of information dissemination were to be expounded. Here Hayek developed the idea (already present in the works of Carl Menger and Ludwig von Mises) of the importance for the workings of a market of knowledge subjectively held and widely dispersed among the individual actors, which actors are separated from one another both temporally and spatially. In this article Hayek took up first the question of what constitutes an equilibrium. He showed that equilibrium is not an inherent quality of the market; it is rather a postulate of neoclassical economics. Equilibrium for the economist is defined as the situation whereby the expectations of the participants in the market are correct. It is therefore a concept suitable for pedagogy, where abstractions are necessary to distill the essence of the subject, but ill-suited for explaining the actual workings of an economy. These academic analyses are not designed to *demonstrate* the manner in which equilibrium pertains, but are instead assertions that there *exists* a series or sequence of economic states that converge to equilibrium. The theoretical model of perfect competition involves a misnomer, since it denies the very essence of the process it seeks to describe. It posits an outcome (equilibrium), which it is the expressed purpose of the theory to derive.[4] Equilibrium analysis is equivalent to the Pure Logic of Choice: both are vacuous tautologies.

---

3. "It is one of the causes of the unique position of economics that the existence of a definite object of its investigation can be realised only after a prolonged study . . ." (Hayek 1933, 131).

4. Hayek repeated this argument more forcefully in "The Meaning of Competition": "if the

For Hayek, equilibrium in the classical and neoclassical sense could only gain validity in two cases: (1) when applied to a single economic agent whose individual acts are conceived as part of a series of acts, or action plans; and (2) when applied to a competitive market with more than one individual, where the actors' subjective data sets are comparable and their respective action plans compatible. (Hayek 1937, 36–40)[5] Thus is equilibrium synonymous with (in fact it is defined as) "correct foresight."

With the concept of equilibrium thus defined, Hayek moved to the more important problem of knowledge. "Equilibrium theorists," by maintaining that in their ideal, "perfect" market "everybody knows everything," have handily dismissed the issue of how, in an actual market, economic agents, possessed of disparate data sets, can upon interaction arrive at a "competitive market solution." As in his 1933 paper, Hayek sought to understand "how the combination of fragments of knowledge existing in different minds can bring about results which, if they were to be brought about deliberately, would require a knowledge on the part of the directing mind which no single person can possess." (ibid., 52)

With this wonderment, Hayek concluded the essay. The advance from the earlier essay was in his acknowledgment that the central feature of the market, which results in the development of subsidiary institutions for the coordination of market activities, is the role of knowledge. This is the reason that neoclassical (equilibrium) theories cannot explain the emergence of institutions: they contain no mechanism for the treatment of the interactions of multiple actors with disparate information sets and noncoincident action plans. In Hayek's words:

> if the tendency towards equilibrium . . . is only towards an equilibrium relative to that knowledge which people will acquire in the course of their economic activity, and if any other change of knowledge must be regarded as a "change in the data" in the usual sense of the term, which falls outside the sphere of equilibrium analysis, this would mean that equilibrium analysis can really tell us nothing about the significance of such changes in knowledge, and would go far to account for the fact that pure analysis seems to have so extraordinarily little to say about institutions, such as the press, the purpose of which is to communicate knowledge. And it might even explain why the preoccupation with pure anal-

---

state of affairs assumed by the theory of perfect competition ever existed, it would not only deprive of their scope all the activities which the verb 'to compete' describes but would make them virtually impossible." (1946, 92)

5. "For a society then we *can* speak of a *state* of equilibrium at a point in time—but it means only that compatibility exists between the different plans which the individuals composing it have made for action in time." (Hayek 1937, 41)

ysis should so frequently create a peculiar blindness to the role played in real life by such institutions as advertising. (ibid., 53)

It was in later efforts at extending the theme of the market as an efficient information and coordination system that Hayek sought to explain the role of knowledge in a competitive market. The price system emerges as a sort of telecommunication network in his 1945 "The Use of Knowledge in Society." Prices are signals; the free-market, competitive economy serves as the mechanism for the efficient transmission of these signals in the service of the allocation of resources. Consistent with the argument of his 1933 article, Hayek here takes to task the advocates of a managed (planned) system, who assume that managed prices are just as efficient as those set by the impersonal device of the competitive market, but are more desirable (and understandable) because humanly designed and administered. The difference between the two sets of prices, those set by the planners and those set by the market, is that competitive prices reflect the outcome of a process of discovery and coordination.

This discovery process is analyzed in "The Meaning of Competition" (1946). It is a fallacy of the dogma of perfect competition that producers "know" the most efficient means of production and the shape of the consumers' demand curve. Consumers likewise are assumed to be omniscient. However, notes Hayek, the fallacy here lies in the fact that these "givens" are in reality not universally known, but are variables to be discovered. The process of discovery is one of learning the facts that the market itself generates. It is a process of extracting information, which information could not perforce have been known at the outset of the process since the actors would have been ignorant as to its very existence. The process of discovery requires that the actors learn not only the prices of commodities and the costs of production, but also the plans and actions of others in the economy; it is this process which leads the economy to a convergence to an equilibrium. This equilibrium is not a point to which the economy is gravitating, for Hayek's system is open. The prices "discovered" by the economic actors in the course of their activities are not even to be viewed as objective "givens," so their "discovery" is but a temporary guideline to action. In short, the competitive price, or the price determined by conditions of supply and demand to be the single market-clearing price for any single good, does not exist as a datum. In fact, in Hayek's scheme, every datum generated is replete with information and disinformation; the actor must arrive at decisions based on his fundamental ignorance. Perfect knowledge is not required; ignorance is in fact a necessary concomitant to action.

The market also serves as a *source* of competition: the attribute of free entry leads to new and ingenious ways of utilizing resources, and promotes the generation of new ideas and new wants and desires. The market *generates* ideas, preferences, technologies, and knowledge previously unknown or unrealized. The pedagogical perfectly competitive market abstracts from interpersonal relationships: "especially remarkable in this connection is the explicit and complete exclusion from the theory of perfect competition of all personal relationships existing between the parties" (Hayek 1946, 96–97).[6] Yet it is the measure of our ignorance of the entire menu of goods and services and their corresponding prices that we fall back on that which we in fact know: those suppliers, retailers, service personnel, and so on of whose constitution we are reasonably certain. In other words, Hayek contends, the competitive market, unlike the perfect competition model, allows a role for "reputation and good will" (ibid., 97). Beyond this, by giving meaning to interactions among the economic actors, the market also creates a venue for contracting arrangements between parties as a means of securing a degree of certainty.

A competitive market by itself, in the absence of a purposeful, constructive force, coordinates activity through the establishment of institutions (Hayek 1933). The market administers its activities through the interactions of individuals with incomplete information about their own wants and expectations and about the wants, actions, endowments, and expectations of the other actors in the system. What the actors perceive are guideposts, institutional frameworks, which serve to channel their activity (Hayek 1937). The convention that is most responsible for the channeling of this activity is the price system. It alone serves as the vehicle by which those possessed of limited information about the activities and workings of the market nonetheless, through interactions with others in similar circumstances, arrive at an orderly outcome. Thus, in essence the competitive market performs the planning function at a highly disaggregated level. "Competition . . . means decentralized planning by many separate persons." (1945, 79) Finally, the discovery process engenders competition beyond that of price. By admitting other attributes of goods and services, it allows discrimination by reputation and other means. By providing a role for contract, the Hayekian market as a process also allows for the establishment of an institution designed to bind interpersonal relationships: it provides for the establishment of the institution of laws.

### The Institutionalist's Contribution to the Debate

The precise constitution of an "Institutionalist" approach is perhaps a central problem in initiating discussion on this topic. Eschewing the simplistic definition of an Institutionalist as anyone who criticizes mainstream economic

---

6. As textual support, Hayek cites George Stigler's *Theory of Price* (1946).

theorizing, it is also difficult to accept the definition implying that all Institutionalists are antitheoretical, meaning antiformalist and antiabstractivist. A more reasonable definition considers the manner in which the individual fits into the economic process.

In an effort to understand the choices presented to the individual economic actor, choices relevant to him from the standpoint of decision making, Institutionalists have sought to describe the various aspects of the market process and the constituents of institutions, and to explicate the situations which have led to its use.

A. C. Pigou, only somewhat of an Institutionalist bent[7] and in his time hardly an antitheorist, was concerned with emphasizing that the market was so constituted (or should be so constituted) as to consider not merely private costs and benefits of any activity, but the social costs and benefits as well. Pigou was certainly well aware that in placing importance on costs and benefits, whether private or social, he would become embroiled in a methodological debate over the correctness of employing concepts not amenable to direct measure. Nonetheless, he felt that monetary measures, serving as proxies, were sufficient to handle the task. More significantly, he recognized the importance in decision making of reconsideration: he was not of a mind to admit that one should never look back and reconsider the choices one had made, but on the contrary was keenly aware of the importance of the admission of error.

John Maurice Clark viewed the market as having to give significant weight to overhead costs, as distinct from the variable costs so important in traditional analyses. One of the areas of individual choice that Clark felt provided a ground for public action was the case of the "complex decision in which many different elements of value are bound together in one act of choice" (Clark 1939, 153).[8] When the actor engaging in market interactions encounters a good of this complex character, Clark insists, he may be unable to make an informed judgment: the limitations of time and availability of

---

7. I ponder whether Pigou would have been more vexed at being considered an *Institutionalist* or an *American Institutionalist*. In either event, surely the *nil nisi bonum* rule can be waived after almost a half a century.

8. Clark listed two categories for public action. In the first he included provisions for (1) defense, (2) protection of person and property, (3) protection of public goods, (4) controlling inheritance, and (5) raising of revenues. In the second category are: (1) prohibition of monopoly, (2) maintenance of competition, (3) protection of "incompetent" individuals, (4) establishment of rules of incorporation, (5) disaster relief and prevention, (6) social insurance, (7) economic guidance (i.e., regulation of public safety in respect to products sold), (8) provision of equality of opportunity, (9) prevention of social costs associated with externalities, (10) provision of goods for which there can be shown to be a free-rider problem, (11) avoidance of negative effects brought about by "neutralizing actions," (12) involvement in the provision for use of unused capacity, (13) protection of the "interests of posterity" (e.g., conservation), and (14) involvement where there exist discrepancies between social and private accounting. (Clark 1939)

information on anything but the completed product force him to reach a decision absent a clear evaluation of the total utilities provided by the composite parts. But Clark admits that the complexities and "confusions" would not necessarily be reduced by political means.

> The political machinery should not supplant the economic but should be used, first of all, to strengthen it at its weakest points and prevent the most obvious abuses, that is, unless we are prepared to go over outright to a socialistic system. (ibid., 153)

Clark's definition of the individual is not markedly different from what one suspects Pigou would have accepted

> Individualism does not assume that the individual is perfectly intelligent, for a nation of such individuals could organize a socialistic state successfully and avoid the admitted wastes of individualism, but it assumes that he has enough intelligence to look after his own interests in direct exchanges better than some outsider can do it for him, and also to learn by his mistakes, thus converting them into essential incidents of the only life worth living: the life of a being who makes decisions and takes consequences. (ibid., 151)

For Clark, the market is an institution that appears to possess an objective existence: "An economic system is an instrument. . . . As an instrument, it is to be judged by how well it serves our ends" (Clark 1949, 52). Further, "the market has its own strong biases, promoting and protecting some kinds of values and relatively neglecting others" (ibid., 50 n. 1).

To take an example, consider the automobile industry. There are many who argue that the problems faced by this industry are tied up entirely with the private costs of technological innovation. This is, however, too simplistic. In the United States, we have socially mandated the placing of extraneous costs, first on the producer and, ultimately, on the consumer. We have mandated legislatively certain social overhead costs (e.g., pollution control, workplace safety, unemployment compensation) and certain other private overhead costs (e.g., liability insurance in the case of product deficiencies). Beyond this, we have institutionally (although not legally) mandated costs for vacation time, health care, supplemental benefits, and even, in some extreme cases, educational benefits. The works of Pigou and Clark provide us with a perception of the significance to the market unseen by other economists working in the mainstream. Their analyses suggest that, absent a willingness on the part of the producers to pay a part of the social and private overhead costs, effective admission to the market disappeared.

The position of Ronald Coase is not dissimilar to that of Clark, and contains elements of Pigou as well. To rectify social problems, specifically problems involving external diseconomies, requires the delimiting of property rights so as to maximize social benefits or minimize social costs.[9] To facilitate this calculation, which objective calculation it is, requires the acceptance of three key assumptions: (1) that perfect competition and perfectly competitive prices obtain, (2) that the environment is atemporal, and (3) that social benefits and costs are measurable. With these stipulations accepted, the problem becomes a trivial one of application of the optimization calculus to the social sphere. The solution is optimal where a solution exists, as it must be, given the preconditions. What remains is for a judicial authority (or other institutionally sanctioned body) to define property rights consistent with the judgment of the economic calculation.

Another way of looking at Institutionalism is through John R. Commons's idea of *industrial goodwill*. Commons, fascinated by the works of Maine and particularly Maitland, saw the legal concept of *standing* as the correct, applicable metaphor. Market participation required standing, albeit the requirement was sometimes placed in abeyance. Keeping "foreign" goods out, except when there could be an indemnification such as a tariff, is an example of standing. Licensure regulations are another. What this type of *purchased standing* suggested to Commons was that participation in the market required compliance with a web of legal and extralegal institutional niceties. Accordingly, to participate in the market was akin to social or political acceptance, or both. The market, in other words, defines the economic community; absent standing, there is exclusion. This defining characteristic of the market precedes consideration of such questions as pertain to the more usual economic problems, questions concerning such mundane matters as costs of production and the price and income elasticities of demand.

## Conclusion

Institutionalists regard the market as having an existence beyond that of the individuals whose interactions define it. They further consider that, given that it is an entity defined as distinct from its participants, with an objective existence, and that it has become anthropomorphized (as the equilibrium theorists are apt to perceive it), it may be subject to similar ills. Note Clark: "experience should be guided by a wise alertness for symptoms of impaired health and vigor in the system" (Clark 1949, 69). For Clark and the other institutionalists, the market is a purposeful institution that can be imposed

---

9. See Roy E. Cordato 1992 for a comparison of the property rights theories of Hayek and Coase.

from without onto an existing political and social structure. As extended by Coase, even property rights can be decided outside of the "market" (i.e., outside of the independent interactions of the individuals comprising the market) based on an objective economic calculation, and imposed costlessly and perforce more efficiently on the market participants. The market is then merely an instrument which can and should be tailored to the provision of socially desirable ends.

For Hayek, the opposite belief holds true. An economy is not an instrument. It is merely a natural outgrowth, defined as a coordination mechanism whose "existence" results from the interactions of individuals in their attempts to meet their subjective needs through the sale and purchase of commodities, services, and such. It is an institution, but one whose existence is not readily understood, and certainly not amenable to contemplation. The Hayekian market has no purpose, social or otherwise. It is neutral. To restrict the actions of its members requires institutions that compel the individual actors to internalize costs while engendering a greater degree of continuity and certainty in their perceptions of the environment. One should not attempt to impose a solution or an institutional form from without, since the bases for the solution will be pragmatic and will inevitably result in a greater degree of uncertainty for the participants. The market cannot be controlled or installed for the purpose of meeting human-designed ends.

A year has now passed since Hayek's death, and for good or ill we believe that the *nil nisi bonum* rule should still be observed.

Considered carefully, the approach of this paper toward Hayek and the Institutionalists is neither critical nor obsequious; it is merely to argue that Hayek's work differed from that of the Institutionalists. This difference is not seen so much in the destined purposes of the two approaches, or even in any manifest assertion of the superiority of one methodological position over another; phrased another way, one's rhetoric was not inherently more persuasive than the other. We merely argue that the two approaches differ in that (1) Hayek's analysis was conceived and generally phrased somewhat on the Kantian level (with the exception of his thesis that legislative or judicial foundations were essential for institutional legitimacy), and (2) the Institutionalists' analyses were somewhat more Hegelian (e.g., observation tempered their confidence in modeling) and pragmatic (e.g., they leaned in the direction of granting legitimacy to institutions on the basis of performance, rather than the manner of their creation).

To paraphrase Addison and Steele's famous eighteenth-century waffle, "there is much to be said on both sides." The principal lessons to be learned are that the "medium (rhetoric) is the message" only in the sense that one approach impresses some while the other impresses others, and that the fury of the "theory versus the institutions" debate was essentially irrelevant. The differences involve the plane of persuasion and a somewhat arbitrary decision to define institutions by their "legitimacy" or by their "instrumental effect."

One could do worse than to end this essay with a quotation from Francis Bacon's *Novum Organum:*

They who have handled the Sciences have been either Empirics or Dogmatists. The Empirics, like the Ant, amass only and use: the latter, like the Spiders, spin webs out of themselves; but the course of the Bee lies midway; she gathers materials from the flowers of the garden and the field; and then by her own power turns and digests them. Nor is the true labour of Philosophy unlike hers; it does not depend entirely or even chiefly on the strength of the mind, nor does it store up in the memory the materials provided by Natural History and Mechanical Experiments unaltered, but changes and digests them by the Intellect. And so from the closer and holier league of these faculty (the experimental and the rational)—which have not been connected—good hopes are to be entertained.

REFERENCES

Clark, John Maurice. 1923. *Studies in the Economics of Overhead Costs.* Chicago: University of Chicago Press.
———. 1939. *Social Control of Business.* 2d ed. New York: McGraw-Hill.
———. 1949. *Guideposts in Time of Change.* New York: Harper and Brothers.
Coase, Ronald. 1960. The Problem of Social Cost. *Journal of Law and Economics* 3:1–44.
Cordato, Roy E. 1992. Knowledge Problems and the Problem of Social Cost. *Journal of the History of Economic Thought* 14 (fall):209–24.
Hayek, F. A. 1933. The Trend of Economic Thinking. *Economica* 13 (May):121–37.
———. 1937. Economics and Knowledge. *Economica* (NS) 4 (February):33–54.
———. 1945. The Use of Knowledge in Society. *American Economic Review* 35 (September):519–30. Reprinted in *Individualism and Economic Order.* London: Routledge and Kegan Paul, 1949.
———. 1946. The Meaning of Competition. Stafford Little Lecture, Princeton. Reprinted in *Individualism and Economic Order.* London: Routledge and Kegan Paul, 1949.
Hill, Polly. 1987. Market Places. In *The New Palgrave.* Vol. 3, 332–34. Edited by John Eatwell, Murray Milgate, and Peter Newman. London: Macmillan.

Marshall, Alfred. 1920. *Principles of Economics*. 8th ed. London: Macmillan.
Perlman, Mark. 1986. Subjectivism and American Institutionalism. In [Lachmann, Ludwig.] *Subjectivism, Intelligibility, and Economic Understanding: Essays in Honor of Ludwig M. Lachmann on his Eightieth Birthday,* edited by Israel M. Kirzner. New York: New York University Press.
Pigou, A. C. 1952. *Economics of Welfare*. 4th ed. London: Macmillan.
Schumpeter, Joseph A. 1954. *History of Economic Analysis*. New York: Oxford.
Stigler, George. 1946. *The Theory of Price*. London: Macmillan.

# C. Essays in Biography

# CHAPTER 14

# The Fabric of Economics and the Golden Threads of G. L. S. Shackle

*My admiration for G. L. S. Shackle having been well articulated, no further explanation of this chapter is really needed. It was written to be delivered at a meeting where he was to be honored, and I chose to present a brief for his future enshrinement in the pantheon of economics heroes. He indicated in his concluding speech how genuinely touched he was by this tribute.*

The title of this chapter is intended to suggest that the long history of our discipline, whatever we choose to tell others, has historically been something different from an efficient linear search for scientific 'cause and effect' first principles. The body of economic knowledge as we know it, I propose, should be imagined as a tapestry, or, better yet, considering our propensity for wiping our feet on the past, as an oriental rug. It is a rug woven by different generations of thinkers and doers, each working within the framework of the facts and ideas of his or her time, and each hoping that from observation and/or excogitation some immutables could be distilled and put to permanent use.

To suggest that we currently enjoy conclusive persuasive evidence that we are now finally on the clear road to success, as implied when we employed that unhappy phrase, 'fine tuning', is universally seen to be an error. It is just that kind of error which seems to sear scholars for a generation or two. Yet to argue the self-denigrating reverse, that in spite of our efforts we have achieved little or no success, is similarly an error. It is best, it seems to me, simply to assert to our numerous, omnipresent critics that we clearly have not been pushed back to 'square zero', and that on the contrary we possess consider-able evidence that we have over the centuries, *including recently,* learned a great many useful things.

But there is more that ought to be said. Fifteen years ago those of us who were serious students of the history of our discipline should not have been surprised when the 'fundamental truths' of the form of macro-economics

---

From *Unknowledge and Choice in Economics* by Stephen F. Frowen (London: Macmillan; and New York: St. Martin's, 1990) 9–19.

prevalent at the time proved to be less than they had been billed. Indeed, anyone (and that should have included all economists who claimed to have been schooled in economic theory) who had read the literature on uncertainty could have expressed—and in some instances did—timely scepticism of that ill-founded confidence.

Thus, it can be argued that *a,* if not *the,* principal utilitarian-type reason for the study of the history of economic thought is to avoid a pattern of cyclical extremes of over-confidence and self-doubt about the subject. Appropriate study of this subfield can give us, *inter alia,* a detailed awareness that the weaving of the rug constituting our disciplinary history not only began long ago, and time and events have broadened and complicated its design, but that the minimum lesson we can offer our less-history-minded colleagues is that as with Mr Justice Holmes's *Common Law* (Holmes, 1881), there is in the old writings of our deceased predecessors a useful record of the 'life of the [economists]', which they dare overlook only at the peril of their continuing credibility.

Let me flesh out this point pertaining not only to the complexity of the pattern, but also to basic changes in the process of its weaving. Schumpeter (1914) possibly drawing on the seminal work by Luigi Cossa (1893), identified the initial era of our discipline as one which had moral philosophy at its centre. It is not especially important to my point whether it was the efforts of Plato and Aristotle or the Church Fathers (and their more peculiarly Jewish antecedents) which marked the beginning of the rug's or tapestry's design. What stands out is that Schumpeter (and possibly Cossa) were of the view that Adam Smith was the last master-weaver of the moral philosophy element in the design. Theirs was a pattern emphasising the integration of moral values, cultural *mores* as they were expressed in the material and service relationships between individual households and whatever communities of which they were a part, and an awareness of what was graspable by the minds of educated men. That 'first' pattern was distinct and included a healthy concern with the unknown and, if one reads the literature with discernment, with what appeared to be an appropriate appreciation of what was unknowable. This is a major point and ought to have been preserved as part of the English scientific method which so dominated much of what later became our discipline. It is a critical part of the original Bacon inheritance, for he himself included the 'unknowable' in his tree of knowledge. It was later writers on science and the scientific method who first eschewed mention of the 'unknowable' and later came to believe that, as such, that category really did not exist. Perhaps D'Alembert's disgust with theological matters and his effective elimination of religion from his tree of knowledge explains in a *de facto* way this critical change. In any event, by the end of the Second World War only a select few among the growing band of economists acted as though they believed that their subject had major areas which were (as the military men say) defiladed (that is, not visible from the standpoint of the observer).

The mercantilist tract writers (as well as Steuart, whose substantial product was far more than a mere tract), were the artists generally held responsible for the next set of designs. And they were followed by those self-conscious sons of the Enlightenment, the Physiocrats. Each of these groups (whatever the differences in their assumptions and conclusions) was not interested in anything so seemingly ephemeral as what was knowable and what was, in principle, beyond man's reason. Instead, each was concerned with trying to identify the mundane socio-economic class relationships involved in trade, the possible and probable ties between those relationships and what both might have to do with that seemingly most secular of all things, the modern nation-state. What they developed, relying in no small part initially upon Baconian observation as well as later on the Descartian *a priorism* method, was a non-Baconian 'amoralisation' or secularisation of their concern and a bundle of purported cause-and-effect regularities (about which they debated all but end-lessly). Believing that they dealt only with material realities or tangibles, what they sought were certain principles which, when translated into custom and/or legislation, would lead to perfectly predictable 'Newtonian' results. Thus, so they said, would the welfare of the 'commonwealth' be enhanced, a position which invariably also seemed to benefit their own group or social class. The emphasis on secularisation or a 'quasi-materialism' is said to have been a good thing; most of my contemporaries think so, and I am aware of their reasons. But something was also lost, and that is a point to which I want eventually to come.

Charles Webster in his study, *The Great Instauration* (Webster, 1975), suggests that the seventeenth century introduced into our current culture the view that with organised inquiry (involving both *a priori* and empirical efforts) scholars could (and should) develop general solutions to the specific social and economic problems, including economic growth, which the community seems invariably to face. His argument appears valid to me. Unlike what happened at such American universities as Harvard and Yale, where the Puritan tradition was preserved, in England the venue was changed from the university setting to Edinburgh and London. There gentlemen- or quasi-gentlemen-scholars created the principles of the classical design of our discipline. The members of that school, each clearly having been well exposed to the philosophy of scepticism, stressed discovery of the *scientific* (that is, the material) explanatory principles initially pertaining to the production but later also including the physical distribution of goods and services. What they ultimately wove was a Cartesian-like pattern, one which seemed simple, straightforward, and sketched in the most sombre of colours. It also included something else inherited from Descartes, namely a conviction that the development of physics-like or Newton-like 'completely explicable' systems were possible for explaining social interactions of which the spectrum of economic activities were a part. Theirs was a design that was taught long past the turn of the twentieth century but in fact actually stayed *in mode* only through the mid-1860s.

It is canon these days to refer to a hiatus in the mode of economic inquiry occurring about 1870, when the innovative economic-rug-weavers moved from a stress on the determinants of production to an equal but somewhat different kind of stress on the formal explanation of the distribution of income (or reward for the provision of economic inputs). But as we look back over our collective shoulders, I think that the achievements of the post-1870 weaver-artisans, those responsible for the 'great marginalist revolution', are more properly seen as the introduction into the grand design of the discipline of a third and even a fourth element, each probably not part of the Descartian legacy. One was subjectivism, in my view, an approach which had as its heart a cognisance of intuition. The other was the relationship between higher and lower order goods, from which there emerges a rather simplified interpretation of the element of time. Another change, no doubt a likely continuation of what had been going on previously, was the introduction of full Descartian rigour, that is the complete specification or 'mathematicisation' of the categories in economics. My view is that, except for the mathematicisation factor, the significant changes in design were more Mengerian than Jevonian. I am prepared to concede that this conclusion may be moot; even so, let us accept it as a minor element of the working basis for the points which I am suggesting here.

In my opening sentence I acknowledged the recent apparent loss of confidence among many of our profession's current hardest working rug makers. No longer able to advise with a confidence born of recent awe-inspiring achievements, they cannot unreservedly offer economic knowledge, particularly as it pertains to the descriptive or predictive efficacy of macro (or, in truth, even micro) models of the functioning of the parts of our economies. If I may be permitted a repetition and an extension of a brief deviation from my basic metaphor, in the 1960s we entered into and rapidly left the 'three-year era' of fine-tuning. We believed briefly that because we had mastered the collection of much concrete or objective historical data (which gave us the necessary firm grip on our 'scientific' generalisations) and because Keynes and Kalecki had purportedly provided us with a universal *a priori* model onto which we could successfully hang past data in order to forsee the full picture of a 'cause and effect' future, we had effective stabilising control of our economic future. The gods, doubtless aware of our *hubris,* wreaked their revenge. We were seen by the citizenry-at-large to have been deluded.

If this misplaced confidence became generally apparent in the late 1960s and early 1970s, the more careful among us had clearly realised the fault much earlier. On the objective or quantitative side readers of Simon Kuznets's 1948 thorough review of the Department of Commerce's work on American national income (Kuznets, 1948) were aware of the faults in the data elements of the design. To many his concern seemed to be more with the observational process than with the theoretical structure, but the truth is that any careful reading of his work also makes clear that he was too knowledgeable a historian to believe that the social accounting entities, which he had much earlier identified conceptually and empirically, were immutable. His conclusion was that the loom used by his own students, those putting the national income pattern into the rug, tended towards 'Procrusteanism', and that, in time, the resulting rigidity would lead to a loss of the appropriateness of their contribution. Not everyone thinks he was right, but there are increasingly those who admit that our national accounting system does not measure what Kuznets originally thought it ought ultimately to measure, the average quantity and quality of household consumption of goods and services (with some reference as well to the problem of the distribution of household income and wealth).

However, for obvious reasons, I am not speculating on the problems of the spinning of 'quantitative-type' golden threads in order to strengthen that aspect of the rug's design. Rather, I want to concentrate on another set of threads, the one associated with Austrian (Mengerian) subjectivism. This latter set is one which the rug or tapestry has long contained, even if it has not been sufficiently stressed in the recent (post-Second World War) training of our econometrically skilled younger colleagues. Obviously, what I have in mind is the strand identified variously as the unknowable element or as the complexity of the time element or very simply as *uncertainty*. We American students identified it all too fully with Frank Knight's *Risk, Uncertainty, and Profit* (1921), but had I read Knight's footnotes as carefully as I did the text, I would have realised that the idea was explicitly presaged by that genius— writing 'before his time'—von Thünen, to say nothing of many other neglected writers whose perception of time went beyond the original 'Newton' model. None the less, what I personally got from Frank Knight was a friendly speculation, offered while we were spending a day walking and talking: 'Given the inescapable fact that it took several millenia to teach man that inanimate objects have no choice and behave according to the simple principles of Newtonian mechanics, how long do you think it will take to teach man that he does have choice and does not behave according to any such simple sets of principles?'

More to the immediate point, however, is the observation that if I had read Keynes on probability as carefully as I had tried to assimilate Keynes on economic planning, I would have been similarly the wiser for it. I first came really to perceive what I had missed and what were inherent in the golden strands of subjectivism and the roles of imagination and intuition when I (as is probably true with many readers) came to the works of Professor G. L. S. Shackle. The seeds may have been in von Thünen, Knight and Keynes, but my perception of the recent blossoming and eventual fruit-bearing of the tree of knowledge came with my discovery of the writings and conversational contributions of G. L. S. Shackle.

Obviously there is a connection between Knight's work and the contributions of George Shackle, even if that connection has more immediacy to me, as an American, than it may have to others. Yet my reference to Knight is, I trust, something more than an expression of my provincialism. In a recent book, another 'American' (we are all immigrants), Jon Elster (1979), has laid out a treatment of intellectual systems linking Knight's and Shackle's perceptions in a way I find pedagogically brilliant.

There is in the self-selection of the group assembled a few years ago at the conference to honour George L. S. Shackle and to whom my remarks were addressed a basis for the judgement that my remarks need not attempt a comprehensive elaboration of his major ideas or a history of their development. But there is also in this same self-selection a need to express an historical concern that those who appreciate his contributions the most should compare their views of what are the 'leading golden threads' in his work so that our collective enthusiasm will serve to record his contribution. This is what I aim to do.

Specifically, it is the variations on his theme of the role of the imagination which I find most exciting. *Imagination,* the term itself, was intriguingly explored by Hobbes (Hobbes, 1651) and one can do worse than turn to Part 1, chapter 3 of his *Leviathan* in order to see the possibilities. None the less, I choose to use the term in a more limited sense, the one employed by James Mill in 1829, when he wrote, 'I am said to have imagination when I have a train of ideas.'

One aspect of Shackle's train of ideas admittedly starts with the selection of a choice among chooseables. But just what does that imply? It is that the spectrum of chooseables depends upon the individual's imaginative powers. Such being so, the individual is limited neither to one moment's imaginative capacities nor to any *single* set of imagined outcomes. The imagination can be an unlimited process; it is the mind in motion.

Thus, the imagination not only provides an ever-changing menu of choices, it can also be used to signal to the chef that the delicacies-in-process have lost their anticipated attractiveness. The consequence is that immediately, if the imagination is in gear, some new suggestions are on the way. The imagination is the master of choices, and it is a master marvellously lacking in constraints. Imagination is the weapon which we use to cope with uncertainty, a weapon which frequently triumphs in the battle between what is wanted, what is perceived (deemed possible), and what eventually happens. In practice, an alert mind, considering the scope of the power of its imagination, need not be overcome by the fact of darkness; it can in its own way contribute to the shaping of coming events. How it arranges its spectrum of choices is perhaps usually the result of what has previously shaped the individual's thinking—that is, his experiences, his reasoning patterns as well as the institutions which condition or 'provide boundaries' for his usual expectations. There are, thus, likely to be quasi-objective observable previous inputs worth studying. Indeed, that is what mastery of the disciplines of psychology and socio-economic institutional history purportedly gives the scholar. So there are ways in which the creative power of the imagination may begin (but only that) to be traced.

What follows a choice or a bounded set of possible choices need not be necessarily 'cast in concrete' either, because with a given act of choice a consequent spectrum of expectations comes to the subjective fore. If checked against later observations some or all of these expectations can be assessed and, if necessary, reassessed. A negative assessment can (and usually does) lead to the recall of the imagination. There is then a new opportunity to produce a revised spectrum of anticipations. So it is that one train of thought comes to be sidetracked, and another train is given the 'green signal'. Obviously, studying psychology and the impact on the behaviour of the individual of socioeconomic institutions (indeed, the whole cultural package), each necessary to reduce the 'boundaries of likely choice' is a heavy burden for any young economist (or thinker for that matter) to undertake. And in the need to know more about the mechanical side of the economic reasoning process, most of our best-trained younger economic thinkers never truly get around to the mastery of all that important semi-factual institutional material. I suggest, however, that when some do get to the point of absorbing vast amounts of that material, they will then have the beginnings (and that is the most they will ever get) of a grasp on how the selection of any particular train of ideas occurs. They will be approaching the process of imagining, which is, as I perceive it, the prior phase of the first step in economic action, the subjective phase preliminary to the making of choice.

Possibly if one studies game theory and particularly if one fleshes out that study with empirical work, as is now being done in what is called 'experimental economics', one might gain systematic (that is, systematic 'Baconian') insights into the *process* of imagining. In the effort, these studies ought not to be confined, however professionally reassuring such a step might appear to be, to simplistic maximisation problems. Other less mechanical objectives should also be kept in mind, for what has separated our greatest thinkers like Pareto and Max Weber from their more typical simple-minded economist and sociologist colleagues was the formers' willingness to observe widely and to expand the spectrum of possibilities (*to imagine big*) as well as to observe widely.

In my review of the many things for which Shackle stands, it is clear that I put even more stress on the originality implicit in his discussion of the nature and place of the *imagination* than on his admittedly excellent discussion of *choice*. This judgement seems to separate my assessment in a small way from the brilliant one made by James Buchanan (1980). In his review of what he calls Shackle's 1979 'distilled vintage' volume (Buchanan's term), Buchanan notes that what the Shackle legacy (Shackle's golden threads, if you will) offers us is a liberation from the traditional perceptions of choice. It is the contribution of subjective choosing as the method of coping with uncertainty which is Shackle's 'greatest' breakthrough. Buchanan likens that capacity to a rediscovery of the application of the relevance of free will (if you please). Free will even more than a perception of the Promethian possibilities of fire, is the principal divine gift to man. Or, to put the matter slightly differently, if choice is the expression of free will, I hold that Shackle's principal contribution has been a fuller understanding of the place of free will in the origins and possibilities of *choice*.

I aver, thus, that it is not *choice,* the noun, but *imagination,* the process, where for our immediate purposes the divine has touched man. This is the precise point which I find in Shackle's treatment—particularly as it is stressed in his most recent book, including specifically the title. And, I might add, it is the same judgement as the one made recently by Peter Earl in his stimulating critique of general equilibrium economics (Earl, 1983), a study I came across well after the time I drafted this paper.

In my view, the implications of Shackle's golden thread is that as we learn more about the process of imagination we will give more order to our understanding of *how* choices are made. It is in *imagining,* even as Hobbes noted in his discussion, where creative thinking and all economic choice processes begin. For economists, the theory of demand should not 'start' with an examination of what transactions reveal about market-place agreements; rather, it actually starts with choices within the mind between a spectrum of imagined possibilities. Or, to put the matter in its harshest form, settling for the final step (revealed preference) just because it is 'quantitatively' measureable is akin to looking for one's keys not where one suspects they have fallen (in the middle of a block in a dark street), but looking for them under the nearest lamp-post because there one can easily see. Relying upon revealed preference may be settling for unnecessarily cold potatoes (*cf.* Oskar Morgenstern, 1972).

In sum, Shackle's golden threads include an important, and virtually novel, emphasis on the role and uses of imagination. But it is an imagination working in its own dynamic time dimension, and that is a theme which he suggests but has yet fully to develop. Nonetheless, what he has offered us as part of our discipline, the fabric or rug recording our thinking, is a new awareness of what others have called *vision*. 'Study the past, observe the present, but imagine the future'; that is as much as one can do; and, as I see it, that is the most valuable part of his message. Imagination is the creative force behind the many and complex aspects of the economic process.

I would be among the last to give up asserting the point that our discipline has greatly benefited from the strong objective materials which have resulted in the impressive large geometric designs woven into the tapestry or the rug. But what Shackle, almost alone among his contemporaries, has urged is concentration on the choice process itself. That process, as I noted above, is imagination. A frequent synonym is *vision*.

If, then, what I write is valid, Shackle is in fine cultural company; for it is written in Proverbs, 29:18, that 'where there is no vision, the people perish'. Attention by economists to the neglected role of imagination—intuition, if you will—undoubtedly offers an opportunity for a comprehensive Descartian empirical research programme. But what Shackle has most clearly already given us on the theoretical side is that rare leavening agent (golden threads?) which makes organic (i.e., living) our discipline's current body of accumulated thought.

REFERENCES

Buchanan, James (1980) Review of G. L. S. Shackle's *Imagination and the Nature of Choice*, in *Austrian Economic Newsletter*, no. 3 (Summer), pp. 10–11.

Cossa, Luigi (1893) *Guide to the Study of Political Economy*, revised by the author and translated from the Italian by Louis Dyer (London and New York: Macmillan, 1876, 1892, 1893).

Earl, Peter E. (1983) *The Economic Imagination: Towards a Behavioural Analysis of Choice* (Armonk, New York: M. E. Sharpe).

Elster, Jon (1979) *Ulysses and the Sirens: Studies in Rationality and Irrationality* (Cambridge, New York, etc.: Cambridge University Press).

Holmes, Oliver Wendell, Jr (1881) *The Common Law* (Cambridge, Mass.: Harvard University Press, 1963).

Hobbes, Thomas (1651) *The Leviathan*.

Knight, Frank Hyneman (1921) *Risk, Uncertainty, and Profit* (London: London School of Economics, 1957).

Kuznets, Simon (1948) 'National Income: A New Version', being a review article on US Department of Commerce, Bureau of Foreign and Domestic Commerce, Office of Business Economics, *National Income and Product Statistics of the United States, 1929–46*, a supplement to the *Survey of Current Business* (Washington, D.C., 1947), *Restat.*, 30 pp. 151–79.

Mill, James, *Human Mind,* as cited in the *Oxford English Dictionary.*

Morgenstern, Oskar (1972) 'Thirteen Points in Contemporary Economic Theory: An Interpretation', *Journal of Economic Literature,* 10, pp. 1163–89.

Schumpeter, Joseph (1914) *Economic Doctrine and Method: An Historical Sketch,* translated by R. Aris (London: Allen & Unwin, 1954).

Schumpeter, Joseph (1954) *History of Economic Analysis* (New York: Oxford University Press).

Shackle, G. L. S. (1979) *Imagination and the Nature of Choice* (Edinburgh: Edinburgh University Press).

Webster, Charles (1975) *The Great Instauration: Science, Medicine, and Reform, 1626–1660* (New York: Holmes & Meier).

CHAPTER 15

## On Thinking about George Stigler
### (*with Charles R. McCann, Jr.*)

*In 1992 I was seated fortuitously next to John Hey, then and now the editor of the* Economic Journal. *In the course of conversation I lamented that no journal was systematically printing obituary notes or essays any longer. Whether or not it was that conversation (or others) that convinced him, the fact is that Hey resolved to restore the tradition. This essay was undertaken with the responsible collaboration of Charles R. McCann, who reads and understands almost everything and also has an ear for whimsy, and I thought his excellent and indefatigable digging up of Stigler quotations and quotations about Stigler was second only to his enjoyment of what we were doing.*

*After saying a few thing about Stigler's "crowd," we go on to discuss first his work in price theory and industrial organization, then his work on public policy, followed by his work on methodology and the history of thought. Part 4 deals with his efforts to enrage academia; Part 5 contains his book reviews, offering some splendid efforts at pricking the pride of most authors; and finally, we end with a synthesis of his credo.*

And still they gaz'd, and still the wonder grew,
That one small head could carry all he knew.
(Oliver Goldsmith, *The Deserted Village*)

George Joseph Stigler (1911–91) was for his time (the period from just prior to World War II until his death), the quintessential 'conservative', if perhaps mordant,[1] professional economics scholar. That he was a professional eco-

*Economic Journal* 103 (July 1993): 994–1014.

The authors wish to thank Moses Abramovitz, Gary Becker, Richard Cyert, Claire Friedland, Milton Friedman, Herbert Giersch, Geoffrey Harcourt, James Kindahl, Allan Meltzer and Herbert Stein for their generosity in offering numerous, always helpful comments on an earlier draft.

1. The quest for this adjective is illustrative of our difficulty in characterising Stigler. Our initial choice of term was 'curmudgeonly', which some of Stigler's most devoted students and a few others thought fitted him to a 'T'. On the other hand, many of his colleagues thought that

nomics scholar, there can be no doubt. Insofar as we can tell, his writings over a fifty year period, comprising no less than 30 books and pamphlets, 130 articles, and 70 book reviews, were generally at the frontiers of the discipline.

Educated at the University of Washington (BBA, 1931), Northwestern University (MBA, 1932), and the University of Chicago (Ph.D., 1938), he served as a faculty member at Iowa State College [later University] from 1936 to 1938, the University of Minnesota from 1938 to 1946, Brown University from 1946 to 1947, Columbia University from 1947 to 1958, and the University of Chicago (where he served as the Charles R. Walgreen Distinguished Service Professor of American Institutions) from 1958 until his death. He received several honorary degrees and *inter alia* the Nobel Memorial Prize in Economic Science in 1982 and the United States National Medal of Science in 1987.[2]

That Stigler was a *quintessential 'conservative'*, of course, rests primarily on the meaning of the term conservative.[3] Stigler defined the term, as applied to economists, as descriptive of 'a person who wishes most economic activity to be conducted by private enterprise, and who believes that abuses of private power will usually be checked, and incitements to efficiency and progress usually provided, by the forces of competition' (Stigler, 1959, p. 524).[4]

---

adjective off the mark; they noted that a curmudgeon is an irascible, churlish person, not at all descriptive of Stigler. They are correct; if that is what a curmudgeon is, it is not the appropriate word. Much searching has unearthed a more precise word. Mordant means caustic or sarcastic, as wit. In Stigler's case, he was invariably quite gentle in dealing with those he thought fools; it was those he thought deserving of his full attention who experienced the treatment. The treatment generally involved a compulsive scepticism used gleefully to burst popularly-held romantic and even professional soap-bubbles. Of course, in retrospect many of those who survived the experience and went on to 'fame and fortune' took rueful pride in exhibiting their intellectual scars.

2. He also served on numerous government boards, was elected to many learned societies, was a director of the Chicago Board of Trade, and served as President of the American Economic Association in 1964. From 1972 until his death he served as an editor of the *Journal of Political Economy*, the house organ of the University of Chicago. (His name appeared as an editor till the April 1992 issue.) His numerous honorary degrees include Doctor of Science degrees from Carnegie-Mellon University (1973), the University of Rochester (1974), the Helsinki School of Economics (1976), and many others. This is, of course, but a partial listing.

3. As Herbert Giersch (correctly) pointed out, it is perhaps more appropriate to characterise Stigler as a classical liberal (in the continental European sense). However, the term 'conservative' as defined herein is so firmly established in American discourse—and was so employed by Stigler as a self-descriptive term—that its use is seen as preferable.

4. Stigler went on to suggest that it was indeed true that 'the professional study of economics makes one politically conservative' (1959, p. 522). One suspects then that Stigler must have been taken aback (to put it mildly) at the suggestion by Joseph Schumpeter (in a review of Stigler's *The Theory of Competitive Price*), that the commencement of Stigler's analysis 'from a schema of "ideal" resource allocation' would better be handled under 'a well-chosen type of socialism' (Schumpeter, 1942, p. 847). Stigler's political conservatism was well-established: remember that he was, after all, a founding member of the Mont Pelerin Society.

We employ the term 'conservative' in a somewhat broader sense, the one in which it is most usually understood, namely the sense of wanting to conserve existing (traditional) ideas and existing (traditional) institutions (insofar as Stigler could mouth the word 'institutions' without flinching).[5]

*Existing* ideas and *existing* institutions. *Existing,* but as of when? As Stigler asserted, whenever given the chance, that he was a disciple of Adam Smith,[6] it may not be too far off the mark to suggest that he harboured a predisposition to think that while economic analysis had surely progressed since 1790 (the year of Smith's death), the framework, including but not limited to value judgements, upon and within which Smith operated should be conserved. Although Stigler did not hesitate in pointing out Smith's errors, he generally favoured that which Smith favoured; he generally opposed that which Smith opposed.[7] Smith favoured free markets (*laissez faire, laissez passer*) and opposed mercantilist (or for that matter any) policies which would have the effect of establishing a detailed network of social controls over economic institutions; Stigler in similar fashion favoured free markets and opposed mercantilist and regulatory policies. Smith favoured policies offering free access to education and distrusted intellectual and economic guilds; for Stigler those selfsame views remained more than merely adequate.

Natural Law institutions which were based for the most part on long-run market forces were for Stigler the best and perforce the most efficient and productive. As for those institutions which were designed as palliatives for short-term emergency situations, they tended to be faddish at best, and truly counterproductive at worst. Stigler's acute dislike for policies which had the effect of disrupting the efficiency of the market, e.g. such things as rent- and price-controls, is well known. His scorn for the policy of price administration and his cogent refutation of the Berle-Means assertion that the modern American corporation was run for the benefit of the managers are less well-known today, even though his acerbic exchanges with the latter's modern apostle, John Kenneth Galbraith, was for a time part of the lore of our profession.[8]

---

5. James Buchanan, in reviewing Stigler's *Essays in the History of Economics,* observed that political economists are more likely to be libertarian (right-liberal) than collectivist (left-liberal).

6. At the bicentennial celebration of the *Wealth of Nations,* held at Glasgow University, Stigler announced that Adam Smith was alive and well at the University of Chicago.

7. See especially Stigler (1976). Fortunately, Stigler was adept at interpreting Smith so as to have him favour that which Stigler favoured.

8. Consider the following: 'Galbraith's notion of countervailing power is a dogma, not a theory' (Stigler, 1954, p. 10). 'It would therefore be premature and even irresponsible to talk in detail of possible policy applications of so tentative and unplausible [*sic*] a hypothesis' (*ibid.,* p. 14). It was not always the case that Stigler had the last word in any argument. Consider the recollection of one who gave as well as he got, John Kenneth Galbraith. As Galbraith related the

The important thing to remember about Stigler is that he had faith in the science of economics, a discipline fashioned on logical principles but declared viable only when empirical testing failed to vitiate those principles.[9] Economics is not a branch of logic, but is rather an empirical science. Stigler's mentor at the University of Chicago was Frank Knight, renowned for his anti-(logical) positivist stance. Despite this situation, because of Stigler's advocacy of empirical testing of economic postulates, in opposition to the more rationalist views of Knight, there is little reason to believe that Stigler intended to be (or indeed that he ever really was) Knight's disciple or that Knight considered him as such. Knight's concept of uncertainty, for instance, did not intrigue Stigler, although he understood it well.[10] Knight's concept of value, however, was another thing; Stigler was intrigued by it, but thought it erroneous. His admiration of Knight centred more on Knight's erudition, and insofar as Knight served as a role model, it was his erudition which counted. Stigler was always far too much his own man, far too independent a person to be a mere sycophantic disciple.

The crowd with which Stigler travelled included early on some of the soon-to-be giants of the Chicago School, including such luminaries as Milton Friedman, W. Allen Wallis, Aaron Director, Kenneth Boulding, and Albert Gailord Hart. Although very much in agreement philosophically with this group, Stigler's positions with respect to the views of others were never compromised. Stigler's reviews of Boulding's 1941 *Economic Analysis* (Stigler, 1941*c*) and Hart's 1940 *Anticipations, Uncertainty, and Dynamic Planning* (Stigler, 1941*b*) were quite neutral assessments: critical where he disagreed and tinted with praise where he was of a mind. His assessment of Samuelson's *Foundations of Economic Analysis* is particularly impressive, and will be discussed in the last section of this essay.

This essay in some senses follows the development of Stigler's interests. Section I deals with theories of price, value, and industrial organisation (the latter being the field for which Stigler was awarded the Nobel Prize). Section

story, Stigler had said on more than one occasion that it was a tragedy of our time that so many had read Galbraith and so few had read Adam Smith. Galbraith replied, the deeper tragedy is that no one much read Stigler at all.

9. His faith in the scientific aspect of economics may be said to have been even more important to him than his faith in Smith. Milton Friedman maintains that his famous methodology essay, 'The Methodology of Positive Economics', owes much of substance to conversations between himself and Stigler.

10. Stigler thought the theory of expectations 'a mirage'. He even suggested in a review article that expectations, their formation and revision, 'depend[s] much more on the accumulation of data (of a type almost impossible to collect!) than on an increase in the versatility of our technical apparatus' (Stigler, 1941*b*, p. 359). This gives some indication of the reason for his aversion to Knight's concept: part of Knightian uncertainty, true uncertainty, is non-measurable. This is anathema to a convinced positivist!

II deals with his life-long interest in matters of public policy, including his forays into the areas of regulation and law and economics. Section III covers his impressive work in the area of economic methodology and the history of economic thought. Section IV deals with his thoughts about the academy he knew. Section V looks at his book reviews, some of the most impressive ever written, and the inimitable style he employed as devastating rhetoric.

Withal, one has always to distinguish between Stigler the mordant wit and Stigler the scholar. The former occasionally got the better of the latter; but even then it was only after something of a bitter inner struggle.

## I. Price Theory and Industrial Organisation

Stigler's achievements in many of the fields in which he wrote were well ahead of their time and so required from him a great deal of ingenuity in arriving at solutions to the problems he himself posed. He seemed to possess an uncanny ability to recognise a problem and an even greater ability to suggest possible solutions.[11] His 1945 'The Cost of Subsistence' may be said to have provided the impetus for later advances in the field of linear programming and its application to problems in economics. The thesis was disarmingly simple: how does one set about determining the minimum cost of obtaining the optimum calorific and nutritional intakes? Stigler, in proposing a solution to this problem, showed his genius not only in identification and analysis, but also in his ability to invent. He first determined the minimum daily allowances of calories, proteins, vitamins and minerals for a typical, 'moderately active' man. He then calculated from a list of 'potential commodities' (a list of foods and their corresponding nutritional values) and corresponding prices the minimum cost of supplying the nutritional needs by first narrowing the list to include the foods which were the most economical in terms of nutritive value,[12] and then by employing an 'experimental procedure' to discern the optimum combinations.[13] An elegant and simple solution to a perplexing problem, a procedure which would take others several years of effort to refine to the point of being applicable to equally challenging problems.

---

11. Much of Stigler's reputation was based on his abilities in this respect, and on the persuasiveness of his analysis. The problems of the discipline tended to become those which had been recognised by Stigler.

12. The surviving commodities were wheat flour, evaporated milk, cheese, beef liver, cabbage, spinach, sweet potatoes, lima beans, and navy beans (Stigler, 1945, pp. 306–7). Certainly this 'diet' gives some indication of Stigler's positivist inclination, for it is not a diet anyone would suggest following day after day.

13. Since 'there does not appear to be any direct method of finding the minimum of a linear function subject to linear conditions' (Stigler, 1945, p. 310).

Price Theory

In his 1939 'Production and distribution in the short run', Stigler argued that the neoclassical economists' preoccupation with the temporal definition of fixed and variable costs was wholly inadequate; accepting the view of Marshall *et al.* that the coefficients of production were variable, the neoclassical approach to production neglected the importance of fixed coefficients in the analysis of the short run. The problem with the fixed coefficient approach which made it inapplicable in its classical version was its failure to account for any but temporal components. For instance, over the short run, 'full adaptability' to changing quantities of variable factors is untenable due to the presence of fixed expenditures; but the law of diminishing returns, to have any viability, requires 'full adaptability of the *form*, but not the *quantity*, of the "fixed" productive services to the varying quantity of the other productive service' (1939, p. 307; emphasis added). Stigler's problem was with the assumption of perfect or full adaptability. One need also consider cost-price relationships and the expectations of future levels and time paths of prices and outputs. *Expectations* play a crucial role in the determination of the entrepreneurs' short-run cost schedules. As Stigler stated the argument:

> If major changes of output are frequent, relative to the life of the plant, and if they are not perfectly anticipated, then the plant existing at any time is in part determined by what the plant was in preceding periods. In other words, if the plant is at all durable and . . . if changes of prices are not fully anticipated, then in general the short-run cost curve will not be the lowest one for that size of plant, and it will not be one of the family of curves on which the conventional long-run curve is based (*ibid.*, pp. 319–20)

Demand conditions and the expectational responses of producers determine the speed with which a firm will alter its productive factors. The long-run cost envelope is a valid determinant of the profit level of the firm only under conditions of stability and certainty.

So much for the traditional theory of price in its analysis of the production decisions of firms! After Stigler, economists could no longer treat the short run as merely a temporal notion. He forced them to recognise the fact that, e.g. the amount of fixed factors of production is dependent on the entrepreneur's valuation of future demand (although the textbooks have yet to catch up). He also, incidentally, opened the field to the use of econometric modelling with his suggestion that lagged expectations were an important determinant of plant size.

In *The Theory of Competitive Price,* Stigler presented a textbook treatment of the subject of (what is now termed) microeconomics. The book itself is actually two works, one covering the methodology of economics, the other taking up the subject of perfect competition. In the methodological presentation, Stigler introduced the necessary conceptual framework, and provided the reader with the necessary analytical tools to allow comprehension of the economic material.[14] The remainder is a pretty standard treatment of price theory and the theory of demand under conditions of perfect competition.

*The Theory of Price* (1946*a*) completed the work begun in *The Theory of Competitive Price* (1942); it extended the analysis to cover imperfect competition, the theory of capital, and the pricing of multiple products. Apparently, though, this was not the venue for the introduction of the new and original concepts which Stigler had been advancing up to this time. A brief four-page section of ch. 9 is devoted to a presentation of the cost theory developed in his 1939 article (previously cited); the remainder of the references to his own studies are (with a single exception) to the historical material in his *Production and Distribution Theories*. But then are textbooks meant to serve as sounding boards for new ideas? More frequently they serve as forums for the presentation of the received wisdom of the past and for the teaching of technical competence.

In an effort to apply economic theory to seemingly unconnected problems, Stigler succeeded, in effect, in creating new and fertile fields of research. His 1961 'The economics of information' for the most part established the field of the same name and stimulated a great deal of interest and research in the economics of imperfect competition and the study of market structure. Again the premise was simple: information was much the same as any other economic commodity, and so could (and should) be handled in much the same way with much the same tools as economists employ to handle the analysis of other commodities. The cost associated with information-collection defines the market structure. Where information is costless, perfect competition is feasible; where not, imperfect competition results. This deceptively simple theory was later expanded (again by Stigler in his 1962 'Information in the

---

14. Schumpeter disagreed with Stigler's advertisement of the book as an advanced economics text. 'I wonder why Stigler calls his book "advanced". Recent refinements are hardly hinted at, and practically everything the modern theorist worries about is conspicuous by absence. It is as an introduction on an elementary level that the book has few, if any, peers—as a text, say, for the undergraduate course in theory . . . ' (Schumpeter, 1942, p. 844). Schumpeter's problem was that 'the intellectual effort it calls for is much below that required, at the comparable stage, from the student of theoretical physics . . . '

Fritz Machlup was more charitable, although a full page of his review was devoted to an enumeration of the problems with Stigler's treatment, including an exhaustive list of the errors of commission and omission (Machlup, 1943, pp. 263–5). A favourite line from this review: 'The second footnote on page 140 is such a "boner" that we had better delete it and blush silently' (p. 264).

labor market') to provide a basis for the theory of labour market search, and served as the basis for many later studies not only of the labour market but also in analyses of the economic function of advertising. Information is a form of capital good: it is producible by an expenditure of effort on search dedicated to its acquisition, and yields a positive product. It pays to continue the search until the point of equality is reached between the expected marginal returns from the continued acquisition of information and the marginal cost of this acquisition. It was in this context of defining information as a producible economic good that Stigler noted that a primary reason for the lack of complete knowledge on the part of the economic actor of market activities is its costliness; the fact that one must come to a decision implies that a local optimum, not necessarily a global maximum, solution may be the best attainable.[15] By an application of his theory of information in conjunction with traditional price theory, Stigler could generate deviations from pure competition (oligopoly, monopoly, etc.) without recourse to alternative, *ad hoc* theoretical specifications.

## Industrial Organisation

While Stigler's early writings dealt with the traditional topics of price theory, namely production decisions and cost considerations, and many of his later writings also concentrated in this general field, including as it does the economics of information, these early forays seem but a prelude to the work he would do in the field he all but founded, industrial organisation.[16] His 1947 'The kinky oligopoly demand curve and rigid prices' marked the first attempt at defining this new area of research, as it struck at the heart of the then fashionable (and ubiquitous still) theory that prices in an oligopolistic market are only flexible downward. After showing empirically (actually anecdotally, through a variety of different examples of oligopolistic enterprises) that the kink in the oligopoly demand curve did not materialise, that in fact price changes within oligopolistic industries were not infrequent as the received theory suggested, Stigler concluded with a statement suggesting that economists be more attentive to industrial behaviour and not simply assume that different market structures require different theories:

---

15. 'From this [the social] viewpoint, the function of information is to prevent less efficient employers from obtaining labor, and inefficient workers from obtaining the better jobs. In a regime of ignorance, Enrico Fermi would have been a gardener, Von Neumann a checkout clerk at a drug-store' (Stigler, 1962c, p. 104).

16. There is of course in the classical economic literature evidence of a concern with industrial regulation and with what may be regarded as industrial organisation. However, the modern incarnation of the concept, the development of the field in an empirical guise, is primarily the result of Stigler. We are indebted to Allan Meltzer for this clarification.

The kink is a barrier to changes in prices that will increase profits, and business is the collection of devices for circumventing barriers to profits. That this barrier should thwart businessmen—especially when it is wholly of their own fabrication—is unbelievable (Stigler, 1947*b*, p. 447).

But empirical testing which led to the falsification of the hypotheses was not sufficient for Stigler's critics; they persisted in their belief that the kink *did* exist, it *had* to! Stigler's reply: take account of the objections and point out to these 'scientists' the errors of their ways:

The objections will be inventoried, but first a comment should be made on one characteristic these defenders of the theory of kinked demand curves all share: the belief that they need not provide evidence to support the theory (Stigler, 1978, p. 190).

Throughout his research in the area of industrial organisation, Stigler highlighted a facet of theoretical analysis hitherto ignored but nonetheless critical in the demonstration of economic hypotheses: that one may arrive at alternative consequences dependent upon the assumptions with which one begins his analysis. He argued that one should not assert *a priori* that a given market is one characterised as perfectly competitive or monopolistic or oligopolistic, but stressed rather that these market structures themselves be deduced from the more primitive assumptions (axioms) of profit maximisation or cost minimisation.[17] This may be termed the *sine qua non* of the theory of industrial organisation: study the behaviour of the enterprise as an economic entity. He put it this way:

A satisfactory theory of oligopoly cannot begin with assumptions concerning the way in which each firm views its interdependence with its rivals. If we adhere to the traditional theory of profit-maximizing enterprises, then behavior is no longer something to be assumed but rather something to be deduced (Stigler, 1964, p. 44).

It was with this understanding that Stigler approached the subject of industrial organisation. In the 1964 'A theory of oligopoly' he tackled the problem of collusion in an oligopolistic market. The difference between his

---

17. Stigler learned. Stigler did not always adhere to this stance. In his *The Theory of Competitive Price*, he opined: 'Competition is a better single *assumption*, even on the basis of realism, than monopoly . . . ' (1942, p. 23, emphasis added). It should be noted that this line, gleaned from the review by Machlup (1943, p. 263) because of the inability to find a copy of the book, did not survive through to the later *The Theory of Price*.

and the mainstream treatments was, as with many of his studies, its empirical nature. It had been assumed in the earlier efforts that in an oligopolistic market, forces worked to generate collusive agreements which were subject neither to alteration nor cancellation. Stability was thought to be a defining characteristic of the oligopolistic market structure. Stigler simply rephrased the thesis. Instead of collusion being the *result* of the structure of the market, collusion became the chief factor in the *determination* of the market structure. Through this reorientation, new and intriguing hypotheses could be entertained, among them being: (a) as the number of firms in an industry is constantly changing, the cost of collusion rises, forcing the industry into a competitive structure; (b) as the product line becomes more heterogeneous, collusion becomes costlier and competition becomes manifest; (c) where collusion can be had at a low cost, monopolistic competition or oligopoly result; and (d) where collusive practices are stable, oligopoly arrangements have the potential for longevity.[18]

## Administered Prices

Clearly Stigler evinced a penchant for the empirical testing of economic hypotheses. Each of the above-listed hypotheses are testable empirically and more importantly are falsifiable. For Stigler, a hypothesis is testable only if falsifiable. But the tests employed themselves must have a certain validity; one cannot impose inappropriate testing procedures upon a given set of empirical data. The theory of administered prices advanced by G. C. Means provides one example of what Stigler felt was poor empirical analysis. Means' thesis, held with a dogmatic fervour, was that industrial price behaviour was 'perverse', i.e., that industrial prices were not responsive to the conditions and dictates of the market. Although Stigler had tackled the issue in his seminal article on the kinked oligopoly demand curve, this new challenge forced a reorientation of effort, an examination of the problem from a slightly different perspective.

In his 1962 'Administered prices and oligopolistic inflation' Stigler dissected the theory of administered prices and found an empty cavity. He noted three problems with the Means' classificatory scheme, to wit (1) subjectivity

---

18. 'The great merit of our theory, in fact, is that it has numerous testable hypotheses, unlike the immortal theories that have been traditional in this area' (Stigler, 1964, p. 59). Cf. the conclusion to which he arrived some years earlier: 'The chief barriers to monopoly, in addition to the Sherman Act, have been the capital requirements of mergers and the tendency of rivals to grow in number and size' (Stigler, 1950a, p. 33). 'We are thus led to "new entry" as the chief defense of competition—a most unseemly reversion to the ruling economic theory of 1900' (*ibid.*, p. 33).

in classification,[19] (2) ambiguity in the definition of frequency of price changes, and (3) lack of a pattern for the price series used. All in all, the Means thesis was supported by poor empirical research and an ill-defined methodology. But the theory would be resurrected again and again, and so would require additional Stigler responses.[20] The next came in the form of a book-length analysis of industrial pricing by Stigler and James K. Kindahl (1970).

One of the problems Stigler and Kindahl discovered in reviewing the Means thesis was in deciding precisely which prices were relevant. Means accepted the series provided by the Bureau of Labor Statistics, which was an index of seller's (reported) prices. Stigler and Kindahl constructed a new series of buyer's (transaction) prices, held to be more indicative of responses to economic conditions, and then proceeded to review the thesis in an attempt to determine whether it held up under this set of pricing data. The thesis failed the test; it could not be shown that, based on the evidence of the transactions prices, such prices were unresponsive to changes in economic activity. Stigler's perceptive conjecture of 1947 had again failed to be refuted empirically!

A second set of problems arose in the definition of 'administered prices'. The problem arose because Means' definition was hopelessly vague (perhaps purposely so) and so was susceptible to reinterpretation as the characteristics of the sample changed. Since the very criterion as to the characteristic of an administered price was so vague and imprecise, it stands to reason that one could not apply testing procedures which would have the effect of isolating specific instances.[21] Using their own standardised definition, Stigler and Kindahl discovered that the Means thesis was unfounded. As they stated in the conclusion to a later study of the same problem:

> The thesis that modern economics has received from [G. C.] Means, whatever he intended, is that perverse or unresponsive price behavior is widespread. Our study, without benefit even of data from a large or protracted recession, contradicts that thesis (Stigler and Kindahl, 1973, p. 721).

---

19. '. . . the classification of price areas is highly subjective, not to say whimsical' (Stigler, 1962a, pp. 2–3).

20. '. . . it is fair to say that economists abandoned the close study of the subject, less because its lack of scientific import was established than because it had become boring' (Stigler, 1962a, p. 1).

21. 'In the absence of a well-defined set of criteria, and rigorously derived implications, no test can be convincing' (Stigler and Kindahl, 1973, p. 719).

Despite its repeated rejection as a viable economic hypothesis, it appears that the motive behind the continued appeal of the Means thesis was that it promoted legislative action. This Stigler had not failed to notice, even mentioning the 'price notification bill' which drafting followed the Senate hearings on the matter of administered prices held in July 1957. Poor analytical techniques, applied to a misformulated thesis, yielding suspect results was to be the basis for unnecessary and counterproductive legislation designed to control a phantom problem. Stigler's reply: 'To turn a governmental body loose on an immense area without even primitive criteria for judgment would be the most reckless of ventures' (Stigler, 1962a, p. 12).

Like considerations applied to Stigler and Claire Friedland's (his colleague in many of his empirical studies) denunciation of the Berle-Means thesis of the divergence in terms of executive compensation between the owner-dominated and the manager-dominated companies. The empirical studies by Stigler and Friedland showed no such divergence, contradicting the earlier findings.[22] What they showed instead was the utter disregard by Berle and Means of the functioning of the economic system. The concluding remark was typical Stigler: 'The main tradition of economic theory was perhaps instinctively recognizing these facts when it continued to work in complete disregard of *The Modern Corporation*' (Stigler and Friedland, 1983, p. 259).[23]

## II. Public Policy, Political Economy, and Regulation

Stigler made many pioneering contributions to the fields of law and economics, the economics of regulation, and other areas within the realms of political economy and public policy economics.

In his work in the area of economic regulation, he set the standard by which others could measure their results, defining the arguments, previously couched in political or legalistic jargon, in economic terms, suitable to allow application of a methodological framework for which positive solutions and testing procedures were available. In their 1962 paper 'What Can Regulators Regulate? The Case of Electricity', Stigler and Friedland showed that it is very often the case—it is perhaps typical—that the policies of regulatory agencies and the very rationale for their existence are not as advertised. Traditional theories of regulation held that regulatory agencies served a public-interest function only in the very early years of their existence, but that eventually they became senescent. While founded with the best of intentions,

---

22. 'Our investigation will support the view that doctrines and theories congenial to an intellectual milieu are accepted quickly and widely, although not necessarily as uncritically as the work of Berle and Means was accepted' (Stigler and Friedland, 1983, p. 237).

23. Although note: 'Almost without exception the lawyers received the book warmly, and often extravagantly' (Stigler and Friedland, 1983, p. 241).

the regulatory bodies eventually became co-opted by the very interests they were designed to regulate.

Never of a (collective) mind to accept uncritically such a sweeping generalisation, Stigler and Friedland took the unusual step of actually putting the hypothesis to the test. The question they asked: Does regulation make a difference in the behaviour of the regulated industry? To answer this question required analysing the effects of regulatory policies and not simply the processes by which they can be adopted and implemented. The effects of regulation are measurable and can be studied by examination of the pricing structure of the regulated industries, through comparative analysis of pricing data before and after the regulatory agencies had been established. The rest is an application of traditional price theory. Specifically, the authors noted that, in the case of the regulation of electricity-generating utilities, where such regulation is designed to bring into line the prices charged for the provision of electricity, the regulators had failed to achieve their stated goals. The pricing structure had remained unchanged after the establishment of a government regulatory body designed to alter it. [24]

Again, Stigler had succeeded in posing questions to which many sought answers: what is the role of the regulatory agency? Who is the beneficiary of the regulatory process? The answers to these additional questions were forthcoming in his 1971 'The theory of economic regulation'. The answers, in typical Stiglerian fashion, again involved the employment of traditional price theory (a mainstay of Stiglerian analysis) to the solution of a supposedly political problem (and one which had always been treated as such). By postulating that firms within industries are profit-maximisers, and that the political system is rational (and hence by extension that the regulatory process is a rational one), regulation of economic activity is simply the result of the prudent use on the part of the enterprise of an available resource (the coercive power of the state as it is applied to the restriction of economic activity) to ensure a profit. Industry regulation, whether it be achieved through direct subsidies, the erection of entry barriers, the promotion of industries manufacturing complementary goods, or the establishment of price controls, is designed and promoted by the industry itself, as the industry discovers that the coercive power of government serves a useful function, namely it has a positive impact on profitability. If the market is neither inherently oligopolistic nor monopolistic, if the supply curve is not inelastic, other avenues must be explored in an effort to keep the total of industry profits from being diluted by the presence of a large (and potentially growing) number of entrants in what is already (to the firms in the industry) a sufficiently competitive market.

---

24. Perhaps this explains the title of Stigler's autobiographical sketch, *Memoirs of an Unregulated Economist*.

The regulatory process promotes subterfuge: the stated purpose of the regulation (usually being for the protection of the consumer and the well-being of the public) is generally not the intended purpose, but the intended purpose can never be made explicit.

In other words, it is in many instances to the benefit not of the *consumers* of the commodity, but of the established *producers* to have the industry regulated. Only in this way (we are assured) can the product be delivered at the lowest possible cost, and, by the way, only in this way (we discover later) can the producers be shielded against unwelcome competitors.

Stigler's 'The optimum enforcement of laws' applied economic-based theories of regulation to the area of law enforcement (following on the path-breaking studies of Gary Becker). He argued in this arena for a set of 'rational criteria', much in line with the positive criteria which guide the economist in his analysis of economic problems, to supplant the normative criteria currently employed (which are capricious at best) in the creation and the enforcement of laws. As with any 'commodity', the acquisition of law enforcement comes at a cost: the amount of law enforcement forthcoming is a function of the resources dedicated to its acquisition. But also as with any commodity, law enforcement is subject to diminishing returns; marginal considerations are important for optimal allocation. The economist could, then, by an application of the principles of price theory, engineer a rational system (at least at the theoretical level) of enforcement. Why then has the system of enforcement not been 'rationalised'? To ask the question is to answer it. What hindered progress in this area was the attitude of the public: the public did not evince an interest in the pursuit of rational criteria in the enforcement of laws, since acceptable norms of behaviour which guide our definition of legality are normative social contrivances, not rational principles.

As policy analysts, economists should attempt neutrality, i.e., they should practice positive economic analysis; value judgments have no place in a discipline seeking recognition and validation as a science. But in any event, should economists feel compelled to take a normative position, they must be prepared to offer policy makers evidence that a proposal is sound and will achieve its intended goals.[25]

> The basic role of the scientist in public policy . . . is that of establishing the costs and benefits of alternative institutional arrangements. . . . A modern economist has no professional right to advise the federal government to regulate or deregulate the railroads unless he has evidence of the effects of these policies (Stigler, 1965*a*, p. 2).

---

25. 'One should reckon among a scholar's achievements not only what he wrought but also what he prevented' (Stigler, 1990, p. 12).

The problem was one which Stigler frequently revisited: no economist, if he is to be worthy of the profession, can or should advocate programmes or policies without a fully documented empirical analysis of the efficacy of such programmes and policies.[26]

## III. Methodology and the History of Economic Thought

It may be said that Stigler had a fascination from the very beginning of his professional career with the history and methodology of economics. Although his definition of the scope of the discipline of the history of economic thought is severely restrictive—'I define the subject matter of the history of economics to be economics which is not read to master present-day economics' (Stigler, 1969b, p. 217)—this did not prevent him from referencing historical episodes and invoking historical analogies in his theoretical work. Indeed, methodological and historical references and considerations are evident throughout virtually all of his writings. His first published article, 'The economics of Carl Menger' (1937), argued for a resurrection of interest in and reappraisal of the economic theories of Menger and the Austrian school. He even went so far as to place Menger's *Grundsatze* on a level with the texts of Smith and Marshall.

Stigler's historical writings on Adam Smith (1971b, 1976), David Ricardo (1953, 1958), Alfred Marshall (1969a, 1990), Henry L. Moore (1962b), John Stuart Mill (1968), Stuart Wood (1947a), Henry C. Simons (1974), and Charles Babbage (1991) (to name but a few) are lucid analyses of the individuals and their beliefs, punctuated by reference to Stigler's own predilections and critiqued in so gentle a manner as to be flattering. His examination of Ricardo led to his questioning whether Ricardo had ever in fact advocated a labour theory of value, a supposition which had heretofore been taken for granted. His review of the career of Simons presented the Chicago economist as a visionary whose goal was the establishment of a decentralised economic system and a utopian social environment designed to promote individual liberty. His essay on Moore shed new light on the founder

---

26. Stigler thought the tendency of many economists to propose or support programmes without proper empirical support a flaw that was pervasive throughout the history of economics: 'One thing did not change at all, however, from the heyday of *laissez faire:* no economist deemed it necessary to document his belief that the state could effectively discharge the new duties he proposed to give to it' (Stigler, 1965a, p. 8). To see that the flaw is present in much economic work even today, one need only consult analyses accepting uncritically the data provided by the U.S. Congressional Budget Office (which the director himself admits is erroneous, improperly calculated, and in many cases involves an improper mixture of disparate data sets). The policy papers drafted by the CBO are little more than studies-on-demand: you tell us what you wish to prove, let us prove it! It is interesting to note that these 'official data' are often cited by left-leaning 'policy institutes' to justify their 'findings'.

of statistical economics, whose work, while important, had sadly been forgotten. To say more about these marvellous essays in biography and intellectual history would be to deny the reader the opportunity to discover them first-hand.

His dissertation, published in 1941 as *Production and Distribution Theories* (and written under the tutelage of Frank Knight), is a historical analysis of price and value theory covering the period of the greatest theoretical advances in the subject. The treatment of the historical material coupled with a trenchant analysis of the theoretical foundations is unmatched.

The two part 'The development of utility theory' is still ranked among the most comprehensive historical analyses of the subject, and continues to be referenced even today.

Within the history of thought (actually the historiography of economics), Stigler sought, as do many historians, to discover the originator of a particular position or idea. We all desire to know from whence came an idea which seems to have at the time altered radically the foundations of a discipline, but which is now accepted as conventional wisdom. Unlike others, he defined 'originality' in a much different way, more in line with the actual evolution of scientific theories. Originality is not to be so limited as to apply only to the first person to express a concept or enunciate a position. It is not enough for an individual to have stated and held to a position; the position itself must be accepted as intellectually valid. Simply having referenced an idea in a footnote or a passing aside does not provide evidence that an author was possessed of a brilliant and incisive mind. As Stigler defined it, 'originality . . . is a matter of subtle unaccustomedness' (Stigler, 1955, p. 295). Originality is a combination of 'temporal priority', non-radicalism (i.e. the ideas do not deviate too far from the mainstream), and relativity to mainstream thought. The originator of an idea must have at his disposal a willing and receptive audience, ready to be persuaded, primed to the acceptance of a new and different point of view. Once the audience is so prepared to accept a new discovery, a brilliant and, dare it be said, a boldly innovative and unorthodox challenge to convention, only then can the expositor of such a position be granted the mantle of original thinker.

To be sure, innovation and originality were for Stigler two entirely different concepts. An innovator is one who advances a new and controversial view or notion; an originator is one who advances such a notion and has it accepted.[27] His discovery stays discovered. The difference of course is that for the originator, the profession has become attuned to the advocacy of novelty, and may even be expecting of it.

---

27. Note that in the case of the linear programming model, Stigler would be considered an innovator, not an originator.

. . . discoveries are dictated by the evolving logic of the science—new ideas are not in the air, as it is often said, but near the surface of the work that has just been completed (Stigler, 1969*b*, p. 226)

To be acceptable, the new ideas will most likely be derivative from those which exist as conventional wisdom or received doctrine. The idea is there, but has escaped notice because the conventional theorists have been attuned to conventional interpretations, not the unusual or the bold. Or it may be that, at long last, the opportunity presents itself for the acceptance of an unusual interpretation of the commonplace; the discipline has become receptive to uniqueness and change.

On the Stigler model, Smith and Marshall and Keynes were undoubtedly visionaries whose novel approaches appeared at the most opportune moments; Mill was a somewhat lesser light, whose ideas were so buried in the conventional structure as to be indistinguishable as innovations.[28] Cournot and Myrdal were innovators, but with ideas too radical or too far removed from the mainstream to be thought of as 'original' (causing their contributions to be relegated in current expositions to footnotes). But even conceding that the discipline is ready for originality, and even though the ideas may be already apparent in the corpus of intellectual output of the time, to gain acceptance of a new idea requires much persuasion, including exaggeration, repetition, and 'disproportionate emphases'. These are the keys to having one's originality accepted.[29]

Stigler advanced the notion that economics as a discipline and profession progressed from the pre-scientific stage (literary heuristics) to the scientific as the subject-matter and the overall concerns of the profession changed. Incomplete knowledge, an ill-defined field of study, the lack of generally-accepted criteria for research, and poor interaction among the 'professionals' define the pre-scientific stage; a secure knowledge base, defined parameters of study (a 'disciplined discipline'), accepted research procedures and methodological frameworks, and agreed-upon criteria for professionalisation define the scientific stage. Those who advocated what may be termed environmental determinism to explain the development of economic theory (a position Stigler declared had been held, at least implicitly, by Wesley Clair Mitchell in his description of the development of economic theory prior to 1870) had to ultimately relax their stance as economics became scientific; the environmental model of theory construction, while a plausible explanation of literary

---

28. Although as Stigler was quick to point out, Mill made many significant, original contributions (Stigler, 1955, pp. 296–9).

29. Moses Abramovitz remarks: 'Well, if that is the way George wants it, that's all there is to it, but it does not strike me as a particularly useful way of doing history.'

economics (pre-utility theory), was simply unable to explain the development
of economic theory after 1870 (Stigler, 1983*b*, p. 533).

According to Stigler, it was not the case that economic theory advanced
as economists attempted explanation of changes in the environment. The
reasoning was straightforward: if the environment generates theories, why
should competing theories exist simultaneously? Marginal utility theory, e.g.
did not arise as a result of attempts to understand and explain contemporary
empirical conditions, but rather because of the rise to prominence of academic
economists whose focus was on the abstract.

> None of the great areas of classical economic literature would have
> gained much from utility theory. . . . Utility theory would have had little
> to say about corn laws and free trade . . . , about central banking and
> Peel's Act, about colonization and overpopulation, about Poor Laws or
> Factory Acts, even about Say's law or taxation.
>
> What utility theory contributed was precisely the values we attribute to
> the academic world and in particular to the academic sciences. . . . The
> method of the classical school had been literary and numerical. Now the
> utility theory obviously permitted and even invited the use of mathemat-
> ics (Stigler, 1972, p. 578).

Despite this explanation for the proliferation of abstract theoretical economic models, Stigler's work throughout emphasises economics as a positive
science. That economics is indeed a science he had no doubt—'to say that
economics is a science is a description, not an encomium' (Stigler, 1946*a*,
p. 3)—and indeed a defining characteristic of a scientific discipline is that it
allows one to distinguish 'generalisations' (with empirical content) (Stigler,
1955, p. 299) which we define as 'laws'. Although knowledge of general
relations is necessary for understanding, empirical testing is a prerequisite for
the explanation of actual behaviour. 'The important purpose of a scientific law
is to permit prediction, and prediction is in turn sought because it permits
control over phenomena' (Stigler, 1946*a*, p. 3). The theories of economists
are not concocted in a vacuum, but are directed at the description and explanation of empirical phenomena, while not necessarily being themselves attuned
to the events and problems of the day.

> The central task of an empirical science such as economics is to provide
> general understanding of events in the real world, and ultimately all of its
> theories and techniques must be instrumental to that task. That is very
> different from saying, however, that it must be responsive to the contem-
> poraneous conditions and problems of the society in which it is situated.
>
> If the problems of economic life changed frequently and radically and

lacked a large measure of continuity in their essential nature, there could not be a science of economics. An essential element of a science is the cumulative growth of knowledge, and that cumulative character could not arise if each generation of economists faced fundamentally new problems calling for entirely new methods of analysis (Stigler, 1983*b*, p. 533).

Theory need be atemporal, divorced from contemporary challenges, in a word 'persistent', if for no other reason than all science would cease to evolve absent a foundation of accepted and timeless belief.

But why bother with the study of the history of economic thought? Again, Stigler's answer was simple and to the point: 'Not only can the study of the history of economics teach one how to read, it can also teach us how to react to what we read' (Stigler, 1969*b*). Need anything more be said on the matter?

## IV. Academia

Stigler never missed an opportunity to engage (and at times enrage) the academy. 'A sketch of the history of truth in teaching' (1973) and 'An academic episode' (1947*c*) are marvelous caricatures of the professions, revealing certain aspects of the nature of academia with just the right amount of satire. Who but Stigler could have traced the consequences of a litigious society working in tandem with a pro-regulatory government on the future of academia? (The result: more government regulation, in this instance the creation of the Federal Bureau of Academic Reading, Writing, and Research.)[30] Is there another who could begin with an empirical observation—that young assistant professors, at the peak of creativity, are saddled with duties that prevent them from achieving in their research, while older professors, who have the most time for research, are beyond creative pursuits—and, looking at proposals for its replacement (in the guise of a South American university ripe for change), lead the reader to the conclusion that it was not so bad after all?[31] 'The conference handbook' (a numerical listing of appropriate comments which have been repeated so often as to be *pro forma*) should be

---

30. 'A fortunate by-product of this reform was the exclusion of communists, classical liberals, foreigners, and men under 36 from the licensed fields of scholarship, and of statisticians from law schools' (Stigler, 1973, p. 495).

31. Proposals included competency examinations, a point system (which had the effect of killing research), a revised point system (to encourage research, but at some cost—one professor 'withdrew a book already in page proof, and published the 19 chapters as 19 articles'), and finally an amendment to allow the chairman to allot points to any professor 'when an offer was received from another university' (Stigler, 1947*c*, pp. 664–5).

employed in many scholarly conferences and papers; it would certainly reduce the tedium associated with so many.

As with his methodological and historical asides, his views on academia are prevalent throughout his works. Consider but these few examples, which need no explanation:

> The writing of textbooks is apparently not a thought-intensive activity: the modal number of changes of *any* sort between editions of a textbook in its discussion of the kinked demand curve is zero (Stigler, 1978, p. 200).

> A final, and rather morbid, observation is that there is a simply enormous amount of unprogressive publication: articles which certainly add nothing to the accumulation of rigorous theory or tested findings (*ibid.*, p. 201).

> A dominant value of the scholarly world is a certain disengagement from the contemporary scene and a search for knowledge more fundamental and durable than that required for practical and immediate purposes (Stigler, 1972, p. 577).

> when economists agree that a movement is inevitable, it is not (Stigler, 1950*a*, p. 34).

## V. Book Reviews

Should anyone seek to inquire as to the proper form and content of an effective book review, the answer should be, look at the examples of George Stigler. Stigler raised the book review to an art form. He was not content with a mere retelling of the central themes or an examination of the author's thesis, which would be a very tiresome exercise indeed (for reader and reviewer alike), and surely not worth the expenditure of a talent such as Stigler's. He was more interested in linking the theme to the fields in which he was interested, in connecting the work to a broader scheme, and in challenging at times the very framework upon which the work was founded. There was no area with which he was so totally unfamiliar as to have no opinion whatsoever, so the range of topics covered by the works reviewed serve themselves to describe the full range to which economic analysis may be employed. The topics very often echoed concerns which had been (or would soon become) the subject of his own research.[32] To understand Stigler, read first not his seminal

---

32. That he completed over seventy book reviews is a tribute to his abilities and range of interests; to the many who suffered his criticism, this was probably more than a few too many.

contributions in the learned journals and published books, but instead peruse his many book reviews; for there lay the essence of Stigler.

Consider but three examples, reviews of Samuelson's *Foundations of Economic Analysis,* Boulding's *The Economics of Peace,* and Simon Kuznets' *National Income and Its Composition, 1919–1938.*

In his critique of Samuelson's now-classic re-appraisal of the foundations of economic theory, Stigler was particularly impressive. Samuelson had set himself the task of discovering 'meaningful theorems' of economics, distinct from vacuous tautologies in that these theorems are falsifiable. Economic propositions must be capable of falsification, as economics is a social science the theories of which must have practical content; examples take the form of first and second order conditions, the signs of which are empirically discernible. But in some instances Samuelson had, in Stigler's view, advanced a series of tautologies, especially in his treatment of utility theory; he had failed to account for (adequately define) consumer tastes. In commenting on the overall work, Stigler's wit again hit the target: the discussion by Samuelson on dynamics should, thought Stigler, be subtitled '"What the Reader Should Know of Differential and Difference Equations." The economics, as usual, is appallingly absent'. Failure to translate the mathematical formulations into prose (which translation Samuelson dismissed as depravity) Stigler reaffirmed showed lack of 'responsibility to the canons of scholarship'.

Boulding's *The Economics of Peace* Stigler described thus: 'As propaganda for a particular set of economic policies, Boulding's book is a successful and, at times, brilliant performance.' Textbooks serve the function of promoting rational discourse; their purpose is to impart to the reader the fundamentals of argument and the proper method of defence, i.e. they serve to teach both logical thinking and the methods of the empirical testing of hypotheses. To this task, Boulding's presentation was unsuccessful. What seemed to annoy Stigler the most was the lack of an empirical basis for the conclusions drawn. But Stigler would not have minded so much 'if the book had been written by an economist of lesser competence and talents'.

Kuznets' study of national income presented a bigger problem for Stigler. While arguing that the work was of high quality—the 'discussion of theoretical issues is balanced and incisive, the interpretation of results far transcends the mere verbalization of tables, and the enormous statistical labours are preformed [sic] (so far as this inexperienced reviewer can tell) with unfailing skill and patience' (Stigler, 1943, p. 528)—important problems, problems the likes of which Stigler would encounter and about which he would crusade throughout his career, remained which marred the presentation. These problems were: (1) the definition of concepts and (2) the measurement of economic magnitudes.

Stigler argued that Kuznets, in advancing a normative concept of income, had violated an unwritten law of economic analysis: economists should be neutral in their employment of concepts. But Stigler decided to refute Kuznets' definition by employing not a logical argument, but an empirical one: the positive definitions considered (but rejected) by Kuznets were much more useful in the examination of sectoral interrelationships and monetary matters. In the area of measurement, Stigler found that even accepting Kuznets' definitions, his measures did not succeed in conveying the concepts for which it had been alleged they were appropriate. The national income series, for example, promoted as serving as a measure of welfare, was simply too vague in its construction, and did not in any event provide an adequate measure of welfare. An interesting review: Stigler praised the quality of the work, while destroying the basis for the credibility of the results.

Other brief examples provide evidence of Stigler's mordant nature. The review of Warren James' *John Rae: Political Economist* began with the statement, 'John Rae is embarking upon his third life, which will probably be little more successful than the previous two' (Stigler, 1965*b*, p. 667).

The review of John Cunningham Wood's *Alfred Marshall: Critical Assessments* was equally critical. Not quite understanding the purpose or the editorial style of the undertaking, and noting that a similar set of assessments of Keynes was forthcoming, Stigler concluded:

> It is interesting to recall that the first edition of Marshall's *Principles* was the vehicle for the reintroduction of resale price maintenance in the book trade in Great Britain. Can the present volumes be the vehicle for the introduction of stochastic pricing? Poor Marshall! Poor Keynes? (Stigler, 1983*a*, pp. 191–2).

Admittedly this sampling is all too brief, and does not do justice to the wit and insight within his reviews of, in some instances, modern classics of economic thought. The hope is that the student of the history of economics will not neglect these important contributions.

## VI. Conclusion

Anyone familiar with the works of George Stigler will recognise the depth of his originality, the rigour of his work, and the vigour with which he pursued it. Those who knew him well (and could take him) found him to be delightful. As for his mordant qualities, such of course is a normative judgment; we rest our case with the evidence presented in the text and footnotes.

Stigler's wit could be devastating. Consider his well-known critique of Overton Taylor's *A History of Economic Thought*. After presenting a lengthy paragraph (consisting of a single, heavily-punctuated sentence), said to be indicative of the style of the work,[33] Stigler announced: 'If the reader can wade through 508 pages of this style of writing with sustained comprehension, which I suspect will put him in a select group, he will be rewarded by some interesting as well as some not-so-interesting pieces of this philosophical background.'

But he could also be eminently charitable in his criticism. His review of Piero Sraffa's edition of Ricardo's collected works is extremely flattering indeed; so much so that, after his review, he wrote a 14-page article detailing Sraffa's editorial brilliance.[34] A rather interesting situation, this disparagement of Taylor and exaltation of Sraffa. Most puzzling indeed, for it is evident that Sraffa did not need the praise, nor Taylor the criticism.

As Milton Friedman so eloquently stated, Stigler's attitude was 'let the chips fall where they may, my task is to be objective, accurate, and interesting'.[35]

REFERENCES

Buchanan, James M. (1965). 'Economists—and economists.' *National Review* (7 September), pp. 777–80.

Machlup, Fritz. (1943). Review of *The Theory of Competitive Price. Journal of Political Economy*, vol. 51 (3), pp. 263–5.

Schumpeter, Joseph A. (1942). Review of *The Theory of Competitive Price. American Economic Review*, vol. 32 (4), pp. 844–7.

33. The paragraph is: 'The *close*, but not always fully realized (or if realized, as it was, if I am not mistaken, by Smith, and even more certainly, I think, by Veblen, although he is always difficult to categorize, then not articulated) interdependence of, and reciprocal set of influences or 'effects' upon one another, of the philosophical (including ethical) system of an economist and— where this can be distinguished, if it ever can—his 'technical' economic theory—to say nothing of the policy positions (attitudes) which were, and could be, but sometimes were absent-mindedly not, associated therewith—is one of the main themes—or, to speak succinctly if only approximately, one of the main beliefs—that pervades and instructs this textbook-treatise of Dr. Taylor' (Stigler, 1961b, p. 426).

34. Some comments: 'Sraffa's edition seems to breathe precision. . . . ' 'The impression of precision is well-founded; I found only one large error.' 'The editorial notes are superb. They seem unbelievably omniscient; they are never obtrusive or pedantical; and they maintain unfailing neutrality' (Stigler, 1953, p. 587).

35. We have eschewed discussion of Stigler the class-room teacher and dissertational supervisor, a theme stressed (in correspondence) by Professor Friedman. The record indicates that Stigler was superb in both dimensions. Surely such a subject deserves a separate article. While many of his students came to appreciate him most only after their student years, virtually everyone who sat through his courses, wrote dissertations under his supervision, or were merely examined by him recalls him vividly. If he was mordant (and he was), he was always effective. Students remember professors for many things; effectiveness should be among the most desired.

Stigler, George J. (1937). 'The economics of Carl Menger.' *Journal of Political Economy*, vol. 45 (2), pp. 229–50.
Stigler, George J. (1939). 'Production and distribution in the short run.' *Journal of Political Economy*, vol. 47 (3), pp. 305–27.
Stigler, George J. (1941a). *Production and Distribution Theories*. New York: Macmillan.
Stigler, George J. (1941b). Review of Albert Gailord Hart, *Anticipations, Uncertainty and Dynamic Planning*, American Economic Review, vol. 31 (2), pp. 358–59.
Stigler, George J. (1941c). Review of Kenneth Boulding, *Economic Analysis*, Journal of Political Economy, vol. 69 (6), pp. 917–18.
Stigler, George J. (1942). *The Theory of Competitive Price*. New York: Macmillan.
Stigler, George J. (1943). Review of Simon Kuznets, *National Income and Its Composition, 1919–1939*, Journal of Farm Economics, vol. 25 (2), pp. 528–32.
Stigler, George J. (1945). 'The cost of subsistence.' *Journal of Farm Economics*, vol. 27 (2), pp. 303–14.
Stigler, George J. (1946a). *The Theory of Price*. New York: Macmillan.
Stigler, George J. (1946b). Review of Kenneth Boulding, *The Economics of Peace*, Journal of Political Economy, vol. 54 (4), pp. 372–3.
Stigler, George J. (1947a). 'Stuart Wood and the marginal productivity theory.' *Quarterly Journal of Economics*, vol. 61 (4), pp. 640–9.
Stigler, George J. (1947b). 'The kinky oligopoly demand curve and rigid prices.' *Journal of Political Economy*, vol. 55 (5), pp. 432–49.
Stigler, George J. (1947c). 'An academic episode.' *American Association of University Professors Bulletin*, vol. 33 (4), pp. 661–5.
Stigler, George J. (1948). Review of Paul Samuelson, *Foundations of Economic Analysis*, Journal of the American Statistical Association, vol. 43 (244), pp. 603–5.
Stigler, George J. (1950a). 'Monopoly and oligopoly by merger.' *American Economic Review Papers and Proceedings*, vol. 40 (2), pp. 23–24.
Stigler, George J. (1950b). 'The development of utility theory. I.' *Journal of Political Economy*, vol. 58 (4), pp. 307–27.
Stigler, George J. (1950c). 'The development of utility theory. II.' *Journal of Political Economy*, vol. 58 (5), pp. 373–96.
Stigler, George J. (1952). Review of Piero Sraffa and M. H. Dobb, ed. *The Works and Correspondence of David Ricardo*, Econometrica, vol. 20 (3), pp. 504–5.
Stigler, George J. (1953). 'Sraffa's *Ricardo*.' *American Economic Review*, vol. 43 (4), pp. 586–99.
Stigler, George J. (1954). 'The economist plays with blocs.' *American Economic Review Papers and Proceedings*, vol. 44 (2), pp. 7–14.
Stigler, George J. (1955). 'The nature and role of originality in scientific progress.' *Economica*, vol. 22 (88), pp. 293–302.
Stigler, George J. (1958). 'Ricardo and the 93% labor theory of value.' *American Economic Review*, vol. 48 (3), pp. 357–67.
Stigler, George J. (1959). 'The politics of political economists.' *Quarterly Journal of Economics*, vol. 73 (4), pp. 522–32.

Stigler, George J. (1961a). 'The economics of information.' *Journal of Political Economy*, vol. 69 (3), pp. 213–25.

Stigler, George J. (1961b). Review of Overton Taylor, *A History of Economic Thought*, American Economic Review, vol. 51 (3), pp. 426–7.

Stigler, George J. (1962a). 'Administered prices and oligopolistic inflation.' *The Journal of Business*, vol. 35 (1), pp. 1–13.

Stigler, George J. (1962b). 'Henry L. Moore and statistical economics.' *Econometrica*, vol. 30 (1), pp. 1–21.

Stigler, George J. (1962c). 'Information in the labor market.' *Journal of Political Economy*, vol. 70 (5), pp. 94–105.

Stigler, George J. (1964). 'A theory of oligopoly.' *Journal of Political Economy*, vol. 72 (1), pp. 44–61.

Stigler, George J. (1965a). 'The economist and the state.' *American Economic Review*, vol. 55 (1), pp. 1–18.

Stigler, George J. (1965b). Review of R. Warren James *John Rae: Political Economist*, *Journal of Political Economy*, vol. 73 (6), p. 667.

Stigler, George J. (1965c). *Essays in the History of Economics*. Chicago: University of Chicago Press.

Stigler, George J. (1968). 'Mill on economics and society.' *University of Toronto Quarterly*, vol. 20, pp. 96–102.

Stigler, George J. (1969a). 'Alfred Marshall's lectures of progress and poverty.' *Journal of Law and Economics*, vol. 12 (1), pp. 181–3.

Stigler, George J. (1969b). 'Does economics have a useful past?' *History of Political Economy*, vol. 1 (2), pp. 217–30.

Stigler, George J. (1970). 'The optimum enforcement of laws.' *Journal of Political Economy*, vol. 78 (3), pp. 526–36.

Stigler, George J. (1971a). 'The theory of economic regulation.' *Bell Journal of Economics and Management Science*, vol. 2 (1), pp. 3–21.

Stigler, George J. (1971b). 'Smith's travels on the ship of state.' *History of Political Economy*, vol. 3 (2), pp. 265–77.

Stigler, George J. (1972). 'The adoption of the marginal utility theory.' *History of Political Economy*, vol. 4 (2), pp. 571–86.

Stigler, George J. (1973). 'A sketch of the history of truth in teaching.' *Journal of Political Economy*, vol. 81 (2), pp. 491–5.

Stigler, George J. (1974). 'Henry Calvert Simons.' *Journal of Law and Economics*, vol. 17 (1), pp. 1–5.

Stigler, George J. (1976). 'The successes and failures of Professor Smith.' *Journal of Political Economy*, vol. 84 (6), pp. 1199–213.

Stigler, George J. (1977a). Review of Adam Smith, *The Wealth of Nations* (Glasgow edition), *Journal of Political Economy*, vol. 85 (1), pp. 235–6.

Stigler, George J. (1977b). Review of John K. Whitaker, *The Early Economic Writings of Alfred Marshall, 1867–1890, Journal of Economic Literature*, vol. 15 (1), pp. 97–8.

Stigler, George J. (1978). 'The literature of economics: the case of the kinked oligopoly demand curve.' *Economic Inquiry*, vol. 16 (2), pp. 185–204.

Stigler, George J. (1983*a*). Review of John Cunningham Wood, ed. *Alfred Marshall: Critical Assessments, Journal of Political Economy*, vol. 91 (1), pp. 191–2.

Stigler, George J. (1983*b*). 'Nobel lecture: the process and progress of economics.' *Journal of Political Economy*, vol. 91 (4), pp. 529–45.

Stigler, George J. (1984). 'Economics—the imperial science?' *Scandinavian Journal of Economics*, vol. 86 (3), pp. 301–13.

Stigler, George J. (1988*a*). *Memoirs of an Unregulated Economist*. New York: Basic Books.

Stigler, George J. (1988*b*). 'Palgrave's dictionary of economics.' *Journal of Economic Literature*, vol. 26 (4), pp. 1729–33.

Stigler, George J. (1990). 'The place of Marshall's *Principles* in the development of economics.' In *Centenary Essays on Alfred Marshall* (ed. John K. Whitaker). Cambridge: Cambridge University Press.

Stigler, George J. (1991). 'Charles Babbage (1791 + 200 = 1991).' *Journal of Economic Literature*, vol. 29 (3), pp. 1149–52.

Stigler, George J. and Friedland, Claire (1962). 'What can regulators regulate? the case of electricity.' *Journal of Law and Economics*, vol. 5, pp. 1–16.

Stigler, George J. and Friedland, Claire (1983). 'The literature of economics: The case of Berle and Means.' *Journal of Law and Economics*, vol. 226 (2), pp. 237–68.

Stigler, George J. and Kindahl, James K. (1970). *The Behavior of Industrial Prices*. New York: National Bureau of Economic Research.

Stigler, George J. and Kindahl, James K. (1973). 'Industrial prices, as administered by Dr. Means.' *American Economic Review*, vol. 63 (4), pp. 717–21.

# CHAPTER 16

## Jews and Contributions to Economics: A Bicentennial Review

*In 1976, when the "Adam Smith Industry" was once again in semicentennial full flower, Dr. Ruth Waxman, the associate editor of* Judaism *asked me to write an essay about economics, presumably about its relationship with Jews and Judaism. I intentionally distorted the invitation and chose to speculate on whether there was a Jewish contribution to modern economics, and by that I did not mean contributions by Jews. My answer focused only on certain contributions made by Russian Jews during the period after 1920. By the time I wrote the essay my father had long been dead—the idea had been the subject of many conversations between us, but I also had had the occasion to talk to Simon Kuznets about my thoughts. As I recall, I chose to take Simon's reactions to be, at best, "quite possible" and, at worst, the Scottish verdict of "case not proven." My thesis was that young Russian Jews, trained first in the Jewish Talmudic tradition and then in the Russian czarist Gymnasium tradition, often turned to Marxism to formulate a theory of history. In the case of my father and Kuznets, emigration to America brought them into contact with two quite different kinds of economic empiricists, and the result was that both immigrants fused all of that training into their unique contributions.*

1776 was the year of American independence. It was also the year of the publication of Adam Smith's *Wealth of Nations.* American independence was the forerunner of the growth of one of the most open, if not the most open, of societies in world history. The publication of the *Wealth of Nations* led to the development of the contemporary discipline of economics. There was considerable social mobility in the American colonies prior to Independence. The economics discipline existed in considerable complexity prior to Adam Smith's second book (the *Wealth of Nations*). In other words, a bicentennial review is simply an artifact; considerable went on before the beginning of this two hundred year period, and there is nothing final about taking a look at the two hundredth anniversary.

---

*Judaism* 25 (Summer): 301–11.

Nonetheless, retrospective viewing has its uses and the two hundredth anniversary of not one but two phenomena encourages us to make broader rather than narrower assessments.

The impact of Smith's work on American economic development is quite clear. Alexander Hamilton, one of the dominant voices at the Constitutional Convention and the first Secretary of the Treasury, was thoroughly conversant with Smith's work and its argument. Moreover, he seems to have been in agreement with Smith's principal conclusions, which were, on the whole, a rather judicious set of insights regarding the relationship of individuals, the production process, and national (and, to a lesser degree, international) economic development. If Adam Smith had any strong views about Jews and economics, I find no record of them. Maybe like the sensitive Scot that he was, he perceived materialism (concern about tangible goods and services) as much a Scottish concern as a Jewish "monopoly." He does mention that Hebrew was not part of the conventional university curriculum and has some harsh suggestions that its exclusion was the result of excessive reliance on Catholic Church doctrinal authorities.

All of us, particularly those who have read long lists of achievements by American Jews, are aware that at the time of the American Revolution there were relatively few Jews in the colonies. True, there were some, and of these only a very small number played a noticeable role in eighteenth century finance and business. The discipline of economics, as such, was not then an academic subject. Its entry into American universities was delayed until the middle part of the nineteenth century, at a time when (and quite unrelated to it) a wave of German-Jewish immigration was beginning to become substantial. Since the middle of the nineteenth century, and particularly since the last two decades of that century, formal economics (as denoted by an academic discipline) has become part of virtually every American college and university. In that same span of years the American Jewish community, having previously seen German Jews replace Spanish-Portuguese Jews as the dominant Jewish type, has seen East European Jews replace German Jews and, then, homogenized American-born Jews with less and less perception of the various cultures of their family's national origin, replace the East European group.

In brief, while this is a bicentennary year, most of the action, both in the case of the economics discipline and in the case of the American Jewish community, has been of relatively recent occurrence. From the standpoint of our interest the concept of "bicentennial" is not signally appropriate; nonetheless, as mentioned earlier, the uses of history (reviews of the past) are there.

This essay, however, undertakes a somewhat more difficult task than simply trying to give a picture of the changing role of Jews in the economics discipline. The key question to which it is addressed is whether there is anything particularly Jewish about American economics—have American

Jews contributed something Jewish to the discipline or have they simply contributed an influence which is similar, perhaps congruent, to the contributions made by others?

I am led to this point by my recollection of a particularly intriguing book review appearing almost thirty years ago in an early issue of *Commentary* magazine.[1] The review was of a collection of essays written by Mr. Justice Nathan Cardozo. Cardozo, then dead less than a decade, was popularly perceived as *the* craftsman in the American legal tradition. Most other reviewers of this volume of collected works virtually outdid themselves in praising the author. They eulogized his judgments, his style, and his attractive (if shy) modesty. Occasionally, these reviewers did mention Cardozo's Jewishness, if only by repeating the story of Mr. Justice McReynold's shameful behavior at the time of the Cardozo nomination hearings and on the day when Cardozo took his seat in the Court. But only Professor Daniel Boorstin, now the Librarian of Congress, went to the heart of the matter (which is my point). Dr. Boorstin noted that the learned Cardozo completely omitted any reference to Jewish sources in these essays. In other words, Cardozo, although seen as a very able Jewish man who made intellectual history while a member of the Supreme Court, gave no indication of his Jewishness in his work. And while Jews (and everyone else) should take pride in what Cardozo did achieve, there is nothing intrinsically Jewish about that achievement, except that (as in Cardozo's case) an American Jew (with a Tammany-tainted father) was given an opportunity, seized that opportunity, and made American (although in no sense Jewish) intellectual history.

## II

Before anyone, Jewish or otherwise, usually can make any contribution to an academic discipline,[2] not only must the discipline, itself, be discernibly established, but the individual has to have sufficient recognition to be read or heard. In other words, individual Jews had to be commonly understood before it could be said that they had made a contribution. As one might expect, the first American Jew to be heard on the subject of economics was from a somewhat assimilated Spanish-Portuguese family. He was Jacob Newton Cardozo (1786–1873), an earlier member of the aforementioned Cardozo family.

This Cardozo, born in New York, was a newspaper man, who spent his career in Charleston, South Carolina. He was in favor of Southern economic development, then largely based on international trade. He was versed in the

---

1. Daniel J. Boorstin's review of Margaret Hall [ed.]. *Selected Writings of Benjamin N. Cardozo* in *Commentary*, 6 (Sept. 1948): 290–92.

2. I grant that some unknown could create a discipline, much as Zeus is said to have created Athena. However, I cannot readily think of an example.

emerging economics discipline and was particularly aware of the economic writings of David Ricardo, an English erstwhile Jew (married to a Quaker), who gets even higher marks as a professional economist than does Adam Smith. Cardozo took issue with some of the ratiocinative details of the Ricardian argument. The details of the difference do not seem to me to be particularly noteworthy, yet it may be significant to point out that even if the essential "efficiency-materialism" (which is central to the concern of all economists, e.g., Smith, or Cardozo) is conceived by many as being "Jewish" in the pejorative sense, one's enemies do not identify the nature of one's contributions. It may be argued that a materialist society is one in which Jews operate relatively easily, only because they do not have to get involved with the intricacies of antimaterialist spiritual (i.e., religious) priorities.

Professor Joseph Dorfman, the preeminent historian of the American economics discipline, describes Jacob Cardozo as, "the only man in pre-Civil War America whose mind operated in that high level of abstraction that characterized the work of Ricardo and his school."[3]

The question is how Jewish was Ricardo's or Cardozo's economics? I have already suggested that there may be those who claim that economics, because it deals with material goods and services, has distinctly Jewish overtones; but I have disclaimed this argument. Economics, as a discipline, has a better claim to Scottish paternity than to Jewish. However, there are those who claim that modern economic analysis, with its reliance upon models and ratiocination, abstraction, and immanent criticism, is "Talmudical" and, by association, therefore, Jewish. What Cardozo, and earlier, Ricardo, had done was to construct models (i.e., explicit rational arguments) as a basis for making public decisions. Many Jews have done this with Talmudical principles: *pilpul* is one example of such a construct. And so those who have opposed these policies, and particularly reliance upon the reasoning involved, have popularly buttressed their offensive by claiming that this abstractionism is culturally alien—even casuistically Jewish. However, when it comes to such careful reasoning, René Descartes was also no mean abstractionist (and I could name several dozen others); Descartes as well as the several others were not Jewish. Thus, I fail to see that abstractionism in any branch of knowledge, including economics, is essentially a Jewish cultural contribution. That Jews, like Spinoza, were good at the logical method does not necessarily say much about the method's origins. My verdict regarding the possible Jewishness of Ricardo's contribution is the Scottish one, "case not proven."

---

3. For a discussion of Jacob N. Cardozo see Joseph Dorfman, *The Economic Mind in American Civilization, 1606–1865* (New York: Viking, 1946), vol. 2. pp. 551–66, 852–62. See, also, the article on Cardozo in the *Encyclopaedia Judaica*, vol. 3. p. 162; Cardozo's credentials as a Jew were more tenuous than his credentials as an economist. Perhaps there is a message in this point.

The more basic principle, and one from which to draw, is simply that in order to make any contribution to economics, individuals have to be identified as economists; thus, if Jews seek to make a contribution, they must first be individually recognized. In practice, such recognition may come easier if the contribution is not initially identified as culturally alien. The resistance of the academic establishment to taking in economics, on the first hand, and to taking in Jews, on the second, has been well documented. Ricardo and Jacob Cardozo did not stress any Jewishness in their economic views; that these views were seriously considered was, probably, achievement enough for any-one—particularly a Jew, erstwhile or active.

## III

It is now a commonplace that Jews migrated to America in a series of increasingly large "waves," and that the process of cultural assimilation was well under way by the time that the third generation of each wave had become mature. These waves were (1) Spanish-Portuguese, (2) German, and (3) East European. As with the migration waves of Jews to America, so later with the admission of Jews to the universities, except that the Sephardic (Spanish Jewish) wave rose prior to the emergence of economics as an academic discipline; indeed, it rose even before the universities became the "corridor to power." The earliest significant appointments of Jews to American economics departments were in the 1880's and the 1890's. In 1888, Edwin R. A. Seligman (1861–1939), scion of the famous New York banking family, was appointed Adjunct Professor of Political Economy at Columbia University, from which he had earlier received a baccalaureate degree in 1879.[4] Seligman's career at Columbia is, itself, from the standpoint of American economics, important. He was one of the founders of the American Economic Association in 1885. He was appointed to one of the first principal chairs in economics (the [Columbia] McVicar Professorship of Political Economy in 1904), which he held until his retirement in 1931. And, even after that date, he was a significant economist insofar as he was the principal editor of the *Encyclopedia of the Social Sciences*.

Seligman had many professional interests. He was widely active in reform causes which ranged from advocacy of progressive taxation to interest in government regulation of industry and working conditions. His economics work focused more on concrete rather than on abstract issues. His taxation analysis and his work in the area of the history of economic thought was relatively unencumbered with esoteric rigor. He was apparently a good under-

---

4. For a discussion of Seligman, see Dorfman, *Op. cit.* vol. 3, pp. 253–56, and the *Encyclopaedia Judaica*, vol. 14, p. 1131.

graduate teacher, and is still best known as an indefatigable discoverer of "forgotten great economists" and as a discriminating collector of early economics tracts. His personal library was donated to Columbia University where it remains as one of the two greatest American collections of early economic writings. In his professional work, he seems to me to have been less rigorous than Cardozo; however, his impact on the profession was clearly greater.

Amongst other things, Seligman was active in the New York City Ethical Culture movement, which, itself, had distinct traditional, social-responsibility Jewish resonances. Some may feel that this social justice reform interest may have stemmed from Seligman's early exposure to the literature of the Prophets. But Seligman's boyhood tutor was no *melamed;* he was actually none other than Horatio Alger, Jr., and it is unlikely that Seligman, the boy, learned much Jewish interpretation of the Prophetic message from that particular tutor. Nonetheless, he had generous views on charity which seem to me to have been as much a part of the American-Christian eschatological tradition as anything else. I conclude, therefore, that it would be disingenuous to conclude that Seligman's economics, reflecting (1) common sense rather than rigorous analysis and (2) a rich American's *noblesse oblige* sense of kindly charity, was significantly Jewish. Historically, it was probably enough (again) that he, a Jew, played a key role in the organizational growth of the discipline, even if his intellectual impact on it was not distinctively Jewish.

The other well-known Jewish economics professor during that period was Jacob H. Hollander (1871–1940), a Johns Hopkins A.B. and Ph.D. (1892, 1894). Hollander, although of Russian-Jewish extraction had married into the affluent German-Jewish Hutzler family of Baltimore; professionally and socially he seems thereafter to have floated on the German wave. When Hollander's young wife died, the family established the Hutzler Chair in Political Economy at Johns Hopkins; Hollander was appointed to that Chair, which he occupied until his death in 1940.

Hollander was one of the more rigorous American economists interested in the classical school. Seligman chose Hollander to write the article on David Ricardo in the *Encyclopedia of the Social Sciences* because he considered Hollander to be the most rigorous of the leading American admirers of orthodox Ricardian economics. There is nothing in Hollander's treatment of Ricardo which stressed any Jewish contribution to the discipline, although Hollander allocated considerable energy in tracking down the Jewishness of Ricardo's paternal family and investigating Ricardo's education, which, Hollander indicated, included two years at the Amsterdam Portuguese Synagogue's *Talmud Torah.* These years were at the end of Ricardo's adolescence. He returned from Amsterdam, so Hollander tells us, spent a short apprenticeship with his father, left his father's home and faith and went to work in the British stock exchange on his own, and married Mrs. Ricardo, who was clearly of non-Jewish origins. Hollander reports that the family did not accept Ricardo's marriage.

But, back to Hollander. In his early years he had a keen interest in the history of the American Jewish community, and, in the 1890's, wrote several monographs on that subject. They were published by the Jewish Historical Society.[5] Hollander was also relatively active in Baltimore Jewish community activities. At the end of his career, he had to cope with a significant increase in overt anti-Semitism. The last of his University Presidents (the geographer Isaiah Bowman), was infamous for his anti-Semitic postures. While it is true that university presidents do not really "make" universities (and, to some extent, university professors do), the historic and unpleasant fact is that part of the Johns Hopkins legend relates to Hollander's self-denigrating attempts to cope with Bowman's prejudices.

On balance, I am disposed to argue that both Seligman and Hollander thought that economics had basically a scientific *wertfrei* character; each was concerned with the origins of economics but thought that it was, if anything, a compound of Jewish and Christian cultural traditions which played the significant part in the development of the subject. Theirs was the usual view of the topic, and both were relatively conventional professors. Hollander clearly had a more active Jewish identification than Seligman, but neither carried anything uniquely Jewish into his professional work.

## IV

Immediately after the first World War several Jews of Russian or East European extraction managed to get appointments to certain economics faculties. Jacob Viner, a native of Montreal but a graduate of Harvard University, was appointed Professor at Chicago in 1925. Leo Sharfman, a Russian born economist who arrived in America by way of Tientsin, was appointed Professor (and later chairman) at the University of Michigan in Ann Arbor. In 1921, my father, Selig Perlman, was appointed to the faculty at the University of Wisconsin where he remained until shortly before his death in 1959. The number of Jews appointed to major faculty positions in economics increased

5. These include:

"Some Unpublished Material Relating to Dr. Jacob Lumbrozo of Maryland," *Publ. Amer. Jew. Hist. Soc.* 1 (1893): 25–39.

"Civil Status of the Jews in Maryland, 1636–1776," Ibid., 2 (1894): 33–44.

"A Sketch of Haym Salomon," Ibid., 2: 5–19.

"Some Further References to Haym Salomon," Ibid., 3 (1895): 7–11.

"The Naturalization of Jews in the American Colonies Under the Act of 1740," Ibid., 5 (1896): 103–17.

"Documents Relating to the Attempted Departure of the Jews from Surinam in 1675," Ibid., 6 (1897): 9–29.

slightly in the 1930's. Professor Simon Kuznets, a Russian-Jew educated at Columbia University under Wesley Clair Mitchell, was appointed to the University of Pennsylvania faculty. Arthur F. Burns, now Chairman of the Board of Governors of the Federal Reserve System, was appointed Professor at Rutgers University. There were other appointments of significance, too, but those that I have mentioned were among the most noteworthy.

There was also great resistance to Jewish appointments. For blatant examples there was the case of Milton Friedman, who, in 1940, was denied a tenured position at the University of Wisconsin for overtly anti-Semitic reasons; also, Professor Paul Samuelson, undoubtedly the ablest graduate of the economics department of Harvard University, was not appointed at Harvard University upon the completion of his doctoral work. Samuelson went "down the river" to the Massachusetts Institute of Technology where he was instrumental in creating a department every bit as distinguished as Harvard's is now, and, quite likely, considerably better than Harvard's was then.

The great influx of Jews into the faculty ranks in economics was after the second World War. By 1960, instances of discrimination against great Jewish economists became all but unknown. The foregoing is not to suggest that discrimination does not still exist; it may well be that the selection of an economics faculty member is not completely stochastic (probabilistic), but certainly a Jew with a modicum of talent is likely to be appointed. Thus, "entry into the theatre" is not presently a significant problem. Whether in this era of compensatory discrimination (in favor of non-Jewish minorities, women, or, perhaps, the young), such a halcyon state will continue to exist, I know not. But, for the moment, it does seem to exist.

In terms of a bicentennial review, the point to be made is that academic economics opened slowly to Jews; generally, it was opened first to Jews of financially established families, and their contributions were not significantly (in the Boorstin sense) Jewish. But was there anything particularly Jewish about any of the contributions of the post-World War I appointments? Thus far I have been rather bearish about anything particularly Jewish in the contribution in the case of the Jews appointed prior to the First World War. I do not argue that either formal economic theory, with its reliance upon abstract analysis, or even concern for Prophetic social reform could not come out of the Jewish tradition; I have merely argued that they could have come from other sources as well. I do think, however, that, in the post-World War I appointment pattern, some of the Jews did incorporate into the economics discipline some elements of clearly Jewish origin. One element in current economic analysis which I think is quite probably of Jewish origin is an interest in defining (including measuring and testing empirically) the problem, within nations, of the rise and fall, as well as the interactions, of economic groups, and of the economic aspects of competition between nations. The approach, as it developed, seems to me to come out of a traditional Jewish fascination with history and its meaning. The Christian tradition in such matters is, in its essentials, teleological; the Jewish is not. To most scholars in the Christian tradition there is some kind of determinism in the process with a promise of a Holy Grail at its end. For those in the Jewish tradition, one studies history for "laws" of action and reaction rather than for discovery of ultimate truth. Whatever concern there was in the East European Jewish cultural tradition for the laws of history came to confront the teleological historicism of Hegel and Marx and blossomed as the revisionist Jewish Marxism of Russia and, later, Poland. It is, when I study it, more easily now seen in its American species as a grafting of a mutated Marxism (inverted Hegelianism), perhaps, but not necessarily, of the Plekhanov variety, onto a "native" American empirical tradition.

Two Jewish economists seem to me to be prime examples of this tradition and their influence on the evolution of American economics is, at the same time, illustrative and indisputable. Both men were clearly products of the Russian-Jewish Marxist pre-1920 crucible. Both, namely Selig Perlman and Simon Kuznets, had a strong grounding (insofar as I understand the significance of their earlier interests) in working out a theory of the relationship between economic causes and historical events. Thus, each, from the first, was interested in trying to explain in economic terms why and how nations grew. Thus, each was interested in "discovering laws of history," and each was exposed to a variety of historical systems prior to developing his own. In my father's case, as a high school student he used the philosophy of the Jewish *Bund* to offset the influence of the Russian Orthodox dogma presented at his *Gymnasium*.[6] His teachers had insisted that he learn the Russian Orthodox historical system, although both he and they disagreed with that system. Those teachers, fearing prosecution, were in no position to offer him an articulated alternative, but, apparently, the alternative he initially found for himself was *Menshevism*. Like many Jews of his generation, he read widely in Marxist revisionism—all the time searching for a *Gestalt* to replace the one furnished in the *Gymnasium*. He came to America in 1907, both a convinced Marxist revisionist (his mentor was the theorist, William English Walling) and a young man in search of an education. In 1908 he was sent by Walling to study with Walling's friends, Richard T. Ely and John R. Commons, at the University of Wisconsin. Perlman's fascination with Ely was all but nonexistent; his fascination with John R. Commons (and, initially, with Commons' colleague, Frederick Jackson Turner) was of much longer duration—

---

6. For a description of the career, including the ideas, of Selig Perlman see Dorfman, *Op. cit.*, vol. 4, p. 395, vol. 5, pp. 395–96 and Mark Perlman, *Labor Union Theories in America: Background and Development* (Westport, Conn.: Greenwood Press, 1976, 2nd edition), pp. 190–210.

indeed, for the rest of his life. Commons was something of a historical-empiricist. His method stressed episodic analysis, and was, I believe, largely a product of Commons' exposure to the writings of two English legal historians (Henry Maine and Frederick Maitland). Perlman became converted to Commons' historical-empiricism and used it to refashion his Menshevik Marxism into an American Institutionalist interpretation of the evolution of the labor movement. It is this economic Institutionalism (a school of thought) and its fascination with the rationing of economic opportunity and the role of property rights which, in Perlman's case, had a relatively obvious Jewish-*Bundist* source. Perlman's product was an alternative to the *Bundist* theory of history, but his question and analytical method were unmistakably of *Bundist* origin.

Perlman's experience with moving from a theologically based historical *Weltanschauung* to a Marxian theoretical *Weltanschauung* and from that Marxian *Weltanschauung* to some form of empirical system characterizes the intellectual development of several other European-educated Jewish intellectual immigrants to America. When these intellectuals were confronted by the relatively system-free empirical thinking found in certain American economics departments (I cite Wisconsin and Columbia as two), they sought to develop new systems in order to interpret the American experience. In Selig Perlman's case, as I note, it was a theory of the development of the American working class. His theory, still under attack by professional economic historians within the economics discipline, has been, nonetheless, the standard organization of the subject since it first appeared over fifty years ago. Its virtues are that it is comprehensive and episodically empirical.

Professor Simon Kuznets,[7] coming from a background similar, but not quite congruent, to Selig Perlman's, came under the influence of another kind of American empiricist, Wesley Clair Mitchell. Mitchell, Professor of Economics at Columbia University and founder of the National Bureau of Economic Research, was an unusually energetic and imaginative quantitative empiricist. In any event, he was much more than a collector of statistical data, because, more than any other economist of his time, he sought to quantify in order to test economic theory. Kuznets, working at first under and then clearly on a par with Mitchell, started by developing a system for measuring various aspects of economic fluctuations. Initially he dealt with cyclical and seasonal fluctuations. Later he went on to analyze trend (as distinct from cyclical) patterns. During the 1930's he broadened what had by then become his system of quantitative economic analysis to the point where he measured and an-

---

7. For a description of Kuznets' career see *Encyclopaedia Judaica*, Vol. 10, pp. 1306–7. His ideas are briefly treated in an explanation of the 1971 Nobel Memorial Prize in Economics by Erik Lundberg in the *Swedish Journal of Economics*, 73 (Dec. 1971): 444–61.

alyzed not only changes in national economic output, but changes in the components of gross output. Kuznets' efforts were put to spectacular public use during the second World War. These technical efforts largely paralleled work done by others (both Jews and non-Jews) in the United States and particularly Great Britain.

However, the most important of the many important contributions of Kuznets' work were not the measurement techniques, but the end to which he was wont to put them. This end was historical interpretation of the economic growth process. Reading Kuznets' Presidential Address to the American Economic Association in December, 1954 is a fascinating exercise in examining the origins of ideas. While denying the present existence of any valid theoretical framework which explained the economic growth process, he disclosed a continuing faith that such a framework could yet be found; indeed, he has continued to seek it since. Even if one such framework, the stages theory of the economic takeoff, postulated by Professor Walt Rostow (originally at Massachusetts Institute of Technology, then in Lyndon Johnson's White House, and now at the University of Texas) which was offered on the basis of Kuznets' work, has been particularly thoroughly attacked by him, his faith persists. Kuznets' attack on Rostow's work is technical. Its ferocity seems to me to reflect Kuznets' judgment that Rostow is close to, but perverting, a truth; thus, the danger. My point is that Kuznets has brought the hunger for a set of laws of historical and economic interaction to American economics. I see that appetite coming from an experience with the Russian (and particularly the Russian Jewish) intellectual climate. Thus, his sense of system stems in perceptible measure from the cultural *Weltanschauung* of the once flourishing intelligentsia, of which the Russian Jewish *Bundist* tradition was one principal flower.

Russian Jewish civilization lacked the empirical tradition that flourished in some American economics faculties, and, when certain young Russian Jews bridged the cultural gap, what they produced was at the same time part of traditional Jewish interest in historicity and a product which came to be incorporated into modern economics.

My view, in sum, is that this interest in developing an intellectual historical system to explain economic relationships, while not necessarily involving Jews as detonators of economic change, does have the Jewish interest in historicity as well as the Jewish East European intellectual experience as one of its points of origin. Because of the career opportunity offered by American economics departments to at least two of these East European-educated Jews, American economics now reflects some aspects of the Russian Jewish intellectual's hunger for an intellectual system and a later American-acquired respect for empiricism.

CHAPTER 17

# An Economic Historian's Economist: Remembering Simon Kuznets

*Vibha Kapuria-Foreman and Mark Perlman*

*I have already written so much about Simon Kuznets's impact on my thinking that it was a joy to try to formulate an intellectual assessment of his many contributions. This chapter has seven parts. After a brief introduction, there is a biographical description; it is followed by analyses of his work on national income, gross capital formation, professional income, and his overwhelmingly important work during the early months of 1942 in reorganizing materiel procurement; next comes a discussion of the development of his work on comparative economic growth and, penultimately, his work in demographic economics; then, finally, an assessment of the impact of his professional contributions.*

*Vibha Kapuria-Foreman, one of my Ph.D. students, impressed me during the period when we were in a seminar as having rare intuition as well as considerable intellectual style. Something of a feminist, a Social-Democrat, and coming from a Brahmin civil servant family, she was precisely the kind of person whose keen interest in Kuznets's work would have likely fascinated him. Alas, they never met. Her dissertation was an essay on the meaning of economic growth; her answer, perhaps derived from analyzing her personal choices, was that for an Indian woman of her generation and education, growth was not measured as much in terms of the quantity of consumption as in the breadth of the spectrum of choices open to her. Generally meticulous in her research habits, she had read virtually everything that Kuznets had written and what had been written about him, and I was delighted to collaborate with her on this essay, written for the* Economic Journal.

Economic Journal 105 (Nov. 1995): 1524–47.

We wish to thank numerous readers whose suggestions we have true reason to appreciate and which we generally took. These include Kenneth Arrow, Richard A. Easterlin, Scott A. Foreman, Milton Friedman, Geoffrey Harcourt, Paul Kuznets, Charles R. McCann, Don Patinkin, and Naomi Perlman.

> A great teacher affects eternity; he can never tell where his influence stops.
> —Henry B. Adams, *The Education of Henry Adams*

## Introduction

Simon Smith Kuznets (1901–85) has been dead for more than a decade. To some that length of time may deprive him of significance, but to others at least a decade is required to really begin to appreciate a man's historical significance. Arthur Koestler held that any rational author would eagerly trade 1,000 readers the year that a book appeared for 100 readers ten years later, and 10 readers a century after the book's initial appearance. So it is, we think, with great historical figures: at the time of their death they are remembered for who they were; it is later that they are remembered for what they really did.

While it could be argued that Simon Kuznets's influence on governmental policy and on the economic history of the world was for fortuitous reasons the greatest of any economist (Joseph, the son of Jacob, was a political scientist, not an economist) in all the past, we will not make that claim. Rather, we will describe him principally as the *exemplar economics empiricist* of the century, and possibly of all previous centuries. He was a man born with some qualities of greatness; he achieved greatness through his imaginative hard work, as one of the architects of the national accounts and conceptualizers of the measurement of capital formation; and he had greatness forced upon him when he and his one-time student and later colleague, Robert Nathan, reorganized the method of materiel procurement during World War II: in four short years the percentage of the gross national product going to the purchase of materiel rose from a mere 4 percent to a mighty 48 percent. What we hope to achieve is to leave our readers with an appreciation of this amazing, imaginative, ambitious, and kindly man—the scholar with indomitable energy, stern self-discipline, and a fragile voice.

Perhaps strangely,[1] Kuznets's 1971 Nobel Award was not for the aforementioned achievement (which still remains all but unknown), but was essentially for a variation or even a reprise of the orchestrated thinking of his earlier work. The committee's comparatively slight delay[2] in recognizing his

---

1. The Nobel Award seems generally to have been given for abstract achievement; for some the quick wartime conversion of the world's greatest economy lies outside the pale of science. *Chacun à son goût.*

2. The initial award, shared by Frisch and Tinbergen, was given very quickly—purportedly before the eventual procedures had been formalized. The second award, given to Paul A. Samuelson, apparently disappointed Erik Lundberg (a key figure on the Nobel Committee recommending the award), who had anticipated that it would go to Kuznets. Insofar as we are aware, the committee makes its awards on the basis of briefs which it commissions. Lundberg,

achievement is nothing compared to the profession's insistent profound ignorance of what Kuznets managed to accomplish in his approximately 60 years of professional work.

This chapter has seven parts. The next, part two, deals with the evolution of his early Bundist thinking and his initial forays into economic data at the National Bureau. Specifically, we examine his collaboration with his teacher, Wesley Clair Mitchell, in the area of Mitchell's prime interest, business cycles. Part three addresses his wartime experience and details the original presentation of his ideas about national income, his experience in implementing these ideas (with his students, Robert Nathan[3] and Milton Gilbert) during the early 1930s, his work on American gross capital formation in the middle and later 1930s, and the culmination of these efforts in his (and Nathan's) reorganization of American war materiel procurement during 1942–43.[4] This section also describes his repudiation of what Milton Gilbert and Gilbert's later associates had done with Kuznets's national accounting system and with the "insider" recognition of his wartime significance. Part four covers his interest in income distribution, wealth accumulation, and comparative economic growth and his subsequent alienation from the National Bureau. Part five deals with Kuznets's ideas on demographic economics. Finally, part six summarizes his standing within the profession during his own lifetime.

## Kuznets's Biography

### The Patristic Legacy

To appreciate the unfolding of Simon Kuznets's interests, some attention must be paid to his patristic legacy. Born into the family of a skilled furrier, Simon's early education was in a Jewish day school, the usual sort of thing for Jewish boys born in czarist Russia. There he learned well the rudiments of elementary education, along with the rudiments of Misnogyd (the legalistic, antimystic branch) Judaism and Jewish history. Like a great many intellectually inclined Jewish boys of the period, he was far more interested in secular

---

dissatisfied with the 1970 Kuznets brief, prepared the 1971 brief himself. Kuznets was granted the third award, in 1971.

3. The administrative and developmental contributions of his student, Robert Nathan, were priceless. Kuznets without Nathan would probably have been no more than another famous "book economist," something akin to William Petty. With Nathan, it was a partnership, something akin to the dual impact of Jesus and St. Paul.

4. For their troubles they left the War Production Board's Planning Committee, although through the intervention of Ferdinand Eberstadt, the investment banker, their method was bought "lock, stock, and barrel" (both literally and figuratively).

topics than Talmudic method. However, it is important to realize that part of this education involved a nonteleological theory of historical events.

By the time he was ready to attend the *Gymnasium,* Russia had entered World War I. He had moved by that time to Kharkov, a city noted for its intellectual life, and he took an interest in discussions of the current social movements. Not the least of these was the Bund, a gradualist Menshevik (Marxian-socialist) but anti-Zionist and essentially anti–religious observance Jewish organization.

One way to grasp the significance of it all is to identify what the Bund opposed. The Leninist Bolsheviks thought that a small band with a will to revolution could and should hasten the coming of Socialism. The Bundists, by contrast, doubtless influenced by Georgi Valentinovich Plekhanov, argued that history had to run its own course. The Bundists wanted reform in Russia; they did not advocate that young Jews flee to the swamps of Palestine and try to create an essentially Jewish economy there. In their Russia, their Jewish-ness was a given; they were so identified on their passports and in every other official way. Moreover, the czarist governments had been wont to use terror-ism (pogroms) against Jewish civilians whenever they feared the rise of other social agitation. The civil atmosphere of Russia (and that included the Ukraine) reeked of an underlying malaise regarding Jews.

Kuznets's official *Realschule* or nonclassical *Gymnasium* education had exposed him to the Russian Orthodox religion's teleological interpretation of history, an interpretation which was founded on what in Britain was called "the Divine Right of Kings." The czar was literally termed "Autocrat of all the Russias." It was at that time usual that boys, particularly Jewish boys of an intellectual bent, would read widely to synthesize their own personal theory of the historical process. We believe that the combination of the Jewish elemen-tary school, with its nonteleological theory of history but with a focus on the Jewish experience, and the Russian Orthodox teleological theory led them to read the forbidden Marxist writers, particularly Plekhanov.[5]

This fascination with the relative distribution of income matured into a lifelong interest in the question of whether an improved relative distribution

---

5. Marxist writings during this period covered a spectrum of ideas. Lenin, with his incisive *State and Revolution* and *Imperialism, the Highest Stage of Capitalism,* was required reading (but agreeing with him was not a requirement). No less required was Eduard Bernstein's revisionism, along with Karl Kautsky's orthodoxy. Bernstein had argued that, contrary to the original Marxian formulation, workers' incomes were rising absolutely, but not relatively; the original Marxian formulation had seen no absolute improvement in incomes being possible. Kuznets seems to have been a moderate; accepting revisionism, with its premise that the historical process had to work itself through, he became interested in the problems of changing distributions of income in the society of his time.

(meaning a movement to household income equality) was compatible with general economic growth. Taken for granted was the stylized fact that during recessions the poor suffered relatively more severely than the rich, and that anything that smoothed out business cycles would help the poor. Also taken for granted was that the absence of recessions would ameliorate such social tensions as existed between Jews and Gentiles.

When Kuznets finished the *Gymnasium,* he entered the University of Kharkov and undertook the curriculum in economics. With the advent of the civil war (after the October 1917 revolution) that university was closed (during Kuznets's second year). Indicative of his thinking was that he wrote two second-year papers, the first on the monetary wages of factory workers in Kharkov, and the second, a more abstract one, on Schumpeter's theory of innovation. The first was published in 1921, and the second, concluding that, while Schumpeter possessed keen insights he really did not have a testable proposition, served serendipitously as the critical link to his American professional career.

With the university closed and the country in civil war, the Kuznets family (father and three sons: Solomon, Simon, and George) escaped via Turkey to the West and emigrated to the United States. The sons[6] entered Columbia University's adult education unit, the School of General Studies. They did well, and Simon, having earned a baccalaureate degree, was admitted to the graduate faculty. In the course of getting his master's degree he had to submit an essay, and he chose to translate the one on Schumpeter. His supervisor, Wesley Clair Mitchell, knew Schumpeter well (Schumpeter had been a visiting professor at Columbia just prior to World War I), and was attracted to Kuznets's analytical skill.

Mitchell, offering Simon a research assistant's position in the newly formed National Bureau of Economic Research, proposed that Simon continue his doctoral studies under his general supervision. This marks the real beginning of their collaboration. But the terms of that collaboration are important. Mitchell trained Kuznets in the methods of quantitative empiricism and, although Simon trained easily, it was not until a few years later that he began to lose his faith in economic theory and in the teleological nature of the historical process. It was the process of this loss of faith in the tenets of Plekhanov Menshevikism which colored all of his later work.

---

6. Solomon also worked at the National Bureau; in addition to his economics training, he also had considerable actuarial experience. Still a young man, he died during World War II. George went on to become a major statistician and was for many decades on the faculty of the University of California, Berkeley.

## Background of and Collaboration with W. C. Mitchell

Kuznets had an inclination toward empirical analysis of economic data before he came into contact with Wesley Clair Mitchell, as evidenced by his work on wages of factory employees in Kharkov. But this inclination was encouraged and stimulated by Mitchell, who was skeptical of the deductive method and argued for the careful analysis of empirical data for understanding economic phenomena. Mitchell introduced Kuznets to his own interest in business cycle analysis and, in 1927, Kuznets joined the research staff at the National Bureau of Economic Research, an association that lasted until 1961.

His dissertation at Columbia, accepted in 1926 and published as "Secular Movements in Production and Prices" in 1930, was awarded the prestigious dissertational Hartshaffner and Marx Prize. *Cyclical Fluctuations* (1926), *Secular Movements in Production and Prices,* and *Seasonal Variations in Industry and Trade* (1933) form a complete whole, analyzing the cyclical, seasonal, and secular patterns in economic data. In *Cyclical Fluctuations,* Kuznets analyzed the cyclical pattern in wholesale and retail trade and presented a theory of the propagation of a business cycle. An original change in consumer demand is magnified both by the speculation of retailers and wholesalers and by the existence of lags and asymmetries in their responses. These lags, as well as the accumulation of unsold inventory at different levels, cause a decline in sales and output, which culminates in a depression.

What is interesting about this thesis is not only the statistical ingenuity in teasing cycles from the raw data, but even more the sophisticated analysis combining the role of expected risk and speculation to weave a theory that relies on disproportionate responses and lags to elucidate the propagation of a cycle.

*Secular Movements in Production and Prices* continues this work, though the interest has shifted to long-term movement or secondary secular movements, later identified as Kuznets cycles.[7] In fitting a trend curve to U.S. data from 1865 to 1925, Kuznets discovered the persistence of these extended cycles lasting 18–25 years (Kuznets 1930, 77–197). He devised a hypothesis relating secondary secular movements to each other and provisionally explaining their propagation in terms of successive changes in prices, wages, profits, and output, as well as redistribution of income between wage and profit earners and between consumption and saving. These movements are prolonged by lags in adjustment and differential response by different sectors

---

7. The goal of *Secular Movements in Production and Prices* is defined as understanding economic growth. However, "It seems advisable to resolve the general problems of economic growth into the narrower question as to the long-time changes which can be observed in various national branches of production and trade" (Kuznets 1930, 4). The analysis of economic growth was his research interest in the post–World War II period.

of the economy. Economic expansion begins to wane due to two factors: a decrease in productivity following the increase in employment and a decline in the rate of growth of the money supply (Kuznets 1930, 207–58).[8]

*Seasonal Variations in Industry and Trade* completes this trilogy, describing seasonal fluctuations and linking them to cyclical and secular movements in the economy. As a chronicle of the behavior of industries and firms at different levels of economic activity, these works are monumental and impressive. As a theory of business cycles that contains both the decision-making process of businessmen and meticulous detail on the structure of industry it is, if not unrivaled, extraordinarily sophisticated and comprehensive. Kuznets's key insight in the whole work is to locate these fluctuations within the structure of the economy rather than relying for explanation on external (or internal) shocks.

Throughout, the goal of the exercise is to discover the causes and costs of business fluctuations and to evaluate alternative mechanisms for dealing with them. This is most explicitly discussed in *Seasonal Variations*. Kuznets outlines the intent underlying his analysis as a guide to policy aimed at reducing fluctuations and a mechanism for evaluation of policies "undertaken to mitigate variations or to offset their undesirable consequences." (Kuznets 1933a, 2.) Upon revealing that the extent of the burden of seasonality on the economic system through surplus commodity stocks, idle equipment, and excess labor supply is significant, Kuznets turns to a consideration of various measures to reduce seasonality. These measures are then evaluated in terms of who bears the burden of seasonality: labor or capital, labor or ultimate consumers, agricultural producers or a public agency. Although he is careful to take no explicit position on these questions, it seems clear that reducing the burden of seasonal changes in employment and income for labor and farmers is of importance.[9]

Kuznets considered *Seasonal Variations* intellectually and conceptually his most polished work.[10] In it he builds upon the discovery that industries requiring a large capital stock tend to react to a cyclical change in demand

---

8. In later work on secondary secular movements, Kuznets related changes in output and business activity to long-term trends in immigration, the rate of net population growth, and capital formation (Kuznets 1958).

9. He deplored the spread of "hand-to-mouth" buying by merchandisers for increasing the variability of seasonal demand, and, thus, the burden of seasonal variations of income and employment for certain social groups. One wonders what he would have thought of "just-in-time" inventory.

10. *Seasonal Variations* saw a complete treatment of the causes and consequences of business fluctuations; this theme was discarded in Kuznets's subsequent work. The research he undertook on income distribution among professionals was first put aside and then became Friedman's project. But his concern with the benefits and costs of income leveling remained with him all of his life.

with disproportionately larger changes in demand for equipment than those employing a small capital stock. If the equipment-producing industry is itself subject to significant seasonal patterns, it cannot easily adjust to unexpected changes in off-season demand, and will therefore maintain significant inventories. These factors introduce a discontinuity between a change in demand and a consequent change in production. This discontinuity serves to magnify cyclical patterns from consumer to producer goods industries and between different branches of sales and production. In addition, it affects the timing of cyclical swings in different branches of economic activity. Finally, these large inventories may fuel cyclical activity by compounding random shocks to initiate a cycle.

### National Income Accounts, Studies in Gross Capital Formation, Professional Income, and World War II

National Income

Kuznets began work on national income accounts in the 1930s.[11] This work formalized the first phase of the institutional measurement of national income and the creation of the American national income accounts, and it was broadened during the mid-1930s when Kuznets took the lead in establishing the Conference on Income and Wealth, an organization which not only met regularly, but also developed an international dimension. Kuznets's approach to and conception of national income are most clearly elucidated in his 1933 article for the *Encyclopedia of the Social Sciences* entitled "National Income."[12] This article is a groundbreaking discussion of alternative uses of national income numbers, as well as a masterly exposition of issues of definition and measurement. Not long after its publication, Kuznets left this topic to work in other areas, and when he returned to it after the war he was much disheartened by what his "child" had become.

Kuznets chose to gauge the volume of the circular flow at the point where income was received by individuals, later arguing that the main intent of the economic system was the provision of goods and services to its citizens. All subsequent choices regarding the inclusion, exclusion, and valuation of items

---

11. This effort includes *National Income, 1929–32* (1934), *National Income and Capital Formation, 1919–35* (1937), *National Income and Its Composition, 1919–38* (1941), *National Product in Wartime* (1945), *National Income: A Summary of Findings* (1946), and *National Product Since 1869* (1946).

12. The actual history of the institutionalization of the effort has been recounted by Kuznets's erstwhile student and longtime admiring colleague, Robert A. Nathan. The article itself was commissioned by his brother, Solomon, who was the principal assistant of the *Encyclopaedia's* editor, Edwin R. A. Seligman.

in the national income totals were guided by this conception of national income. National income is then the sum of wages, salaries, rent, interest, dividends, and such, as well as all production for self-consumption and compensation in kind. The rest of "National Income" is devoted to answering questions regarding the treatment of individual items within the total and different distributions of national income among regions, industries, functional shares, and persons. Kuznets confirmed that the distribution of incomes between *service income* (wages, salaries, and entrepreneurial income) and *property income* (rent, interest, and dividends) had remained roughly stable over the period for which estimates were available (1850–1928), with the share of wages and salaries rising slightly and that of entrepreneurial income falling within the service income total. Kuznets's concern with the distribution of income is revealed by his devotion of almost half of the article to this topic, with a substantial portion devoted to an analysis of personal income distribution and alternative measures of income inequality.

Among those who read the drafts of the *Encyclopedia of the Social Sciences* article was Paul Webbink, then an administrative assistant to Senator Robert Marion LaFollette of Wisconsin. Webbink, much impressed with what Kuznets had laid out, drafted a resolution, which the U.S. Senate passed in June 1932, directing the new secretary of commerce to provide national income estimates for 1929, 1930, and 1931 through the Bureau of Foreign and Domestic Commerce (BFDC). The new secretary, Daniel Roper, was unable to find anyone at BFDC to undertake this task and turned (as many had done before) to Wesley Clair Mitchell. Mitchell suggested Kuznets, who had been hired in 1930 as professor of statistics at the University of Pennsylvania.

Kuznets was, of course, sympathetic to the idea, but he did not want to take leave from Pennsylvania at that point in his career.[13] He agreed to some discussion, however, and, serendipitously, met in Frederic Dewhurst's Commerce Department office a former favorite student, Robert Nathan, who was seeking federal employment. Kuznets arranged that Nathan and another erstwhile favorite Pennsylvania student, Milton Gilbert, be hired. Initially the two worked nominally for Martin, although they reported biweekly to Kuznets.

---

13. In conversations with Perlman after Kuznets's retirement from Harvard, he marveled at the collapse of anti-Semitism in American universities in the late 1940s. Perlman's recollection is that his Penn appointment was in statistics because the economics department did not want immigrant Russian Jews. Later, after Kuznets was voted an appointment at the Johns Hopkins University, Isaiah Bowman, the articulately anti-Semitic president, threw a spanner into the works and offered Kuznets a salary much lower than had been informally discussed. George Heberton Evans, the chairman of the Hopkins Department of Political Economy, told Perlman that Kuznets never replied to the Bowman letter—he neither declined nor accepted. After Bowman's retirement, Kuznets chose to reply to Bowman's written offer indicating that the salary was the sole impediment. Bowman's successor, the eminent biostatistician Carol Reed, amended the offer satisfactorily, and Kuznets accepted the post.

Together (with only a secretary or two), and under Kuznets's supervision, they prepared the estimates in record time. Much of Nathan's effort went into persuading governmental bureaus to gather piggyback national income data on their other field surveys. By 1934, Nathan was heading the office. (See Nathan 1994).

During the late 1930s, the office created additional national income estimates for the United States and extended them successively backward in time. Of these efforts, the most comprehensive is *National Income and Its Composition, 1919–1938*, published in 1941. This exhaustive exploration is marked by a thorough definition and description of concepts and methods, presentation and analysis of results, discussion of the underlying data, and a commendable effort not only to compare these estimates with those of others, but also to measure the reliability of the estimates. *National Income and Its Composition* is useful to us because it can be employed for comparison with the official Department of Commerce estimates prepared (mainly) by Milton Gilbert in the early 1940s[14] and with concurrent British estimates by J. E. Meade and Richard Stone.[15]

The Kuznets method of defining and measuring national income differed from the Department of Commerce method in significant details,[16] but the major difference was the approach they took to national income. These differences were most distinctly apparent in Kuznets's review of the new Department of Commerce Series published in the *Survey of Current Business*.[17] To

---

14. Gilbert took over the national accounting program in 1941.

15. The Meade-Stone framework was explicitly Keynesian. It relied on the division of the economy into three sectors (five accounts) and double-entry bookkeeping; the accountants made pragmatic judgments of valuation on the basis of data availability. Meade and Stone defined national income, output, and expenditure at factor cost, with the last corresponding to our familiar $C + I + G$ schema (See Meade and Stone 1941 for details). Output was conceived as the sum of accumulation and consumption, and was valued at market prices when these were available, at cost when market prices were unavailable (government sector), and ignored when neither market prices nor quantity of output was available or estimable (household production). Net national income (Meade-Stone) differed from national income (Department of Commerce) in including imputed rent on owner-occupied housing, corporate income and excess profits taxes, capital outlays charged to current expense, and inventory revaluations, and in excluding social security contributions of employers and interest on federal debt. See Stone 1942 for details.

16. Kuznets included (but the Department of Commerce excluded) imputed rent of owner-occupied houses, relief payments, an adjustment for gains on inventory holdings, social security contributions of employees, and interest on federal debt. On the other hand, Kuznets excluded (but the Department of Commerce included) government savings and corporate income and excess profits taxes.

17. The response to this criticism was by Gilbert et al. Kuznets insisted that explicit assumptions about the goals of economic activity must precondition choices regarding the point at which the circular flow should be measured, as well as questions of inclusion and valuation. Thus, he repudiated the official U.S. national income accounts when they were presented in 1947

Kuznets, national income estimates were a "summary and appraisal notion rather than an analytical entity" (Kuznets 1933b, 205). Such an appraisal requires an understanding (on the part of the accountant) of the goals of economic activity and some mechanism for defining and evaluating social productivity. In the absence of these criteria, national income will be a meaningless total and the accountant will have no justification for distinguishing yields from costs or for the choice of appropriate levels of aggregation. Therefore, some concept of a socially accepted definition of productive activity must be antecedent to any definition of national income and must guide all subsequent choices regarding the treatment and valuation of particular entries. Kuznets was well aware that this method was contingent upon the existing social structure. "Being conditioned by the institutional setup of the family and of economic society, the line between economic and noneconomic activity shifts from country to country and from time to time" (Kuznets 1933b, 209). The conditional character of national income appraisal necessitates explicit assumptions and consistent treatment of all questions of scope on the basis of these assumptions.

Thus, Kuznets was critical of Gilbert et al. because the new series demonstrated an absence of any consensus regarding the end result of economic activity undergirding the accounts. Such a consensus is essential because the treatment of, say, government as a producer or ultimate consumer flows from it. If the true purpose of economic activity is production, then decisions regarding the treatment of various items will differ from the decisions made if the accepted end purpose of economic activity were consumption.

Kuznets maintained that in the new series decisions had been made solely on the basis of expediency. Such solutions might have been appropriate if the institutional character of the economy remained frozen, but he felt that such solutions distorted our view since these items were themselves subject to change. Thus, the exclusion of the services of housewives constituted a large and variable omission from national income. Similarly, the inclusion of all costs of business activity and all government services[18] as part of the final product introduced an element of double-counting—an element that made a

---

as an integrated set of accounts (cf. Milton Gilbert, George Jaszi, Edward F. Denison, and Charles F. Schwartz 1947). Kuznets's views are in Kuznets 1948. The Gilbert et al. team replied respectfully but in great disagreement with Kuznets's position (Gilbert, et al. 1948).

18. Kuznets evaluated the contribution of the public sector in terms of the payments made for its services. This method was adopted in order to ensure consistency with the valuation of output of the private sector and because of its sensitivity to short-term fluctuations. Further, in deriving the net value of production, the value of all services "sold" by government to business was deducted as being intermediate in nature.

mockery of "national income" as that term has been employed by past investigators and also rendered impossible attempts at comparison over time.

Although the Gilbert version of the accounts has been refined over time, their essential structure has remained unchanged since 1948. While revisions of the national accounting structure to account for new questions and problems have periodically been suggested, such revisions would make consistent comparisons difficult. The accounting structure is not fluid or flexible enough to answer questions regarding the impact of environmental expenditures, depletion of natural resources, increased consumption, costs of crime and commuting, and so on. Periodic reformulations of the national income accounts, most recently to include the value of home production and natural resources, reflect the inadequacy of this (or any) accounting system for answering questions regarding the success of the economy in satisfying the needs of its consumers.

One final element of Kuznets's national income work remains to be considered. During the period shortly before World War II, Mitchell suggested to Kuznets that, as he had been so occupied with the capital formation studies, he accept Milton Friedman as a colleague in his research on changes in income distribution, particularly as they related to certain professions. That work was published in 1945. Kuznets's own work was published as *National Income: A Summary of Findings* and *National Product since 1869,* in which he reported the discovery that the ratio between consumption and income remains nearly constant when cyclical changes in these two variables are ignored. This constant average propensity to consume (APC), rather than a decreasing APC as suggested by the Keynesian model, led to reformulations of the consumption function by Duesenberry (1949), Modigliani and Brumberg (1954), and Friedman (1957). Friedman's comment about Simon's influence on his own work (cf. Kuznets and Friedman 1945) is revealing not only about the creative role that Simon played, but also about the standards of intellectual integrity that Kuznets (and Mitchell, too) held:

> Simon played a very significant part in our book. Only part of it was used by me for my thesis, not the whole of it. Moreover, my experience with Simon in connection with that book was the basis for my great admiration of him as a human being. . . . [My] book was kept from being published for something like five or six years by the opposition of one of the directors of the National Bureau to our discussion of the role of the American Medical Association in restricting entry into the profession and thereby raising the relative income of physicians compared with dentists. There was enormous pressure on Mitchell and also on Kuznets from members of the board to avoid the dispute and simply eliminate the

material that gave rise to it. Both Mitchell and Simon displayed complete devotion to the protection of intellectual freedom and fought the battle through to the end when the manuscript finally got approved by a narrow margin. I recall how many long memos Simon and I drafted during that period in answer to the criticisms of Mr. N————, the director who objected. (Letter to Perlman from Friedman, dated December 30, 1994)

## Measuring Capital Formation

Kuznets came to work on American capital formation in a roundabout way. In the early 1930s, the Poughkeepsie New York Life Insurance Council undertook a survey of capital formation in the United States. Its purpose was to advise its constituents, the large American insurance companies, where to invest the flow of funds coming into their coffers. Professor Jacob Viner, an economist at the University of Chicago and the author of two empirical studies of Canadian international trade relations, agreed to undertake the investigation, but his efforts came to naught because he was effectively seconded to advise Henry Morgenthau, Jr., then appointed as Roosevelt's secretary of the treasury. Again Wesley Clair Mitchell was consulted, and again he suggested Kuznets.

It was in this context that Kuznets seems to have discussed (but hardly endorsed) what is properly credited to John Maurice Clark, the "accelerator principle." But his most important contributions were his decision to measure not net but gross investment and to locate, industry by industry, just what firms were doing.

*National Income and Capital Formation, 1919–1935* (1937) was the preliminary report of a study undertaken by Kuznets for the NBER at the behest of the Committee on Credit and Banking of the Social Science Research Council. It provides estimates of gross and net national product, and their distribution by industrial origin and type of income, as well as between consumption and capital formation. *Commodity Flow and Capital Formation* (1938) was the expanded version of this study and contained detailed notes on sources and methods. Being envisaged as the first of a series of studies, it focused on gross capital formation as a flow of physical capital, with its financing left to later investigation. The study provides annual estimates, in constant and current prices, of the volume of durable capital goods, construction, and net changes in inventories from 1919 to 1935. In addition to providing estimates, Kuznets also examined trends in totals and subcategories, noting, for example, that net capital formation provided a small and relatively volatile share of net domestic product, with the volume of consumer outlays being a large and stable component of the total.

## War Work

In 1942, Kuznets went to work at the Planning Committee of the War Production Board.[19] The planning committee was chaired by Robert Nathan and was engaged in the analysis of long-term production planning. Committee members analyzed trends in civilian production and their relationship with national income and gross national product in order to estimate the economy's productive capacity and to locate areas of slack that could be switched over to the munitions program. They also evaluated industrial capacity and the availability of materials, labor, and other resources in an attempt to gauge limits to military and total production in the U.S. economy. "These studies, largely the work of Simon Kuznets, were directed to bringing production objectives into line with the ability to produce and they led to specific recommendations that had far reaching effects on the magnitude and composition of the Nation's production program." (U.S. Government, Bureau of Demobilization, Civilian Production Administration 1947, 240).

Upon its establishment, the committee's first assignment consisted of reviews of the total munitions program, of the relationship between shipping needs and munitions objectives, and of the feasibility of the aircraft program. In addition, the committee was also involved in the details of controlling and directing the flow of materials to firms, as well as in the scheduling of production for maximum utilization of plant and equipment. "The Planning Committee was distinctive among governmental planning groups for its vigor in seeking to get its recommendations implemented. As many of its recommendations touched on important organizational and personal interests, this prodding for action resulted in opposition to the committee by a few affected individuals in the Services and within the WPB itself."[20] (U.S. Government, Bureau of Demobilization, Civilian Production Administration 1947, 240).

The Kuznets-Nathan wartime work was responsible for both an understanding of the productive capacity of the U.S. economy and its reorganization to meet the needs of war. In addition to analyzing the feasibility of production targets, they estimated how and where the economy could readjust

---

19. The War Production Board had been founded in January 1942 by order of President Roosevelt, with its chairman, Donald M. Nelson, having "the power of general direction over the war procurement and production program" (U.S. Government, Bureau of Demobilization, Civilian Production Administration 1947).

20. For example, General Somervell, commanding general of the Service of Supply, was "not impressed by either the character or basis of the judgments expressed in the reports [of the Planning Committee] and [he recommended] they be carefully hidden from the eyes of thoughtful men." Memo to Robert Nathan, in (U.S. Government, Bureau of Demobilization, Civilian Production Administration 1947, 287).

to achieve these targets. For example, using national income and capital formation data, they were able to arrange for the expansion of national output by $17 billion in 1942.[21] (Perlman 1987, 144). In addition, Kuznets and the Planning Commission were directly involved in the reorganization for increased efficiency of military procurement and production. Thus, for example, in a report to the board in January 1943, Kuznets discussed the submarine problem and the need by merchant shipping for adequate escort as a major issue in decisions regarding the composition of the munitions program and the priority given to various items in production. (U.S. Government, Bureau of Demobilization, Civilian Production Administration 1947, 538). Finally, they had the unenviable task of explaining ". . . the impossibility of providing all of the items set forth in the president's list of specific objectives, and at the same time producing everything else then called for under the programs of the Army, the Navy, the Maritime Commission, and Defense Aid." (U.S. Government, Bureau of Demobilization Civilian Production Administration 1947, 276).

## Interest in Economic Growth

By the end of the 1930s, Kuznets was less interested in business cycle causes and measurement than he was in general economic growth. This shift estranged him somewhat from the Mitchell-Burns perception of the National Bureau's grand role; by the end of World War II, Kuznets was moving into a new research area, related to business cycles but mainly through the tie between changes in income and growth. The Conference on Income and Wealth and the SSRC Committee on Economic Growth were his research theaters for the remainder of his career. The principal key to his fascination with economic growth was not technological (although he was fascinated with that, too), but rather the size distribution of income. The relationship between social change and income equality was his continual question—and he was never satisfied with the answers he found.

Kuznets defined economic growth as a sustained increase in per capita or per worker product, most often accompanied by an increase in population and usually by sweeping structural changes. A major part of Kuznets's work on growth consisted of an examination and analysis of the characteristics and patterns of modern economic growth with a view to understanding its nature and causes and making it more readily comprehensible and achievable. Only then could the worldwide distribution of income be made more equal.

---

21. In a 1941 GNP of $125.3 billion and a 1942 GNP of $159.6 billion. *1947 Statistical Supplement to the Survey of Current Business*. Washington, D.C.: US GPO 1948, 7.

This concern is most apparent in his presidential address to the American Economic Association in 1954. "Economic Growth and Income Inequality" discusses the nature and causes of long-term changes in income distribution with a view toward understanding changes in income inequality with economic growth. This gem of an essay begins by evaluating data for the United States, the United Kingdom, and Germany, and tentatively concludes that there is long-term stability followed by some narrowing of income inequality. An attempt at explanation considers first the forces making for increasing inequality as growth progresses and then describes certain factors counteracting these forces. This leads to a hypothesis about the pattern of income inequality in developing countries, later called the Kuznets U hypothesis: an initial increase followed by a decrease in inequality of income distribution. This prospect disturbed Kuznets, because an increase in inequality of distribution of an already low average level of income might imperil growth or give rise to authoritarianism. "How can either the institutional and political framework of the underdeveloped societies or the processes of economic growth and industrialization be modified to favor a sustained rise to higher levels of economic performance and yet avoid the fatally simple remedy of an authoritarian regime that would use the population as cannon-fodder in the fight for economic achievement" (Kuznets 1955, 25)?

The address was prescient in warning against assuming that Western patterns must be followed in underdeveloped countries as they grow and that increased income inequality is a precondition for growth because it allows the upper income groups to save. Kuznets argued that this may be a false expectation because the upper income groups may invest their savings unproductively (in real estate or abroad) so they generate little domestic growth. Thus, to him potential economic growth could not be used as a justification for continued or increased inequality.

Kuznets was deeply interested in the role of technological change in initiating and accelerating economic growth. These technological changes bring about vast changes in the patterns of production, consumption, employment, birth, and death. But to Kuznets technology was not the key; that role was reserved for institutions. "Even if the impulse to growth is provided by a major technological innovation, the societies that adopt it must modify their preexisting institutional structure. This means substantial changes in the organization of society—an emergence of new institutions and a diminishing importance of the old. Changes will occur in the relative position of various economic and social groups" (Kuznets 1966, 6). He thus ascribed differences in the speed of absorption of technological innovations to the difficulties that different societies encounter in making the necessary institutional adjustments. This, then, required a widening of the normal scope of economic investigation to include analysis of technological, demographic, political, and social factors.[22]

The importance of political and social factors is also reiterated in his Nobel Memorial lecture, "Modern Economic Growth: Findings and Reflections" (1972). Here the limited spread of modern economic growth among the underdeveloped world is ascribed to the difficulties of making the ideological and institutional transformations necessitated by the adoption of modern technology.[23] Economic growth entails almost continuous changes in the relative position of various groups and trades in society, and this generates conflict. "Only if such conflicts are resolved without excessive costs, and certainly without long-term weakening of the political fabric of the society, is modern economic growth possible" (Kuznets 1972, 319).

Kuznets's quest was for an understanding of the nature of economic growth. He believed that an extensive study of the records of economic growth of many nations over long periods of time would yield knowledge of the wellsprings of growth. Thus, he catalogued the aggregate changes and structural shifts in demographic and economic data of countries undergoing modern economic growth. Preliminary reports of the results of this activity were presented in a series of articles titled "Quantitative Aspects of the Economic Growth of Nations," published in *Economic Development and Cultural Change* over the period 1956–67. Parts of these were revised and updated in *Economic Growth of Nations* (1971). This volume, along with the earlier *Modern Economic Growth* (1966), provides a survey of most of Kuznets's findings in the area of economic growth.

These publications detail the results of mapping economic growth in terms of its level and variability and its relationship to changes in population, in productivity, in patterns of the industrial source of national product, in employment, in the use of national product for consumption and capital formation, and in the distribution of income. Each investigation has certain common characteristics: he explains what he intends to examine and why, defines concepts, and describes the problems of definitions, as well as the problems caused by the quality of the data. Then the patterns revealed in the data are presented and tentative hypotheses about correlations are put forth.

---

22. "If we are to deal adequately with processes of economic growth, processes of long-term change in which the very technological, demographic, and social frameworks are also changing—and in ways that decidedly affect the operation of economic forces proper—it is inevitable that we venture into fields beyond those recognized in recent decades as the province of economics proper. . . . Effective work in this field necessarily calls for a shift from market economics to political and social economics (Kuznets 1955, 28).

23. This lack of growth is also, Kuznets said, a result of the policies of developed countries.

But these hypotheses are comprehensive; each possible explanation is investigated until only a few remain that warrant further investigation and confirmation.

Kuznets had high expectations for a theory of economic growth. Such a theory had to explain the economic regularities he had documented as well as incorporate the role of cultural and institutional factors. In addition, it had to demonstrate the impact of differing initial conditions on economic growth and explain how growth spreads (Kuznets 1959, 109–17).[24] He was particularly skeptical of "partial theories" that might explain little and provide misleading policy advice. Further theoretical inquiry and empirical investigation were necessary for the formulation of a general theory of economic growth;[25] much more data in both economics and other social sciences were required for the formulation of such a theory. He was highly critical of Walt Rostow's presentation of a theory of economic growth based upon a specification of stages and turning points. Rostow's "The Take-Off into Self-Sustained Growth" (1956) and *The Stages of Economic Growth* (1960) present a theory of economic growth in several stages, each stage characterized by the achievement of levels and rates of growth of economic variables. Kuznets criticized this theory, contending that it did not clearly (empirically) characterize stages or leading sectors and made meaningful analysis impossible. But "my disagreement with Professor Rostow is *not* on the value and legitimacy of an attempt to suggest some pattern of order in the modern economic growth experience of different countries. On the contrary, I fully share what I take to be his view on the need to go beyond qualitative and quantitative description to the use of the evidence for a large number of countries and long periods, in combination with analytical tools and imaginative hypotheses, to suggest and explain some common patterns but also, I would add, the major deviations from them" (Kuznets 1965, 233). Kuznets's argument was merely that Rostow had not succeeded in this endeavor: Rostow's theory did not clearly characterize stages and his description of the takeoff did not accord with the observed pattern in currently developed countries.

Some reviewers of Kuznets's work have argued that neither Rostow nor Kuznets was likely to be successful in this quest. Paul Hohenberg expressed skepticism about the feasibility of Kuznets's approach toward a theory of economic growth; aggregative quantitative data, he claimed, are liable to be insensitive to changes in stages and to turning points. Further, quantitative approaches that specify levels of, say, capital formation or investment without focusing on the relationship between capital formation and the initiation of

---

24. See also "Economic Growth and Income Inequality" (Kuznets 1955).

25. In Economic Growth of Nations (1971) Kuznets argued for a bureau devoted to this quest.

economic growth are unlikely to be very productive. "No amount of patient and imaginative marshaling of data can compensate for the failure to consider explicit mechanisms by which modern economic growth may be initiated, propagated, and sustained" (Hohenberg 1966, 418).

This has tended to be the dominant criticism of Kuznets's research. Denison expressed reservations about his method, arguing that "marshalling of statistical evidence to establish patterns is exceptionally informal" (Denison 1967, 1327). Similarly, Robinson (1961) was "dubious" that the construction of a model could occur only after the collection of a sufficient quantity of empirical data; she was wary of the kind of dogmatism that resulted from facts without theory, just as Kuznets had warned of dogmatism resulting from theory without facts.

A different type of review is one of *National Income and Its Composition* by George Stigler (1943). Stigler began by praising the work: "The discussion of the theoretical issues is balanced and incisive, the interpretation of results far transcends the mere verbalization of tables, and the enormous statistical labors are performed (as far as this inexperienced reviewer can tell) with unfailing skill and patience" (Stigler 1943, 528). He then chose to focus on three contentious issues: the choice of net welfare income as the appropriate measure of national income, the measurement of government's contribution to national income, and the mechanisms used to gauge the accuracy of the estimates. Only the first will concern us here. Stigler found Kuznets's use of a normative concept and his abandonment of the "neutrality of the economist towards the ends of economic activity" troubling. In addition, he argued that other definitions of national income were more useful for analysis and that the "net welfare income" concept was as subject to flaws as the alternative concepts. Thus, Stigler denied the legitimacy of Kuznets's insistence upon establishing a normative framework around his empirical analysis.

On the whole, however, reviewers tended to highlight Kuznets's technical mastery of his statistical material and his use of data to attempt to understand and explain the underlying economic processes. Robert Lekachman's review of *Economic Change* asserts, "Mr. Kuznets combines the tremendous technical virtuosity for which he is justly celebrated with keen theoretical insight into the sociological and philosophical implications of his economic devices. . . . The general reader has an exceptional opportunity . . . to accompany . . . one of the sharpest economic minds among us on a number of explorations which sketch the present limits and the future possibilities of the almost science of economics" (Lekachman 1953, 21). Similarly, Phyllis Deane notes

Two features of the Kuznets approach are well illustrated here. The first is the exhaustive care he takes to define his terms, clarify his concepts and expound an analytical framework even before beginning to manipulate the data. The second is his way with figures. Most of the statistical data he has to hand are extremely crude and sketchy. Kuznets sifts this rough material with the delicate patience of the archaeologist. By a process combining remorseless logic, indefatigable cross-checking and bold judgement he extracts the evidence for a coherent and consistent picture out of what often seems the most unlikely material. All this is done, however, without losing sight either of the inaccuracies of the underlying statistics or of the fact that the statistical results can never yield more than a bare skeleton that requires a political and social covering to give it meaningful shape. (Deane 1967, 112)

Then there is Hohenberg, reviewing *Economic Growth and Structure:* "A brief review cannot do justice to Kuznets's numerous insights, nor to the ingenuity with which he cajoles conclusions from data while remaining fully conscious of their imperfect and tentative character" (Hohenberg 1966, 417).

Kuznets's own reviews of the work of other economists were based upon his perception of the appropriate methodology when studying business cycles and economic growth.[26] His reviews tend to be critical of other people's work on the following two grounds: inadequate use of statistical data to support hypotheses, and inadequate use of analysis to go beyond purely empirical results. Thus, in reviewing Schumpeter's *Business Cycles,* Kuznets focused on Schumpeter's assumption regarding the distribution of entrepreneurial ability among the population, his theoretical model of business cycles, and the schema employed to classify different cycles. "The critical evaluation above of what appear to be important elements in Professor Schumpeter's conclusions . . . yields disturbingly destructive results. The association between the distribution of entrepreneurial ability and the cyclical character of economic activity needs further proof" (Kuznets 1940, 270). Kuznets finds that the theoretical model "does not yield a serviceable statistical approach." Finally, "the rigid relationship claimed to have been established among the three groups of cycles cannot be considered, on the basis of the evidence submitted, even tolerably valid; nor could such validity be established without a serviceable statistical procedure" (ibid.). In summary, he finds links establishing the relationship between primary concepts and observable characteristics of business cycles absent in this book.

Michal Kalecki (*Essays in the Theory of Economic Fluctuations*) is chided because he overestimated the empirical validity of his inferences.

---

26. We have already seen how his review of Gilbert et al. spelled out the kind of empirical work he expected and his insistence upon a judgment of the end goals of economic activity before "positive" analysis of the economic data could commence.

"Careful consideration reveals that the empirical generalizations advanced rest upon limited data and somewhat loose criteria as to what constitutes stability or association; and the final conclusions are, at most, interesting suggestions of uncertain validity" (Kuznets 1939, 806). Alvin Hansen's *Business Cycles and National Income* is admired for its concise and clear discussion of business cycles, but the lack of a statistical basis for the analysis is criticized: "It is difficult to see how a theory can be judged unless its empirical referent is clearly defined and the outstanding characteristics of that referent are established" (Kuznets 1951, 968). Kuznets lamented the absence of empirical evidence in the section devoted to multipliers and accelerators and concluded that he did not find "much evidence in this volume of the urge to fit models to the observed reality, and gauge their weight. Surely, the time has come for these analytical tools . . . to be tested within the framework of empirically observed cyclical processes" (ibid., 959).

On the other hand, Gerhard Tintner is praised for conducting a good empirical investigation but criticized for limited economic analysis of the results (Kuznets 1936). While reviewing John Partington's *Railroad Purchasing and the Business Cycle*,[27] although Kuznets does not doubt the validity of the conclusions, "one tends to regret that . . . no attempt has been made to supplement the inductive test by an analytic consideration of factors making for interrelationship between railroad buying and the business cycle" (Kuznets 1931, 233). Overall, Kuznets's empirical method demanded a judicious mix of economic analysis and statistical data, each supporting conclusions and hypotheses for the succeeding steps in the inquiry, and his reviews censured investigations that omitted either of these two essential elements.

## Demographic Economics

In all of Kuznets's professional work there was such a conscious effort to derive interpretations from the data, rather than to use data as a test for some excogitated hypothesis or other, that it may seem presumptuous to suggest that, withal, he came to every bit of data examination with a certain kind of mindset. We have already indicated that not only did his *Bundist* interests give him a commitment to certain kinds of economic policy, but also when he looked at the data he came to realize that the policies he had earlier imagined as optimal were quite probably counterproductive.

When it came to his work on demographic economics, the role of predisposition seems to us to have been somewhat different. He was, himself, an immigrant, and one lucky enough to get into the United States before the

---

27. This study was an attempt to test the thesis that variations in railroad purchasing have influenced American business cycles.

barriers were raised in 1925. And like all Jews of his generation, the Holocaust was a peculiar personal horror for him, even by the standards of general horror perceived by others.

Although we admit that the role of personal motive, even when it is used as an explanation by the person, himself, may be problematic, when it comes to Kuznets's views on population and economic choice, his personal experiences give some ring of authenticity to explanations of his position. When we look over the many essays he wrote within the ambit of demographic economics, they focus on two major themes: (a) the role of migration, and (b) the impact of population growth on economic development.

From the standpoint of chronology, he wrote first in the area of migration, where his work with his University of Pennsylvania colleague, Dorothy Swaine Thomas,[28] an eminent sociologist, resulted in his editorship of a massive three-volume work in 1955, *Population Redistribution and Economic Growth: United States*. The topic of migration continued to interest him to the end of his life, and he was particularly responsive to the work of Oded Stark, but the bulk of his creative ideas were on the relationship between population growth and economic change.

After World War II, Kuznets's view of fertility control policies deviated from the more popular attitude among academics. The "baby boom" of the later 1940s and 1950s had reinforced the latent Malthusianism (cf. Perlman 1975) among both academics and the educated laity. Kuznets's skepticism was expressed at a Universities-National Bureau of Economic Research conference on economic development and population in 1958, with the proceedings being published in 1960. The essence of his thought, an essay, "Population Change and the Aggregate Output" (Kuznets 1960, see esp. 326–30),[29] started with an examination of a growing population from the varied standpoints of production, saving, and consumption. He speculated that a larger labor force encourages output growth not only through enhanced opportunities for specialization, but also through an increased opportunity for technological advance. This last was an ingenious argument. Its premise was that high-quality intellectual talents were very unequally distributed in society, with those having great originality being never more than a fraction of 1 percent of the population. What mattered greatly in terms of economic growth was not the presence of a talented individual so much as the ease with which one talented individual communicated with all the other similarly talented

---

28. In an era when there were few women academics and even fewer great ones, Dorothy Swaine Thomas stands out. Her doctoral dissertation on "Fertility and Business Cycles in Sweden" was seminal. She also chaired the Social Science Research Committee's Committee on Migration Differentials.

29. The foregoing paper was atypical; it was data-shy.

individuals in a given period of time.[30] Similarly, what retards the development of some countries is the massive proportion of children as well as the small number of trained, greatly talented adults and the absence of ease of communication between them.[31] Thereafter, whenever Kuznets turned to discussion of the relationship between population growth and economic development, he amassed considerable data and drew from them his generalized observations (or perhaps used them defensively).

His later analysis generally either pointed to sociological questions pertaining to institutional constraints and incentives, or to compositional changes in populations. It was not the rate of growth of the population that was important, but rather its age structure and the communications between what to some seemed trivially small shifts in order to tie the behavior of one subseries with its impact on economic development.

Toward the end of his professional life, Kuznets published several books of selected essays. What is impressive is that virtually all of his work in the period starting in the 1960s was on demographic change and economic advancement. This interest in population change, size distribution of income, and the infrastructure, largely communications, speeding the transmission of basic and developmental research in applied economics was ever-present.[32]

Prototypical of Kuznets's method of analysis is a May 1967 paper he presented at the University of Indiana, "Economic Capacity and Population Growth" (Kuznets 1973, 49–93). Replete with statistical data reflecting FAO estimates of food requirements for the period 1968 to 2000 and even more

---

30. It is appropriate to draw the inference that what made sixteenth-century Firenze so productive intellectually was the proximity of a small number of highly talented writers and artists.

31. His critics were Richard Quandt, who used some calculus to give sense to the Kuznets argument, but seemingly missed the point of Kuznets's exercise, and Milton Friedman. Friedman, with whom he had worked at the end of the 1930s, resulting in Friedman's seminal dissertation, *Income from Independent Professional Practice* (1945), thought it useful to create a sort of a procrustean matrix, where logic of categorization was the focus. In his formal reply, Kuznets, sensing a professional nakedness without his usual covering of empirical data, avoided immediate confrontation, merely remarking, "the aim of this paper is to suggest problems for further research, and that the claim of validity for any of the speculative suggestions, if made, is intended as an irritant, not a sedative . . ." (1960, 351).

32. *Modern Economic Growth: Rate, Structure, and Spread,* published in 1966, has nine essays. The second is "Growth of Population and Product"; the fourth is "Distribution of Product and Income"; and the eighth is "Economic and Social Structure of Underdeveloped Countries." His *Population, Capital, and Growth,* published in 1973, contains ten essays, of which the first, "Population and Economic Growth"; the second, "Economic Capacity and Population Growth"; and the third, "Economic Aspects of Fertility Trends in the Less-Developed Countries," were explicitly demographic in approach. And in 1979 a third set, *Growth Population, and Income Distribution,* extended much of the demographic detail found in the essays in the earlier books to studies making rural-urban, past-present, and north-south comparisons.

detailed data on growth of food production for selected periods from the mid-1920s until the mid-1960s, it also draws heavily on opinions of various empirically minded scholars about the capacity of the earth to produce, particularly if available and anticipated new technologies will be accepted by economically retarded regions. The paper has three parts: (1) Capacity to Produce (with Special Emphasis on Food); (2) Technological, Economic and *Social* Aspects of Capacity to produce (emphasis added); and (3) Summary Comments.

Turning to the last, there are nine numbered points: (1) "the available and tested knowledge and the known natural resources are adequate for sustaining the projected population number at moderately rising standard of living" (1973, 90); (2) growth in food production should not absorb all of the available resources; (3) if the natural or expected population increase is checked, there is no reason to believe that there will be an adverse change in living standards; (4) it is likely that land reform is necessary to create a social atmosphere conducive to technological reform associated with increased food output; (5) "we have no inventory of the known political and social resources and their capacity for change. This aspect of the future is therefore usually presented as a 'challenge' in response to the promise extended by the technocratic potentials . . ." (1973, 91); (6) adaptation to the necessary technocratic changes will be determined by each country, and that is on what the scholar's eye must be trained; (7) short-term palliatives through foreign trade (imports) may screen failure of local development; (8) long-term improvements may be jeopardized by cyclical fluctuations associated with the weather, and one part of local government concern should be to counter short-term declines in living standards; and (9) even within countries, and particularly within LDCs, inter-area differentials may develop because of poor means of transport and communication.

His concluding paragraph states it all—substance and concern for method.

> My own judgement is that neither wholesale calamity—widespread starvation and devastating epidemics—in the populous less-developed countries, nor widely successful social and political modernization permitting a rapid and effective exploitation of the large technological and economic potentials which many of them possess will eventuate. But it is a judgement that does not reflect tested experience in a recognizable explicit fashion. The prospects for change in the social and political structure of the less-developed countries and in the framework of international relations can hardly be explored by the methods of economic and quantitative analysis; they require data and tools that are beyond the scope of this paper. (1973, 93)

In sum, although Kuznets regarded himself and was regarded by others as both a statistician and an economist, his interests in demographic economics—migration, size distribution of income, changing age compositions of populations in industrialized and in industrializing economies, and the roles of saving and social infrastructure—led him in the course of his career to an increasing concentration on what would in another decade have been called sociology. Perhaps that is true of many economists—particularly those of an era when they knew many languages, the history of many countries' institutions, and the complex influences of culture on reason.

## Assessing Kuznets's Impact

In his lifetime Kuznets's achievements were quickly and thoroughly recognized. In 1949 he was president of the American Statistical Association. In 1950 he received from Princeton the first of about a score of honorary degrees and the like. In 1954 he served as president of the American Economic Association, also receiving its once most prestigious award, the Francis A. Walker Award, in 1977.[33] We have already mentioned his Nobel Prize in 1971. Besides that, he was honored with memberships in numerous academies, both in the United States (e.g., the American Philosophical Society and the American Academy of Arts and Sciences) and abroad, as well as affiliating memberships with such recognized academies as the Royal Society.

His professional academic career included three principal appointments: at the University of Pennsylvania (1931–54), at Johns Hopkins University (1954–60), and at Harvard University from 1960 until his death (he retired in 1971). Of course there were also many short-term academic assignments. But in some senses the critical professional affiliations of his life were with the National Bureau of Economic Research (1927–61) and the Social Science Research Council. The council funded his work on income and wealth and his work on economic growth, and drew upon his wisdom for its Committee on China.

Kuznets was not only an indefatigable worker himself, but was also an imaginative and somewhat hard-driving organizer. As an "elder statesman," his usual second question (the first was invariably about his visitor's life, spouse, and children, often by name) was, "What are you working on these days?" At his seventieth birthday party one of his Harvard colleagues mentioned that after that question was levied, Kuznets would listen closely, and more often than not "his gaze would focus in, the corners of his mouth would tighten, and a patient scorn would tint his face." Others report that after that

---

33. Thereafter the award was discontinued; apparently the Association's leadership felt that its significance had been superseded by the Nobel Prize in economics.

first question, he would put the invariable second, listen closely, his eyebrows would arch slightly, he would smile piquantly, and then ask, "Have you found anything that you didn't expect?" Of course, if you had, the "hour was made," and he would start a series of marvelous speculations as to why new things had turned up.

Kuznets's self perception was accurate—he knew his worth, but he also recognized enthusiastically the originality of others. If he had great scorn for some in the profession, he also expressed deep admiration for others—not only for Mitchell, but also for such as Henry Ludwell Moore, the statistician. There was a personal warmth that softened frequently the harshness of his skepticism.

Kuznets's interests embraced many national concerns. He was keenly interested in Chinese development, having spent some time immediately after World War II in Nanking trying to work out a national accounts system for the Chiang Kai-Shek Kuomintang government. Like a great many ex-Bundists he had nothing but deep hatred for Leninism and Stalinism. In the late 1930s, like many Jewish emigres, he worried constantly about the rise of Nazism. After World War II he was even more concerned about refugee problems, and particularly about the capacity of Israel to absorb Jewish refugees.

This interest flowered into a project, which the Maurice and Laura Falk Foundation of Pittsburgh initially largely underwrote. The original Falk Project for Economic Research in Israel (after 1963 known as the Maurice Falk Institute for Economic Research in Israel) involved great talent, including originally an active blue-ribbon American Advisory Committee (among others there were Daniel Creamer [who had been the initial research director], A. D. H. Kaplan [Brookings], Isador Lubin [the New Deal Commissioner of the federal Bureau of Labor Statistics], and Kuznets, who was its chairman), and a lengthy list of brilliant Israelis, of whom Don Patinkin was one of the earliest. Kuznets took special care to work closely with the project-cum-institute, attending meetings so long as he was physically capable, and giving close professional and social attention to the economists who were affiliated. Kuznets enjoyed a truly remarkable relationship with the talent assembled. As with the original Conference on Income and Wealth, Kuznets led the group into ever more critical research projects. While Kuznets had outstanding graduate students, to us, at least, his comparative advantage was working with scholars who were on the edge of becoming fully mature. And in no area was he more appreciated than in this Israeli connection.

Like many of his generation, he was appreciative of a wide variety of literary, artistic, and musical achievements. His knowledge of history, sociology, political theory, and particularly mathematical statistics was deep. Although he usually looked as though the wind would blow him over, he was said to be an aggressive tennis player, and for as long as he could he not only smoked fine cigars, but his personal influence was such that those about him did, too—not so much to get accustomed to his smoke, as to his style.

Having noted the wealth of his recognition, let us return to our assessment of him. From an academic standpoint he was the exemplar economic empiricist of his generation; Mitchell was his teacher, but Kuznets was culturally even broader than his mentor. We think that his (and Nathan's) war achievement explains the overwhelming superiority in numbers of U.S. materiel in 1944 and 1945. In some senses, what went on before was the essential prologue, and the Allied victory was in a specific way the consequence.

Yet, when in 1950 he was to get his honorary degree from Princeton, he and his wife, Edith (Handler), met none other than Jacob Viner on Nassau Street. (Viner, you will recall, had not finished the task of measuring capital formation.) Viner, ever peppy and acerbic, said, "Simon, what are you doing here?" Simon replied that Princeton was giving him an honorary degree. Viner's next statement speaks reams: "Whatever for?" Academics often forget to realize that their own world is not front and center. Kuznets, ever an American Institutionalist, thought otherwise; his real world was not Cartesian modelling, but cognition and inference. His historical legacy was the system for monitoring national output, income, and, to some degree, consumption. From the standpoint of method, his legacy was simply the reiteration of Euclid's point about Royal Roads and knowledge. So much of his original work later became canon and in the process lost its identity as his that, more than anything else, simple academic honesty requires us to remember his creativeness and his thorough integrity.

### BIBLIOGRAPHY

Deane, Phyllis. Review of *Economic Change,* by Simon Kuznets, *The Economic Journal* 77 (March 1967): 111–12.

Denison, E. F. Review of *Modern Economic Growth,* by Simon Kuznets, *American Economic Review* 57 (December 1967): 1326–28.

Duesenberry, James. *Income, Saving, and the Theory of Consumer Behavior.* Cambridge, Mass.: Harvard University Press, 1949.

Friedman, Milton. *A Theory of the Consumption Function.* National Bureau of Economic Research, no. 63. Princeton, N.J.: Princeton University Press, 1957.

Gilbert, Milton, George Jaszi, Edward F. Denison, and Charles F. Schwartz. "National Income and Product Statistics of the United States." Supplement to *Survey of Current Business* 27 (July 1947): 1–54.

———. "Objectives of National Income Measurement: A Reply to Professor Kuznets." *The Review of Economics and Statistics* 30 (August 1948): 179–97.

Hohenberg, P. H. Review of *Economic Growth and Structure,* by Simon Kuznets, *Journal of Political Economy* 74 (August 1966): 417–18.

Kuznets, Simon. "Money Wages of Factory Employees in Kharkov in 1920" (in Russian). In *Materials on Labor Statistics of Ukraine,* 2d issue. Kharkov: Central Soviet of Trade Unions, Southern Bureau, Division of Statistics, July 1921.

———. *Cyclical Fluctuations.* Westport, Conn.: Hyperion Press, Inc., 1926.

———. *Secular Movements in Production and Prices.* New York: Augustus M. Kelley, 1930.

———. Review of *Railroad Purchasing and the Business Cycle,* by John Partington, *Journal of the American Statistical Association* 26 (June 1931): 231–33.

———. *Seasonal Variations in Industry and Trade.* New York: National Bureau of Economic Research, 1933a.

———. "National Income." *Encyclopedia of the Social Sciences.* Vol. 11. New York: Macmillan, 1933b, 205–24.

———. Review of *Prices in the Trade Cycles,* by Gerhard Tintner, *Annals of the American Academy of Political and Social Sciences* 185 (May 1936): 241–42.

———. *National Income and Capital Formation 1919–1935.* New York: National Bureau of Economic Research, 1937.

———. *Commodity Flow and Capital Formation.* New York: National Bureau of Economic Research, 1938.

———. Review of *Essays in the Theory of Economic Fluctuations,* by Michal Kalecki, *American Economic Review* 29 (December 1939): 804–6.

———. "Schumpeter's Business Cycles." *American Economic Review.* 30 (June 1940): 257–71.

———. "Discussion of the New Department of Commerce Income Series," *The Review of Economics and Statistics* 30 (August 1948): 151–79.

———. Review of *Business Cycles and National Income,* by Alvin H. Hansen, *American Economic Review* 41 (December 1951): 967–71.

———. "Economic Growth and Income Inequality." *American Economic Review* 45 (March 1955): 1–28.

———. *Population Redistribution and Economic Growth: United States, 1870–1950* 3 vols. Philadelphia: American Philosophical Society, 1957–1964.

———. "Long Swings in the Growth of Population and in Related Economic Variables." *Proceedings of the American Philosophical Society* 102 (1958): 25–52. Reprinted in *Economic Growth and Structure: Selected Essays.* New York: W. W. Norton & Co., 1965.

———. *Six Lectures on Economic Growth.* Glencoe, Ill.: Free Press, 1959.

———. "Notes on the Take-off." In *The Economics of Take-Off into Sustained Growth,* edited by W. W. Rostow. New York: St. Martin's Press, 1963. Reprinted in *Economic Growth and Structure.* New York: W. W. Norton & Co., 1965.

———. "Population Change and Aggregate Output," in Universities-National Bureau Conference for Economic Research (1960). *Demographic and Economic Change in Developed Countries.* Princeton: Princeton University Press, 1965, 324–39; discussion following, including: Richard Quandt, 329–45; Milton Friedman, 345–50; and Kuznets's reply, 350–51.

———. *Modern Economic Growth: Rate, Structure, and Spread.* New Haven, Conn.: Yale University Press, 1966.

————. *Economic Growth of Nations.* Cambridge, Mass.: Belknap Press of Harvard University Press, 1971.

————. "Modern Economic Growth: Findings and Reflections." In *Le Prix Nobel en 1971.* Stockholm: Bonnier, 1972.

————. *Population, Capital, and Growth.* New York: Norton, 1973.

————. *Growth Population, and Income Distribution.* New York: Norton, 1979.

————. "Recent Population Trends in Less Developed Countries and Implications for Internal Income Inequality" in *Population and Economic Change in Developing Countries* NBER, no. 30. Chicago: University of Chicago Press, 471–511, 515; discussion following by Albert Fishlow, 511–14. 1980.

Kuznets, S., and Milton Friedman. *Income from Independent Professional Practice.* New York: National Bureau of Economic Research, 1945.

Lekachman, Robert. "A Virtuosi Economist." Review of *Economic Change,* by Simon Kuznets, *New Republic* 129 (August 10, 1953): 21.

Lundberg, Erik. "Simon Kuznets' Contribution to Economics." *Swedish Journal of Economics* 73 (1971): 444–61.

Meade, J. E., and Richard Stone. "The Construction of Tables of National Income, Expenditure, Savings and Investment." *The Economic Journal* 51 (June–Sept. 1941): 217–22.

Modigliani, Franco, and R. Brumberg. "Utility Analysis and the Consumption Function." In *Post Keynesian Economics,* edited by K. K. Kurihara. New Brunswick, N.J.: Rutgers University Press, 1954.

Nathan, Robert R. "GNP and Military Mobilization." *Journal of Evolutionary Economics* 4 (1994): 1–16.

Perlman, Mark. "Some Economic Growth Problems and the Part Population Policy Plays." *Quarterly Journal of Economics* 89 (1975): 247–56.

————. "Political Purpose and the National Accounts." In *The Politics of Numbers,* edited by William Alonso and Paul Starr. New York: Russell Sage Foundation, 1987.

Robinson, Joan. Review of *Six Lectures on Economic Growth,* by Simon Kuznets, *Journal of Political Economy* 69 (February 1961): 74.

Rostow, W. W. "The Take-Off into Self-Sustained Growth." *The Economic Journal* 6 (March 1956): 25–48.

————. *The Stages of Economic Growth.* Cambridge, Mass.: Harvard University Press (1960): 17–35.

*Statistical Supplement to the Survey of Current Business, 1947.* Washington, D.C.: U.S. Government Printing Office, 1948.

Stigler, George. Review of *National Income and Its Composition,* by Simon Kuznets. *Journal of Farm Economics* 25 (May 1943): 528–32.

Stone, Richard. "The National Income, Output and Expenditure of the United States of America, 1929–41." *The Economic Journal* 52 (June–Sept. 1942): 154–75.

U.S. Government, Bureau of Demobilization, Civilian Production Administration. *Industrial Mobilization for War: History of the War Production Board and Predecessor Agencies.* Vol. 1. Washington, D.C.: U.S. Government Printing Office, 1947.

CHAPTER 18

# Introduction to Fritz Machlup, *Essays in Economic Semantics*

*This second edition differs from the first in two respects. My introduction, written after Fritz's death, says a few new things about him, particularly about his activities during the last two-plus decades of his life. It also explains why this edition contains two additional essays—one on a confrontation with Paul A. Samuelson (and, to a lesser degree, Frank Knight) on the subject of mathematics in economics and methodology and the other a survey of his thoughts regarding the comparability of social sciences and the physical sciences, particularly physics and chemistry. Finally, I survey the spectrum of reviewers' and my own assessments of the initial edition.*

My remarks in this prefatory note cluster about two poles. The first involves some discussion of the first edition of the book, its reception, and Machlup's views. The second concentrates on some additional materials we have added in this edition to round out certain aspects of Machlup's views. I conclude by offering some of my own observations.

### 1. The Book's History

Presented to Machlup on his 60th birthday in 1962, the first edition was a collection of his own essays. It was an effort on the part of several of his students to honor Fritz in an unusual way. By collecting and reprinting a few of his straight-forward principally pedagogical (as distinct from his mainly research) efforts they wanted to mark particularly that aspect of his many-sided influence. Their choice, perforce, had to be extremely limited, and what resulted was a selection clearly designed for an audience of American graduate students. That their gift became something of a derivative classic speaks volumes of their prescience as well as an indication of Machlup's historical significance.

Machlup lived and worked at full pace into his 83rd year. He was only a

*"Introduction to the Second Edition"* Fritz Machlup *Economic Semantics*. New Brunswick, Transaction Publishers, [1963] 1991, 2d ed., vii–xxi.

mere 60 in 1962, when Professor Merton Miller, leading the aforementioned students, presented this gift. Selection of material to be included was made from what had been written earlier, what Machlup was interested in then, and in one case something that had not previously been published in English. What were possibly the richest of his pedagogical-research products, his final work on the economics of knowledge and the knowledge industry, *Knowledge and Knowledge Production, The Branches of Learning,* and *The Economics of Information and Human Capital,* were still well in his future. In a very real sense, these final, very lengthy studies, supplement as well as complement what his students had chosen because, if his audience for those last volumes were scholars at large (rather than graduate students), he was writing from a lofty paternal lectern—as an elderly seer teaching the adults of his old age the body of learning he had been taught as well as what he had discovered as an autodidact, throughout a long life.

From early on Machlup had wanted to be a professor of economics, but initially fate did not seem likely to afford him that opportunity. By the time he did secure a true professorial appointment (in the United States, at Buffalo), he had already absorbed a feeling for the importance of the kind of empirical details usually required of market-place outsiders—what many academic self-styled intellectuals consider the crassest type, namely profit-hungry entrepreneurial businessmen. Thus, if his professional career was built in good part on the traditional foundations of an academic training at an Austrian *Gymnasium* and then at the University of Vienna under Professor (*ordinarius*) von Wieser, generally, and afterwards under Professor (*honorarius*) von Mises and the von Mises circle (including Hayek, Haberler, Morgenstern), particularly, it also included the battering of a non-academic experience, as well. As a Jew (indeed, one with a slightly confused lineage[1]), Machlup was not in any real sense during the 1920s and 1930s, specifically, eligible for a regular academic appointment—if they were rare in the United States, they did not exist in Austria. For this reason (if not for others, as well), Machlup, while still a graduate student, created a firm in the paperboard business. Perhaps like Ricardo, he was led by his mind in one direction, and by his observations in another, to delineate between what it was rational for a business man (qua businessman) to do, and what from time to time he (fun-loving and aesthetic,

---

1. Machlup was a natural child, something which he took even greater pains to explain in his last year than he had ever taken pains previously to conceal. When John Chipman wrote his splendid biographical entry for the 1979 Biographical Supplement of the *New Encyclopedia of the Social Sciences,* according to a recollection of my last visit with Fritz (in Vienna in 1982), he suggested that Chipman explicitly mention this point. Whatever—Chipman's text carries the message implicitly. As I had always been impressed, but puzzled, with Machlup's combination of a passionate respect for social traditions and his extreme willingness to tolerate eccentric behavior, this element in our last long conversations explained something significant to me.

fiercely logical and diligent Fritz) actually did. In any event, he was a product of those two cultures (academia and the market place).

These aspects of his academic and non-academic experiences show up in this volume. The essays reflect mostly the early evolution of the history of his economic thought between his training under von Mises and his final massive efforts concerning the knowledge industry.

The book, originally published by Prentice-Hall in 1963, was reprinted in 1967 and again in 1975. A desire, decades later, for a new edition shows a rare continuity of interest.

## 2. The Contents of This Book

*The first edition.* At first sight, the book has 11 essays. Closer examination suggests that it really has only "ten," with two being quite short and accordingly less substantive. The first (really one of the two "halves"), written especially for the first edition, simply contains Machlup's effort at trying to provide a rubric. His choice, obviously, was economic semantics. It is mainly in this very brief essay where he makes his case for *general* philological rigor, and even there Machlup's ability to see several sides to every question can be observed. It is not a profound writing; it leans heavily on patristic quotations from Malthus and Senior rather than on insights, any explicit reasoning, or even the assembling of episodic data. Had Machlup, instead, leaned on John Stuart Mill's views on the advantages of ambiguity (the less preferable alternative to an ambiguous statement might be no statement), he could have had a patristic (surely that describes J. S. Mill's role) view giving the alternative conclusion. Also, this essay eschews any consideration of institutional considerations which might explain why a phrase, created for one time and/or place, was insufficiently descriptive, directly or by analogy, of a second, similar phenomenon found in another time and/or place.

We were thus left with the "ten and a half" reprinted articles—articles originally printed between 1934 and 1960. One was translated and appeared in English for the first time in this volume.

The next four essays deal with imprecision as found in the usage of such word combinations such as *statics and dynamics; equilibrium and disequilibrium, structure and structural,* and *micro- and macro-economics.* Machlup thought the unifying tie in his treatment of these four was economic methodology, particularly insofar as methodology offered the most obvious key to the differences between the deductive and the empirical methods. Besides showing each author's methodological preferences, he also thought that the choice and usage of words revealed the quality of a writer's deductive abilities.

Letting these asides pass, the essays show several things. The 1959

"Statics and Dynamics: Kaleidoscopic Words" opens with reference to five previous such essays.[2] Within such a framework he proceeds to show, often with quotations, how no less than 38 different more-or-less modern economic theorists have used the two words. These range from Comte and Veblen, both Keyneses, both Clarks, to Samuelson, Patinkin, Baumol, and himself (interestingly, Allais, Arrow, Hurwicz, and Debreu are not included); Schumpeter the younger is quoted against Schumpeter the older, however. From these examples he constructs his own generalizations regarding the way that the terms were bent for creative as well as rhetorical purposes. In all, it is a fine exercise in comparative *explication de texte*.

The next is a 1958 essay, "Equilibrium and Disequilibrium," in which the rhetoric, that is the order of presentation, is reversed. It starts with his generalizations regarding the usages of the terms, and then in the final segment shows how a variety of writers in the international trade subfield have employed the concepts. If the older Schumpeter differed from his younger self (as noted immediately above), in this case J. E. Meade flipped and then flopped back again. Here what Machlup seems intent upon showing is not the inconsistency of usage, but the problems of specifying adequately as against the problems of inadequate specification.

A second 1958 essay, "Structure and Structural Change: Weasel-words and Jargon," comes next. It sets out a 10-point check list to help would-be users of the two terms identify the "clearer meanings." It then moves to a 9-point list of vulgar usages of the terms. The essay concludes with six illustrations of the use of the term to postpone (perhaps to occlude) just what the author was saying scientifically and what he was implying normatively.

The fourth of these essays, "Micro and Macro-economics: Contested Boundaries and Claims of Superiority," appeared first in 1960. As I reread it, it is an exercise in intellectual orientation, rather than an exercise in definition. I was his colleague during the period, and I can recall the debate which went on at Johns Hopkins. Machlup had taught three theory courses; (1) the theory of relative prices, (2) the theory of relative incomes, and (3) methodology. While he was expressly impressed with Don Patinkin's fusion of the traditional Walrasian general equilibrium analysis with the Keynesian disequilibrium system, *Money, Interest, and Prices*,[3] he was less enthusiastic about the

---

2. Four of these are contained in this collection. The omitted one is the 1950 "Three Concepts of the Balance of Payments and the So-called Dollar Shortage."

3. Patinkin's book, a reworking of a brilliant dissertation, managed to explain much of the Keynesian model in terms of Walrasian general equilibrium. Two things are particularly worth historical note about the book: Patinkin explained the Keynesian disequilibrium model in general equilibrium terms, and what Patinkin thought was required for that explanation shortly became the discipline of modern macroeconomics. The book is not so much the first modern treatment of macroeconomics as it was a definition of what modern macroeconomics encompassed.

compression of applied topics including fiscal policy, monetary policy, and employment policy into the Ann Arbor *macroeconomic* theoretical, mold, as designed sequentially by Richard Musgrave (1959) and Gardner Ackley (1961). However, when Evsey Domar left the Hopkins to go to M.I.T., the faculty voted to offer the vacated position to Musgrave, and Machlup, ever ready to admit those with whom he differed, enthusiastically accepted the choice. I see this essay as part of Machlup's effort to express, if not to clarify, his thinking about micro- and macroeconomics.[4] In it he reveals his antipathy for "persuasive definitions," a kind of elusive rhetoric which seemingly permeated Musgrave's work. Machlup thought such definitions were the kind of thing honorable and intelligent men had to take extraordinary care to avoid. Not so much for reasons of their sneaking in implicit value judgments consciously or unconsciously, but because their doing so made most systematic economic analysis impossible. At Hopkins the relationship between him and Musgrave was brief; Musgrave came in September 1960 and twelve months later Machlup had left for Princeton, where his responsibilities were not in the micro-macro theory fields but in international trade and finance.

The ensuing "two and a half" essays relate to a "debate in the journals" with Richard A. Lester. It started with the second of the essays (as presented), one which was published in 1937 shortly after Machlup had accepted his appointment at the University of Buffalo. He was then perceived (both by himself and others) as a prototype Austrian economist. "On the Meaning of the Marginal Product" is an expository treatment, really a textbook statement. Nonetheless, it served as a classificatory personal label for the immigrant, Machlup, and when given the opportunity Machlup, "the theorist," decided to do battle with Richard A. Lester, "the empiricist," albeit one trained at Yale under Fisher. In March 1947 Lester's article, "Shortcomings of Marginal Analysis for Wage-Employment Problems," purported to show that few if any of the firms that he had studied appeared consciously to model their policies along the lines of conventional marginal analysis; therefore, such analysis was, at best, irrelevant, and certainly in that sense wrong. Machlup's reply in

---

4. Machlup's political positions were a mixture of (1) his conviction that in the end the market's truths, unvarnished supply vs. demand, were bound to prevail, and (2) his warm humanity which suggested that weak parties entering the market were well-advised to try to ameliorate their condition politically. We had, as might have been expected, many extended conversations about the "good and bad" of trade unions; I recall Machlup asserting that in the long haul unionism, if it was successful, "distorted" the natural outcome (a *bad thing*) but that he, himself, would join a union (a *good thing*) if he could, and particularly if he felt that he faced a monopsonist. I think that the record shows that Machlup used his role as a union leader in the American Association of University Professors effectively to speed the upward movement of the salaries of well-known professors (the skilled workers, if you please). Characteristic of his warmth and sense of social equity, he set up the AAUP Committee T (the one on salaries) to benefit all of the professoriat.

September 1946 (Machlup had been editing the *Review* for part of the period of the War and he was in the position to undertake the reply to Lester if he wanted to, and he wanted to) attempted to show that Lester's empirical methods were too crude to justify any conclusions, he thought that what underlay the problem is not what business men said that they did but what they logically had to do if they wanted to remain in business. Self-description, Machlup averred, was not usually a reliable source of scientific description. Except for a brief (4-page) 1955 half-essay, printed here as "Reply to Professor Takata," there is no mention of several sequels to the Lester-Machlup *Methodenstreit*. Such there was, however; one case was its choice as the topic selected by Machlup for his 1967 Presidential Address to the American Economic Association. By that time Lester and he were colleagues at Princeton; the verve of Machlup's language suggests that he felt that there remained need for continued battle.

The remaining three essays in the original edition were grouped under the rubric, "Semantic Issues in Macro-economics and Economic Policy." They deal with several of the hot topics of the post-war decades. His 1943 essay, "Forced or Induced Saving: An Exploration Into Its Synonyms and Homonyms," however, is as illustrative of the era as it is of the topic. It was a time when journals carried clarifying, what Bacon called light-casting (as distinct from fruit-bearing) articles, and here Machlup was trying to eliminate what one TV series more recently called "mushy-headedness." It is a measure of the advance in the method of argument to note the more limited time-applicability if greater sophistication, but also the greater caginess, in the second essay in this section, the 1960 "Another View of Cost-Push and Demand-Pull Inflation." The last essay, "Disputes, Paradoxes, and Dilemmas Concerning Economic Development" is far more an essay on the futility of planning economic development than it is on semantics, albeit on the semantics side it has merit. What seems trenchant about these last essays is Machlup's desire to combine the precision of academic scholarly discipline with the kind of messiness of the political world and the active material market place. If economic semantics, as seen in academe had a strong transcendental side, Machlup seems intent on showing that economic semantics could be considered in the forum, as well.

*The second edition*. Machlup was a many sided person. For this and other reasons we are including in this second edition two major additions. One is a reprint of the session on methodology at the 1951 annual meeting of the American Economic Association. It contains several essays, one each by Frank H. Knight, Kenneth E. Boulding, and Paul A. Samuelson, as well as Machlup's response. Machlup had organized the session, his choice of these three prominent theorists was made in pursuit of his pedagogical plan.

Three additional volumes of collected Machlup essays appeared in 1964,

1974, and 1978. The first dealt with his work on international trade and finance; the second and third[5] included much material on his views relating to methodology. Nothing contained in them, however, put forth so starkly his underlying concern about the limits to the role of Cartesian thinking in economics. For this reason, we have chosen to put his 1951 response, particularly to Samuelson, within the contextual setting of the session in which it was delivered.[6] The other addition is an article, "Are the Social Sciences Really Inferior," he wrote for publication in 1961 in the *Southern Economic Journal*.

His choice of the reporting of his session on methodology for the 1951 American Economic Association meetings in New York is revealing. It starts with a short Machlupian statement distinguishing methodology from comparative methods. First, Kenneth Boulding (in some sense then only approaching the zenith of his career at Michigan) was invited to give his views under the rubric, "Implications for General Economics of More Realistic Theories of the Firm;" they involved a defense of theorizing, generally, and the use of some maximization methods, specifically. Boulding's approach reveals his developing interest in organization, communication, and control theory. His comments are divided between static and dynamic theorizing; he gives marginal analysis all its points on the former, and he urges the theory of organization for the latter.

Frank H. Knight (then nearing the close of his brilliant career at Chicago), using as his title, "Institutionalism and Empiricism in Economics," gave what he, himself, termed, "A Few Brief and Hasty Observations on the Topic Printed in the Program." It dealt in good measure with the roles of uncertainty or the unknowable and of human intent in economic thinking. His remarks on institutionalism explicitly abstracted from the quantitative approach associated with Wesley Clair Mitchell, clearly damned Veblenian "diatribes against any 'meliorative trend' and insistence upon colorless mechanism," and strongly disassociated any personal approval for the kind of thing that John Rogers Commons had been doing.

It was Paul A. Samuelson's essay, "Economic Theory and Mathematics—An Appraisal," which served to focus the session on Machlup's concept of methodology. It served as the real target of Machlup's rebuttal. Quoting Willard Gibbs' "only speech" before the Yale faculty, albeit a statement of

---

5. Indeed, the title of this collection was *Methodology of Economics and Other Social Sciences*. It contained 26 essays of which only the first appears for the first time. I draw particular attention to this first essay; Machlup, the advocate of semantic discipline, almost "gives up" and nearly admits that "*Mrs. Malaprop Takes Over:*" "Methodology," as such, has come to mean in practice not only what it ought to mean (criteria for the selection of methods), but a description of the "cookbook-approach" to particular methods.

6. See Machlup 1978 for many of his articles on methodology; of these, one was published in 1936 and another in 1951, the remaining two dozen were published after the 1951 meetings.

four words: "Mathematics is a language," Samuelson went on to improve it in three words: "Mathematics is language." Samuelson continued with wit and imagination to drive home his point—mathematical knowledge may not be necessary or even sufficient for a contribution in economic theory, but it is overwhelmingly desirable.

I eschew summarizing Allan G. Gruchy's comment, but Machlup's is what we are here for. It is a frontal consideration of Samuelson's underlying view that without mathematics most (really, virtually all) work in future economic theory is impossible. It is a statement about epistemology; it should be seen as such. Machlup thought mathematics, at best was *a* language; and there were some things which all languages could not express equally well. Mathematics was clearly unsuited to express certain emotions, etc. His views, as given in a brief form, explain why in his last years Machlup despaired of the direction most academic economics was taking and tried to recapture ground by trying to integrate economics with other branches of learning.

His 1961 essay on the social sciences is a broad, sophisticated, and many-faceted comparison of that body of knowledge,[7] generally (and implicitly of economics, specifically), to knowledge in the physical sciences, particularly physics and chemistry. Machlup's comparisons include, (1) invariability of recurring situations, (2) objectivity of observations, (3) the capacity to use controlled experiments to verify (sic) hypotheses, (4) exactness of measure, (5) numerical quantification, (6) existence of mathematical constants, (7) use of predictability of future events as a test, (8) rigorousness and acceptability of specialized scientific language, and (9) average competence of professionals. The result of this multi-faceted comparison is a mixed verdict—two comparisons are irrelevant, four suggest "no real difference," and three suggest inferiority to the natural sciences. True to his nature, he ends the essay with a discussion of the "Crucial Question: 'So What'?"

## 3. The Book's Initial Reception

When the first printing of the first edition of the book initially appeared, an unsigned review in the *Economist* gave it generous space but devoted most of the space to summarizing his argument with Lester. It concluded by noting that Machlup, for all of his "political views (extreme liberalism)" was still offering "a trenchant criticism of loose usages, even if it annoys some of his readers. Some very respectable economists are found guilty of semantic im-

---

7. Machlup suggests that the list could include more than Sociology, Cultural Anthropology, Social Psychology, Human Geography, Demography and Population Theory, Ethnography and Ethnology, Political Science, Economics, History, and International Studies, but that there is also so much overlapping, that it could also be said to include less.

propriety; now they have been warned to behave better in future and so have we all" (*Economist* 1964, p. 1007).

More scholarly reviews appeared in three other journals. Kurt Klappholz, writing in *Economica,* gave the LSE-Karl Popper School's judgment; it was not favorable. Although his review contained several detailed criticisms, the main point was that "a preoccupation with the 'meaning of terms' tends to encourage futile methodological approaches . . . verbalism and [Popperian] essentialism." Popper, Klappholz points out, noted "that . . . physics which worries hardly at all about terms and their meaning, but about facts instead has achieved great precision." Moreover, Machlup (whom Klappholz writes, "is not an *apriorist* after the manner of Mises . . .") gets thrown because in one of his essays he asserts on the one hand that equilibrium is not an operational concept, yet, on the other hand, he concludes that one can "verify" the appropriate theoretical predictions. *Verification,* from the standpoint of the LSE-Popperian crowd, was not "the name of the game in town;" it was *falsification.* Machlup's efforts were not successful, and "the deficiencies of the subject could be better remedied by a greater concentration on its explicanda rather than on the meaning of terms" (Economica N.S. 1965).

In the *Journal of Political Economy,* Don Gordon gave more of a summary of the contents of the book. While Gordon commented on Machlup's reputed prowess as a teacher and even as a theorist, he disagreed with Machlup's rationale for the book and concluded that viewed *ex post* semantic confusion was really in and of itself not much of a problem. The problem was theoretical confusion. There is an apocryphal story about a conversation between Hans Bethe and Nils Bohr. In inviting Bohr to give a 'name lecture' at Cornell, Bethe implored him to speak clearly. Bohr's reply was that the problem was not his speech, it was his thinking.

Professor Terence W. Hutchison, who had recently been engaged in fierce journal debate with Machlup, was asked to review the book in the *American Economic Review.* His assessment, featured as the opening review in that issue, was presented in three long paragraphs. The first dealt swiftly with the pedagogical virtues of the book—the initial set of essays was not only the best, "but all graduate students of economics would do well to read them."

In the second paragraph Hutchison raised the ghost of his own differences with Machlup. The issue involved the relevance of empirical testing of theories, particularly since Machlup seemed unclear ('ambiguous' was the word) about whether he felt that empirical testing could prove a theory erroneous or merely irrelevant.

The third paragraph states that the third part of the book, although "[containing] models of how economic policies should be discussed by academic economist . . . [they] are not especially concerned with semantic issues . . .". Alas, unlike Machlup, Hutchison was never a businessman, and does not realize that advertising is built on the premise of roses smelling differently when sold under other names. Words do matter.

## 4. Some Concluding Remarks

This collection offers even now, almost a third of a century later, things of value and of interest.

The *organization* of the essays, using the materials of the history of thought as intellectual evidence combined with assertive definitions and chains of syllogisms, remain among the finest examples in the economic graduate student curricular literature. As such, Machlup remains a "living" teacher.

As essays in the history of economic thought, these also offer splendid starting places for further analysis.

Machlup's policy views, particularly seen in the last essays of the first edition, are, as phrased, more time- and place-bound than his subjects warrant, but even they are pedagogically relevant in this time (1989–90).

Machlup's defense of abstract theorizing, as seen in his debate with Lester, is probably of more historical interest than of current value. J. A. Schumpeter is said to have remarked that Lester had the argument, but that Machlup won the debate. There are many, including specifically Terence Hutchison, who have held that Machlup's 'victory' reflected more Lester's incompetence than Machlup's competence. Perhaps, it was Machlup's desire to go over that ground again which led him to take up the topic anew in his 1967 American Economic Association presidential address.

During his last years Machlup, the abstract theorist, came to despair of the ultra-abstraction of formal, mostly advanced algebra, formulations of economic relationships. For most of his career, however, he stood for the Carl Menger Austrian tradition (Carl, but not Karl [the son], was also anti-mathematical), which favored use of the syllogism and verbalized abstraction, but not the headiness of easy mathematical transformations. As we have already seen his concern with this topic had led him to organize a blue-ribbon panel for the 1951 American Economic Association meetings. As I have already noted, some of his considerable writings on the topic were collected and published (he records, at my suggestion) in 1978 under the title, *Methodology of Economics and Other Social Sciences*.

But, let us consider the basic topic—economics and semantic discipline. Machlup, unlike Humpty-Dumpty, preferred to believe that words should not be allowed to mean anything that the writer wanted them to; nor did he assign higher values to arcane words that should be "paid extra." Words, in his view, should be tools, and it was a sloppy workman who neglected his tools by not keeping them as sharp as was expedient. Yet, Machlup argued as though he believed that philological imprecision resulted from ignorance of etymology, inadequate care given to literary style, and individual arrogance. And, while much can be said for understanding etymology, does the point that in one era a word had a particular association bind it to mean the same thing later on?[8] Perhaps because he lived in early 19th century Britain long before the Reform Act, Ricardo may have appropriately posited that only land was in fixed supply, but should the classical economists' hijacking of that word *rent* preclude Pareto's choice of the same word *rent* to apply to any force of the factors in short supply later on? Should there be a verbal analog to Fisher's Ideal Index Number which handles the weighting both forwards and backwards?

One can, of course, assert that the "mis-usage" of words may not only be the result of carelessness and ignorance, but it can also be a reflection on organic changes in thinking. Indeed, Machlup knew this, and one of his wonderful teaching skills was to misunderstand purposefully a student's language to lead the student to things the student had not realized were there— like Molière's M. Jourdain, many of Machlup's students found after he had finished with them that their thinking was deeper than they had ever imagined.

Earlier I indicated that the crowning achievement of Machlup's career was probably the scope of his final 8-volume project on learning and knowledge, and particularly the execution of the first 3 (the ones he completed). Now I suggest that these essays represented the initial phase of Machlup's thinking about the nature of learning and economic knowledge, but that that initial phase was incomplete. What seemed pedagogically straight-forward and effective during most of his career was on reflection more a set of questions than it was a set of answers. The final major project was his effort to present *both* a better set of questions as well as of answers. It is a pity that they are not available, particularly in an inexpensive edition.

REFERENCES

Ackley, Gardner (1961). *Macroeconomic Theory.* New York: Macmillan.
Gordon, Don (1964). Review of F. Machlup. *Essays on Economics Semantics. Jour. Pol. Econ.* 72, 103–04.
Hutchison, Terence W. (1956). "Professor Machlup on Verification in Economics." *South. Econ. Jour.* 22 (April) 476–83.
———. (1964). Review of F. Machlup. *Essays on Economic Semantics. Amer. Econ. Rev.* 53, 1104.

---

8. The origins of the word *fornicate,* for example, suggest only that prostitutes plied their trade in the basements of public buildings—fornix refers to the *vaulted* areas.

Klappholz, Kurt (1965). Review of F. Machlup. *Essays on Economic Semantics*. *Economica N.S.* 32, 101–02.

Machlup, Fritz (1952). "Issues in Methodology: Introductory Remarks." *Amer. Econ. Rev. Supp.* 42 (May), 35 ff. "Discussion," *ibid.* 69–73.

———. (1955). "The Problem of Verification in Economics." *South. Econ. Jour.* 22 (July) 1–21.

———. (1956). "Rejoinder to A Reluctant Ultra-empiricist." *South. Econ. Jour.* 22 (April), 483–93.

———. (1964). *International Payments, Debt, and Gold*. New York: Scribner's.

———. (1967). "Theories of the Firm: Marginalist, Behavioral, Managerial." *Amer. Econ. Rev.* 57 (March) 1–33.

———. (1976). *Selected Economic Writings of Fritz Machlup*. Edited by George Bitros. New York: New York University Press.

———. (1978). *Methodology of Economics and Other Social Sciences*. New York: Academic Press.

Musgrave, Richard A. (1959). *The Theory of Public Finance—A Study in Public Economy*. New York: McGraw-Hill.

Patinkin, Don (1956). *Money, Interest, and Prices: An Integration of Monetary and Value Theory*. Evanston: Row, Peterson.

CHAPTER 19

# Harvey Leibenstein

*I first met Harvey Leibenstein in September 1947, just after both of us had joined Princeton as instructors. After our second meal together, I realized that he had the spark of genius, and before I left Princeton I made exceedingly bold and told as much to the department's chairman, E. Stanley Howard. Over the years we kept in contact, both professionally and socially. In 1988 Klaus Weiermair, York University (Canada), proposed that we organize a one-week conference at the Villa Serbeloni in Bellagio (Como, Italy) on one of Harvey's most original ideas, "X-efficiency." By the time the conference was held in 1990, Harvey, having been disastrously injured in an automobile accident, could no longer participate, but Klaus and I edited the volume as a Festschrift (see Perlman 1990). It contains my opening essay, describing the crucible that had contributed to his X-efficiency idea. Later Warren Samuels, editing a series of volumes on great economists of this century, asked that I expand that essay to cover all of his work. This chapter is what Samuels published. In 1994 I spoke at both Harvey's funeral and the memorial service Harvard held in his honor. My talk at the latter again traced the development and marveled at the originality and breadth of his research. It was a somewhat depersonalized presentation; however, I chose to close with an anecdote about him.*

*When I told him in the autumn of 1947 that I had been disappointed in what I found at Princeton, he said that while he was not as put off as I seemed to be, he did realize that the "Princeton Greats" were not all that he had anticipated them to be. He continued, "You know, before I came here I was teaching at 'Illinois Tech,' and I imagined that Princeton, being the big time, would be much better. But, the truth is that there are a couple of young fellows there who are really every bit as good as the 'greats' around here."*

*"And who might they be?" I asked.*

*"A couple of guys you have never heard of—Herb Simon and an Italian named Franco Modigliani."*

From Warren J. Samuels (ed.). *New Horizons in Economic Thought*. Aldershot, Hants, U.K.: Edward Elgar, 1992, 184–201.

Parts of this essay have been adapted from Perlman (1990).

**Introduction**

Harvey Leibenstein was born in Russia in 1922. Brought as a small child to Montreal, he received his initial education there. After a brief period at Sir George Williams University, he transferred to Northwestern University where he was awarded a BS in 1945 and an MS in 1946. He was at Princeton University from the autumn of 1947 until 1951, when he finished his doctoral studies. After ascending through the various professorial ranks at the University of California, Berkeley, from 1951 until 1967, he accepted an appointment at Harvard as the Andelot Professor of Economics and Population. He retired from Harvard some time after 1987 when it became apparent that the serious injuries he had received in an automobile accident precluded any early return to his normal teaching and research activities.

Recognized from an early stage as possessing both an original mind and considerable technical qualifications, Leibenstein was awarded numerous fellowships throughout his professional career.

**The Evolution of Leibenstein's Thinking**

In *Who's Who in Economics* Leibenstein described his contribution as:

> The microeconomics of human fertility, and X-efficiency theory (the non-allocative aspects of inefficiency). The latter attempts to develop a mode of analysis which relaxes the maximization assumption of conventional micro-theory, and substitutes postulates under which individuals are non-maximizers when there is little pressure on them, approaching maximizing behavior as external pressure increases. Behavior according to convention is an important aspect of this approach. Also, current research involves the application of the prisoner's dilemma paradigm to normal economic behavior. (Blaug, 1986, p. 508).

The Legacy of His Training

One can easily see in Leibenstein's work evidence of the influence of certain teachers. The impact of two of his Princeton professors, Oskar Morgenstern and Frank Notestein, was apparent, particularly in the 1950s. Perhaps Morgenstern's influences lasted even longer, shaping Leibenstein's perception of what theory was about ('providing a framework for understanding'), the role of subjectivity[1] in contrast to 'objective rationality', and a taste for the kinds of demonstrations now associated with game theory and/or with experimental economics.

## His Taste for Economic Theorizing

Morgenstern's scholarly impact was clear in Leibenstein's 1950 graduate-student essay, 'Bandwagon, Snob, and Veblen Effects in the Theory of Consumers' Demand', published in the *Quarterly Journal of Economics,* well before he had completed his doctoral degree. This article, establishing Leibenstein's professional reputation for facile analysis, revealed the complex intertwining of ideas and exposition which has marked his contributions as having both a strong and an original strand. Although Leibenstein started that article with an incorrect Morgenstern assertion, that the market demand curve cannot be a summation of individual curves, the point of his effort was to show how one could construct a market demand curve illustrating *interdependent* as well as independent consumer preferences. In the process, Leibenstein differentiated goods wanted for the direct utility services they provide from goods wanted for ancillary (self-identification) reasons.

This differentiation was achieved by suggesting (but not performing) an experiment; different consumers were initially to be asked how much of a particular good or service each wanted at a variety of prices. Each consumer was then asked how much he/she would take if others' preference schedules were made known. Leibenstein conjectured that if an individual augmented his previously independently derived demand for any good, upon learning that others shared his preferences, that good had a 'bandwagon' quality. If that same bit of knowledge led to a reduced desire for the good, the result was a 'snob' effect. There was also the possibility of a *Veblen effect* which suggested that consumption *per se* of a good might carry some form of special prestige rather than utility; as such it was slightly different from the snob effect.

One important contribution was his proposed ingenious method of iterative questioning so that dependence or independence of response could be assured. It anticipated much of what is now occurring in the new sub-field of experimental economics.

That article laid out the Leibenstein argument in two modes: one was literary, as in the Marshallian 'main text' form; the other was geometrical, as in the Marshallian footnote but also as in the Joan Robinson main text style.

## His Taste for Observational Generalizing
## Close to the Level of Fact

His dissertational effort was in the Notestein tradition (Leibenstein, 1951). Notestein's interest was in problems, not in analytical or theoretical models. Notestein, personally interested in the question of what he was convinced were too high birth rates in most parts of the world, depended not upon abstract analysis but on careful generalization as his research method. He is best known to a generation of American demographers for his attachment to the Demographic Transition hypothesis [in industrialized societies increases in life expectancy (lower death rates for every cohort group) precede lower fertility (and birth) rates by about a generation].

## His Work on the Micro-economics
## of Human Fertility Decisions

Leibenstein's 1957 book *Economic Backwardness and Economic Growth* was an outgrowth of the published version of his earlier dissertation, *A Theory of Economic Demographic Development* (1954).[2] Here again, the Morgenstern-Leibenstein interest in the interdependency of individual preferences, manifested in a desire for personal (household) economic improvement, holds centre-stage. For reasons of brevity it suffices to note that understanding both the role of individual motivation and the fact that there are limits to human understanding about oneself (to say nothing about others) are clearly the points of entry into this work.

Leibenstein's approach involved studying in splendid detail the objective biological and economic factors which could shape fertility decisions. Yet he went beyond them to study the very nature of the reasoning behind the decision-making process. This work is well-recognized for his ideas about the institutional shifts from regarding more children as the pay-off for previous prosperity-inducing decisions to a more 'modern' situation where the responsibility of educating and otherwise preparing children for life in an industrialized society became costly, indeed overwhelmingly so. Later, in 1974, he was to attack the Chicago/Becker New School of Home Economics for its excessive reliance upon full specification and clear (read 'logical') reasoning in the case of fertility decisions. Leibenstein's position, as I interpret it, was not an attack on logic *per se* but on the belief that the logical method was mechanistic. In his view, reasoning itself was a process costly in many dimensions, and how rigorously or even extensively one used the process was itself a separate decision.

The book received full and even lengthy and favourable reviews in the *American Economic Review* (Hamberg, 1958), in the *American Journal of Sociology* (Whitney, 1958) and in the *Annals of the American Academy* (Buck, 1958).

During this period he also worked with Walter Galenson on topics of national production functions[3] (a professional activity considered fashionable during the 1950s). Conventional wisdom, challenged by them, was that backward countries (a term then used without embarrassment) with high levels of disguised unemployment (that is, underutilized, particularly low-wage labour) were well-advised to introduce labour-intensive manufacturing methods (Galenson and Leibenstein, 1955). Rather, it was suggested by the two of them that *if these LDCs wanted to enter international markets,* it would be wiser to look for state-of-the-art technology.[4] In retrospect, it is clear that this conclusion was consistent with the point that individual motivation was the key to competitive economic performance; if the absence of individual motivation was a general problem, then, of course, capital substitution for labour made greater programmatic sense. What showed up was a pattern of differential national productivity increases. That was *the* phenomenon of the time.[5] But underlying their whole analysis was the premise that empirical evaluations (by their nature *ex post*) provided a kind of knowledge that could not be expected to exist *ex ante*.

Leibenstein's 1960 book, *Economic Theory and Organizational Analysis* (1960a), reflects his mind in mid-passage as it moved from concern with the practical parameters of rational maximization in fertility decisions and decisions relating to the embracing of the fruits of industrialization as compared to the traditional fruits of pre-industrial social wealth, to questions of how firms producing goods and services in the industrialized market operated. He seems to have been organizing intellectually what others had written, and what he made of it.[6]

## The Development of the X-Efficiency Theory

Leibenstein's later and best-known contribution was his work on X-efficiency, a concept he introduced to explain the internal operation of firms, particularly under some external stress, although effective internal leadership, perhaps motivated by the Veblenian instinct of workmanship, could result in the same outcome.

### What Is the X-Efficiency Theory?

Among the most recent efforts Professor Leibenstein made to expound his ideas about X-efficiency theory, was the description he wrote in *The New Palgrave* (Leibenstein, 1987b). The 'concept' of X-efficiency, he writes, is one thing; the 'theory' explaining it is another.

The concept refers to a regularly observable phenomenon. It is that firms not only perform their productive functions with considerable 'preventable' waste, but that if one looks only at the 'molecular' unit (that is, the firm) one misses an important area of preventable waste. It is the interactive, but somewhat constrained, economically bargained decision-making among 'atomistic' individuals within the firm.

X-efficiency theory is an effort to explain this phenomenon at all levels. This loss to the firm (deviation from the 'optimal') is not only a result of technical (that is, technological) incompetence (refusal to abandon outmoded equipment and systems as well as other manifestations of psychological inertia or cultural or individual sloth); it also is a result of an inability and/or an unwillingness to achieve (or is perhaps a breakdown of) organizational fully specified (contractual) relationships and obligations, rights and responsibilities, co-ordination and focus.

In Leibenstein's words (1987, pp. 934–5):

> X-efficiency theory represents a line of reasoning based on postulates that differ from standard micro theory. . . . The postulates of the theory . . . [are:]
>
> [First:] *Relaxing Maximizing Behavior* such that it is assumed that some forms of decision making, such as . . . habits, conventions, moral imperatives, standard procedures, or emulation, . . . can be and frequently are of a non-maximizing nature. . . . not depend[ing] on careful calculation . . . Other decisions attempt at maximizing utility. In order to deal with the max/non-max mixture we use . . . [the] psychological . . . Yerkes-Dodson Law, . . . at low pressure levels individuals will not put much effort into carefully calculating their decisions, but as pressure builds they move towards more maximizing behavior. At some point too much pressure can result in disorientation and a lower level of decision performance.
>
> [Second:] *Inertia:* . . . functional relations are surrounded by inert areas, within which changes in certain values of the independent variables do not result in changes of the dependent variable.
>
> [Third:] *Incomplete Contracts:* . . . the employment contract is incomplete in that the payment side is fairly well specified but the effort side remains mostly unspecified.
>
> [Fourth:] *Discretion:* . . . [the] employees have effort discretion within certain boundaries, and . . . top management has discretion with respect to working conditions and some aspects of wages. [The relationship between] the employees on the one side and management on the other . . . jointly determine[s] the outcome. Thus, . . . [there is] a latent Prisoner's Dilemma problem . . . In general the Prisoner's Dilemma problem solution will be avoided . . . [because] a system of conventions which depends on the history of human relations within the firm is likely to lead to an outcome that is usually intermediate between the Prisoner's Dilemma outcome and the optimal solution. . . . for every effort option that employees choose the firm will want to choose the minimum wages and working conditions . . . Similarly, for every [working condition level] the firm chooses, the employees will want [their minimum tolerated working-condition-level]. This . . . [would be] the Prisoner's Dilemma outcome, which . . . is not likely . . . However, this adversarial-relations problem between employees and managers is compounded by

another free-rider problem. Every employee has a free-rider incentive to move to the [his tolerated] minimum level . . . even though he or she might want others to work effectively. . . . overall effort would be reduced to the minimum if they all followed their individual self-interest. Clearly, . . . individual rationality cannot solve the Prisoner's Dilemma problem. Something akin to 'group rationality' . . . is required to achieve an improved solution.

. . . conventions should be viewed as solutions to multi-equilibrium, coordination problems, and . . . can provide superior solutions to the Prisoner's Dilemma outcome. . . . A coordinated solution is superior to an uncoordinated outcome. However, the various [possible] coordinated solutions . . . need not be equally good. . . . [E]ffort . . . and working-conditions conventions can bring about a non-Prisoner's Dilemma solution. . . . Thus, the effort convention is a coordinated solution . . . superior to uncoordinated individual behavior. Similar remarks hold for managerial decisions. Of course, the . . . [minimum-working condition level] has to be viable in the sense that it must represent a long-run profitable outcome, although not necessarily the maximum profit level.

There is a difference between the creation of a convention and adherence to it. . . . [C]reation may come [from] . . . leadership of some managers, . . . some employees, or . . . some initial effort levels being chosen arbitrarily. Once established, a convention reduces the flexibility of employees' behavior. Thus, new employees will adhere to the convention, and possibly support it through sanctions on others.

Although stable to small changes of its independent variables, an effort convention need not stay at its initial level indefinitely. The concept of inert areas suggests that a large enough shock can destabilize a convention. Once destabilized it is no longer clear whether the dynamics of ready adjustment will lead to a superior or inferior situation for both sides, or a situation under which one side gains at the expense of the other. Such considerations (and fears) help to stabilize the convention.

. . . [U]nder low-pressure conditions the postulate of non-maximizing behavior . . . explains why firm members may stick with their conventions and impose supporting sanctions even in situations where they would be better off not doing so. Non-calculating, situation-response behavior helps to shore up the convention-solution to the Prisoner's Dilemma problem, and to shore up the persistence of nonoptimal conventions . . . [and] helps to explain the existence and persistence of X-inefficient behavior.

I draw on some of his other writings to expand the foregoing material. His emphasis on micro-micro analysis put the spotlight on the reaction of 'atomistic' individual motivation to various kinds of constraints. As noted, within every economic unit there are numerous individuals, each of whom prefers 'to do his/her own thing'. But what can be said about that 'thing'? It is a compromise between what the individual accepts as something with which he/she is culturally comfortable, which he/she personally prefers, and whatever must be done if the job is to be retained and/or the firm is to survive. What is true of workers as individuals is comparably true of management as individuals and even owners as individuals. Thus, those employing the X-efficiency thesis (unlike most economists) recognize the profession's basic unit, the firm, as a molecular *aggregate,* made up of individualistic atoms compressed under various kinds of pressure.

Under *usual* conditions these molecular aggregates operate at less than maximum efficiency because there are abounding disparate atomistic individual motivations (incomplete contractual specification permitting greater choice by the worker; inertia leading to the ignoring of rule-breaking; and/or the nature of the job allowing more or less personal discretion which permits individuals to choose their levels of effort). Under certain *unusual* conditions, particularly those arising from changes in external pressures, such as price competition from other firms, the firm is forced to reduce costs. The freedom for these disparate motivations to interact is then reduced, and the pressure to develop a lower cost system is increased. The very economic survival of the firm may require that what individuals *like or ought* to offer in the way of output gives way to what they feel they *must* offer. This shift to *unusual* conditions, whatever may precipitate it, means that management decides that neither it nor the workers can be left to follow former procedures. It could also mean that the owners (shareholders) can come to the same conclusion about management.

All of this goes beyond a mere power struggle. X-efficiency theory also states that even under pressure there are inert areas surrounding the existent levels of effort. These inert areas reflect the disutility of effort; the benefit to be gained by the change must exceed the cost of changing, or else the effort level will remain the same. Leibenstein defines 'inert areas' as areas of choice which are left untouched for a variety of very different reasons ranging from a sheer inability to penetrate to the high costs of penetration. There are, however, problems of bargaining standoff. These come under the game theoretic Prisoner's Dilemma rubric.

Under *usual* conditions firms produce[7] and consume without much serious attention to leakages in the output stream. Insofar as the *usual* output varies from the *unusual* or 'might-have-been', assuming identical cost inputs are the same for the two contrasting sets of conditions, we can estimate quantitatively X-inefficiency, or the amount lost by the firm because of the impact of this aspect of worker and management individualism. That loss is X-inefficiency; or to put the matter the other way around, we can identify and estimate this 'X-efficiency gain' as the product of stringent pressure.

One point of X-efficiency theory is that firms do not maximize mechanically because each firm's managers are not completely in command of the full spectrum of the decision-making process. Management must cope with each worker's motivation preferences, and in some instances the latter are so complex, even at points contradictory, that a 'best' outcome is no more than management's collective (but no less subjective) conclusion that it has done as much as it can (and whatever that was) it was good enough to keep the firm economically afloat. *'Firms do not maximize because true maximization requires a level of control not consistent with "Free Will".'* Leibenstein's work on X-efficiency surfaced in the *American Economic Review* in 1966 under what *ex post* was a transitional title, 'Allocative Efficiency vs. "X"-Efficiency'. It drew heavily on the work of many scholars trying to identify the losses in potential growth due to various kinds of traditional misallocations by management. These, Leibenstein concluded, were quantitatively trivial, 'frequently no more than $^1/_{10}$ of 1 percent' (Leibenstein, 1966a, p. 397). But growth fluctuated much more than that small amount. What caused it? The answers, X-inefficiency as well as X-efficiency, are mentioned in passing, without any effort at definition except the implication that they are due to 'managements [not] bestirring themselves sufficiently, [unless] the environment forces them to do so'.[8] His data were drawn largely from LDCs, with considerable emphasis put on episodic reports. His conclusion reflects an early formative state of the theory (Leibenstein, 1966a, pp. 412–13):

> [There are] three reasons for X-inefficiency . . . These are (a) contracts for labor are incomplete, (b) the production function is not completely specified or known, and (c) not all inputs are marketed or, if marketed, are not available on equal terms to all buyers.
>
> . . . [F]or a variety of reasons people and organizations normally work neither as hard nor as effectively as they could. In situations where competitive pressure is light, many people will trade the disutility of greater effort, of search, and the control of other people's activities for the utility of feeling less pressure and of better interpersonal relations. But in situations where competitive pressures are high, and hence the costs of such trades are also high . . . [t]wo general types of movements are possible. One is . . . towards greater allocative efficiency and the other . . . involves greater degrees of X-efficiency. The data suggest that [often] the amount to be gained by increasing allocative efficiency is trivial while the amount to be gained by increasing X-efficiency is frequently significant.

In the years that followed Leibenstein expanded his X-efficiency theory, partly in response to comments on it and partly due to his desire to differentiate it from the work of others.[9] In 1975 the *Bell Journal* published a more polished rendition of the theory (Leibenstein, 1975a). *Inter alia*, it also distinguished Leibenstein's theme from Herbert Simon's idea of firms maximizing within areas of bounded rationality and the Cyert–March thesis that firms found it irrational (uneconomic/?) to fight currently dominant institutions (City Hall/? and certainly unions).

Two of Leibenstein's books (1976a and 1978a) came out in the late 1970s with the apparent intention of trying to lay out his whole thinking in detail. As I read them, the first was a major effort at locating his ideas within the profession's general perception of economic theorizing. The second book was an application of X-efficiency theory within the stream of development economics. *De gustibus non disputandem est,* but the tightness of the applied argument found in the latter has, for me at least, a special appeal.

In 1978 he published two particularly sharply focused articles on his theory. One, a reply to the voice of price-theory orthodoxy, Professor George Stigler, lays out in good natured (if biting) prose—almost matching Stigler's own style (Stigler, 1976)—Leibenstein's abhorrence of attempts to fit his theory into the Procrustean bed of the *original* Marshallian price system legacy (Leibenstein, 1978c), something Stigler had thought desirable to do, citing the high cost of individuals' foregoing their preference for leisure as they were driven to excise X-inefficiency.

The other is Leibenstein's assertion of the X-efficiency theory 'while standing on one foot' (1978b): 'In a budgetary permissive environment the looser the [*effort responsibility consequence* for any firm member i], for all i on the average, the greater the degree of X-inefficiency (i.e., the excess of actual over minimum cost).'

His general efforts, in my opinion, reached a more condensed, if not a new or higher, plane in his 1979 article, 'A Branch of Economics is Missing: Micro-Micro Theory' (Leibenstein, 1979a). There he discusses five important elements in his theory:

- *Selective rationality (degree of maximization deviation).* This relates to individual decisions regarding the degree to which deviations, reflecting a variety of inner and external pressures, from the firm's goals occur. These are spelled out and then diagrammed.
- *Individuals are basic decision-making units.* Each individual joining the firm gets all sorts of signals from his peer group, from the hierarchy, and from historical influences.
- *Effort discretion.* Of course in addition to all of these signals (or,

perhaps underlying them), are a set of economic pressures on the firm.

* *Inert areas.* Here habit takes over. Unless the firm's goals are dominant to the point of pure dictatorship nothing changes.
* *Organizational entropy.* The management must struggle using centripetal integrative energy against the centrifugal individualistic forces. Failure can occur.

In a second article published in 1979, he used tabular presentation, employed elsewhere, to contrast his theory (1979b). This is worth reproduction (see Table 8.1).

After 1979 Leibenstein wrote several other books and essays. Some were additions, emendations often prepared as response to comments in journals (1980a, 1980b, 1981b, 1981c, 1982a, 1982c, 1983a, 1985a 1985b). And some tied X-efficiency to other theoretical *Gestalt* such as the economic theory of contracts (1982c), game theory (1981d, 1982c), and the general theory of organizations and management (1987a). The degree of refinement increased, but the general outlines had been laid out earlier. Much of this work was in response to criticisms levied by both 'orthodox' neoclassical economists and some fellow heterodox types. Roger Frantz (1990), writing in the posture of assessing these criticisms, categorizes them under four headings: (a) assertions that X-efficiency theory can be subsumed under rent-seeking behaviour; (b) that the employees' leisure is one of the output products of the firm; (c) that in practice management is the residual claimant for undistributed profits; and (d) that X-efficiency theory can be subsumed under a theory of property rights. His last book *Inside the Firm: The Inefficiency of Hierarchy* (1987a) received mixed reviews: James D. Hess (1989) wrote that he shared Leibenstein's dissatisfaction with neoclassical orthodoxy, but he could not accept Leibenstein's formulation of an alternative; yet John Kenneth Galbraith (1988) shared the dissatisfaction common to Hess and Leibenstein and appeared to accept much of the latter's answer.

**TABLE 1.  X-Efficiency Theory and Neoclassical Theory**

| Components | X-Efficiency Theory | Neoclassical Theory[10] |
| --- | --- | --- |
| Psychology | Selective rationality | Maximization or minimization |
| Contracts[11] | Incomplete | Complete |
| Effort[12] | Discretionary variable | Assumed given |
| Units | Individuals | Households and firms |
| Inert areas[13] | Important variable | None |
| Agent-principal | Differential interests | Identity of interests |

## Leibenstein's 'Pigeon-Hole' in the History of Economic Thought

### Reflecting the Marshallian Influence

Although neoclassical economics is associated these days with Hicks–Samuelson–Solow, Leibenstein basically draws on the original Marshallian approach, albeit with some of his criticisms. The Marshallian and Pigovian level of abstraction was intentionally lower than that employed by Hicks, and for the most part by Samuelson and Solow.

What Marshall thought economics was all about was how men in their ordinary pursuits of livelihood made decisions; he deliberately eschewed formal exposition, noting that intangibles were critically apparent in that decision-making process. Formal exposition, as seen by Marshall, was relegated to footnotes, where it did not interfere with the flow of his thinking but could be used as an explanatory device.

Leibenstein's thinking as well as his pedagogical preferences seem to parallel Marshall's. Moreover his method (choice of rhetoric) has that same quality of episodic empiricism (with a historical dimension). He shies away from the formalism of simple (purely rational) maximization, as found in mathematics, not only because it requires specification where specification (of intangibles) is impossible, but also because it employs a level of abstraction which negates the purpose of the analysis. Neither for Marshall nor for Leibenstein is a reasonable man necessarily logical; their man, having a mind influenced by cognition as well as imagination, lives in a dynamic and disequilibrating world, and does his 'level best' (which is a good measure short of perfect). Their reasonable man bases his decisions on habit, on his incomplete and otherwise imperfect subjective perceptions of his internal (cf. superego) pressures, and on what he must bend to because of the superiority of forces he cannot easily manage (or manage at all).

In the development of the history of economic thought Marshall's preferred example of the firm in competition was supplanted by firms in some other relation to the market. It is often forgotten that his *Principles of Economics* was essentially an unfinished product, and that Marshall clearly noted in its 'Mathematical Appendix' that conditions of increasing returns not only vitiated his simple competitive model theoretically, but also *in actual fact*. This point is commonly credited to Piero Sraffa and was popularized by Joan Robinson. But her method was far more abstract than Marshall's generally was. In terms of preferred rhetoric Edward H. Chamberlin's was closer to the level of observed fact; Leibenstein's rhetoric (where he has the space) is also close to the level of observed fact. However, in deference to the *mores* of our profession at the time of his own graduate training, Leibenstein usually lays out his argument *in the text* in geometric (formal) terms—Mrs. Robinson's impact.

In his *Beyond Economic Man* (1976a), Peter J. Kalman co-authored with him a formal statement of the theory, employing much of the rhetoric of symbolic logic: 'Toward a Mathematical Formalization of X-Efficiency' (pp. 273–282, 291).[14]

What makes Leibenstein's work on population and on X-efficiency theory so 'Marshallian neoclassical' is something else as well. It is the role of attitude and how it is generated (created, manipulated and handled by incentive systems). Leibenstein's interest in individuals' motivations is central to his perception of the whole economic process—not only of production but also of distribution. Men, Leibenstein concludes, do not and often cannot maximize; Marshall put the point in another way when he remarked that economics was the study of man in the ordinary business of making a living.

Other economists have offered somewhat separate reasons for man's failure to maximize: (a) maximizing is perceived as economically too expensive (cf. Herbert Simon's costs of information and 'satisficing'); (b) maximization is theoretically impossible—absent *ex ante* perfect knowledge, there is no path to *ex post* optimization (cf. G. L. S. Shackle's 'uncertainty'); (c) the capacity to maximize is a limited resource—differential personal endowments or capacities create entrepreneurs and innovators (cf. Cantillon's and J. B. Say's 'entrepreneur' and Schumpeter's 'innovator'); (d) many have no taste, much less a penchant, for efficiency (cf. J. M. Clarke's 'an irrational passion for rationality'); and (e) the underlying contradictions within the specifications of the social contract and the government contract (cf. Thomas Hobbes, 1651; and Cyert and March, 1963).

However, Leibenstein suggests that, given sufficient market pressure, the individuals in the firm suppress some of their contrary or inconsistent motivations and are likely to get closer to the maximization process. This switch is one which seems to require the assertion of one set of priorities over all others—that is, the assertion of one set of individual preferences, cleaned up of its internal contradictions, over all the others. Survival pressures, to paraphrase Dr Johnson, 'powerfully clarify the mind'. *A measure of the presence of X-efficiency may be an inverse measure of personal liberty.*

## As Part of the Morgenstern-Austrian Tradition Influence

There is also a neo-Austrian underpinning to Leibenstein's perception of theory. One key Austrian element is the role of subjectivity in the decision-making process. This element was perceived in the role of the consumer, whose tastes for consumer goods, according to Menger and his two 'students', von Wieser and Böhm-Bawerk, provided the 'first cause' for all economic activity.

Professor Wesley Clair Mitchell, in his Foreword to the English edition of von Wieser's *Social Economics* (1927, pp. ix–xii), puts his finger on the exact point. If things occur in the mind, how then does the mind operate?—a problem which von Wieser (and his group) eschewed, but which von Neumann and Morgenstern tried to handle as the mini/max. Leibenstein's X-efficiency theory leads us back to the wilfulness (that is, subjectiveness) of each of the parties in any economic activities. Leibenstein adds that given *sufficient* pressure, one man's decisions (the imposition of his ordered and consistent preferences) can and often will replace the others' subjectiveness with that decision, which in operation thus becomes interpersonally 'objective'. That management's decision can be said to be the 'entrepreneur-in-action'. Otherwise the entrepreneur, like everyone else, is quiescent, and production proceeds without much reference to the elimination of efficiency—the state of Leibenstein X-inefficiency.

It has recently been fashionable to categorize most modern economic theorists in sequential sets of pigeon-holes. One early division is between those studying tendencies towards equilibrium and those focusing on disequilibrium. Clearly Leibenstein's work fits better into the latter category.

So much of the former category draws upon the equilibration mechanism of Walrasian *tâtonnement* that it is pertinent to mention that X-efficiency theory not only eschews *tâtonnement* as meaningful in the interactions between the various individuals making up the firm, but seems to deny the simple rationality that Walras's and Pareto's general models required. Given outside pressures, individuals are driven to communicate according to comparative status, not according to negotiated interactions. The metaphor is not Walras's *tâtonnement;* it is Pirandello's *Six Characters in Search of an Author* (for author, read some compelling force like Hobbes's *Leviathan*).

But I think one can say more. The leading 'neo-Austrian' of our time, Professor Hayek, has of recent years come to see the importance of economic conventions as signalling systems or communications devices. Communications devices are precisely what Hobbes identifies as language itself. Language is partly what Hayek calls 'institutions', borrowing (knowingly or otherwise) the precise phrase John R. Commons used almost a century ago (cf. Perlman, 1986). The impact of these conventions/institutions is one of the external pressures which can force firms to diminish their levels of X-inefficiency. X-efficiency theory requires communications or signalling within the firm. That is what the theory is largely about.

Morgenstern and Hayek came from the same mould. That they were different in the end merely indicates that the mould is at the starting point. But were they so different? Morgenstern was, it may be unnecessary to recall, Hayek's successor at the Vienna Research Institute which they both left in the 1930s—the one to go to the London School of Economics, the other to

Princeton. The linkage of Leibenstein to Morgenstern is clear; the linkage of Morgenstern and Hayek to the Austrian-subjectivist tradition is also obvious. The linkage of Leibenstein to the original Menger formulation is not clear; but there is a link to the Austrian post-Menger tradition. And that is where I would fit in Leibenstein.

### Reflecting the 'Adam Smith Problem'

During the latter part of the nineteenth century there developed, particularly in Germany, great interest in purported contradictions between Smith's view of man as seen in his *Theory of Moral Sentiments* and in his *Wealth of Nations* (cf. Viner, 1926). In the former, man was perceived as usually having a gregarious nature (a 'herding' kind of 'animal'), and capable of continuous detached self-judgement of his actions, as planned and also with regard to likely consequence. In the *Wealth of Nations,* single-minded, efficiency-conscious 'economic man' emerged totally supreme.

X-efficiency theory can be presented as an effort to identify the active relationship between these two aspects of man. Why? Because Leibenstein's work on economic development as well as on X-efficiency theory explains the internal and the external pressures which cause man-in-the-production process to choose between what he would like to do (the Austrian subjective factor), what he thinks he ought to do (Smith's detached observer), and what efficiency considerations, under certain conditions, force him to do (the compromises he must make with true maximizations, in so far as he can grasp the latter).

I believe that his X-efficiency theory goes beyond this important point. It also explains what efficiency considerations cannot force him to do, and why. That is the rubric of inert areas. In this sense Leibenstein goes beyond Smith and *das Adam Smith Problem.*

In sum, perhaps one of the more useful ways to classify Leibenstein's contribution to economic theory is to note that in its initial grasp it was Marshallian neoclassical, but almost immediately he came to challenge the assumptions of simple rational maximization. He is not part of the Walrasian mathematical, purely logical neoclassicism. And in so far as this last is the mainstream of our time, his work has to be seen as part of contemporary heterodoxy.

NOTES

1. Part of Leibenstein's dissociation from both Marshallian and Hicks-Samuelson neoclassical economics reflects the impact of Morgenstern's own brand of Austrian

economics. In the flow of ideas early Austrian economics came to stand for many things: The role of the subjective, the importance of demand from which was derived supplies of consumer goods and supplies of higher order goods, resistance to mathematical formulations, a strong preference for 'free markets' and an opposition to socialism, etc. Morgenstern was intellectually very independent and differed greatly from many of his contemporary 'Austrians'. For one thing, he was from early on interested in quantification and headed a private research organization studying business cycles, albeit he was there as Hayek's successor. For another, he came to represent one type of formalism—the mathematics involved in the point theorem and game theory. What stands out about Morgenstern's brand of Austrian economics was its concern with how choices were made, particularly on the demand side. While not all the questions on which Leibenstein has written have that as the dominant theme, his work on interdependence of consumer choice, human fertility and, derivatively, X-efficiency theory do.

2. Interest in the determinants of fertility choices persisted. Whether it was the source of his interest in X-efficiency theory or has merely paralleled it is unimportant. But much of Leibenstein's bibliography comes under the heading of demographic economics, as such (cf. Leibenstein 1962, 1964, 1974b, 1974c, 1975b, 1975c, 1976a, 1976b, 1977a, 1977b, 1978a, 1979c, 1980b, 1981a).

3. Macroeconomics was emerging during the post-Second World War period. It turned attention to the work done on aggregate national constant-returns-to-scale production functions by Paul Douglas and Charles Cobb.

4. Part of the professional reaction they encountered was that this approach was exactly the hard-line 'little-or-nothing-for-consumers' policy which Stalin had pursued. Both men had always been anti-Stalinist. Their conclusions, implying that there was a hard logic to Stalin's cruel investment policy, came as something of a surprise. Many first reactions found expression in strong (if irrelevantly derived) criticism of them. Leibenstein spent a great deal of time refuting critics (cf. Leibenstein 1958, 1960b, 1962, 1963, 1966b).

5. Note the date; it was the era of fine-tuning. In that period the concept of an American annual productivity increase of about 4 percent was accepted almost as a given. Fabricant and others spoke of growth cycles having replaced business cycles.

6. A 1962 article, 'Notes on Welfare Economics and the Theory of Democracy', seems to me to have reflected a more original and formative type of thinking. In it he introduces the concept of 'consent areas', a forerunner (?), albeit negatively phrased, of what later he was to term 'inert areas'.

7. I see no reason why X-efficiency theory should not be adapted to the purchasing and consuming activities of the household. Indeed, what is amazing to me is the number of times Mitchell's 'backward art' has been republished and cited, without anyone mentioning the underlying rationality conditions (cf. Mitchell, 1912).

8. The X-factor might well have referred to the unknown or residual factor in trying to explain the 'high' American annual productivity growth rate. In the course of my work I have found many claims to being the first to note that 'unexplained residual'. I am inclined to credit Professor Abramovitz with having been 'the last' to have discovered the unexplained phenomenon; thereafter it 'stayed discovered'.

9. Cf. Leibenstein 1969, 1972, 1973, 1974a, 1977c, 1980a, 1980b, 1981b, 1981c, 1981d, 1982a, 1982b, 1982c, 1983a, 1983b, 1985a, 1985b.

10. '[W]e [have] ended up with the unalloyed jewel known as the market in general equilibrium. In such a market the firm becomes a trivial and indeterminate entity. If price of inputs and outputs are known, and if the menu of techniques that translates inputs into outputs is known, then the firm can be presumed to behave quite mechanically' (Leibenstein, 1979b, p. 128).

11. Contracts are incomplete and can be asymmetrical—payment is specified, but work effort is not (ibid., p. 130).

12. The effort variable is 'made up of . . . (A) activities chosen, (P) the pace of carrying out the activities; (Q) the quality of activities, and (T) the time sequence aspect. Assuming that A, P, Q, and T can be assigned values, we can then visualize the vector APQT as an effort point' (ibid., p. 130).

13. 'We posit the existence of a psychological *inertial* cost of moving from one [effort] position to another. Thus an individual who finds himself in one effort position may not move to a superior effort position because the inertial cost is greater than the utility gain. Inertial cost should be viewed as a personality characteristic. An individual who is a maximizer would have zero inertial costs' (ibid., p. 130).

14. A much earlier effort at formal exposition was made by William S. Comanor and Leibenstein (Comanor and Leibenstein, 1969).

REFERENCES

Abramovitz, Moses (1956), 'Resource and Output Trends in the United States Since 1870', Occasional Paper 52, New York: NBER.

Blaug, Mark (1986), *Who's Who in Economics: A Biographical Dictionary of Major Economists, 1700–1760*, Cambridge, MA (2nd edn).

Buck, Philip W. (1958), Review of Leibenstein's *Economic Backwardness and Economic Growth: Studies in the Theory of Economic Development*, in *Annals of the American Academy of Political and Social Science*, 318, 185.

Comanor, William and Harvey Leibenstein (1969), 'Allocative Efficiency, X-Efficiency, and the Measurement of Welfare Losses' *Economica*, N.S. 36, (143), 304–9.

Cyert, Richard M. and J. G. March (1963), *A Behavioral Theory of the Firm*, Englewood Cliffs, N.J.: Prentice-Hall.

Fabricant, Solomon (1958), 'Basic Facts on Productivity Change', Occasional Paper 63, New York: NBER.

Frantz, Roger S. (1990), 'Ex-Ante and Ex-Post Criticisms of X-Efficiency Theory and Literature', in Klaus Weiermaier and Mark Perlman (eds.), *Studies in Economic Rationality: X-Efficiency Examined and Extolled*, Ann Arbor, Mich.: Michigan University Press, 43–62.

Galbraith, John Kenneth (1988), Review of Leibenstein's *Inside the Firm: The Inefficiency of Hierarchy, New Republic*, 198, 42.

Galenson, Walter and Harvey Leibenstein (1955), 'Investment Criteria, Productivity, and Economic Development', *Quarterly Journal of Economics*, 69, 343–70.

Hamberg, D. (1958), Review of Leibenstein's *Economic Backwardness and Economic Growth: Studies in the Theory of Economic Development*, in *American Economic Review*, 48, 1020–3.

Hess, James D. (1989), Review of Leibenstein's *Inside the Firm: The Inefficiency of Hierarchy*, in *Journal of Economic Literature*, 27, 641–3.

Hobbes, Thomas (1651), *The Leviathan*.

Leibenstein, Harvey (1950), 'Bandwagon, Snob, and Veblen Effects in the Theory of Consumers' Demand', *Quarterly Journal of Economics*, 54, 183–207.

———. (1951), 'Toward a Theory of Demographic Transition', a doctoral dissertation submitted to the Department of Economics, Princeton University.

———. (1954), *A Theory of Economic Demographic Development*, Princeton, N.J.: Princeton University Press.

———. (1957), *Economic Backwardness and Economic Growth: Studies in the Theory of Economic Development*, New York: John Wiley.

———. 1958), 'Underemployment in Backward Economies: Some Additional Notes', *Journal of Political Economy*, 66, 256–8.

———. (1960a), *Economic Theory and Organizational Analysis*, New York: Harper.

———. (1960b), 'Technical Progress, the Production Function and Dualism', *Banco Nazionale Lavoro*, 13, 345–60.

———. (1962), 'Notes on Welfare Economics and the Theory of Democracy', *Economic Journal*, 72, 299–317.

———. (1963), 'Investment Criteria and Empirical Evidence—a Reply to Mr Ranis', *Quarterly Journal of Economics*, 77, 175–9.

———. (1964), 'An Econometric Analysis of Population Growth: Comment', *American Economic Review*, 54, 134–5.

———. (1966a), 'Allocative Efficiency vs. "X-Efficiency"', *American Economic Review*, 56, 392–415.

———. (1966b), 'Incremental Capital–Output Ratios and Growth Rates in the Short Run', *Review of Economics and Statistics*, 48, 20–7.

———. (1969), 'Organizational or Frictional Equilibrium, X-Efficiency, and the Rate of Innovation', *Quarterly Journal of Economics*, 83, 599–623.

———. (1972), 'Comment on the Nature of X-Efficiency', *Quarterly Journal of Economics*, 86, 327–31.

———. (1973), 'Competition and X-Efficiency: Reply', *Journal of Political Economy*, 81, 765–77.

———. (1974a), 'Comment on Inert Areas and the Definition of X-Efficiency', *Quarterly Journal of Economics*, 88, 689–91.

———. (1974b), 'An Interpretation of the Economics Theory of Fertility: Promising Path or Blind Alley?', *Journal of Economic Literature*, 12, 457–79.

———. (1974c), 'Socio-economic Fertility Theories and Their Relevance to Population Policy', *International Labour Review*, 109, 443–57.

———. (1975a), 'Aspects of the X-Efficiency Theory of the Firm', *Bell Journal*, (Autumn), 580–606.

———. (1975b), 'The Economic Theory of Fertility Decline', *Quarterly Journal of Economics*, 89, 1–31.

———. (1975c), 'On the Economic Theory of Utility: a reply to Keeley', *Journal of Economic Literature*, 13, 469–72.

——— (1976a), *Beyond Economic Man*, Cambridge, Mass.: Harvard University Press.

———. (1976b), 'The Problem of Characterizing Aspirations', *Population and Development Review*, 2, 427–31.

———. (1977a), 'Beyond Economic Man: Economics, Politics, and the Population Problem', *Population and Development Review*, 3, 183–99.

———. (1977b), 'Economic Theory of Fertility: Reply to Cullison', *Quarterly Journal of Economics*, 91, 349–50.

———. (1977c), 'X-Efficiency, Technical Efficiency, and Incomplete Information Use: a Comment', *Economic Development and Cultural Change*, 25, 311–16.

———. (1978a), *General X-Efficiency Theory and Economic Development*, New York: Oxford University Press.

———. (1978b), 'On the Basic Proposition of X-Efficiency Theory', *American Economic Review Papers and Proceedings*, 68, 328–32.

———. (1978c), 'X-Inefficiency Xists—Reply to an Xorcist', *American Economic Review*, 68, 203–11.

———. (1979a), 'A Branch of Economics is Missing: Micro-Micro Theory', *Journal of Economic Literature*, 477–502.

———. (1979b), 'The General X-Efficiency Paradigm and the Role of the Entrepreneur', in Mario J. Rizzo, *Time, Uncertainty, and Disequilibrium: Exploration of Austrian Themes*, Lexington, Mass.: Lexington Books, 127–39; Israel M. Kirzner's 'Comment', 140–51.

———. (1979c), 'Comments on "Fertility as Consumption: Theory from the Behavioral Sciences"', *Journal of Consumer Research*, 5, 287–90.

———. (1980a), *Inflation, Income Distribution and X-Efficiency Theory*, London: Croom Helm.

———. (1980b), 'Notes on the X-Efficiency Approach to Inflation, Productivity and Unemployment', in Burton Weisbrod and Helen Hughes (eds), *Human Resources, Employment and Development*, vol. 3: *The Problems of Developed Countries and the International Economy*, Proceedings of the Sixth World Congress of the International Economic Association held in Mexico City, 1980, 84–96.

———. (1981a), 'Economic Decision Theory and Human Fertility Behavior: a Speculative Essay', *Population and Development Review*, 9, 381–400.

———. (1981b), 'The Inflation Process: a Micro-Behavioral Analysis', *American Economic Review*, 71, 368–73.

———. (1981c), 'Microeconomics and X-Efficiency Theory', in Daniel Bell and Irving Kristol (eds), *The Crisis in Economic Theory*, New York: Basic Books, 97–110.

———. (1981d), 'X-Efficiency Theory, Productivity and Growth', in Herbert Giersch (ed.), *Towards an Explanation of Economic Growth*, Symposium 1980, Kiel: Institut für Weltwirtschaft, 187–212.

———. (1982a), 'On Bull's-Eye-Painting Economics', *Journal of Post Keynesian Economics*, 4, 460–5.

———. (1982b), 'The Prisoners' Dilemma in the Invisible Hand: an Analysis of Intrafirm Productivity', *American Economic Review Supplement*, 72, 92–7.

———. (1982c), 'Worker Motivation and X-Efficiency Theory: a Comment', *Journal of Economic Issues*, 16, 872–3.

———. (1983a), 'Intrafirm Productivity: Reply [to M. Shamid Alam in ibid.]', *American Economic Review*, 73, 822–3.

———. 1983b), 'Property Rights and X-Efficiency: Comment', *American Economic Review*, 73, 831–42.

———. (1985a), 'Comment [on the *World Development Report, 1984*]', *Population and Development Review*, 11, 135–7.

———. (1985b), 'On Relaxing the Maximization Postulate', *Journal of Behavioural Economics*, 14, 5–20.

———. (1987a), *Inside the Firm: The Inefficiency of Hierarchy*, Cambridge, Mass.: Harvard University Press.

———. (1987b), 'X-Efficiency theory', in John Eatwell, Murray Milgate and Peter Newman (eds), *The New Palgrave*, vol. 4, pp. 934–5.

Mitchell, Wesley Clair (1912), 'The Backward Art of Spending Money', *American Economic Review*, 2, 269–81.

———. (1927), 'Foreword' in Friedrich von Wieser, *Social Economics*, trans. A. Ford Hinrichs with a Preface [*sic*] by Wesley Clair Mitchell, New York: Augustus M. Kelley, reprinted 1967.

Perlman, Mark (1986), 'Subjectivism and American Institutionalism', in [Lachmann, Ludwig M.], *Subjectivism, Intelligibility, and Economic Understanding: Essays in Honor of Ludwig M. Lachmann on his Eightieth Birthday*, ed. Israel M. Kirzner, New York: New York University Press.

Perlman, Mark (1990), 'The Evolution of Leibenstein's X-Efficiency Theory', in Klaus Weiermair and Mark Perlman (eds), *Studies in Economic Rationality: X-Efficiency, Examined and Extolled; Essays Written in the Tradition of and to Honor Harvey Leibenstein*, Ann Arbor, Mich.: University of Michigan Press, pp. 7–25.

Stigler, George (1976), 'The Xistence of X-Efficiency', *American Economic Review*, 66, 213–16.

Viner, Jacob (1926), 'Adam Smith and Laissez Faire', in John Maurice Clark *et al.*, *Adam Smith, 1776–1926*, lectures to commemorate the sesquicentennial of the publication of *The Wealth of Nations*, Chicago: University of Chicago Press.

Whitney, Vincent Heath (1958), Review of Leibenstein's *Economic Backwardness and Economic Growth: Studies in the Theory of Economic Development*, in *American Journal of Sociology*, 64, 105–6.

# Part 3
# Labor Problems and Institutions

# A. On Labor Union Theories

# CHAPTER 20

# Assaying the Five Theories of the American Labor Movement

*During the three-and-a-half years I spent at Cornell's Industrial Labor Relations School my principal assignment was to write a book on theories of the American labor movement. I suspect that Leonard Adams, the school's research director, really wanted a book (a) offering a completely new or revised theory, (b) attacking my father's A* Theory of the Labor Movement, *or, not quite as good, (c) attacking its critics. What came out was none of these three. I offered no more than a taxonomy of then-available theories and some analysis of the paradigms from which they stemmed. It was the kind of thing I have since chosen to do in all of my work in the history of economic thought. When it was published I realized that my father was happy with the fact that I had not attacked his critics; my former colleagues at Cornell attributed the fact that I had not attacked his ideas to my "immature dependency" upon him; and no one else has since offered any ideas on the topic that were not present when I did the study. This chapter summarizes the five formative types of labor union theory. I still think it a journeymanlike effort—thoroughly competent, but surely no masterpiece. Yet, it remains interesting to me, because it was my first studied effort to show how the Patristic background (the "subculture," if you will) shapes scholars' thinking about a "factual" institution.*

We have implied in our earlier discussion that unionism is a multifaceted institution in which each observer will perceive unique characteristics. We have suggested that the literature from its inception until the New Deal can be clustered in five groups and we have examined the theories underlying each of these groups. In organizing our material in this manner we have given this study its framework.

Each group of theories concentrates upon a single facet of unionism and deals with questions intended to illuminate that facet. Thus the observer will tend to be attracted to that theory which best explains the particular aspect of the institution in which he is most interested.

---

From *Labor Union Theories in America: Background and Development.* Westport, Conn.: Greenwood Publishers, (1958), 1976, 2d edition, 214–41.

But what shapes his original interest? What makes him more sympathetic to the discussion of one aspect of unionism than to another? The answers to these queries generally are to be found in an examination of his background. What are the prevalent social, ideological, and economic patterns found in the society about him? Has he been trained in a specific academic discipline? Has his thinking been influenced by the creed of any social movement? No less significant will be his personal willingness to challenge the explanations that have been given to him and thence to reason inductively or deductively to his own conclusions.

Each of us will accept in each theory only as much as we are prepared to consider relevant in the questions that the respective theory asks. And the questions posited by that theory are directly related to the theory's basic assumptions or postulates regarding social structure. We can, therefore, with some confidence stress the relativism of the theories, emphasize that from each theory comes its own set of insights, and consider each theory as but an elaboration of one set of premises as they affect a particular question.

We are concerned now with questioning the relevancy for current use of each of the five groups of theories. We seek to provide an over-all view of the five theory groups, and to explain why certain of the theories appear to have lost, at least for the present, their usefulness. In brief, we are concerned with assessing the value of the early literature and suggesting why some writings now seem less significant.

Our discussion will consist of five divisions; the first is a recapitulation of the five groups of interpretations, which we will regard rather as five distinct theories: the moral-conditioning theory, the social-revolutionary theory, the psychological-environment theory, the economic-welfare theory, and the social-institution theory. The second division is a brief comparison of their salient features. The third is a short examination of one major implication of the methodology involved in this study. The fourth part provides a synoptic digression on the meaning of the New Deal to unions as it might be seen from the vantage point of a proponent of each theory; and the fifth and last part presents what seems to us to be the most useful combination of theories for understanding unionism.

## Synthesizing the Theories

### The Moral-Conditioning Theory

This is an ethical, not a historical, theory of unionism. It assumes that unions can be organized by right-thinking individuals who, by using persuasion, will inspire individual workers to improve their ethical behavior. These leaders do not have to be themselves workers, but can be and often are self-appointed social reformers from all kinds of backgrounds, particularly the pulpit or the professorial chair. They consider that the value of unions lies in their ethical consequences, which can be judged at the social and the individual level.

At the social level, unions are considered essentially educational institutions which teach habits of propriety, self-restraint, and decent self-expression. Through unions, workers are enabled to rise to the point where they can be permitted to have the controlling voice in industrial decisions. Ultimately, the factory will enjoy the benefits of full representative government (producers' co-operation) in every aspect of its activity. Quite naturally, day-to-day union policies are to be determined in the light of their educational implications.

The individual will be attracted to unionism because it is a schooling institution designed to help him to help himself to realize his maximum personal potential in the factory, just as the church and the public school are there to perform similar functions in his religious and political activities.

## The Social-Revolutionary Theory

This theory, in its many forms, is based on what is believed to be a dispassionate, scientific understanding of the historical process. Technological advances in production techniques have caused changes in the relationships between the bourgeois, property-holding classes and the working, propertyless classes. Inevitably and increasingly, the *bourgeoisie* has exploited the workers. One way in which the workers frequently, if not always, retaliate is by forming unions. Thus the immediate cause of unionism is class conflict; the immediate cause of class conflict is bourgeois exploitation of the working class; and the immediate cause of this exploitation is technological changes in production techniques. It then follows that unions are caused originally by technological advance.

What specific unions do at any one time in any particular situation depends upon the union leader's appreciation of the historical process. Unions acting in ways that further the revolutionary ends of the working class are considered to be acting wisely. Unions that accede to the demands of their bourgeois employers or that temporize their revolutionary purpose in favor of shortsighted pecuniary and nonpecuniary concessions are thought to be useless and undeserving of their historical sanction. Ultimately, only the Socialist theorist who comprehends the full historical consequences of any given act can be trusted to judge between the good and the bad. And it is unanimously agreed that any union leader who tries to make peace with the bourgeois employer is a faker and a traitor.

According to this philosophy, unionism is a device useful in the workers' class war against the *bourgeoisie*. But when a Socialist society is achieved, unionism will have to develop a new purpose, since its old one will have been completely fulfilled. Unions in the Socialist state would continue to organize the workers, but to increase productive efficiency rather than to promote class warfare.

Why would a worker join a union? Because in a capitalist society it gives him, as a member of the working class, protection from bourgeois exploitation, and because it offers him a chance to play a progressive role in the historical process. Every informed and loyal worker understands that the historical process is the law of destiny. Through his union, the worker can help to shape the future. What about the worker who refuses to help the revolutionary cause? He is either uninformed or selfish—in both instances he has to be salvaged by a program of vigorous reorientation.

Two things stand out in this revolutionary theory: its teleological nature and its dependence upon a "proper" understanding of the historical process. The former stimulates moral certainty and confidence in the future. The latter creates dissension in the ranks, since any human action or program of intended actions, regardless of the ostensible motives involved, encourages speculations about the "real" consequences. As a result, the revolutionary theory has had numerous advocates, each of whom has tended to give his own interpretation of the historical meaning of any action.

### The Psychological-Environment Theory

This theory grew out of the psychologist's interest in human behavior as affected by physical and cultural stimuli. By and large, it is conceded that some human responses are instinctive or unlearned, while others are conditioned by ethnic or cultural traditions. Only in the sense that the psychologist, with his emphasis on science, admits the importance of historical experience on cultural developments might this theory be considered historical.

Adherents to the psychological theory view unionism as a movement controlled by the interaction of three factors: (1) the cultural lag associated with technological change, (2) the effects of economic insecurity on the attitude of workers, and (3) the manifestations of certain basic human instincts, which vary according to the ethnic or cultural group to which the worker or group of workers belongs.

At any given time union policies are decided by the members' understanding of the evil confronting them. Whether their reaction is a moderate one (leading to negotiation) or a violent one (leading to revolution) depends upon the three factors mentioned above. Individuals who believe that workers form unions for psychological reasons imply that an employer, aided by a skilled and experienced psychologist, can within certain broad limits control the nature of worker response (union policies). Whether or not unionism will continue indefinitely into the future depends upon the nature of the interaction of the three factors, with the possibility that experienced psychologists can affect the course of events. Veblen evidently believed that they could not, and predicted that industrial disorder could not be prevented. His conviction of the inevitability of unending blind conflict was not shared by others who agreed with his general point of view.

This theory suggests that the worker is attracted to unionism because of certain drives about and within him. It also implies that an employer, by using a conditioning program or by a successful educational policy, can influence the individual worker so that he becomes antiunion rather than pro-union. It is not difficult to see why a form of this theory has often been adopted by personnel administrators attempting to break a union.

## The Economic-Welfare Theory

There are those who believe that general dissatisfaction causes workingmen to band together and to develop institutional controls that will guarantee greater job security, higher wages, and improved working conditions. Of the various methods used by workers to achieve these ends, collective bargaining has in recent history produced the quickest and the best results. Hence the union, the most efficient administrative unit for carrying on collective bargaining, becomes the most important unit in the labor movement. This is primarily an economic theory, for it is based on the idea that unions are the least costly way to achieve certain objectives, but the theory has its historical implications in its reliance on historical records to demonstrate why collective bargaining has been more successful than mutual insurance or legal enactment in improving the worker's lot.

According to this theory, union policies are determined by a rational ordering of the goals chosen by the union, combined with a rational estimate of the efficiency of various alternative solutions. Since the decisions that must be made often involve highly technical considerations, it follows that unions should rely upon trained experts. This implies that a sympathetic trained expert can provide a considerable part of the day-to-day union leadership.

Whether or not collective bargaining will remain the means of negotiation most favored by the labor movement is uncertain, and it is probable that if some other means becomes more economical, the usefulness of the trade-union as the prime working-class unit might become less than that of a political labor party.

Many persons who maintain this point of view feel that legal enactment will prove superior to collective bargaining as a means of handling such economic problems as unemployment, industrial accidents, and superannuation. They criticize the unwillingness of the labor movement to abandon its historical commitment to unionism, as an irrational dedication to an ineffective institution. Implicit in this criticism, of course, is the belief that unions are not social ends in themselves, but merely administrative devices.

## The Social-Institution Theory

In this approach to unionism, unions are considered to have an importance in the western European democratic social structure quite apart from their ability to raise wages and improve working conditions. Unionism is the technique through which social inferiors band together to secure social and industrial rights. Once having secured these rights, workers use unions to protect themselves from the effects of rigorous market competition, which through history has been intensified by the growth of markets (bringing once separate communities into direct economic competition) and changes in production techniques (resulting in competition among the workers in any one area). Thus unionism has been both an offensive and a defensive institution, but invariably it has intended to promote the social interests of its membership. This approach to unionism developed from a study of historical records showing how specific workingmen sought to protect their jobs. These records were found in court trials for conspiracy and in the development of job customs or working rules in particular trades or industries.

The primary intent of union policies, according to this theory, is to protect job opportunities for the group of workmen concerned. As a rule, the older a union gets, the more it tends to draw on its own historical experience. In other words, it tends to rely upon the "common will," as interpreted by union leaders. Consequently, unions are reluctant to follow the advice, however well intentioned, of outside well-wishers and experts. Unions generally attempt hegemony over a limited job territory only, having discovered by experience what limits are most effective. In Anglo-American countries, unions pursue policies intended to give to job possession the type of property rights already guaranteed to real estate and chattel ownership. In this sense, when workers bargain collectively they are acting in the tradition of the barons at Runnymede and the Protestant reformers of the sixteenth and seventeenth centuries.

Social-institutionalists assume the existence of social pluralism. The union exercises hegemony over job rights, just as the state does over civil rights and the churches do over religious rights. Unions, according to this theory, are therefore an inherent and essential part of modern representative democracy. Their primary justification rests on the social role they play in giving order and stability to an important phase of community life and to a lesser, although still important, extent on the economic role they play in maximizing workers' gains.

## Comparing the Theories

These five groups can be compared and contrasted. Doing so points out the ways in which different writers treated the same or similar aspects of trade-unionism. It also serves to emphasize that for the most part the writers within each of these theory groups were concerned with distinctly different matters. Some emphasized normative standards which they felt unions should adopt; others merely tried to explain what unions did. This variation of emphasis makes a systematic comparison somewhat difficult, yet it also serves to underline the value of understanding the intellectual media in which the theories grew.

Two contemporary writers (1, 3) have suggested a useful set of four questions, discussed in the following sections, that bring out the principal comparisons.

1. *What were the original causes of unions?* Technological change and the upsetting of values and relationships cause unions to develop as agencies for *revolutionary* change or as agencies formed by workingmen who feel a *psychological* need to band together. Growth of the market, bringing the intensification of competition and the need for stabilizing controls, was the main cause of the development of unions in a representative democracy, according to the *social-institution* theory. A rational comparison of the net-cost advantages of unionism, group self-insurance, and political action in augmenting labor's share of the national income largely explained the rise of unionism, according to the *economic-welfare* theory. Spiritual poverty caused by economic misery led to the *moral-welfare* approach to unionism and the stress it put on the moral aspect of unionism.

Thus three factors emerge as causes: technological change, market competition, and the desire to improve the workingman's lot. Elements of each factor are probably present in each theory, but so great are the variations of emphasis that they serve to differentiate the theories from one another.

2. *What considerations should control policies?* For those who regard unions as *moral-conditioning* institutions, the significant factors in the union's determination of policy are the ethical consequences. Those who regard unions as *revolutionary* believe that union policies should be largely determined by the anticapitalistic results to be obtained. If unions are considered to be *economic-welfare* institutions, a rational analysis of the economic costs and the benefits gained by union action will be taken as the explanation of most tactical decisions of the labor movement, although it will be understood that miscalculations are possible. When unions are considered primarily as *social institutions,* the common will (embodied in written and oral union traditions and expressing the group's desire for social recognition and power) is thought to be the main determinant of union policy. The theory that regards unions as

products of *psychological environment* holds that there are three factors—cultural lag, economic insecurity, and human instincts—determining union policies; it implies that something can be done to control the collective response to the three stimuli.

Of great importance in the history of unionism is also the influence of men outside the union movement. The *moral-conditioning,* the *revolutionary,* the *psychological-environment,* and the *economic-welfare* theories all agree that "outsiders" (nonworkers) should help to steer the labor movement. Only those who believe that unions are *social institutions* attempt to explain why there is an inherent distrust in union circles of the outsider or expert, even though the expert is sympathetic and produces results. The explanation they offer is that no one outside the unions can generally interpret the common will in a fashion satisfactory to the regular membership.

3. *What will be the future of unionism?* When unions are considered as products of the environment, there may be no future for unionism if employers use skilled and experienced laboratory psychologists to solve the problems of the workingmen. Should the employers not use these experts—or, according to Veblen, should the experts fail—unions would continue as protest institutions. The *economic welfarists* also indicate that the future of unionism is uncertain, and that straight participation in politics may be the best course for workers to take. The *social-institutionalists,* on the other hand, stress that there are areas of democratic community activity, such as religion and industrial production, which are not suited to the usual forms of political control. Thus in a democratic society enlightened private-interest groups, of which unions are one, will have a continuing function to perform. Both the *moral conditioners* and the *revolutionaries* predict that unions will play ever greater roles in industry in the future. In the end, they say, workers will run the factories and make all industrial decisions.

4. *Why does unionism appeal to the worker?* According to those who believe that unions are *social institutions,* unionism appeals to the typical worker because he feels insecure and unable to hold his own in his daily struggle for economic security. This "scarcity consciousness of the manualist," to use Selig Perlman's phrase, explains why most workers will exchange some of their personal freedom for the "community protection" of the union. The *social revolutionaries* and *psychological environmentalists* believe that workers join unions because of rebellion against exploitation and poor living conditions. A realization that he can strengthen his moral position or maximize his economic position explains, according to the *moral conditioners* and the *economic welfarists,* why the worker joins a union.

In each instance the explanations are not mutually exclusive, and this question (almost ignored except by Hoxie, Tannenbaum, and Perlman), points up least satisfactorily the significant differences between the theories.

## A General Theory?

We have found that the literature can best be understood by employing a fivefold theoretical classification. Thus there are five theories—each with its own set of postulates and its own range of interpretations. Each theory raises its own set of questions, and develops an appropriate set of answers. Yet the questions and the answers are meaningful only to those who appreciate the relevant postulates. For this reason, the postulates are of critical importance. They serve to focus attention on one or another facet of unionism. And they serve to classify different writers.

Within each theory there tend to be differing interpretations. But the variation between these interpretations is of an altogether different order from the wide differences between the theories. In the former case there is agreement on the postulates; in the latter there is not. With such an agreement, it is possible for different writers to come to some sort of integrated understanding. They are communicating in the same language, asking much the same questions, considering similar answers. Ely's and Ryan's works are compatible; as are those of Adams, Commons, and Perlman. Even the various "scientific Socialist" writers (the Marxians) understood one another's arguments, although full agreement on details was not forthcoming. Veblen, Hoxie, Parker, and Tannenbaum all had a common bond. Such differences as existed merely reflected individual estimates or values imputed to one or another of the general factors considered.

But where there are separate sets of postulates, the task of integrating the five theories becomes nearly if not completely impossible. The sole common denominator for all five was that each discussed unions. And there the common features end. Some discussed unions as they have been; others discussed unions as they should be. Some discussed unions within the context of a capitalistic society essentially private in character. Others considered unions under social arrangements of quite another character.

Therefore in approaching the literature one cannot lay too great a stress on the differences in postulates. They create the theories, they separate them, they give to each its particular tone. For that reason it is useful to summarize them as they apply to each theory.

1. The *moral-conditioning theory* subsumes the desirability of producers' co-operation and thereby the ownership and control by workingmen of the factories in which they are employed. Unions, therefore, are devices to prepare the workingmen in a given factory for the responsibility of owner-managership.

2. The *social-revolutionary theory* purports to be scientifically teleological. As such, it postulates economic determinism and the ultimate abolition of all forms of private ownership of the means of production. Unions, conse-

quently, serve to marshal the working class for the day when the nonproductive *bourgeoisie* will be overthrown. Then production decisions will be made by disinterested experts. And then the workers in a given factory will work for the good of society as a whole—not merely for themselves or their exploiters.

3. The *psychological-environment theory* stems from an estimate of the causes of maladjustment of workers within a socially disoriented world. Great emphasis is put on the unhappiness of the individual. Hence unions and union policies reflect socially the individual workman's felicific calculus of misery, degradation, despair, and unhappiness. It further implies that under some conditions controls can be developed. Improve the adjustment of individuals, it seems to say, and the picture will change.

4. The *economic-welfare theory* is based on the critical assumptions that labor wants only to improve its material lot (maximizing its returns), and will do so rationally by employing the least-cost means. Thus unionism can be *the* economic way to achieve a given end; it can also be otherwise. Unionism is used when it is economically efficient; other more desirable means will be used when they prove more economic than unionism. In any event, there is nothing deterministic about social organization—workers may or may not be inherently maladjusted. What can be believed, however, is that workers will strive to get as great a net material return as possible.

5. The *social-institution theory* posits both the existence and ethical desirability of groups within society generally and among workers specifically. It further hypothesizes that workers are concomitantly members of many groups, and that in most organized social activities the individual achieves self-expression, material security (that is, the right to property), and moral realization only by joining with others. Democratic government or control is achieved through the interaction of responsible groups or factions, to which the individual belongs by free choice or because of some psychological or economic necessity. Thus democracy in industry, as in all other sectors of society, can be attained only through collective bargaining of some sort. Unions are the collective-bargaining instrument in industry. From all of this it follows that unionism is not a transitional instrument to a new and better world, but a part of the new and better world. Unionism and industrial democracy are indistinguishably interrelated.

From this comparison it is apparent that irreconcilable differences between the postulates exist. This is particularly so when each set of postulates is pursued to the extreme. And because every theory must rest firmly on postulates, it becomes evident that one cannot construct a general theory that will include all the conflicting theories discussed in this book. Thus there are five theories, not one grand one. But this is no cause for despair. Each theory provides insights of a kind, and as such can lead to the understanding of different aspects of the subject. And the empirical work done in the name of any one theory often contains information that will be useful to scholars or others concentrating upon another theory.

In sum, theorizing about unions and the labor movement is like theorizing about all other living institutions. The truth is larger than the mind; the mind can only benefit by making use of the results of varied approaches to the truth. This is the justification for any study of the history of ideas; it is also the reason for this comparative study of the theories of unionism.

## The Great Depression and Thereafter

A convenient point at which to terminate any discussion of the early trade-union theory is the Great Depression, when for the first time the whole structure of American industrial society became a matter for serious governmental reconsideration. By 1933 economic activity had fallen to the point where virtually all sectors of the American community were willing to reassess the theory and the practice of the previously predominant "old order." That old order had not been sympathetic to the rise of trade-unionism, and had emphasized individual rather than collective bargaining. If it had at times produced high wages and rising standards of living, these had been the products of basic, impersonal economic forces and of employers' unilateral decisions—although, to be sure, the specter of unionism and the need to meet economic competition frequently prompted the employers' moves.

The Great Depression marked the end of one era in the government of American industrial society. It was a time when it was universally admitted that individual bargaining was insufficient—when a national illusion that the ruggedly individualistic worker could cope with the vicissitudes of the business cycle and the vagaries of employer attitudes was shattered. Yet if an old belief had been destroyed, just what would replace it was not necessarily immediately apparent. In historical perspective the New Deal was a melting pot of ideas, speculations, and theories—a mélange of influences striving to reshape the American mold. And the five theories of unionism, too, were put into the melting pot.

For the sake of intellectual curiosity it is interesting to review some of the New Deal programs as they were proposed, in order to associate them with each of our five theories. At the same time it is also of interest to indicate where the "end product," the post–Great Depression American trade-union movement, deviated from the lines suggested by the theories. In other words, where do the theories fit into later developments? In this fashion it is possible to estimate roughly some aspects of the current relevance of the theories.

1. *The moral-conditioning theory.* In its purest form this theory found its earliest expression in the National Industrial Recovery Program. Section 7a of that Act, later spelled out as the Wagner Act, sought to establish through

enlightened governmental leadership, more than through a program of punitive measures, the copartnership in production of management and labor. Labor, in this case, was encouraged to seek self-expression through union organization. That the NRA—a halfway house on the way to factory and industry councils—failed, first functionally and then legally, is beside the point; what is significant is the emergence of an action plan based on the type of thinking urged initially by educators and reformers of the stamp of Ely and Monsignor Ryan.

The other elements of the New Deal program intended to help those who cannot help themselves—child labor laws, minimum wage-maximum straight-time hourly pay laws, aid to impoverished students and youths, and particularly the assertion of federal responsibility for the old, the very young, the ill, and the indigent—also may have borne the stamp of the type of thinking propounded in this theory. The spirit of charity, once effectively the symbol of the humane rich, was written into law and acquired a professional priesthood of civil servants.

Yet if the New Deal contained these program elements, it is even more apparent that much of what this theory had to offer was rejected. Producers' co-operation, the key to this theory, was virtually forgotten. The wage system was not abandoned; in fact, it emerged from the Great Depression as dominant as it had been in the twenties. Even "labor banks," perhaps the closest most American unions got to achieving one form of managerial status, disappeared. And where unions continued to handle large sums of investment funds, greater reliance was put on the usual market channels. By the fifties, the avowedly pro-capitalist firm of Merrill Lynch, Pierce, Fenner & Beane enjoyed a staff (advisory) relationship with many onetime socialistic unions.

The general view of unionism as a ladder to higher educational achievement and greater moral protection also seems to have waned. The change may be due to a diminished need, as a result of expanded public educational opportunity, and to the effects of increased social mobility. The latter has also led to less self-conscious *noblesse oblige,* a change that may be more apparent than real, but which nonetheless results in fewer self-designated "friends of the workingman."

Most of all, there is little mutualism seen in industrial relations today, unless it is the pseudo-mutualism which every seller must perforce find in any buyer. What prevails instead is a market or business bargaining relationship, more geared to positive "deals" than to normative standards. Labor now considers itself as good as management; and fewer managements act as though they honestly believed themselves the protectors of their employees.

In sum, the major failing of the moral-conditioning theory was simply that it did not foresee the actual course of development of American unionism. On the industrial scene its major themes, that is, producers' co-operation, leadership from the "upper classes," and full social co-operation between economically competitive groups, did not materialize. The type of reform which did occur, and which was advocated by Ely and Monsignor Ryan, was not of the union movement. The role of unions was incidental and subordinate. The Ely-Ryan approach was not validated by the postdepression union movement, if it was validated at all.

2. *The social-revolutionary theory.* If one can abstract from the dogmatism of the Socialists and Communists, one can see many aspects of their earlier thinking written into the law and the customs of the land.[1] What they had preached had been the leveling of economic benefits, the taking away of their economic advantages from the aristocrats of management and labor, the brotherhood of the industrial and agricultural worker, and the nationalization of enterprise in order to prevent cyclical unemployment and victimization of the worker. Moreover, they had sought to make the government the critical instrument in the social process, and to awaken worker interest in governmental programs of significance to him.

At first glance, the record does indicate developments along these lines. For a time there were active political coalitions between farmer and union groups, which had action programs supported alike by rural "individualists" and the urban quasi-proletariat. Nor should one minimize the leadership exerted by unions, and particularly by the CIO leaders, in state and national politics. Especially in New York, Michigan, and California, labor played a dominant, if brief, role.

More specifically within the trade-union field, stimulation and even protection was given by the government, through the National Labor Relations Board, to the new industrial type of union comprised of those unskilled and semiskilled industrial workers who theretofore had been unable to secure recognition for themselves. By "running interference" for these industrial unions, the government indirectly aided the CIO revolt against the *status-quo,* jurisdiction-minded AFL leadership. Within ten years several of the large industrial unions, notably those of the steel, auto, and rubber workers, had become pacesetters in American industry. The development of government ownership reflected yet another aspect of the revolutionary theory. The large western dam projects, the Reconstruction Finance Corporation, the Tennessee Valley Authority, and the Commodity Credit Corporation are but a few of the more obvious examples of what the 1912 right-wing Socialists, at least, had

---

1. The dogma tripped them; it became for some more important than the goal of heightened living standards and levels of social opportunity. For they condoned not only cunning, but also outright deception and avoidable violence. No wonder that as time progressed the ranks of the Marxists became bitterly divided between social-democratic moderates and dogmatic "actionists."

longed to see. And even if one will grant that most of the changes were not the result of direct Socialist activity (the Socialists had never claimed that history needed them to accomplish its inevitable purpose), it may still seem clear that the social-revolutionary theory foretold much about future developments.

But this is not the case. The truth is that economic class lines are not rigid in America. Economic misery has not increased. And Marxism depended upon the rapid development of class consciousness among the proletariat as the cornerstone of its theorizing. Insofar as this did not occur, socialism failed to provide the answer.

Even public ownership—the simplest and most direct step toward the "new society"—proved to be no panacea. All the industrial-relations problems known to private industry remained evident in the governmentally owned sector. Moreover, the right to strike, guaranteed to private industry's employees, is virtually denied to public employees. Unions are today no closer to engaging in direct political action—that is, becoming part of one party's political machine—than they were in 1912.[2]

From evidence of this type one may safely conclude that the social-revolutionary theory did not dominate. Assessed historically, it even played a minor role.

3. *The psychological-environment theory.* Several developments during the two decades since the depression can be listed as active validations of this theory. During the depression the prevailing misery caused by unemployment led to a popular realignment of social values. One important change was the new faith in collective bargaining as the means to prevent individual and group distress. The exposures publicized by the La Follette committee hearings on employer infringements of worker civil rights did much to awaken the public conscience and to reorient opinion regarding unionism.

The reaction of employers, too, is of importance. Although in the twenties many employers believed that worker morale depended upon high wages and pleasant physical working conditions, the new thinking emphasized "humanism" in industrial relations. It is not for bread, or even butter, that men work; rather do they want to be treated as significant personalities. In short, one version of the new gospel preached the necessity for worker expression, even through unions. Let the worker have a voice, let him ask his own questions, voice his own demands, and this act of self-expression alone, regardless of what he is given, will do much to make him happier. And a

---

2. It is important to note that Gompers' "political voluntarism" did not preclude engaging in politics. Unions have always taken an active role in political fights, particularly on the local (municipal) level. But they have never concluded a blanket alliance with a national party machine; endorsement of leading candidates and some limited financial aid has been the extent of their political action.

happy workman can, with proper managerial supervision, become a more productive worker.

Thus "human relations in industry," an awkward title for much that comprises humanistic industrial psychology, became a source for a certain type of union recognition. Some of those who studied the effect of factory environment on worker attitudes noted that high wages, pleasant physical working conditions, and short hours were insufficient without an instrument for "upward communication." Something else was needed, and unionism was suggested. But the suggestion carried implicitly, if not explicitly, the message that the union could be manipulated. "Management gets the kind of unionism it deserves," was the articulated slogan. What was meant but often left unsaid was that a smart employer could outmaneuver any union.

A survey of the record since 1932 leads to the conclusion that this theory has much to commend it as an explanation of developments. It does not require ingenious reinterpretation to see positive evidence of its influence. Where previously it had been argued that unionism was the reaction to economic misery, it is now said, as we have already noted, that it is the controlled humanistic element in environment, as expressed in contrived attitudes, that gives employers "the kind of union they deserve." Thus, with modifications, the old theory seems to stand.

Notwithstanding the "validity" associated with this theory, it really explains only how to control worker response, not the social purpose to be served by unionism. "Treat a man right, and he won't hate you," is the message. But if this indicates indirectly, for the employer's purposes, why a man joins a union, it does not tell what that man's own reasons are for joining or not joining. Quite the contrary, it merely implies that under certain conditions, an employer utilizing certain techniques can "wheedle" cost-reducing, tension-eliminating co-operation. In its application, therefore, this is an "employers' theory." It explains possible, but not sufficient, conditions for unionism.

The disciplines of psychology and sociology are doing much to fill the gaps in our knowledge of the limits of effective "use" of unions by employers. As yet, however, research is principally on the narrative or observational plane, although some experiments, such as Elton Mayo's historic Hawthorne study, have yielded theoretical conclusions about motivation. It is to be hoped that in time additional findings will fill more gaps, so that this theory can become fully operational. Nevertheless, the psychological-environment theory, because of its assumptions, will most probably always be management-oriented—that is, a means to serve employers' ends. As such it does not have a broad enough application to cover most of the aspects of the kind of unionism that has developed during the last twenty-five years. It may explain why employers think that they should "tolerate" unions; it does not explain much more.

4. *The economic-welfare theory.* The many ways used to achieve economic benefits for workers during the liberal-reform period of the thirties is the significant point in assessing the effect of this theory. Where the method of legal enactment was believed to produce better results than the method of collective bargaining, the former was used. Witness, for instance, the complex of social-security laws and benefits, the use of national minimum-wage legislation for workers too weak to organize unions, and the use of federal and state authorities to obtain union recognition and prevent victimization of individual workers.

On the other hand, where collective bargaining purportedly worked best—where it was the more economic method—it was embraced and endorsed, even to the point of making strong unions actively oppose some of the efforts of the public authorities intent upon helping those workers unable to help themselves.

A spectacular instance of the shift from one method to another was the AFL endorsement of minimum-wage legislation in 1937. Previously the AFL had opposed minimum-wage fixing because it feared governmental intervention, but in 1937 the leaders of the AFL, having become all too aware of the threat of factory migration to low-wage areas in the South, reversed themselves and sought to have the government do for their members what they themselves had been unable to do. Granted that this was being done in the name of underpaid southerners, nonetheless Messrs. Green and Woll knew how desirable for their own ends the natural consequence would be.

During World War II, when governmental policy made money-wage increases unlawful, unions sought fringe benefits to get "more and more and even more" for their members. And when after World War II taxation on personal money income remained high, the use of fringe benefits was expanded in order to maximize the net take-home earnings of labor.

While it had become apparent that the method of legal enactment was preferred for most social-security benefits, it was no less obvious that labor pressure on Congress alone could not effectively expand the federal program. Thus unions used collective-bargaining pressure upon large employers, and won concessions resulting in supplements to the regular social-security benefits, knowing full well that the employer would then have particularly strong economic incentives to join forces with unions in pressing for increased coverage through the national system. This technique was tried first for pensions and later for supplemental unemployment insurance. In both instances, as in all the cases previously mentioned, the goal was an increased share of the national product for organized workers; the selection of the appropriate means had become essentially a problem in the economics of alternatives.

We have repeatedly noted Barnett's postulate that unionism was generally believed by workers to be the most economic means of increasing their share of the national dividend, and that as long as this conviction prevailed, unionism had a future. The old organizing cry of "Join the CIO [in order to] win a 10-cent hourly increase" is essentially a confirmation of this view. The opinions of Dunlop (2, pp. iii–v) and Ulman (4, pp. 594–604, esp. 601 and 603–4) that unions serve primarily to achieve material goals in an economic fashion are further elaborations of the theory developed by Barnett. The very fact that their research has appeared, written as it was long after Barnett had sung the swan song of unionism, is at the same time indicative of the reasserted vigor of "his" theory and an indication that his 1931 assessment was untimely and wrong.

Although there is much in the economic-welfare theory to commend it as the explanation of the post-1932 trade-union movement, it does lack at least one important element. Just as Barnett failed utterly to see the noneconomic driving force in unionism at its most critical hour, so this theory today still overemphasizes the calculating aspect of the trade union movement. American workers have frequently not acted as this theory predicted that they would. They have not been as calculating or as "rational" as they should have been if they were trying to maximize their net advantage. Instead they have often chosen to fight lost battles and sacrificed more where by abandoning their union they could have sacrificed less and achieved the same result. This point is discussed further in the following section.

5. *The social-institution theory.* The industrial-relations field was staked out in the United States in the thirties and forties not by government civil-servant "surveyors" alone, but also by self-interested "communities" or pressure groups. If the Wagner Act gave the "workers' communities" the license of freedom and recognition of "full" citizenship, the "gift" was viewed by the government only as desirable, not as essential to American social order. Thus unions could not rely on the government; although they could use the government, they had to rely on themselves. In this sense the postdepression decades, a period when organized groups "found themselves," saw one group in particular exert pressure upon society, or upon the general community which makes up political subdivisions such as the state and the nation. It saw the rapid rise of unions and union pressure. But all of this did not develop in an orderly fashion. One union community was opposed by another; all union communities, by blocks of business and professional interests. Consequently a retrospective view yields a picture of factorial dissension and continual bickering—control by pressure rather than by logic.

The fact (not the theory) of social justice seems to be to give to the lion the lion's share. But some erstwhile lions, such as the old AFL unions, were forced to learn that to hold their own they had to develop strength in more parts than the larynx. The social-institutional theorists can point to the flux of group organizations during the postdepression decades, to the claims voiced by each regarding its right to hegemony (in other words, the property concept), and to the patchwork of jurisdictional divisions which resulted, as examples of their correct understanding of the American social process. The result was not simply increased economic benefits; it was the assertion of the property rights of first-class citizenship by several groups. And even when these assertions brought the small community into conflict with the state, the method of resolution was one of trial by combat—and the state, as represented by the NLRB, often came out second best. Within the "house of labor" the new industrial groups forced the "old guard" first to reform itself, and then to give to what had been considered rival and dual unions the stamp of legitimacy.

Increased emphasis on grievance procedure as well as on union security clauses is another example of the application in positive practice of this theory, which stresses the property rights of citizenship. The workers' ownership of job opportunities and the union's right to recognition and continued existence were the goals; the only appropriate means inevitably was, in the last analysis, the procedure of collective bargaining—either over the bargaining table or by group pressure put on the three governmental branches. Great significance was attached to the means, since it was believed that without the existence of a means of group expression, no economic gains, regardless of their size, were secure. Thus this theory emphasized that economic benefits alone were less important than the job right, viewed in all of its complexity— apprenticeship rules, seniority rules, stint rules, and so on.

The record of willingness of union membership to strike and thereby forego economic benefits for the cause of union security is additional telling evidence of the insight which this theory yields. The number of examples of member dedication to the cause of the union is certainly high enough to corroborate the point. In fact, the New Deal and Fair Deal decades serve as excellent examples of unionism as a way of life for social or bargaining inferiors.

Yet even when unions turned over to the civil government the responsibility for the administration of any programs, they frequently lacked confidence in the fairness or understanding of civil government; there was a belief that the handling of the area was directly affected by the strength of the union, standing as watchdog. Thus what the social-institutionalists point to in the two decades after 1929–32 are not the pure gains economically "won" by unions, but the increased scope of collective bargaining, the moves toward representative democracy in industry, and above all, the establishment of the right to the job as defined and guaranteed by the group as an integral part of the constitutional rights to life, liberty, and property.

With all of this, the social-institution theory seems unable to explain some of the things to which the economic-welfare theory gives insight. The rush to unionism since 1932 can be only partly explained by a devotion to industrial democracy per se. It must also be admitted that union ranks swelled because unionism proved during the period to be the most efficient instrument for securing higher wages and better working conditions. Our conclusion is simply that this theory may explain much of the hard core of unionism, but it does not entirely explain the great waves of union growth after 1933. For example, it does provide an understanding of the jurisdiction issue, in that it explains why unions have pressed claims long after the cause seemed hopelessly lost. It even explains why some unions will not negotiate such claims. But it does not by itself provide an explanation of membership lethargy, antiunion political activity by union members, and the like. These, too, are part of modern unionism and need explanation. For the "complete" explanation, one cannot turn to any single theory.

**Toward a Reasonable Eclecticism**

In any work dealing with the history of ideas, it is incumbent upon the author to make every effort to deal as objectively as possible with the thoughts and sentiments found in the data he examines. It is also desirable for him at some point to make clear his own views, even if he feels confident that he has made an objective analysis. In this postscript we outline very briefly our position. We do so with no apologies—it is included merely to make the picture complete.

As already noted, for most purposes we find the economic-welfare and the social-institution theories most valuable in giving insight into American unionism. Thus we acknowledge an intellectual dualism which, for reasons indicated earlier in this chapter, should not and possibly cannot be harmonized into a unified theory. Nevertheless it may be possible to explain our position by referring to the same ambivalence in complexity and multiplicity of goals in the American cultural environment.

The American heritage emphasizes social opportunity and material advancement. There are two goals: one of social self-realization or recognition, and one of ease in getting additional goods and services. These goals are not uniformly complementary or uniformly interchangeable. Which goal one seeks is determined by considerations of the time and by the impact of contemporary events. So it is with American workers and unions—they want the social prestige of job ownership and the social security it affords; they also want to get material things as effortlessly as possible.

Job security via job ownership is obviously important, but under some conditions workers seem to become hypnotized by the belief that job security can be achieved more effectively through legal enactment and the resultant due process. But in a contracting market workers are perforce brought to realize the full meaning of unionism to job ownership. After impressive instances of victimization, they are extremely conscious of the necessity for unions to stand as guarantors of the job right. Seniority, seen in this light, has the overtones of a political right, and remains the heart of unionism today.

Under other conditions the ease of getting and holding increased real wages tends to minimize the general need for job security. Here it is not relative poverty alone that seems to make workers willing to agitate for more material things. Often a belief exists that there is little chance of prolonged unemployment as a result of a demand for more—a belief that one can get another job quickly. In this event, union-guaranteed job security may be forgotten, and the union may be simply the best (least-cost) mechanism to get material results. An example of this is the case of some tugboat pilots who, knowing the value of their irreplaceable skill, use their union boldly and simply as the most effective instrument to "hold up" metropolitan communities such as New York City, rather than as an essential to industrial democracy. When instances of victimization are rare, when the job market is full of opportunity, when workers feel their mutual interest is easily evident to all, then the commitment of workers to unionism and collective bargaining may be limited to unionism's getting them what they want more economically than some other means. At such times the economic-welfare theory seems to us to be the best explanation of union behavior.

But this discussion is not to say that one's choice of theories can be made by a simple determination of the state of the business cycle or the prevalence of fairness in industrial discipline. For some workers there is never sufficient job security—to them the need for union controls over the job is omnipresent. These men, to our mind, represent the inevitable adherents of the social-institution theory. To them the *right* to the job—jurisdiction, if you will—is always the critical question. And only unionism can provide a satisfactory answer. They are over the years the backbone of the trade-union movement.

Yet the bulk of union membership probably does not at present share this concern. After fifteen years of unrivaled prosperity, many of the rank and file may have forgotten the historical mission of elevating workers to the rights of full industrial citizenship. Instead they are concerned with material plenty in the here and now. This has been an increasingly evident phenomenon since 1946; and, as we have already indicated, is best explained to us by the economic-welfare theory. By implication, the economic-welfare theory also explains why it is difficult for American labor to stay organized, since the goal of achieving material wealth may appear at times to be attainable most easily by agreeing to well-paying yellow-dog contracts. Hence this theory can and does indicate why unions fail during periods of prosperity as well as during depressions.

Whether an American union in a particular situation and at a given time reflects the economic-welfare or the social-institution theory depends upon what its policy makers seek. But a knowledge of these theories of unionism can provide an appreciation of some of the implications of the choice.

We find two of the five theories most useful today. Yet we do not wish to imply that any of the others will never have more than curiosity value. Were the American cultural environment to change, it seems obvious that our preferences might have to be modified. If American social life were more frequently and more strongly motivated by Christian ethics, for example, the moral-conditioning theory might have appeal. Similarly, if the Great Depression had led to greater economic stratification and thence to revolution, a variant of the revolutionary theory might have seemed particularly meaningful. Or if we thought that the "invisible hand" was really under the control of a human engineer (or a Madison Avenue advertising shark), our ideas would be considerably different, and would make the psychological-environment theory more useful. But because we do not hold any of these three sets of postulates to be currently relevant, the theories which they support do not appeal to us.

Yet if a theocratic national dedication such as Moral Rearmament were to occur, brought about by some natural, scientific, or military catastrophe, the usefulness of the moral-conditioning theory could increase. Similarly, if owing to an economic or military defeat a "proletarian" movement should develop in the United States, then the value of the social-revolutionary theory might also grow. Needless to say, such changes do not presently appear likely.

REFERENCES

1. Dunlop, John T., "The Development of Labor Organization: A Theoretical Framework," Chap. 7, pp. 163–93, in Richard A. Lester and Joseph Shister, *Insights into Labor Issues*. New York: The Macmillan Co., 1948.
2. ———, *Wage Determination under Trade Unions*. New ed. New York: Augustus M. Kelley, 1950.
3. Taft, Philip, "Theories of the Labor Movement," Chap. 1, pp. 1–38, in *Interpreting the Labor Movement*, "Industrial Relations Research Association Publications," No. 9, 1952.
4. Ulman, Lloyd, *The Rise of the National Trade Union: The Development and Significance of Its Structure, Governing Institutions, and Economic Policies*. Cambridge, Mass.: Harvard University Press, 1955.

CHAPTER 21

# Labor Union Theories

*When Albert Rees commissioned the economics articles in 1963 for the* New International Encyclopedia of the Social Sciences, *he asked that I write an essay on labor union theories. Alert to the point that labor economics cum industrial relations was being dropped from economics department curricula, not only did I survey all the major literature (that is, surveying materials not covered in my* Labor Union Theories in America: Background and Development*), but I tried to explain how and why the dominant group of economists saw labor unions mostly as an undesirable impediment to the optimal competitive market system. The concept of segmented labor markets was just being introduced. This was really the last essay I wrote on labor union theory.*

## Theories of the Labor Movement

There are three principal groups currently developing theories of unionism. The communist group, primarily located in the Soviet Union, is concerned with how unions can increase productivity in communist societies. To them unions are workers' morale agencies, and it seems irrelevant whether the state or the plant management (*in loco* employer) dominates the organization.

Most Western neoclassical economists who are concerned with unions focus on the effects that worker-controlled monopolies will have on factor prices, levels of employment, labor mobility, technological change, and profits. Hence they view unions as logical constructs, units intent on maximizing gains for all or only some of their members—much as a business firm (also a construct) is supposed to operate. They are not usually interested in exploring the forces that bring unions into being and keep them operating effectively.

The third group includes most of the well-known Western labor union theorists. They attempt to explain workers' historical behavior regarding wages, hours, working conditions, and job rights by answering all or most of four questions: (1) Why did unions come into existence? (2) How do unions

---

*International Encyclopedia of the Social Sciences.* New York: Macmillan, 1968, vol. 8, 516–23.

choose their goals and tactics? (3) What explains varying individual worker attitudes toward unions? (4) What is the impact of national cultural and legal experience on worker organizations? In other words, these writers study the historical records of institutions.

Each of these three groups is discussed separately below—the third group first because chronologically it first developed the bulk of labor union theory.

## The Western Historical Tradition

Originally the central questions about unions were why and how socially inferior bargaining groups managed to redistribute wealth and gain recognition. Answers were first furnished by theologians and philosophers, historians and economists. Later, as the newer disciplines of psychology and sociology developed, they, too, influenced the analysis of unionism. All had in common an interest in the dynamic nature of workers' group identification and organization. I have discussed the relationship of the disciplines to the theories more fully elsewhere (M. Perlman 1958).

## The Revolutionaries

In the western European tradition, interest in union theory stemmed originally from the study of Marx's law of historical materialism. From it was fashioned a theory of revolutionary unionism which, in its many forms, is based on a supposedly scientific understanding of the historical process. Technological advances change the relationships between the bourgeois or property-holding classes and the working or propertyless classes. Inevitably the bourgeoisie, motivated by profits, exploits the workers, and workers frequently retaliate by forming unions. Thus, the proximate cause of class conflict is bourgeois exploitation of the workers, which in turn is caused by technological change.

What a specific union does in a given situation depends upon its leaders' appreciation of the historical process. Unions that further the revolutionary ends of the working class are considered to be acting wisely. Unions that accede to the demands of bourgeois employers or that temporize with their revolutionary purpose, perhaps because of misleadership, are thought to be useless and undeserving of historical sanction. Only the socialist theorist, who can comprehend the full historical consequences of a given act, can be trusted to judge what is good and bad. These theorists consider any union leader who tries to make peace with a bourgeois employer to be a "faker" or class traitor.

According to this philosophy, unionism is a useful device in the workers' class war against the bourgeoisie. But when a socialist society is achieved, the role of unionism is indistinct. Some Marxist writers believe that the workers' organizations should not materially change their personalities. Others, discussed below, believe that a whole new set of objectives is essential.

Two discordant elements of the revolutionary theory stand out: its teleological nature and its dependence upon "proper" understanding of the historical process. The former gives certainty and confidence in the future. The latter creates dissension among the theorists since any human action or program, regardless of the alleged motives involved, encourages speculations about the "real" consequences. Advocates of the revolutionary theory have therefore each tended to give his own interpretation of the historical meaning of any action. These writers can be divided into three general categories: the right wing, the left wing, and the anarcho–syndicalists (M. Perlman 1958, chapter 3).

The right-wing theorists embrace political gradualism, like Bernsteinian revisionism. They agree that unions should represent the class interest of all workers (including particularly the less skilled) and should keep a steady economic pressure on employers for improved benefits and for the peaceful nationalization of industry. They advocate industrial unionism on the economic front (unions organized by industries or by geographic areas) and a labor party embracing gradualism on the political front. Where unions have become craft-particularistic, right-wing theorists urge constant education or "boring from within" to reorient them to their true historical purpose. The best-known American theorists in this tradition were such American Federation of Labor (AFL) socialist–pragmatists as Max Hayes, Nahum I. Stone, Victor Berger, and Norman J. Ware. All agreed that in the American context, craft-particularistic unions were ideologically misled, but nevertheless historically legitimate, representatives of the working class.

The left-wing theorists saw unions sometimes as the "protecting shield" and sometimes as the "avenging sword" of the working class. To them the particularistic craft unions, which they believed all AFL constituent organizations to be, were traitors to the working class and to the *deus ex machina* of history. Despairing of changing the AFL unions, this group formed "dual unions." Among the American leaders in this tradition were Daniel De Leon and William Z. Foster; both advocated political action and urged the development of aggressive, socialist-dominated unions as the main revolutionary instrument in bourgeois society.

The third or anarcho–syndicalist subcategory is often confused with the left-wing revolutionaries because both groups urged violence in bourgeois societies. Although both opposed craft-particularistic unions, they differed in their interpretation of the teleological nature of Marxism and of historical causation. The anarcho–syndicalists, lacking faith in the inevitability of the historical process, urged sabotage, duplicity in dealing with employers and public officials, assassination, and physical violence to bring about the disorder which they believed essential for the development of true freedom. The best-known American theorists in this group were William Trautmann, Vincent St. John, and William D. Haywood.

The impact of such revolutionary theorizing has not been great in the United States. Many of the egalitarian and social welfare programs advocated by the revolutionaries, particularly the right wing, have become part of American public policy. However, these changes were not brought about by the realignment of class structure which the revolutionaries considered essential to the fruition of their plans.

### The Historical Empiricists

Although the Marxians raised questions providing the most intriguing discussion, Sidney and Beatrice Webb used analytical methods that were the most widely admired. They went beyond the old Marxian question of why history should be dominated by worker organizations and asked how British workers had historically formed their organizations. The Webbs' theory involved a new social science method, combining the patient fact collection of the German historical school with cautious, bit-at-a-time analysis. Their labor union theory was based on British labor history but goes beyond the recording of its facts to present generalizations. Since the Webbs were among the earliest British Fabians, it is not surprising to discover that their intellectual method incorporated political norms.

The Webbs noted that British unionism had, over time, developed several doctrines, each in response both to the workers' desire to form their own continuous associations for improving wages, hours, and working conditions and to the key institutional features of a particular time (1897). Initially, when unions were small, weak, and at the mercy of employers and unsympathetic judges, workers embraced the self-interested doctrine of vested interests. They used the "method of mutual insurance," implying mutual help within the workers' group according to the self-insurance principle. The group was kept small in order to enhance job opportunity, and just large enough to spread the risk.

Later, as unions became stronger, successful attempts were made at bargaining with employers. In these instances the doctrine of vested interest was replaced by a market-price oriented "doctrine of [equilibration of] supply and demand." The method of mutual insurance gave way to a newer "method of collective bargaining." This was a bilateral arrangement which postulated worker solidarity but which could produce the flexibility sought by workers intent on improving their collective lot. The great shortcoming of this type of unionism was its parochialism—it gave benefits to the strong, that is, to those needing help the least.

Ultimately, the Webbs believed, unions would turn to a third, broader theory, namely a "doctrine of the living wage," applying to all workers, not just to the strong among them (S. Webb 1918). This doctrine would be presented through the "method of legal enactment," which was national in scope and parliamentary in means.

The Webbs favored the third doctrine as well as the third method. Indeed, so strong was their endorsement of these that there is a danger of assuming that they deprecated the others. On the contrary, they implicitly noted the usefulness of both the other methods and at least the doctrine of supply and demand. Even in a socialist state there would be a need for workers in advanced and profitable industries to bargain bilaterally with employers so that new and higher standards could be set where economically possible.

The burden of the Webbs' normativism fell on their moral condemnation of what they considered to be an all-too-frequent union device, restriction of numbers—restricted entry into the trade and the union (S. Webb 1919). They condemned it as parochial, selfish, and inefficient. Rather, they endorsed another device, "the common rule," a minimum working standard.

It is hard to overemphasize the impact of the Webbs' work. It was soundly based on fact, where the earlier Marxian thinking was conjectural history at best. It advocated reasonable evolution where some Marxists suggested violent revolution. And most important, it did not present a teleological face, which practical men distrust.

The Webbs have had severe critics. Some have pointed out the influence of their inarticulated norms, namely a moral commitment to social efficiency (S. Perlman 1928); others have noted their anticapitalistic (anti-free-market) orientation (Cummings 1899); and some have even seen a coloring of history in their selection of episodes. Nevertheless, their monumental studies provided the groundwork for most of the later labor union theory.

Although there were several earlier American theorists of the labor movement, the impact of the Webbs' work on John R. Commons and his subsequent reformulation of it mark the beginning of the most important American school. Using the Webbs' research techniques, Commons and his students at the University of Wisconsin fashioned a general Spiethoffian theory of the development of the labor movement. It is built in large part on extending the concept of private property to include job rights and on analysis of the effects of geographical expansion of the product market on factor-market (particularly wage) relationships.

Commons believed that unionism was a protective device for social and economic inferiors, who had to be protected from the impersonal rigorousness of the market. He took care to point out that this impersonality was caused by the growth of the market (leading to transactions between strangers) and by technological change. Commons did not believe in natural harmony; unlike the Webbs he had little hope for the development of social consensus on economic matters. Rather, he put his faith in the functioning of countervailing large groups, which he thought would be able to fashion acceptable modi vivendi with good faith and a modicum of luck.

## Contemporary Theorists

The best-known (and the most controversial) theory of labor unions was presented by Selig Perlman, who was Commons' student and collaborator and the first holder of the John R. Commons chair in economic research at the University of Wisconsin (where both Commons and he did most of their academic work). Perlman, a Russian-Jewish *émigré*, had in his youth been a Social Democratic *Bundist* (a Jewish right-wing Marxian socialist). Commons' influence on his thinking led him to shed his earlier Marxian conclusions. In the Commons–Perlman approach, unions are considered to have an importance in the western European democratic social structure quite apart from their ability to raise wages and improve working conditions. Unionism is the technique by which workers band together to secure social and industrial rights. Having secured these rights, workers use unions to protect themselves from the effects of market competition, which through history has been intensified by the growth of markets (bringing once separate communities into direct economic competition) and changes in production techniques (resulting in competition among the workers in any one area). Thus unionism has both an offensive and a defensive characteristic, but invariably it was intended to promote the social interests of its membership rather than the needs of an abstract "working class." The Commons–Perlman approach to unionism devolved from a study of historical records showing how specific groups of workingmen sought to protect their jobs. These records were found in court trials for conspiracy and in the development of job customs or working rules in particular trades and industries.

According to Commons and Perlman, the older a union gets the more it tends to draw on its own historical experience. It tends to rely upon the "common will" as interpreted by union leaders. Consequently, unions are reluctant to follow the advice, however well intentioned, of outside sympathizers and experts. Unions generally attempt hegemony over only a limited job territory, having discovered by experience what limits are most effective. In Anglo-American countries, unions pursue policies intended to create property rights in job possession similar to those already guaranteed to ownership of real estate and chattels.

Although there are some differences between Commons' and Perlman's ideas, it is erroneous to think that the two men were ever in conflict. However, it must be realized that Commons, unlike Perlman, was not particularly interested in developing a general theory of unionism.

Perlman's theory drew heavily on the historical generalizations of Max

Weber and Werner Sombart. From Sombart he took an appreciation of the role of psychology in explaining both the *Zeitgeist* and the individual's reactions to changes in economic opportunities.

Perlman took care to define the confines of worker group loyalty because he did not believe that in the American context there was any "class" loyalty as such. Rather, the ambit of such loyalty was set by the manual workers' innate fear of factor-market competition for the job. Perlman's phrase "dynamic job-consciousness" sought to explain the changes made by technology and market expansion in a once tightly defined craft concept of job ownership. The "manual worker" (an ideal type in the Weberian tradition) was the key to Perlman's theory of unionism. These workers, he felt, were willing to trade a purported freedom of contract for a small share of the collective voice controlling job ownership because they had little faith in their ability to survive in the junglelike factor market in which they sold their services. Perlman emphasized that the diffusion of wealth, and unfavorable worker experience with industrial self-government, made American workers and labor movements reluctant to embrace abstract social experiments like socialism (S. Perlman 1928). Later in his life, after the Nazi holocaust, Perlman added that even mature labor movements appeared unable to resist highly nationalistic leaders; indeed, they did not always try. At no time was he sanguine about colonial labor movements' abilities to resist the appeals of nationalistic or socialistic reformers.

The traditional Marxians, the Webbs, Commons, and Perlman had much in common in their labor movement theories. Each tried to explain the development of the labor movements of western Europe, North America, and Australasia. Where Marx had first asked "why organization?", the Webbs added "how does organization work?" Commons and, particularly, Perlman reformulated the basic questions to "under what conditions will a labor movement develop, and what specific rational and historical factors shape its development?"

There have been several vigorous criticisms of the Wisconsin theory. Some have disliked its selection of the parochial, American ideal-type union, with its limited social objectives, arguing that Perlman "liked" or "approved" of that type of union's particularism (see Hardman 1950; Laski 1948, pp. 221–222; 1950, pp. 37–40; Sturmthal 1953; Gulick 1948, vol. 1, pp. 294–297, 300 ff.; Gulick & Bers 1953). Others have felt that the theory was applicable only to nonexpanding industries (Meyer & Conrad 1957) or to already industrialized and capitalistic societies (Kerr & Siegel 1955).

Criticism from the last point of view has resulted in several interesting discussions, most of which are not presented as formal theories. Two of these were written by John T. Dunlop. The first (1948) summarized both the questions earlier theorists had discussed and what he thought were the shortcomings of their work. He argued that individual theorists had neglected some of the dynamic economic roles in the development of the labor movement played by changing technology, product-market and factor-market forces, public opinion, and the government. Subsequently Dunlop (1958) further clarified his dissatisfaction with labor movement theory. The key to this analysis is an interest in the process by which production and distribution decisions are made by firms within society and by society itself (cf. Moore 1960). He relegated the labor movement to a role somewhat different from the one that had become traditional. Unlike earlier writers who viewed the labor movement partly as a political and social force, Dunlop directed his attention exclusively to the processes of decision making in the allocation of labor. Consequently, unionism in his framework varies in importance among countries and requires a subtheory of labor movements. Where unions play an important industrial role (for example, in bipartite collective bargaining), their significance is great; where they play only a political role, their significance is less.

## Communist Tradition

At the turn of the century, in response to public opinion, the tsarist government attempted to set up "legal unions," which anticipated both Italian fascist unions and American company unions. As substitutes for genuine unionism these organizations were not successful, and in 1905 the Soviet of the Workers Deputies of St. Petersburg was founded. In October of 1905, at the time of the granting of a constitution, the first Russian Trade Union Conference was held, made up of 26 Moscow unions and 10 from other localities. With the failure of the Russian revolution of 1905, the reactionary government reasserted its authority, and in 1907 the police claimed to have disbanded 107 unions and exiled or imprisoned their leaders.

In March 1917 the Petrograd soviet reappeared in the central role and, together with revolutionary soldiers, declared a strike. The following month 82 such local soviets were represented at the first Soviet Conference meeting in Petrograd. Two months later a Russian Trade Union Conference was held whose 220 delegates represented a total membership of nearly 1.5 million workers. Within the organization there was a strong Menshevik, or Social Democratic, opposition. Bolshevik leadership was far from assured of support from the renascent older trade unions. From this distrust of the older group emerged both the Leninist policy toward unions and, later, the Leninist theory of unions. Lenin made an important speech in January 1919. His views were later circulated in 1921 and appeared as "The Task of the Trade Unions." Lenin was concerned with the deterioration of factory equipment during World War I, which aggravated the country's previous backwardness. He sought to improve production facilities and wanted the unions to abandon all policies which directly or indirectly hindered production. In both his 1919 speech and his reformulated views, he endorsed Taylorism, or scientific management.

Taylorism as Lenin knew it gave the workers virtually no voice in the handling of industrial problems. Nonetheless, Lenin sought to provide a place for union activity in the general framework of a scientifically managed industrial system. Trade unions were to discipline the workers, on the one hand, and be a quasi-public watchdog over managerial efficiency, on the other. The union was to minimize production loss and eliminate discrimination against particular workers, rather than improve wages generally or even improve working conditions for the workers in a given plant or area.

After Lenin's death the government union system, which Lenin originally urged, was taken up by Leon Trotsky. Trotsky wanted the state to control and eventually absorb all unions. He was opposed by Michael Tomsky and the functional leaders of the trade unions. Up to the time of his dismissal as head of the trade union's executive committee in 1929, Tomsky held strongly that the unions should occupy an independent place in the development of industrial policy. A third or middle view, popular within the party itself, held that the union should be apparently independent but actually controlled by party cells within it.

With the gradual sidetracking of Trotsky following Lenin's death, the first view ceased to be an important issue. The second view, Tomsky's, obtained until the New Economic Policy (NEP) yielded to the first five-year plan. Thereafter the third, or party, plan became official.

Under the NEP there was a tripartite control arrangement with three supposedly equal parties: the plant manager, representatives of the local unions, and representatives of the party. The manager was usually chosen by the party, and the leaders of the local unions were chosen by popular acclamation—which in practice also meant by the party. This troika arrangement continued for some time. Yet it is clear that by 1930 the unions had ceased to count; plant managers were in fact in unchallenged charge of all plant activity, and the trade unions had lost their voice in policy determination. By World War II the unions themselves seemed to have become primarily interested in increasing productivity through the Stakhanovite and the Udarniki movements. They were also concerned with providing rest resorts for deserving workers and the processing of a few types of grievances against unpopular plant managers. The best-known theorists of Soviet unionism have been Lenin and A. Lozovskii, who became the party's semiofficial spokesman.

## The Neoclassical Approach

Although most neoclassical economists have concentrated on the economic effects of wages and of particular union policies, such as strikes and secondary boycotts, several have also written on union power to affect the rate of technological change within the firm and the right of licensure (entry to the trade) [see Hicks 1932; Friedman 1962]. Until fairly recently the typical neoclassical analysis of unions concentrated upon the conditions under which a union would raise the wages of its membership at the expense of employers or other workers (Simons 1944; Machlup 1952). Now, however, attention has turned to the various alternative goals which unions can maximize. These include wage rates, wage payments, and employment levels as possible goals of the membership as a whole or of a dominant (even if minor) fraction of the membership. Moreover, these models admit a different selection of goals by a given union at different stages of the business cycle and during different phases of a long-term technological development. Different assumptions are also made about the price elasticity of demand for the product, and there has been recognition of the importance of treating each firm within an industry differently for tactical reasons. Finally, the impact of tax provisions, among other factors, leads to different types of wage payments—as in the case of pensions and nontaxable services such as health benefits.

The recent emphasis on statistical measurement has increased our knowledge of the effects of unionization on wage rates. Some economists have held that the gains made by one group of workers have been offset by a rise in prices or by a decline in the earnings or employment of others (Friedman 1962). Other writers, not necessarily rejecting that finding, have emphasized the "possible" result; one "guesses" that the "average effects of all American unions on the wages of their members in recent years will lie somewhere between 10 and 15%" (Rees 1962, p. 79).

One of the best summaries of the neoclassical position concludes simply that the direct effect of unions on the economy is detrimental but that the total social effect of unions (going beyond considerations of prices, wages, and the allocation of resources) turns the conclusion on its head (Rees 1962, pp. 194–195). This judgment, however, merely reflects the dichotomy within the field of Western labor union theory. One group of theorists approaches the topic from the institutional and historical position, while the other approaches it from the standpoint of economic theory.

BIBLIOGRAPHY

Alexander, Robert J. 1962 *Labor Relations in Argentina, Brazil, and Chile.* New York: McGraw-Hill.
Bauder, Russell S. 1943 Three Interpretations of the American Trade Union Movement. *Social Forces* 22:215–224.
Cartter, Allan M. 1959 *Theory of Wages and Employment.* Homewood, Ill.: Irwin.
Commons, John R. (1899–1913) 1913 *Labor and Administration.* New York: Mac-

millan → Contains essays and speeches previously published in various publications.

Commons, John R. 1919 *Industrial Goodwill.* New York: McGraw-Hill.

Croce, Benedetto (1900) 1922 *Historical Materialism and the Economics of Karl Marx.* London: Allen & Unwin; New York: Macmillan. → First published as *Materialismo storico ed economica marxistica.*

Cummings, E. A. 1899 A Collectivist Philosophy of Trade Unionism. *Quarterly Journal of Economics* 13:151–186.

[Dridzo, Solomon A.] (1934) 1942 *Marx and the Trade Unions,* by A. Lozovskii [pseud.]. New York: International Publishers. → First published as *Karl Marks i profsoiuzy.*

Dunlop, John T. (1944) 1950 *Wage Determination Under Trade Unions.* New York: Kelley.

Dunlop, John T. 1948 The Development of Labor Organization: A Theoretical Framework. Pages 163–193 in Richard A. Lester and Joseph Shister (editors), *Insights Into Labor Issues.* New York: Macmillan.

Dunlop, John T. (1949) 1953 *Collective Bargaining: Principles and Cases.* Rev. ed. Homewood, Ill.: Irwin.

Dunlop, John T. 1958 *Industrial Relations Systems.* New York: Holt.

Friedman, Milton 1962 *Capitalism and Freedom.* Univ. of Chicago Press.

Gulick, Charles A. 1948 *Austria From Hapsburg to Hitler.* 2 vols. Berkeley: Univ. of Calif. Press. → Volume 1: *Labor's Workshop of Democracy.* Volume 2: *Fascism's Subversion of Democracy.*

Gulick, Charles A.; and Bers, Melvin K. 1953 Insight and Illusion in Perlman's *Theory of the Labor Movement. Industrial and Labor Relations Review* 6:510–531.

Hardman, J. B. S. (1950) 1951 From "Job-consciousness" to Power Accumulation. pages 146–157 in Industrial Relations Research Association, *Proceedings of Third Annual Meeting.* Chicago: The Association.

Hicks, John R. (1932) 1964 *The Theory of Wages.* New York: St. Martins.

Kerr, Clark; and Siegel, Abraham 1955 The Structuring of the Labor Force in Industrial Society: New Dimensions and New Questions. *Industrial and Labor Relations Review* 8:151–168.

Kerr, Clark et al. 1960 *Industrialism and Industrial Man: The Problems of Labor and Management in Economic Growth.* Cambridge, Mass.: Harvard Univ. Press. → A second edition was published in paperback in 1964 by the Oxford University Press.

Laski, Harold J. 1948 *The American Democracy: A Commentary and an Interpretation.* New York: Viking.

Laski, Harold J. 1950 *Trade Unions in the New Society.* London: Allen & Unwin.

Lenin, Vladimir I. (1902) 1961 What Is to Be Done? Volume 5, pages 347–529 in Vladimir I. Lenin, *Collected Works,* 4th ed. Moscow: Foreign Languages Publishing House. → First published as *Chto delat'?.*

Lenin, Vladimir I. (1919) 1921 Scientific Management and Dictatorship of the Proletariat. Pages 177–199 in John R. Commons (editor), *Trade Unionism and Labor*

*Problems: Second Series*. Boston and New York: Ginn. → First published in Russian.

Lenin, Vladimir I. (1921) 1945 The Task of the Trade Unions. Volume 23, pages 503–518 in Vladimir I. Lenin, *Collected Works*. New York: International Publishers. → First published in Russian.

Machlup, Fritz 1952 *The Political Economy of Monopoly: Business, Labor and Government Policies*. Baltimore: Johns Hopkins Press.

Meyer, John R.; and Conrad, Alfred H. 1957 Economic Theory, Statistical Inference and Economic History. *Journal of Economic History* 17:524–544.

Moore, Wilbert E. 1960 Notes for a General Theory of Labor Organization. *Industrial and Labor Relations Review* 13:387–397.

Pen, Jan (1950) 1959 *The Wage Rate Under Collective Bargaining*. Cambridge, Mass.: Harvard Univ. Press. → First published as *De loonvorming in de moderne volkshuishouding*.

Perlman, Mark 1958 *Labor Union Theories in America: Background and Development*. Evanston, Ill.: Row, Peterson.

Perlman, Mark 1960 Labor Movement Theories: Past, Present, and Future. *Industrial and Labor Relations Review* 13:338–348.

Perlman, Selig (1922) 1950 *A History of Trade Unionism in the United States*. New York: Kelley.

Perlman, Selig (1928) 1949 *A Theory of the Labor Movement*. New York: Kelley.

Reder, Melvin W. 1960 Job Scarcity and the Nature of Union Power. *Industrial and Labor Relations Review* 13:349–362.

Rees, Albert 1962 *The Economics of Trade Unions*. Univ. of Chicago Press.

Simons, Henry (1944) 1948 Some Reflections on Syndicalism. Pages 121–159 in Henry Simons, *Economic Policy for a Free Society*. Univ. of Chicago Press. → First published in Volume 52, No. 1 of the *Journal of Political Economy*.

Sturmthal, Adolf 1953 *Unity and Diversity in European Labor: An Introduction to Contemporary Labor Movements*. Glencoe, Ill.: Free Press.

Taft, Philip 1952 Theories of the Labor Movement. Pages 1–38 in Industrial Relations Research Association, *Interpreting the Labor Movement*. Madison, Wis.: The Association.

Webb, Sidney 1918 *The Works Manager To-day: An Address Prepared for a Series of Private Gatherings of Works Managers*. London: Longmans.

Webb, Sidney 1919 *National Finance and a Levy on Capital: What the Labour Party Intends*. London: Fabian Society.

Webb, Sidney 1920 *The Root of Labour Unrest: An Address to Employers and Managers*. London: Fabian Society.

Webb, Sidney; and Webb, Beatrice (1897) 1920 *Industrial Democracy*. New ed. London and New York: Longmans.

# B. Labor History

# CHAPTER 22

# Labor in Eclipse

*Shortly after my Harvard book on the International Machinists was pub-*
*lished, John Braeman wrote requesting that I contribute an essay on the*
*decline of unionism in the 1920s. My work on the machinists, particularly,*
*illustrated my father's kind of craft-oriented unionism, the kind of thing where*
*job property rights were front and center. Accordingly, my interpretation, as*
*laid out in this chapter, if not modeled completely on the experience of the*
*IAM, surely was strongly influenced by what had happened there and how*
*Arthur O. Wharton, the international president, had salvaged what he could.*

*When I wrote this chapter the American labor union movement was in its*
*heyday, and I thought that the kinds of problems it had faced in the 1920s were*
*well in the past.* Sancta Simplicitas!

## I. The Question

Unions symbolize many things. They are protective organizations designed to
stabilize employment and working conditions. They are business organizations designed to improve the economic, social, and possibly the political
fortunes of their members, their leaders, and various groups in general society. They are reform organizations working with an eye to specific or even
general social problems. They are even simple cluster organizations that serve
personal and social purposes such as education, insurance, and lobbying. And
not infrequently, they are social-movement organizations grasping for an
ethos; and if they are able to define it, they give such expression to that ethos
as is meaningful to their function, their members' aspirations, and to the time.

It is common to note the decline of American unionism in the 1920's. At
the beginning they were (relatively) large; at the end they were small. At the
beginning they expressed confidence (if not exactly assurance); at the end,
they were cautious. At the beginning they had many plans and dreams; at the
end they concentrated simply on survival. Perhaps the topical word is frustra-

---

From *Twentieth Century America*, J. Braeman, R. H. Bremmer, and D. Brady (eds).
(Columbus, Ohio: Ohio State University Press) 1968, 103–45.

tion. By the end of the 1920's they seemed barely able to hang on to their members, let alone raise the banner and march into battle.

But stress and adversity do have a very few advantageous products. As one catastrophe piles on another, the natural or rational thing for a unionist to do is to seek what he needs through some means other than unionism. By the same token, those who must deal with labor will develop other ways to organize and control their employees. If, at the end, there is something that adversity has not completely destroyed, the very hardiness of that something demands respect and investigation. Thus, this essay has, as one of its purposes, the indirect goal of identifying the hardy element of American unionism that survived the period of trial.

"The use of history," Emerson claimed, "is to give value to the present hour and its duty." Dean Inge put the point even more directly when he commented that "our chief interest in the past is as a guide to the future." For these reasons particularly, the opportunity to look at "labor in the eclipse" (by which was certainly meant "unionism in the eclipse" in the 1920's) is a chance to see the significance of the changes in the light afforded by today's events.

This essay is organized about several points. First, we look at the decline of unionism from 1920 to 1930 in quantitative terms. Second, we ask what caused the decline, not so much because we are interested in identifying the crucial individuals or the critical moments, but because we want to know what factors were operative. Third, we ask what unionism had come to mean to its members by the end of the period, or, was there an emergent ideology that seemed to stand out more and more as the other faces of unionism shriveled and were cast aside.

Finally, we consider the eclipse experience in the face of our own knowledge of what came later and what seem now to be the problems. What did the experience reveal about the American worker, the American employer, and their thoughts about each other? What did it tell us about the economics of unionism, about the role of economic growth, and even about its attitude toward itself?

## II. The Decline

### Measurement of the Decline

The vintage year of trade union membership was 1920, when there were 5,047,800 members. This number was almost twice as large as the membership figure of 1913 (2,716,300), and the ratio was even better than the 1915 figure (2,582,600). Membership had swelled because of wartime prosperity and because the federal government had encouraged unionism in war industries. It had grown because the 1916 Adamson Act, giving the railway unions legislatively directed concessions, suggested to many workers that unions could accomplish meaningful achievements.

The prosperity had continued throughout 1919, and the glow of success continued to suffuse the unions. Yet there were sophisticated observers who saw blight setting in. And they were right. They suggested that the easy wartime wage gains, the rapid upgrading of personnel, the generous resolution of grievance disputes, all characteristic of the war and postwar periods, were not likely to continue. They also believed that the antiunion crusades of many individual employers and such employer organizations as the National Metal Trades Association were likely to be resumed with a vigor that would astound the forgetful union rank-and-file.

Even when the informed observers mentioned that unionism's gains had been geographically concentrated in the larger cities, at railroad division centers and in the Northeast and Midwest, that the citadels of antiunionism had not been cracked, the analysis fell on deaf ears.

Professor Leo Wolman has done much of the authoritative work regarding the size of union membership. His figures show that by the end of the period (1930) membership had fallen to 3.4 million; by 1933 it was to fall to 3.0 million. Table 1 gives Wolman's figures. Examination of it suggests that the great losses were between 1920 and 1924. Thereafter, there were either fairly small gains or relatively small losses.

Wolman's figures are estimates made by a reasonably skeptical mind, and although they suffer from some almost obvious shortcomings, they are still the best we have available at this time. He got them from the AF of L or the railway unions organizations, and the figures represented the number that each union used as a basis for its representation claim (and tax) in the roof organization. Here we run into the first difficulty. Unions paid a representation tax to the AF of L (if they were affiliated). The amounts they chose to pay were governed by several considerations, only one of which was their actual membership. The other factors included the state of the affiliate's treasury and whether and how much the affiliate wanted to influence AF of L policy.

Another problem of measuring union size is more thorny. Union policies regarding definition of membership have always varied widely. Some hold that an individual can be counted for internal representation purposes by his local only if he is currently dues-paying (usually delinquency of three to six months is permitted in order to allow for the inexperience of local treasurers); others are quite lax about internal representation matters and base their estimates of membership really on the size of per capita payments to the national (international) organization that the local makes. The impact of these differences in union policies and practices makes estimates of the relative sizes of different unions subject to irregular distortions.

Dr. Wolman's figures for 1920–21 represent a possible overstatement of

**TABLE 1. Reported Union Membership**

| | | IAM | | | | |
|---|---|---|---|---|---|---|
| | | Absolute | | Annual Change | | % Deviation of |
| Year | Total Wolman* | Wolman† (000) | Perlman‡ (000) | Wolman | Perlman | Wolman's Figures from Perlman's |
| 1913 | 2,716.0 | 71.0 | 74.0 | . . . . | . . . . | −4.2% |
| 1918 | 3,467.0 | 143.6 | 229.5 | . . . . | . . . . | −37.8 |
| 1919 | 4,125.2 | 254.6 | 331.4 | 77.3% | 14.4% | −23.2 |
| 1920 | 5,047.8 | 330.8 | 282.5 | 29.9 | −14.8 | +11.7 |
| 1921 | 4,781.3 | 273.6 | 206.9 | −17.3 | −26.8 | +13.2 |
| 1922 | 4,027.4 | 180.9 | 148.3 | −33.9 | −28.3 | +12.2 |
| 1923 | 3,622.0 | 76.4 | 104.7 | −57.8 | −30.4 | −27.0 |
| 1924 | 3,536.1 | 71.7 | 79.6 | −6.2 | −25.9 | −9.9 |
| 1925 | 3,519.4 | 71.4 | 72.0 | −0.4 | −9.5 | −0.8 |
| 1926 | 3,502.4 | 71.4 | 71.6 | 0 | −0.9 | −0.3 |
| 1927 | 3,546.5 | 72.3 | 71.0 | +1.3 | −0.9 | +1.0 |
| 1928 | 3,479.3 | 74.5 | 69.0 | +3.0 | −2.8 | +8.0 |
| 1929 | 3,442.6 | 77.0 | 71.6 | +3.4 | +3.8 | +7.5 |
| 1930 | 3,392.8 | 78.0 | 69.4 | +1.3 | −3.1 | +12.4 |
| 1931 | 3,358.1 | 77.6 | 63.6 | −0.5 | −8.4 | +22.0 |
| 1932 | 3,144.3 | 70.7 | 58.9 | −8.9 | −7.4 | +20.0 |
| 1933 | 2,973.0 | 75.0 | 61.1 | +6.1 | +3.7 | +22.7 |

*Wolman, *Ebb and Flow in Trade Unionism*, p. 16
†*Ibid*, p. 177
‡Perlman, *The Machinists: A New Study in American Trade Unionism*, p. 206.

true membership numbers. That is, did union leaders' confidence in their ability to hold onto their wartime gains lead them to report inflated figures either because they believed that the losses were temporary or because they feared that employers would become more aggressive if convinced that unions were losing worker appeal?

A comparison of Dr. Wolman's figures for the International Association of Machinists and the figures that developed from my own research in the IAM's general secretary-treasurer's office records is interesting in this connection. Wolman's figures in Table 1 for 1920 exceed my own by almost 50,000 members (11.7 percent). In 1923 his figures were 27 percent too low. But as will also be gleaned from column 7 of Table 1, the relationships are not consistent in amount or even in direction. Annual changes in membership, columns 5 and 6 of Table 1, also illustrate how neither the quantities nor their signs (plus or minus) illustrate stability between Wolman's figures (those given to the AF of L) and my own (coming from the IAM's confidential files). Any survey of the IAM history of the period will suffice to explain how the pressures mentioned above influenced its payments to the AF of L (which Wolman relied upon). The decade was one of general retrenchment, although after 1926 (when a civil war within the IAM was resolved), there was a small regular increase through 1930. After 1930 the Great Depression served to cut union membership, even though the IAM (for one) permitted unemployed members to maintain their affiliation at the monthly cost of only ten cents.

## Implications of the Numerical Decline on AF of L Policy

Not all sectors of American industry were identically affected by the loss in membership. Dr. Wolman's figures in Tables 2 and 3 show some interesting points.

**TABLE 2. Percentage of Employees Organized by Selected Occupation\***
**(Having over 100,000 Employees)**

| | 1920 | | 1930 | |
|---|---|---|---|---|
| Occupation | Number (000) | Percentage Organized | Number (000) | Percentage Organized |
| Bakers, bakery workers | 127 | 21.2 | 181 | 10.8 |
| Barbers | 183 | 23.3 | 261 | 19.0 |
| Blacksmiths, forgemen, and ham- | | | | |
| mermen | 295 | 17.6 | 148 | 3.0 |
| Brick & stone masons | 139 | 50.0 | 170 | 49.4 |
| Carpenters and joiners | 892 | 40.5 | 934 | 32.3 |
| Compositors, linotypers, etc. | 140 | 46.4 | 184 | 39.6 |
| Electrical workers | 190[1] | 6.1† | 605 | 22.8 |
| Locomotive engineers and firemen | 201 | . . . ‡ | 168 | 96.4 |
| Machinists, millwrights, | | | | |
| and toolmakers | 934 | 33.9 | 774 | 8.9 |
| Mail carriers | (91) | (24.8) | 121 | 75.3 |
| Molders, founders, and casters | 124 | 43.4 | 105 | 19.1 |
| Painters, decorators, and paper- | | | | |
| hangers | 344 | 29.1 | 557 | 18.7 |
| Plumbers & gas and steam fitters | 214 | 33.5 | 244 | 17.5 |
| Stationary engineers | 242 | 12.4 | 256 | 12.5 |
| Stationary firemen | 144 | 19.9 | 159 | 5.1 |
| Schoolteachers | 752 | 0.8 | 1,044 | 0.5 |
| Teamsters & chauffeurs | 926 | 11.9 | 1,273 | 7.7 |
| Waiters and cooks | . . . . | . . . . | 959 | 4.5 |

\*Sources: 1920 data from Leo Wolman, *Growth of American Trade Unions 1880–1923* (New York: National Bureau of Economic Research, 1924), pp. 155–57; 1930 data from Leo Wolman, *Ebb and Flow*, pp. 222–23.

†Pertains only to telephone operators

‡Data rejected as unreliable (i.e., well over 100 per cent unionized).

**TABLE 3. Principal Divisions of Industry,
Percentage of Trade Union Organization Among Employees**

| Division of Industry | 1910 | 1920 | 1930 |
|---|---|---|---|
| Mining, quarrying, crude petroleum and gas production, total | 27.8% | 39.6% | 22.4% |
|   Coal mining | 36.8 | 50.9 | 33.0 |
|   Other mining | 14.9 | 13.9 | 3.3 |
|   Quarrying | 7.8 | 5.8 | 4.4 |
|   Crude petroleum and gas production | . . . . | 24.4 | 1.0 |
| Manufacturing and mechanical industries including construction, total | 11.4 | 22.2 | 12.2 |
| Transportation and communication | | | |
|   Transportation, total | 19.5 | 39.6 | 22.1 |
|     Motor and wagon transportation | 4.5 | 11.7 | 6.2 |
|     Steam railroads | 27.6 | 53.2 | 38.6 |
|     Street railways | 23.6 | 50.0 | 57.6 |
|     Water transportation | 33.2 | 80.9 | 30.4 |
|   Communication, total | 9.0 | 19.9 | 7.7 |
| Service industries, total | 2.0 | 4.9 | 3.2 |
|   Clerical service | 1.7 | 8.6 | 5.4 |
|   Commercial service | 0.8 | 1.0 | 0.8 |
|   Professional service | 3.1 | 4.6 | 3.6 |
| Domestic and personal service, recreation and amusement | 2.2 | 4.2 | 3.0 |

Source: Lee Wolman, *Ebb and Flow,* p. 118.

Among the occupations only one, mail carriers, showed an increase in percentages of workers organized. Most showed substantial declines; the declines were relatively small only in a very few. It is quite clear that the mail carriers were not affected by the private-employer animus against unionism.

Table 3 tells much the same story. Generally, the percentage of workers in unions fell. The sole exception was among street railwaymen. Again, their activity has to be explained as a special phenomenon, namely, situations where the employer was occasionally a public authority or a private corporation fearful of violence and the possibility of franchise cancellation.

Usually, the skilled were the bulk of union membership, but it is clear also that the bulk of skilled workers was generally (but not always) non-unionized.

Nor were all American unions affected in the same way by the general downswing. If we rely on Wolman's figures (and in the absence of any others, we must), the pattern is quite interesting and can be concluded from Table 4, which purports to show the strength of the various voices in the ranks of organized labor. What stands out is the relative growth of the building-trades

**TABLE 4. Relative Importance in Organized Labor of Principal Groups of Unions by Reported Size of Membership**

|  | 1910 | 1920 | 1929 | 1933 |
|---|---|---|---|---|
| Mining, quarrying, and oil | 12.8% | 8.7% | 7.9% | 11.9% |
| Building and construction | 21.4 | 17.6 | 26.7 | 19.6 |
| Transportation and communication | 22.5 | 24.9 | 25.9 | 20.5 |
| Clothing | 4.6 | 7.4 | 6.3 | 11.3 |
| Paper, printing, and bookbinding | 4.2 | 3.2 | 4.7 | 5.1 |
| Metals, machinery, and shipbuilding | 9.2 | 17.0 | 6.1 | 6.1 |
| Textiles | 1.0 | 3.0 | 1.0 | 0.5 |
| Food, liquor, and tobacco | 5.7 | 3.6 | 1.9 | 1.9 |
| Public service | 2.7 | 3.2 | 7.2 | 10.0 |
| Total percentage and identified | 84.1 | 88.6 | 87.7 | 86.9 |

Source: Wolman, *Ebb and Flow*, pp. 87, 88, and 91.

unions' role and the relative stability of the transportation and communication industry (where increases in union membership on the railroads were offset by growth of such non-union sectors as the telephone- and automobile-connected operations).

On the whole, the AF of L was dominated by the building-trades unions. Internecine conflict between them may occasionally have immobilized policy-making, but usually theirs was the biggest voice. That voice was given its timbre both by the relative size of its respective membership and by the seniority rights its representatives enjoyed in the AF of L executive council. The railway unions were not then (nor are they now) AF of L affiliates. The largest metal-trades union was the IAM, but until 1926, when its international president (William A. Johnston, a "radical") was replaced, the IAM had virtually no positive impact on AF of L policy. The mineworkers union, led by the redoubtable John L. Lewis, was isolated both because Lewis was unpopular and because of organizational weakness. Basic steel and the auto industries were unorganized, and consequently, they had no voice in the AF of L council. The typographical union was strong in the newspaper sector; yet its membership was not large. The lithographers were even relatively more unionized but even smaller in absolute numbers.

What I have suggested, then, is that American unions really had only three possible stable points of focus; the railway operating brotherhoods (outside of the AF of L), some parts of the printing industry, and the building trades. The operating brotherhoods had difficulties with several managements, but by 1926 had managed to get the managements to develop a program of governmental intervention that assured unions basic continuity; they usually represented the vast majority of the eligible workers, although certain large railroads were exceptions. The building trades unions (which I identify as the citadel of the AF of L), on the other hand, generally had to depend upon co-operation of the many small contractors in the industry who could, if they were willing, pass on the costs of wage benefits (changes in the factor market) to their customers. Since factor markets (where the agents of production were hired) and the product markets (where the products were sold) were both local, it was not hard to maintain union stability unless the local contractors were vehemently antiunion. Many of them were, it should quickly be added. But where a desire to work with the building-trades unions existed, the employers, whose earnings were often tied to a fraction of labor cost, profited and did not substitute machinery for labor. Yet in spite of this unique factor/product relationship, Wolman found that between 60 and 68 percent of all carpenters were *not* union members during the period 1920–30. Seventy to almost 80 percent of electrical workers were *not* union members. Other similar figures could be cited for the plumbers, painters, plasterers, and so forth. So the decibel level of the building-trades unions' voice in the AF of L councils was tempered by a general knowledge that they were not really in control of their own sub-industries.

## The Pattern of Decline

At the end of World War I union leaders were aware that their greatest strides had been made in industries where the sympathetic attitude of the Wilson administration had been economically most easily expressed. They had few illusions that the antiunionism of the pre-Wilson period on the part of many employers had really been changed during the war. Moreover, they were also aware that the swelled ranks of their organizations contained many workers who believed that unionism and union membership provided benefits without sacrifices.

Their decision was to try first to convert by talking what had been the antiunion citadels into a more agreeable attitude. The Wilson administration staged two postwar labor-management conferences. Both were unsuccessful, or as one writer summarized the record, were dominated by Mr. Gompers' eloquence and Judge Gary's (U.S. Steel Corporation) silence.

Labor unions also tried to combine their resources to force recognition by U.S. Steel, *a* (if not *the*) bastion of the open shop. The "Great Steel Strike" of 1919 lacked many virtues as such operations go; principal among them was victory. And from that time on, it was apparent to any discerning mind that the prewar antiunion sentiment was once again going to be the rule (cf. Table 5).

In some of the areas where unionism had gained strength during the war, it became weak afterward simply because the sub-industries vanished; munitions manufacture is an excellent example. Yet many munitions firms turned

**TABLE 5. Principal Defeats of American Labor Unions, 1920–30**

| Year | Industry | Union | Issue | Remarks |
|---|---|---|---|---|
| 1919 | Steel | AF of L interunion group | Recognition | Union kept out of industry. |
| 1920 ff. | Coal | Mineworkers | Wage cuts, grievances, and recognition | Union generally pushed out of industry. |
| 1921 ff. | Building trades in New York and Chicago | Building trades | Wages | Racketeering became an issue, and unions lost public confidence. |
| 1921 | Maritime | International Seamen's Union | Against wage cuts and three-watch system | Union pushed out of industry. |
| 1921–22 | Meatpacking | Meat Cutters and Butcher Workmen | Against wage cut | Union pushed out of industry. |
| 1922 | Railroad | Shopcraft Unions | Wage cuts and refusal of representatives to arbitrate | Unions generally defeated; rise of B&O plan. |
| 1927 | Textiles | Textile workers | Recognition and wages | Union largely kept out of industry. |

to manufacture other things and did not vanish. Here the record shows frequently the impetuousness of the members, unaccustomed to the real sacrifices that maintaining a union requires, and the inability of the officers to restrain the demands *and remain in office.* The men demanded wage increases to compensate for the loss of overtime and forced the leadership to condone strikes when negotiations failed. The strikes also failed. They were expensive, exhausted the unions' pecuniary reserves, and left the employers angry, the members disillusioned and frustrated, and the leadership, if anything, discredited. Such was the story in the International Association of Machinists; it can be repeated if one looks in the records of many other unions. What needs to be added, of course, is that management in these firms lost whatever enthusiasm or patience it had for unions and pursued open-shop policies.

The AF of L leadership was only too well aware that the union movement lacked the money resources to win by fighting the employers. So, it proposed conciliation once again. At the 1923 Portland, Oregon, meeting of the AF of L executive council, the famous Portland Manifesto was issued. Its offer was for labor to eschew governmental intervention and thereby to reject even the barest trace of socialism. The corpus of socialism had been rejected years before. The key phrase in the message was "The continuing clamor for extension of state regulatory powers under the guise of reform and deliverance from evil can but lead into greater confusion and more hopeless entanglements." Labor, so the Manifesto promised, would work directly with management, and a new era of peaceful industrial relations was promised. If the Manifesto represented the outstretched hand of organized labor, business did not rush to grab it. In fact, business ignored it.

Business even ignored the orders of the governmental board administering labor conditions in the one industry where the law seemed to require an appreciable willingness to abandon unilateral decision-making, i.e., the railroads. The shop-crafts unions were not happy with what the governmental officials ordered, and they were even more astounded when the railroads refused to comply. The courts upheld the railroads' right to intransigence, and the 1922 strike began. It ended in union defeat. Disaster was averted only because a very few of the railroads' managements were basically not anti-union; President Willard of the Baltimore and Ohio worked out with the shop crafts a compromise productivity program that several unions accepted as a means of salvaging something, if only continued recognition.

## Some Limited Successes

Some unions, particularly those in the garment industry, went more willingly up the road of joint responsibility for productivity improvements and cost control. Meyer Pearlstein, an officer of the International Ladies' Garment Workers' Union in the Cleveland market, was one who showed how unions could work sympathetically with employers in the face of the latter's problems. Few employers, however, offered the reverse.

One exception to that last generalization was the railroads, not to the shop-crafts unions but principally to the operating brotherhoods. The Transportation Act of 1920 had proved a failure; the railways dishonored it when it had served their immediate purpose to do so, and it brought them no peace when they needed it. Because of the work of a Chicago attorney, Donald Richberg, the two sides (union and management) did work out their differences and presented jointly a plan to Congress to reform the handling of labor disputes on the railroads and the allied transportation intermediaries. Congress passed the plan in 1926; it was strengthened by amendment in 1934 and continues to be the predominant legislation in the field. It looked most satisfactory in its first two decades of operation; since then, its results have seemed less and less attractive.

Unionism, as I have suggested, was on the defensive virtually everywhere. The railroads seemed to be the one exception, and they were only partially so.

## III. The Decline as Explained

There is an understandable temptation to explain decline as a result of poor decisions, bad timing, or villainy of key individuals. Although it may be true that any or all of these factors may play a significant role at a critical moment in history, yielding to the temptation to explain everything by resort to one or more of these three factors seems to me to be erroneous. The decline of American union growth during the 1920's can be partly explained by these factors, but there were other factors as well. In this section I want both to suggest some of them and to consider how they affected the others, mentioned earlier.

### Causes Associated with General Economic Growth

*Different rates of growth of specific industries.*—A principal problem of American union leaders was that the industries in which they were relatively strong tended to grow more slowly than those where they were relatively weak. Thus growth worked against the interests of unionism.

Another way to consider the same point is to note that there were three major shifts in the characteristics and composition of the labor force during the period. The biggest, the shift from the farm to urban employment, will be discussed later, but it worked against the interests of unions. Second, the proportion of the labor force occupied as manufacturing operatives or as white-collar and service workers (types for which unionism had had previously little or no appeal) grew significantly. And third, women played an increasingly important role in the labor force and they, too, had rarely been enthusiastic in large numbers about unionism.

Some older industries were replaced (harness-making by auto repair shops or concert gardens by radios). Others were destroyed by law (brewing and saloon-keeping). And some were weakened simply by the force of new inventions as local transit companies gave way to private automobiles.

On the whole, as I have suggested, industrial growth was greatest in the areas where unionism was weak, and somewhat less in the areas where unionism was relatively strong.

*Technology.*—We have already suggested that new industries came into being and hurt established industries. Behind this change was often a radical shift in technology that induced a demand for a completely new kind of labor. It was this change on the production line, a shift away from traditional to assembly-line production, rather than the AF of L's "inability to absorb industrial workers" that caused the problem. It is a frequently repeated error to claim that the AF of L consisted only of craft unions. In the first place, there were actually several industrial unions of the AF of L even before 1895; in the second place, very few of the predominantly craft unions were really completely craft-organized or even craft-dominated. And finally, craft unions had since 1895 rarely withstood the opportunity to take on production workers, if the latter could be incorporated without pain or expense. An example of this was the Machinists' absorption under its aegis of the production workers in "its plants."

Nonetheless, the AF of L's problem was aggravated during the 1920's when there was a general shift in American industry from the traditional methods of production to mass production or assembly-line organization. The product market, as Adam Smith might have observed, had grown, thus permitting (even encouraging) work specialization, with each employee performing a small number of carefully defined tasks. A vast output of product at a low unit cost resulted. What also resulted was each worker realizing that he was no longer a "wheel" (much less a "big wheel"); what he had become was a "cog". Whether this change actually destroys the self-esteem of a new worker is a topic open to debate. It seems that it did do much to destroy the self-perception of craftsmen accustomed to the previous patterns of production. The unions' traditional strength had been among craftsmen, and this shift had significance for American unions in a variety of ways; among these was the stepped-up recruitment of new types of workers, generally women or migrants from rural areas. These new types saw in the factory an opportunity to get good wages providing she or he did as each was told. These women workers and "green hands" competed quite successfully with older craftsmen, since, working with machinery and intense management supervision, they could produce products that sold widely for less than the craftsman-produced products. The traditional workers, whether they were truly craftsmen or only thought they were, had often offered to bring the women and green hands into their unions in order to police the job-opportunity area, but the latter were not to be fooled; they well understood that the unions' interest in them might result in improved rates of pay only in the short run. In the long run there would undoubtedly result fewer jobs for them. Union leaders seemed completely unable to break through to these new types of workers. Indeed, they were largely unable to do so until the mid-thirties when the combination of a harrowing depression experience plus federal government aid sufficed to do much that was necessary.

*Different rates of regional growth.*—What is true of industries is similarly true of regions. Textiles, as an industry, did not fare badly during the 1920's; but New England textiles did. Thus, in so far as the New England mills were the unionized sector of the industry, the textile union fared miserably. The Textile Worker's Union tried to organize the growing southern textile industry, but failed to do so. It failed because of the hostility of the southern employers, who often used the local police forces as veritable extensions of their own plant guards. Employer groups in one region after another, forced by competition even when they were not led by evangelical antiunionists, came to embrace the open-shop movement, often known as "The American Plan," the "Anti-boycott League," or simply the "Open Shop Movement." And as the change occurred, regions as well as industries became known for their antiunionism. Southern Ohio, Detroit, Los Angeles, the South, the Mountain States, all were bastions of this antiunionism; inasmuch as many were also economically expanding areas, the impact on the American union scene of their attitude was large and, over time, expanding. Even in large cities where unionism had strong roots, trouble mounted; public investigations showing racketeering in New York City and Chicago undermined public, and certainly worker, confidence in the building trades unions, to cite but one example.

The point here is not subtle, but nonetheless it is often missed. If the less-unionized areas where the antipathy toward unionism was strong grew much faster than the areas more favorable to unionism, then unionism after a time became *on the average* (throughout the nation, defined as comprising both areas) relatively weaker in terms of its total or over-all strength than it had been "in the beginning." It was just this kind of differential regional growth that did occur in the 1920's. Consequently, economic growth as such worked against union success during the decade.

## Causes Associated with Employer Attitudes

It is apparent that employers, on the whole, thought that they could operate their plants without unions. But it would be an error to conclude that employers had learned nothing from unions. Quite the contrary, many of them realized that unions played a positive and significant role in industrial government. However, these employers believed that there was a preferable substitute for a union playing this role, and they set about creating the substitute.

Unions, they reasoned, improved pay, reduced hours, provided grievance procedures, and offered an opportunity for potential leaders to identify themselves. They, as employers, would do these things, and even outdo the unions. Pay increases would be generous rather than niggardly. Hours would be voluntarily reduced. Personnel administrators would be hired both to prevent grievance situations from developing (by not hiring proven trouble-makers) and to smooth other obvious inequities where shop committees (without any outside "agitators"—like union representatives) suggested they existed. Finally, promotion would be given to almost anyone; no more was the bright worker to be passed over while a not-so-bright relative of an executive was promoted.

The emphasis was on the appearance of consideration for workers' feelings. Employers emphasized the necessity of creating "an atmosphere of appreciation" for their employees. Promotions came easily, and in many instances there was marked improvement in the communication of workers' dissatisfactions. The personnel administration movement emphasized the advantages of the carrot over the stick, and many workers agreed to accept the pecuniary and other enrichments at the expenses of loyalty to what appeared to them to be an unneeded protective device, the union. Employers agreed to pay high pay rates and to give lavish benefits; it was useless for unions to point out that the workers so rewarded only enjoyed a portion (and often a small portion) of the outcome of increased productivity.

These employer policies are usually identified under the rubric of "welfare capitalism." But they include the scientific management movement inspired by Frederick Winslow Taylor and improved upon by H. L. Gantt and Frank and Lillian Gilbreth. There is also the personnel management movement, one phase of which was developed by Clarence Hicks at the Colorado Fuel and Iron Company and later at Standard Oil of New Jersey, and another phase coming out of the work of Edward Filene in Boston. What these plans had in common was a conviction that the functions that unions performed could be better done by employers, and if they were done by employers, the employer was justified in all senses in keeping unions and unionists off of his property.

All of this, of course, is not to suggest that many employers really had to be convinced that they could perform union functions better than unions could. Many were initially just basically antiunion. Many of the things they offered were given simply and obviously with the intention of weaning workers' affections away from unions. Very often, the employer was not particularly subtle: unionized workers were immediately discharged, and nonunionized workers were made welcome. Any worker who advocated unions was considered a traitor to the firm and was not only discharged but frequently blacklisted in the industry.

One other point on this topic should be added. Rapid technological change, of which there was much, involves not only new machinery and new methods of assembly but also new methods of supervision. During the 1920's American industry, as will be mentioned again later, turned on a large scale to variant forms of Taylorism or "scientific management." One of the original tenets of scientific management was to deal with workers on an individual basis. But that alone was not enough to stop unionism. What scientific management usually preached, and what was even more injurious to the cause of unionism, was the insistence that management stood responsible for determination of worker methods; the individual workers were not to be consulted on how to do the job—they were to be told. Of course, over time some of the rougher edges of scientific management were smoothed off. But during the 1920's the technological change associated with mass production and scientific management worked to the detriment of unionism for no other reason than that the unionism available was a product of an earlier kind of industrial organization.

## Causes Associated with Government Policy

There can be no question but what Wilson's New Freedom incorporated enough of the *élan vital* of the old Socialist-Populist reforms that socialism itself never recovered from the impact. In addition, the patriotic frenzy associated with World War I was channeled from anti-Kaiserism to anti-Bolshevik activity. In so far as the Lenin revolution kindled an interest on the part of American workers, the xenophobic charge of subversive radicalism had to be faced. The raids staged by Attorney-General A. Mitchell Palmer were not discriminating in their targets. Hard as union leaders tried to disassociate their organizations from those that Palmer and others categorized as subversive, the efforts rarely succeeded.

One can also point to other activities. Frequently, state governors used the National Guard to break strikes. Even the attorney-general of the United States under President Harding, Harry Daugherty, gratuitously injected the federal government into the ill-fated shop-crafts strike in 1922. His reasons for doing so can only be explained by his desire to help employers in their avowed battle for the open shop and even for the abolition of unions.

Later it became apparent that unions did need the positive support of governments. In so far as this is true, the lack of any positive prounion position on the part of national, state, or local governments (to say nothing of an antiunion position) explains well the relative loss of union influence during the period.

Another very important reason why unions declined relates to the difficulty union leaders had in reaching prospective members. There were legal factors that must be cited. The "yellow-dog contract" was upheld by the United States Supreme Court in a famous case involving President John Mitchell of the United Mine Workers and the Hitchman Coal and Coke Company. That case stood as a precedent and increased the already great difficulty that unions invariably had when, in order to talk to "the men," private property had to be crossed.

A recent study has also suggested that there was a systematic attempt on the part of former President Taft to put conservative (even reactionary) lawyers on the bench while he was Chief Justice of the United States Supreme Court in the early 1920's. These men, if the charge is true, had a predilection for issuing injunctive orders against union organizers or leaders. The courts, never particularly sympathetic to unions, became markedly unsympathetic during the 1920's.

## Causes Associated with the Effectiveness
## of Union Operations

*The Economics of Decline.*—Decision-making in unions is a topic all too frequently overlooked by students of labor history. There are many facets of it that should be analyzed: (1) Who makes the decisions? (2) What are the economic, political, social, ideological, and personality factors influencing the decision-maker? (3) What is the role of timing as apart from the substantive characteristics of the decision? (4) Who opposes the decision and why?

Generally, the rule is that in an atmosphere of optimism and expansion it is relatively hard to make a blunder, and that in an atmosphere of pessimism and contraction one can only choose the least bad (there being no really happy) outcome.

Unions are basically political organizations, where the popularity of the leader counts more, particularly in the short run, than his economic insights or moral excellence. However, it is necessary for us to consider the basic economics of union policies as they developed in the 1920's. Essentially, union leaders have the traditional business concern, namely, how to balance expenditure with income over some type of time period—usually longer than a year and usually shorter than the typical seven to eight years of a business cycle. Union revenue comes mainly from dues and assessments. Unions spend for personnel to conduct union business (usually termed business agents or union representatives, but also lawyers, pickets, and members on strike). There are massive economies in scale vis-à-vis many of these personnel. One representative can handle a great many contracts, but only superficially as to details. If the union employs a large number of representatives in any specified area or industry, each can specialize on a few aspects of the union-employer or union-member relationships. Specialization here, as in Adam Smith's pin factory, creates true productive efficiency.

During the massive decline in membership during the 1920's, unions, on the whole, suffered diseconomies. As their memberships diminished, their revenues fell. As the revenues fell, they could afford fewer agents and, even then, often had to settle for less well-qualified individuals. The cost of organizing (in terms of gross and particularly net gains) became heavier and heavier. The economic burden of union business became larger for each member, i.e., a larger share of the cost of union representation had to be collected from each member. Bad as that might have been during the mid-1920's, when most businesses flourished, by the end of the period the revenue situation was desperate. What naturally had to result was the curtailment of services and a reduction in the amounts that unions could pay to each of its employees.

I believe that my own studies of the Machinists' experience yield relatively typical conclusions. The program least resistant to outside pressures was the business agent system. The organizing and the strike programs during the period involved served the majority of members' interests only indirectly, and were therefore cut back radically. The IAM had to make all labor rates (possibly, but not probably, labor costs) more uniform in an area and an industry because such a change would work to the advantage of the strongly unionized segments of the industries in which IAM members worked. To accomplish this result, employers had to be approached and potential members convinced. Whenever possible, strikes were avoided; but the IAM still occasionally had to authorize walkouts for organizing purposes.

As the depression deepened, per capita allocations fell, and per capita resources fell even more. More and more members maintained a nominal tie to the union by buying "unemployment stamps," which was from the standpoint of the national organization a poor substitute for the usual per capita tax. In such an economic setting the union machinery worked inefficiently or not at all. The conclusion to be drawn is that the efficiency of union activity is worst in depression. It is often not very good during a period of decline, either.

**TABLE 6.  IAM Grand Lodge Expenditures on Selected Service Programs**

|  | Per Capita Expenditures | | |
| --- | --- | --- | --- |
| Year | Organizing | Business Agents | Strike Allocations |
| 1921 | $1.26 | $0.68 | $4.33 |
| 1922 | 1.14 | .82 | 4.19 |
| 1923 | 1.22 | 1.31 | .80 |
| 1924 | 1.04 | 1.25 | .59 |
| 1925 | 1.46 | 1.29 | .37 |
| 1926 | 1.55 | 1.35 | .27 |
| 1927 | 1.62 | 1.38 | .19 |
| 1928 | 1.39 | 1.41 | .86 |
| 1929 | 1.79 | 1.31 | .44 |
| 1930 | 1.58 | 1.35 | .13 |
| 1931 | 1.45 | 1.42 | .18 |
| 1932 | 1.05 | 1.30 | .11 |
| 1933 | .76 | 1.01 | .02 |

Sources: M. Perlman, *The Machinists: A New Study in American Trade Unionism*, pp. 220, 223.

Inasmuch as American unions were depressed throughout much of the 1920's, their record is, in terms of how well they performed their usual functions, less than excellent.

*Communication problems.*—But the size-of-operation factor was not the only one. There were also some very significant social factors. The enactment of Prohibition closed the saloons, where previously a union organizer could contact a large number of men over a relatively short period of time. Before the close-down, if an organizer agreed to stand sponsor for a round of drinks, he usually could expect a reasonably friendly hearing, even if no outright decisions to join were made on the spot. The closing of the saloons, without any logical successor, made it much harder for union organizers to operate. Bad as that situation was, it was made more difficult by the wide sale of automobiles, such as Ford's Model T. Workers not only did not remain in the saloons where they could be contacted, but they didn't congregate at parks or picnic grounds as was the usual pattern for a summer's Sunday prior to World War I. Instead, many workers packed picnic baskets, the children, and the wife and toured the countryside. Union organizers had a difficult job tracking them down, and when they found them at home, the organizer had frequently to contend with the on-the-spot expression of the wife's fears.

### Causes Peculiar to Labor Leadership

Other factors that must be included in this consideration of the causes of decline include several important points regarding union organizations themselves. The old leadership was unwilling to retire and be replaced by younger men. Retirement was not a common feature of life after World War I. Though it was true that the span of life had increased, people were generally not aware of the implications of this with regard to business, government, universities, or even unions. The traditional leadership became less energetic as the men themselves passed sixty-five years of age, to say nothing of the biblical allotment for life.

Yet in many unions there were vigorous struggles for leadership. These struggles occasionally resulted in the installation of younger officers. But invariably, these installations followed a bitter political fight, and did not end it. John L. Lewis retained control of his union (even though charges of fraud flew), but an entire sector of it became disaffected. In the case of the Machinist's Union, the traditional leader, J. J. O'Connell, was defeated by William A. Johnston in 1911. Johnston never managed to consolidate his victory and finally was himself forced out in 1925. His successor, A. O. Wharton, pursued a very cautious policy intended to consolidate the organization. Whereas Johnston had advocated large-scale organizing, Wharton advocated other policies intended to solidify support of the leadership within the organization at the expense of growth in numbers.

Many of the old-time Socialists, who had been active in unions, lost their zeal for unions as an aid to socialism primarily because union leadership disavowed socialism in order to escape the xenophobic charges mentioned earlier. Many of these socialist-radicals became bitter critics of unions and both believed and preached that the union leaders were traitors to the working class generally and to their own members specifically. In some instances it seems quite true that local union leaders were "bought out" by employers and that the local leaders sacrificed the economic interests of their members for bribes, either pecuniary or psychological. Moreover, the dangers of racketeering, always present where power can be concentrated, gripped several important unions in metropolitan areas.

## Causes Associated with Indifference or Hostility of Potential Members

There is no reason to believe that all workers are predisposed in favor of union membership. The abstract or general reasons why some like it have been analyzed in one of my early books, *Labor Union Theories in America*. Professor Selig Perlman has synthesized in his *A Theory of the Labor Movement* what he calls the typical (or "Tom, Dick, and Harry") unionist mentality. Professor Frank Tannenbaum, to cite someone else with another view, also has some insights on the topic of the conservatism of unionists.

But the important point is that unionism does not appeal to a lot of individual workers. Some view it as a blanket smothering the fires of their personal career ambitions. They have faith in their own ability to deal man-to-man with their employers or their immediate representatives, the supervisors. Some feel that the unions' omnipresent shibboleths, "seniority" and that what is good for the group averages out for the good of the individual, may only be correct in theory; and these people do not care about seniority (they are young) or the group (they are industrial transients or casuals). For these individuals unionism *per se* is not good; and if the employer offers them a good personnel policy, they are more than just satisfied.

Other workers are anticapitalist. They look to real proletarian revolution or to widespread political reform. Unionism might appeal to them; American-type unionism generally did not. In the 1920's specifically, they rejected the capitalism-accepting, wage- or job-conscious-oriented unionism of the AF of L. Most of these embraced IWW-ism or the various organizations that the communists (including myriad splinter groups) spawned, baptized, buried, and resurrected. A few were Social Democrats who did not want to "bore from within" (the tactics of the Communists), but preferred to support the method of legal enactment. Hence they put their energies into lobbying for "security by legislation" rather than working for "security by collective agreement."

But if adversity has its problems, it also presents some opportunities. Lack of resources precludes opportunities to make big (or even many small) decisions; but the time not so spent can be diverted to some thinking. The 1920's was such a period. In the next section, we are concerned with the evaluation of the philosophy or theory of American unionism which emerged quite clearly during the decade 1922–32.

## IV. The Eclipse as It Affected Refinement of Labor Union Theory

What Happened to Socialism

At the turn of the century and for about a decade thereafter there seemed to be developing a stable variety (as well as several unstable competitors to it) of socialism within the rather amorphous "labor movement," and even within its much better defined unit, the trade union movement. Max Hayes, representative of the Printers' Union, in one AF of L convention after another challenged Gompers' antisocialist leadership. Hayes's strength was never enough to topple Gompers or even to threaten his antisocialism. But it was enough to give hope that in the near future there lay the possibility of socialist success.

Hayes's socialism (and he was typical of those who influenced the unions most) was not intellectually rigorous. It merely emphasized the brotherhood of man (modified to exclude lesser breeds like the colored, orientals, and perhaps East Europeans) and stressed the necessity of industrial unionism.

The election of 1912 not only presented a breach in the ranks of the Republicans, it also presented a renovated Democratic party. Woodrow Wilson's platform included a great many social reform planks. When Wilson was elected, he believed (as did a majority of the Congress) that a mandate for reform had been given. The New Freedom (as his program was called) absorbed many of the ideas that the Socialists had espoused. Thus at the same time Wilson was adopting many of their objectives, he was giving erstwhile Socialists a reason to vote for one of the established parties. Many Socialists seized the opportunity; the obvious result was a decimation of the socialist ranks. Public interest in socialist reforms as such became weaker. And because of the pacifist sentiment found among many socialist leaders, America's growing participation in the Allies' military efforts intensified public antipathy toward them. It often spilled over to cover socialism, as well. And the unions, like most institutions in a democratic society, tended to absorb the prevailing sentiment (whenever possible). The shift served to confirm and even exacerbate the unions' support of Gompers' antisocialism.

But within the union movement there was also after World War I a change in attitude toward the brotherhood-of-man concept, as it applied to unionism. The great increases in unions' ranks during World War I occurred in war industries (building, shipbuilding, munitions, and textiles) and on the railroads. The attempts to make these increases permanent generally failed in the former group. A bitter lesson was learned. Though there were advantages to large numbers (emphasizing the brotherhood of man) in a given union, the disadvantages often outweighed the advantages. The sense of individual identity got lost, and many of the new members were at best halfhearted in their enthusiasm for unionism.

Moreover, the conditions that brought about the increase in unionism—principally, prosperity—actually served as a substitute for unionism in many industries. If an individual was badly treated by his employer, he could get another job easily; employers knew this was so and consequently tended to be more considerate in their treatment of their employees. If an employer refused a pay raise, another employer, short of labor, usually agreed to the demand unless the demands were beyond the pale. Employers knew this to be true also, and consequently were relatively generous in granting pay raises. It is perhaps wise to add that pay raises were often granted in a variety of ways; overtime was increased, rates were hiked, and upgrading of positions (promotion) was easy. In any event, the sense of solidarity of workers and the belief that unions should be the sword of the working class did not come to be a popular doctrine, and many of the worst social conditions that might have been expected to drive workers to unionism were alleviated by the impact of labor shortage. It was a case where reform was accomplished by the action of the market rather than by pressure group activity.

Yet there were those who felt these should have been popular doctrines. The history of the left-wing labor movement during the 1920's is an interesting one. However, it attracted little mass support, and if it has a colorful history, much of the color is in the literature (principally in ballads) it produced.

## The Benefit/Cost Theory

There is another theory of unionism, quite "economics"-oriented. This theory, made somewhat popular by Sidney and Beatrice Webb in England and by Professor George E. Barnett in this country, suggests that unionism is an institution that workers embrace when it serves to achieve easily the ends they want. In so far as unions lead to pay raises, job security, and status, workers will embrace them. It is quite apparent that at the beginning of the 1920's, many workers thought that unions could bring them the things they wanted. They supported unions' programs in the steel industry, in the metal trades, in the transportation field, and elsewhere. However, it soon became apparent that unionism was far from successful in these areas. Better deals could be made if one dealt directly with a welfare-oriented employer (i.e., an employer believing in the American Plan). Thus it was logical for workers to reconsider the old question regarding the usefulness of union membership. Professor Barnett, for one, came to conclude that political enactment was a preferred means for providing economic and job security. In his well-known presidential address to the American Economics Association in 1932, "American Trade Unionism and Social Insurance," he rang the death knell of unionism.

## The "Wisconsin" or "Commons-Perlman" Theory

A third theory of unionism argued that unions alone could provide the necessary job security that workers needed. It was this theory that was most thoroughly developed during the 1920's. If it was synthesized by an academician (as indeed it was), his synthesis was grasped eagerly by many of the leaders of American union organizations. When Miss Florence Thorne brought out Samuel Gompers' autobiography (she was certainly the editor, and probably the ghost writer), she used this theoretical formulation to explain Gompers' objectives. This theory, best known as the Wisconsin, or Commons-Perlman, theory, explains the development of unionism as an attempt by job-conscious workers to stabilize their "ownership" of work opportunity. The theory was developed in Professor Selig Perlman's *A Theory of the Labor Movement*. Miss Thorne incorporated the theme in her work.

What this brand of unionism suggested was that unionists were a special kind of people. They were essentially pessimistic about opportunity, but were willing to accept the mores of a capitalist society, provided that society would modify its concept of ownership to include not only land but jobs too, and then argued that unions had to exist to guarantee rights to jobs.

It would be an error to suggest that this "Wisconsin" theory of unionism was universally accepted. It would also be an error to suggest that all unions' activities could be explained by it. However, the years of disaster between 1920 and 1933 did serve to produce more evidence of the kind upon which Professor Perlman had based his analysis. Later, as conditions changed, other ideas of unionism appeared. The economic-benefit theory was certainly apparent during the New Deal renaissance of unionism. Yet the period of eclipse, namely, the 1920's, did produce something durable, if only a theoretical formulation.

Professor Robert F. Hoxie had earlier described American unions in his book *Trade Unionism in the United States* as principally "business-oriented." His notion of a business union was a union dominated by a passion for business-like efficiency. His use of the term was meant to suggest that American workers had become imbued with the businessman's mentality, which he thought particularistic rather than ideological. Unlike the Barnett kind of formulation, Hoxie's stressed the place of ideology. Thus, although in his view the typical American union was benefit/cost analysis-minded, this aspect or concern was subordinate to a more pervasive consideration: "What was its attitude toward general social reform?" General social reform, he concluded, did not "pay off," and for that reason American unions tended to eschew all opportunities to improve the lot of the public generally and of the working class in particular. There were those who claimed that the job-conscious theory of unionism was simply a rendering of the business-unionism that they believed Hoxie described. Such a conclusion was not warranted. The union theory that emerged attempted to explain not only why unions had to exist (according to the Hoxie formulation, if "no-union" paid off better than any union, then no-union would be used) but it also tried to explain the reason for the essential conservation of labor organizations—namely, the dependence upon the concept of property.

## V.  A Retrospective View

### Summary

At the outset we considered some of the many things unions can do. In brief, they serve as protective organizations, business organizations, reform organizations, simple cluster organizations with specific purposes, and the working face of a social movement. In two of the substantive sections of this paper we have considered the record and some of the reasons for it. Let us now very briefly ask what, if anything, provided the services that unions sought to furnish.

*Protective aspects.*—Though it is said frequently that in the 1920's employees had to depend upon the employers' favor, which is implicitly no protection at all, there were then (as now) two elements that kept some (even many) employers from being capricious and overbearing. The first was custom; for if an employer is overly greedy or immoral, his reputation suffers, and a poor reputation can in time hurt him. The second was the market; for if an employer drove away employees by his inconsiderateness, he had to replace them with others who required training, and training cost him money. Thus, in principle, there were checks on the employer. In the face of the record, however, these checks were ineffective. So there was no substitute for the relative job protection unions offered. In other countries arbitration was used: it didn't usually work well, but it was something. Here there was all but nothing. By the end of the 1920's the idea of giving unionism a try (i.e., preventing employers from throttling it) was gaining popularity.

*Business aspects.*—What raised wages and handled such grievances as were processed was some employers' willingness to see that it was the ratio of value added to labor cost that was important rather than simple hourly or weekly rates of pay. America became an even higher wage economy than it had been because the scientific-management people and those influenced by the personnel administration movement had relatively open minds regarding wages and career opportunities. Although the economic position of many workers did not suffer consequently, not as much can be said for their political and social rights. Companies dictated what products they had to buy (each major auto manufacturer's employees learned by violence what would happen if they bought a competitor's products). Companies dictated what friends they could not have (union sympathizers, for example). As for the efficiency of the system, morality and market allocation do work; but they work neither quickly nor thoroughly. However, if one considers how inefficient unions became (as suggested in the discussion), the difference between the abstract forces of conscience and cost (on the one hand) and external union representation (on the other) were not great. Neither worked well, and by the end of the period, it was clear that unions possibly might work economically, but only if given an opportunity to grow. Not all employers agreed, as was to be expected, but the trend was in the direction of trying unionism—if only to forestall more radical possibilities.

*Reform organizations.*—Although there have always been many socialist and other reform unions, they have not prospered in American soil, fertilized as it has been by federalism and only slightly irrigated by the traditional astringent interpretations of common-law precedence over liberal Constitutional construction. American unions operated best when the reforms they proffered were grafted on to the native vines of increased real wages and property rights, including the right to a job unless objective (rather than subjective) factors interfered. The good economic life was preached before all else. Utopian reform, such as it was, came via the political area—i.e., the New Freedom and the New Deal; and later, the Fair Deal, the New Frontier; and now, the Great Society. Unions have in the past (and even more recently of the last decade) offered themselves as pilots for the nation in its sailing forward (we always seem to claim to be progressing in that direction); but success has not been great, and general reform, as such, has been left to the political parties or interested minority groups. The unions' role in national politics has varied. In 1924 (as in 1964) unions "could" support only one candidate. But always the problem remains—are the gains possible in the face of victory worth the losses probable in the face of defeat. Throughout the 1920's the general weakness of the federal government in matters of economic policy tipped (or perhaps should have tipped) the balance in favor of nonparticipation in political contests. Such a conclusion was similarly warranted if state government was similarly weak in economic policy matters. The reverse conclusion may now be the case because of the expansion of state and federal policy-making activities. But even where governments are active economic-policy formulators, just how unions will line up is not always clear. Yet if unions have not been leaders, neither have they been the stalwart opposition. What union leadership has had to learn is how to steer a middle course— one that neither embraces unnecessary or too soon membership-dividing reforms nor destroys the union's reputation for imaginative equity (where injustices previously existed).

*Cluster aspects.*—The lesson of unions performing non-job-connected functions for the members was not an easy one to master. Unions provided insurance benefits, ran banks, and tried to supplement their members' educational opportunities. Each of these activities had program and business aspects. How popular the programs were, of course, depended in good part on the abilities of the leaders and the cultural and personal interests of the members. The business side, however, was influenced not only by these considerations but also by some purely objective elements. Insurance programs have a technical side involving an understanding of "area of risk," "nature of risk," abandonment or protection of "individual equity," and so forth. If unions learned anything in the 1920's, they learned that although these programs could be popular with the membership and although they could provide an otherwise unmet service, technical (even professional) competence was needed. If it was to be had, some control had to be taken from the normal leadership and given to specialists. In the 1920's this transfer was on a few occasions successful; witness the early attempts at union medical clinics and homes for superannuated members. In some instances, the attempts were signal failures; the IAM, to cite one union, failed in its effort to run job-creating firms, an actuarially sound insurance program, a bank, and even a buyers' co-operative.

*Social movement aspects.*—If the period of the 1920's showed anything clearly, it showed that there was no effective substitute for unionism as the voice of workers protecting their job- and wage-gains. Although it is true that many workers did not like the terms in which these gains were protected, it was clearly apparent that the solution lay in revising the unions' policies rather than in developing an alternative institution. The need for brevity does not permit elaboration of this point, but it can be found in much of the labor literature on scientific management, personnel administration, and in the partial "successor" to both, the "human relations" approach.

## The Key Problems at the End of the Period

Obviously the most important problem that faced American labor at the end of the 1920's and at the beginning of the New Deal was how to increase the size of its ranks. How could unions organize—should they be industrially oriented, should they be large, should they have national or local control, should they be job-conscious or economic reform–conscious? Disagreement about these factors led ultimately to the formation of the Committee for Industrial Organization.

A problem of almost equal importance was how to overcome employer hostility. In an effort to overcome it, unions came to accept the role of continual governmental intervention in labor disputes—even in purely juris-dictional matters. This idea was first proposed by Democratic Senator Robert Wagner of New York and later was administered, with both pro- and antiunion consequences, by the National Labor Relations Board. The extent to which unions and the labor movement should endorse one political instrument, the national Democratic party, was a natural result of unions relying on govern-mental intervention. In 1936 John L. Lewis, perhaps the most dynamic labor leader of the inter–World War period, abandoned his traditional membership in the Republican party to campaign not only for President Franklin D. Roose-velt but for the candidates whom Roosevelt had endorsed. Lewis' later disillu-sionment was swift and complete. But the question of unionism's political alliances remained afterwards.

There was also the problem of replacing old leadership. In many cases by this time, the old-timers were dead. A new generation appeared and replaced some of the stalwarts by then in the pantheon of unionism. Not all the new leaders were permanent, but many established great reputations and records. Tied up with, but by no means tied to, this problem of leadership was the evil of racketeering elements in many union organizations. It is not hard to cite an impressive list of unions that had fallen prey to greedy individuals who used the control of the labor market that unions could exercise for their own selfish ends.

Finally, there was the problem of accumulation of revenue. The unions ended the period with small treasuries, little hope for financial improvement in a situation, and levels of operation far below anything approaching optimal effectiveness. Left to their own pecuniary resources, it was probable that most unions could not achieve very rapid improvement in their situations. This is one of the reasons that explains the turning to governmental assistance.

### Significance of the 1920's for the 1960's

There are several ways in which the 1920's throw light on the present labor movement. The recent variety of rates of growth and of technological change in the various sectors of American industry and the shift from unionized to nonunionized areas and industries in the country have great similarities to the situation in the 1920's. If the personnel management program of the Standard Oil Company was used then as a model for antiunionism, the unwillingness of the personnel of the International Business Machines Corporation to join unions today has some points of similarity. In the one case, of course, the management was patently antiunion; in the present case the management cannot be patently anything; but the fact is that the workers now have not elected to use unionism as the preferred method for representation of their interests.

Whereas earlier industry grew most rapidly in open-shop localities like Detroit, Cincinnati, or Los Angeles, today the most rapidly developing industrial areas are the Southeast and the "desert states" of Arizona and New Mexico. If the areas that grow fastest economically are antiunion, the portent for union growth is perforce discouraging.

If high real wages plus regular increases without union pressure made workers happy in the 1920's, the same formula seems to work today. Whereas once production operatives, greenhands and/or women workers, seemed hostile to unions and no formula for organizing them seemed to work, so today many white-collar workers remain hostile—or, at best, indifferent—toward unionism.

Once again, unions have the problem of maintaining adequate revenue. The costs of representation have climbed increasingly as dependence upon economists and lawyers, rather than lay bargainers, has increased. The membership of one union after another has shown a reluctance to increase union revenue; and where they have agreed to do so, the agreement has often been accompanied by marked dissatisfaction with the personnel who demanded it.

Again, we have problems of allegedly jaded leadership. In the past few years several key union leaders have lost control of their organizations. But the problem of leadership is not simply a question of its jaded quality. Federal and state legislation has worked to make unions "more democratic." Leaders are no longer able to restrain impetuous rank-and-file dissidents. If it was purportedly the intent of those who framed the legislation to make unions democratic, frequently that end was achieved at the cost of union stability.

It is on the philosophical, ideological, or theoretical level where unionissm today best parallels unionism in the 1920's. Critics of the AF of L in the 1920's derided the philosophy that the leading AF of L unions embraced, namely, job-consciousness. Today, among the most active and successful unions are those that appear most to lack the reform idealism, so dear to the hearts of those who study the labor movement. The teamsters, the operating engineers, and even the dying railroad brotherhoods, all are principally concerned with their own parochial interests—principally, the protection of job rights. There are those who decry this emphasis and urge the labor movement to stand for something more. Nonetheless, a reading of the history of the 1920's suggests that it is this very parochialism that is the hard core of the labor movement. At least, it is arguable that that aspect has not changed.

SELECTED BIBLIOGRAPHY

Barnett, George Ernest, "American Trade Unionism and Social Insurance," *American Economic Review,* XXIII (1933), 1–15.

Galenson, Walter. *The CIO Challenge to the AFL: A History of the American Labor Movement.* Cambridge, Mass., 1960.

Gompers, Samuel. *Seventy Years of Life and Labor.* New York, 1925.

Gregory, Charles O. *Labor and the Law.* New York, 1961.

Harrington, Michael, "The Retail Clerks," in *Studies of Comparative Union Governments for the Center for the Study of Democratic Institutions,* ed. Walter Galenson. New York, 1962.

Holland, Thomas, "The Labor Management Conferences." 1950. Privately circulated.

Horowitz, Morris A., "The Structure and Government of the Carpenters," in *Studies of Comparative Union Governments for the Center for the Study of Democratic Institutions,* ed. Walter Galenson, New York, 1962.

Hoxie, Robert F. *Trade Unionism in the United States.* New York, 1917.

Kaufman, Jacob J. *Collective Bargaining in the Railroad Industry.* New York, 1954.

Kramer, Leo, "Labor's Paradox: The American Federation of State, County, and Municipal Workers, AFL–CIO," in *Studies of Comparative Union Governments for the Center for the Study of Democratic Institutions,* ed. Walter Galenson. New York, 1962.

Lecht, Leonard A. *Experience under Railway Labor Legislation.* New York, 1955.

Mason, Alpheus Thomas. *William Howard Taft: Chief Justice.* New York, 1965.

Perlman, Mark, "Democracy in the International Association of Machinists," in *Studies of Comparative Union Governments for the Center for the Study of Democratic Institutions,* ed. Walter Galenson. New York, 1962.

———. *Judges in Industry: A Study of Labour Arbitration in Australia.* Carleton, Victoria, Australia, 1954.

———. *Labor Union Theories in America: Background and Development.* Evanston, Ill., 1958.

———. *The Machinists: A New Study in American Trade Unionism.* Cambridge, Mass., 1961.

Perlman, Selig. *A Theory of the Labor Movement.* New York, 1949 printing.

———, and Taft, Philip. *Labor Movements.* (*History of Labor Movements in the United States, 1862–1932,* Vol. IV.) New York, 1935.

Rayback, Joseph G. *A History of American Labor.* New York, 1959.

Romer, Sam, "The International Brotherhood of Teamsters: Its Governmental Structure," in *Studies of Comparative Union Governments for the Center for the Study of Democratic Institutions,* ed. Walter Galenson. New York, 1962.

Rothbaum, Melvin, "The Government of the Oil, Chemical, and Atomic Workers' Union," in *Studies of Comparative Union Governments for the Center for the Study of Democratic Institutions,* ed. Walter Galenson. New York, 1962.

Sayles, Leonard R., and Strauss, George. *The Local Union: Its Place in the Industrial Plant.* New York, 1953.

Seidman, Joel, "The Brotherhood of Railroad Trainmen: The Internal Political Life of a National Union," in *Studies of Comparative Union Governments for the Center for the Study of Democratic Institutions,* ed. Walter Galenson. New York, 1962.

Stieber, Jack, "Governing the UAW," in *Studies of Comparative Union Governments for the Center for the Study of Democratic Institutions,* ed. Walter Galenson. New York, 1962.

Taft, Philip. *The A.F. of L. from the Death of Gompers to the Merger.* New York, 1959.

———. *Organized Labor in American History.* New York, 1964.

———. *The Structure and Government of Labor Unions.* Cambridge, Mass., 1954.

Tannenbaum, Frank A., *A Philosophy of Labor.* New York, 1951.

Ulman, Lloyd, "The Government of the Steel Workers' Union," in *Studies of Comparative Union Governments for the Center for the Study of Democratic Institutions,* ed. Walter Galenson. New York, 1962.

Witte, Edwin E. *The Government in Labor Disputes.* New York, 1932.

Wolman, Leo. *Ebb and Flow in Trade Unionism.* New York, 1936.

# CHAPTER 23

## Unionism and Community Values

*This is a chapter drawn from the Harvard book on the International Associa-*
*tion of Machinists. The book had three parts: the first two dealt with the*
*episodic history of the union's Grand Lodge (the parent administration) and a*
*quantitative and organizational analysis. The last (third) part offered general-*
*ization essays on the union's association with the employers, with other*
*unions, and with the general (political) community.*

*Writing during the heyday of American unionism (the late 1950s), I*
*believed that unions were too conscious of their public profile and too little*
*aware of the need for internal morale building. I surely did not foresee the*
*coming impact of environmentalism, of general capital substitution through*
*computerization of production, and of the impact of the internationalization of*
*product and factor markets associated with the speed of jet travel and tran-*
*sistorized communication.*

To what degree can a union be independent of the community to which it
belongs? In other words, "can a union afford to ignore public opinion?" Or
even, "should a union reflect the value systems of its members or the value
systems of the community at large?" This chapter attempts to put a discussion
of these questions in the context of the history of the IAM.

Before turning to the questions we have raised, it is desirable to consider
two basic points. First, popular opinion, as the term is generally used, is
frequently only a rhetorical phrase used by those who do not wish to identify
the source of their views. When put to a test, the alleged popular opinion
appears to be little more than the convictions of a few individuals. Second,
union policy is usually more than the prejudice of a leader; it is generally the
result of a serious conviction on the part of union leadership and its bureaucratic machine that some particular purpose is best served in a particular way.
Because unions are made up of numerous individuals and factions, developed
policies usually represent workable compromises. Consequently, in those in-

From *The Machinists: A New Study in American Trade Unionism* by Mark Perlman (Cambridge, Mass.: Harvard University Press, 1961) 269–87.

stances where it can be said that a union has a consistent policy, what is meant is that either all factions are more or less content with the devised program, or that one faction within the union has managed to become dominant. Naturally, it does not follow that a union policy need be morally right or economically sound. It suffices simply that it represents, possibly, in the short run, the most practical approach in terms of the alternatives open to union leadership. Putting this matter in another way, most union policies generally require some degree of membership cooperation. No leader, irrespective of his moral failings, would try to implement an unpopular policy, if he could equally easily implement a popular one.

This chapter considers three aspects of the problem of the relationship of the IAM to the community at large. The first part considers the attitude of the grand lodge toward political activity on the national level; the second is concerned with the grand lodge's attitude toward certain "social menaces"; and the third is an estimate of the present position of the IAM in modern American community life.

## The IAM and Political Action

In the previous chapter we discussed why the IAM concentrated on collective bargaining. In this chapter we are considering the obverse side of the same question, namely, why has the IAM changed its attitude from time to time toward political action. Generally the IAM's attitude has been based on three separate considerations: social, economic, and political. The social consideration is the desire to improve the social structure of the United States quickly and efficiently. No better way for this seems to exist than reform of some governmental policies and legislation. The second consideration, the economic, involves an estimate of the advantages to be gained by political activity as compared with collective bargaining activity. In other words, for a given amount of resources expended on political action, will the results be better, equal, or less than the results from collective bargaining? The cost of engaging in a political campaign can be relatively easily determined. And if the candidate is fully committed and will give you whatever you need or want, it might be worth calculating the odds. What we are suggesting is that when the cost of a political program is approximately the same as the cost of a collective bargaining program, the union will choose whichever produces better results; but, if the cost of a political program seems to be very, very small and the possible gains tremendously large, even though the calculated probability of victory is also small, the union may be willing to gamble. Finally, a union will engage in political activity up to the point where its return compared to its cost is about the same as a comparable input–output relationship would be in collective bargaining activity. We call this the economic analysis of political action, because it is based on a belief that the union will use political activity as an alternative, where it is economically feasible. Unlike the social approach, which assumes political action to be the *sine qua non* of progress, the economic approach makes the choice of a policy simply a question of the more satisfactory alternative.

The third or "political" reason for the IAM's engaging in political activity on the national level, relates to its own internal political process. So long as the national political arena is important, and only the grand lodge can cope with it, engaging in national political action may have the effect of increasing grand lodge authority and strength. No less important, of course, is the opportunity that engaging in national politics furnishes the personal ambitions of various grand lodge leaders. They become, in short order, national figures mentioned in the newspapers, and are consulted by other national leaders.

These three factors constitute the basis of our analysis of the reasons for IAM political activity. In citing them, we have indicated some of the ways in which political action can be used advantageously. For instance, with friends in the government it is possible to change the public policy with regard to collective bargaining. An example of this occurred during the Wilson administration, when support from the White House helped the IAM and other unions to gain such recognition as was contained in the Clayton Anti-Trust Act. Again the same thing occurred during the Roosevelt administration, at the time of the passage of the Wagner Act.

The disadvantages of this reliance upon politics for social engineering are of course legion. The government which passed the Clayton Act was unable to enforce the act; that is, an unsympathetic Supreme Court held the relevant clauses of the act to be meaningless and therefore invalid. The prounion Congress that passed the Wagner Act later became antiunion and passed the Taft-Hartley Act. A third reason why resort to politics has not been successful relates to the "tarring" of the organization. For example, if the IAM chooses to support a Democratic candidate or a Democratic slate of candidates, and the Republican candidate or that slate of candidates wins the election, the IAM is "tarred" and can in the future only look forward to reaping the results of its miscalculation. For this reason, the IAM has frequently eschewed social reform by political action. The reasoning expressed at different times is discussed below.

The political disadvantages of involvement in national matters are fairly easy to comprehend. Frequently, engagement in national political life involves decision making that divides the IAM. For instance, how does the IAM feel about extending reciprocal trade powers to the President? On the one hand, national foreign relations require that imports into the United States be expanded and that tariff laws be softened, on the other hand, reductions in the tariffs on IAM-produced equipment will lead to short-term, if not long-run, unemployment for IAM members. It is no answer to say that the IAM need not have an official opinion in these matters; frequently engagement in political life requires that stands be taken even when it would be preferable to remain silent. This naturally leads to division within the IAM. Some members fear the effects of the given piece of legislation more than they fear the effects of no legislation; other members, motivated by a strong sense of public responsibility, wish their organization to come out categorically for a particular measure even if it means some loss to other IAM members.

It is apparent that each year the factors must be weighed anew. At one time it may be socially desirable to engage in political activity simply for an ideological reason. Regardless of the economic cost, it is the responsibility of free men to take a political stand in favor of issues, popular or otherwise. At the same time the economic costs must be clearly viewed, and the individual must compare the advantages gained with the costs incurred. It does not follow that if the advantages seem small and the costs great, that the union should refrain from political activity. To do so would be to say that the economic factor is all-important, which it is not; and it also disregards the element of chance in a great return on a very small investment. Free men because they value their freedom, may not look at short-run costs; instead, they will be concerned with larger issues which may, as in the case of the third factor, divide the union politically.

In reviewing the history of the IAM's attitude toward politics, it is useful to point out that the social approach was most popular during the early administrations and the Johnston administration. During the Talbot–Creamer–O'Day period the "Southern influence," with its dedication to moral improvement, implied an interest in national political questions. This influence, and that of the old "Knights of Labor," made the membership of the IAM particularly eager to discuss all sorts of social topics. For instance, in 1890 there was an editorial in the journal which said,[1] "We have always looked forward to the day when the working people of America would rise up in their own might and shake off the political yoke of all parties and place a representative from their number in the chair of Washington." This was not an isolated, Socialistic outburst; quite the contrary, it was the expression of the desire on the part of the "common men" for turning the government over to one of their own. From 1895 through 1896, the journal discussed the important question of the day, the free coinage of silver.

Starting in the period, 1898–1899, the interest in Socialism grew rather rapidly. For instance, at the 1899 convention there was a proposal that the local lodges should educate their members in the problems of the "class struggle," so that it would be easier to combine to advance class interests, in order to take over the government of the country.[2] Instead, the law committee recommended that the IAM should stimulate the political education of its members to understand their political rights, and to use the ballot intelligently in their respective political parties, so that the government might be for and by the people and not simply exist as a tool to further the strength of management. At the 1901 convention, there was a resolution, rejected by the committee and by the convention itself, that the machinists' union declare itself for Socialism. The wording of the proposal concluded: "be it resolved that the machinists in international convention assembled, unqualifyingly declare themselves in favor of Socialism, the cooperative commonwealth, as being the means whereby the worker will ever obtain the full fruits of labor." The Resolutions Committee recommended that the motion be rejected because as it said, "the time [was] not quite opportune for the adoption of such a measure." However, by the 1903 convention the Socialists were beginning to develop more strength. Their increased prestige was undoubtedly associated with the falling prestige of the anti-Socialists, particularly O'Connell. The change was brought about first by the relative failure of the NMTA strike and by the change in the government attitude toward unionism. At the 1903 convention the preamble of the constitution was changed to stress the existence of a class struggle, and to encourage members' activities along the lines of restoring the control of the government to the people, and using the national resources for the common welfare of all the people.

Two years later, at the 1905 convention, the Socialists actually proposed that every union meeting should devote some time to the study of Socialist theory. This proposal, again perhaps reflecting an upward change in the fortunes of the O'Connell group, was not endorsed. During these years a considerable debate on the question of political activity, viewed as a social responsibility, raged in the journal, probably because it was popular in many other circles in the American community. Besides, D. D. Wilson, the popular editor of the journal, himself appears to have been actively sympathetic to the Socialist cause. Finally, in 1911 with the defeat of the O'Connell group, the IAM seemed to have embraced the doctrine that there was a basic social responsibility to participate in political action. At that time it seemed to most observers that the IAM was exhibiting its interest in Socialism; however, the election of President Wilson was to show that the interest in political activity and social reform contained within it an element of economic analysis. That is, the leadership of the IAM quickly turned from the support of Socialists to the support of the New Freedom and Wilson. This change was further developed during World War I when Wilson and his administration consciously furthered the interests of IAM.

After World War I the leaders of the IAM were appalled by the possibility that American railroads would be turned back to their antiunion employers. They preferred to have the railroads remain in friendly governmental hands, as had been the case since the seizure in 1917. President Johnston became one of the leading officials of the Plumb Plan League and sought Congress' endorsement of the plan to nationalize ownership of the railroads. It would seem that Johnston's reason for advocating political control of the railroads was based as much on economic considerations as it was based on a belief in Socialism. By the time the Plumb Plan was debated, it was apparent that the government had made the life of unionists on the railroad relatively easy compared to what had transpired previously. Anyway, whatever Johnston's motivation, he took an active role in national politics. At the 1920 convention, he announced that all the evils facing unionism could be remedied without force, if the ballots were properly and intelligently used. At the same time, Johnston took care to dissociate his views from those of the political radicals of the hour. Also, in 1920 the IAM donated one cent per member to the AFL's national partisan political campaign fund, organized to elect pro-labor members of Congress.[3]

The period, 1920–1924, when the railroads set out systematically to destroy their shopcraft unions, and the government stood idly by, served to convince Johnston that there was no hope in using either of the two established political parties. As a result he took an active part in the Progressive Party campaign of the La Follette–Wheeler ticket. It is possible that Johnston was convinced that political action was a public responsibility, regardless of the possibility of success. It is further possible that he actually believed that the La Follette–Wheeler ticket had a real chance of success, and for the amount of resources that the IAM devoted, its possible returns would have been tremendous. More likely, Johnston's position was the result of his personal belief that the leader of the IAM was a national figure, and that it was incumbent upon him to take a stand. In any event, he and the general executive board succeeded in getting the IAM to endorse the La Follette–Wheeler ticket. The resulting defeat did not strengthen Johnston's position within the union.[4]

Arthur Wharton succeeded to the presidency at a time when political action had been more or less thoroughly discredited. It is equally true that the method of collective bargaining had not proved to be very successful, but compared to political action, it was certainly superior. Wharton appeared to avoid all political activities. This does not mean that the IAM was indifferent to political questions. Quite the contrary, the IAM subscribed to *Labor*.[5] It also favored public unemployment insurance plans, despite the opposite stand of the AFL.[6] Emmet Davison, the general secretary–treasurer, was an active political figure in the Democratic Party of Virginia.[7] And there were many others who maintained active political careers. Our point is simply that Arthur Wharton, on the whole, felt neither the urge as a citizen to engage in a political career in a big way, nor did he believe that the method of legal enactment (that is, systematically engaging in politics to solve one's problems by enactment of laws) "paid off." That he himself may have had doubts, is contained in a memorandum he sent out in 1937. Noting that the Democratic Party was trying to raise $200,000 to clear its debts, he informed the council members that he had personally contributed $200 and reminded them that the IAM itself had not contributed anything to Roosevelt's 1932 or 1936 campaigns. He concluded with the statement that "there are few of the larger labor organizations that have not made some contributions." He asked the council to reconsider its previous position.[8]

When General Vice-President Fechner was asked to become a member of the Roosevelt administration, Arthur Wharton saw no reason to dissuade him. However, Fechner was not allowed to function within the IAM while holding and carrying out the responsibilities of national office. Earlier, we indicated that in our judgment Arthur Wharton miscalculated the importance of governmental activity in shaping the development of American industrial relations after 1935. Fortunately, there were within the organization those who saw in the Roosevelt administration staunch support, and who were willing to engage in politics in order to maximize the IAM's position. Wharton managed to maintain nominal control of the organization, although it is apparent that his voice became less dominant in the private circles of leadership.

Both Harvey Brown and Albert Hayes realized that the day of relatively complete eschewal of political activity had passed. The government played far too great a role in the practice of American industrial relations, and the destiny of the grand lodge was far too dependent upon the role it played in the relationship with the government to permit the leaders of the IAM to be indifferent to general political questions. In other words, the political approach made it mandatory to engage in political activities, regardless of whether there was some ideological basis for so doing. It is entirely natural for the IAM to take a stand with regard to national political office and candidates, and, moreover, the IAM has even found it mandatory to have opinions on such diverse questions as pension rights, health plans, international trade issues, and foreign affairs. Whether in the long run IAM participation in political matters will prove divisive remains to be seen. It is highly probable that some negative effects will be observed.

The long-run consequences of the post-1935 developments have been to strengthen the grand lodge at the expense of local autonomy. Once the federal government chose to play a dominant role in the allocation of jurisdiction as well as the handling of certain grievances (i.e., unfair labor practices), it became almost certain that the grand lodge's powers would have to be augmented. The grand lodge, alone among the organizational units within the IAM, is equipped to handle the problems of federal government relationships. This is not to suggest that problems of state and local government relationship cannot exist, and that they are not best handled by state conferences or local lodges. But insofar as the national picture is concerned, grand lodge interest in political activity has certainly come to stay. The costs may be very great, the advantages may grow comparatively less, but as far as one can see, there is little likelihood of a return to the attitude expressed by Wharton during the latter part of the 1920's, when he in effect announced that political activity was an incubus sucking untold financial resources as well as considerable membership loyalty from the IAM.[9]

Whether in the long run the IAM can afford to be fully identified with one political party, namely, the Democrats, remains to be seen. Recently it is true that the Republican party has leaned over backward to gain union support. Should at some time either major political party stop courting labor, as would be the case if certain segments within the Republican Party were to become dominant, then the IAM would have to reconsider its whole method of political participation.

In brief, the IAM's attitude toward political involvement has at different times reflected one or more of the three determinants. Generally, the economic approach (comparing the costs and the returns of using politics and other approaches) seems to have been the most important, although the roles of the other two, social reform, and national recognition, are far from negligible. In a market society, which to a great degree America is, it is natural that the economic approach should be the principal one. But one should not sell the idealism of social reform short; granted it has been dominant only at intervals, but its presence at other times may be strong enough to influence actions, if not to motivate them. The third approach, that concerning the union's concept of its own political importance as a national institution, has become, if anything, more, rather than less important as the union has become larger and as the grand lodge has achieved greater interorganizational importance. Considered analytically, however, it is the economics of using political means, which basically conditions the IAM's policies. So long as the important relationships remain the ones between employers and the union, the IAM will favor the direct collective bargaining approach over that of legal enactment.

## Public Relations and Social Menaces

No problem has been harder for the IAM to master than that of handling dissident internal groups. Within the IAM there is a wide range of opinion regarding the desirability of extending union benefits to what are considered marginal or "inferior" groups. Facing this dilemma has been postponed on many occasions, when compromises have been found, as in the 1895 revision of the constitution, when the anti-Negro clause was technically deleted. Again, at the turn of the century the benefits of unionism were extended to specialists, but only after they had in fact been admitted. Even then, there were long debates prior to the formal action, and when the action was taken, it represented a compromise. Viewed from the inside, the lengthy arguments and the repeated ballots resulted in the optimum practical resolution, because by the time the "outsiders" were accepted, they came in with few, if any, complaints. Viewed from the outside, the delay in final action was both discriminatory and shortsighted.

To the members, the marginal group is a menace and has to be treated with suspicion. The burden of assimilation of an "inferior" group obviously rests upon the institution which competes with them. It is fairly easy for social reformers to urge that unions accept all individuals who apply for membership. However, if those who join the union are unwilling to adapt to the union's customs, the union will be weakened by their affiliation. A second point not to be overlooked is that the acceptance of an "inferior" group often results in the development of schisms in the union. For instance, it seemed reasonable to believe that accepting Negroes as members would have resulted in the secession of many southern white members. On the other hand, the union was forced to a choice; if did not accept Negro members, the Negroes would have no alternative but to try to undersell the union and take jobs away from union members; if it did accept them, the disaffected white members would try to undercut the union's position and destroy it. The union could only select the lesser evil, realizing the while that this selection represented a very unsatisfactory resolution. Nothing better illustrates this point than the long series of debates between 1893 and 1948 on the subject of admitting Negroes to formal membership. The point was repeatedly made that unless the Negroes were admitted, the union would suffer economically. Yet, when the vote was taken, the majority of the convention delegates regularly voted to retain the discriminatory clause. They did so, not only because several of them sincerely objected to the inclusion of colored members, but because they feared even more the actions of the die-hard anti-Negro members.

In Chapter II we discussed how the anti-Negro clause was shifted from the constitution to the ritual in order to keep it from public view. We could have added that the clause was also used to keep out Orientals (Chinese), but the point was that the ritual had become the declaration of principle for the southern locals. O'Connell had little use for the ritual as it was practiced.[10] To him its historical origins made it seem somewhat unnecessary, particularly since the IAM contained many Roman Catholics to whom the whole business was distasteful. O'Connell noted on several occasions that the ritual was greatly in need of revision and, more to the point, could be dispensed with entirely (as was actually the case in several lodges), without detrimental effect.

In November 1918, it may be recalled in another context from Chapter

VII, District Lodge 46 (Toronto) sought to amend the ritual through referendum vote, in order to strike from it the offending whites-only clause. This use of the referendum instrument was challenged immediately, and the issue was put before the general executive board. President Johnston and all the members of the board, except General Secretary–Treasurer Davison, supported the Toronto proposal.[11] Nonetheless the issue was not voted upon. Instead, at the 1920 convention the matter was considered, and after considerable debate the IAM's position was left unchanged.[12]

No further move was taken to amend the ritual with regard to the race point until the 1936 convention, where the majority of the Committee on the Ritual recommended that the whole matter be turned over to the discretion of the executive council. The committee's minority report proposed the elimination of the offending clause in order to facilitate the organization of New York City transport workers. The convention was unwilling to authorize either line of action; instead, it tabled both reports. Thus by the 1930's the ritual had become more than anything else a racist declaration. Its original purpose of creating a sense of moral dedication seems to have been all but lost, although to be sure some aspects of the ritual, like the taking of the obligation (agreeing to abide by the customs and rules of the craft), were still presented with simple dignity.

At the 1940 convention the whole question was again raised, when it developed some legal overtones.[13] New York and Pennsylvania had passed Fair Employment Practices Acts, which many delegates felt made the retention of the offending clause illegal. Among these delegates, there was some division as to the most desirable course of action. Some, like Anthony Ballerini (San Francisco Local Lodge 1327), believed that the IAM ought to take Negroes in and say nothing about it. Others said that the Fair Employment Practice Commissions laws were probably unconstitutional, and that the IAM should test them. Still others asked that the executive council determine the policies to be followed in the different state jurisdictions. General Secretary–Treasurer Davison, who was a southerner, told the convention that it did not really much matter what was voted; each local would probably do pretty much as it wanted anyway. The convention chose to retain the offending clause, and to authorize the executive council to make a test case of the Fair Employment Practice Commission laws, if thought wise.

Throughout the twenties, the thirties, and the mid-forties the IAM executive council piously announced that the IAM was not opposed to the employment of Negroes in industry; it merely did not want them as members. This position, of course, fooled no one and, when during World War II President Roosevelt appointed a President's Committee on Fair Employment Practices, it was inevitable that complaints would arise. They did. As early as 1941 Mark Ethridge, chairman of the President's Committee, wrote to the executive council citing reports about discriminatory treatment against Negroes in the San Francisco and Los Angeles areas. Davison replied for the council saying that it "is familiar with the general conditions throughout the country, and knows that there are many thousands of Negroes employed in defense industry, and that there have been for a number of years many thousands of Negroes employed in industry connected with the machine industry that are represented [*sic*] by the IAM. It is not now, and never has been the policy of the IAM to interfere with the employment of Negroes in industry." This answer, as might have been expected, satisfied neither Ethridge, nor those who had complained to him. The executive council then told the two locals in California against whom complaints had been filed (Local Lodge 68 and District Lodge 727) to act in accordance with the President's executive order. What that meant is not clear. From later records, it appears that District Lodge 727 accepted the Los Angeles Negroes as members, and that Local Lodge 1327 "saved the day" by admitting the San Francisco Negroes.[14] It is also clear that had Local Lodge 1327 not acted, there would probably have been a full discussion of the matter on the floor of the United States Senate.

During the war some Negro workers in St. Louis applied for membership. It was granted to them, but later withdrawn "as soon as it was discovered."[15]

The issue of dropping the whites-only clause was again fully debated at the 1945 convention, after the Committee on the Ritual voted 10 to 3 to recommend dropping the clause.[16] The matter was put to a roll call vote and was defeated 2173 to 1958. As the vote suggests, the debate was vigorous and bitter, with many speeches based completely on cultural atavisms.

Late in 1947 the executive council, on its own motion, moved to amend the ritual and to eradicate the race clause.[17] It did so, it explained to the membership, because the passage of the Taft–Hartley Act had made it necessary. Later it became clear at the 1948 convention that there were even more proximate causes.[18] At that convention, held in Grand Rapids, Indianapolis Local Lodge 511 argued that the executive council was *ultra vires* in taking the previous action. General Vice-President Melton then explained why the council had been forced to act. In two cases before the National Labor Relations Board it had come out that the ritual barred Negroes.[19] In one case the employer argued that the bar was reason to decertify the IAM as the representative of his employees; in the other case the teamsters' union suggested that it, rather than the IAM, should be given the certification. Although these cases had been much earlier, the passage of the Taft–Hartley Act had left the executive council with no option; it had to remove the clause. The Committee on the Ritual rejected the Indianapolis lodge's contention and recommended that the convention uphold the action.[20] Several bitterly anti-Negro speeches were then made from the floor; but the convention upheld the committee.

For a while there were a few all-Negro lodges chartered. In 1954 the executive council ordered such practices to stop, even though several of the Negro lodges protested.[21] Nonetheless, the council thought that the good of the organization required the abandonment of any form of racial exclusion. In practice, it is necessary to add, many lodges even in 1958 were reluctant to give up the old practice, although some, even those in Georgia, have abided by the law and are admitting members irrespective of race. The executive council supported the application of the sleeping car porters' union, an overwhelmingly Negro organization, for affiliation with the Railway Labor Executives' Association.[22]

What caused this situation to change in 1948? We have recounted the exact incident which caused the executive council to change the union policy without recourse to convention vote, but an analysis reveals three factors emerging; one was the attitude of the country as exemplified by the policies of the National Labor Relations Board, which refused to permit the IAM to discriminate as it had done for the past sixty years. The second was a realization that the union's policy, based on an old premise that the IAM was a craft union and that there were few skilled Negroes, was outmoded, and that it was no longer possible to maintain it except at great cost to the union itself. The union leadership realized that not only the National Labor Relations Board but also many locals within the union found the policy to be distasteful and would either ignore it (thereby weakening the union's internal structure) or would actually seek affiliation elsewhere. The third reason for changing the policy, reflected growing confidence of the IAM leadership in the shaping of IAM policy unilaterally. Previously, leaders had been voted out of office for less. However, since 1926 no member of the administration had ever been successfully disciplined by the rank and file. Twenty-two years of such success gave the IAM leadership a type of confidence which it could not have had at any previous period.

What then did the IAM leadership do? First, it deleted the offending clause from the ritual. Second, it permitted the establishment of colored locals, giving to colored machinists of ability some opportunity for leadership recognition. Third, it later moved to incorporate these colored locals into the established "white" locals. Thus, it quickly engineered not only the *de jure* shift, but it set out to convert this shift to a *de facto* one as well. Within a few years the shift was complete; and what the leadership had been unable to do as late as the 1945 convention was accomplished, without reference to popular membership opinion, by executive council action within three years.

It is fair at this point to ask whether the method of accomplishing this reform was democratic. Quite obviously, the duly elected convention delegates had repeatedly refused to take the action which the executive council believed both right and necessary. Thus, in a very real sense the executive council's action was undemocratic because it did not meet with the type of formal membership approval which it traditionally required. On the other hand, the earlier refusal to take in members because of their racial antecedents was also in a very real sense undemocratic, as the term is used. The leadership's earlier refusal to take the type of action which it successfully carried through in 1948, may be considered under this line of reasoning to be nothing less than support for a basically immoral, as well as undemocratic, doctrine. Certainly, it was contrary to the established moral code of the land; that is, contrary to the federal Constitution, as amended. This type of argument, however, is useless because it fails to comprehend the dynamic forces which motivate our society as well as those forces which govern union decisions. The executive council acted because the social forces requiring its action had grown to a point where they could no longer be ignored; at the same time the executive council had previously failed to act because the social forces preventing it from acting were too strong. In other words, the IAM moved when it became mandatory for it to do so. Delay would have greatly weakened the organization. Conversely, an earlier decision by executive council action would have also weakened the organization.

To act or not to act, and if so, how, when, and action by whom, are the problems of every democratic society. One of the characteristic errors in popular thinking is to confuse representative democracy with a pure democracy. Virtually all civilized institutions, if they are democratic at all, are run through some system of representative government. It is important to recognize that a society is governed not by the will of the majority, but by the will of the majority of the representatives. Selection of the representatives should under optimum conditions reflect in some way or other the confidence of the rank and file. One is then left with the question of whether one group of representatives is better qualified than another to deal with specific questions. Of course, there is a legal answer; quite frequently one group of representatives is selected to handle policy questions, while another group is selected to administer the policy. So viewed, it is entirely reasonable to conclude that the convention should have amended the ritual, rather than turning the job over to the executive council. However, to pursue one legal argument further, it is necessary to realize that the executive council exercises the prerogative in matters of ritual between conventions. This point should be stressed; in most matters the referendum is the instrument for handling the prerogative. However, the ritual cannot be changed by referendum action. Therefore, it is incumbent upon the executive council to handle problems concerning the ritual between conventions. In any event, there is some legal basis for the executive council's acting as it did. Whether the executive council had full moral sanction to make the decision is a matter of opinion; those who believe that the original basic policy was immoral, may support the action taken by the executive council. Those who believe that the decision rested upon an analysis of its strengths and weaknesses, will conclude that taking the decision at the time it was taken, was wise because to have done so earlier, or not to have done so in 1948, would have been excessively costly in both instances. However, the point that does stand out is that the representative assembly (the convention) seemed unable to take a decision which was probably economically wise and certainly morally sound.

The "menace" of radicalism has also touched the IAM. Radicalism can be understood in two senses; one refers to the beliefs of those who harbor unpopular or heretical thoughts. The other, the type with which we are presently concerned, refers to a coordinated heresy. That is, it refers to a group of heretics sharing the common belief and conviction that the union should be converted, irrespective of the technique, to their basically different viewpoint. For many years, the IAM has had many highly individualistic members, each of whom felt entitled to his own view. At no time in the union's history has there been any real attempt made to make these individualistic heretics conform. On the other hand, from time to time, these heretics have "gotten together" and tried to shape IAM policy. On such occasions the IAM, in order to protect itself, has had to take steps against them. The IAM has not been opposed to radicalism, so much as it has been opposed to conspiratorial radicalism. Again, this would not present much of a problem, were it not for the fact that the conspiratorial radicalism which emerged in the IAM emerged in other sectors of society at the same time.

During World War I, American Socialism went into a major decline. Reasons for this are relatively clear. Wilson's New Freedom drew from the old Socialist ranks many of those interested in moderate social reform. On the other hand, the internationalism which characterized the old Socialist movement became swamped with patriotic fervor. Those who embraced the belief that all men were brothers, were accused of loving "Huns" as much as they loved good, red-blooded Americans. The Socialist movement was rent by this situation. The result was a super-patriotism on the part of many of those who had previously embraced Socialist doctrine. At the end of World War I, the United States, influenced by the specter of Communist success in Russia, became more sensitive than ever to conspiratorial radicalism of a left-wing variety. The raids, conducted by United States Attorney–General Palmer, are part of our national history. Within the labor movement, both in left-wing unions like the IAM and in right-wing circles like the one surrounding Gompers, great effort was made to stress the differences between nonconspiratorial (home-grown, individualistic) radicalism and the type which was killing authorities, confiscating all property, and destroying churches abroad. International President Johnston was swept along in this tide. He was not a great admirer of the Soviet Union, primarily because he had some knowledge of the brutality of its leaders.[23] On the other hand, he was regularly charged with having "un-American sympathies." This being the situation, he was particularly sensitive to developments within his own organization which seemed to betoken the growth of radical interests.

In earlier years the union had had to take steps against those members who sought to destroy the union by excessive factionalism. These were the groups who refused to abide by the majority decision when votes were taken. These were the groups who embraced dual unionism, in the eyes of unionists, the greatest of all sins. Johnston, influenced by the antiradical sentiment rampant in America, became convinced that any person who embraced the Soviet brand of Socialism (Communism) was for that reason alone a threat to the IAM. Consequently, he directed that those identified with Russian Socialism should be charged with insurrection. The history of the trial in Toledo and the subsequent appeal at the Detroit convention is referred to in Chapter IV. The outcome of the episode was a modification of the Johnston position. He was unable to discipline his "enemies," the Toledo "reds," successfully. When Johnston left the presidency, his successor, first by executive fiat, and then by regular convention and referendum action, outlawed Communism in the IAM. The IAM, in other words, declared that membership in any Communist organization was grounds for expulsion from the IAM. The reasons for its taking this action lie in two areas. One was a true fear that the Communists were trying to take over. The other reflected a public relations attitude.

Wharton, for reasons quite different from the ones developed by Johnston, concluded that it was socially desirable for the IAM to go on record as opposed to Communism. These were different from the ones developed by Johnston because they reflected an impersonal estimate of the situation. No one charged Wharton with being a radical; on the other hand, Johnston, because of his earlier political career, was believed to be one. Neither Wharton nor Johnston were political revolutionaries; in both cases they had had some Socialist interests, but these interests reflected a traditional American Populism. Wharton, however, had never played a significant role in the Socialist movement, as had Johnston; consequently, it was not necessary for him to be "more Catholic than the Pope" nor "more royalist than the King." Nonetheless, Wharton supported the executive decree outlawing Communism in the IAM, and at the 1928 convention that executive decree was incorporated into the basic IAM law through regular convention and referendum processing.[24]

As a result of the Wharton action and the steps taken by the convention, several individuals, who during the late 1920's and during the 1930's were charged with Communism, were convicted and suspended from membership.[25] Occasionally, after having assured either Wharton or the executive council or both of their true reform, they were readmitted to membership. In any case during the period, 1930–1935, there were a few instances of disciplinary action.

When the mass production industries were organized, in many cases by individuals against whom the charge of Communist affiliation could fairly be applied, the IAM was not overly squeamish in accepting their support. It was only when these same members, more true to their political affiliation than they were to their union membership, turned against IAM leadership, that the IAM leaders brought charges of Communist radicalism against them. In due course they were suspended, and their influence was eliminated. The Communist trials in Minneapolis in 1938 and in Seattle at the Boeing Plant during the period, 1940–1942, were held for different reasons. The Minneapolis situation reflected the development of an antiadministration cabal.[26] Action was taken against the leaders, Harry Mayville and William Mauseth, because they had set out to provoke a dispute. Mauseth sought to turn the Minneapolis machinist organization over to the CIO. The executive council brought him and twenty-nine others to trial, during which Mauseth and his associates sought a court order forbidding General Vice-President Nickerson and any other grand lodge personnel from issuing what were termed slanderous statements. Only three of those brought up on charges bothered to offer any defense at the trial, which was conducted in Minneapolis by the executive council. Those three were exonerated; the rest were found guilty and expelled. The record is replete with demonstrated arguments against the program advocated by the local leaders; the result was obvious, they were expelled.

The trials in Seattle were brought about because of war department pressure.[27] The military became quite concerned with evidence of subversion in the Boeing Plant. It is now fairly clear that the subversion came both from right-wing seditionists, particularly German *Bundists,* as well as from left-wing Communists. The IAM, because of its constitutional provisions barring subversives, agreed to the FBI request to bring charges against the ring leaders and expel them from the union. Once expelled from the union, they could easily be fired, and the danger of sabotage would be past. Parenthetically, it is worth adding that the company was also asked to get rid of the *Bundists.* The IAM administration made a thorough study of the situation, brought charges against sixty members, most of whom were convicted. In 1948, reflecting the emergence of a new fear, the convention denied membership to Nazis, Fascists, and any others who supported totalitarian forms of government.[28]

One other major example of radicalism is worth considering. This was the situation in San Francisco, where the leadership of Local 68, undoubtedly radical in its political views, had entrenched itself. The struggle to discipline the leadership is described in Chapter V.

One can well ask whether the IAM was "justified" in its antiradical measures. A truly democratic society generally permits a wide range of opinion. Were those who were expelled from the IAM merely exercising their citizens' prerogative? Or were they actually conspiratorial as charged? Again the answer rests upon some basic opinions. If the IAM were truly in jeopardy, it was probably justified in eliminating the "revolutionaries." If, on the other hand, the revolutionaries were merely sacrificed to provide a "clean record," there is some reason to doubt the justice of the action. The history of Communism in the American labor movement probably confirms the view that there was real danger to the IAM, and that the IAM's action was not taken simply to gratify some popular and prejudiced opinion. Whatever may be the criticism of the arbitrariness of the IAM action, it is worth pointing out that the union proceeded only after some form of a trial. Generally these trials were fairly run, and the defense was given every opportunity to be heard. At the same time that the IAM was taking these steps, other institutions in the country such as school systems, universities, and the government were facing similar problems. Those interested in comparative processes might point to the care which the IAM exercised to ensure fair hearings, and use the IAM's record as a basis for comparing the record established by the other institutions named. The general conclusion is that the IAM's attitude toward radicalism has a factual basis. Furthermore, the IAM is justified in establishing measures to protect itself. Finally, the IAM's record in trying subversives compares favorably with the record of society at large.

### The Place of the IAM in Modern Community Life

As unionism has become more secure because of continued economic prosperity and the protective attitude taken by the federal government, many social leaders have come to recognize the importance of union cooperation in civic administration. Not only are union leaders asked to address civic functions, university seminars, and even public testimonial dinners, but they are asked also to lend their support to desirable public movements. During the two world wars, the IAM made gifts to agencies helping to entertain soldiers and sailors; it also publicized war bond drives.[29] For instance, some time during World War II and the years thereafter, many Community Drive leaders came to recognize that union cooperation often resulted in greater collections. Therefore the IAM, in common with many other unions, was frequently asked to endorse charitable drives. Sometimes the IAM responded for several reasons; for example, the March of Dimes was not only a worthy cause, but because of its association with President Roosevelt, it appeared politic to support it. In other cases, the IAM refused to lend support for similar reasons. In a few instances, the IAM was eager to give spot relief where it was needed; examples of this would be donations to the Red Cross for help in flood or disaster areas, contributions to help unionists abroad, or even contributions to deserving individuals. As the IAM became more established and wealthier, it agreed to play a larger role in community life. In the international foreign affairs field, the IAM was able to make a major contribution (discussed in Chapter V). Here it should be noted that the international president expanded the efforts which the IAM made overseas, extended its economic aid to sister organizations, and used the knowledge gained by its activities to advise political officials in Washington of developments in labor union fields.

The executive council took stands on several issues in which it felt that it had an interest. It initially opposed compulsory military training in 1945; it endorsed the Marshall Plan "with the understanding that it will not adversely affect our domestic economy"; and it directed local lodges to appoint committees to publicize cancer detection programs. In contrast, the council once declined to start a "College Scholarship Foundation" because "it was agreed that no matter how worthy it was, the fact remained that [such an effort] would not be [possible or] workable under the Association's laws and structure."

The executive council thus became more than the representative of machinists in industrial life; it became a voice in public affairs. Therefore it was natural that the council became "public-relations-conscious," and within a few years the public relations director became an important administrative aid to the international president and the executive council. This change is particularly significant, when it is realized that the traditional attitude toward the administration of the IAM policy had been internal; that is, the important opinion was that of the members, not what the public believed the policy to be. Increased dependence upon a public relations program indicated a significant shift in emphasis.

It is important to add that the development of an executive council public relations program caused some readjustments in the area of grand local lodge relationships. So long as the executive council eschewed public policy pronouncements, it could, and did, caution locals to refrain from speaking out on nonunion matters. But when the executive council switched its policy, not only was it harder to claim that only strictly union matters were to be considered on the local levels, it was hard to avoid friction over how issues were to be considered. If the executive council considered cancer detection to be a worthy cause for support, how could it claim that some other non-union-related drive, supported by local leaders, was not to be helped. The abandonment of the tradition harking back to Wharton's day of no involvement in nonvital questions, meant the opening of another area of conflict among the various levels of organization in the IAM.

Whether this shift in emphasis will continue, remains to be seen. So long as unions play an ever-increasing role in public life, it is hard to imagine the council abolishing its public relations interest. On the other hand, public relations emphasis, and attention to general public attitudes and problems, draw resources from other uses. It is important for an institution which must play both an internal or private role, and an external or public one, to strike a balance between the two. The strength of the IAM must rest upon the loyalty of its membership, but its influence will depend in good part on the wisdom of the executive council in the handling of its "public role."

NOTES

1. IAM, *Machinists' Monthly Journal*, 1890, pp. 194–5; 1896, pp. 414–15.
2. IAM, *Proceedings* 1899, pp. 350–1, 362, 1901; p. 653; 1903, pp. 434, 552, 570, 637; 1905, pp. 62–3; 1907, p. 14; 1920 pp. 6, 10–14, 37.
3. IAM General Executive Board, Proposition 299 (Feb. 21, 1920).
4. IAM, *Proceedings*, 1924, pp. 15ff.
5. See Chapter IV.
6. IAM Executive Council, Minutes, Nov. 16–24, 1931.
7. His candidacy was endorsed by the executive council when he ran for Congress in 1942; EC, Minutes, May 13–26, 1942.
8. IAM Executive Council, Proposition 441 (May 3, 1937).
9. EC, Minutes, Sept. 10–29, 1928.
10. *MMJ*, 1907, p. 969.
11. GEB, Proposition (Nov. 29, 1918).
12. IAM, *Proceedings*, 1920, pp. 207, 219, 385–6, 582; 1936, executive session (undated and not printed with regular proceedings); 1940, executive session, Sept. 27, 1940 (not printed with regular proceedings).
13. EC, Minutes, Dec. 3–12, 1940; July 18–24, 1941; Jan. 26–31, 1942.
14. IAM, *Proceedings*, 1948, closed session Sept. 21, 1948 (not printed with regular proceedings).
15. EC, Minutes, Dec. 9–17, 1943.
16. IAM, *Proceedings*, 1945, closed session Nov. 3, 5, 1945 (not printed).
17. *Circular* 487, Dec. 11, 1947.
18. IAM, *Proceedings*, 1948, closed session, Sept. 21, 1948 (not printed).
19. Norfolk and Southern Bus lines and Texas Motor Freight lines. NLRB Hearing, Case 16–R–2223, pp. 3232–3242 (Apr. 9, 1943).
20. See Note 18.
21. Letter to all grand lodge representatives and auditors, special representatives, business representatives railroad and airline general chairmen, from the general secretary-treasurer (Jan. 18, 1954).
22. EC, Minutes, July 30–Aug. 3, 1951.
23. GEB, Minutes, Apr. 5–16, 1921.
24. IAM, *Constitution*, 1929: Art. XXI, Sect. 2 and 3.
25. Case of Tim Buck: EC, Proposition 87 (Apr. 18, 1928); case of H. G. Price: EC, Proposition 84 (Mar. 5, 1928); 136 (June 5, 1930); case of William Simons: EC,

Minutes, Feb. 4–11, 1929; case of C. E. Webber: EC, Proposition 102 (May 14, 1929).

26. EC, Minutes, Sept. 14–Oct. 3, 1936; Sept. 13–19, 1937; Dec. 13–17, 1937. See also Cellar File 2, folder 55, and EC, Proposition 578 (Feb. 18, 1938).

27. See Chapter V.

28. IAM, Proceedings, 1940, closed session (not printed).

29. For instance, a gift to Father Flanagan's Boys' School was refused because such action was *ultra vires* of the council: EC, Minutes, Nov. 16–21, 1942; Nov. 17–Dec. 5, 1947; Jan. 15–27, 1951.

# CHAPTER 24

# The Impact of Government and the Social Climate on the Rise and Fall of the American Steel Industry, 1920–1980

*Bela Gold, one of that rare breed—an empirical economist with an engineering training and a capacity for generalization—became an expert on the American and Japanese steel industries. Having worked for Robert Lind (of Middletown, USA, fame) he wanted to include in a book, written with some Case-Western Reserve associates and me, a chapter on the economic sociology of the heyday and the subsequent decline of the big and small U.S. steel industry. What I wrote divided the history into five periods: (1) 1900–20, the era of managerial dominance; (2) 1920–40, the decades of struggle for union recognition; (3) 1940–45, the war period when the War Production Board had to solve the problem of maintaining a supply of workers; (4) 1940–60, the period of union heyday, but also a time not only when foreign competition was entering the product market, but also when a new kind of international travel and telephonic communications were effectively erasing the time-space barriers of what had been geographically protected markets; and (5) 1960–72, the period of "consequences," when social and governmental concern shifted from labor-management relations to concern about the social cost of environmental degradation.*

*Given my traditional focus on the problems of Genossenschaft (in the case of unions, the need to maintain member solidarity), I focused on the relationship between the federal government and the Steelworkers' Union. I stressed Harry Truman's dependence on Phillip Murray and the Steelworkers' Union and its subsequent use of governmental intervention, including the Method of Legal Enactment, as a means of getting wage and fringe benefits. The union was confident of its handling of affirmative action, but time was to show that legislation requiring massive investment in environmental cleanup equipment plus the speed of jet travel, as well as transistorized communications, made foreign steel very competitive in the American market. The union*

From *Technological Progress and Industrial Leadership: The Growth of the U.S. Steel Industry, 1900–1970* by Bela Gold, William S. Peirce, Gerhard Rosegger, and Mark Perlman (Lexington, Mass.: D. C. Heath, 1984) 609–31.

*did not realize the power of capital substitution. Our study was done in the 1980s, when the major steel firms were tottering. We realized that foreign competition with improved techniques had to be matched; we were even aware of the success of the American mini-mills, but we were writing at the nadir of the industry's fortunes. My study led me back to the views espoused at Wisconsin by Ed Witte and my father, namely that union and industry reliance on governmental intervention, if heady at times, was poisonous at others. It ought to be minimized.*

Governmental intervention in an industry may take many forms, among them antitrust actions, establishment of standards for labor relations, or direct and indirect subsidization, as well as taxation. It is not surprising that the history of the steel industry is replete with such occasions, particularly when one considers the steel industry's purportedly key role in the U.S. economy.

## Major Developments by Periods

### 1900–1920: The Era of Managerial Dominance

The early part of this period seems clearly to have been dominated by the formation of the U.S. Steel Corporation, at the time considered to be the largest private economic combination effort in the history of the American economy, if not in the history of the Western world. The stories of why Elbert H. Gary and his associates with the help of J. P. Morgan thought it essential to the survival of the profitability of other firms in the industry to buy Andrew Carnegie out and obtain his promise never to return to the industry make for fascinating reading (Gras and Larson 1939). Gary and his group created a billion dollar corporation (actually $1.1 billion) and in so doing created the prototype of modern U.S. monopolistic industry. The U.S. Steel Corporation, particularly after it had constructed its large plants in northern Indiana, by sheer size dominated the industry. Table 1 illustrates the sales and capacity of the various major firms in the industry in 1910 at ten-year intervals between 1910 and 1950.

What about federal antitrust intervention? Such size by its very existence attracted the attention of all parties committed to antitrust, antimonopoly, and antibigness. Efforts made to prosecute U.S. Steel under the antitrust laws began in 1912 and were ultimately unsuccessful in 1920.[1] The prosecutors were unable to persuade the courts that the price leadership that U.S. Steel apparently exerted was the result of overt collusion. Furthermore, the 1945 dictum of size per se (enunciated in *United States* v. *Aluminum Company of America*) was far in the future.[2]

It is erroneous to assume that because the federal government's prosecu-

**TABLE 1.   Total Sales of Leading Steel Companies, 1902–1950 (millions of dollars)**

|                  | 1902 | 1910 | 1920  | 1929  | 1940  | 1950  |
|------------------|------|------|-------|-------|-------|-------|
| U.S. Steel       | 560  | 704  | 1,757 | 1,502 | 1,076 | 2,956 |
| Bethelem         |      | 26   | 276   | 350   | 603   | 1,445 |
| Republic         | 24   | 28   | 76    | 81    | 305   | 882   |
| Jones & Laughlin |      |      | 149   | 127   | 153   | 487   |
| National         |      |      |       |       | 158   | 537   |
| Wheeling         |      |      | 100   | 85    | 93    | 185   |
| Youngstown       | 3    | 18   | 95    | 163   | 144   | 404   |
| Inland           |      | 10   | 52    | 69    | 142   | 459   |
| Armco            | 1    | 3    | 34    | 70    | 112   | 439   |
| Crucible         |      | 19   | 68    |       | 78    | 148   |
| Pittsburgh       |      | 12   | 28    | 40    | 35    | 118   |
| Sharon           |      |      |       | 23    | 22    | 135   |

Source: G. G. Schroeder, *The Growth of Major Steel Companies, 1900–1950* (Baltimore: Johns Hopkins Press, 1953), pp. 216–227.

tors were unable to prove their case against U.S. Steel that the company was not aware of the dangers of such federal intervention. Surely differences in the behavior of the U.S. steel industry from that in Germany (where a cartel was not only legal but was encouraged by the government) and that in Britain suggest that the threat of federal intervention may have had some indirect but nonetheless significant effects.

Managerial dominance was also manifested in the pricing policy followed by U.S. Steel,[3] the Pittsburgh-Plus system. That system originally added the freight cost from Pittsburgh to the customers' final destination irrespective of whether the material was actually fabricated in Pittsburgh. Later multiple points were used, largely as a result of Federal Trade Commission actions.[4] Indeed, there is considerable evidence, particularly in the work done by Fetter (1931), to the effect that the steel prices from the new bases were lowered even beyond the affirmed transportation formula in order to forestall certain kinds of competition. It became a fascinating policy as well as a theoretical issue involving several leading economic theorists.[5] However, the government did not win an antitrust case against this practice until 1948 (against the cement industry),[6] although the system was severely criticized by the Temporary National Economic Committee (U.S. Federal Trade Commission 1941).

There is some evidence that one of the many motives for the establishment of the U.S. Steel Corporation was to slow down rates of technological change because Carnegie's aggressiveness on that score served to make all of his competitors nervous about costs. But it was in the area of labor relations where managerial dominance seemed to be most manifest and government intervention most neglected.

Henry Clay Frick, with the probable connivance of Andrew Carnegie, had managed to drive out of their plants the old Amalgamated Union of Iron and Steel Workers. The drama of the 1892 Homestead strike antedates the beginning of our analysis, but the memory of it lingered.[7] What they had done was emulated by most of the other firms. Perhaps the most bitter effort to drive unionism out was the bitter strike in 1913–1914 of the Rockefeller-owned Colorado Fuel and Iron Company (Perlman and Taft 1935, pp. 335–341). Like many other strikes, it was brutal; what was outstanding about it was not so much the eager collaboration of the Colorado governor with the company but the intensity of the bad press that resulted. It was the time of the election of Woodrow Wilson as president and, drawing on an earlier proposal to sponsor a federal study of U.S. labor relations, Wilson threw his support behind the establishment of the tripartite U.S. Industrial Relations Commission (Perlman 1958, pp. 279–300). Frank Walsh, chairman of the commission, lost no opportunity to pillory John D. Rockefeller, Jr., and the leadership of the Colorado Fuel and Iron Company. Indeed he lost no opportunity to indict and damn what seemed to be the intransigence and insensitivity of the leadership of U.S. industry, the steel industry in particular. Although the commission produced a great many trained labor economists and a great deal of printed evidence, it produced neither legislation nor any overt public move to rehabilitate unionism. Moreover, the advent of World War I not only turned public attention to other matters but also gave certain market advantages to traditionally low-paid workers such that their real living standards increased.

There is clear evidence that employment in the steel industry during the period in question was organized on the principle of using different immigrant groups who were antagonistic to each other or incapable of communicating with each other. In this way the industry prevented the development of unions or other forms of worker combination.

Immediately after World War I, the American Federation of Labor made an ill-fated effort to reorganize the steel industry.[8] Although it had a friend in the White House, the AFL was essentially unable to bring Judge Elbert Gary, president of U.S. Steel, to the bargaining table. Gary's stand in favor of the open shop resulted in a complete failure to open discussions. In the end the unionization effort was judged a clear failure and the efforts were abandoned.

In some senses the silences of Judge Gary typified the absolute dominance of management during this period. In other senses, these same silences drew not only public attention to the absoluteness of management's control but also to the essential irrationality of it. One of the issues that drew considerable attention during the 1919 strike negotiations was the continued existence of the twelve-hour-day, eighty-four-hour week required of furnace workers.

Such a regimen offered a twenty-four-hour respite every fourteen days for the workers, but the price of shifting from working days to working nights was a period of twenty-four-hour duty on alternate weekends.

The length of the working day in U.S. manufacturing industry had fallen considerably by 1919; it was in the steel industry, however, where managerial resistance to such a change seems so callous. The need for 168 hour-per-week manning of the mills doubtless presented problems faced infrequently by other manufacturing industries. Thus it is simplistic to assert, as many did and have, that the steel industry's management was motivated only by overt indifference or callousness. But it is also clear after the fact of the change that there were abundant alternatives, some of which seem to have been simultaneously more humane to the workers and at least as profitable to the owners. It was, accordingly, on management (whose reason for being was to keep the labor force happy and productive while maintaining or increasing profits) where the responsibility should have been and was pinned. Although such judgments are patently subjective, it is a rare student of the period who does not conclude that the harsh criticism (or even more) was deserved.

## 1920–1940: End of Employer Hegemony

After the collapse of the 1919 unionization drive, and probably influenced by President Harding, Judge Gary and U.S. Steel finally agreed to abolish the twelve-hour day. What replaced it was the three-shift eight-hour day. The eighty-four hour week was replaced by the forty-eight-hour week, with one day, not in sequential weeks the same day, off. But these changes came about as a result of feelings and personal judgments within the corporate hierarchy. There is no evidence of any impact of worker pressure.

The period was one when the managements began to be increasingly aware of the costs to productivity of unimaginative, intransigent, and traditional views. As a result of the Colorado Fuel and Iron strike, the Rockefeller interests introduced William Lyons Mackenzie King and Clarence Hicks into the formulation of their labor relations policies (Giddens 1955, pp. 333–360). Hicks's suggestions, adopted particularly in the Standard Oil Corporation, reflected the view that "companies get the kind of labor relations they deserve."

The historic work done by Frederick Winslow Taylor for the Bethlehem Steel Corporation, later popularized by Justice Brandeis as scientific management, came to embrace not only work analysis and worker training but also motion and time study and experimentation with various kinds of incentive high-pay schemes. This is an interesting chapter in the history of U.S. industrial relations, but the truth is that if management lost its total hegemony, what management yielded to was not worker pressure (however much the public might have been sympathetic, and that is a complex story) but to the allegations of professional expertise on the part of efficiency (industrial) engineers (Nodworny 1955; Filipetti 1953).

The collapse of industrial production during the Great Depression not only led to a renewed rise in support for governmental assistance in the formation of a cartel in the industry, a cartel capable of allocating market shares as well as establishing minimum prices, but it also led to widespread concern with the arrogance of leadership of most large industries, steel included.

The first Franklin Roosevelt administration moved quickly to give the industry the cartel that it seemed so desperately to need to survive in periods of low sales or almost no sales. The National Industrial Recovery Act, giving industries the right to set up pricing schedules and market shares, was passed within the first hundred days of Roosevelt's assumption of office in March 1933 (Lyon et al. 1935). That act also identified U.S. public policy as supporting the establishment of unions, particularly in industries seeking federal assistance for their own survival. Whatever may have been the letter of the act or the intent of its sponsors, there is virtually no evidence that the leadership of the steel industry was willing to enter into serious negotiations with representatives of all of the workers in the industry.

The National Industrial Recovery Act, apparently unsuccessful in its general purposes and certainly unsuccessful in its specific purpose of encouraging unionism, was declared unconstitutional by the Supreme Court. Nonetheless the principle, first, and the process, later, of encouraging the development of unionism was institutionalized. The 1935 Wagner-Connery Act, formally entitled the National Labor Relations Act, spelled out in detail not only the rights of workers to form unions but went beyond and established a quasi-judicial agency, the National Labor Relations Board (NLRB), the duties of which were to assure workers the exercising of these rights. As is so often the case, not all the signals were the same. At the time that the federal government had given a green light to the union organizers, there was another development that impeded fast movement—struggles within the AFL. John L. Lewis and several of his colleagues in the United Mine Workers, certain of the leaders of the clothing and garment workers, and the potential leaders of unions in the so-called mass production industries refused to recognize the traditional jurisdictional rights of the great majority of the AFL constituent membership (Galenson 1960; Taft 1959).[9] In due course the Lewis group defected and/or were expelled, and a new labor organization, the Congress of Industrial Organizations, was established.

Lewis, with one of his UMW vice-presidents, Philip Murray, undertook the organization of the U.S. steel industry. Philip Murray, who in time proved to be as charismatic a leader as John L. Lewis, surrounded himself with aggressive organizers. The managerial leadership of the steel industry appeared to respond to the organizing drives with their conventional bitter hostility (Galenson 1960, pp. 84–122). But the political climate had changed, and the leadership of the U.S. Steel Corporation in particular no longer seemed certain that the costs of fighting unionization were not greater than the benefits received while keeping the union out.

After some secret negotiations with Lewis, U.S. Steel, led by Myron Taylor, at the beginning of March 1937 signed a contract with the Steel Workers Organizing Committee (SWOC) not only guaranteeing recognition to that group but also tying that recognition to a substantial pay increase.

SWOC's success with most of the other major steel companies was short of immediate; their leadership was neither as confident as was U.S. Steel's of their capacity to raise wages nor as convinced of the inevitable loss of costly antiorganizing strikes. Violence continued to occur when SWOC's organizers appeared in the various communities where steel was produced. But the bastion had fallen, and it seemed merely a matter of time before the other steel corporations, faced by the aggressive and personally brave activities of the SWOC organizers, one by one ended the "Little Steel Strike of 1937," if only by giving SWOC-inspired pay increases. What then occurred was continuous and unwilling conversations between the various companies and the SWOC representatives, conversations mandated by the NLRB. The frequent and consistent interventions of the NLRB on the SWOC side was no small factor. It is also likely that U.S. Steel's leadership's strong views about standardization of labor costs throughout the industry contributed to the inevitable (Reynolds and Taft 1956, pp. 45–65; Stieber 1959, pp. 4–11). And whatever time that otherwise might have been required was further reduced by virtue of the companies' return to profitability and by the market pressures associated with the rearmament engendered by the outbreak of World War II.

During this period, the greatest impact of government intervention into the industry's development was the NLRB's regular intervention into the labor factor market. This intervention was not simply in terms of the encouragement of exclusive recognition of SWOC. It also involved the publicity given to company violence and produced a new attitude toward the use of the billy club by local police. Public enthusiasm for unionism may have peaked around 1936–1937. Certainly the slough of right-to-work legislation after 1939 suggests that the arrogance of unions and union leaders came to be regarded by many as not much different from the traditional arrogance of managements and managerial leaders (Killingsworth 1948). But the capacity of local police to bully seems to have begun to diminish. In this respect, local government lost much of its traditional power, a point too frequently overlooked. It suggests things not only about the loss of immediate social and civic status of local management as it affected the exercise of police power but even more the penetration of national legal standards. Doubtless national unions, equipped with real capacities for public relations, organizers with a willingness for some forms of martyrdom, and an apparent capacity to deliver the vote were both a cause and a consequence of this change, a change the institutionalization of which is popularly associated with the civil rights struggles of the 1950s and 1960s but whose foundations were really identified and laid two decades earlier.

### 1940–1945: Maintaining the Industry's Labor Force

The war brought with it regulations affecting all industries, particularly in the form of wage and price controls. The steel industry was a key industry in the wartime situation, and intervention took the form of wage and price concessions necessary to ensure cooperation with the war effort from management and labor. The delay on the part of the large steel companies in coming to agreements with the union (absent the success with U.S. Steel's SWOC contract) effectively conflicted with the federal government's wage-freezing wartime policies. These policies were administered by the federal War Labor Board (WLB). In order to encourage production, in April 1941 the WLB developed a "catch-up program," which allowed wage increases and thus gave management a way to attract workers; at the same time it also gave checkoff of dues rights to the union. Termed the "Little Steel Formula," this policy became for the moment the solution to the simultaneous needs to raise steel workers' wages in order to prevent mass defection from the steel mills to other wartime industries where pay rates were higher and to grant recognition to the union. If the bastion fell in 1937, the war against unionism seemed ended in 1941. To the combined impact of the SWOC and the NLRB must be added the wartime interventionary impact of the WLB, a point too frequently ignored.[10]

Within a couple of years (1943), the Little Steel Formula was not enough. Early in 1943, the general counsel of SWOC, Lee Pressman, presented to the WLB a long list of new demands. Workers were again leaving the industry, and the union, sharing an obvious management concern, proposed a variety of pay increases that logically should have been, but were not, construed to have violated the federal wage-freeze program. Certain employer services, particularly health insurance, were consequently introduced as tax-free benefits to workers; thus technically they were not considered to be additions to their wages. In time that list, which included supplemental unemployment benefits, vacation pay, the guaranteed annual wage, and supplemental pensions, served as the blueprint for not only the steel workers' future negotiations with the managements of the industry but also the negotiations of virtually all other unions with managements in their industries.

But the great 1944 change proved not to be the wage award but the establishment of a joint management-union effort to work out cooperative inequities in the wage systems. Stieber (1959) has detailed the background of this effort and explains why in his view the 1945–1947 cooperative wage study was a success. That it led to relative compatibility of attitudes seems likely; that it removed part of the responsibility for efficiency from management also seems likely.

Government intervention during World War II was primarily directed to maximizing industrial output. Essential to that effort was mature intervention into the labor market, designed to make it possible for the industry to maximize output. Draft deferments, extra gasoline rations, and other kinds of inducement played important roles. The important point, one often overlooked, was that the federal government became intimately involved in the wage negotiation process, an involvement that was to prove in the following period to be irreversible.

## 1945–1960: The Postwar Period

*1945–1960: Wage-Price Relationships, Strikes, Profits:* Immediately after the Japanese surrendered in August 1945, the federal government, probably unwisely, cancelled, on short notice, many of its war material contracts. The letdown in such production as coal, in large part inevitable because of worker fatigue, not only exacerbated the European and Japanese misery during the cold winter of 1945–1946 but led to what later proved to be an ungrounded fear of a major reduction in family earnings. The standard work week, which had been increased during World War II to forty-five hours, reverted to forty hours. Workers were aware that irrespective of the official statistics, there had been a major price inflation during the war. The consequence was that the steel workers (among others), egged on by President Truman's voiced view that job and wage security were likely key postwar issues, demanded large wage increases, increases meant to compensate for what some thought were the niggardly authorizations given during the war years. The companies had asked for key price increases, a request that was denied in November 1946 (Dulles 1966, pp. 346–354; Hogan 1971, pp. 1613–1616). A four-week strike began on January 21, 1946, and ended after a presidentially appointed fact-finding board recommended a new contract ultimately giving the workers much of what had been initially demanded, and consequently the price control authorities gave the companies what they wanted. The domestic and the international elasticities of demand for steel, most of which had to be produced in the United States, since the production facilities in Europe and Asia were largely destroyed by the war, made it economically possible for the industry to pass on the costs associated with generous wage increases, providing that the price control authorities went along. They went along.

This was a period of widespread strikes, and the steel strike was probably less bitter than some. Congress, no doubt responding to antiunion sentiment, passed the Taft–Hartley Act in 1946, which contained a provision for processing strike situations in essential industries. When the president deemed a strike dangerous to the public interests (that is, in an essential industry), he was directed to appoint a fact-finding committee, the duties of which were to investigate the terms and causes of the dispute and report them to the president. Each fact-finding committee was given ample time to do its work, and during that term striking was prohibited. After the committee made its report to the president, according to the legislation, the president was not only to send its report of the facts to the Congress but also then to identify his recommendations for legislation or whatever else was needed to resolve the strike. In practice, the president did not establish these fact-finding committees until after strikes had begun. Thus, it was only after the parties had reached their own peculiar levels of intransigence that the president came to intervene. And invariably the fact-finding committee not only reported a set of facts, it also suggested (even though it was mandatorially forbidden to do so) what the resolution of the strike ought to be. These were the formulas that became the industry's rules. So it was that the role of the federal government became confirmed in the collective bargaining process. Bipartite bargaining was replaced by tripartite bargaining.

Strike situations in 1947, 1949, 1952, 1955, and 1959 were invariably resolved through the intervention of presidentially appointed labor negotiators, chosen to resolve each crisis. The 1952 crisis in particular was of greatest interest because President Truman, relying on what he thought were his Korean wartime powers, nationalized the steel industries in order to maintain production. The steel managements immediately appealed his nationalization order, and every level of the federal courts up to and including the Supreme Court upheld the company's position.[11] Ultimately, the by-then usual tripartite negotiated settlement was reached.

The obvious question is whether the industry, specifically, and the public, generally, realized what the insinuation of the federal government into the cost allocation activities of the industry meant (Gregory and Katz 1979, pp. 583–642). The answer is far from simple.

There were many pressures in the country at the time. The interwar isolationist views failed to reappear after the Japanese attack on Pearl Harbor, but there was considerable doubt regarding the posture that the United States ought to take toward Stalin's Soviet Union. Now, long after the events, it is easy to forget the many efforts made by the Roosevelt and Truman administrations to coordinate economic rehabilitation activities with the Soviet Union, efforts that were invariably declined, and usually declined rudely. Within the labor movement generally and within the steel workers' union specifically, there was bitter division regarding U.S. cooperation with the Soviet Union. The election of 1948 offered a pro-Soviet candidate, Henry A. Wallace. Part of the disciplinary process within the Democratic party was the elimination of Wallace's admirers, many of them prominent in the various far left-wing segments of organizations identified with that party. The Congress of Industrial Organizations, but only after bitter debate, voted to drive out its pro-Soviet groups. Not the least bitter part of that effort involved Philip Murray's decision to eliminate his general counsel, Lee Pressman, a far left winger, who had been in a truly major sense Murray's idea man, particularly with regard to wage packages.

No evidence suggests that Murray was not totally convinced of the need to tighten the anti-Soviet leadership of the union. But I am confident that help from the White House, particularly with regard to the wage and fringe benefit concessions in the triennial bargaining sessions, irrespective of passing bitter moments, was perceived as a necessary reward for Murray's personally politically expensive moves. Moreover, within his labor union, Murray (and many other centrist or right-wing labor leaders) were great vote collectors for the Democratic party. This point lost no relevance after the 1952 election defeat because the party comeback, particularly in the Congress, was swift. Thus, industry also became saddled with governmental wage intervention for reasons that had nothing to do with the manufacture of steel. Rather it had much to do with discipline within the Democratic party.

Throughout this period the demand for steel and steel products was at record high levels. Such demand led to price inelasticities and ultimately to the rationing of product among customers. By the early 1950s, it was apparent that the U.S. steel industry did not have the capacity to produce as much as the domestic market plus foreign demands required. Certain customers became identified as favored; certain product lines became identified as high priority.

Among the most favored customers were the U.S. automobile manufacturing firms. They consumed vast quantities of rolled steel. Because the demand for their products was reasonably inelastic, they were able and willing to pay premium prices for the steel products they needed. In order to protect that portion of its market, the U.S. steel industry moved to shuck off other customers, particularly less sophisticated and less profitable product lines.

The auto industry, made conscious of its dependence on continued production in the steel industry by virtue of the strikes of 1947, 1949, 1952, and 1956, became worried about the repetition of shortages as negotiations with the steelworkers' union approached in 1959. The automobile companies made the first of many moves to stockpile not only sufficient U.S. steel to meet their demands if a steel strike were to develop, but they began to develop business relationships with foreign (non-U.S.) steel manufacturers lest the probable steel strike of 1959 last long enough for them to exhaust their stockpiles.

Thus it was that the steel industry began to suffer from foreign imports. Early in the 1950s, the U.S. steel industry was only too ready to tell some of its smaller and less important customers to import product from abroad, particularly when the products seemed to be of a low order of sophistication. But by 1959 both management and the union, perceiving that the most favored customers were looking abroad for more as well as less technologically sophisticated products, became frightened about the costs to the industry of their triennial head-on collisions. Neither the union nor management saw any way in which the government through any action that seemed either constitutional or politically acceptable could help the situation. The 1959 strike was traumatic, and the lesson learned was to try to prevent strikes if at all possible.

One such effort was the establishment of a bipartite Human Relations Research Committee; the purpose was to reestablish bipartitism, and its efforts probably helped avoid a 1962 strike. Domestic economic recession and an industry-wide willingness to realize the end of the international halcyon period also were present, however.

There is more to the story. Although the 1950s was a period of relative price stability, there was widespread concern about a tendency toward price inflation. The oligopolistic nature of the steel industry, with its alleged bilateral (really trilateral) labor negotiations, seemed to set the stage for an inevitable drift toward inflation. The argument was put forth, and generally accepted, that wage increases in the steel industry led to price increases in that industry. Price increases in the steel industry led to intermediate product increases in all other industries. And as the chain of that syllogism was forged, the conclusion was that if wage increases in the steel industry could be absorbed without price increases, the inflationary impact on the U.S. economy would be significantly reduced.

During this period governmental intervention into the wage negotiation process for political and for economic reasons became all but institutionalized. Early in the period, the idea was clearly to improve the real living standards of the steelworkers. By the end of the period, the government was likely less concerned with the real living standards of steelworkers than it was with the probably critical position of price increases in the steel industry (associated in some major way with wage increases) and their impact on the inflationary drift within the United States (Eckstein and Fromm 1959). But communication of the newer concern invariably conflicted with the all-too apparent and immediate cost of strikes or labor unrest. Economists suggesting a national wages policy were simultaneously given a courtesy hearing and then asked if they knew how to bell the cat. They did not.

1945–1960: Internationalization and
National Interdependency

This time period duplicates the previous one, but the interpretation is from a somewhat different standpoint. The previous section dealt with government's domestic role and its impact on the steel industry. This section deals with the government's role as the formulator of international policy and its consequent impact on the industry.

Immediately after World War II, the federal government undertook relief and rehabilitation efforts. Interest focused on feeding the displaced populations of Europe and Asia and on cooperating with the rehabilitation of the industrial systems destroyed by the war. Loans were made to former allies, but they proved to be insufficient to alleviate the economic collapse caused by the wartime destruction. In 1948 Secretary of State George Marshall announced at the commencement exercises at Harvard University broad plans to participate in the economic reconstruction of Europe and Asia. Initially, certain of the East European countries, in particular Czechoslovakia, asked to be included, but after the relevant message was received from Moscow, the Marshall Plan became a plan devoted to the economic recovery of Western Europe and Japan. About the same time, President Truman extended the principles of the Marshall Plan for economic reconstruction to an open-ended program for the economic development of poor and/or less-developed countries. Truman's Point Four Program, like the Marshall Plan, committed the federal government to help friendly nations to develop their industrial base.

It is one of the ironies of history that most countries believe that the cornerstone of their economic development must be a domestic steel industry. As a consequence, insofar as the U.S. government received requests for immediate aid in industrial development, a large share of those requests focused on the development of domestic steel industries. In many instances the federal government complied. It offered generous loans designed to make it possible for the industrialized nations of Western Europe and Asia as well as some less-developed nations to develop steel production. The U.S. steel industry, doubtless influenced by what seemed to be an eternal inelasticity of foreign demand for its products, offered technological assistance in steelmaking capacity in other parts of the world. There seemed to be no end to the generosity of the U.S. government in helping now-friendly nations develop their industrial base, particularly their capacity to manufacture steel products.

Forgotten was the U.S. tradition of protection for its steel industry, a tradition existing from before 1820 until World War II. America, historically the proponent of trade protection, became the evangelist for free trade. Forgotten also were the historic advantages of scale that the U.S. industry had enjoyed over the various European countries' industries by virtue of the immense size of the U.S. domestic market. The United States, once possessor of the largest market without trade barriers, became the advocate of a European Common Market.

Probably not forgotten but surely unimagined was the likely capability of foreign producers to market vast quantities of sophisticated steel (or steel alloy) products. Some Americans surely were aware of German and other European technical capacities, but these same Americans seemed unaware of the brief time span involved in the expansion of the European scale of output to a point going well beyond Europe's own domestic demands so that there was going to be a sizable export residual. Other Americans, conscious of our own capacity problems (cf. Broude 1963) were willing, even eager, to let others make the less sophisticated products (such as steel rods and wire), not realizing that the sophistication learning curve was short and steep. Finally, still other Americans, worried about military (particularly Korean war) requirements, showed explicit eagerness in having the Japanese help out.[12] In all too brief a time, helping out started becoming taking over.

Perhaps because of the U.S. steel industry's sanguineness regarding the eternal inelasticity of demand for its products, there seems to have been no discussion of what turned out to be the long-run consequences: a vast expansion of steel-making capacity throughout the world during the period of high demand. The domestic industry consequently was faced with a choice between immediately expanding existing older, technologically less modern facilities and the longer tasks of constructing completely new plants. The former was frequently chosen, adding immediate capacity but delaying modernization.

Americans, dominated in their thinking in the 1950s by the historical traditions of domestic demands for steel in every country consuming all of that country's usual steel-making capacity, and by the historical record that sophisticated steel products could be produced by only a very few countries, were inexplicably oblivious to the vast increases in capacity occurring abroad and the implications that a brisk demand for entry into foreign markets (including specifically the U.S. domestic market) was in the offing. This short-sightedness was further complicated by a crippling unawareness of the extent to which it had lost the kind of Andrew Carnegie-like intuition about the possibilities of speedy and profitable basic R&D. Viewed retrospectively, U.S. smugness set the industry riding for a fall. Yet if the industry was unaware of what was going on abroad and the implications, it was heavily occupied in endless negotiations with federal authorities who urged capacity increases but who were unwilling to cooperate in legalizing (much less popularizing) the need for higher profits or the need to lower labor costs as a necessary source.

Two additional factors should be considered. The more important is that the costs of shipping ores and finished products were falling because such technological changes as vast ocean-going carriers serving tidewater mills and the widespread use of the post-World War II massive rubber-tired highway truck (making land-side delivery much cheaper than the previous railroad service) were quickly implemented. Steel produced near Yokohama (from ores shipped by large carrier from the west Australian coast), then shipped by sea to the East and West Coasts as well as a Great Lakes port, and then transported by truck to the customer made the previous U.S. system, heavily based on rail transport, less competitive. True, the new transportation system took a few years to work out, but the cost differences became if not in fact, in prospect, quickly realized.

Changes in communication technology also made foreign producers more competitive. Telephonic communication and airplane travel became increasingly more efficient, such that once seemingly distant producers could be contacted easily and could show up quickly for negotiations. Warehousing and service centers were effectively established. The previous propinquity factor, something that made U.S. customer-supplier relationships more or less personal, began to decline in importance. Price advantage and the capacity for foreign suppliers to respond quickly also took their toll of the U.S. industry's ability to protect its home market. What occurred might well have been imagined; it would have been harder to imagine how fast the changes, one after another, piled up.

This was, nonetheless, the period when some U.S. research and development was again encouraged. The exhaustion of the Mesabi Range led to technological changes that introduced pelletization into the manufacture of basic steel. The discovery of rich ore beds in Newfoundland led to the implementation of an old plan to improve the navigability of the St. Lawrence River for large (ore-carrying) ships. In sum, the period of 1945 through 1960 was the apogee of U.S. internationalization. Free from doubts about effective limits on its capacity to compete successfully, full of the spirit of brotherly generosity, the American people, its government and, in this case the steel industry, rushed to its hour of economic reckoning.

## 1960–1972: Consequences

The decade of the 1960s, in spite of the growing frustration with U.S. inability to achieve military dominance in Southeast Asia, was a period of faith in the capacity of the society, usually through legislation, to improve not only its domestic welfare but also the welfare of the world. In spite of the fast-growing recognition that there was likely to be a surplus of iron and steel manufacturing capacities throughout the world and in spite of a stunted recognition that some U.S. consumers of steel were increasingly starting to turn to foreign suppliers, the leadership of the steel industry was faced with demands for improving the quality of U.S. domestic life by reduction of air and water pollution, historic concomitants of the production of their product. Whatever investment funds were available for the renovation of the industry, a significant portion of those funds were mandated for the production of clean air and clean water rather than cheaper iron and steel. The Environmental Protection Act might not have imposed such crushing burdens in the 1950s when the reality of the inelasticity of demand for the product was significant. But by the time the Environmental Protection Agency began to require the mandated investment, the steel industry had to choose where it was going to spend less. The historic fact is that by 1960 wages in the steel industry were among the highest in any other U.S. industry, resulting from the government's intervention in the wage-setting process. By the early 1960s, the steel industry had been spending vast sums not so much for competitive modernization as for necessary replacement of old facilities and for meeting customer demands for higher quality. Also by the mid-1960s, the industry was not spending enough on research and development to maintain its historic technological leadership.

That was not all. The same legislative alliance that produced the Environmental Protection Agency as an institutionalized organization for improving the quality of consumers' lives also produced the Occupational Safety and Health Administration, similarly an expensive, mandated operation designed to improve significantly the quality of workers' on-the-job lives.

Thus, its limited capital resources were faced with multiple compelling demands, with decisions influenced more by governmental requirements than by managerial preferences. Economists are enamoured of saying money spent on one program cannot be spent on another. I would argue that in spite of the evident truth of this statement, the critical questions were not the desirability of these programs but the standards mandated, their timing, and the amounts of investment monies diverted from too-long postponed R&D.

### Analyzing the Lessons

This section analyzes the governmental function. It involves both generalization and abstraction—generalization because it draws on an overview of the historical experience narrated immediately previously, abstraction because it attempts to draw on the rich theoretical literature suggesting that intervention is not merely a matter of momentary political whim or of historical caprice. Governmental intervention occurs not only on the product side, the side affecting prices and interfirm product competition as well as imports, but also, both historically and analytically, the greater role of governmental intervention has been on the factor market side, such markets as may be identified with labor, with technological change and the rights to the special benefits given to inventors, the problems associated with the reduction of transportation costs, the complexities associated with capital accumulation, the vagaries associated with provision of pure water and air, and even the kind of atmosphere to appreciation or lack of appreciation offered to risk-taking entrepreneurs.

## Conflicting Pressures about Objectives

The important generalization is that the fear of, or the presence of, governmental intervention has been management's constant companion since 1902. The intensity of concern with monopolistic pricing policy prior to World War I may have diminished after 1920. It reemerged in an additional form during and after World War II when the issue was not freedom to penetrate price floors but freedom to penetrate price ceilings. One almost omnipresent reason for managements' concern was the federal consequences of industry's pricing decisions.

Another concern was the question of oligopsony in the labor market. No competent reading of the history of the steel industry's labor relations can lead to any conclusion but that without the NLRB and the WLB, the unionization of the industry would have taken a different course. Those who believe that "as U.S. Steel goes, so goes the industry" have forgotten the record. Elbert Gary may have been the leader in the open shop movement, but it was not Myron Taylor but the WLB that secured the union's checkoff victory in the quest for union security. Management's concern after 1935 regarding its labor market relationships had solid foundations; the union it dealt with was a bedrock pillar of the Roosevelt-Truman Democratic party.

A third concern was the belief that market-tightness increases in steel prices tended to drive up the U.S. aggregate price level. Thus, any post–World War II managerial pressures for labor-cost containment got mixed with public pressures for price ceilings. The bullying tactics employed by President Kennedy and his attorney general (the threat to harass the companies' leadership with personal income tax audits) do not make for pleasant reading. Nonetheless they do serve to explain the collapse of one set of managerial efforts to combat federal bossing. And if nothing else, they reveal governmental contradictions: if profits are to be constrained, where is the capital for real modernization and expansion to come from?

Finally, the view that the steel industry should be an instrument in rebuilding the war-destroyed industries in Europe and Japan and that it should also be an instrument in the development of steel industry competence (if not steel industry competitiveness) in developing economies again was a White House concern that prompted federal intervention in the industry's foreign activities.

## Means and Objectives of Governmental Intervention

There are certain analytical sets or matrices favored by economists endeavoring to explain the reasons why governments otherwise committed to laissez-faire intervene in economic market activities. At their best, these reasons offer the necessary organizational pigeonholes that make retention of a complex subject feasible; at their worst they distort understanding. Nonetheless, their virtues are sufficient to justify their inclusion here:

1. Scale economies for blast furnace and some related operations in this industry are such that the classic model of competitive industrial organization is inapplicable. Moreover the consequent results (market concentration) make anything like competitive pricing unlikely. Thus governmental intervention occurs to prevent oligopolistic price setting, even when such price setting is logically necessary (but politically untimely) to permit economic growth and/or international competitiveness. This is one form of the public utility set of reasons for rate setting.

2. Policies encouraging weaker parties to band together so that the bargaining power of the stronger parties can in some way be countervailed. This is the rubric under which support for unions by the NLRB and the WLB entered the scene.

3. Using the taxing power, including administrative tax rules for depreciation, of the various levels of government to shape and reshape the relative quantities and costs of labor and capital goods employed. With the possible exception of a weak taxation of wartime profits during World War II, thus is the plane of competition set. Here is where intervention in this industry was most unsuccessful. It now has resulted in a legacy of disrupted investment schedules and the current presence of an outmoded plant.

4. Extension of the market leading to larger-scale sales, historically a key to economic success. This is the market-extension–scale of production set. Here the intervention after World War II, largely devoted to encouraging development of a modern larger-scale European steel industry, seems to have been clearly counterproductive from the longer-term U.S. viewpoint.

5. Governmental concern with the social costs and social benefits of decisions taken by private parties, particularly manufacturing concerns. The technical word is *externalities;* it covers not only a set of cost allocations but also complexities of the ordering of social priorities.

6. Governmental concern about the uses of protection (in whatever form)

versus the advantages of free trade is both a means and an objective of a variety of its social responsibilities. Its relevance to the steel industry prior to 1880 or after 1970 may be great. It seems essentially irrelevant to our period, 1900 through 1960. Since 1960 dumping may well have become a crucial problem.

7. Finally there is the dilemma of the shortness of human life and the length of life of societies and corporate business enterprises. Only the wisest of people have time horizons extending beyond five or ten years. Traditionally corporations had time horizons comparable to those of the wisest of people, but in recent years it seems apparent that the time horizon of most corporate managements has shrunk to less than five years. But societies and their governments do expect to endure, and many industry decisions probably should be made in terms of decades. One of the major reasons for governmental intervention, however it can be effected, into the long haul calculations of those aware of their reasonably imminent business mortality is the fact that the day of economic judgment is, if not the next annual meeting, surely the annual meetings of two or three years away. To help reverse such an overemphasis on immediacies, it would be helpful for government to explore the extent to which its own tax policies as well as broad economic conditions involving interest rates and fluctuations in economic activity have contributed to such policies.

## Assessments

Has public monopoly power (such as use of governmental corporations like British Steel) proved to be innocuous compared to private oligopoly power? Surely some of the problems of private monopoly power persist when the monopolist ceases to be private but becomes purportedly a representative of the public, albeit one with his own bureaucratic self-interest. Is there a means of minimizing public monopoly power, particularly when the courts eschew whatever responsibility they may purport to have regarding the review of administrators' findings?

The governmental capacity for coping with deflation and insufficiency of demand seems to have been well demonstrated in the last half-century. Is there a governmental capacity to deal with inflation and insufficiency of supply, particularly when we live in a democratic society where the interests of the have-nots have a great many more votes than the interests of the haves? If in the past the interests of the managements of large firms were overrepresented, and labor's demands that it get respectable wages were too seriously considered, have we now come to the point where the interests of the consuming public, invariably demanding such low prices that saving for investment is all but impossible, are no longer paramount—particularly from the standpoint of the national interest in safeguarding future development?

The instrument of tax policy has perhaps been somewhat less flexibly used than its possibilities offer. Perhaps the move should be to regenerate or reindustrialize the steel industry by virtue of generous tax (including excise and tariff) policies. Finally events in the U.S. steel industry are not simply the product of its own choices or even the product of the choices of the U.S. government and public. What happened in Japan is so complex a story that it defies easy explanation. Once isolated in a corner of the world, an able people sought recognition by conventional twentieth-century imperial military methods. Subsequently defeated in war but with it ambitions remaining, it achieved its old objectives by positive institutional policies and accelerating development of its industrial competitiveness. The role of the United States was essentially passive. Historically, the United States was the one great domestic market in the world. Whether it was Washington's enthusiasm or not that timed the development of the European Common Market, it was European self-interest that most clearly brought it about. As a consequence, the U.S. steel industry was no longer the only such national industry to envision emergence of a large domestic market. That we had forgotten in the meantime how to protect that market may be another story. But the economies of scale, which the United States alone had once enjoyed, were clearly becoming available to others as well.

If we want to have effective U.S. competitors, we have to create incentives and minimize deterrents to their development. To cut down the Judge Garys with their arrogance and insensitivity may have been a historic necessity, but to believe that management can maintain effective competitiveness effortlessly—without aggressive efforts to control costs, advance technologies, and seek market advantages—seems contrary to the lessons the record suggests. Worse, governmental policy was not even neutral; it actively restricted profits (capital accumulation), it did little to sponsor R&D over the long haul, it encouraged high labor costs through jawboning and its tax treatment of fringe benefits, and it implemented EPA and OSHA programs with excessively high targets within overly short periods.[13] The record may not be *the* manual for disaster, but it could be *a* manual for it.

NOTES

1. *U.S.* v. *U.S. Steel Corp.*, 251 U.S. 417 (1920). Also see ibid., 223 Fed. 55 (D.N.J. 1915).
2. *U.S.* v. *Aluminum Co. of America* (ALCOA), 148 Fed. 416 (2 Cir. 1945).
3. For a general, if not hostile, discussion see Whitney (1958, pp. 260–264).

4. U.S. Steel Corp. Docket 760, 8 FTC 1 (1924).

5. The more conventional theoretical view is in Machlup (1949). The heterodox view can be found in Clark (1939). Clark's general view about the nature of effective competition is laid out neatly in his article, "Toward a Concept of Workable Competition."

6. *FTC v. Cement Institute*, 333 U.S. 683 (1948).

7. For a very brief history of the 1892 strike see Commons and Associates (1918, pp. 495–499).

8. Cf. Perlman and Taft (1935, pp. 461–468). Also note Interchurch World Movement (1921).

9. It is fashionable to identify the conflict as between the skilled or craft unions and the industrial unions. The fact is that among the leading traditionalists were such industrial unions as the teamsters and such unskilled building trades unions as the hodcarriers and even the Pullman porters' union. The essential citadel of craft unionism was really in the railroad industry, an industry operating essentially under different laws and different personalities.

10. Broude (1963) concentrates on post–World War II steel industry–government relationships.

11. Cf. *Youngstown Sheet & Tube Co. v. Sawyer*, 343 U.S. 578 (1952).

12. Involving World Bank financing and U.S. sponsorship of a Japanese productivity center.

13. Lewis 1959.

REFERENCES


Broude, H. W., 1963. *Steel Decisions and the National Economy.* New Haven: Yale University Press.

Clark, John M. 1939. *The Social Control of Business.* 2d ed. New York: McGraw-Hill.

———. 1940. "Toward a Concept of Workable Competition." *American Economic Review* 30 (June): 241–256.

Commons, John R. and associates. 1918. *History of Labour in the United States.* New York: Macmillan.

Dulles, Foster Rhea. 1966. *Labor in America.* 3d ed. New York: Crowell.

Eckstein, Otto, and Fromm, Gary. 1959. "Steel and the Post War Inflation." In *Study of Employment Growth and Price Levels.* Study Paper No. 2 U.S. Congress, Joint Economic Committee.

Fetter, Frank A. 1931. *The Masquerade of Monopoly.* New York: Harcourt, Brace.

Filipetti, George. 1953. *Industrial Management in Transition.* Homewood, Ill.: Irwin.

Galenson, Walter. 1960. *The CIO Challenge to the AFL: A History of the American Labor Movement, 1935–1941.* Cambridge: Harvard University Press.

Giddens, Paul H. 1955. *Standard Oil Company (Indiana): Oil Pioneer of the Middle West.* New York: Appleton-Century-Crofts.

Gras, N. B., and Larson, Henrietta M. 1939. "Elbert H. Gary and the United States

Steel Corporation, 1901–1938." In *Casebook in American Business History.* New York: Appleton-Century-Croft.

Gregory, Charles O., and Katz, Harold A. 1979. *Labor and the Law.* 3d ed. New York: Norton.

Hogan, William T. 1971. *Economic History of the Iron and Steel Industry in the United States.* Volume 4. Lexington, Mass.: Lexington Books, D.C. Heath.

Interchurch World Movement. 1921. *Supplementary Report on Steel Strike.* New York: Harcourt, Brace and Howe.

Killingsworth, Charles C. 1948. *State Labor Relations Acts: A Study of Public Policy.* Chicago: University of Chicago Press.

Lewis, B. W. 1959. "Economics By Admonition." *American Economic Review Proceedings.* (May): 384–398.

Lyon, Leverett S., Homan, P. T., Terborgh, G., Lorwin, L., Dearing, C. L., Marshall, L. C. 1935. *The National Recovery Administration: An Analysis and Appraisal.* Washington, D.C.: Brookings.

Machlup, Fritz. 1949. *The Basing-Point System.* Philadelphia: Blakiston.

Nodworny, Milton A. 1955. *Scientific Management and the Unions, 1900–1932: A Historical Analysis.* Cambridge: Harvard University Press.

Perlman, Mark. 1958. *Labor Union Theories in America.* Evanston, Ill.: Row, Peterson.

Perlman, Selig, and Taft, Philip. 1935. *History of Labor in the United States, 1896–1932.* New York: Macmillan.

Reynolds, Lloyd J., and Taft, Cynthia H. 1956. *The Evolution of the Wage Structure.* New Haven: Yale University Press.

Stieber, Jack. 1959. *The Steel Industry Wage Structure: A Study of the Joint Union-Management Job Evaluation Program in the Basic Steel Industry.* Cambridge: Harvard University Press.

Taft, Philip. 1959. *The A.F. of L.: From the Death of Gompers to the Merger.* New York: Harper.

U.S. Federal Trade Commission. 1941. *The Basing Point Problem.* TNEC Monograph 42. Washington, D.C.

Whitney, Simon N. 1958. *Antitrust Policies: American Experience in Twenty Industries.* Volume 2. New York: Twentieth Century Fund.

CHAPTER 25

# An Analytical Theory of Labor
# Arbitration in Australia

*Schumpeter (and others) have written that often a man's most original work is done when he is at the beginning of his career. This chapter, one of the first I published, synthesized my theories about the operation of the old (pre-1954 Boilermaker Decision) Australian Arbitration Court. The distinction I drew between the way courts were supposed to operate and the way that legislatures operate had the kind of neatness that theorists appreciate. I wrote before Brown v. Board of Education, as well as the plethora of decisions which characterized not only the Warren but all other American Supreme Courts until recently. Who knows—the shift to Republicanism in the national administration as well as the Congress may make my views timely again.*

*Whatever else, this essay reflects the catholicity of training I had received as a student—catholicity as to subject, to method, and to purpose. If the first chapter in this book is intended to show how I analyzed my formal training, in high school, in college, and in the postgraduate years, this essay reveals how I applied that training. It is something of an unconscious portrayal of how I explain things.*

I

Modern free society, emphasizing popular welfarism, has sought palliatives, preventatives, and finally remedies for industrial unrest. Of the many panaceas contemplated, arbitration has been one of the most popular. Australasia, it is almost unnecessary to note, has led the world in this type of social experiment. This essay, which concerns the day-to-day operation of the Australian arbitration system, develops a hypothesis relating to the role of the public official in the arbitration process. Briefly, the intent is to present a general thesis summarizing the conclusions of several Australian industrial studies covering the period 1920–1950,[1] to compare the thesis with a contemporary American discussion in a cognate area, and, finally, to consider some of the inherent implications.

---

From Mark Perlman, *Sydney Law Review* 1 (1954): 207–12.

1. See M. Perlman, *Judges in Industry; The Role of the Australian Arbitration Court* (1953).

The delicate question of the place for private organizations in democratic society is one which has long fascinated certain political theorists who are dissatisfied with what they term superficially abstract discussions of the sovereignty of the State or of the law. For instance, Otto von Gierke noted the issue in 1902:[2]

> Jurisprudence has to do with social institutions only insofar as they are active in law, and must, therefore, necessarily proceed in a one-sided fashion. For legal activity is only one side of collective life, and by no means the important side. Jurisprudence must remain conscious of this one-sidedness. It must also bear in mind that the active powers of the social organism come to light beyond law in all movements of force or culture and realize their most powerful effects independently of law, or even in opposition to law.

A splendid opportunity for observation is afforded by the almost half-century history of the federal Arbitration System, where public authorities representing a State, limited in powers, and an inarticulate public have attempted to deal with employers' associations and trade unions. It is not necessary to review the history of the legislative background of the system, nor even to investigate the judicial peccadillos of Arbitration and High Court claims for legitimate jurisdiction, for the interested student to realize how difficult has been the task of the public authorities. They, dressed in the robes of the bench, have had to yield a product which is largely enforceable only with the co-operation of the interested litigants.

Fortunately, the disputants have some observable immediate needs and do not approach the arbitration tribunals with ungovernable and inarticulate hostility. And, if the governmental officials are able to formulate awards which, in one way or another, take into account the parties' needs, the problem of compliance is considerably minimized. Thus, the basis of the argument of this essay is that the parties' dependence upon the public representatives (as seen in the judges and later in the conciliation commissioners) is the key to the relatively successful operation of the system. Implied is the assertion that it is not alone respect for the law, but imperative need, that brings the organic social groups of employers and employees to formal litigation.

What are the causes of such a need? Obviously a disproportionately strong or unbalanced bargaining relationship makes the weaker side seek out the public's representatives as a protector. Similarly, a distaste for the chaotic

---

2. *Das Wesen der menschlichen Verbande*, inaugural address upon assuming *Rektorat* at the University of Berlin, October 15, 1902: quoted from John D. Lewis, "The *Genossenschaft*-Theory of Otto von Gierke" (1935) 25 *Univ. Wisconsin Studies in Soc. Sci. and Hist.* 156.

state of chronic struggle leads the parties to a willingness to settle for a system intended to bring peace,[3] although how much a particular truce agreement is desired depends inevitably upon underlying economic and political factors. Another, perhaps more complicated, cause is to be found within the "personality" of the group *(Genossenschaft)*, or "group-will". For in their development groups often reach out and absorb so many members that factions develop. As a result the organic group finds itself incapable of peacefully resolving internal conflict. In these instances, if the larger unit is to survive, either an internal bargaining compromise must be developed or an appeal to some external authority for settlement must be made. Yet in the first instance general dissatisfaction can develop as logically as general agreement: in the latter, a poorly engineered solution is possible.

Hence it follows that the business of the arbitrator facing two groups of litigants is not only to come forth with a solution to the immediate problem brought by them to him, but also, if possible, to handle it in such a way that it is applicable to their individual needs. In one sense, then, the terms of the settlement must be within the range of expectation.[4] Equally as important, however, is the process of or procedure in achieving settlement, since a set of terms may become unsatisfactory if in its presentation it is compromised.[5]

## II

The Australian arbitration system has long intrigued American observers.[6] The lack of effective punitive powers at the Court's disposal suggests the existence of another source of strength. It proceeds logically from the foregoing discussion that this strength is essentially associated with the pattern or role of the judges and conciliation commissioners in fulfilling the demands of the parties. For instance, where a union is composed of two major factions, one wanting long weekly working hours because its members are paid by the piece (tally) and live away from home, and the other wanting a shorter working week because its members are paid by time units (weekly wage), the case presented to the authority is naturally rather ambiguously formulated. Similarly, where there is great fear of "cutthroat" competition (sweating), the employers will prefer a strong disciplinary authority, even though it means a

---

3. According to Thomas Hobbes this is the first law of nature *(Leviathan* pt. i, c. xiv).

4. *Cf.* A. C. Pigou, *The Economics of Welfare* (4 ed.) 452–53.

5. E.g., ends and means are, of necessity, related. The theory of economic *tâtonnements* is a too often neglected area of study.

6. V. H. Clark, *The Labor Movement in Australasia* (1960); M. B. Hammand, "Wage Boards in Australia" (1915) 29 *Q.J. of Economics;* Carter Goodrich, "The Australian and American Labour Movements" (1928) 4 *Economic Record* 193.

diminution of their own prerogatives.[7] Conversely, where each party is closely knit, the need for the stabilizing interference of the public authority, as well as the tolerance of him, is correspondingly diminished. Thus in the case of a relatively compact entity, like a craft-oriented union,[8] or one with a concise economic program easily evident to the rank and file, or an employers' federation in a "horizontally-organized" industry, the role of governmental experts is less creative in scope.

The judges of the Arbitration Court have not been slow to respond to the calls for assistance. Some, like Mr. Justice Higgins, have sought to extend the advantages of planning or social engineering to the provinces of industrial relations. Higgins, J., had included in the original Arbitration Act a provision for the establishment of industrial common rules applicable to all parties which his court thought to be interested. Although this provision was invalidated by the High Court,[9] his intent remains on the record. In another instance, he implied that it was "right" for him to determine that the differentials for the skilled be cut in order to transfer income to the unskilled and thereby permit a living wage for all.[10] This type of reasoning or conception of his role appears to have had a "legislative" flavour, and the judge is tempted to write into the "law" by enlarging the realm of judicial notice and by summoning evidence on his own motion to adopt his own set of ethical commitments.[11] One student of the Court's policies felt that judges like Higgins have tried to put themselves in the vanguard of social reforms to the "grievous embarrassment of the country".[12]

Generally we can note on the part of many other judges, too, a willingness to set standards for industry. From their pens and judgments have flowed a widening series of judicially-legislated decrees, including the principles of

---

7. See my *Judges in Industry* for an examination of the industrial alignments in the pastoral and stevedoring industries, cc. iii and v. Essentially the important factors are the elasticity of the demand curve, the short run mobility of the factors of production (particularly labor), and the economic geographic organization of the buyers' market.

8. *Ibid.* c. iv. Reference is to the Amalgamated Engineering Union.

9. *Whybrow's Case* (1910) 11 C.L.R. 311, 16 A.L.R. 513.

10. 3 C. Arb. R. at 32.

11. "Give (the workers) relief from their materialistic anxiety; give them reasonable certainty that their essential material needs will be met by honest work, and you release infinite stores of human energy for higher efforts, for nobler ideals. . . ." (from H. B. Higgins, *A New Province of Law and Order* (1923) 37–38). Also, ". . . but in order that the Court may effectually carry out its primary program of settling and preventing industrial disputes, it has to provide for the just treatment of employees, and it has to find and to state what it thinks to be the proper standards for such treatment. The Court (however) has nothing to do with theories for the reconstruction of society on some new economic basis—for example, the ending of the wage system. . . ." from H. B. Higgins, "The Australian Commonwealth Court of Conciliation and Arbitration" 1924 speech at Oxford University and privately reprinted (Melbourne, 1925).

12. M. A. Rankin, *Arbitration Principles and the Industrial Court* (1931).

the basic wage, of quarterly adjustments, of annual leave with pay, and of long service leave. And while it is true that s. 51, pl. 35 of the Constitution prevents the Parliament from handling directly these topics, it does not follow, as so many Australians imagine, that such matters could not have been handled by direct negotiation between the employers and the unions. What has developed is a belief that the judges and commissioners should *administer* industry, that they must for reasons of social efficiency assume a legislative mantle, or, in the words of one judge, they must function as the "economic dictators" of Australia.[13] Thus, there has developed an approach to the arbitration process—a theory of the role of judge-legislator which, for want of a better term, we call *"administrative* arbitration".[14] It predicates parties needing judges with figuratively strong hands and keenly imaginative eyes. "It is the principal duty of this Court," commented Drake-Brockman, J., in 1935,[15] "to prevent and settle industrial disputes. This Court is only in a minor degree a court of law. Its legal functions are practically limited to the interpretation and enforcement of its own awards. Its main activities are directed to the making of awards, which is a legislative function. . . ."

## III

Unlike Higgins, J., a few judges have resisted the forces which compelled them into a quasi-legislative (*administrative*) function. Their product, although still "unbound" by normal judicial standards, is, compared with the *administrative* variety of arbitration, constrained; they have tried to narrow the allowable area of judicial notice and have restrained the temptation to call for and introduce evidence on their own motion. Instead, they have left the initiative to the litigants, and where the parties have been able to present adequately their positions, the end-product has been generally acceptable. For instance, in one case O'Mara, J., in delivering judgment noted that he personally disagreed with the conclusion that the evidence presented to him suggested, but that he felt bound to abide by it.[16]

This approach to the arbitration process tends to be devoid of articulated

---

13. See *Sydney Morning Herald,* October 17, 1947.

14. We use the adjective, "administrative", in order to carry the connotation of "administrative law"—by it we also imply something of a legislative nature.

15. *Australian Rlys. Union* v. *Victorial Rlys. Commissioners* (1935) 34 C. Arb. R. 15.

16. "The Unions have asked for the rescission of the provision which enables employers to take apprentices in the trades of mechanical engineer (etc.) . . . in the proportion of one to one. Their advocate, however, concedes that some dispensation from the proportions of one to three or one to two might be allowed and I have redrawn the clause in a way which conforms to his suggestion. *I would have limited the proportion as at present, but I have deferred to (his) suggestion. . . .*" 57 C. Arb. R. at 280 (italics added).

social goals and is, by way of contrast, thereby somewhat less inspirational. As a young man Kelly, C. J., once penned his sentiments on this topic:[17]

> As I conceive them, there is in the function of an Industrial Court no room for experiments such as may originate in the realm of politics or in the fertile field of sociological ideals. The Court is constituted to remedy injustice. The injustice must be proved in terms of facts and of the recognized rules of human like and fair dealing. These will, of course, vary as civilization progresses; but until they are accepted by the community as part of the regulative code for its transactions, they must be treated by the Court as not having emerged from the regions of social idealism. The Court has no right to assume the role of reformer. Having discovered an injustice, however, it is bound to devise a remedy. But the remedy should be sufficient for its purpose and nothing more, for further interference by the Court is unwarranted and, in my view, beyond the limit of its jurisdiction.

And in yet another instance, Dethridge, C. J., noted that his judgment was not to be considered the end of the matter, and implied that the issue could be resolved on bases other than his determination.[18]

This second theory of arbitration we term "*autonomous approach*", since it implies that the relationship between the parties and the system is essentially one of independence. As a political philosophy, it resembles the views of James Madison in the *Tenth Federalist Paper*. It seems to favor direct negotiation between the parties at the expense of a controlled or planned relationship.[19]

---

17. *Public School Teachers' Case* (1934) 13 S.A. Ind. R. 18.

18. "This Court is not to be influenced by political considerations, but it cannot ignore economic conditions merely because they have been created, partly or wholly, by political or governmental action, even though that action might be considered by some people to have been ill-advised or too far-reaching. . . . In any event, this Court cannot prevent a State Government or Legislature from continuing to grant a 44-hour week to its own employees, or from requiring it to be granted by all public bodies under its control, or by persons desiring to make contracts with such Government or public bodies involving the employment of workers. This Court has not power to prevent any person or body from granting to his or its own employees the 44-hour week, nor has it any power to prevent any person or body from requiring a condition in contracts that the contractor shall grant the 44-hour week . . ." *Amalgamated Engineering Union* v. *Alderdice & Co.* (1927) 24 C. Arb. R. 755, 789.

19. It should be clear that not all industries even in the United States are in a strong enough economic condition to weather the vicissitudes of "unassisted" collective bargaining. By and large the partisans of group autonomy and *autonomous* arbitration assume sufficient economic resiliency to permit a relatively great degree of unfettered bargaining. In any case these practitioners tend to refrain from direct intervention until the parties have clearly formulated their

In this discussion we have sought to avoid the terminology of "pro- and anti-labor" officials: obviously, it follows, *a priori,* that the official who says to a relatively weak or poorly organized union, "it is essentially up to you", has the effect *in the short run,* at least, of being unfriendly. It does not follow that such is the long-run case, although admittedly account must be taken of economic and political considerations. The major point, however, has been to discuss the arbitration system in the light of long run developments and to see its implications in terms of the growth and behaviour of responsible social groups. Before, however, turning to this topic, it will be useful to consider a discussion of a cognate American question.

## IV

In the United States collective bargaining is not as anarchistic as many non-Americans imagine. Not only have Congress and its administrative agency, the National Labor Relations Board, defined public policy on many points, but long-term relationships between employers and unions have developed patterns of industrial jurisprudence. Generally, these patterns are found within the negotiated joint agreements, as well as with the unions' working rules and the policies unilaterally determined by the employers.

The joint agreements or collective contracts are usually negotiated on a one- to five-year basis. Within the life of the contracts questions of interpretation arise, which are often eventually settled by recourse to a formal, although private, arbitration process. In addition, the contracts often provide for the eventual arbitration of individual worker grievances directed at company actions. And, in a few instances, the contract provides for arbitration of unresolved issues in the preparation of new contracts.[20]

Functionally American labor arbitration falls into two sets of categories: first, as already noted, there is arbitration under existing contracts as differentiated from the arbitration of new contracts. And, second, there is arbitration by a semi-permanent tribunal where the same individual or individuals handle all cases until dissatisfaction or other disruption develops. Compared with

---

positions and realized that a bi-partite developed compromise is not possible. The *autonomous-minded* official not only views his positive role as a substitute for direct bi-partite negotiation, but above all he limits his participation to ruling on the evidence prepared for his notice by the litigants themselves. By and large he is reluctant to base any part of his decision on his own personal knowledge of the situation; if the parties want something to be considered, it is their responsibility to point it out to him.

20. This is the case in some of the garment trades where the unions dominate the scene and where union leaders have used the arbitration system as an entering wedge into the production side of the industry. Cf. S. Perlman, "Jewish-American Unionism, Its Birth Pangs and Contributions to the General American Labor Movement", 31 *American Jewish Historical Society* (1952), 311 ff.

these "permanently umpired" systems are those of an *ad hoc* nature, involving a new tribunal for each individual or set of cases. The first arrangement in the umpired industries has gained considerable popularity where there is fear of protracted economic struggle involving bankruptcy or where considerable litigation has developed or threatened to develop over the course of the life of some previous contract.

Arbitrators are usually drawn from the ranks of lawyers specializing in labor law, from amongst economists or other academicians, or occasionally from governmental employees. The preponderant number of cases are prepared and presented by legally-trained advocates. The reliance on the legal profession has often been the cause of charges of excessive legalism. This feeling has been accentuated by the formality of proceedings which, particularly in cases of *ad hoc* procedure, takes place. In fact, there has been a spate of literature on the proper procedural role of labor relations arbitrators.[21] And while this question stems from disagreement over procedural techniques, it relates basically to the level of intervention desired or even tolerated by the parties.

Two American arbitrators, dealing in different segments of "big" industry, provide students with philosophical formulations that, when seen against the relevant industrial backgrounds, illustrate excellently the dichotomy developed above. In 1940 United States Senator Wayne L. Morse (then a professor of law at the University of Oregon) held the "permanent", although part-time, position of arbitrator in the west coast longshore (stevedoring) industry. The litigating parties consisted of a militant, somewhat embittered, union, headed by the ubiquitous Harry Bridges, and an employers' association that had with obvious reluctance been forced to grant recognition and concessions to the union. The leaders of the two groups reflected the basic social

---

21. E.g. G. W. Taylor, "Effectuating the Labor Contract Through Arbitration", paper presented to the National Academy of Arbitrators, Washington, D.C., January 14, 1949; and an opposing view, J. Noble Braden, "Current Problems in Labor-Management Arbitration" (1951) 6 Arb. J. (N.S.) 91 ff. Professor Taylor (Wharton School, University of Pennsylvania) suggested *inter alia* that arbitration awards inevitably shape the relationships between the parties, that the arbitrator must fashion his award so that it falls "within the area of expectation", that, if necessary, the arbitrator should "sound out" the parties (employ mediatory tactics), and that the arbitration process is, in reality, no more and no less than an opportunity to bring about a meeting of the minds. Dr. Taylor relied on his extensive and successful experience as a "permanent" arbitrator, and his long service on governmental labor boards. Mr. Braden (a principal figure in the private American Arbitration Association), along with several others, vigorously opposed the *Taylor*-view, and held that it virtually stripped the arbitrator of his claim to rigorous impartiality. The American Arbitration Association held a conference on March 1, 1949, in New York City to discuss the differing concepts. A summary of these proceedings was prepared by J. Noble Braden, "The Functions of the Arbitrator in Labor-Management Disputes" (1949) 4 Arb. J. (N.S.). While the proponents of the two views undoubtedly understand each other, the "great debate" continues.

antagonisms. In short, it was not the type of situation conducive to "a meeting of the minds."[22] Thus, it is not surprising to find Professor Morse having expressed a typically *autonomous*-view:[23]

> My chief criticism of labor arbitration as it functions in many cases is that too few arbitrators have grasped the full significance of arbitration as a judicial process. Too many arbitrators still take judicial notice of interests and facts not established in the record of the hearings. Too many arbitrators still try to apply the principle of compromise in their decisions. I think I understand their good intentions and motives, and their desire to please both sides, at least a little bit. But when they yield to the principle of compromise they wrong not only both parties to the dispute, but they impair the effectiveness of arbitration as a judicial method of settling labor disputes. . . .
>
> I am satisfied that if we followed a less technical and formal system of procedure in our cases, it would be impossible to confine the arbitrator's decision to the record made by the parties. As I have indicated before, I am convinced that there is but one way to try a case on its merits, and that is to try it on the basis of the record made before the arbitrator. That record must be an orderly record. The parties must be guaranteed that only relevant and material evidence will go into the record. They must be protected in their right to cross-examine those who submit evidence against them. They must be given an opportunity to present their cases in an orderly fashion, and an opportunity to answer their opponent's case in an orderly fashion. Such guarantees involve both substantive and procedural rights. In fact, I know of no way of protecting the parties in respect to such rights, except in accordance with the generally accepted rule of court procedure, which we apply in all of the arbitration cases under the longshore contract. An arbitrator is bound by the language of a contract, and he has no right to reform or amend it. . . .

While it seems an eminently fair judgment to conclude that this view, analogous to that of Dethridge, C. J., Kelly, C. J., or O'Mara, J., was intended to protect the arbitrator by clothing him in the socially recognized robes of impartial judicial propriety, what is more significant is the under-

---

22. *Cf.* the classical American anecdote of the union representative who said: "We don't know what we're going to ask, but it will be one hell of a lot." To which the employers' representative is said to have replied, "Regardless of what you ask, you won't get that much."

23. W. L. Morse, "The Scope and Limitations of the Arbitration Process in Labor Disputes", *Proceedings*, International Longshoremen's & Warehousemen's Union, Third Annual Convention, April 6, 1940. Quoted in E. W. Bakke and C. Kerr, *Unions, Management, and the Public* (1948).

standing of the background and its relationship to a particular socio-political philosophy.

A second American illustration involves the views of Mr. Harry Shulman, Sterling Professor of Law at Yale University. Professor Shulman has been for many years umpire of the Ford Motor Company–United Automobile Workers (C.I.O.) contract. The parties, in this instance, concluded their first joint agreement in 1941, when the Company did a sudden *volte-face* and recognized the union as the bargaining agent for its employees. At the time all of the important company policies were determined by the Founder-President, Henry Ford, who demanded and received unquestioning obedience from his subordinate officials. Thus, when the shift was made, it was complete and the "new order" had many appearances of starting off *tabula rasa*. The inference is that any company official who thwarted Professor Shulman in the latter's necessary duties was seeking *economic decapitation* from the head office.

Also, in this instance, the union has had severe factional disturbances, particularly evident in the giant (80,000 member) River Rouge (Detroit) Ford local (branch). Many of these union issues were related to "pure" union politics (including a series of internal political squabbles), but others related to alleged racketeering, and such festering sores as the (anti-Negro) racial prejudices of some of the rank and file. Thus, the union leadership, too, has generally been most willing to "co-operate fully" with the umpire.

In the light of this background, it is not surprising to find that the parties looked for substantive, as well as procedural, suggestions from the arbitrator. Their attitude found its reflection in Professor Shulman's views:

> Some speak of the 'grievance procedure', with beguiling metaphor, as the judicial branch of the industrial government. Its function is thus thought of as that of ascertaining and enforcing rights and duties under the collective agreement. To be sure, that is one function. But it is a subordinate one. The primary function of the grievance procedure is to ease and advance the co-operation of the parties in their common enterprise—to maintain the continuity of joint endeavor which the collective agreement only initiates.
>
> The grievance may have to be denied, of course. But the denial will sit better and be more conducive to future co-operation if it is made after honest and serious consideration, and if it is explained in a manner designed to elicit sympathetic understanding rather than to provoke animosity by naked insistence on 'legal right' or 'prerogative'.[24]

---

24. H. Shulman, "The Settlement of Labor Disputes", 4 *The Record of the Association of the Bar of the City of New York,* (1949) 17, 19. Italics added.

Although Professor Shulman has elsewhere generalized his view,[25] this writer still holds that most basic to the question are the economic and political factors that condition the parties' behaviour.

The relevance of including these American examples goes beyond a mere comparison of mutual national experiences. While showing a similar problem facing an industrial society, purportedly pledged to a system of "free" collective bargaining, and one where the state takes a vital role, the American experiences again illustrate that the key variables in the industrial relations picture are the needs of the parties. The socio-political philosophies of the arbitrators must find sympathetic responses there if the systems are to work. One implication is that the system must seek out the right man, but that a good man may not be able to work in all systems.

## V

Having discussed the existence (meaning) of a procedural dichotomy, with substantive effects, in the matter of labor arbitration, as well as its probable cause, the final step is to speculate a little. For instance, if the needs of the parties are the key variables, can an arbitrator satisfy the same two litigants over time during which their needs, simultaneously, change? Or what happens if one desired the *administrative* approach, and the other the *autonomous?* In the first case, the answer undoubtedly lies not only in the intellectual agility of the arbitrator, but in the degree of extremeness of the litigants' and his own views. For it is only proper to note that our distinction has been developed in polarized form—the weakness of any theoretical discussion.

When the parties want the "judge" to approach the problem in opposing ways the need for agility is even more increased. In fact, it may be so great that no one can fill the role. The history of the Arbitration System's unhappy experiences in the Australian coal and stevedoring industries illustrates this conclusion only too vividly.[26]

---

25. *Ibid.,* p. 22: "With this conception of arbitration, questions as to whether an arbitrator should mediate or 'socialize' with the parties are idle talk. Where the situation permits it, he will do both; where the situation does not permit, either because of the nature of the case or the character of the parties, he must do neither. As previously stated, there are cases which present an issue for determination not symptomatic of any wider trouble nor pregnant with serious implications for the parties' future whichever way the decision goes. The decision may reflect on the arbitrator's intelligence and be quite displeasing to the losing party, but it relates to a single instance and will not shake the relationship. Attempts at mediation in such a case, particularly in *ad hoc* arbitration, is quite undesirable. It reflects upon the arbitrator's courage. It wastes the parties' time. And it unduly glorifies compromise over insistence upon the right."

26. See M. Perlman, *op. cit.* c. v; and an, as yet, unpublished manuscript of Professor K. F. Walker, Professor at University of Western Australia (Perth). (The latter manuscript has

Another aspect to be considered is the implication that this province of investigation and control belongs not in the juristic realm, but in the area of politics or political economy. Perhaps that is why the bench has since 1926 been occupied by what in America is termed "practitioners of labor law" (in contrast to general or the other more traditional types of legal practices). Similarly in the United States, the non-legal talent in the area of industrial relations tends to be specialists in *empirica,* rather than their more rigidly abstract (deductive) colleagues. It is possibly not enough, however, to say that the Arbitration Court really is not a court, because that implies a more static concept of the juridical process than need be taken. Yet, if it is not a court (in the usual narrow sense), what is it?

Obviously it is a quasi-juridical agency operating in the twilight zone between the purely legislative and purely judicial processes. It is the agency, set up on the frontier of a system of social control, charged with "civilizing" what Mr. Justice Higgins so nicely hailed as a "new province of law and order". Yet, as it has felt its way along, is it possible that it has inhibited more progress than the order, which it claims to have initiated, is worth? Many critics of the Court so believe. They argue that the judges have, in the hope of "civilizing" the entrepreneur, seriously diminished his vitality. Others, like the late Maurice Blackburn, think that the System has made Australian unions mere "agents of the state", and reduced thereby their usefulness to the membership.[27] Another view is that the Court has not destroyed the stamina of the entrepreneurial "class" or of the trade unions, but has merely filled in a void, created by economic factors (shortage of water resources, available capital, and high transportation costs), or by the irremedial exhaustion of two major wars, or by misguided social policies *vis-à-vis* immigration, etc. Thus, it is said, if Australia is not fulfilling her potential it is not due to the Court or the System, but to more basic factors. This writer does not, for the most part, share these critical views; having been educated largely in American schools, he believes that the Australian national development is little short of phenomenal, when compared to the development of other one-time colonial areas. This debate over the effects of the Arbitration System, while containing many aspects of validity, is merely the local adaptation of the endless controversy, "order v. progress". At the moment it is possible that the Australian entrepreneur needs something of a shot in the arm, a condition which is said to prevail in many British countries. Times do change, however.

The barons, bargaining collectively at Runnymede, are said to have forced on John Lackland the innovation of personal property rights. It took the

been submitted as a doctoral dissertation at the Harvard University, Cambridge, Massachusetts, U.S.A., and contains *inter alia* a detailed history of industrial relations in the coal industry.)

27. M. Blackburn, *Trade Unionism: Its Operation Under Australian Law* (1950).

"law" several centuries to digest the new concept: it is debatable whether some political theorists have absorbed it yet, which is, perhaps, just as well, since the change continues even now. The individual rights which the barons sought are analogous to the collective rights or type of hegemony sought currently by the unions. The implication is that the "new" area of "collective" rights remains relatively uncharted.

One added embarrassment is that while thoughtful individuals can indicate their desires and long-run needs, that process is not simple for a group. In spite of the willingness of some over-enthusiastic members to synthesize articulately these demands, the latter often remain on an effective level, relatively undefined. Here the historical record of tactics employed, invoking intra- and inter-group negotiations, as well as the long relationships with governmental agencies, can be most helpful in synthesizing the group's strategy. It is undoubtedly in these reports that the answer to queries about group-will (*Genossenschaft*) lie, as well as an excellent evaluation of conscious institutional controls, like the Arbitration System. In other words, studies in sociological jurisprudence may stem from an historical estimate of the relation of group tactics to group strategy. "But whether one embraces a one-sided cult of hero-worship or revels in a one-sided collective picture of history," wrote von Gierke,[28] "still one can never overlook the fact of a continual interaction between the two factors. At all events, the community is something active."

---

28. *Op. cit.*, p. 149.

# Bibliography

**1951**

a. "The Australian Arbitration System: An Analytical Description." *Arbitration Journal* 6:168–76. Also appeared as a University of Hawaii Occasional Paper, Honolulu: University of Hawaii, 1951.

b. Review of *Bonds of Organization: An Appraisal of Corporate Human Relations,* by E. Wight Bakke, *Journal of Business* 24 (January): 73–74.

**1952**

a. *Labor, Trade Unionism, and the Competitive Menace in Hawaii.* With John B. Ferguson. Honolulu: University of Hawaii Industrial Relations Center.

b. "Organized Labor in Hawaii." *Labor Law Journal* 3:263–75.

c. Review of *The Australian Party System,* by Louise Overacker, *Industrial and Labor Relations Review* 6:447–48.

**1953**

a. "An Industrial Problem—Australia's Longshoremen." *Labor Law Journal* 4:462–73.

b. Review of *Reflections of an Australian Liberal,* by Sir Frederic Eggleston, *Political Science Quarterly* 58 (September): 439–41.

c. "Australia" (Proceedings of the Industrial Relations Research Association), *Monthly Labor Review* 78 (June): 591–92.

d. Review of *Studies in Australian Labour Law and Relations,* by Orwell de R. Foenander, *Industrial and labor Relations Review* 6 (July): 609–10.

**1954**

a. *Judges in Industry: A Study in Labour Arbitration in Australia.* Melbourne, London, and New York: Melbourne University Press.

b. "Wage Regulation in Australia." *Labor Law Journal* 5:25–30.

c. "An Analytical Theory of Labor Arbitration in Australia." *Sydney Law Review* 1:207–12.

## 1955

a. Review of *Relation of the State to Industrial Action and Economics and Jurisprudence*, by Henry Carter Adams. With an Introductory Essay by Joseph Dorfman. *Industrial and Labor Relations Review* 8:439–40.
b. Review of *The Australian Federal Labour Party, 1950–1951*, by L. F. Crisp, *Industrial and Labor Relations Review* 9:498–99.
c. Review of *Scientific Management and the Unions, 1900–1932: A Historical Analysis*, by Milton J. Nadworny, *Industrial and Labor Relations Review* 9:671–72.

## 1957

a. "Economic Growth and Government Wage Regulation: The Australian Problem." *Annals of the American Academy of Political and Social Science* 310:123–32.
b. Review of *The Response to Industrialism*, by Samuel P. Hayes, *Industrial and Labor Relations Review* 11:301–2.

## 1958

a. Review of *The Response to Industrialism, 1885–1914*, by Samuel P. Hays, *Industrial and Labor Relations Review* 11 (January): 301–2.
b. *Labor Union Theories in America: Background and Development.* Evanston, Ill.: Rowe Peterson.

## 1959

Review of *The Development of Australian Trade Union Law*, by J. H. Portus, *Industrial and Labor Relations Review* 13:132–34.

## 1960

a. "Labor Movement Theories: Past, Present, and Future." *Industrial & Labor Relations Review* 13:338–48.
b. "Sumner Huber Slichter." In *Dictionary of American Biography, 1955–1960*, 585–87. New York: C. Scribner's Sons.
c. Review of *Studies in Income and Wealth, Vol. 24*, Princeton University Press, for the National Bureau of Economic Research. *Schweizerische Zeitschrift für Volkswirtschaft und Statistik* 98:362–64.
d. "Economics of Metropolitan Medical Care," *Public Heath Reports* 77 (May): 388.

## 1961

a. *The Machinists: A New Study in American Trade Unionism.* Cambridge, Mass.: Harvard University Press.

b. Review of *Industrial Conciliation and Arbitration in Australia,* by Orwell de R. Foenander, *Industrial & Labor Relations Review* 14 (July): 621–22.

**1962**

a. *Democracy in the IAM.* New York: Wiley.
b. "Commentarios Sobre el Trabajo 'La Evaluacion del impacto economica de las actividades Sanitarias.'" *Boletin de la Oficina Sanitaria Panamerica* 52:40–45. "Methods of Evaluation of the Contribution of Health Programs to Economic Development: Discussion of Atilio Macchiavello's Paper, 'Evaluation of the Economic Impact of Health Activities.'" September 30, 1961.
c. Review of *The Pennsylvania Manufacturers' Association,* by J. Roffe Wike, *Business History Review* 4 (June): 131–33.

**1963**

a. *Human Resources in the Urban Economy,* (ed.). Washington, D.C.: Resources for the Future.
b. "Economic Aspects of the Health Industry in Dynamic Societies." *American Journal of Public Health.* 53:381–91.
c. "The Economics of Human Resources in the American Urban Setting: Some Concepts and Problems." In Mark Perlman, ed., *Human Resources in the Urban Economy,* 1–20. Washington, D.C.: Resources for the Future.

**1964**

a. "Some Economic Aspects of Public Health Programs in Underdeveloped Areas." In *The Economics of Health and Medical Care.* Proceedings of the Conference on the Economics of Health and Medical Care, May 10–12, 1962. Ann Arbor: University of Michigan Press.
b. Review of *The Economics of Labor,* by E. H. Phelps Brown, *Industrial & Labor Relations Review* 17 (January): 320–22.

**1966**

a. "Measuring the Effects of Population Control on Economic Development: Pakistan as a Case Study." With Edgar M. Hoover. *Pakistan Development Review* 6:168–76.
b. "On Health and Economic Development: Some Problems, Methods, and Conclusions reviewed in a Perusal of the Literature." *Comparative Studies in Society and History* 8:433–48.

**1967**

a. *Health Manpower in a Developing Economy.* With Timothy D. Baker, M.D. Baltimore: Johns Hopkins Press.

b. *Contemporary Economics and Selected Readings.* (Edited with Reuben E. Slesinger and Asher Isaacs). Boston: Allyn and Bacon.

**1968**

a. "Labor in Eclipse." In J. Braeman, R. H. Bremmer, and D. Brady, eds., *Twentieth Century America,* 103–45. Columbus, Ohio: Ohio State University Press.
b. "Theories of the Labor Movement." In *New International Encyclopedia of the Social Sciences,* Vol. 8, 516–22. New York: Macmillan.

**1969**

a. "Editor's Note." *Journal of Economic Literature* 1:iii.
b. "Government and Economy: How Much Intervention?" In Judd Teller, ed., *Government and the Democratic Policy,* 67–74, ff. New York: American Histadrut Cultural Exchange.
c. "Rationing of Medical Resources: The Complexities of the Supply and Demand Problem." *Sociological Studies in Economics and Administration.* Monograph 14 of the *Sociological Review,* 105–19.

**1970**

a. "Cost/Benefit Ratio of Population Planning." In Dong-A Ilbo, *Population Planning and Economic Development,* being a report on an international conference held in Pusan, Korea, February 25–28, 6–13.

**1971**

a. *Carter Goodrich.* Memorial. Pittsburgh: University of Pittsburgh.
b. "Union Negotiations, 1971: Whither?" *Monetary Indicators* March 26, 1971.
c. "Some Comments on the American Productivity Growth Rate." *Monetary Indicators* November 12, 1971.
d. "The Trend in Physician and Hospital Bills." *Monetary Indicators* November 19, 1971.
e. Review of *Health Manpower Planning in Turkey: An International Research Case Study,* by Carl F. Taylor, Rahmi Dirican, and Kurt W. Deuschle, *Economic Development and Cultural Change* 19:490–94.
f. Review of *Medical Care Use in Sweden and the United States: A Comparative Analysis of Systems and Behavior,* by Ronald Andersen, Bjorn Smedby, and Odin Anderson, *Journal of Economic Literature* 9:1224–26.

**1972**

a. "Some Reflections on Theorizing about Industrial Relations." In Norval Morris and Mark Perlman, eds., *Law and Crime: Essays in Honor of Sir John Barry,* 181–209. New York, London, and Paris: Gordon and Breach.
b. "On Health, Population Change, and Economic Development." In Mark Perlman, Charles Levin, and Benjamin Chinitz, eds., *Spatial, Regional, and Population Economics: Essays in Honor of Edgar M. Hoover,* 293–310. New York, London, and Paris: Gordon and Breach.
c. "Economics Libraries and Collections." In *Encyclopedia of Library and Information Science,* vol. 7, 345–63. New York: Marcel Dekker.
d. Review of *The Rise of the United Association: National Unionism in the Pipe Trades, 1884–1924,* by Martin Segal. *Industrial and Labor Relations Review* 25 (Number 4): 578–80.
e. Review of *West German Reparations to Israel* by Nicholas Balabkins and *The German Path to Israel* edited by Rolf Vogel. *Conservative Judaism* 24 (Number 4): 80–83.

**1973**

a. "Comments on 'Consumption Values of Trade Unions.'" *Journal of Economic Issues* 7:303–5.
b. "Communications, The Editor's Comment." *Journal of Economic Literature* 11:56–58.
c. "Editor's Comment: On the Classification of Economics Materials." *Journal of Economic Literature* 11:898–99.
d. "Model for Hospital Micro-costing." With Larry J. Shuman and Harvey Wolfe. *Industrial Engineering* (July 1973): 39–43.

**1974**

a. "Introduction" and "Economics of Health and Medical Care in Industrialized Nations." In Mark Perlman, ed., *Economics of Health and Medical Care,* xiii–xx, 21–33. New York: Halsted Press.
b. Review of *Population Change, Modernization and Welfare,* by Joseph Spengler, *Journal of Economic Literature* 22:1372–73.
c. "Family Health in Urban Migrants." National Council for International Health. *Health of the Family,* 51–54. International Health Conference, October 16–18, held at Reston, Va.

**1975**

a. "Economics of the Family: Marriage, Children, and the Human Capital." *Demography* 12:549–56.

b. "The Editor's Comment: The 1975 Kiel Conference on Economics Bibliography." *Journal of Economic Literature* 13:1320–21.
c. "Some Economic Growth Problems and the Part Population Policy Plays." *Quarterly Journal of Economics* 89:247–56.

**1976**

a. "Jews and Contributions to Economics: A Bicentennial Review." *Judaism* 25:301–11.
b. "Foreword." In Michael C. Keeley, ed., *Population, Public Policy, and Economic Development*, vi–vii. New York: Praeger Publishers.
c. Review of *The Great Instauration: Science, Medicine, and Reform 1626–1660*, by Charles Webster, *Journal of Economic Literature* 14:1289–91.
d. Review of *Studies in the Colonial History of Spanish America*, by Mario Góngora, *Journal of Economic Literature* 14:898–900.

**1977**

a. "The Changing Modes of Data in Recent [Economic] Research (with Naomi W. Perlman)." In Mark Perlman, ed., *The Organization and Retrieval of Economic Knowledge*, 197–229. New York: Halsted Press.
b. "The Editing of the *Economic Record, 1925–1975*." In J. P. Nieuwenhuysen and P. J. Drake, eds., [Wilfred Prest]: *Australian Economic Policy*, 218–30. Melbourne: Melbourne University Press.
c. "Introduction." In Mark Perlman, ed., *The Organization and Retrieval of Economic Knowledge*, 1–11. New York: Halsted Press.
d. "Orthodoxy and Heterodoxy in Economics: A Retrospective View of Experiences in Britain and the U.S.A." *Zeitschrift für Nationalökonomie* 37:151–64.
e. "Economics and Health." *Tribuna Médica* (A Weekly Newspaper Sent to All Physicians in Spain) December 16.

**1978**

a. "Considering the Future of American Health Care Capital Funding: A Working Paper." With Gordon K. MacLeod. In Gordon K. MacLeod and Mark Perlman, eds., *Health Care Capital: Competition and Control*. Proceedings of the Capital Investment Conference Sponsored by the University of Pittsburgh, 379–97. Cambridge, Mass.: Lippincott, Ballinger.
b. "Discrepancies of Supply and Demand in the Labor Market: Sectoral, Regional and Professional—Causes and Cures." In Herbert Giersch, ed., *Capital Shortage and Unemployment in the World Economy: Symposium*, 159–60, 329–30. Tübingen: Mohr (Paul Siebeck).
c. "Labor Movement." *World Book Encyclopedia* 12:6–17.

d. "Reflections on Methodology, Persuasion, and Machlup." In Jacob S. Dreyer, ed., [Fritz Machlup]: *Breadth and Depth in Economics*, 5. Lexington, Mass.: Heath.

e. Review of *The Last Great Subsistence Crisis in the Western World*, by John D. Post, *Journal of Economic Literature* 26:120–23.

f. Review of *Knowledge and Ignorance in Economics*, by T. W. Hutchinson, *Journal of Economic Literature* 26:582–85.

g. Review of *William Beveridge: A Biography*, by José Harris, *Journal of Economic Literature* 26:1079–81.

h. Review of *Ethics and Society in England: The Revolution in the Social Sciences, 1870–1914*, by Reba N. Stoffer, *Journal of Economic Literature* 26:1447–49.

**1979**

a. "One Man's Baedeker to Productivity Growth Discussions." In William Fellner, ed., *Contemporary Economic Problems, 1979*, 79–113. Washington, D.C.: American Enterprise Institute.

b. Review of *Historical Studies of Changing Fertility*, edited by Charles Tilly, *Journal of Economic Literature* 16:120–23.

c. Review of *On Revolutions and Progress in Economic Knowledge*, by T. W. Hutchinson, *Zeitschrift für Nationalökonomie* 39:225–420.

**1980**

a. "Prices, Technological Change, and Productivity in the American Health Care Industry." In William Fellner, ed., *Contemporary Economic Problems, 1980*, 227–62. Washington, D.C.: American Enterprise Institute.

b. Review of *Corn, Cash, Commerce: The Economics Policies of the Tory Governments, 1815–1830*, by Boyd Hilton; *Political Economists and the English Poor Laws: A Historical Study of the Influence of Classical Economics on the Formation of Social Welfare Policy*, by Raymond G. Cowherd, *History of Political Economy* 12:299–302.

c. Review of *Worker's Control in America: Studies in the History of the World*, by David Montgomery, *Journal of Economic History* 40:656–59.

d. Review of *Daniel DeLeon: The Odyssey of An American Marxist*, by L. Glen Seretan, *Journal of Economic Issues* 14 (Sept 1980): 804–07.

e. Review of *Imagination and the Nature of Choice*, by G. L. S. Shackle, *Journal of Economic Literature* 18:115–18.

f. Review of *Labor and the Law*, by Charles O. Gregory and Harold A. Katz, *Journal of Economic Literature* 28:648–51.

g. Review of *Malthus*, by William Petersen, and *Population Malthus: His Life and Times*, by Patricia James, *Journal of Economic Literature* 28:1100–1103.

h. Review of *The Rise and Fall of Economic Growth: A Study in Contemporary Thought*, by Heinz W. Arndt, *Journal of Economic Literature* 28:1558–59.

i. Review of *Research in Health Economics: A Research Annual,* by Richard M. Scheffler, *Southern Economic Journal* 47:562–65.


## 1981


a. *Health, Economics, and Health Economics.* Edited with J. van der Gaag. Amsterdam, New York, Oxford: North-Holland Press.
b. "Some Economic Consequences of the New Patterns of Population Growth." In William Fellner, ed., *Essays in Contemporary Economic Problems: Demand, Productivity, and Population,* 247–79. Washington, D.C.: American Enterprise Institute.
c. "[Valedictory] Editor's Note." *Journal of Economic Literature* 19:1–4.
d. Review of *Population Change in Developed Countries,* by Richard A. Easterlin, ed., *Journal of Economic Literature* 19:74–82.
e. "Professor Clarifies Economic Talk." *The Pitt News,* March 25.
f. Review of *The Dynamics of Industrial Conflict: Lessons from Ford,* by Henry Friedman and Sander Meredeen, *Journal of Economic History* 41:441–42.
g. Review of *The Ownership Theory of the Trade Union,* by Donald L. Martin, *Journal of Economic Issues* 15 (December): 1099–1102.
h. Review of *The Origins and Development of Labor Economics: A Chapter in the History of Social Thought,* by Paul J. McNulty, *Journal of Economic Literature* 19:1083–85.
i. "Schumpeter as a Historian of Economic Thought." [Reprinted from Frisch, "G. L. S. Shackle as a Historian of Economic Thought."] In Warren J. Samuels, ed., *Research in the History of Economic Thought and Methodology: A Research Annual,* volume 1, 113–30 (Schumpeter) and 223–28 (Shackle). Greenwich, Conn.: JAI Press.
j. "Schumpeter as Historian of Economic Thought." In Helmut Frisch, ed., *Schumpeterian Economics,* 143–61. Eastbourne, East Sussex, England: Praeger. [Also reprinted in Warren J. Samuels, ed., item listed immediately above.]


## 1982


a. "Opportunity in the Face of Disaster: A Review of the Economic Literature on Famine." In Kevin M. Cahill, ed., *Famine,* 75–81. Maryknoll, N.Y.: Orbis.
b. "Patterns of Regional Decline and Growth: The Past and What Has Been Happening Lately." In William Fellner, ed., *A Study in Contemporary Economic Problems, 1982,* 1–56. Washington, D.C.: American Enterprise Institute.
c. Review of *Hospital Costs and Health Insurance,* by Martin Feldstein, *Journal of Political Economy* 90:872–79.
d. Review of *The Economics of Population Growth, Population Studies,* and *The Ultimate Resource,* by Julian Simon, *Population Studies* 36:490–94.

**1983**

a. "Human Resources and Population Growth." In Paul Streeten and Harry Maier, eds., *Human Resources, Employment and Development.* Vol. 2: Concepts, Measurement and Long-Run Perspective. Proceedings of the Sixth World Congress of the International Economic Association held in 1980 in Mexico City, 167–80. London: Macmillan.

b. "Tres Clases de economistas." [A translation by Manuel Siquenza of "The Tensions Between Abstraction and Generalization: The Uses of Economics."] *Papeles de Economia Española* 16:275–78.

c. Review of *Population Change and Social Policy,* by Nathan Keyfitz, *Population and Development Review* 9:727–30.

d. Review of *The History of the A.C.T.U.,* by Jim Hagan. *Industrial and Labor Relations Review* 37 (Number 1): 128–29.


**1984**

a. "Collective Bargaining and Industrial Relations: The Past, the Present, and the Future." In William Fellner, ed., *Contemporary Economic Problems, 1983–84,* 287–322. Washington, D.C.: American Enterprise Institute.

b. "Governmental Intervention and the Socioeconomic Background." In Bela Gold, et al., *Technological Progress and Industrial Leadership: The Growth of the U.S. Steel Industry, 1900–1970,* 609–31. Lexington, Mass.: Lexington Books.

c. "L'audience de Malthus aux Etats-Unis Comme Economiste," being a translation of "Malthus's Economics and Its Early American Reception." In Antoinette Fauve-Chamoux, *Malthus, Hier et Aujourdhui,* Congrès international de démographie historique/CNRS mai 1980, 117–25. Paris: Editions des CNRS, 1984. Being the Proceedings of a 1980 Paris Conference on the 150th anniversary of the birth of Thomas Robert Malthus.

d. "Perlman on Shackle." In Henry W. Spiegel and Warren J. Samuels, eds., *Contemporary Economists in Perspective,* 579–90. Greenwich, Conn.: JAI Press.

e. "The Role of Population Projections for the Year 2000." In Julian L. Simon and Herman Kahn, eds., *The Resourceful Earth,* 50–66. Oxford: Basil Blackwell.

f. Review of *The Baby Boom Generation and the Economy,* by Louise B. Russell, *Journal of Economic History* 44:224–26.


**1985**

a. "A Coming Inflection in the American Economic Policy?" In [Horst Klaus Recktenwald] *Staat und Ökonomie Heute,* edited by Horst Hanusch, Karl W. Roskamp, and Jack Wiseman, 135–45. Stuttgart and New York: Gustav Fischer Verlag.

b. Review of *History of the Human Gamble,* by Reuven Brenner, *Journal of Economic Behavior and Organization* 6:395–98.

**1986**

a. "Perceptions of our Discipline: Three Magisterial Treatments of the Evolution of Economic Thought." History of Economic Society Meetings, May 1985, George Mason University, Fairfax, Va. *Bulletin [of the History of Economics Society]* (Winter): 9–28.
b. "Subjectivism and American Institutionalism." In [Ludwig M. Lachmann], *Subjectivism, Intelligibility, and Economic Understanding: Essays in Honor of the 80th Birthday of Ludwig M. Lachmann*, 268–80. Edited by Israel Kirzner. New York University Press.

**1987**

a. "Are Five Billion [People on the Earth] Too Many?" *San Diego [California] Union* August 9. Later syndicated.
b. "Concerning Winters of Discontent: Does Methodology or Rhetoric Contain the Answer to a Possible Malaise?" *International Journal of Social Economics* 14:9–18.
c. "An Essay on Karl Pribram's *A History of Economic Reasoning*." *Revue Economique* 38:171–76.
d. "Political Purpose and the National Accounts." In *The Politics of Numbers*, edited by William Alonso and Paul Starr, 133–51. New York: Russell Sage.

**1988**

a. "Foreword." In Arthur F. Burns, *The Ongoing Revolution in American Banking*, v–x. Washington, D.C.: American Enterprise Institute.
b. *The Fundamental Issues in the Controversy of the [Macroeconomic] Policy Paradigms: Policies, Theories, and Underpinnings.* A working paper published by the Institut für Weltwirtschaft an den Universität Kiel.
c. "On the Coming Senescence of American Manufacturing Competence." In Horst Hanusch, ed., *Evolutionary Economics: Applications of Schumpeter's Ideas*, 343–83. New York: Cambridge University Press.

**1989**

a. "Comment" on Philip T. Hoffman, "Institutions and Agriculture in Old-Regime France." *Journal of Institutional and Theoretical Economics* 145:182–64.
b. "Comments I" on Stiglitz's *The Economic Role of the State*. In Stiglitz, Joseph E., et al., *The Economic Role of the State*, 89–106. Oxford: Blackwell.
c. "Foreword." In James H. Cassing and Steven L. Husted, eds., *Capital, Technology, and Labor in the New Global Economy*. Washington, D.C.: American Enterprise Institute.

## 1990

a. "Demographie et Fiscalite." *Le Figaro* (Paris), June 8, 1990.
b. "Die Bienen-Fabel: Eine moderne Würdigung." In Friederich A. von Hayek, Mark Perlman, and Frederick B. Kaye, *Bernard de Mandevilles Leben und Werk*, 65–107. Düsseldorf/-Darmstadt (FRG): Verlag Wirtschaft und Finanzen GMBH. (Ein Unternehmen der Verlagsruppe Handelsblatt). Being an interpretation of Bernard de Mandeville. *Fable of the Bees: Or, Public Vices Publik Benefits* [London, 1714].
c. "The Fabric of Economics and the Golden Threads of G. L. S. Shackle." In Stephen F. Frowen, *Unknowledge and Choice in Economics*, 9–19. London: Macmillan and New York: St. Martin's.
d. "Introduction." (With Arnold Heertje.) In Arnold Heertje and Mark Perlman, eds., *Evolving Technology and Market Structure: Studies in Schumpeterian Economics*, 1–13. Ann Arbor, University of Michigan Press.
e. "Preface," "Introduction" (with Klaus Weiermair), and "The Evolution of Leibenstein's X-Efficiency Theory." In Klaus Weiermair and Mark Perlman, eds., *Studies in Economic Rationality: X-Efficiency Examined and Extolled. Essays Written in the Tradition of and to Honor Harvey Leibenstein*, 1–6, 7–26. Ann Arbor: University of Michigan Press.
f. Review of *Breaking the Academic Mould: Economists on American Higher Learning in the Nineteenth Century*, edited by William J. Barber, *History of Political Economy* 22 (Summer 1990): 406–8.

## 1991

a. *Capital Markets and Trade: The United States Faces a United Europe*. Edited with Claude Barfield. Washington, D.C.: American Enterprise Institute.
b. *Political Power and Social Change: The United States Faces a United Europe*. Edited with Norman Ornstein. Washington, D.C.: American Enterprise Institute.
c. "Early Capital Theory in the Economics Journals: A Study of Imputed Induced Demand." *Economic Notes* 20:58–88.
d. "On the Editing of American Economic Journals: Some Comments on the Earlier Journals and the Lessons Suggested." *Economic Notes* 20:159–72.
e. "Fraternity, Free Association, and Socio-Economic Analysis." Being part of a Symposium on the French Revolution and the History of Economic Thought. In Warren J. Samuels, ed., *Research in the History of Economic Thought and Methodology: A Research Annual*, vol. 8. Greenwich, Conn. JAI Press.
f. "Introduction." In Fritz Machlup, *Essays in Economic Semantics*, 2d ed., vii–xxi. New Brunswick, N.J.: Transactions Press.
g. "Two Concurrent Explorations of the Frontiers of the Economic Science." In *Colloque International: "J. A. Schumpeter et J. M. Keynes"*, 29–43. Paris: Centre National d'Enseignement a Distance de Vanve for the Universite de Droit, D'Economie, et de Sciences Sociales de Paris.

h. Review of *The Management of Labor Unions: Decision Making with Historical Constraints*, by John T. Dunlop, *Journal of Economic Literature* 29:111–12.
i. *Horst Claus Recktenwald. A Memorial.* (Privately printed.)

## 1992

a. *Entrepreneurship, Technological Innovation, and Economic Growth: Studies in the Schumpeterian Tradition.* Edited with Frederic M. Scherer. Ann Arbor: University of Michigan Press.
b. *Industry, Services, and Agriculture: The United States Faces a United Europe.* Edited with Claude Barfield. Washington, D.C.: American Enterprise Institute.
c. "Harvey Leibenstein." In Warren Samuels, ed., *New Horizons in Economic Thought*, 184–201. Cheltenham, Gloc. (UK): Edward Elgar.
d. "Agenda für die Zunkunft der Mikroökonomen." (Translated into German from an article, "Agenda for the Microeconomists' Future.") In Horst-Klaus Recktenwald and Horst Hanusch, eds., *Ökonomische Wissenschaftin der Zukunft: Ansichten führender Ökonomen* (*Economic Science in the Future: Perspectives by Eminent Scholars*), pp. 303–21. Düsseldorf: Verlag Wirtschaft und Finanzen.
e. "Understanding the 'Old' American Institutionalism." *Revue d'Economie Politique* 102:281–95.
f. Review of *Essays on the Intellectual History of Economics*, by Jacob Viner, *Journal of the History of Economic Thought* 14:116–18.
g. Review of *The Economic Problems in Biblical and Patristic Thought*, by Barry Gordon, *Judaism* 161:106-8.

## 1993

a. "On Thinking About George Stigler." With Charles McCann. *Economic Journal* 103:994–1014.
b. "George Lennox Shackle." *Review of Political Economy* 5:270–72.
c. Review of *Eminent Economists*, by Michael Szenberg, *Journal of the History of Economic Thought* 15:330–33.
d. "Rhetoric and Normativism: An Idiosyncratic Appraisal from the Standpoint of the History of Economic Thought, A Review Essay." Being reviews of *The Rhetoric of Reaction*, by Albert O. Hirschman, and *If You're So Smart: The Narrative of Economic Expertise*, by Donald N. McCloskey, *Methodus*, 5 (June): 129–39.
e. "Series Editor's Note." In Shigeto Tsuru, *Japan's Capitalism: Creative Defeat and Beyond*, 267–70. Cambridge: Cambridge University Press.
f. Review of *Stabilizing Dynamics: Constructing Economic Knowledge*, by E. Roy Weintraub, *Journal of the History and Philosophy of Science* 60, no. 4 (December 1993):669–71.

**1994**

a. "Introduction." In Joseph A. Schumpeter, *History of Economic Analysis*, xvii–xxxix. London: Routledge, [1954] 1994.
b. "Foreword." In Charles R. McCann, Jr., *Probability Foundations of Economic Theory*, ix–xi. London and New York: Routledge.
c. "Introduction." with Yuichi Shionoya. In Yuichi Shionoya and Mark Perlman, eds., *Schumpeter in the History of Ideas*, 1–3. Ann Arbor: University of Michigan Press.
d. "Commentary." In Yuichi Shionoya and Mark Perlman, eds., *Schumpeter in the History of Ideas*, 125–27. Ann Arbor: University of Michigan Press.
e. "Introduction." With Yuichi Shionoya. In Yuichi Shionoya and Mark Perlman, *Innovation in Technology, Industries and Institutions: Studies in Schumpeterian Perspectives*, 1–6. Ann Arbor: University of Michigan Press.
f. "Remarks to the History of Economics Society Pertaining to the Reprinting of Schumpeter's *History of Economic Analysis*." Presented at the History of Economics Society meetings, June 1994, Babson Park, Mass.

**1995**

a. "The Population Summit: Reflections on the World's Leading Problem." *Population Development Review* 21 (June): 341–49.
b. Review of *Economic Thought in Spain: Selected Essays of Marjorie Grice-Hutchinson*, by Laurence S. Moss and Christopher K. Ryan, eds., *Journal of the History of Economic Thought* 17 (Spring): 166–67.
c. "An Economic Historian's Economist: Remembering Simon Kuznets." With Vibha Kapuria-Foreman. *Economic Journal* 105:1524–47.
d. Review of *The Nature of Economic Thought: Essays in Economic Methodology*, by Johannes Klant, *European Journal of the History of Economic Thought* 2 (Spring): 227–29.
e. "What Makes My Mind Tick." *American Economist* 39:6–27.
f. "Foreword." In Kofi Kissi Dompere and Mansur Ejaz, *The Epistemics of Development Economics: Toward a Methodological Critique and Unity*, ix–xi. Westport, Conn.: Greenwood Publishing Group, Inc.
g. Review of *Theorists of Economic Growth from David Hume to the Present: With a Perspective on the Next Century*, by Walt Whitman Rostow. In *Research in the History of Economic Thought and Methodology*, vol. 13, 277–83. Greenwich, Conn.: JAI Press.

**1996**

a. *The Character of Economic Thought, Economic Characters, and Economic Institutions: Selected Essays by Mark Perlman*. Ann Arbor: University of Michigan Press.

b. "Varieties of Uncertainty." With Charles R. McCann, Jr. In Christian Schmidt, ed., *Uncertainty in Economic Thought.* Cheltenham, Glos., U.K.: Edward Elgar.

c. "Introduction." Edited with Ernst Helmstädter. In *Behavioral Norms, Technological Progress and Economic Dynamics: Studies in Schumpeterian Economics.* Ann Arbor: University of Michigan Press. Forthcoming.

d. "Introduction." With Enrico Colombatto. In Kenneth Arrow, Enrico Colombatto, Mark Perlman, and Christian Schmidt, eds., *The Rational Foundations of Economic Behaviour.* Proceedings of the IEA Conference held in Turin, Italy. London: Macmillan. Forthcoming.

e. Review of *Aging and Old Age,* by Richard A. Posner, *Population and Development Review.* Forthcoming.

f. "Harvey Leibenstein as a Pioneer in Our Time." With James W. Dean. *Economic Journal.* Forthcoming.

g. "Keynes's Economic and the Meaning of Uncertainty." With Charles R. McCann. In O. F. Hamouda and B. B. Price, eds., *Keynesianism and the Keynesian Revolution in America: Memorial Volume in Honour of Lorie Tarshis.* Cheltenham, Glos., U.K.: Edward Elgar. Forthcoming.

h. "Putting the 'Harcourt Problem' into a Framework." In Philip Aretis, Gabriel Palma, and Malcolm Sawyer, eds., *Essays in Honor of Geoff Harcourt.* Vol. 1, *Capital Controversy, Post Keynesian Economics and the History of Economic Theory.* London: Routledge. Forthcoming.

i. Review of *Joseph Alois Schumpeter: The Public Life of a Private Man,* by Wolfgang E. Stolper, *Zeitschrift für Nationalökonomie.* Forthcoming.

j. "Some Aspects of Our Western Heritage." In B. B. Price, ed., *Ancient Economic Thought.* London: Routledge. Forthcoming.

k. "Assessing the Reprinting of Schumpeter's *History of Economic Analysis.*" In *Joseph A. Schumpeter, Historian of Economics: Perspectives on the History of Economic Thought.* Selected Papers from the History of Economics Society Conference, 1994. Edited by Laurence S. Moss. London: Routledge, 15–20.

# Index

Abramovitz, Moses, 24, 233, 246, 281, 297n, 376
Abstinence, 149, 151, 152
Ackley, Gardner, 23, 353
Adams, Henry B., 319
Adams, Henry Carter, 242
Adams, Leonard, 383, 391
Adamson Act, 420
Adolph, Robert, 107, 108
Agency for International Development, 25
Alger, Horatio, 312
Allen, Robert Loring, 180, 185, 190n, 199
Allias, Maurice, 352
Alonso, William, 207
Altmeyer, Arthur, 239
Altruism, 103
Aluminum Company of America, 470, 488
Amalgamated Union of Iron and Steel Workers, 472
American Academy of Arts and Sciences, 343
American Association of University Professors, 353n.4
American Economic Association, 22, 50, 56, 142, 146, 146n.6, 164, 164n.21, 186, 228, 242, 282n.2, 317, 334, 343, 354, 358, 440
*American Economic Review*, 23, 24, 52, 55, 146n.6, 246n.4, 357, 364, 369
American Enterprise Institute, 26, 27
American Federation of Labor, 395, 398, 399, 407, 421, 423–26, 427–28, 429–30, 437, 438, 445, 454, 472

*American Historical Review*, 238
American Institutionalism. *See* Institutionalism
*American Journal of Sociology*, 364
American Medical Association, 330
American Philosophical Society, 343
American Plan, 431, 440
American Revolution, 308
American Statistical Association, 218, 343
Amherst, 51
Anarcho-syndicalism, 407
Anderson, Benjamin McAlester, Jr., 68
*Annals of the American Academy of Political and Social Science*, 49, 52, 364
Anti-Boycott League, 431
Aquinas, Thomas, 70, 71, 72, 134, 138, 193
Arbitration Court (Australia), 7, 491–503
Arena, Richard, 28
Aristotle, 66, 75, 133, 136, 188, 193, 196, 272
Aristotelianism, 71, 121, 130, 133–34, 136, 138, 139, 197
Aronson, J. Richard, 55, 56
Arrow, Kenneth, 23, 137, 319n, 352
Ashley, William, 77, 250
Augello, Massimo, 180
Auspitz, Rudolf, 77
Austin, John, 107
Australia, 6, 7–10, 21n.13, 30, 491–503
Austrian school, 65, 67, 69, 70, 72, 76, 80, 84, 147–48, 174, 176, 275, 350, 353, 358, 373–75, 376
Ayers, Clarence, 231